OPENING DOORS

THE UNTOLD STORY OF CORNELIA SORABJI

REFORMER, LAWYER
AND CHAMPION OF
WOMEN'S RIGHTS IN
INDIA

RICHARD SORABJI

I.B. TAURIS

LONDON · NEW YORK

Published in 2010 by I.B.Tauris & Co. Ltd
6 Salem Road, London W2 4BU
175 Fifth Avenue, New York, NY 10010
www.ibtauris.com

Distributed in the United States and Canada Exclusively by Palgrave Macmillan
175 Fifth Avenue, NY 10010

ISBN: 978 1 84885 375 1

A full CIP record for this book is available from the British Library
A full CIP record for this book is available from the Library of Congress

Library of Congress catalog card: available

Typeset in Perpetua by Integra Software Services Pvt. Ltd., India
Printed and bound in Great Britain by CPI Antony Rowe, Chippenham

DEDICATION

To my sister, Francina, and the memory of our father and aunts

CONTENTS

LIST OF
ILLUSTRATIONS

INTRODUCTION

Cornelia Sorabji (my aunt) had a life of opening doors. Opened doors are ones that have been shut and the first door, which was opened to Oxford University, had been slammed shut on a woman prize-winner in 1888. Next to be opened was the door closed to woman sitting Oxford's law degree. Then Cornelia opened the door of the first woman to plead in a court of the British Empire. Next her campaign opened the door for the first woman lawyer with a post in the British Raj. Finally she opened a door for Indian women who had never seen the outside world since their childhood.

These women had been Hindu or Muslim child brides and often child widows and they found themselves in charge of estates, magnificent or dilapidated, often in remote jungles of India. Cornelia was wholly Indian, but, unlike them, was a Christian Parsee. The all-male British Raj had responsibility for these women, but could never see them face to face, because, sometimes from the age of four, they disappeared for ever behind the 'curtain' or purdah, and never saw a male again other than their husband. The all-male Raj could only interview a curtain, never knowing who was behind it, while relatives were killing their children to get their estates or thrones. Cornelia's knowledge was unique of what was happening to these women who sat behind the purdah, the purdahnashins. Unique too was what Cornelia wrote privately about the all-male élite of the Civil Service, their quarrels, friendships, passions, wisdom, blindness, strengths and weaknesses. In public, she observed the public schoolboy etiquette of never telling, but her diaries and letters to confidants reveal the other side. Then there was her unusual attitude to Gandhi, whose movement was eventually to wreck her social work, and her remarkable confrontation with him in his extraordinary person.

I knew Cornelia in the Second World War, as striking in old age as she had been beautiful when young. She always wore brilliant sarees, even in the darkest days of the Second World War. She tried to do for her boy nephew what had been done for her in the London of 1892, introducing him to the excitements of London's legal inns and courts in the vain hope that he too would become a lawyer. I wanted to write a biography, based especially on her personal papers, of which I possess some,[1] and partly on my knowledge of her as her nephew. She gave an account of virtually every day of her life, written in up to three versions over 50 years. It is partly in a personal diary, in some years in a work diary too, in most years in letters to family or a series of confidants, with a few extra notebooks thrown in. It reveals the cliff-hangers, the agonies, the triumphs, when they came, and for ever the uncertainties, as she never knew what would happen next.

Only some of her life story is well known. There was her father converting to Christianity at risk of his life, her mother's intense belief in multi-cultural friendship and assistance, the mixed rivalry and support she felt in relation to her siblings (my father and aunts). All these explain a great deal about her feelings and aspirations. When she reached Oxford as a student in 1889, there was the unexpected celebrity arising from the scholarship denied her, on the grounds that she was a woman. The substitute scholarship was funded by aristocratic English ladies, among them Florence Nightingale. She arrived, to her astonishment, as one of Victorian England's darlings in the salons of Oxford and London with Oxford's leading academic Jowett, the political luminaries Arthur Balfour and Margot (later Asquith), the Poet Laureate Tennyson and the Royal Family. In 1892, she was the first woman to sit the Oxford law degree, championed by Jowett in the teeth of the examiners' violent objections to a woman, though she could not receive the degree for another three decades. Back in India in 1894, she embarked on a ten-year campaign to get the British to give a woman a legal job. She had at first to content herself with legal briefs from the Indian Princes who ruled directly in the so-called Princely States. They were not so biased against a woman lawyer, but gave her idiosyncratic missions such as defending an elephant. From 1898 a tumultuous love affair almost wrecked her and her campaign. But her unrelenting ten-year effort led suddenly, against all odds, to the overriding of the redoubtable Viceroy, Lord Curzon. He, like almost everyone else, had thought a woman should not be employed. But in 1904 through Lord Curzon's superior, the Secretary of State for India, she was given an anomalous appointment to the prestigious Indian Civil Service, which was then staffed almost entirely by Britons. There followed immediate and spectacular success from 1905–1922 in breaking through cultural barriers, gaining the secluded women's confidence, resolving their problems and sometimes in carrying out daring rescues from imminent death. The women's estates and palaces were spread over the jungles of north east India and Cornelia's exotic travels to visit them, as well as what she found there, are central to the story. Like no one else she penetrated into their beliefs, attitudes and customs, cherishing the good ones, and devising a new educational approach to modify those that disadvantaged them. This led to nine years of acclaim and then nine years salted with male Civil Service jealousies.

After her retirement in 1922, she went to London where the English bar had at last been opened to women. She was able to study and qualify and she returned to India in 1924 as its first woman barrister. The opposition was more intense amongst lawyers against a woman who might, as a pleader, defeat men publicly in argument. But her scholarly legal opinions, which did not threaten men, were acclaimed and she even defeated one of the most prominent male barristers of India. She made excursions back to the Princely States and learnt how secluded women fared if they appealed from their princely rulers to British supervisory justice. In 1927, the unhappy misappropriation of her special knowledge for anti-Hindu purposes by a bigoted American writer, Katherine Mayo, helped to wreck her legal work. Her reaction was from that year to intensify her social work, which advanced from helping secluded women to enlisting them as helpers with a social conscience for their poorer sisters. But the immediate counter-activity of Gandhi's followers, not authorised by him, was to wreck her social work as well. Her unusual attitude to Gandhi led to her interview with him, which encapsulated their differences of character and belief. Her opposition to Gandhi resulted in a lack of recognition for her achievements in India. But after a brief period of embarrassment in the late 1920s, she was recognised in England and was still working with the Secretary of State for India in the desperate years of the Second World War. She had served under, and interacted with, seven Viceroys, was a close friend of two of them and of their wives, of two of the Secretaries of State, and of King George V and Queen Mary. But she felt herself at least as much a friend of the Indian secluded women whom she had helped.

She wrote her own excellent autobiography, *India Calling*.[2] But because of its sensitivity, she suppressed half of the details. Her three-year exile starting in 1901 from India to England to scotch a love affair is concealed, and to preserve the concealment, her encounters at that time with such leading cultural figures as G. F. Watts, Bernard Shaw and the serpentine Mrs Patrick Campbell are deliberately mis-dated. Yet it was thanks to her presence in England that her campaign for a job finally succeeded. Neither of her two love affairs is mentioned. Nor, except in the most oblique way, are the quarrels with certain British officials and their retaliation. Omitted too is any mention of the young suspect Nogen, her ward, whom Cornelia defended from a charge of terrorism, and rehabilitated against her colleagues' objections, only for him to confess the charge 12 years later to the Viceroy. Her tragic entanglement with the agenda of Katherine Mayo is missing, as is the wreckage of Cornelia's legal work which resulted partly from that and partly from anti-woman bias in the legal profession. As for the stories of her beloved women behind the curtain (purdahnashins), some are totally concealed, as is one of her most daring rescues at Ramgarh. In other cases, some stories about the women are publicly told, but the women's identities are concealed. Their lives are cut up into little episodes scattered through her public writings without names or with assumed names. It is only the personal papers which reveal that the stories often belong to the continuous life narratives of the same few people, which makes more sense of them, although concealment was necessary at the time, in order to protect identities.

As regards her own family she concealed things too. Her father's heroic conversion to Christianity carried an unhappy consequence which only he was happy to reveal. The indiscretions with men on the part of her older sisters, Zuleika and Pheroze, powerfully influenced Cornelia's own conduct, with unforeseen consequences, but the indiscretions are missing from her published work. The despair of her next youngest sister, Susie, at the painful illness which seemed to threaten the establishment of her schools is edited out of Cornelia's biography of that sister, who is presented as ever confident. Her feelings of jealousy in relation to her youngest sister, Alice, are very honestly told in her diaries and have been noticed by other writers, but are not available in her publications. Her relations with her brother Dick, my father, were even closer and he forms an integral part of her story.

Besides deliberate concealment, there are sometimes, chiefly as regards the early period of work in the Princely States, small variations between the original diary entry or letter and the literary account written up to 40 years later. This can be due to a memory slip, to the wish to protect identities, or to a tidying up for literary or other effect. In some cases it can be due to an incomplete knowledge at the time of the original entry of what the facts would turn out to be, so one cannot always be sure that the earlier account is more accurate. On the whole, the accounts tally and these less conscious variations do not significantly change the picture of Cornelia's life as the deliberate concealments do. More important are the differences of addressee among the unpublished accounts. Writing to a close friend about her wards, Cornelia sometimes gave her first impression of their startling predicaments in exotic terms that might seem to distance them. But by the time she reported to the British her official findings on the same situation, her accounts could hardly be more sympathetic to her wards, or more knowledgeable about their problems and prospects.

Cornelia's selectivity in her *published* work makes it essential to consult her unpublished papers and some writers have achieved good results from doing so. The most comprehensive use of papers to date has been that of Suparna Gooptu. In her book on Cornelia she has laid the groundwork,[3] wisely making a selection from the huge collection of materials. She has presented Cornelia's public life in concise form and made sympathetic use of selected private letters.[4] She has also achieved something very important. Suparna rejects such attitudes as 'Cornelia is a feminist; hooray!', or 'Cornelia is an imperialist. Let us ignore her!' Indian history contains individuals who do not necessarily fit into stereotypical categories.[5] And Suparna has opened the door to looking at the complexity of an Indian pioneer without having to use political pigeon-holes. There are other good writers too who have pointed out that Cornelia's multiple affiliations defy stereotyping.[6] But I shall not normally comment on the growing academic literature on Cornelia, however valuable. I want to write a more personal sort of book.

For this purpose I need to draw not only on Cornelia's official and professional papers, and not only on a selection of her more personal ones, but on all fifty years of the personal papers already mentioned, both letters and diaries, some of each being in my own collection. I also draw on my knowledge of Cornelia and her family and of what they said about her. It is the personal records that reveal the drama of her life. They also uncover major events which she deliberately concealed. They help to explain how she succeeded in obtaining a legal post after ten years of opposition to a woman from 1894–1904, and they exhibit her success in the first ten years of that post from 1904–1914, before renewed opposition to a woman made it a struggle. These ten relatively unopposed years alter the balance of good will and opposition in her story, as does her recognition in England in the Second World War from 1939 onwards. The personal papers also make it possible to fill out the story of her family, both parents and siblings, and of their impact on her, and to reconstruct the stories of her wards. Her wards' stories bring out the nature and continuity of her work more fully than the scattered episodes she committed to print.

It is on Cornelia's work in India for the disadvantaged women behind the purdah that I want to focus, tracing the narratives of some of the estates and her rescue operations, because I see that as the centrepiece of her life's work. Her background and preparation[7] paved the way for her campaign for a job and for her enthralling 18-year career working for purdahnashins up to the age of 54.[8]

Equally, her return to India after retirement until the age of 63[9] bears on the same theme. For, insofar as that later work was successful, it developed her earlier work and developed it in interesting ways, to help disadvantaged Indian women and protect her wards' estates. No one else ever visited hundreds of secluded female households and discussed with them their most intimate problems year after year for 18 years. Cornelia provides primary source material on a closed society of 100 years ago which has been swept away.

The personal account of her life and career still provides many glimpses of the wider background of India. The predicaments of her secluded wards were one aspect of India,[10] along with their customs, beliefs and attitudes.[11] Another aspect was the colour of her travels through Indian jungles and deserts to visit her remote estates,[12] and of life first among the gardens of Poona,[13] then in the bazaars and on the lawns of Allahabad[14] and after that in the pomp and ceremony of the British administration in Calcutta.[15] She was always conscious of her own Indian costume and of that of others. The British-run Indian Civil Service was another aspect of India, and the Service will be described both in its strengths[16] and in its weaknesses, although the weaknesses will be different from those usually attended to. The quarrels and harassment[17] not only reveal what Cornelia had to overcome, but also are a side of the Indian Civil Service never revealed in public even by Cornelia, but recoverable from the privacy of her diaries and confidential letters. Yet another aspect of India was sporadic terrorism against the British.[18] I shall tell the story of Cornelia's dealings with two self-confessed terrorists, both of whom were rewarded after their confessions.

In her retirement, Cornelia came to be involved in the new landscape of Gandhi's India, and this is where her ability to surmount obstacles began to falter. Cornelia was opposed to Gandhi. She was startled by his new disobedience to law. She had been a friend of an earlier nationalist, Gandhi's guru Gokhale, and had seen the equally law-abiding nationalism of Tagore.[19] That, along with the perspective of her women wards, which was incompatible with Gandhi's, as well as her faith in her British supporters, helps to explain Cornelia's opposition to him.[20] She shared some ethical beliefs with Gandhi, but was not able to appreciate the whole remarkable range of his ideals. Nonetheless, her personal confrontation with him reveals much about his own character and attitudes as well as about hers.[21] Moreover, the enormity of the task of making a single country out of India is clarified by Cornelia's familiarity with constituencies very different from those to which Gandhi appealed directly: the purdahnashins and[22] the Indian Princes.

Cornelia's acceptance of two things that were to be swept away can seem pathetic in retrospect, the British Empire, and, in its gentler aspects, the system of seclusion or 'purdah' for women. This acceptance distanced her from movements that were actually going to shape Indian history. But at that time, after ten years of effort, she had found it was only through the post she got created by the reluctant British that she could bring help to Indian women. She did bring the first and only legal protection and support to hundreds of vulnerable women and children, and she did so from the position of being an outsider herself, a woman among males, an Indian among the English, a Christian among Parsees and a Parsee among Hindus and Muslims.[23]

The 1890s, when Cornelia was young, were a long way from the Independence Movement of the 1920s. She had tried every door into the legal profession to help women, including the courts of Maharajas, who were at least less prejudiced than the British against woman lawyers. But with British domination of the legal system, there was no realistic way for her to bring legal help to Indian women, if she could not persuade the British to give her entry.

Often we have only Cornelia's word for what happened and she may be wrong. Only occasionally do I have any way of querying her account of vulnerabilities in a closed society of a century ago. Some of her claims are about horrifying things: murders, intended murders, death threats, unrelenting maltreatment of wives and heinous conduct on the part of certain individuals both British and Indian. She stood up impartially to what she saw as maltreatment of her wards from whatever direction it came. I should not be taken as endorsing her allegations or her lesser criticisms, but as giving them the expression that she often could not give them in her public writings at the time.

I shall not only use Cornelia's personal papers. I shall also often borrow her words and also provide quotations from published and unpublished work. She was very good at describing scenes and also at expressing her own feelings, especially in her diaries, with astonishing honesty. Publication of some of her diaries and letters was her wish, as she told her family and the man who was her dearest beloved.[24] She also left money in her will for a biography, but the draft was not accepted for publication.

THE AUTHOR'S INDIAN BIRTHRIGHT

To their little nephew, born in England in 1934, Cornelia and her sister Alice emphasised the romance of Princely India which they knew a little boy would like. Tantalisingly removed from his Indian heritage, this is what the author duly emphasised to his schoolfriends, and the romantic picture he painted influenced them in turn. Yet Alice herself had reservations in her novels about the influence of the English on Indian Princes, and my adult view has become very different from my childhood view of India. My view of Gandhi is also different from Cornelia's view of him and I hope that another book of mine in preparation on Mahatma Gandhi and his world, so different from that of the Princes,[i] may even make some amends for Cornelia's hostility to that giant. But some of my schoolfriends continued to see me in the romantic guise I adopted as a child. My poet schoolfriend, Jon Stallworthy, went on to write a poem after our student days seeing me as an Indian Raja whose birthright he had stolen by reaching the Indian subcontinent before I did. He spoke of 'a cabin trunk belonging to your aunt'. It was the cabin trunk of the much-travelled Cornelia still in my possession. In my childhood it contained turbans, my father's Persian fez which Cornelia so much liked him to wear, and strips of saree materials for play acting. I quote Jon's poem with his permission from *The Critical Quarterly* 5, 1963, p. 1326.

The Birthright

Richard Sorabji – five light syllables
return me to the playground where we met,
bronze hand to plaster hand, pitching marbles;

two seven-year olds, one in a secret
chrysalid dream of India, and one
whose India was the map's pink silhouette.

You peel me time-past like an onion,
transparent year by year. Riding to school
howdah-high in a tunic and turban -

plump as a pigeon egg your turban jewel -
you call me to your side, caparison
with tiger skins my starveling bicycle.

The gold umbrella, like a subject sun,
haloes you to Durbars where you mount,
last of the Moghuls, the Peacock throne -

a cabin trunk belonging to your aunt.
'Fetch my lord a golden sword, and let his wrist
be royally falconed for the wildfowl hunt.'

---

i Richard Sorabji, book in preparation, tentative title, *The Stoics and Gandhi: Modern Experiments on Ancient Values*.

Strange, that to your country I come first:
stranger, to find myself no stranger now
to the pulse of paddles and the Jhelum mist

garlanding willows and a sword-fish prow.
Your evening, Richard, fills my lap with light:
most prodigal of rajahs, to add now
to your boyhood gifts that of your birthright.

ACKNOWLEDGEMENTS

I am very grateful to Soli Sorabjee for reading my chapter on legal practice, Chapter 17, and to Suparna Gooptu for looking at my two chapters on Gandhi, Chapters 20 and 21. I am grateful to Suparna Gooptu more personally for showing me Writers' Buildings, where Cornelia had her office during her main career, the third storey room in the Calcutta High Court to which Cornelia was confined when a woman was not allowed in the bar library, the bar library itself, now full of women, the interior of Government House, Calcutta, where Cornelia was for many years the only Indian woman entertained, and Warren Hastings's house, which Cornelia so often tried and failed to obtain for social service for her purdahnashins. My special thanks go to my daughter, Cornelia Sorabji, to Rajeshwari Sunder Rajan and to Janet Morgan, all of whom read and commented on the entire manuscript and gave me the benefit of the most astute and expert advice. I thank my wife, Kate Sorabji, for reading the whole manuscript with an eye to readability. I benefited greatly from helpful comments by Liz Friend-Smith at Tauris. I am most grateful to David Godwin for recommending the book to Penguin India from whom I gained some further helpful comments. I gratefully acknowledge the help of Balliol College Library in giving me access to letters of Cornelia to Benjamin Jowett, of Dr David Pat Shui Fong for permission to reproduce his photograph of Tajhat Palace, of Dr Keith Hannabuss and Brian Foster for the photograph of a modern Balliol concert and of the British Library for permission to reproduce their copy of a photo in Cornelia's papers of herself with Blair's hourse and buggy. I am grateful to Mr Dinesh Gupta, Registrar General of the Allahabad High Court, whose photograph of Harrison Falkner Blair enabled me to identify the one that Cornelia kept in her own papers. The publication of this book by I. B. Tauris has been assisted by grants from the Scouloudi Foundation and the Jowett Copyright Trustees.

MAP OF INDIA

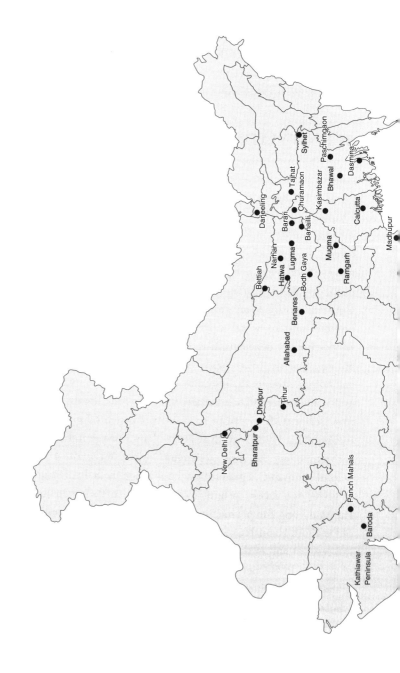

Darjeeling
Sylhet
Tajhat
Churamaon
Paschimgaon
Kasimbazar
Bhawal
Dasmina
Barari
Bahalili
Calcutta
Namhar
Hatwa
Lugma
Mugma
Madhupur
Bettiah
Bodh Gaya
Ramgarh
Benares
Allahabad
Tirhur
Dholpur
Bharatpur
New Delhi
Panch Mahals
Baroda
Kathiawar
Peninsula

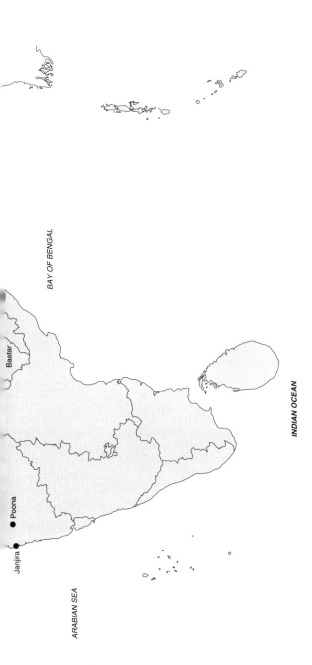

BAY OF BENGAL

Bastar

Poona

Janjira

ARABIAN SEA

INDIAN OCEAN

FAMILY TREE

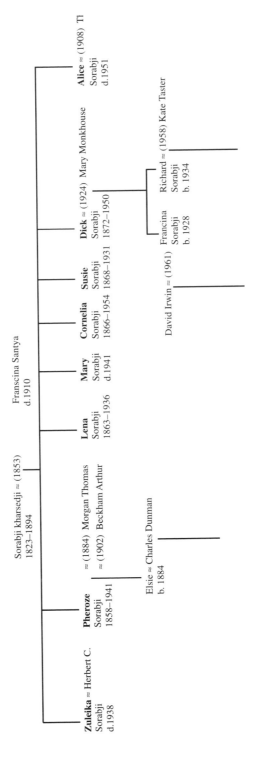

Sorabji kharsedji ≈ (1853)   Franscina Santya
1823–1894   d.1910

Zuleika ≈ Herbert C.
Sorabji
d.1938

Pheroze   ≈ (1884) Morgan Thomas
Sorabji   ≈ (1902) Beckham Arthur
1858–1941

Elsie ≈ Charles Dunman
b. 1884

Lena
Sorabji
1863–1936

Mary
Sorabji
d.1941

Cornelia
Sorabji
1866–1954

Susie
Sorabji
1868–1931

Dick ≈ (1924) Mary Monkhouse
Sorabji
1872–1950

Alice ≈ (1908) Tl
Sorabji
d.1951

David Irwin ≈ (1961)

Francina
Sorabji
b. 1928

Richard ≈ (1958) Kate Taster
Sorabji
b. 1934

PART I

PREPARATION AND BACKGROUND FROM 1866

CHAPTER 1

PARENTS AND FAMILY AND MOVE TO OXFORD

Cornelia Sorabji, the one who would interpret East and West to each other: that was how Benjamin Jowett, Oxford's leading figure, described Cornelia, when she came from India to Oxford in 1889. Nobody could foresee then that she would be Oxford's and India's woman pioneer in law, nor that she would record unique knowledge of the life of secluded women and of the daily workings of the British Raj. She was wholly Indian, a Parsee, beautiful and beautifully dressed in Indian sarees, but otherwise brought up in India by her Indian parents in English style.

Born on November 15th 1866, she was only 22 when she landed in England on September 19th 1889. She was coming up, in much heralded circumstances, as a student to Somerville College, Oxford's first women's college, then only ten years old. Writing home about her arrival, she said, 'How I do hope all will be successful.'[1] When I first read those words of 1889 after Cornelia's death in 1954, I wanted to assure her, 'All will be successful.' But after reading the daily account of her life over 50 years and more, I now know that her story is more complex. She herself was to say wistfully in old age, 'I think of my first visit, so young and full of life.'[2]

PARENTS AND FAMILY

Cornelia's family provide part of the context for understanding her. Not only had she absorbed her parents' beliefs and values, but all her life she was to be reacting to her sisters. Her brother Dick will be described as her story unfolds, because he shared her life at Oxford and was to share a house with her when they both got back to India. But her parents and six sisters need more introduction, starting with her father, Sorabji Kharsedji.

FATHER

Cornelia's father (my grandfather) was born 187 years ago in 1823, when Napoleon was only two years dead. Sorabji lost his father at the age of 13. His oldest sister's husband, Cawasjee, became his faithful and much loved guardian. Cawasjee was a cousin who had been brought up by Sorabji's mother when orphaned. Sorabji Kharsedji suffered near-martyrdom from his fellow-Zoroastrians in Bombay (Mumbai) when he converted to Christianity at the age of 16. His story is no less heroic for involving a feature which Cornelia omitted when she wrote about her parents in a book called *Therefore*. But the omitted feature is honestly told in a simple and straightforward way by Sorabji Kharsedji himself in his own unpublished account of his life. [3]

He had six surviving sisters, but was the youngest and the only surviving son out of seven boys, in a Parsee family in Bombay who were practising Zoroastrians. History was to repeat itself, since his son Dick was to be the only surviving boy out of three, with seven sisters. The Parsees had fled to India from the Muslim invasion of Persia in the ninth century CE. Sorabji Kharsedji's position as the youngest and only surviving son after so many losses made him the apple of his parents' eye, cared for by six older sisters, all married. According to his own account, nothing was too good or too expensive for him and his slightest wish was fulfilled with prodigal lavishness.

His first language was Gujarati, but as a relative of the Zoroastrian High Priest, he learnt the scriptural languages Pahlavi and Zend as well as Persian. As an extra precaution for his physical safety, his adoring mother took him to a Catholic chapel and had him kiss a silver image of the baby Jesus and place it in the arms of a statue of the Virgin Mary, while she said, 'Ave Maria'.

Sorabji Kharsedji's education included several false starts. At seven, he went to a Gujarati school to learn reading, writing and arithmetic, then very briefly to Dr Wilson's controversial proselytising Missionary college, to learn English, but only for two months as he did not like it, and asked to be transferred to learn business. When he did not like apprenticeship to a merchant in the opium and silk trade with China, he moved again to a more literary occupation as an apprentice to newspaper editors, the second of whom edited a reforming paper, *Chabook* or *The Whip*, which criticised the Parsees' treatment of the poor. Although that encouraged radical ideas, Sorabji, aged 12, was entirely on the side of his paper's vigorous protests when two Zoroastrian boys from his former college, Dr Wilson's, were converted to Christianity.

Conversion had been disallowed by the British East India Company until about 1820 as disruptive to trade, but then it had been allowed and an aggressive type of conversion was sometimes practised involving denigration of other religions. This was true of some conversions of Bombay Zoroastrian school children. The first two happened in 1835–6 with another in 1839, and they caused riots.[4] The convert of 1839, unlike Sorabji Kharsedji, regarded Zoroastrianism as Satan's religion. But although they had abandoned their religion, both were proud of their ethnic identity as Parsees,[5] or descendants of ancient refugees from Persia, an identity which passes through the father's side of the family. Zoroastrians did not proselytise at all, and in practice conversion separated people from their families. This background explains why the Parsees were already very sensitive to conversions, and why so many were willing to make attempts on Sorabji Kharsedji's life, when they could not dissuade him.

There was an even worse feature, the one that Cornelia does not mention. Sorabji Kharsedji had a wife of his own age, having married her when he was between five and six. He calls her fair and beautiful. It is easy to imagine why Cornelia left this out. Such early marriage was exactly what she saw in the case of Hindus as causing the most terrible hardship to wives, who were supposed to be married at a similarly early age between four and eight. She did not think the practice could be cured by legislation, but she did think that it should be changed by education. The hardship caused to Sorabji's devoted wife may have been less than that which Cornelia was seeking to alleviate in Hinduism. Zoroastrianism allowed, Hinduism at that time normally forbade, remarriage to women. But Cornelia's father found his wife's pleas excruciating, and the hardship caused was a downside to the conversion whose heroic character was only now about to begin.

The conversion came about in the following way. In 1840 at the age of 16, to avoid returning to commerce with his uncle, Sorabji Kharsedji undertook to learn English, and as Dr Wilson's school was banned by Zoroastrians, he enlisted at the Robert Money School with Mr Valentine of the Church Missionary Society as tutor. Conversions in this school were not sought in the same way. One day, a teacher set Sorabji Kharsedji the wrong homework, and when he was as a result unprepared, called him a fool. Sorabji struck the teacher on the head, dislodged the folds of his turban, and was reported to Mr Valentine. He expected punishment and prepared defiance, but Mr Valentine took him entirely by surprise. He talked to him lovingly and gave him to read Christ's Sermon on the Mount. He felt that Mr Valentine showed the qualities of forgiveness found in the Sermon, whereas he, Sorabji, was unworthy. So he enlisted in Bible classes, as well as his two evenings a week in lectures on Hinduism and Zoroastrianism.

Sorabji wanted his wife to accompany him to the classes, but she entreated him with tears and sobs to desist, and asked how his Gospel could allow him to abandon and dishonour his mother and family. His mother in consultation with his guardian, Cawasjee, arranged to send him out of harm's way to the mercantile uncle in China. He was heir to this uncle as well as to his father and would have inherited a fortune from both, but this he gave up. The day before he was due to sail, he slipped out to Malabar Hill to find the school principal, and then onward, at his advice, to Mr Valentine at the Mission House by a circuitous route. But over 200 Parsees crowded round the Mission House gate, and 30 to 40 broke in and came up to the first floor bringing Sorabji's mother and wife, whose lamentations were too heart-rending for Sorabji Kharsedji to describe even 50 years later. When their persuasion failed, those below carried Sorabji off bodily to a waiting carriage, but Mr Valentine appealed to the bazaar master, who was passing, and who took Sorabji down to the police court at Mazagon. There a magistrate bound over a dozen Parsees to keep the peace and allowed Sorabji to remain in the police court house, where a Muslim lady lived who urged him to keep to his new faith. But about 40 Parsees hid in neighbouring buildings with a view to carrying him off, and the servants of the Muslim lady warned against accepting food from Mr Valentine's servants. Instead, Mrs Valentine cooked his food and Mr Valentine brought it over twice a day.

After a month, the police superintendent with 12 horsemen dashed up and whisked him back to Mr Valentine, where he was able to stay guarded by his tutor who slept beside him for safety. But every week, his mother would visit with his wife or a sister with food offerings and much weeping. Friends also brought him food purported to come from his mother, but Mr Valentine had it tried on a dog, which died of poison.

After four months, his mother persuaded him to visit her at a sister's house, not bringing his usual two police escorts, in case the Parsees got excited. He was carried in Mr Valentine's palanquin with only its four carriers for company. A crowd of 2000 Parsees mobbed the house, and though he escaped through the back door to the waiting carriers, they were stoned by volley after volley, until the palanquin broke and the wounded carriers dropped him and fled. He was opposite the European General Hospital and he knew where to find the sentry and ran straight there. But the sentry took him to be a fugitive from justice and pointed his bayonet. By chance, two passing Scottish missionaries recognised him and took him by the arm and carried him off.

The next plan in 1842 was to send him far away to Ahmedabad to stay with the English commissioner at Sircage and work as a catechist for the Society for the Propagation of the Gospel, and there he was safe for a while. But when he went one day without protection to look for a book on his own, he was seized and gagged. A faithful servant followed and discovered that Sorabji Kharsedji was taken to jail, where a jailer was bribed to put him in a cell. The English Commissioner then disguised himself as a jailer and rescued him, but Ahmedabad was no longer safe and Sorabji Kharsedji returned to Mr Valentine in Bombay.

In the most dramatic attempt on his life, he was pushed out to sea in a boat without provisions or oars, but he was washed up into a creek and rescued by fishermen several days later. He was woken up by water dashed in his face, and found Goanese men from Mahim on the Bombay coast bending over him. They sent a message concealed in a hollow reed to alert his English friends.

After that in 1844, when he was 21, he made a complete change of scene. He had already been baptised. He never expected that his wife would be restored to him, although a friend attempted to secure that in the civil courts, but expected that she would be given in marriage to another. Nine years later he was himself to remarry and go on to start a family. For the present he was attached to the Bishop of Bombay as interpreter on the Bishop's country tours with a surgeon round villages as far afield as Baroda (Vadodara) and at least some of the time stayed in the Bishop's Poona home. He then moved on to Nasik (Nashik), to help run an orphanage under the Church Missionary Society and establish a Christian colony and an industrial settlement which trained rescued Arabian and Abyssinian child kidnap victims.[6]

He was ordained much later in 1878 when the family had moved to Poona, and after that he worked, first as an 'honorary' missionary, for the Society for the Propagation of the Gospel and the Church Missionary Society. This unpaid status fell short of the conditions on which another of the Zoroastrian converts, Nowroji, had insisted, with Dr Wilson's backing, of full equality with English missionaries with full evangelistic power and liberty, and of the payment of 375 pounds a month that Cornelia records for English missionaries in 1893.[7]

Cornelia remembers her father as a scholar in his study, stooped, wearing Persian dress and hat. His scholarly work included membership of the committee for translating the Bible into Gujarati. He was reconciled with members of his family, some of whom came to stay. It was a point of pride with him, with Cornelia and with his other daughters to call themselves Parsees, that is descendants through the father's side of refugees from Persia, and to wear their sarees in Parsee style, despite not now being Zoroastrian by religion. He interacted too with the Zoroastrian High Priest and persuaded him to agree in print that an important part of the Zoroastrian scripture, a body of law called the 'Vendidad', was an addition to the text interpolated later. Cornelia was home in time to see him before he died in 1894, but Dick, whom he had not seen since 1886, did not get back from England until 1896.

Cornelia was very broken by her father's death, as she tells Lady Hobhouse:[8]

'My dear Father went from us on the 14th August, and we are unspeakably deso-late without him. I cannot realise it even now, and one thinks and thinks and longs. Alas! Sleep is the happiest time of one's existence, for one can then even hear his voice and touch him and look upon him; of course there is the waking: but even then one goes through one's day the stronger somehow for that blessed imagination which has stood in the place of memory. The worst pity of it all, how-ever, is that he did not live to see my brother alas! – and for the last five years and more he has seemed to live only to look on him once again. In truth none but the Infinite Pity can suffice for the Infinite pathos of human life. But it was that very Infinite Pity which did it all – I cannot understand – it is too great a mystery.'

Cornelia repeated this in the 14 page booklet she wrote, 'How an Indian Clergyman died',[9] in which she treated his death as a model for others.

Twenty five years later in 1919, in consoling her friend Elena, Cornelia wrote about the loss she still felt.[10]

'I feel as if it were only yesterday that my own father died (so little do the years efface memory). Though it was 25 years ago that he left me. And I cannot prom-ise that one's longing for the beloved dead gets less poignant with the years. But I can tell you from my experience the blessed fact that the years *do* bring them nearer. In some subtle heartward way, they *are* with us whenever we send out our yearning and desolation and need and *trust*, to seek them.'

MOTHER

Cornelia's mother, Franscina Santya, grew up in the Nilgiri hills.[11] She had lost her own mother when young and, according to one report, was at first brought up by missionaries. That would account for her perfect English and her Christianity. Lady Ford, wife of a British colonel, got to know her on her summer visits to the cool of the hills, while her husband Sir Francis Ford stayed down in the plains as Colonel of his regiment. Having lost her own daughter, she virtually adopted Franscina Santya from her twelfth year around 1844–5, which Franscina's step mother willingly allowed, and taught her English ways.

Cornelia and her siblings were later to speak English as their mother tongue and with the exact accent of the English establishment.

Cornelia's mother was born a Hindu and is so described in Lady Hobhouse's appeal for funds for Cornelia and in a well-informed account of 1891.[12] The broad, determined features in her photograph[13] are distinctive and I once mistakenly conjectured that she might instead have originated as a member of the Toda tribe who live in those hills, but later abandoned that conjecture for want of evidence. Further unreliable specifications assigned Cornelia's mother's mother variously to the Chamars or tanners, a category of Dalit (then called 'Untouchables'), or to Rajput stock.[14]

Around 1850, when Franscina was 17, Colonel Ford's regiment moved to Nasik, the very same town where Sorabji was helping to run the orphanage and industrial settlement. There the couple met and married in 1853. Sorabji Kharsedji was able to build a house in Nasik called Rusul Bagh.[15] The first five daughters were born there and Lady Ford's name, Cornelia, was given to the fifth daughter. The Fords returned to England and Lady Ford was in Tunbridge Wells. Much later she received the eldest daughter in 1885 and Franscina in 1886. But

3. Cornelia's mother (extreme left) with her school, 1876–1909, in grounds of the Poona home. Her father (inset).

before that, the Indian family had to move from missionary to Government work, in order to earn enough money. They went in 1867 briefly to Sholapur, where Susie was born in 1868, then to Belgaum, the birthplace of the last two, Dick (1872) and Alice (1873), and then to Poona by 1874, Cornelia's eighth year.

FAMILY LIFE IN POONA

In Poona, Cornelia's parents took a house at 80 Civil Lines with a garden behind, and a porch and a creeper in front, which climbed to the roof.[16] The house was still intact with many of the family furnishings on my visit a hundred and thirty two years later in 2008. The grandfather clock was there, along with the beds, pictures of Versailles on the walls and the original stained glass windows, some Victorian, some Art Nouveau. The upright piano had been converted to a writing desk. By the porch stood the family's two-wheeled carriage of wood and brass with shafts for the horse. The ornate banisters up to the first floor were unchanged, and a first floor room stretching the full depth of the house had stained glass on the balcony in front and in the bathroom behind.

Before the family came to Poona, their father had taught the children history, English literature and mathematics. But in Poona, the house was spacious

4. Cornelia's childhood home, Poona: the family clock with her great niece, Cornelia.

5. Cornelia's childhood home, Poona: the family carriage still at the porch.

6. Cornelia's childhood home, Poona: verandah of her parents' bedroom.

enough to set up a school. They called the house 'Langrana House',[17] the Parsee
family name of Sorabji Kharsedji, and the school 'the Victoria High School'.
It started in 1875 with seven pupils of all ethnic groupings and both genders,
Cornelia, aged 9, being one of the first seven. Three years later she was helping to teach. The children would easily have fitted at first into the 18 rooms of
the house. But eventually it grew to nearly 400 pupils and the parents built a
substantial stone school house and dining room, which still stand in the garden.
To one side of it was added the thatched bungalow for the infant Parsee school,
the only building taken down, but it is recorded in the photograph of Franscina
Sorabji and her teachers (see photo on page 9). The instruction, lasting from
nursery up to University, was in English, except at the infant Parsee school,
which used Gujarati. When Franscina had retired from teaching, the house and
school were sold in 1909 to the Ritz Hotel, whose two careful owners have
preserved so much of the original.

The family also acquired a holiday bungalow in the woods in Lanowli
(Lonavla), where the children would tent under the trees, build play houses, or
swing from branch to branch and play hide and seek.[18] Cornelia described the
holiday bungalow as somewhat like the Belgaum bungalow of her early years.
Both were:

> 'single-storied bungalows with deep verandahs, set in gardens of flowers and
> shady trees. I remember chiefly the *Champak*, white-limbed, adorned with the
> exquisite ivory-petalled flower that held a golden secret in the bottom of the
> cup; and the tall straight teak trees beside our tennis court, lighted with spiral
> candles when in bloom; … *quisqualis*, a tangle of pink, red and white, the blaze
> of tomato-coloured flowers in crisp bunches, the Indian honeysuckle which
> grew along the wall beside my room, the "Elephant-creeper", great bell-shaped
> lilac flowers which covered the wide porch.'[19]

There were still timbered Parsee bungalows in the woods at Lanowli, and
still gardens bursting with flowers in Poona on my visit in 1988. After leaving England, Cornelia resumed annual visits with her ageing parents to their
holiday woods in Lanowli, and she described to Jowett exploring the Buddhist
caverns sculpted in antiquity amongst the forests with their fireflies.

> 'I landed the end of April and we spent all May encamped on the outskirts of a
> great Indian forest – our summer home, among the hills. I wish you could see
> our hills with their great weird caverns, and their lovely huge woods, and their
> wild and simple grandeur. The trees are so large one can house oneself among
> the branches, and they hold out friendly arms to each other, so that if one would,
> one could walk the whole forest stepping from tree to tree. Then at night they

are gorgeous, our forest trees, lit up with innumerable fireflies – dear little things with green lights in their tails, but marvellously luminous.

'They have often guided us across the hills on dark nights and over danger-ous ground. Some of the caves close by where we were encamped are famous Buddhist remains. We climbed the hills to some, one morning, which date back to *200 B.C.* The largest cave was a good bit larger than Balliol Hall, and the roof and sides were ornamented with most perfectly carved episodes from the life of Buddha and early *Rishis* – all worked into the solid rock – and a great image of Buddha sitting under a lotus leaf presided over things in general at one end of the Hall.

'We had a long climb and the air was fresh, and –must I confess it? – we ate an excellent breakfast under the shadow of the great Buddha himself. However, he smiled on us serenely the while, and judgment has not yet overtaken us, so we hope that he has pitied our weakness and forgiven us'.[20]

The children were brought up English in one way and international in another: English, in that they spoke English, learnt the alphabet by rhymes (A was for 'Appaji Bapaji') and had English nursery rhymes and stories, though their mother made up Indian versions for Indians. They had English furniture, as did many Parsees, and English plates and cutlery, but their food was often Parsee. They were made to learn Marathi, the language of the Hindus, and they were told about their own Persian origins. They knew the religious obli-gations of others, and people exchanged delicacies with their mother at the time of their diverse religious festivals. People of all races and religions came to consult her, and Hindus, Muslims and Parsees were introduced to her English friends. The two Mysore bulls who drew the family wagon were dis-tinctively Indian. Their games were mixed, though to a large extent English. They were for ever playing with their Zoroastrian neighbours next door in Poona, the Candy family,[21] who had them to stay at their holiday retreat in Mahableshwar where they went riding. Hindus and Muslims lived in another part of town in houses with very different arrangements, courtyards, little furniture, and for better off Hindus, separate women's quarters.

The family discipline was English, with an elder sister appointed in lieu of a governess for each younger sister. Cornelia fell under Mary.[22] The official governess had been sacked after leading Susie, aged seven, and two English children, one nine and one six, to a broad path in the woods in Mahableshwar called 'Tiger Path'. They left their pony tonga or trap outside the woods, prob-ably where the polo ground now is. But when a tigress unexpectedly appeared, holding her cub in her mouth, the governess fled back to the tonga, leaving the three little children. The tigress put down its cub and growled at them, but the nine-year-old had the three link hands and outstare the tigress, who picked up its cub again and turned back into the forest.[23] Cornelia would have liked to be part of Susie's adventure.

The family all sang and the children all played European music. On first arriving in England, Cornelia discussed what music she had left behind in Poona.[24] Alice accompanied everyone impromptu on the piano,[25] while Pheroze played the organ[26] and Dick kept a piano for the whole of his life. On her return to India, Cornelia mentioned playing Chopin, Schubert and Beethoven, and she taught classical music at the Poona school.[27]

In Poona, Cornelia's mother founded two more schools besides the two in the family's grounds. They were for Hindu children who spoke Marathi and Muslim children who spoke Urdu. Both schools were free, being intended for the poor, and were run first by the eldest daughter Zuleika and then by Lena and Susie. In the Hindu and Muslim schools it was difficult at first to promote the idea of education for girls, which would mean postponing the safety of seclusion behind the curtain or 'purdah'. For Muslim girls it was all the more difficult because boys were attending as well as girls. There were to be initial difficulties even in the absence of boys at another school, the High School for Indian Girls, opened in Poona in 1884. Although this was not run by the family, one sister, Mary Sorabji, was asked to teach there from the opening, and she has left a description of how at first only twelve pupils, two of them widows, were brave enough to attend and in order to take them to school, they had to hire an old horse-drawn carriage with an *elderly* coachman accompanied by an escort of female servants.[28]

Besides founding the four schools, Cornelia's mother provided some of the only teacher-training in the Bombay Presidency. In 1882, she gave evidence on women's education to Sir William Hunter's Government Commission on Indian education, and in 1886 she made the fund-raising tour to England for her schools. Someone told Cornelia that she did not know what eloquence was until she heard her mother speak,[29] and later Cornelia on first arrival in England basked in her mother's popularity.[30] Cornelia's father, left behind in 1886 to look after the schools, wrote, 'I feel as though I had lost my right hand. Often when I have been in need of her wise counsel and prompt action, I have been forced to wait and hesitate.'

As well as teaching, her mother did social work in the villages around Poona. This proved particularly important at times of famine and later of plague, when she took into her household children, orphans and widows.

The plague was the real bubonic plague, the cause earlier in Europe of the Black Death and of the Plague of London. It came over in 1896 with rats in ships from China. Franscina's knowledge of the villagers' beliefs was invaluable, as she visited stricken regions with her family and school staff. Having first instructed her own servants, she then got the agreement of villagers to the measures which were so unpopular when carried out compulsorily. Feelings had been inflamed by British soldiers polluting idols and cooking pots by washing them in disinfectant. She herself helped disinfect, showed how to deal with rats and persuaded them that digging up their floors for reasons of drainage was not for the purpose of finding the family valuables which orthodox Hindus buried there. Nor could the removal of corpses by officials not of their caste possibly affect rebirth. But she found many corpses hidden from the compulsory inspections in bundles of clothes in the laundries. Objections about plague-stricken cows or horses in the house were almost as great. When the plague serum arrived, she went from house to house in the city persuading people they were not being injected with Christianity. She also helped to convince the authorities that different communities should be allowed to make their own arrangements, and have their own segregation camps.[31] Even so, Cornelia writes, a man was shot dead in Poona in the belief that he was the plague officer.[32] The school's chief Muslim woman teacher was taken to the plague shed and died in a single day, and her three orphan boys, once out of segregation, became permanent members of the Sorabji family household, featuring thereafter as 'the chicks' in the accounts of family life.[33]

This experience of plague was relevant to several members of the family. In 1898, Cornelia's sister Mary had a butler in Baroda, a Christian, whose child died of plague. Its parents were segregated and the coolies simply dropped the child's coffin. Mary, who had to leave her bungalow and have a course of innoculations, had the world's work to get the coffin carried at all, until she found some mission convert boys.[34] Dick appealed against the death sentence on one or more of the 14 Cawnpore (Kanpur) rioters, who had killed six policemen when attacking the huts in which plague victims had been isolated.[35] Cornelia learnt a very great deal towards the health care of her future clients, and one of her earliest literary stories is a story of plague, which shows an intimate knowledge of it.[36] But she underwent much anxiety, changing the culpable official in her story from a civilian to a tea planter, so as not to antagonise the Civil Service.[37]

Writing from England, Cornelia gives a picture of family personalities back in Poona. When her mother founded the new school for Muslims in 1890, she imagines that her father would have seen all the difficulties, but her mother would have said, persistent and calm, 'It must be done,' and, behold, it was done. Dick used to repeat his mother's phrase, 'Do it: that's the thing to do.' School prize-giving was a big feature of life. As Cornelia imagines it, Father is anxious that the ceremony should not be too long. Mother assures him that the girls will get it right. He recruits Zuleika and Mary to repeat his message. But Mary worries like her father, while Zuleika pleads that they cannot displease the parents who want to see the schoolchildren shown off, and then shows Father a deceptively short version of the programme. Lena, the thin one, asks, 'What does it matter?' None of the family is left with any time to eat, including Susie who arranges all the music and flowers.[38]

Cornelia speaks of a certain type of isolation of the family, but it was not a loneliness. Never was there a home of those days, she says, to which more people came of every race and condition, nor between which and other homes and people there was more traffic. She was rather speaking of 'an invisible circle' drawn round the family which brought them very close to one another, and which made it untypical of the Indian home of the period.[39] They were wholly Indian, yet brought up and educated English and Christian. This had no isolating effect except, as will be seen, in respect of marriage prospects.

In 1906, after 12 years as a widow,[40] Cornelia's mother retired and returned to her first married home in Nasik. Lena, who in 1896 had been in charge of the vernacular teaching, had since at least 1902 been virtually running the main English language school, apart from a recuperation period in England in 1904–1905. The Poona house and school was sold off in 1909, which is when it became the Ritz Hotel. But by that time Susie's plans to replace all the schools from scratch had all borne fruit. Meanwhile, in retirement in Nasik, their mother still took in orphans and had people to meals right up to her death at the age of 76 on October 24th 1910.

SISTERS

Cornelia's sisters very much shaped her life. The first two, Zuleika and Pheroze, she took as a warning, because they both got into difficulties with men friends. Pheroze married, but her daughter may have been conceived before wedlock.[41] Zuleika became attached to a man of whom the family strongly disapproved. Five years later she went on to do something so bad that in Cornelia's eyes 'only death could cure it'. I shall attempt to discover what the bad thing was in Appendix 1. For the moment, I will only say that Cornelia tried to avoid their fate by befriending only older men. This worked very well in her student days with Jowett, Grant Duff and Lord Hobhouse. But, we shall see, it almost scotched her career before it began when she tried the same policy in Allahabad.[42]

The third sister was the ever reliable Lena, who gave Cornelia so much support as headmistress of a school within Cornelia's area of operation in Bengal,[43] attended Mary and Dick in their depressions[44] and took over her mother's main school by 1902 and Susie's during 1923.[45] The fourth was Mary, who had acted as Cornelia's governess when she was small. They had still not quite escaped the relationship of Cornelia being wrong footed by Mary, when she shared Mary's flat in 1936–1939.

Cornelia was the fifth, but Susie, the sixth, was the one who did most for her mother's teaching projects in Poona. When her mother's schools were being closed on her retirement in 1906, the other sisters who had been helping gave up. But Susie, at the age of 34, and in appalling health, had made the most astounding fund-raising trip on her own to America, finishing up in the Rockefeller's New York mansion and President Theodore Roosevelt's White House, and she secured the money to start up new schools to carry on the work. Her main school, St Helena's, was flourishing with 3000 girls in its centenary year in 2008. It fell to Cornelia to abandon her own floundering work and go to Poona to ensure the continuation of Susie's school in 1931 when Susie died. The contrast between the admiration for Susie's work and the opposition to her own must have given her pause for thought. It was then that Cornelia gave up her main projects in India and her strenuous lecture tours in America just before and after this time seem to emulate Susie's.

The next child was Dick, who is part and parcel of Cornelia's story. But the youngest, Alice, gave Cornelia the most pause for thought. Cornelia may have started off as Alice's governess and protector of studies. She was delighted when Alice gained matriculation (admission) into Bombay University at 14, two years younger than herself, and became Bachelor of Science, with far more marks than any man in the examination. Cornelia went on to be the admonisher who criticised Alice for failing medical exams in London and for taking out educational loans to continue, warning her that she should not apply for work unsupervised by a superior. She was not prepared, then, for Alice to prove as successful as herself in almost every sphere: as a professional in medicine, as attracting the interest and friendship of the Viceroys for her social work, in her reputation for courage in the hair-raising dangers of the Afghan frontier, in her ability to run a hospital single-handed and even as a literary writer. She was pretty, where Cornelia was beautiful, and later stately, where Cornelia was formidable. In some spheres she surpassed Cornelia's aspirations, being sought out of the blue in marriage to a distinguished older Englishman, and being loved for her medical work, instead of being for ever opposed and even sabotaged, as would happen to Cornelia. Moreover, Alice had a cheerful and relaxed nature. She was not seeking to be the pioneer and had no particular interest in the praise which she received. This difference is very apparent in some of the photographs of Cornelia and Alice. Cornelia is always impeccable; Alice seems to have thrown her clothes on cheerfully. We shall encounter a number of situations in which Cornelia could not help feeling either jealous or worthless in comparison to her youngest sister and others in which her decisions, for example on seeking marriage, were a response to feelings about Alice. Sometimes there was direct competition on fund-raising for projects, and often political disagreement.

Cornelia's history cannot be understood without a fuller picture of the sisters to whom she was reacting. This is most of all true of Alice, whose success needs to be described, in order to see what made Cornelia so anxious. But each of the sisters had her own history. Those histories will make more sense, when the various encounters with Cornelia through her career have become familiar, and I shall present them in Appendix 1.

CORNELIA'S FIRSTS AT BOMBAY UNIVERSITY

Cornelia's father taught his first two daughters up to matriculation standard for the University of Bombay, but matriculation was refused to them as women. However Cornelia, with Mary as her appointed teacher, gained matriculation as the University's first woman at the age of 16. Cornelia then had to attend Deccan College in Poona, which was part of the University. As the only female among 300 males, she had to withstand hostility from the non-Parsee students. They played practical jokes on her, slammed classroom doors in her face and tried to keep her out of lectures. But her success was continuous. She completed the five-year Latin course in one year, gained a College scholarship each year, won the Havelock Prize and the Hughling's Scholarship of Bombay University for the highest candidate in the first Arts exam. In 1887, she was one of four students in Bombay University to win first class honours and was the top student in Deccan College. So she very much hoped to win one of the Government of India scholarships for that year to continue her studies in England.

Meanwhile in 1888 she saved some money by accepting an appointment to teach English Literature, again as the only woman among males, as Dakshina Fellow at Gujarat College, Ahmedabad. Aged only twenty one, she described her experience as follows. 'I do not like to recall my first lecture; but the men behaved well. One rather dreaded contest was all I have to record, and a little sarcasm cured the men. I found them docile and very appreciative'. After 3 months she was promoted for 6 months to Acting Professor of English, a role usually reserved for the College Principal. But meanwhile the hoped-for scholarship was denied her. The authorities objected that she was a woman, and that the creators of the scholarships had not envisaged that a woman could win.

7. Cornelia awaiting the restored scholarship to Oxford, 1889.

CORNELIA'S MOVE TO OXFORD

Nonetheless the doors to England and Oxford were opened from another side. A question was raised in the House of Commons by Sir John Kennaway, whose home at Escot in Devon Cornelia was repeatedly to visit. She would come to know him as 'Father of the House' – Parliament's longest-serving member. His long white beard, almost a badge of office, was said to have been the inspiration for a famous rhyme, a 'limerick', by Edward Lear, 'There was an old man with a beard, …'.[i] He spoke both as a senior member of the House of Commons and as one whose family had been in the forefront of the British conquest of India. The Secretary of State for India replied that the story of the scholarship denied was indeed true, but that the scholarships were not yet open to women.

Once the denial of the scholarship was known in England, Lady Hobhouse, whose husband had been Law Member of the Governor General's Council (later the Viceroy's Council) in India, wrote a letter to *The Times* on April 13th 1888.[46] She thereby rallied a number of prominent people to create a substitute scholarship for Cornelia after all. One of them was the founder of modern nursing, Florence Nightingale. The support of Florence Nightingale was natural, because,[47] although she had made her name much earlier when reducing mortality rates in the Crimean War of 1854–6, she had since 1864 agitated by correspondence for the improvement of health in India. In 1885, she had been occupied with a request to advise on a sanitation text book to be used especially for helping secluded women in India, and later in 1897 she was to be in close correspondence with one of the English nurses who was helping with the bubonic plague in Poona at the same time as Cornelia's mother.

CORNELIA'S ARRIVAL IN ENGLAND

Cornelia reached England after a rough 35-day voyage from India at 5.30 on the morning of September 19th 1889.[48] Dick, her younger brother, was there to meet her. He had gone to England for his schooling three years before and

---

i In one version:

 There was an old man with a beard
 Who said, 'It is just as I feared.
 Two owls and a wren,
 Three rooks and a hen,
 Have all made a nest in my beard'.

had in the meantime entirely changed in appearance. So when at 9.30 the tug brought him with an older lady to take Cornelia ashore at Liverpool, she was the only passenger who did not recognise the tall person waving on the dock as her brother. She tells her family in India of her surprise at his maturity:[49]

'I *was* so pleased to see Dick. He looks so big and strong – a head and shoulders over me. I have not got over his size yet and have quite succumbed to it. He took me in hand at once: saw about my luggage. … He has a man's voice and air – and I feel so small next to him and so befriended. He talks and behaves like a gentleman, but is as cheeky to me as Alice is' (the youngest of the family). 'He wears a small sporting moustache – Lena' (she tells an older sister), 'please put on a veil. Indeed, I blushed inwardly at kissing this stalwart youth. I think he still regards home with his old affection and he is not at all spoilt with the attentions he has been receiving. His change of plans' (not to try for the Indian Civil Service exam) 'stun me – but Father has telegraphed consent, so we must just hope all is for the best'.

Two days after her arrival on September 21st, Cornelia visited her sponsor, Lady Hobhouse, in London. Lady Hobhouse showed Cornelia a piece about her, asking for contributions, in a magazine for Society ladies, *The Queen*.[50] It had Cornelia's striking photograph as the frontispiece. But Cornelia was still taken by surprise a week later when the editor of a magazine called *Echo* said she had had the desire of her life in being introduced to her, because Cornelia's graduation had made her a heroine. She thought the editor was joking and felt small, and she was to feel similar disbelief when two weeks into her first term as a newcomer to Oxford, an 'at home' (reception) was given in Oxford for people to meet her. Her photograph was sent by the hostess, Miss Weld, to her uncle, the Poet Laureate Tennyson.

Before the Oxford term started, Cornelia had a role to perform as a sister six years older than her brother Dick. He, born on July 11th 1872, had moved from being a 'day boarder', aged 14, at Dulwich School in 1886[51] to boarding at the South-eastern College, Ramsgate. His guardian at Ramsgate had reported, 'Dick has neither first class nor even second class abilities.' His formidable sister went down to the school to 'act the inspector' and 'insist on being made acquainted with all he is being taught'. She wanted him 'examined in his classes by his own masters in my presence'. Arriving there on October 11th, she got a much more favourable report from the master with whom Dick was living. The master's wife had cared for Dick like a mother and they both became very friendly with Cornelia too. Nonetheless, she thought that other masters were leaving Dick to teach himself, so that he was behind except in Latin and Greek, and she asked for a 'weekly report in each subject'. Within a year, she would arrange for him to leave and would help him, through her new contacts at Oxford University, to get in as a fellow-student at Oxford in a man's college, Balliol.

CHAPTER 2

THE OXFORD UNIVERSITY OF BENJAMIN JOWETT 1889–1892

Two of England's universities, Oxford and Cambridge, were six hundred years old in 1889 (now over seven hundred). Standards in Oxford had slipped earlier in the nineteenth century. But Jowett restored them in his Oxford college, Balliol, when he selected pupils by examination instead of through old networks. With the support of the Prime Minister William Gladstone, he also made Balliol the leading college for training young men to go out as administrators to India. He knew the leaders of Victorian society at the time and through his students and the teachers he appointed he helped to mould contemporary attitudes. It was Jowett's Oxford to which Cornelia was coming up-soon to become his special confidant.

Cornelia was also coming up to an Oxford hall, Somerville Hall (from 1894 Somerville College). For the last ten of the six hundred years there had been halls in Oxford for women students, of which Somerville, was one of the first two, founded in 1879, three years before Cornelia became the first woman to matriculate in Bombay University. Cornelia was coming from a family of female educationists to a pioneering hall for university women.

AUTUMN TERM 1889: SOMERVILLE AND JOWELT

On October 15th 1889, Cornelia arrived in Oxford for the first day of term at Somerville. She was to read English literature, completing the Anglo-Saxon part of the course in two terms. This subject had not been her original wish. As she tells in her later autobiography, *India Calling*,[1] her mother, unusually, was proud of having seven daughters as well as a son and had encouraged them (at least the younger ones) to suppose that there was some piece of work for India that would be especially theirs.[2] Cornelia had formed her ambition at the age of eight or nine through a visitor to her Poona home, though she did not on arrival in England see it as practical. Her mother had received a distraught Rani, who arrived in a carriage drawn by two white bulls. She was a widowed Hindu lady who lived behind the veil or curtain, and so, not being able to negotiate with men herself, had entrusted all her private property, her dowry, to a paid male manager. She had just discovered that he had got her to assign the property to himself 30 years earlier by getting her signature on a blank piece of paper and had been living in the house she had asked him to get built for herself. There was no redress. Cornelia, who could hear some of the conversation, was told by her mother that if she wanted to help the many women like that in India, she should, when the time came, ask to study law. Her youngest sister, Alice, had formed a corresponding ambition to become a doctor, according to the same later reminiscence. Cornelia's main desire was still to study law, as she wrote to Lady Hobhouse from Ahmedabad in 1889, explaining that she had already been asked to give legal help to a lady from Kathiawar. Sir William Markby had also written to Miss Shaw Lefevre in her last year as the first Principal of Somerville Hall, saying that Cornelia should study law.[3] When Cornelia arrived in England, she began to receive conflicting advice, and so briefly considered Alice's option of medicine, but was urged against that by more than one English adviser, as Alice herself was to be later. The consensus for the moment was that Literature would have to be Cornelia's path as a subject suitable for women.

Somerville Hall had, apart from some cottages, two main buildings and Cornelia, having come from India to chilly Oxford, was put with nine other new girls in the new building because it was heated with hot air. She was also allowed the privilege of a fire in the morning to dress by and to burn all day. She arrived at 11.30 in the morning and the Principal, Miss Maitland, newly appointed at the age of 40, took her over to the new West building. Her room had a dormitory bed, in one corner. She put up her books and photographs of home with her six sisters. There was in another corner a chest of drawers with a bookshelf. There was a small stand for basins and jug for washing, a hanging press, a writing table, the fireplace with mantelpiece and a lovely window. There was a looking glass on the wall, two blackwood chairs and an easy one. There was a kettle and hob for making tea, and for parties she would spread a bright saree on the bed.

Later that day there was tea in the drawing room and a chat round the fire, and then dinner in the West Building with the Resident Tutor, Miss Pater, sister of the author of *Marius the Epicurean*, who[4] often visited.

In the first week, Cornelia describes her typical day. She would be called at 7.10, the maid would make the fire and she would dress hurriedly. At 8 the bell rang and there would be prayers with Miss Pater and reading by the house tutor. Breakfast offered hot and cold ham, fried fish or eggs, bread and butter and jam, with tea, coffee, or cocoa. The food was on a side table and each girl helped herself. They would read for half an hour while their rooms were cleaned, and then the house would be quiet until lunch, while the girls read in their rooms, or went out to lectures, where they were segregated from men. Some lectures were given near Somerville in special rooms only for ladies arranged by the Association for Promoting the Higher Education of Women. But women could go to lectures with men, if accompanied by a chaperone, usually a paid older lady from the city of Oxford, and there they would sometimes sit within earshot in a separate room. Cornelia also read in town in Duke Humphrey's beautiful medieval library, which was her idea of heaven.

Lunch in Somerville was self-service over a one and a half hour period, and after lunch women went to further lectures, or to take a walk, to play outdoor games, or to garden, Cornelia to buy books. Then she would study back in Somerville until tea at 4.30 typically in the drawing room, though by the second week she had given tea to Miss Maitland in her room. After tea the girls would study again in their own rooms, except for the one or two who had a further lecture or coaching session, or who took their exercise then.

At 6.45, the dressing bell rang for dinner. Some girls wore low-neck dresses, but Cornelia wore a saree at all times and was very insistent on this. At the second bell, Miss Pater would take different girls in to sit next to her each night; senior students would take in junior students, and they were waited on by serving staff. After dinner they would have music in the drawing room and 'be social' until 8 or 8.30, followed by a further study period, and from 10 to 11 there was a calling hour with the girls giving supper parties to each other in their rooms. Occasionally, the girls had a dance after dinner, prettily dressed up, but with only ladies from outside present, and no men apart from husbands of members of Council.

Cornelia had neuralgia all her life, and her fellow students were very kind in giving her massage and fomentations. She also tried coca with great success, but under strict instructions to limit its use. Most of the ten girls in her group remained friends for life. In friendly banter, one caricatured Cornelia with an 'Indian Princess and other stories' pose, while others, referring to her intended Honours degree, characterised her photograph as having the look of 'Honours or Westminster Abbey: pass or die'. Somerville had many student societies and Cornelia took a leading part in debates with the other women's colleges and enjoyed a cabaret at one of them. Robert Browning was the poet of choice at that time and Somerville had a Browning Society. The next term, The Browning Society read his *Strafford*, which she also saw performed, or over-performed, by the son of the great actor Henry Irving.

Already by the fifth week, some of the most prominent people in Oxford had called for her at Somerville: not only Tennyson's niece, Miss Weld, but others who would play a role in her life: Sir William Markby, the Reader in Indian law who had been a judge in the Calcutta (Kolkata) High Court, Sir William Hunter, former editor of the multi-volume *Imperial Gazeteer of India* and now Director of Oxford's Indian Institute, whose Education Commission had interviewed Cornelia's mother and who was to entertain her in his magnificent house outside Oxford, and Mrs Max Mueller, wife of Oxford's most famous Sanskritist. She had also called on, and become friends with, the widow of T. H. Green, who had been Oxford's greatest moral philosopher and was more widely known to that generation because of his portrayal as 'Mr Gray' in the acclaimed novel *Robert Elsmere* by Mrs Humphry Ward. Several of these were prominent supporters of Somerville. Cornelia did not yet know how crucial her Oxford contacts would be for her later career. But one caller more than anyone was about to change her life.

As Cornelia left lunch, she records in the fifth week, Miss Maitland ran after her to bring her into her drawing room to see Mr Jowett, the translator of Plato, Master of Balliol College, and leading source of administrators in British India. A cabinet member who was a friend of Jowett had sat with Cornelia at lunch, and now with an elderly Reverend, they had a discussion on Indian politics. Cornelia describes Jowett as a dear old man and all of them as clever. Jowett apologised for not calling at her own building, but explained he was always so busy. But he did give her, along with Miss Maitland, the first of many invitations to be his guests at the next Balliol concert and dinner. Jowett set great store by the Balliol concert and had paid out of his own pocket for an organ in the Dining Hall, so that concerts could be held there. When he left, Miss Maitland took Cornelia in her arms and said, 'My child, this is a great honour.'[5] Cornelia had no idea what she meant. But the support she received in Oxford was to account for some of her faith in Britain in the dark days of later life. Without the contacts she was given with eminent people, she would never have surmounted the colossal obstacles placed in her path.

On the appointed day, Miss Maitland wore black satin with rubies and Cornelia wore a green saree. At Balliol, Jowett came forward to meet them.

8. Benjamin Jowett of Balliol College, Oxford,
photo presented to Cornelia with autograph.

The cabinet member and his lady were there, and the poet Julian Grenfell
took Cornelia in to the 'tip-top' dinner. After dinner, they went down past
the cloaks and overshoes for the concert across the quadrangle. The Master, as
she called him, for the first time gave her his arm: 'allow me, Madam, to conduct you across in safety.' So she released her hold on her skirts and got them
soiled. They put on gowns and went in to the very crowded Hall. The Master
was received standing. The musicians, mostly students and ex-students, strings
and piano, were ranged on the dais where the dons had eaten at high table, and

for the first time Cornelia admired the organ opposite, the present from the Master, and the oil portraits round the walls of successive masters, including Jowett. When there was German, Jowett translated it for her, as she could not understand all, and she singled out the arrangement of 'It came upon a midnight clear' as being by the father of a friend.

The following week, Cornelia was invited to dinner by one of Oxford's two Nettleships, Henry, Professor of Latin and older brother of Richard Nettleship, the Balliol philosophy tutor whom Dick was to know. She went in a bath chair, something that could be hired from the Feathers, a seventeenth century inn in premises that still stand not far from Somerville at the corner of Keble road. Throughout dinner, Nettleship talked about Greek and Roman antiquities and then philosophy. She admired the classical figure holding up the candlesticks and the huge glass mirrors which she imagined were found in most Oxford houses.

Her other chief host that term was Sir Monier Monier-Williams, who had defeated Max Mueller for the chair of Sanskrit, but who later came to feel supplanted by him. Dinner parties typically included entertainments, and on this occasion there were scenes acted before supper and songs sung after. She also saw Sir William Markby again when he called at Somerville and escorted her through the snow to her first early English and Anglo-Saxon exam in the second week of December. Cornelia had not seen frost or snow before, much less the skating that went on in the beautiful grounds of Worcester College. She also experienced for the first time the itchy chilblains which people got on their toes, ears, or fingers every winter before houses were uniformly heated.

When vacation started in the second half of December, Cornelia and Dick both moved to London, sooty at this time of year. They had many people to stay with, because their mother had made so many friends on her lecture tour, fund-raising for her Poona schools in 1886, which was when Dick started his English schooling. That was also how the family was known to Sir John Kennaway, who raised the question about Cornelia in the House of Commons. But Cornelia's first hostess in London, Miss Manning, had a different connexion. As secretary of the National Indian Association, she had met Cornelia on a visit to Bombay, and she used her home as a clearing house for Indian students arriving in Britain.[6] She had helped Lady Hobhouse to organise the fund for Cornelia. So she was well placed to offer Cornelia her main London base at this time and was very kind to her in innumerable ways, often nursing her through colds and advising her what to do. Later in the vacation, Cornelia visited the

Hobhouses, and other visits she made in company with Dick. Dick was still wearing a moustache and Cornelia thought he looked 'swell' and 'a bit of a masher', but she persuaded him to shave it off, in case he looked too old when applying to Oxford.

On the way back to his school in the third week of January 1890[7], Dick stopped off in Oxford and met both the bushy-bearded Henry Nettleship and the handsome, moustached William Hunter[8] at Miss Weld's, where he was very much at home. Miss Weld showed him possible lodgings, Nettleship offered to help him all he could, while Hunter asked him to lunch, and next day he had an interview with William Markby, who advised him in detail and very kindly. Then Cornelia sent the 'poor little chappie' back to school, an expression Dick (my father) was to use of me going off to boarding school nearly 60 years later.

SPRING TERM 1890: THE FIRST WOMAN TO READ LAW

For Cornelia in this, her second, term, there was a decisive change affecting her whole career. On February 23rd 1890, she wrote home, 'I am to read law: the desire of my heart is accomplished, and to have, I hope, an extra year at Somerville.' She was to be the first woman to read law in Oxford. William Markby was to be her tutor, and so she would be taught in his and Jowett's college, Balliol. The meetings with her new supporters were already bearing fruit. The first plan was that William would create a special undergraduate course for her, to include Hindu and Muslim law, and she would sit the same examination papers in law as candidates for the Indian Civil Service. But the plans were to evolve.

In Anglo-Saxon and Gothic, she had had a bear-like tutor, Dr Wright, who actually wrote a 'Thank you' in red ink on her essay, but growled, 'There, you've got what I seldom give, but the better you do your papers, the more I'll scold you, till you get to perfection.' He had also offered to come to Somerville to make up for lectures missed through influenza. She now had to confess the change of plan to Dr Wright. He replied, 'Blessed is the man who expects nothing, for he will get it.' He said he was used to being disappointed, but this was the severest cut of all. He had not the slightest doubt she would have got a first class degree in English. He had had such hopes and would have devoted to her all his spare time. Nonetheless, he wished her all speed in her new school, and, though she was abandoning Philology, he endorsed the wish (this in Latin): 'May you live and prosper and flourish'.

Jowett was very sympathetic about Cornelia's influenza, and when she spoke of her anxieties, he said, 'But that was your *influenza* self, not your real self, I am sure; and that will comfort you when you recall its oppressive depression'.

Lady Markby asked Cornelia to stay with them for a few days to recuperate and sent a carriage to bring her up to lunch in their beautiful grounds and house, the Pullens, overlooking Oxford and its colleges on the top of Headington Hill. The grounds were still there in 2009, although only the coachman's lodge (Elmgate cottage) is still standing. The interior walls were cream with a deep terracotta dado painted by Lady Markby herself. In reminiscence of India, she grew bamboos, the red jasmine quisqalis, red love-lies-bleeding and 'lovely blue and white Indian creepers tumbling down the wall from the roof'. In the well near the windows opposite, she grew lotuses.

Dick's fortunes were changing as well. He left Ramsgate in mid-April and came to study for Oxford admission, 'Responsions', to be held at the end of September. He was to stay with the Markbys until he could find lodgings, which he eventually did in Little Clarendon Street in Wellington Villa, a house which Cornelia could see from her Somerville rooms. William Markby had got Dick the best tutor in Oxford for coaching in Greek and a little maths, Evelyn Abbot, also of Balliol, whose co- edited ancient Greek grammar was my introduction to Greek 55 years later and is still in print 119 years later. Dick was jubilant after his first lesson with Abbot, and in August he was happy to move when, because of Abbot's ill health, he had to take his later lessons not in Balliol, but at Abbot's home at Ripon in the North of England. If he passed, he would study for the Honours degree in Law, and here Markby gave Cornelia further advice. She should make Dick give her summaries of the lectures he went to. What Cornelia did when the time came was to show him her summaries of the law lectures that they both attended.

Markby learnt that Cornelia was making summaries also of his own book, *Elements of Law*, also still in print today, and he told her, alarmingly, to send the notes to Balliol unchanged. To her relief, he wrote, 'I think these notes show that you have appreciated more than I could expect on a first reading of the portion of the book to which they refer.' He wrote his comments on her copy of his book. She was to be examined next term in the summer of 1890 after less than one term of study, but he said that she was not to work in the Easter vacation more than five hours a day.

In the Easter vacation, Cornelia made a final trip to Ramsgate before Dick's departure on April 18th, partly to say goodbye to the couple who had cared for him at the school. By now she found them like brother and sister to her and they were on terms of mimicking Cornelia and getting her to admit to her former touch-me-not self. Dick looked extremely smart in red and white cricket cap and blazer. Nonetheless, there seem to have been problems, probably of a racial sort, with some of the boys, and he had had to choose his companions carefully.

The Oxford term had finished in March with a dinner party at the Hunters' magnificent house, Oakenholt, which still stands under Wytham Woods, three miles from Oxford above the road to Eynsham. Cornelia wore her salmon pink saree with a gold and silver border worked by her sisters Mary and Lena. She was seated at Jowett's left and told him about Dick's plans for Oxford admission.

She went on to spend some time in London, where she was given[9] the first of her many visits to the House of Commons, to hear the debate from the ladies' gallery. She was struck by the ceremony in which top hats were worn and doffed with a bow to the Speaker of the House on entry and again to each individual speaker. At the close, the sergeant called, 'Home, home, who goes home?', meaning as a bodyguard for the Speaker.

She also visited Monier-Williams in his London home and compared him with his rival, Max Mueller, to whose Oxford house at 12 Norham Gardens she was invited so often. Monier-Williams had founded the Indian Institute and obtained Government scholarships to Oxford for Indians, but now felt unappreciated. Cornelia speaks of Max Mueller as 'genial, delightful, imaginative, friendly, poetic, taking, young (in thought), romantic in appearance, carrying with him the zephyr of fairy land and the gnome's store of knowledge'. Monier-Williams she described as 'soured, discontented, austere, melancholy, shrivelled up, cynical, uninteresting, calm for the other's enthusiasm, prosaic for the other's poetry'. Each was jealous of the other. Max Mueller would not support Monier-Williams' work and Monier-Williams had gone off to London and was too chagrined to come down to Oxford.

OTHER WOMEN PIONEERS IN ENGLAND: PANDITA RAMABAI AND RUKHMABAI

Cornelia was only one of three women pioneers to come from India around this time. Another had been a family friend from Poona, Pandita Ramabai. Most unusually for a Hindu woman of that time, Ramabai had been a formidable scholar of sacred Sanskrit texts and had disputed with male Pundits and even more surprisingly had been accepted by them. More controversial was her continuing to travel alone and lecture on the texts after marriage and widowhood. But her travels took her to Poona, where she met Cornelia's mother, Franscina, and stayed to listen to her ideas at the family school which Franscina ran in Poona. Franscina inspired Ramabai to do two things, according to Cornelia.[10] One was to have controversial consequences. The plan was for Ramabai to visit England. It was arranged for her to stay in a Christian community at St Mary's Home, Wantage, 14 miles from Oxford. Cornelia's mother herself stayed there at the same time as Ramabai on her visit in 1886, and so did Cornelia's sisters, Pheroze and Mary. The startling development was that Ramabai was there converted to Christianity and baptised. When Cornelia went there by train, chaperoned by Miss Pater, at the beginning of June 1890, to give a class and a lecture, Ramabai had already been gone a year. But Cornelia and the family stayed in close touch with her.

Ramabai had returned to India in 1889 and that was when she followed Franscina's advice again and founded a widows' home, along with a school. But then, her conduct as a Christian was seen as intolerable. She was accused of converting her students to Christianity. Cornelia's letters home of 1890 to 1891 express sympathy in response to her mother's reports. Cornelia spoke admiringly of Ramabai, apart from some competitive words when she was briefly worried in 1890 that Ramabai was competing with her sister, Mary, for the headship of the High School for Indian Girls in Poona. When Cornelia's father died in 1894, Ramabai brought the widows from her widows' home to put flowers at his feet. In 1897, Cornelia reported that Ramabai, like her own mother, helped at a time of famine and plague in Poona, bringing 50 women and children from stricken districts to her home and school. In 1900, Cornelia reported again on Ramabai's 'wonderful work'.[11] Ramabai was later to lend premises for the school of Cornelia's sister Susie.[12] Cornelia eventually spoke of her as the ideal model, achieving by her practical work more than even the best male reformers had been able to achieve.[13] And one of the very last things Cornelia did on retirement before leaving India was to visit Ramabai to see round her work.[14] 'The Widow's Home', she reported, 'was now part of a village settlement, which included schools, an industrial and domestic training centre, and a rescue home'.[15]

With another woman from India, Cornelia had prickly relations. They were fellow-lodgers for a time in the London house of one of Cornelia's sponsors, Miss Manning. Rukhmabai was a pioneer rebel against the status of orthodox Hindu women.[16] She had earlier been sent to prison for challenging the system of childhood marriage by denying conjugal rights to the husband to whom she had been married off in childhood. These two Hindu-born pioneers were doing what Cornelia would seek to do from outside Hinduism by the even more difficult route of becoming a lawyer, namely to improve the lot of women.

Rukhmabai was now, from 1889–1894, studying medicine at the London School of Medicine for Women. Her studies were supported by the fund set up by a heroine of Cornelia's, Lady Dufferin,[17] and her registration was sponsored by none other than Miss Manning.[18] In these circumstances Cornelia saw her as a potential rival. Rukhmabai was to return to India as a doctor after qualifying in 1894 and was to become head of a Poona hospital. She had written in September 1889 to welcome Cornelia to England, and Miss Manning had commended Rukhmabai to Cornelia in December 1889 as gentle, earnest, anxious to learn and as not having had Cornelia's educational advantages and she arranged that they should see each other, later even staying in her house together. This powerful lady's arrangements seemed to be steering Cornelia towards a less glamorous profession in literature, and this may have intensified Cornelia's wish to outdo Rukhmabai. Cornelia was uncharitably wary and disliked Rukhmabai's referring on every occasion to her (Cornelia's) advantages and perfect English. She even suspected her of copying her choice of saree colour. She declined to contribute funds to a proposed ladies' association, saying that Rukhmabai would do better to give support to Ramabai, but suspecting that she would not want to play second fiddle. Throughout her life, Cornelia stayed aloof from women's movements, and in this she was like another heroine, Florence Nightingale.[19] Cornelia did, however, recognise Rukhmabai's pluck in coming alone to hear a grand lecture by Lady Dufferin in Oxford on medical aid for India, and back in Poona in 1895 she acknowledged that Rukhmabai had been very nice when she called and was received by her sister Alice, since Cornelia herself had a fever. Finally in *India Calling* in 1934,[20] Cornelia was to write of her in terms that for Cornelia constituted high praise:

> 'An unusual and fine character, silent and almost stolid, . . . Rukhmabai returned as a doctor to India, and has served her country with ability and dignity, . . . unemotional and untouched by the hysteria of politics or "Women's Rights"'.

SUMMER TERM 1890: OXFORD'S SUMMER DELIGHTS

The next term in June, there was a party in the elegant Codrington law library at All Souls College in Oxford, possibly the most formal environment in that formal university. Max Mueller took Cornelia into a secret reading room in the library and then surprised the guests by appearing with Cornelia up above and shouting down to them.[21]

> 'Then we went into tea in the lovely library. It seemed almost desecration to eat and drink in it. Dear old Blackstone[i] sat in his wig at one end of the hall looking on. The Markbys and all the nicest Oxford people were there. The library is the best Law and History library in Oxford. Professor Max Mueller took me into the secret little reading room. Such a lovely quiet retreat with the world shut out and the law books gazing down on us in improving dustiness. Then we looked up the Oriental corner and saw his translations, and finally he said, "Now we shall surprise the guests", and he led me up a staircase and we were by the Hall books almost on the shelves looking down on the people. We shouted to them and I really believe the greater number thought we had performed gymnastics to get up there. Professor Max says he thinks they will let me read there. Won't it be jolly? We met Sir William Anson, the Warden of All Souls and a great law man. He said, "I am proud of our faculty since a lady joined us. I used to be quite jealous of History because it had so many attractions for ladies, but I am greatly repaid by the one to whom it was our honour to open our Schools" '.

Cornelia would soon get her invitation as the only woman allowed to read there.

Her law lectures in her first summer term were by Markby in All Souls and Montagu, also called the octopus, in Oriel College. She was afraid to ask questions in Markby's lectures, so wrote her questions down. She was, for law lectures that no woman had attended before, allowed comparative freedom in the matter of being chaperoned. Markby chaperoned her to All Souls, and she 'chaperoned herself' to Oriel. But she had earlier had an inquisitive professional chaperone. And a chaperone was needed in the second year to accompany her to the dentist. This role the Principal of Somerville, Miss Maitland, played herself,[22] and Miss Maitland also visited in Christ Church, so that Cornelia could go to tea there with Dick's undergraduate friend Richard Burn,[23] who was to spend his career in the Indian Civil Service and start a continuing family friendship. Cornelia could visit Dick in his own rooms, since he was her brother and not in a college with other men or 'bipeds', and she could walk with him, but no other girl could join them. For some reason, the names given to male and female students were 'biped' and 'animal', the two parts of Aristotle's definition of human. Girls could not normally go on the river without a lady chaperone, but an exception was again made for brothers, so that Dick was able to punt Cornelia on the River Cherwell in the summer term. In

---

i A statue of the 18th century lawyer.

addition, Miss Maitland, as Principal, was able to ask Dick to Somerville to play tennis, and the next year, Dick could be Cornelia's chaperone at the lectures they attended jointly.

Besides tennis and punting on the river, there were other summer term delights. On the first of May, the choir of Magdalen College traditionally sang a hymn to the dawn at 5 in the morning from the top of Magdalen tower and then threw its caps and gowns over the parapets. In the street below there were competing whistles and trumpets, supposedly commemorating the Puritans who had objected to such a hymn as pagan. Dick and Cornelia attended independently. Later that week, a party of Somerville girls took an all-day picnic, 25 of them in a four-horse dray. Cornelia was practising to sing in Mendelssohn's *Elijah*. And around the end of term, when gardens were at their loveliest, there were no less than four garden parties, of which the one that used the Codrington library in All Souls was only one.

SUMMER VACATION 1890: MARGOT TENNANT AND THE WAIT FOR EXAM RESULTS

Cornelia's first law exams were held on June 10th 1890. The three and a half months of Oxford's summer vacation had elapsed before she heard any reactions. But by the end of August the outcome was to be dramatic. At first she heard from Montagu,[24] and only on her Jurisprudence, that her papers were far above the average. He wrote a special report, saying that her papers showed the most surprising facility, thought, and knowledge, and that she was a most satisfactory pupil.

After that there was a wait, and she stayed in Oxford for some time, accompanying Dick. They went up again up to the Markbys, and walked back with arms full of flowers and fruit along the river below and across the University Parks. On July 31st, Cornelia started a great tour of friends in Scotland and the North of England, arranging to spend part of each day on study, before returning to London to work in the British Museum Library.

The most notable stay in Scotland was in late August at the Glen, Inverleithen, a house Cornelia describes as being in the style of a French chateau. Her hostess was one of the most discussed young women of society and later on a national figure. Margot Tennant (later Asquith) was a friend of Jowett's, who was expected at that time to marry the future Tory Prime Minister, Arthur Balfour. But this she firmly denied to Cornelia, and she actually went on in

1894 to marry the future Liberal Prime Minister, Herbert Asquith. Later in 1901,[25] she was to tell Cornelia that no one else could have suited her like Mr Asquith, though she did not feel so at first. The family were friends and strong supporters of the Liberal Prime Minister, William Gladstone. Their principles were clear from Cornelia's first day, when they played cricket after tea with their footmen.

> 'After tea they played *cricket with the footmen* in the cricket field below the house. I need hardly say they are Gladstonians, Home-Rulers. Margot looked charming in her short skirts and red bodice. She *is* so pretty. I must show you her photographs when I get home. A boyish face with sharp features. Dark, curly, brown hair, pretty, large eyes, a small little figure, bright and fairy-like in every move. She is one of the women of the day – wonderfully clever and brilliant, a friend of Gladstone's and Jowett's. Indeed, there is hardly any literary or political gun who does not adore Margot. Gladstone has written verses to her. So has Symonds. So have most people. It is rumoured she is to marry Balfour, but she told me it is not true. I am glad, for I do not like Balfour.'[ii]

Margot was mischievous from the start, and when she was at home, the gardeners and dairymen locked up the houses, but she jumped through the dairy window, drank six glasses of cream, and handed some out to the others, making a dreadful mess in the process. She then confessed so sweetly that nobody could be angry. This was an early sign of the mischievousness for which she was later famous. In 1890, she displayed a serious side. She had long tête-a-têtes in her boudoir, 'the dovecot', with Cornelia, sometimes about the life and death of her serious-minded sister Laura, to whom Margot had been deeply attached. The boudoir had round a corner a tiny chapel with a stained glass window and prayer desk. Cornelia remarked of Margot, 'I cannot think how she keeps as pure and beautiful as she does with all the temptations she must have.' Margot asked Cornelia to set her a reading course in philosophy. Only serious talk was allowed in the house. The same was true, she told Cornelia, among the Souls, an elite society of which Margot was a leading spirit, although she denied it, along with Balfour, the future Viceroy Curzon and Brodrick, who later as Secretary of State for India would override Curzon on the subject of Cornelia's employment.[26] The society had been formed in 1885 by members of the aristocracy who had intellectual and aesthetic interests. There are various accounts of why the society was so named.[27] But the explanation that Margot gave to Cornelia was that at a party given in

---

ii By the time she met the charming Balfour, Cornelia had changed her mind.

London (by Curzon in 1889), where she was one of the few women invited, each person was given before dinner some verses about themselves printed on the back of the menu. Curzon's versification broke off unfinished with the excuse that each *soul*, in the sense of individual, was calling for the consommé to be served.

The same week as Cornelia's visit to Margot Tennant, wonderful news arrived. Cornelia was free, if she wanted to take the risk, to drop the undergraduate degree in law, and to study for the BCL, or Bachelor of Civil Law, which was a postgraduate degree, despite being called by the name of Bachelor. Indeed, most men took it only after legal experience as barristers in London. Miss Maitland, William Markby and Lady Hobhouse all approved the risk.

Dick also met with success. He passed his Responsions in September and went on to pass the Balliol College matriculation, which was considered harder than that of other colleges. He did his additional subjects and his unseen translation so well that at his two-minute oral examination, the examiners said, 'That is quite enough, thank you Mr Sorabji. Your papers have been very satisfactory' and Mr Abbot said that no one else would have done what Dick did in the time. He was to embark on law, with extra subjects to give him extra marks.

AUTUMN TERM 1890: LECTURERS AND LEADING VICTORIANS

They returned to Oxford in October and Dick walked for the first time in cap and gown. Cornelia's lecturers gave her the special attention of coming to interview her, except that Dr Dicey was too shy to interview her in Somerville Hall alone, and did so in Miss Maitland's rooms. Markby said to her lecturer Dr Grueber, 'Though Miss Sorabji is present, I cannot refrain from telling you that she has great legal aptitude and indeed you will find the very lecturing to her a pleasure.'

Some of Cornelia's new lecturers in law were, or were to become, influential figures in the affairs of the Empire.[28] Later this would become true of Thomas Raleigh, whose move to the Viceroy's Council in India was to affect Cornelia's career. Already Professor Bryce had been a member of the cabinet and was to rise higher. A. V. Dicey and Sir Frederick Pollock were to be on opposite sides in the debate on bringing together the countries of the Empire in a Colonial Conference with a permanent secretariat.

Dicey brought his sister to a lecture because he was too shy to ask Cornelia to tea himself. Cornelia described him by saying, 'Mr Dicey is a mind in suit and trousers which hang loosely onto 'contracts' which compose that mind. He shuffles, but takes flying leaps when he has new ideas on contracts.' When Mr and Mrs Dicey had Cornelia to lunch with Henry Nettleship, it emerged that Dicey had been with Nettleship in Germany as a young man and lived in constant fear of his moral sense being invaded. He used to fear the effect of music on his morals and would tear Nettleship away from concerts to the safer pursuit of sipping coffee.

Chaperoned to discuss her lecture timetable with Dicey on the first day of term in January 1891, she found him as full of knowledge, clear, uncouth, badly dressed and unwashed as last time, but also as kindly. She said she did not want to go to Mr Raleigh because he was sleepy and phlegmatic, nor to Pollock, as he was uninteresting when in cap and gown. But Dicey said she should go to Pollock as the only jurisprudent and to Bryce for Roman law, while Raleigh became her coach. All were described by her as monomaniacs.

She had encountered Pollock the previous term when he too lectured on contracts. When a meeting with him was arranged in Merton College, she had been full of anticipation because she had gleaned her most valued researches from his writing on contracts. In had walked what looked like a shy undergraduate whom Cornelia had seen in the All Souls law library, and said, 'I'm Pollock'. He had chaperoned Cornelia to Corpus Christi College, where he was lecturing on the origins of the Common Law. She waited at the porter's gate while he arranged his magnificent robes, and then he conducted her in, warning her that it would be dry. The lecture was indeed dry and scrappy and she was greatly disappointed. Now, in January 1891, she found his lecture not so dull, but he still asked her, 'Dull lectures, aren't they?' He approached with extended hand and lifted her umbrella, things that she would never have expected from a professor. She asked, 'are there books I could get it from?' But that was taken as a criticism. He asked her to informal instruction in his rooms, and when she did not come, asked her again after another lecture, striding after her down the High Street and then discoursing on a French writer. He was to become a life-long friend and she sought and valued his advice on law in her career in India.

She had a discussion of Roman law with Dr Grueber, with his heavy German accent, whom she described as pouncing. After a lecture, he walked part of the way back to Somerville with her, arguing, because they disagreed on the origins of customary law. They were under one umbrella and he in cap and gown. Her fellow students said that such company was improper, and they said the same of

Markby's accompanying her. The Gruebers she later invited to a tea party with others in her Somerville rooms and she was to be invited back to tea.

Despite having tried to evade Thomas Raleigh, she now found him delightful. He was Scottish,[29] and had lived in Oxford with Ruskin the former Professor of Art in Oxford. He had stories of Ruskin's insanity and the difficulties of persuading him to eat. Cornelia's friends called Raleigh the 'stout youth', and considered him acid and heavy. But at least they declared themselves pleased that his coaching made the clever Cornelia feel a fool. Like Pollock, he too invited her to lunch in All Souls, in his case on a day when those receiving doctorates were lunching there in their coloured robes.

Compliments on work were always carefully graded in Oxford, but this autumn term Cornelia did well. She had a lifelong penchant for finding overlooked cases, and she was thanked for finding some her tutor did not know, while two of her examination papers were said to be better than any man's.

This term, she was twice invited to dinner with Brodrick, the Warden of Merton College. The resulting friendship was important because it was Brodrick's brother who was later able to secure for her the job she most wanted. Cornelia had right away got to know other members of the family, and invited back to tea Miss Brodrick who was the Warden's cousin.[30] On her second visit to Merton, she took particular trouble. She dressed in her green velvet bodice and pale blue saree, and wore maidenshair and white chrysanthemums, after having her hair done at Hetts, the hair dresser. She sat between Brodrick and another barrister, Sir Harry Cunningham, who was staying with Brodrick, and she criticised the Contract Act. After egging her on, Sir Harry said, 'I was the Secretary to the government which drew it up.'

Jowett was as always the central figure in Oxford, and as Master of Balliol he personally read essays set by himself to Dick, who was now in his college. Jowett asked Cornelia to at least five occasions in the eight weeks of term, although she was too tired for one of them, and new, stricter rules at Somerville confined the girls to one dinner out per week. One invitation was to meet Miss Stanley, a sponsor of Girton College for women in Cambridge, spirited, white-haired, 80 year old relative of the explorer. At 9, Jowett left them together while he went to chapel. Miss Stanley was reading Xenophon to compare his travels with Stanley's. As Miss Stanley could not suffer fools gladly, she had had engraved on a card, 'Suffer the foolish and stupid ones to enter into thy rest, O Lord.'

On a memorable Sunday, Jowett brought up Arthur Balfour, the future Tory Prime Minister, to Cornelia in his drawing room. At the time of her visit to

Margot Tennant, she had been opposed to Balfour, but now she viewed him as a hero and was against the Liberal Prime Minister Gladstone. 'Dear Balfour', she wrote, 'He is dark and handsome. . . . His smile is a thing of beauty and a joy for-ever, and he has the sweetest manner'. They talked for half an hour on Indian things and principles generally – on how to adapt the best in other civilisations while respecting their own identity. He was charmed with her dress and glad she was a conservative, and he said one met in her the love for the old coupled with the reasonable desire for progress and moderate progress so harmoniously coupled.

After one of Jowett's Balliol concerts, her frequent host Sir William Hunter joined them and Cornelia said rather grandly that Hindus lacked the moral courage to reform the marriage laws which penalised women (those against which Ramabai and Rukhmabai were working). Hunter replied by asking if she had the moral courage to marry. He was not urging marriage on her as a woman, but marriage in order to reform the conditions they were discussing, as she herself later explained. But she was still offended at the time, perhaps partly because he spoke in the hearing of undergraduates.

In November, she got her invitation to be the first woman to use the Codrington law library in All Souls. She went in by a private entrance and through noiseless doors and passages to an inner room with a blazing fire. There she had silence and the cream of the books. The librarian always had more coals piled on for her, but when she later found that he removed books from the men readers if she wanted them, she stopped asking for books that were out.

The autumn term was the term for fires. The Somerville girls taught her how to toast muffins at the fire, and she studied with her feet on the fender in front of the fire, sitting in a hired arm chair, with her paper in her lap, while outside there raged sleet, cold, mist and damp. When the snow came, Cornelia took a guest to the roof of the domed Radcliffe camera in the heart of medieval Oxford for a view of the wintry buildings, and on to hear the choir singing in Magdalen College.

CHRISTMAS VACATION 1890: PHEROZE AND ALICE IN WONDERLAND'S FATHER

In mid-November, shortly before the Christmas vacation, Cornelia's recently widowed elder sister Pheroze arrived from Poona, with her little girl, Elsie, and Cornelia's new friends had Pheroze to parties. She was invited by Miss Weld, the Hunters, and above all Jowett who asked Pheroze to his house and a Balliol

9. A modern Balliol concert.

concert. Cornelia also had a tea party for many friends in her room with the
help of two of the girls who served. She had made her room still more exotic
with a saree as a dado as well as one on the bed. She had also decorated the
room next door, putting two rooms together.

Pheroze was persuaded by Cornelia to wear a saree on her last day in Oxford
and Lady Markby said she looked charming. The borders of sarees were an
important feature and a year or more later Cornelia made Pheroze a crewel
border with shamrock on black, while Pheroze made Cornelia a border of
little flies in shades of faded rose. Cornelia herself was then writing to Poona
for a border of gold and silver on white velvet ribbon. Black and red velvet
borders were recommended to her sister Mary, if she should come over to
England, and full instructions were sent on bodices being another shade of the
same colour as the saree, tight fitting, one of them at least being velvet and on
how many sarees she should bring.[31] Later she was to wear the shot silk that
shows different colours with different angles of light, with which Dick's home
was eventually to be cushioned.[32] All this was in contrast to the family practice
in Poona, which was to wear Western dress, and she expressed the wish early
on that they would all wear sarees.[33] Cornelia's Indian 'draperies', as she called
them, were part of her armoury. Yet at the same time, as the photographs of

her show, she liked to wear not the tight Indian bodice she recommended to Pheroze, but elaborate English blouses under the saree.

Cornelia, Pheroze and Dick were all in London at different addresses over the Christmas vacation of 1890–1891. The widowed Pheroze was seeking to learn singing as her new living and found lodging with two music students from the Royal Academy of Music. Elsie, though disrupted by the sudden loss of her father and the move to England, was affectionate and entertained with her own singing and dancing, with the games she taught, her misspelled verses, and the French recitation she supplied Cornelia for her later visit to France.

In mid-December, London was wrapped for days in a thick yellow blanket of fog, turning one day to inky black. The canal in Maida Vale, where Miss Manning lived, was frozen and there were ice floes in the River Thames. Dick rejoiced and went skating. The fog was followed by snow inches deep with drifts that slowed the traffic. Dick and his friend Hugh Vickers piled into Miss Manning's house for them all to study Roman law together. Christmas for Cornelia and Dick was with the family who were putting up Dick, and Cornelia described him as excelling at impromptu acting and games. After Christmas,[34] a ten-acre lake had frozen at Norwood and Cornelia, in a party of ten, began to learn to skate.

Her main visit at the start on the new year, while Dick went back to the family friends up North, was the first of many to the country estate of her champion Sir John Kennaway at Escot in Devon. Her stays in beautiful English country houses were one of the features of her reception in England. She was met at the station by the 16-year-old Gertie Kennaway and taken the long drive to the estate which Gertie's great grandfather had bought with a fortune made in India. There was still an Indian room with Indian pictures and Cornelia thought the entrance hall rather Indian in style. She was welcomed in to a further room with a huge log fire by both the parents. There was to be skating, a big lunch party with many friends and admirers of Cornelia's mother and post-Christmas celebrations for the villagers with a Christmas tree and presents.

Cornelia returned to Oxford in January 1891 before the vacation had ended and stayed at 94 St Aldates, the home of George Romanes, the investigator of human and animal minds, still commemorated by an annual lecture. They had met at a dinner, where he talked animals to Cornelia, and his wife had invited Pheroze and Cornelia to a party. The Romanes' house was a former almshouse, had oak panelling, carved mantelpieces and windows all looking onto Christ Church. The house still stands and may, as many of the nearby houses still do, have its original panelling. Cornelia was able to work undisturbed in the All

Souls library, because everyone was out skating, including her Principal, Miss Maitland, who skated the mile or two up to Godstow, while the water pipes in Somerville had burst with the ice.

Cornelia was woken by the bell of Christopher Wren's Tom Tower in Christ Church and went across the road on Sunday to hear Dean Liddell preach in Christ Church Cathedral within the college. Liddell was co-author of the still standard ancient Greek dictionary and father of the Alice of *Alice in Wonderland*. Having been invited to the Deanery more than once, Cornelia described his face lovingly as 'beautiful, clean shaven, of a type seldom seen now, refined and impressive. Hair, snow white, clings to the little black cap that protected his dear learned head from draughts'. Elsewhere she calls him 'tall with the most beautiful and most dreamy of refined faces'. 'The Dean's head is one of the grandest old age can produce.'[35] His sermon was commemorating Christchurch worthies who had died during the vacation, and Cornelia felt that he, 'standing on the verge himself of the invisible, sounded most impressive and pathetic as he spoke of those beyond the threshold'.

The Dean had the reputation of being 'frightfully rude', but she had never found him so. On her visits to the Deanery, his wife and his daughters had been very well dressed, a comment which makes it likely that Cornelia had met the daughter for whom the *Alice* books were written. But Liddell did not care for the Christchurch mathematics don, Dodgson, who had written them, because his interest in taking professional photographs of little girls was considered unhealthy. Cornelia's friend Miss Weld had been the model for Dodgson's famous photograph of Little Red Riding Hood. Dodgson told Miss Weld fascinating stories and made her hunt for presents. Cornelia was told that the title *Through the Looking Glass* was chosen because one model would allow no more than her reflection to be photographed.[36] Before term started, Dicey and Jowett talked with her about her work. She had done better than the men in her citing of cases and better than most of them in last term's exam as a whole.

SPRING TERM 1891: MORE VICTORIAN ADMIRERS

By the spring term of 1891, Somerville's gymnasium had been completed over the vacation, and Cornelia had a gym costume made. She was elected, not for the last time, president of Somerville's 'Sharp Practice' impromptu debating society and secretary for the term of the Literary Society and of the Southwark

Knitting Society which collected clothes for the poor. She also joined in founding a secret society, 'The Turned Worm'. At-Home receptions in Somerville
sometimes admitted men and sometimes not, but when they did, she was able
to include not only her distinguished supporters but also Dick and his friends
Vickers and Burn. At the end of term in Somerville, the members of the new
hall in fancy dress gave the other hall supper in the new gym. Cornelia was
dressed as Mephistopheles in red cloak, wings and hat with peacock's feather,
corked moustache, eyebrows and tights. This was followed by comic songs and
an all-girls dance.

Cornelia describes Dick's gait and attire. He strode after her one Saturday
evening in cap and gown, with a slight stoop, head forward, piles of notebooks
under his left arm and a camel's walk. This latest pose was considered the last
thing at Balliol. Later that term during the boat races, she saw him in St Giles in
white flannel trousers with Balliol colours in his cap and coat, hands in pockets,
running as hard as he could go towards the Balliol barge on the river to support
the college rowers.

This year, the son of the actor Irving again took the title role in the production of the Oxford University Dramatic Society, which was of *King John*,
a better play, Cornelia comments, than *Strafford*, but he exaggerated his part,
and at the University College Glee Club later that term she was to see his performance hilariously parodied. Cornelia, however was to see the real thing in
London more than once in 1892 – Henry Irving and Ellen Terry, the two leading actors of the time, in *Henry VIII* and *King Lear*.[37]

One new pair of friends made this term was Sir Henry and Lady Acland
whom Dicey asked her to meet at tea. Acland had been Regius Professor of
Medicine since 1857 and had created the University's first science museum.
Before science was on the curriculum, it concentrated on medical science, and
was lodged in the houses adjoining his own at 40 Broad Street, where the new
Bodleian library now stands. Many of his exhibits were kept in the house itself.
The Acland Hospital in Oxford is named after him.[iii] She described him as a
sweet old man with a refined face and hair like a poet's.

On Sunday mornings, Cornelia would hear the Church bells. She liked best
going to St Giles Church just outside Somerville, to the Gothic University
Church in the centre and to the cathedral. There were beautiful choirs in the
cathedral and in several other colleges, all in medieval settings with light passing
through stained glass windows. There were several other churches she visited

---

iii Built in the Banbury Road in 1897, its site has now been moved to Headington.

too, and one Sunday she went to three. In the University church this term, there was a University sermon by Charles Gore, not yet a bishop, on a day when the dons processed in robes while the organ played the voluntary. And next term, Gore was to give the very unconventional Bampton lectures which led to his having to resign the Principalship of Pusey House, a recently founded theological centre in Oxford. He argued that Christ, on being incarnated, emptied himself of divine attributes such as omniscience and became subject to human limitations. Cornelia attended all of the lectures in fascination and reported the content home.

Jowett's invitations remained the most important to her. She was asked, with Miss Maitland, to dinner one Saturday to meet the Lord Chief Justice, Lord Coleridge. Lady Coleridge, Cornelia reported, was young. She wore a pale green chiffon dress to the neck with a sea green train, and glistened with diamonds. Lord Coleridge she described as having a splendid head, close-shaven face, and pointed nose and chin. 'Oh! The beauty of his face and the wisdom of his years'. Cornelia wore her white silk with green velvet bodice and lilies of the valley to her throat, while Miss Maitland wore blue velvet with primrose front and her best jewels. Cornelia was taken in to dinner by Sir Montstuart Elphinstone Grant Duff, and they sat next to Lady Coleridge and Jowett. Grant Duff, a barrister, had been Undersecretary of State for India, and Governor of Madras, and upon retirement had concentrated on literature. He was to become a fellow of the Royal Society just before it shed its Humanities section, and a trustee of the British Museum.

The next day, Grant Duff called on Cornelia at Somerville and she showed him round her building. That evening, she went again to Jowett for coffee with the same dinner guests and had a good talk with the Lord Chief Justice. Mr Justice Wright, who was also there, 'was so *very* nice. He is ugly and clever'. He spoke of Dick, whom Jowett had praised the previous night, and said that if Dick should want any help about being called to the bar (in other words becoming a barrister), or about work in London, he would be delighted to give it. He told Cornelia that Grant Duff had said that she combined the highest qualities of the West with the grace and poetry of the East more perfectly than anyone whom he had ever known or imagined. At 9, she went to Balliol chapel sitting between the Lord Chief Justice and Grant Duff and thought she had never heard anything more lovely than Pergolesi's *Stabat Mater*.

To the last Balliol dinner and concert of the term Jowett invited Dick as well. Dick was in black and white dinner costume, while Cornelia had the same white and green with hyacinths to her throat. Her neighbour on one side

(Lord Sandford) was nostalgic for the Oxford of his Balliol youth 50 years earlier. There were then no trams, no perambulators–the solid and well-sprung
baby carriages of the later time– no married dons, and above all – this for
Cornelia– no ladies' colleges. However, she sat by Jowett all evening and at
the concert he said, 'Your brother is doing excellently, Miss Sorabji– he could
not do better. Have you any more brothers like him to send us? I should like
to have them.'

In the spring vacation 1891, Cornelia travelled with a chaperone to the French
Riviera, to join Mrs Darling, the sister-in-law of her adoptive-grandmother
Lady Ford. Mrs Darling liked to be called Cornelia's 'English Mother'. It was
on this trip that the customs officers at the Italian border refused to believe that
the silks in Cornelia's luggage were sarees like the one she was wearing, and
not, as they asserted, imported goods. She tells the tale in *India Calling*.[38] They
were adamant, so she was forced, with a chaperone, to prove it in a customs
shed by dropping her saree to her feet with a pull of the wrist. The customs
men were delighted. 'Do it again,' they cried.

Dick meanwhile had gone to stay with his friend Vickers in the North.
Cornelia, so confident in some things, was easily embarrassed in others. She
thought Vickers' mother, who had come to be an English mother to Dick, was
common and loud, and was embarrassed at having her visit Somerville next term.
Dick, to whom such a view would always have been alien, did not even understand the objection, and protested that the angelic home life Mary Vickers led
should be reason enough for liking her. Cornelia was also embarrassed by Dick's
lodging being opposite a butcher, a dairy and a second rate boot warehouse, and,
travelling in France, she felt a certain liberation at feeling free to go into cheap
shops. There was a contretemps with her sister Pheroze too at Cornelia's thinking it would be more respectable for her to *teach* singing than to sing, especially
in opera. In each case, Cornelia had an over-developed sense of respectability.
This oversensitivity was quite different from the knowledge of etiquette which
she required for staying in grand houses, and which had been imparted to the
family presumably by Cornelia's adoptive grandmother, Lady Ford.

SUMMER TERM 1891: OXFORD FESTIVITIES

Cornelia's summer term started with 15 lectures a week, as Dicey was giving
extra ones, although the load returned to six after a while. Both she and Dick
proved to be very good in logic, Dick especially so. His tutor said he had a

logical mind, and, after his exams, that he must have studied whole systems of logic. He passed another exam at the same time, Moderations in Divinity, and was now set to proceed on his law course for final examination in two years' time, supplemented by additional subjects.

Lady Dufferin, the former Vicereine of India, who had established hospitals and medical funding there, came from London to give a lecture on medical aid for India. Special trains were run from London with saloon carriages, and the talk was given in Christopher Wren's Sheldonian theatre which can accommodate 850 people. Lady Dufferin's work was especially relevant to Cornelia's future career and within six years by 1897 Cornelia would be on one of the Dufferin committees for continuing that work in India.[39] As Vicereine from 1884–1888, Lady Dufferin had been asked by Queen Victoria to look into the hardships suffered by Indian women.[40] She established a fund for helping women all over India. The organisation, with committees in a number of cities, was called 'The Association for Supplying Medical Aid to the Women of India'. Lady Dufferin was especially interested, like Cornelia, in the health of *secluded* women. Among other activities, she funded the training of women doctors, nurses and midwives who could visit secluded women behind the *purdah*. We have seen that Rukhmabai, whom Cornelia had been treating as a potential rival, was supported for her London medical training by the Lady Dufferin Fund. It was also Lady Dufferin who had asked Florence Nightingale to advise on a sanitation textbook for India.

Cornelia had an invitation to Lady Dufferin's lecture and wore an apricot silk saree with a bronze bodice. Acland, as Oxford's Regius Professor of Medicine, provided tea afterwards in his house opposite, and Cornelia had a nice long talk with Lady Dufferin there. After dinner, Dick and she were invited to the big party for Lady Dufferin at the Hunters' country house. Cornelia introduced Dick to Lady Dufferin and to her mother. This was the beginning of Cornelia's friendship with Lady Dufferin.[41]

Max Mueller had been at that party and had found a quiet ante-room in which to talk with Cornelia. He also asked Dick and Cornelia to his party to meet Grant Duff at which all the dons were robed because the Vice-Chancellor was present. The Vice-Chancellor asked to be introduced to her, and Grant Duff took her into dinner and cheered her up about her decision to study law, as against Miss Manning's contrary advice. Lady Grant Duff very sensibly came up and said that her husband had made her quite long to see Cornelia, and that he was charmed with her on his last visit to Oxford. She appears to have taken no further precautions against her husband's fascination with Cornelia. Cornelia invited her to tea in Somerville, and was asked to visit them in London.

It was a season for bonfires on river picnics and bonfires in Somerville. At the end of term bonfire party, Cornelia helped with the ceremonial burning of an effigy of Miss Cobbe, an anti-vivisectionist said to have opposed the practice and teaching of science for women.

The summer term finished with the usual series of parties in beautiful college gardens, and after the Merton College garden party, Cornelia sent home a summary account of the mentors who had been assembled there. The egotistical Warden of Merton with his 'I think' (this was the brother of her later benefactor, Brodrick); Professor Max (Mueller),

> 'with his splendid head and courtly ways, affectionate sallies and old world allusions; dear old Jowett, with his biting sarcasm and open contempt of shows of all sorts, ever kind to me in his incisive little ways - has not once snubbed me; beautiful Sir H. Acland, stolid but kindly; Sir William Markby, dramatic; and social Sir W. Hunter; antiquated anatomy Mr Dicey, who sidled up to claim me as his pupil. I cut the stout youth Mr Raleigh[iv] for standing where he could vigilate me; the "octopus", Monty'.

SUMMER VACATION 1891: ROWING FROM OXFORD TO LONDON

Back in London the vacation started with Dick and Cornelia attending Pheroze's singing soirée. By the end of the vacation she had many singing engagements, and her different sarees, lavender, or heliotrope with darker plush bodice, are lovingly described.

Cornelia was invited to the first of many parties by the Speaker of the House of Commons, Lord Peel, on the Commons Terrace. She had sat on his right at one of Jowett's concert dinners in the term just ended. She sipped iced coffee on the terrace to the sound of the splash of oars and the noise of the city distant. Lord Elwe, to whom she was introduced, told her that Jowett was the only male of whom he was afraid. This was a typical reaction. Some 35 years later, a Mr Patrick told Cornelia that the Balliol undergraduates used to see Cornelia go into concerts with the Master and watch her lack of fear with amazement and envy. They themselves, he said, shivered at the breakfast parties to which they were bidden.[42]

---

iv Another later benefactor.

Lord Hobhouse took her to hear a trial before the Lord Chief Justice, another person met at Jowett's. They were seated in the Chief Justice's, not in the strangers', gallery. Lord Coleridge wore a pretty wig, according to Cornelia, and his summing up was masterly, clear, and literary, though one-sided. He used unsparing satire and the plaintiff looked subdued. The jury decided unreservedly for the defendant.

The next two days, Hobhouse took her to the Privy Council. He had briefed her on the case which was Indian, an appeal involving Maratha history, and he introduced her to some of the judges. Six months later, Hobhouse was to take her to Lincoln's Inn, one of the medieval colleges for barristers, to see the library, where he got her permission to read, along with the barristers' mess where they lunched, and the chapel.[43] This was no doubt how Cornelia was inspired to do some of the same things for her nephew 52 years later, when he was nine, the age at which her own career plans were formed.[44]

Cornelia and Dick both returned early to Oxford to study,[45] she staying in Somerville's cottages, and Dick started to teach her sculling on the river, an art which she was to continue enjoying back in India. There was a trip along the River Cherwell and another up the Thames to the village of Wytham, where Dick turned out to be very well known to the old lady who served strawberries and cream. All this was in preparation for a great row together with two others down the Thames from Oxford to London as far as Richmond in three days, for which Miss Maitland's permission had been obtained.

On the morning appointed for the row, there was a nasty drizzle and Cornelia thought of turning back. She took the tram in the direction of River Thames, but it was held up in St Giles by a flock of sheep. 'I had begun to ruminate on a possible fine day, for an old woman in the tram had exclaimed as a flock of sheep crossed our path and delayed us, "Good omen that for them as is starting on an hexpedition." ' The tram dropped her at the central crossroads at Carfax and she swung into her 'late-for-lecture' walk. At Salter's boat house at Folly Bridge, the boat was not yet out and Dick was not yet there. But he appeared in his boating clothes and looked a 'swagger', taking a boating expedition in charge which he very much enjoyed. The other two were another brother and sister, Mr and Miss Amos, but Cornelia thought Dick by far superior to Amos, and his sister too asked where Dick had got his thoughtfulness and gentlemanly manners. Cornelia was 'really proud of him' throughout the trip.

It looked thundery when the double sculler was produced, called the crocus and promptly renamed crock. But the sun appeared and the two boys started the rowing, with Cornelia steering. They thought of writing a book – 'Down the river without a chaperone'. They were exploiting the rule that sisters could be chaperoned by brothers, but what was unusual was that after Clifton Hampden on the first day the girls got a turn rowing, which was increased by Dick each day until Cornelia did ten miles on the third day. Here the chaperoned ladies were rowing but on a different trip with Dick's friend Burn Miss Maitland and a don's wife as chaperones were persuaded to tow the boat, and this inspired a cartoon in *Punch* called 'Uses for Chaperones on the river'.[46]

At Clifton Hampden, they lunched in a cove and visited the lock keeper's house where Dick played the lady of the house a tune on the cracked piano. At intervals, the boys tried towing as an alternative to rowing, which resulted in running aground, entanglement in hawthorn bushes and collision with boats being towed the opposite way. The first night was spent at the Swan Inn at Streatley, the second after tea in Henley at the Old Bells Inn at Hurley and the third night at Shepperton.

Soon after, on a visit with Dick to Ireland, they had much conversation with family friends of their mother, and Dick challenged Cornelia's Toryism with attacks on the British Government of India and support of the recently formed Indian Congress Party. 'That beggar of a Dick', she wrote, 'is a ranting Liberal and Congress-lover'. He also, like most of her friends, believed in Gladstone's Liberal policy of Home Rule for Ireland. 'Dick, little wretch', she wrote later,[47] 'is, I believe, a Home-Ruler, and I know he is radical to a degree'. But it was Cornelia, whose Toryism was exceptional in her circles. Gladstone, now in his fourth term as Prime Minister, had made Home Rule for Ireland the centrepiece of his programme, an idea that was later to be echoed in India's Independence Movement.

AUTUMN TERM 1891: START OF THE FINAL OXFORD YEAR

On return to Oxford for Cornelia's final year, the news was that Jowett was very ill indeed, although he was to last another three years. He dictated his sermon, saying that perhaps it was the last one, and asked forgiveness for his many failings, but left this to God. Jowett's orthodoxy on doctrines about Christ had always been in question, at a time when one had to *repudiate* other sects,[48] and his salary as Professor of Greek had earlier been withheld for this reason.[49] Now, near death, he revealed how far his open-mindedness had progressed. So far from engaging in repudiation, he found examples of God's goodness in *all* religions and sects, even non-Christian ones. To his listeners he said: 'think of the best thoughts of all ages and you will get some idea of the ideal God has put before us: the love of others, to forget self and division'. He was not without hope of recovery, and he did in fact recover. But he said that in crises, life appeared in true proportions, and he expressed his own uncertainty about what religious truth to believe. He looked to the best thoughts of all ages to find God's ideal for us. He expressed perplexity, asked for God's light: 'Lighten Thou us, O Lord, with thy true and undimmed light, especially now when good men of all religions and sects get near to Thee, and we know not how or where to turn.'

Cornelia was starting her last year at Oxford and Dick his second. Dick had new rooms in Museum Terrace. He chaperoned Cornelia one day the short distance to the gates of Somerville, which at that time was not allowed even to brothers, and they both got a certain frisson from his threat that his identity as brother might not be recognised.

Cornelia wrote a mock trial with different parts to entertain Somerville, but lost a debate in which she supported capital punishment, a subject on which Dick was all his life passionately on the other side. Amidst floods and river fogs, she succumbed to a severe cold with fainting fits. Miss Pater and the girls looked after her, and Miss Maitland came to see her inhale medication. Dick acted as her postboy, collecting the letters she wanted posted. She was still unwell when Dick and his friend Vickers arrived to demand coaching for the term's law exam in Balliol, and Miss Pater allowed all three to sit in the library.

In October, Cornelia published in *The Nineteenth Century* for the first of many times. She had called her article 'Social India', but the editor renamed it 'Stray thoughts of an Indian girl'. There was nothing stray about it, because it set out a belief that she was to hold and put into practice all her life. Her article addressed the topical question of the woes of child marriage in India, and already she formulated her view that legislation on its own was ineffective and what was needed was education. What she meant, or came to mean, by education will only become clearer in Chapter 12 when it is seen how she was actually to carry it out by gaining the loving trust of her women clients. The two interesting exceptions she was to allow of legislation preceding education will emerge in Chapters 18 and 19. There would be many struggles before she reached that point. But she knew that her family might not agree with her view, and her letters show that it did indeed prove controversial and that her sister Mary went into print to defend her. It has been argued that Cornelia's view was a riposte to Rukhmabai, who had called for legislation in a famous article just a year earlier.[50] But it can also be said that Cornelia's premium on education as against legislation was in line with the views of Florence Nightingale.[51]

Raleigh called at the end of term with a carefully graded report. He said Cornelia's style of work was uncertain, so that he could not predict a first or second class. She was preparing in two years for what usually took four or five and often with legal practice.

Back in London, Cornelia went for Christmas to the Grant Duff's beautiful home at York House in Twickenham, the house in which Queen Anne had been born. There was an elm avenue and the drawing room had a Moorish archway. Grant Duff gave her for Christmas a ruby from his collection and was later to give her an amethyst to match one of her sarees. The following day, she had him to herself walking from after lunch until 5, and he made her a speech: 'I can't imagine anyone so young who has so ideal a life before them. In the way of knowledge your heart's best desires are being fulfilled; moreover you are about to give the result of it all to God and humanity. More than once it will fall to your lot to be a pioneer. In Oxford your life is perfect. In every way you meet and know more of the people worth knowing in the highest senses than anyone of your age, and what is nicest is that we all love you, and each one must like you better than the last.'

Nine months later Cornelia was to write that she had a penchant for old men and that her three favourite men were Lord Hobhouse, Mountstuart Grant Duff and Jowett.[52] Indeed, she positively disliked compliments from young men and shunned them throughout her time in Oxford, as much as she liked compliments from the right old men. This may have been a reaction to the vulnerability to younger men of her two oldest sisters, to which I will return.[53] Certainly she explicitly contrasted herself with her sister Pheroze as one who confined her affections to old men.[54] But five months later again in February 1893, Miss Manning was to say that she should not let old men admire her as she did, and at a party interrupted her conversation with an older one to bring up young ones whom she found boring.[55] Cornelia seems naively to have thought that friendship with older men would always be safe. She was to find otherwise in a dramatic way, as will be described later.[56]

In the new year of 1892,[57] the vacation continued with a trip to stay with her Somerville friend Alice Bruce whose father, Lord Aberdare, provided Cornelia with three new supporters or friends. First, his nephew was there who was later to marry Cornelia's confidant and friend, Elena Richmond, the recipient of the largest number of her letters. Secondly, there was his son, Alice

Bruce's younger brother, who would later become, as General Bruce, a friend and visitor with Cornelia's own sister, Alice, on the Northwest frontier with Afghanistan. Thirdly, on her next visit, Cornelia was to meet the father's son-in-law, Mr Whately,[58] who was to secure for her a solicitor's training in London and remain her own solicitor for the rest of her life. Alice Bruce and Dick were to finish up 46 years later one street apart from each other in Oxford, she at 54 Sandfield Road, and in old age Cornelia with Dick and family would visit her there.

SPRING AND SUMMER TERM 1892: TRAUMA AND TRIUMPH OF THE FINAL LAW EXAM

The spring term of 1892 started two weeks late, in order to protect students from an influenza epidemic. Jowett was now well enough for Cornelia to walk with him and to sit with him at another Balliol concert. He encouraged her about remembering enough for her final exam, saying that we have more memory than we realise or is good for us. Dick had moved into Balliol rooms, but Cornelia could not at first see them because she needed Miss Maitland as a chaperone even to walk across a Balliol quadrangle. She did, however, see them in the end, and Dick had arranged for Pheroze to sing in Balliol in the presence of Jowett. This may have been the occasion of Jowett's question to Dick. He asked, 'How many sisters do you have?' When Dick said, 'Seven', Jowett replied, 'Like Homer: Homer had seven sisters'.[59] Whether the incident was before or after his illness, Jowett must have been suffering from Spoonerism. What Homer had was seven *cities*, in the sense that seven cities claimed to be his birth place.

In her final term of summer 1892, Dick took Cornelia on the river as a mode of relaxation before the exam. The finale was to be dramatic.[60] A week before the exam, she was dining with Jowett when he asked if it would make a difference to her if she sat the exam not in the Examination Schools with the men, but privately, supervised by Miss Maitland in Somerville. She said indeed it would make a difference, because that might enable people to say that she had not sat at all. Why could she not sit with the men? Because, said Jowett, the London examiner for the BCL refused to examine a woman. But since Cornelia felt that way, a decree must be obtained from the University Council, which met on the eve of the examination. The motion, as she recalls in 1934, was 'That Cornelia Sorabji be allowed to sit for the BCL examination', although she then describes it, implausibly, as a motion before the much larger body of Congregation. Jowett's letter reporting that Oxford had granted the decree reached her at 4 p.m. the day before the exam and she shrieked, 'so that it was good to hear her'. Even then, her devoted and well-meaning tutor Dr Grueber walked in a great state of excitement into the Somerville garden, where she was rejoicing with her friends and urged her that she need not sit the examination because the decree from Oxford University was enough. His red hair was flowing against the pink chestnut blossoms and Cornelia remembered wincing at the disharmony of colour, which matched the disharmony of sentiment.[61]

> 'Soon after, my Roman Law Tutor was to be seen walking up the drive towards the West Building where I lived. He was greatly excited, his red beard shone in the sunlight and his red hair was flying in the wind; he carried his hat in one hand and a badly-rolled umbrella in the other. I was in the garden with my special College friends, who were rejoicing with me at the conclusion of an anxiety which they had shared, and I remember wincing, as at a false note in music, at the colour of Dr Grueber's hair against the pink spirals of the chestnut trees – a terrible disharmony. "Miss Sorabyi" (as he always called me), said he, "you need not sit for that examination". "But why?" "You have your decree. That is enough for a life time. You need go no further. The University of Oxford" (and the thrill in his voice was awesome) "to pass a decree like that! . . ." '.

She arrived at the examination schools in the formal white tie, then required of all candidates, to find lawyer candidates positively ancient compared with herself. She described herself as walking to the funeral pyre:[62]

> 'I followed the clerk to my place in the wake of the ancient Fathers to the funeral pyre. I was not at all frightened. I was quite calm outwardly, but very curious as to what would happen, half fearing I would have to scratch (i.e. retire because I knew nothing), half despairing. But I thought of the dear little service at St Giles, and of its being Whit-Monday,[v] and how my dear Number 80[vi] and other people were thinking of me, and of the good wishes of my friends, for I had received a huge budget of such that morning, and as I thought of all these things, I clenched my left fist hard and wrote for my very life. The papers were *very* difficult and they gave us stiffest things in my nicest subjects, so that I felt I could not have done myself justice. But I know a power outside mine was helping me, for my pen wrote so many things that I did not think I knew.'

---

v When Christians were first inspired to spread the Gospel, having miraculously acquired foreign tongues.

vi The home address.

She heard that night that she was to be called for an oral examination (viva) the next day and, as she describes it, the London examiner, Professor Nelson, did for her.[63]

> 'It was that brute of a Nelson who lost me my last chance. He did not want me in at all and made the fuss about the exam which eventually gave me my decree, and when I was on for viva, he bullied my life out. He was brutal enough to other men who shook before him and he tried the same on me together with horrid jeers. I turned and rent him before I left, for Professor Dicey had told me that something in his book on Private International Law was questionable. I said in answer to a question which introduced this point, "Some writers think so-and-so, but it's wrong". He looked as if he'd like to kill me, but he only jeered and asked reasons, which, having ready, I hurled at his head'.

She was given neither a first class degree, nor a second class, but, to her bitter disappointment, a third. There were no first class degrees awarded, and only two seconds, both gained by men who had been working at it for years. But at least the pass counted when in 1920 women were at last allowed to receive degrees, and in 1922 she was able to collect the degree she had passed 30 years earlier.

> 'I am only *3rd class* and this is a frightful disappointment, for I hoped for a second and should have got it, but for my abject stupidity. The world in general seeks to console me. They say I ought to be proud of it and all the rest. But I am conceited enough to feel it'.

She now felt she was turning her face for ever on the happiest time life could have for her, but her mentors still had many words of encouragement. She had her tutors and Jowett to a farewell tea. Raleigh invited her for lunch in his rooms. She paid a last visit to the Max Muellers. She had lunch with the tutor, possibly Raleigh, who had been most supportive and understanding and had a long evening talk with him under the cedars, in which she was given rules for her conduct in life, not divulged on this occasion.[vii] But most help-ful of all were her two visits to Jowett. First he had talked to the examiners and told her that they thought her very clever and found it incomprehensible that she had amassed so much knowledge in so short a time. She had curious powers of assimilation and a wonderful memory for case law. But that made her not a good candidate for examination purposes, because she knew too much. These qualities would make for success and excellence in after life, so

---

vii But his views on her employment as a lawyer were to become relevant later: Chapter 4.

that she should not regard her class of degree as an indication of her powers. But they had to fit her into preconceived standards of how to answer questions, and she was outside these standards by the very fact that her work was non-mechanical. She could not, however, answer questions sufficiently well to satisfy a higher class.

A few days later, he had her to his study for a quiet talk. 'He gave me courage and counsel,' she says,

'for the future. The things he said will always remain with me. Nothing put in his quaint terse way could fail. He wrote two little notes, one to the India Office and one to his friend Miss Nightingale[viii], and then I said a farewell and the dear courtly old gentleman kissed my hand, as he gave me my benediction: "God bless you, dear". Alas, that I may never see him again in those distant days when I revisit Oxford haunts. I crept downstairs into the Broad, but I had felt the nearness of the Unseen'.

She described Jowett as having tiny footsteps, tiny handwriting, a tiny voice with staccato speech and as lacking the puff to blow out candles at a dinner party game.[64] As a keepsake Cornelia had from him a lock of Robert Browning's hair set in a crystal.[65] A few letters between her and Jowett survive,[66] and she tells of some of them in a memoir she wrote for *The Nineteenth Century* in 1903. In 1892, he wrote with prescience, 'Everybody who undertakes an enterprise like yours must necessarily have many phases both of exaltation and depression.' She felt that Jowett had revealed to her a better self, which would hardly have existed, if he had not compelled it.[67]

On leaving Oxford she decided, 'If I live to be an old lady, I mean to buy a house in Oxford, that my bones may rest there.' In fact, it was to be Dick who finished in Oxford, while she was to choose London, the place she went on to next, to gain some legal experience.

---

viii Florence Nightingale

CHAPTER 3

LONDON: GLAMOROUS INTRODUCTIONS AND LEGAL EXPERIENCE, 1892–1893

C ornelia moved to London in the hope of securing practical experience in law. She was to be given even more glamorous introductions than she had received in Oxford, and she was welcomed by a firm of solicitors who gave her a training in methodical attention to documents which was to stand her in good stead on many occasions in later life.[1]

GLAMOROUS INTRODUCTIONS: THE POET LAUREATE, A LEGENDARY NURSE AND THE ROYAL FAMILY

Cornelia settled in the empty London house of Mrs Darling, her former hostess, on the French Riviera.[2] Very shortly afterwards in early September 1892, Jowett arranged for Cornelia and Dick to go and visit his old friend the poet laureate, Tennyson, at his home on the Isle of Wight. After swearing them to secrecy, Tennyson read them the not yet published poem, 'Akbar's dream'. The poem celebrates the Moghul Emperor's toleration of all religions, which Tennyson thought put to shame England's monarchs of Akbar's time. He wanted to check with Cornelia and Dick his many Indian allusions. Regrettably, Cornelia's letter home about the visit is missing from the collection because it was taken and published elsewhere in the style of a newspaper interview probably in a missionary publication in India.[3] Cornelia was annoyed because she already had a wish that her letters should be published some day.[4] But brief descriptions are supplied in her *India Calling* and by Dick, who wrote:

'I shall never forget my visit to the great poet at Aldworth. The house is hidden away behind trees, so that you do not see it on entering the gates, till a bend in the drive suddenly discloses it. From the garden terrace you can see forty miles of country stretching in billows to the sea. My first sight of him was in his old English garden which his daughter-in-law had planned for him. He did not at first like the idea of its preparation, but when it was ready and its straight and prim rows of dear, sweet-scented old English flowers were in bloom, it was his favourite spot. He had on the black cloak and the large wide awake hat with which his portraits have made everyone familiar. He was charming to invited guests, though he was somewhat forbidding to unexpected strangers. He had a deep musical voice and a world of kindness in his face. I shall never forget his reading of "Akbar's Dream". The poem was still in manuscript at the time, and as he read, he explained the thoughts which had led to the words.'[5]

Very shortly after the visit, Cornelia wrote to Tennyson to ask if he would consider writing a poem for the dedication of the new school building in her mother's school in Poona. Tennyson's daughter-in-law replied that he had hoped he might do the poem, but was not well and had to decline. He wanted her to know that this was not from want of interest in her mother's wonderful work. A month later Tennyson was dead, but a fortnight before he died, Cornelia was told, he had been talking about their visit and regretting that he could not write the verses for the Victoria High School.

The family sent Cornelia a ticket for the funeral on October 12th 1892, in Westminster Abbey, and Cornelia described the funeral to her parents, culminating in Tennyson's own poem, 'Crossing the bar'.[6]

'And now I must tell you all about the funeral. The Hallam Tennysons sent me a "mourners'" ticket, which was most kind of them. I was privileged above friends of long standing and was with the family in the Chapter House and had the privilege of doing honour to the dead Laureate in the Mourners' procession. I took off from office and found my way easily to the Abbey, which is quite close. What the papers say about the crowds waiting for admittance is true. The Mourners went through the Dean's Yard by a *quiet* entrance into the Chapter House. The dear Master of Balliol was there and we had a nice little talk while we waited. He is kind enough to want me to go up to Oxford to see him. Agnes Weld came in deep crepe of course: she feels her uncle's death very much. And there was old Miss Tennyson (his sister) there too, who could scarcely walk. The pall bearers were soon summoned and the procession formed silently, calmly. The coffin looked like the emblem of *Victory* more than of death and so I doubt not it meant to him who had passed into the Invisible. Slowly we filed through the long cloisters, past rows of the visitors who waited to follow up the Mourners, and as we entered the nave, the organ played Chopin's Dead March, and just then the sun came out and caught the Union Jack and the lovely white pall and the laurel wreaths and lit it all up as if the Father smiled upon the mortal remains of that truly Inspired of his children.

'Then followed the beautiful service and what shall I say of the anthem? "Crossing the bar" was *exquisite* – you heard his whole thought in it – the dying away of the life as night sank. The gentle bearing of it out to the boundless Deep in answer to that "Clear Call"– just a little regret that the tide had to bear him – but then the glorious assurance in the Finale, rising to joyousness, a foretaste of the meeting with the Pilot. … And all was still. It was perfect, the plaintiveness, the calm, the whispering of the waves, the momentary struggle, the Beatific Presence. Add to all that the impressive coffin and the bearers and the deeply veiled Chief Mourner and the beautiful Abbey, and the consciousness that the greatest of the dead rested in that little Poets' corner, and I don't know when I have felt what I felt then. I wish you had been there. It is a memory that will rest with me.

'The mourners next followed the coffin to the grave. And we stood by while those incomparable sentences were read, ending with a glorious burst of praise, "Holy, Holy, Holy", as the last rites ended and the sacred Dead was forever put out of sight. Surely in the near Presence of the Trinity the Poet himself must have rejoiced to think that his sorrowing widow and his many friends could "give thanks" even at the saddest moment of all. His wish was fulfilled. There was no "sadness of farewell" when he embarked.

'Professor Huxley and Sir John Evans[i] took care of me in the crush around his grave. Sir John is the husband of a Somervillian and he saw me and asked if he might protect me one side and if he might see me to my cab. Then I heard a kind voice behind, "and will you allow me to take care of you this side? A crush is so awkward for a lady", and Sir John introduced me to the owner of the voice, *such* a dear old man with white hair. He said the Master had asked me to meet him at Balliol, but I was not able to go'.

Jowett's other great introduction was to Florence Nightingale,[7] the legendary nurse who had contributed to Cornelia's scholarship to Oxford.[8] Cornelia described her as '*such* a sweet creature, the dearest old lady in the world with the brightest of faces and the rosiest of cheeks and such a twinkle in her eye. Nevertheless, she is never well and was in bed when I saw her'. She had her flowers round her, birds singing in her aviary and was full of questions about sanitation and health projects in India. 'Talking to her was like breathing fresh mountain air. It made me feel so strong for what might be in the future for me, and she put her hand on my head and blessed me when I was coming away and said, "I am sure God is sending

---

i T. H. Huxley, Darwinian scientist; Sir John Evans, archaeologist father of Arthur Evans, the excavator of Knossos.

you to your work, my child. Don't be afraid. Go in his strength. He will bless you and use you to work his purpose," and she kissed my hands and my forehead.'

When Cornelia next visited Jowett, they sat in his study after lunch facing a picture that Cornelia had often noticed. It was of a young girl standing in early Victorian dress beside a pedestal on which sat an owl. Jowett pointed and said, 'Would you recognise that for the little old lady in a frilled nightcap whom you saw last week?' Cornelia was silent, not knowing what to say. 'When she was like that', said Jowett, 'I asked her to marry me'. Cornelia was struck dumb, and Jowett concluded, 'It was better so.' Later, a cousin of Nightingale showed Cornelia a confirming entry in Nightingale's diary: 'Benjamin Jowett came to see me. Disastrous!'. Cornelia told the story to some Americans and retold it in *India Calling.*

During this period, Cornelia had time to visit the House of Commons with the Speaker's daughter for a debate on the Irish question, and to hear Gladstone and Chamberlain, though Balfour only smiled in response to taunts as if he were in a drawing room. Mrs Gladstone said to Cornelia that if she wanted to hear good speaking, she should go the night Mr Gladstone was on.

In 1892, Cornelia also met for the first time Princess Mary of Teck, later to be Queen Mary, wife of George V, and a life-long supporter of Cornelia. Queen Mary was much later to remind Cornelia of their meeting.[9] It was due to the friendship of their mothers. The Duchess of Teck had heard with enthusiasm about the Poona schools, when Cornelia's mother visited England in 1886, and had invited Cornelia's mother to call on them in White Lodge, Richmond Park.[10]

Cornelia was also to be presented to Queen Victoria and this had caused much reflection about the right saree for the occasion. The required dress at Court was white. But Cornelia got the Queen's permission to wear a colour.[11] In the event she wore pale pink crepe silk with a sort of cinnamon velvet and gauze bodice, and a pink border sent from Poona. She kissed Queen Victoria's hand, who said she had heard of her and was very pleased to see her, and as she curtsied to the Duchess of Connaught, the Duchess said, 'Don't you remember me, Miss Sorabji – how do you do?' When the Duke had been commander in chief in Poona, two of his children had helped to fell a tree in the drive of Cornelia's mother's house.[12]

DICK UNDER JOWETT IN OXFORD

Dick was progressing towards his BA Law finals and Jowett told Cornelia that he was a very clever man. On a visit to Balliol, Cornelia visited Dick in his new rooms there and a letter home from Dick of October 17th 1892 is included in the collection.[13] He had moved from the Garden Quadrangle to a set of rooms in the Front Quadrangle that had been lavishly designed for Lord Selborne's brother, but was currently unoccupied. He writes that Gladstone was due to speak in the Shedonian Theatre at 2.30 on Monday and one would have to be there early to get a seat. This was probably the occasion on which he had to climb the Sheldonian's railings to hear him.[14]

Richard Nettleship, the Balliol philosophy tutor and brother of Cornelia's friend, had just died. A climber, he died at the age of 46 from exposure to cold and exhaustion on Mont Blanc, reaching for the hand of each of his companions before he expired. Dick knew him because Nettleship took the Balliol roll call every morning and Dick's son was to know his dry book on Plato when it was set to Oxford students sixty years later. Balliol College was a closely knit community. Nettleship had earlier edited the posthumous work of another of Balliol's dozen teaching fellows, Jowett's star pupil, T. H. Green, who had died in 1882. Green had developed Jowett's unorthodox thoughts on the essence of Christ's teaching. Jowett was overcome several times in preaching the memorial sermon after the second premature loss of a philosophy tutor.

CORNELIA'S LEGAL INITIATION IN LONDON

Cornelia wanted some kind of legal experience in London for herself. Lawyers in England were divided into barristers, such as Dick was to become, and who alone in those days could plead in court, and solicitors who prepared the legal documents. Cornelia was not yet seeking either role but was gaining experience in a solicitor's office. She was very lucky as a woman to be allowed to do that, and one prominent lawyer said that he would like to see his clerk's face if Cornelia, as a woman, called with a document in his chambers. But not only had the Bruce's son-in-law, Mr Whately, introduced her to a leading firm of solicitors, Lee and Pemberton, at 44 Lincoln's Inn Fields close to Lincoln's Inn, but she immediately proved invaluable to them.

She described Mr Whately as tall, dark, slight, young-looking, handsome, Government House aide-de-camp style. On the first day, the other clerks, male, looked shy and miserable. Whately introduced her to his fellow- partners, showed her the ropes and asked her to draw up an agreement for the sale of a house, which he checked at intervals. Soon they were just bringing papers and saying, 'Will you please advise our client?', and they wished she were not leaving in six months. The Pemberton partners started having her to lunch and to their club. When she was ill with a cold, the partners said they could not do the work without her, and called on her with their wives. On her return, five partners came to see her in the first hour. She in turn benefited all her life from the rigorous record-keeping she learned from Lee and Pemberton. Lord Hobhouse tried to pay off her 50 guinea apprenticeship fee, but Lee and Pemberton returned it to him, saying that she was as useful as three men.

CRITICISMS OF MISSIONARY SOCIETIES AND ATTITUDES TO CONVERSION

Some of Cornelia's time in London was taken up with battles against missionary societies. Though Cornelia's family was Parsee by birth, they were Christians by religion, as we have seen.[15] Many of the family friends who welcomed Cornelia were members of the Church Missionary Society, with and for which her father had often worked,[16] and her champion, Sir John Kennaway, was its President. But Cornelia was herself extremely suspicious of the Society and the priority she thought it gave to converting Indians. Conversion was the subject which had already got the family friend Ramabai into trouble when she was accused of converting her pupils. Cornelia's own attitude to her Hindu and Muslim clients in India was to be the very opposite to that of missionaries, and but for that she could not have done her work at all. She wanted to preserve their religious beliefs and customs, but to gain their confidence so that they would revise those aspects concerning health, education, legal security and so on which put them at such a disadvantage. For her, much more than for the other members of the family, Christianity was a private faith, without which she would never have endured the trials that were to come. The widespread interest in conversion in England is illustrated by a story which Cornelia tells in *India Calling.*[17] To a lady who was seeking to convert her she replied that she was a Christian already, at which the lady replied, 'But you *look* so very heathen.' I am sure that Cornelia found this as hilarious as anyone else. When someone asked Cornelia, 'Are you saved?', she replied, 'No, but my sister, Susie, is.'[18]

Cornelia's father and mother both sought to convert people[19], but her mother's approach at least was nuanced. Her mother's main school, the Victoria High School in Poona, was partly supported by the Church Missionary Society, but with very strong reservations on their side, because she did not put conversion to Christianity first. Her attitude was rather one of intimate knowledge of all the faiths and valuing them, while showing her own Christianity, and in the main school including Christian belief in the programme. She would also help the surrounding villagers with their needs and tell them of the Christian Gospel.[20] Hence in 1889, Cornelia can still in a letter home express the wish, which was that of her parents, that all India might one day be Christian. But the help given to people by her mother was never conditional, as some wanted, on their hearing the Gospel. Another thing that was missing was the idea that other faiths were evil, and that people *must* be converted. We have seen that she and her older daughters ran extra schools in vernacular languages, one for Hindus using Marathi, one for Muslims using Urdu, as well as one using Gujarati for Parsee infants who would go on to the main school. The Church Missionary Society was anxious that none of their money should support the vernacular Hindu and Muslim schools, where no conversions could be expected.

The reservations of the Church Missionary Society become clearer from the limitations they placed on funding the Victoria High School. They made a deal with Cornelia's mother when she came over to England to raise funds in 1886. If she would give fund-raising lectures, the proceeds would go to the Society's general funds, not to her school, but she was free when lecturing to interest individuals in funding her school as well. She did indeed raise private donations for the main school. She raised enough to buy the land, and a Miss Ashlin propped up the infant Parsee school, while the boys' dormitory in the main school was paid for out of her husband's savings. The Society made a limited contribution of 200 rupees a month, or less than 20 pounds.[21] Given this background of mixed funding, Cornelia disputed how much of the property on the site the Society could claim to own, and how much it should contribute to running the school.

For this purpose, Cornelia used her new legal training and demanded to see the Society's secretary. She argued that her mother, and the two daughters currently helping, Lena and Susie, worked without pay and were overworking while all the new building was going on. The secretary protested that the Society's contributors actually complained about the Victoria High School because it was not missionary. Nonetheless, the Society offered an extra 70 rupees a month, or 5 pounds, to prevent overwork during the period of building, on condition it was used only to give relief in connexion with her mother's work for the main school. Later, Cornelia secured a contribution from the Society of half the building fund.

Cornelia's confrontation with the Church Missionary Society produced a backlash, even among some kind but zealous family friends and supporters whom she liked and continued to like personally, the Kinnairds, whose family had founded an affiliated missionary enterprise, the Zenana Mission, for which Dick and his bride were to work many years later.[22] The Kinnairds' reaction to Cornelia helps to make clear their difference of attitude. They asked her whether she was true to the (missionary) cause. One of them said that Cornelia's mother had given the school over to yet another affiliate of theirs,[23] knowing her family was unsafe because, as they strangely put it, Christianity did not run in the family as hereditary. Their gift was seen as giving them rights, but not responsibilities. It was taken to mean that they and the Church Missionary Society did not have to meet the full costs of the school, because it was known as Mrs Sorabji's school, and not as a school in which she acted as the Society's agent. Cornelia was even criticised for contemplating doing secular work for disadvantaged Indian women, instead of missionary work, and also for having taught in a men's school.[24]

Different family members had different attitudes to conversion. Dick's later support for the Kinnairds' Zenana Mission did not mean that he shared their attitude. When Susie died, her most devoted Zoroastrian helper, Naja Kabraji, at her grave announced her conversion to Christianity.[25] But Susie would not, while alive, have been helped by her conversion, she thought, and another sister, Alice, urged Naja to delay her decision.[26] In contrast with this caution, Susie had earlier announced that she hoped to convert Parsee pupils in her school, and she made sure that every child had a Christian Bible, as well as singing Christian hymns.[27]

Cornelia's sister Alice had a robust, but qualified, view. She was to run with her husband, Theodore Pennell, a fully missionary hospital on the Afghan frontier. They did everything together,[28] and he insisted on preaching the Christian Gospel both in the bazaar and before giving treatment in the villages and in the outpatients department of the hospital.[29] Though he was loved by Muslims, Hindus and Christians alike for the thousands upon thousands whom he cured with equal devotion, he continued to be stoned when preaching in the bazaar and survived earlier attempts on his life only because there was always someone to say, 'don't kill the Doctor Sahib.' He wanted India to become Christian, but he wanted conversion to be based on the example given by Christian lives. He had a very large number of converts, including a mullah who survived his head being axed for having converted. Although conversion exposed the converts to reprisals, Theodore shared every bit as much of the danger. Moreover, although he admired the good qualities of the tribesmen, the life of blood feud from which he sought to convert them is one which it is hard for his readers to admire even as much as he did. Alice supported conversion only for those Hindus and

Parsees who had abandoned orthodoxy, as will become clearer from one of her novels, *Doorways of the East*, to be discussed below.[30]

Cornelia, by contrast, and her sister Lena in her role as a scrupulous head-mistress, were at one extreme in the family. Cornelia actually suspected mis-sionary societies and avoided any Christian teaching in her work. But she did make some amends for her attitude, when, in *India Calling* in 1934 she praised the good work of the Oxford Mission to Calcutta.[31] In her political dispute with Gandhi in 1932, she also pressed on his attention the work of missionary societies for Dalits ('Untouchables', as they were then called).[32]

Suspicion of her mother's school as not genuinely missionary was to have a sad outcome. In 1907, Cornelia's mother had retired and made a deed of gift of the school buildings to the Kinnairds' missionary group and hence to its affiliate, the Church Missionary Society, hoping that that would guarantee the future of the school. But in 1909, the Society sold the school buildings while Cornelia's mother was still alive and transferred the proceeds to a Bombay school of theirs. Her mother's work was re-established only by the extraordinary feats of fund-raising of Cornelia's sister Susie that will be described in Appendix 1. All Cornelia could do was to make sure that the main school which Susie was to found in 1908 was better protected when Susie died in 1931.[33]

Nonetheless, Cornelia's legal efforts for her mother's schools, during her training in England, had at least gained a temporary relief in costs. It was now 1893 and, with her legal practice completed, she sailed home to join the Poona family, full of hopes and uncertainties about the future.

PART II

TEN YEAR CAMPAIGN FOR A LEGAL POSITION, 1894–1904

CHAPTER 4

WOMEN'S RIGHTS IN PRINCELY STATES AND ALLAHABAD 1894–1899

On returning from London to Poona, Cornelia had difficulty establishing a legal career. In the Princely States of India, where princes ruled under British supervision, only appeal courts were run by the British. In those states, Cornelia was allowed to move from preparing legal cases to pleading in court. But when she transferred to Allahabad in British India with Dick, promises to let her plead in court were broken. After five years of frustration from 1894–1899, she sought a different type of legal role in British India. She tried to establish the need for her services by rescuing, at extreme personal peril, a secluded Rani in a Princely State from imprisonment and probable death.

THE RETURN FROM LONDON TO POONA

Cornelia had returned from London to join her parents and her sisters in their Poona home in 1893. The orphan boys or 'chicks' were there whom her mother had rescued from the plague. Cornelia taught the enlarged family boating, as well as joining in tennis and badminton, and the trips to the cottage at Lanowli. She taught music at her mother's school and was as involved as anyone in the prize-giving days.

In 1894 their father died, and Mary was the one who sang to him as he was dying.[1] Dick, who had been away in England since 1886, could not return until 1896 after passing his bar finals, and so to his sorrow never saw his father again.

CORNELIA'S ANXIETY: WOULD THE SISTERS DEPEND ON DICK AS BREADWINNER?

In 1895, Dick tried for the Indian Civil Service exam and had the disappointment of not passing. Unlike Cornelia, he did go on to pass his bar finals at Lincoln's Inn in London and to be called to the bar at Lincoln's Inn on April 29th 1896, in the same batch of nine candidates as Jinnah, who was later to found Pakistan.[2] But Dick's failure to pass the Indian Civil Service exam weighed heavily with Cornelia. She seems to have been expecting too much of Dick. Certainly Jowett had predicted, 'There will not, I consider, be any difficulty about his getting into the Civil Service.'[3] But the admission of Indians to the Indian Civil Service at this time was almost nil. There had been a very few cases before 1892. But since then things had become, if anything, harder, and Dick was competing in England with Englishmen over the most prized examination of all. In 1892, there were created two services lower than the Indian Civil Service, a Provincial Service in which Indians could rise only as high as Deputy Collector, below the most coveted post for Indian Civil Service beginners,[4] and a Subordinate Service, in which Indians could hold only the rank of Munsiff, or local judge for legal cases involving small sums of money, or Tehsildar, a sub-collector for a sub-district. A concession was the further provision to allow very slowly for the promotion of Indians into the Indian Civil Service, but only after they had made a success of the Provincial Service, and not in such a way as to impede the promotion promised to Englishmen already appointed to the Indian Civil Service. Even twenty years later in 1915, there were only 63 Indians in the Indian Civil Service, or 5 per cent of the total.[5]

Cornelia, the champion of women, revealed how insecure she felt about the prospects of women when she described the seven sisters as 'a parcel of womenfolk'. The only security, she felt, lay with the one boy in the family, and that, she believed, was now jeopardised. She wrote to Lady Hobhouse, whose husband was so high in the legal profession, looking for a way out:[6]

> 'Our horizon has sadly changed since yesterday, and it is all that horrid I.C.S. list, news of which reached us only yesterday. I will not disguise the fact that it was a terrible disappointment to us that Dick did not get in, his final try. . . . We are so frightfully anxious, because he's our only boy you see, the only one to do good work in the world and bring honour to Father's name, and we, alas! are now only a parcel of women-folk at home – and at a crisis like this miss my dear father more than ever.'

By 1900, Cornelia had completely changed her view. She then thought that Dick was already better off in the law than he would have been in the Indian

Civil Service, where he 'might have become a soured, cynical clerk, forgotten in a far away district. So that disappointment is early *blossoming.*' Nonetheless, in the end it was Cornelia who got attached to the Indian Civil Service, though as an anomaly with no particular rank, but some of the privileges of high rank. But this belongs to a later part of the story.[7]

As soon as Dick returned to Poona, Cornelia thought him the life and soul of everything. He spoke at his mother's school, and he had a strong line in writing skits and songs both to raise money for the school and for entertainment at home.[8]

10. The graduates back home, 1896: impeccable Cornelia (seated) with Dick and hastily robed Alice.

CORNELIA'S FIRST JOB: FEMALE EDUCATION – IN A JUNGLE

Cornelia herself had been warned back in London that it would not be easy for a woman to break into the legal profession in Bombay even in a solicitor's office. Inquiries on her behalf by Lord Reay had received the answer that men clients would not want to explain their quarrels to a woman, and that legal clerks would also object.[9] Indeed, on her arrival, a job proposed to her with some English solicitors fell through. She discovered later that the Chief Justice of Bombay had opposed it.[10] So, in summer 1893, she tried instead a post for furthering the education of women, offered by the Gaekwar of Baroda, who was far ahead of his time in seeking reforms for women in his state.[i] Cornelia came to feel that the time was not yet ripe for success. Baroda, where the education was to be promoted, was a Princely State (its capital now called Vadodara), governed by the Gaekwar, not directly by the British. One third of India was still ruled by Indian princes, subject only to the veto of a British political agent or 'Resident'. Cornelia lived in a large, remote house by the jungle, and in danger of burglars. Indeed, she was burgled while on tour and was advised to carry a revolver. She summed up the problems to Jowett:

> 'I know no one here and live in a great solitary house, all by myself with the *jungle* stretching almost all round it and a river flowing close beside it. . . . I have to be guarded every night by a watchman (- who probably is a retired member of the *thief* caste – but at that one must wink). . . . My duties are mostly what I make them, but the direction of female education in an arrear [area] about as large as half England is a pretty big order, especially when things are hopelessly chaotic. In this town itself, there are a college and twelve schools under me – and I have to inspect them and note abuses, and make suggestions and reforms. The official writing to be done is considerable. Then there are plans of all sorts to make or examine, and I find it necessary to make translations into the vernacular (Guzerati and Marati) for their literature here is of the raggedest, so that I am fairly busy, and after all there is not much time to grieve the loneliness. The Maharajah is most anxious to be *un-Eastern* in his care for the women and girls in his State. We have just had *four lakhs* of rupees sanctioned (£40, 000) for the building of a college, and some of our schools are for *Zenana* ladies only, quite separate from the schools for children, but it is so hard to get them to look upon the acquisition of knowledge as something other than *a sin*'.[11]

---

i As early as 1902, 1904 and 1906, he passed laws allowing remarriage to Hindu widows, prohibiting infant marriage and offering free compulsory education.

PREPARING LEGAL CASES VERSUS PLEADING IN COURT

Cornelia also thought that the officials she had to deal with were dishonest. So it was with relief that she stopped after eight months. But she did learn a lot about the position of women in the Princely States and she was offered a number of legal cases by women as a result of her educational tours into the Kathiawar peninsula. By the end of the time, she was also at last offered a job in a solicitor's office nearer home in Bombay, Framji and Moss.[12] Cases to prepare for women in the Princely States began to come to her quite fast, although it was difficult to collect the evidence for them, given the restrictions under which the women lived. A well- known Indian judge reformer, Mr Justice Ranade, offered to chair a lecture by Cornelia on the need for women lawyers, in which she was able to announce her availability.

At the same time, Cornelia confessed to Lady Hobhouse that she wanted to go beyond the solicitor's role of preparing cases behind the scenes. She would like actually to plead in court.[13] This was to prove an impossible ambition for a woman. But in hopes of qualifying, she applied to take the Bachelor of Laws exam in Bombay, the nearest big legal centre to Poona. Having already passed the Bachelor of Civil Laws in Oxford, she felt disbelief when she found her name not on the list on December 20th 1895, and she had indeed been failed. The next year, on January 6th to 8th 1896 she found she had got only a pass, and not a first or second class.[14] She was further told that only a man, not a woman, could plead in the British courts on that basis, for want of a female precedent.[15] She could not know that 100 years later in 1988 a new portrait of her would be hung alongside that of Justice Ranade in the ground floor reading room of Bombay University's library tower. For the moment she had to content herself with work in the Princely States, usually preparing cases, but occasionally appearing in court.

FIRST APPEARANCES TO PLEAD IN COURT: DEFENDING AN ELEPHANT

One appearance to plead in the Princely State of Panch Mahals (Five Districts) greatly disappointed her because of its frivolity.[16] She was visited by an outrider from the Raja's palace, with a crooked sword in Kathiawari style, and asked to defend an elephant which had been deprived of the sugar palm grove bequeathed to it. After her initial visit, the Raja sent a carriage and pair and outriders with drawn swords to take her to the palace for the official hearing. The caparisoned elephant, named Folded Rosebud, stood in the courtyard, and they walked past the sentries in red and gold, who saluted with a 'present arms'. There was a great English bulldog which she patted at the top of the storey-tall flights of gleaming steps and who followed her into the Hall of Justice. The bench consisted of the Raja himself swinging on a swing with a musical box beside him playing 'Champagne Charlie is my name'. As Cornelia approached, the Raja declared, 'Your request is granted' – before she had said a word. Cornelia was indignant: she wanted to plead the case. That too was granted, but the Raja then dictated that whoever denied the elephant its grove was to be trampled to death by wild elephants. 'Are you satisfied?' he asked. As she returned down the steps, she asked the Chief Minister what was going on. 'His Highness long ago decided', the Minister replied, 'that he would never understand the complexities of the law. He therefore hit upon a simple device. If the dog likes the defence counsel, the case is won. If not, not'.

FIRST APPEARANCE OF A WOMAN TO PLEAD IN COURT IN BRITISH INDIA

In one case Cornelia was allowed to plead in a British court. This was another door opened and she was celebrated in the press as the first woman ever to do this in British India. She was allowed to plead not as a lawyer, but as a 'person for the defence of the accused'. She pointed out that British legal wording would allow a woman to act for the defence in a murder trial in her own home town of Poona, which was under British jurisdiction. Mr Crowe, the judge, checked with the Bombay High Court, which had to allow that 'person' did not exclude woman and so Mr Crowe heard her plead in his Sessions court with courtesy, on July 1st to 3rd 1896. Cornelia's lady, who was accused of murdering her woodcutter husband, had appeared from behind the croton bushes in their Poona garden and thrown herself at the feet of Cornelia's mother. Cornelia was able to prove that her lady could not have killed her husband on the night alleged, because the overnight storm would have washed away the pools of blood. The murderer was in fact a fellow woodcutter who was in debt to the victim.[17]

11. Cornelia back in Poona, 1896 (seated, with Dick and Alice standing).

BRITISH COURTS IN THE PRINCELY STATES: FURTHER APPEARANCES TO PLEAD

Most of Cornelia's appearances to plead were not in British India, but in the Princely States. There, there were courts known as agency courts, where subjects of these states could bring grievances to British adjudication through the political agent if application in the princely courts had failed. At this stage, Cornelia did much of her work for secluded women in the Kathiawar courts, in the first instance in princely courts - she was often in Wadhwan - and, on appeal, in agency courts centred on Rajkot in Gujarat. The case of which she was proudest took a very long time because it involved an appeal to the Viceroy, and was not finally successful until 1906. It concerned a senior Rani, or to give her the title proper for that region, a senior Thakurani. On the death of her Hindu husband, she had had to flee from the quarters where his other wives lived, and indeed three or four royal wives from each of four generations. Polygamy was then allowed to Hindu men for the purpose of producing a son. The Thakurani was escaping a plot to murder her, and for 30 years she had not been paid the allowance that her husband had left her. Cornelia first appealed to the court of the ruling step-grandson who, following his father, was unapologetically withholding the money. From there she had to appeal through the British political agent to agency courts and eventually to the Viceroy. Cornelia later contrasted the success of this appeal with what she regarded as cover-ups by the political agents in the later years of the British Raj. When the verdict in favour of her Thakurani was announced, a message purportedly from the ruling step-grandson offered reconciliation and a garment to be worn next to the lady's skin. Her waiting woman held it back to show Cornelia, who had it chemically analysed. It was poisoned and would have killed the Thakurani. When the widowed Thakurani finally got the full arrears in 1907, she chortled. But she nonetheless wanted little of the money for herself, except for the costs of a pilgrimage to Hardwar (Haridwar) and her funeral expenses. The rest she allocated to her married waiting woman and husband, and to the new son of the offending step grandson. When Cornelia asked, 'Are you not angry with him?', she replied, 'When others hurt us, God resents it for us.'[18] Cornelia took this answer over from the Hindu Thakurani as part of her own Christian belief and had a number of occasions on which to say it.

It was during this period that Cornelia's defence of a client provoked a murder attempt on her. She saw a man slipping over a wall with a Kathiawar weapon, and called out, 'Careful. There is no foothold,' at which the man disappeared as fast as he had appeared.[19] In another attempt, a packet was sent to her breakfast table from the palace she was investigating which caused her to faint immediately. Chemical analysis showed that her life had been spared only because of her practice of breakfasting out of doors.[20]

So far Cornelia's attempts to defend women in the Princely States had proved difficult. The Maharajas were more friendly to women lawyers than the British, but defending an elephant was unsatisfying, gaining evidence on behalf of women was difficult, and the British appeal system was slow. Increasingly, it looked as if, despite British hostility to women lawyers, pleading in *British* Courts in *British* India would be the way to help women.

The uncertainty of her position, compared with her earlier assured place in England, still weighed on Cornelia and fostered a certain jealousy of Alice who was now enjoying her student days in London. She writes, 'I feel so odd, as if I were dead and my place taken by another. She (Alice) is doing all the things I did and is evidently very happy.' She found it particularly difficult to share her closest friends with Alice, when she could no longer see them herself, and writes, 'The good God make me willing to part even with Nell[ii] to her.'[21]

Cornelia's experience in Kathiawar enabled her to write a magisterial account in *The Nineteenth Century* of the needs of secluded women.[22] There was a much more dramatic case in the Princely States still to come, but that was nearer Allahabad, where she was to move next. Dick was not able to plead as a barrister in Poona, as he was not enrolled there.[23] So he decided in 1897 to move to Allahabad, and Cornelia went with him. Allahabad was the capital of what was then called the Northwest Provinces, and later came to be called the United Provinces (UP, now Uttar Pradesh). It was also to become for a while perhaps the greatest centre for law in India. As well as Dick, who was a barrister, two Indian lawyers of vakil rank were promoted to practise as barristers in the High Court there. One, slightly older than Dick, was Motilal Nehru, the father of the man who was to be India's first Prime Minister, Jawaharlal Nehru. Another was Sir Tej Bahadur Sapru, four years younger. They were both to become leaders of the Indian Independence Movement. Jawaharlal Nehru's sister, Nan Pandit, was to remember how good Dick was to her as a child,[24] and Cornelia spoke warmly of her when she was adult.[25]

BROTHER AND SISTER MOVE TO ALLAHABAD

Cornelia and Dick arrived in Allahabad on March 18th 1897 and for a few initial weeks took rooms, sometimes together and sometimes apart. Cornelia's first impression of the Allahabad market was of a quaint oriental place, with shops much more primitive than in Bombay or Poona. It swarmed with beggars and grubby children. Cornelia and Dick 'poked about' among the grain, and Cornelia watched

ii Nell was a very close Somerville friend, née Martin.

people being shaved in the street, and bargaining.[26] Later, she drove the dog cart through the city to the market on market day, her groom holding an umbrella over her and clearing the way with well chosen insults to individuals in their path.[27]

> 'Here were carpet sellers beating out their glorious coloured wares, here yellow- and blue- and red-garmented cotton cleaners, sitting by an upright "harp", twang, twang, a mountain of driven snow behind them, here pyramids of brass gleaming in the sunshine, here the wax worker tracing his pattern on the indigo blue table cloth, a brush his only implement, his eye and imagination his only guide, now a dyer lifting the heavy masses of moist drapery out of the transforming pan.'

And on arrival at the market, despite her groom's incantation, 'imps of the evil one, dancing shameless in the path of the Presence', she accepted the offer of one of the imps, a boy of nine, who said, 'I will be your guide in the market place.' That way she learnt how one got the basic price for the goods on offer and how disputes were settled by the one who had bought the stall traditionally associated with justice.

By April 5th, Dick had arranged to rent their home together in an elegant part of town at 10 Edmonstone Road, a pretty yellow bungalow with 'a wealth of orange-gold honeysuckle festooning the porch'. The garden, tended with the assistance of those children who had had the audacity and charm to win in the daily offer of services, had spacious grounds. It included orchards, a tennis court, and a secluded well near the servants' quarters.[28] This was to feature in Cornelia's story later.[29] A well was essential to the luxuriant gardens of Allahabad, and Dick had earlier had one dug for the family's holiday cottage in Lanowli. A later house of his in Allahabad was even called 'the high well house', because it had a quaint old ruin rising high above the well, robed in creepers which twice a year were decked with masses of white and pink antigonum in 'cascades of beauty'. Dick shared Cornelia's love of flowers and he wrote of the later garden:

> 'My rose garden is at the side of my house, so that people do not see it unless I specially take them to it. No one wonders at my vases being full of sweet pea and larkspur and phlox and such, because those grow in front where they are readily seen, but when they see bowls of roses, they say, 'where did you get those lovely roses?'. And then with pride I show them my miniature rose garden. ... My gardener's favourite colour is crimson, and bowls of these deep red blooms delight my eye and brighten my rooms'.[30]

On April 15th they moved in. By May, the heat required a coolie to pull the punkah fans or curtains. Dick went to a large number of auctions for furnishings, and he made two unsuccessful purchases of sickly horses through trying

12. Dick and Cornelia's shared house in Allahabad, 1897–1901.

to economise. Cornelia arranged the rooms, leaving the flower arrangements to Dick, although at first they could not afford grass seed for the lawns.[31] On my visit to 24 Edmonstone Road in 1989, the grounds of number 10 were still there with the address carved on the original stone gatepost, but they were owned by a newspaper and the yellow bungalow had first become a hospital and then been pulled down.[32]

SOCIAL LIFE IN ALLAHABAD

On their second day in Allahabad, they had called on a senior English judge, Harrison Falkner Blair, and his wife, who were charming to them, and advised them on housing. The Falkner Blairs returned the call on March 25th, and further advised them on the 27th about the documents Dick needed in order to be called to the Allahabad bar as a barrister. In April, Cornelia asked Mrs Falkner Blair about Dick's joining the gym, and she said her husband would propose Dick, though she had to chivvy to get him elected a year later. The Falkner Blairs had them to dinner twice in April.[33]

Their other early host was the Bishop of Allahabad. It was a cathedral town, and Cornelia and Dick attended regularly. Dick threw himself into cathedral work, playing cricket for the cathedral, singing in the choir and entertaining Christian workers. He also went out for the Bishop to the Christian village of Muirabad, opened a library and sat on a commission to investigate workers' grievances, while Cornelia did some teaching in the school there.[34]

The town was very sociable. There was tennis and badminton, although they moved to the courts in the Park, since their own was not well marked out. There were polo and gymkhanas, with 'at-home' receptions at the polo ground. There was much walking round the Park, drives to the Jumna Bridge and to Fort George above the river. In the summer, there was sculling on the river. There were many garden parties, some with fireworks, and many dances, some in peoples' homes, or in their marquees or their floodlit grounds, and regular ones at Mayo Hall, where Dick sometimes put up the decorations. Cornelia danced 'The Washington Post' with Dick. Dick's undergraduate friend, Richard Burn, was on the committee of the club and it invited Dick to attend until such time as they balloted on his membership. Dick and Cornelia promptly arranged an evening's entertainment there, with Dick doing a sketch and Mrs Falkner Blair bringing Cornelia along. Dick was also called on to recite at private dinner parties.[35] Dick's other long- term friend, besides Burn, was his fellow lawyer Wallach, an Englishman who always enlivened Dick with a wit and style that reflected his Bulgarian origins. In 1919, he was to return to England a little before Dick and become a Privy Council lawyer.[36]

Some parties were on a grander scale. The Lieutenant Governor of the Northwest (later United) Provinces had 'at-home' – receptions – in the pretty grounds of Government House, with gorgeously apparelled Rajas among the guests. And in 1898, there were two special farewells, one to the retiring Lieutenant Governor, Sir Antony MacDonnell, who was to play a role in Cornelia's later story,[37] and one to the retiring Chief Justice of Allahabad.[38]

The party for the Lieutenant Governor was given at Muir College, the handsome college built through a former Lieutenant Governor, Sir William Muir, where Dick would later teach. It happily combined Sicilian capitals with a Moghul-style tiled dome and stone lattices. On my visit in 1989, the stonework of the sand-coloured colonnades was unimpaired. There was a magnificent marbled hall, and the shuttered lecture rooms were still ornate. The party was given by Indians, the Pundits of the sacred city of Benares (Varanasi) and landowners grateful for the Lieutenant Governor's famine relief measures in 1896–1898. The college was beautifully illuminated with 'festoons of brilliance' along the drives, many coloured lights over the gateways, tiny rows of 'butties' picking out the terraces and lighting over the Lieutenant Governor's whole route from Government House. There were fireworks, speeches and supper in the tents and Mr Falkner Blair gave Cornelia introductions to some of the Rajas. Little did Cornelia foresee that she might later suspect MacDonnell of being an enemy.[39]

The party for the retiring Chief Justice was given by Indian vakils, pleaders of the rank below barrister, which was the commoner rank at that time for Indians. It was held in the gardens of Kushru Bagh under the stars among the tombs of emperors, tombs with minarets and Persian inscriptions. The filtration tanks were lit and there were reflections in the water. Cornelia and Dick went with two of the judges' families, the Falkner Blairs and the Knoxes. Cornelia wore an evening blouse of red silk shot with pink, the sleeves and trimmings red, the front pink veiled with white crepe silk, the saree pink. Mrs Falkner Blair had Cornelia photographed. The ladies' dresses were pretty. There were fireworks, the best band, the cleverest jugglers, the nicest champagne, strawberries and cream. Again, Cornelia did not foresee that the choice of the next Chief Justice would matter so much.[40]

Allahabad is at the sacred confluence of the Rivers Jumna and Ganges, and on February 10th 1899, Blair took Cornelia to her first Mela, a gathering on the banks of 10,000 pilgrims.[41] On this occasion she was taken by surprise and horrified by the thousands of fakirs. Some of them were selling bottles for collecting holy water from the Ganges, or ashes to eat made of cow dung. They were absolutely naked, hair matted, covered with ash or coloured powder, some with arms permanently extended and atrophied, some on spikes, others shrivelled with nails curling down their arms. In 1936, she was to go to the much bigger Kumbh Mela, held in the same place only once every thirteen years or so, and that time, though avoiding the ascetic fakirs, she appreciated the learned sadhus and positively enjoyed talking to the pilgrims.[42] I myself was to go with a Pundit host in 1989, when 3 million pilgrims had already assembled and 25 million were expected 11 days later. We were offered Ganges water to drink from earthenware pots, and though I only sprinkled myself, the pilgrims waded in their clothes out into the Ganges, shoulders bared, collected the water in bottles, and, according to our Pundit host, drank straight from the river, the women returning with their bright saris held aloft in a rectangle to dry. My own conversations were with swamis and Sanskrit scholars, whom I was asked to address in a huge marquee on the importance of Sanskrit, of which my knowledge was confined to the common root words of Greek and Sanskrit. As we drove away at dusk from the temporary city-encampment, we could not take in all the things that people were carrying for sale, the ingenious vessels in which they were carrying them, the temples, tents, moving neon lights, brightly decorated bicycle rickshaws, none motorised, and all with an unimaginable gaiety.

THE BROTHER AND SISTER LAWYER TEAM

Dick and Cornelia soon became known as a brother and sister lawyer team, and although only Dick was allowed to plead, they prepared the cases together. Dick first went to the High Court on April 26th 1897 and rented an office, then

13. Dick, the young Allahabad barrister, 1890s.

two days later went for the first time in robes and soon was going daily, and he got his first cases surprisingly fast in May.[43] On February 11th, he undertook an appeal in a murder case from the Cawnpore (Kanpur) riots. His client had been condemned to be hanged, but on March 22nd 1898, Dick got him reprieved and was complimented in open court for a bold new line of argument by the outgoing Chief Justice.[44] The case involved the recent Cawnpore riots over the Government's measures for controlling plague.

Dick also helped his future prospects by giving an inspiring lecture to the students at Muir College, where he would later be employed, on university life and what students should be like.[45]

CORNELIA'S CAREER AS A PLEADER SABOTAGED

Although Dick was so soon successful, Cornelia's experience was very different. The pass in the Bombay Bachelor of Laws should have enabled her to plead at the level of vakil anywhere in India. But in 1897, she applied three times to the High Court in Allahabad to practise, and, as a woman, was refused three times. On May 15th, however, she was told that she could practise, if she passed their special exam. She passed the exam on January 19th, including the language examination in Urdu, even though she was being examined by some of her most violent opponents. She knew she passed the Urdu, because the examiner told the law examiners and the Registrar. But then a trick was played on her. They had not examined her in the complex ancient Persian script called Shikasta, because it was archaic and obsolete, and so they deemed that she had not passed in Urdu. So she studied for another year, simultaneously improving her Urdu every day, and had passed the examination, including the new requirement, by February 3rd 1899. But meanwhile something else had happened. A new Chief Justice had been appointed. Cornelia had hoped it would be Harrison Falkner Blair, but the man appointed was Sir Arthur Strachey. His direction to the jury in the 1897 trial of the nationalist leader Tilak had given him prominence, but came to be considered unfair even by some of the British. Strachey came to stay with Falkner Blair, and his very first remarks to Cornelia at a dinner given by Falkner Blair were ominous: 'If you appeared before me, how could I scold you?' His wife went on to warn Cornelia that there were appalling and insuperable difficulties about appointing her. In the event, on April 4th 1899, the court was split three against three, with Falkner Blair, Aikman and Knox voting for Cornelia, and Burkitt, Bannerji and Strachey against. Because the votes were equally divided, Strachey as Chief Justice added his second casting vote against. This use of the casting vote was questioned three days later by Aikman and Falkner Blair at a further meeting for which they called, but the query was rejected. The Bengali judge, Bannerji, who voted against Cornelia, clearly felt awkward, and came to see her for two and a half hours. But Cornelia confronted him and the Chief Justice, who, however, went on to re-emphasise his opposition by pointing out to her that even outside the High Court no magistrate would now be willing to go against the High Court's decision. In fact he went out of his way to bring that about, because he contacted the District Magistrate and told him that it would be disrespectful to the High Court if magistrates' courts employed Cornelia after all.[46] The bar library, which consisted of all the barristers sided with Cornelia, so Dick was able to tell her, and thought that the High Court had made a promise that it had now broken.[47]

At the time of the next vacancy in 1901, Lord Hobhouse told Cornelia that the Privy Council thought that Falkner Blair would get the job of Chief Justice.[48] If that had happened, she might still have been enrolled as a vakil or barrister, and her whole life story, and perhaps the future of women vakils and barristers, might have been different. But by then it would have been difficult for Falkner Blair to bring this about.[49]

By this time, the 'stout youth' tutor, Raleigh, who had been so supportive to Cornelia in Oxford had been appointed as the Legal Member on the Viceroy's Council and was in Simla (Shimla), so she consulted him. But Raleigh too was not keen on her appearing in court. So she asked why, instead of inclusion as vakil on the rolls or barrister at the bar, there should not be a post of legal adviser on women and infant wards of court in British India. She also wrote, but without effect, to Mr La Touche, the Chief Member on the Board of Revenue, Cornelia's eventual employer, which was responsible for the Court of Wards, and later it proved that he had been put off by the High Court decision. Raleigh was not very favourable about this either when talking to Falkner Blair. But Strachey, who would not be affected by such a post, proposed that Cornelia should collect opinions on whether such a post would be useful and she learnt from her enemy.[50] Raleigh went on to be very helpful about collecting opinions.[51] So now for Cornelia, half way through her ten-year campaign, the idea of pleading in court was shelved and she had set herself the new goal of getting a special post created.

DEFENDING SECLUDED WOMEN: PERILOUS RESCUE FROM TIHUR FORT

Within four months of her rejection, Cornelia was engaged in one of her most hair-raising investigations involving the rights of secluded women. Although her two trips took place in a Princely State and not in British India, the welfare of the lady in question had originally been arranged by the local British district officer of the rank of Collector,[iii] and the trips vividly revealed the need for a post such as she had proposed, given that no one but a woman, and therefore no one in the British Raj, could visit women behind the curtain to find out what was happening to them. Her second visit involved her most dangerous, though not her only, kidnap rescue of a secluded woman. Having written an account of the episode in letters, she took the opportunity of converting one set of letters into an article in *The Nineteenth Century*.[52]

A Brahmin priest came to find Cornelia, having heard of her power to help from a Hindi newspaper. As priest to a certain Rani, he had repented of his part in her marriage, and so had gone to Allahabad to find the now legendary brother and sister 'ballisters'. The Rani owed her jeopardy to having been married off to a mentally deficient ruler, a Thakur or Raja in the remote town of Amapur. The Rani's priest confessed to Cornelia that he had conspired with the deficient Raja's priest to conceal the Raja's mental condition, and it was the two priests who had arranged the marriage. The Raja had no such royal ancestry as his educated wife, who came from a ruling family, that of Ullwar near Calcutta. Rather, he had been adopted into the ruling family from the lowlier circle of the local ministers of the dowager Rani.

For the first year of marriage, while the dowager Rani lived, she greatly valued the new wife and gave her a record sum as wedding gift or 'seeing-of-the-face' gift. But the scheming ministers had got the priests to carry out a secret second marriage, within hours of the first, to a girl from their own circles, with a view to getting their own way when the old dowager Rani died, as she soon did. Unsurprisingly, as the first two children of the first wife were sons with prior claim to succession, they died, one, according to Cornelia, smothered in tobacco fumes, another plunged in boiling water. But, being educated,

---

iii Collector is the second rung up the ladder of the Indian Civil Service described in Chapter 10, p. 1.

the Rani had written to a British Collector for protection when expecting her third child. Collectors in the Indian Civil Service had responsibility for whole districts, which were sometimes huge, and rose to this position as the second rung on the highly selective ladder of the service.[53] The Rani's third child turned out to be a son as well and the Rani begged the Collector to investigate, while exonerating her husband from the murders because of his mental condition. The Collector interviewed her through a screen and had her removed to the supposed safety of Tihur fort,[iv] five miles further off, where the child was born, with an allowance of 800 rupees a month and a guard of Indian sepoys from the British Collector's headquarters. Unfortunately, the fort was by now bat-infested, the sepoys were paid by the deranged ruler and regarded her as his prisoner, and the allowance had been stopped two and a half years ago, after she visited Cawnpore for medical help, even though she had done so with her husband's permission, and her medical attention had called for 200 rupees a day. The British Collector's successor knew nothing about the case and regarded the Princely State as outside his jurisdiction. Meagre provisions were supplied to the Rani by a Brahmin, also mentally disadvantaged, but loyal. But the local village was forbidden to let her have provisions and he had to get them from a distance. At night, the Rani guarded her son, who was now 8, with a pistol.

Cornelia decided first to go and see if the report was true. The priest who came to see her wanted her to carry a gun because there were so many bad people in those parts. Instead she inquired about a British police escort, but that was denied on the grounds that the journey was not official. She reached Orai[v] by train at midnight on August 17th 1899, with a nurse (ayah) and a head servant (khansama), only to find that the Rani's priest had been obstructed in his efforts to secure the promised palanquins to carry her further. Cornelia travelled in palanquins a great deal. They were boxes on poles and very uncomfortable as they did not allow her to sit upright without banging her head on the lid and in the present case were even more cramped as she had to carry her valuables with her.[54] It took two hours on the cold railway platform and then the following morning to secure the palanquins, and consequently Cornelia did not reach Jalaun,[vi] 13 miles along the road, until 2.30 in the afternoon, and could not leave for the next leg of the journey until 10 in the evening.

---

iv Cornelia's published versions, but not her letters, call it Sihar, by way of disguise.
v Her published version disguises this as Raio.
vi Disguised as Launaj.

At Jalaun, Cornelia suffered 'agonies of thirst'.[55]

'I did not dare venture well water, but I sucked a sour lemon. I shall be grateful to the little yellow sour lemon all my days: had several of 'em in my lunch basket and they were my only drink for four hot days of journeying.'

It was not quite her only drink because there was at Jalaun a Tehsildar, an Indian Sub-collector of the local sub-district which included Tihur. His sepoys (armed men) arrived just as Cornelia was about to move on.

'One of them at my request brought me the loveliest draught of fresh milk (a stirrup cup, as my foot was in the palanquin. The bearer could not find any). I drank two mugs full and felt the muscles of my throat moist again'.

The Tehsildar's men escorted her only a little of the way out of Jalaun, and once they had turned back, the bearers of her palanquin put her down every ten minutes and finally refused to move further through the dark unless she entrusted her valuables to their tender care. She overcame that, but there were other troubles.[56]

'Oh, the hideousness of that night: roads awful, men insolent and the torch, oh! the torch. It annoyed every nerve of me: the brilliance and the heat and the smell of the oil. I told the torch bearer to precede the procession. The bearers *insisted* on his walking by the open palanquin, so that the wind blew the heat and smoke into my face. They saw that it annoyed me and refused to move an inch unless the man was just in that position were t'would most inconvenience me to have him. I suppose it was their sole method of retaliation for my refusal to be robbed.'

Cornelia nodded off during the night and woke up with the oil torch out, and everyone asleep in the middle of a bare wilderness. After directing them, from her knowledge of maps, to the nearest village,[vii] bribing the village watchman for lamp oil, securing three hours' rest and promising extra pay for an early arrival, she got the bearers to press on to Madogarh[viii] by 8 a.m. But this was in Princely territory governed by the Raja, and the priest who had accompanied her decided he had better conceal Cornelia's purpose by telling the local doctor that Cornelia was herself a doctor. To maintain that disguise, she had to examine the doctor's patients and pretend medical knowledge. Eventually, she insisted that the doctor must bring the officer in charge of the police station (Thanedar), so that she could get a pass to enter Tihur fort, still some hours

---

vii Disguised as Dale Buna.
viii Disguised as Damhogarh.

away. The police officer was uncertain whether to please the British authorities or the Raja, and the pass he supplied was initially defective, but Cornelia insisted on correction.

She finally reached Tihur fort at noon, but was denied entrance by the guard at the outer moat, along with the nurse and head servant. But again the guard was uncertain what to do, having sent for instructions both to the nearest British town and to the Raja, and not yet having heard from the Raja. Her peremptory orders, identification of the guard's commanding officer, production of the Thanedar's note, and the bluff that she would report non-compliance to the Tehsildar at Madhogarh, slowly led to compliance. She was admitted through a series of moats, walls, overgrown courtyards, filthy passages, and up dark stairs to the damp and crumbling roof terrace where the Rani lived amidst damp, dirt and disrepair. The Rani, a little fat, fair woman with glossy hair,[57] promptly laid her head on Cornelia's feet, wept, thanked God, and called her her sister and her salvation. Her boy had only a woman's saree to wear and had never had his hair cut.

Cornelia spent much of the day hearing her story. But she had to start her return that night, although she had to parley with the palanquin bearers for three hours, perhaps because everyone was awaiting the Raja's decision. Eventually, she got the guard on her side and forced the palanquin bearers. They set off only at 11 at night, but she had confirmed the truth of the story.

The next journey in October was much more dangerous, because the Raja's people were fully alerted. She had been in touch with the Rani's mother in Cawnpore, who was not allowed by the Raja's family to see her daughter. On hearing from Cornelia, the mother had sent a maid servant and provisions to her daughter, but the hostile Tehsildar at Jalaun had not given them a pass to enter the fort. The mother had also applied to the British to authorise a rescue kidnap and this had been granted. Cornelia was warned more than once that the Raja's people planned to kill her and the Rani en route and kidnap the boy. Justices Falkner Blair and Knox told her to take a guard and she wrote to the Inspector General of Police, Mr Grierson Jackson, to ask for one, but he was on tour and she got no reply. The Raja's people meanwhile sent an agent to Allahabad to persuade Cornelia to turn against the Rani and were even angrier when she refused. She took with her three servants, a nurse (ayah), a head servant (khansama)[58] and a henchman (chaprassi), and she packed chocolate and biscuits for the desert.

Dick and Falkner Blair were away, so she left final messages elsewhere.[59]

'Saturday was spent in preparations. There was the very strong presumption that I would never return and there were naturally *last things* to do and say. I wrote my final words with a lump in my throat and made all business arrangements with a Collector, asking interviews for the next morning, and then I had a warm bath and turned into bed for a couple of hours. . . . I wrote a note to the Chaplain at the Cathedral, kind Mr Hatchett, saying that if I did not send a message by wire or otherwise by the following Thursday, he was to understand that my head was on that threatened charger, and he should find a sealed packet in such and such a place, to break the news to my people, etc. Sunday morning I went to Cathedral, and what I thought would be my last celebration'.

Arrived at her railway stop at Orai, Cornelia had an introduction from her legal friend Justice Knox in Allahabad to the British District Superintendent of Police, who was very helpful. But he had to bow to the Tehsildar at Jalaun, and Cornelia speaks of 'all the weary ache and impatience of that day'.[60] The Tehsildar was very hostile to the Rani, said her throat should have been cut, refused a proper guard, never supplied any of his own armed men as he had been got to promise, and yielded only one palanquin. But well into the night, 13 miles further along the route, the next Tehsildar, to whom she had written, had two palanquins waiting, and 30 bearers to do the carrying in relays. Speaking in Urdu, she persuaded the bearers to get her to the fort by morning, which they acknowledged they could do by taking a very rough short cut. Even so, Cornelia woke up in the middle of the night surrounded by strange villagers, to find that the bearers, whether by accident or not, had wandered into the Raja's territory at Rampura. She identified the village watchman, had her headman seize his arm and commanded him to show them back onto their route, which in his astonishment he did. Cornelia's henchman had meanwhile been sent by the slower route to Tihur and told to listen for any gossip about plots from the Raja's side.

At the fort by 8 a.m., she was determined to return the same day. But the Rani asked for a week to prepare. She wanted to take on their clandestine escape a golden umbrella and a brocade cover for the top of her palanquin, along with old halberds, gold maces and silver spears, to bribe assailants, and a hookah, a water-cooled smoking tube, as well as the necessary sloppy food and the personal cooking vessels required by custom. Cornelia had eaten neither dinner the night before nor breakfast that morning. After finding something to eat, she made a complete check of the many unused rooms, to rule out the accusation that the Rani had concealed treasure.[61]

'Oh! the steep and unclean stairs and the – odours; and oh! the *bats*! A nightmare! *Flights* of them coming from everywhere. I had disturbed them, you see, as I walked up the narrow staircase and here they were, wheeling round and round, a-flapping about my head and ears, at my elbow – *clouds* of them shut in with me, and, ah! the filthiness under foot. I put my draperies over my head and rushed up blindly! Yes, I own it! No army of dacoits[ix] did I fear, nor man, nor beast – but *bats*!'

No sooner was Cornelia rid of the bats than her henchman came to say that the assassination team was awaiting them on the regular cart road at 7 that evening. She had no guard and so had to persuade the recalcitrant bearers and the Rani to start earlier and by a different route, without revealing the reason.

Cornelia got the Rani and boy with their goods down to the courtyard in her own suitably screened palanquin and let the 30 bearers in to take her outside the gates. But her head servant then reported that the Rani absolutely refused to depart in anything but the heavy, lumbering, worm-eaten royal palanquin. In order to protect the Rani's purdah while swapping palanquins, Cornelia ordered the bearers and fortress guard inside the gates and locked them in before they could think, and then transferred Rani, boy and accoutrements, screened under the brocade cover, from the light palanquin into the royal one, as required. Then she let the astonished guards and bearers out. The problem now was the weight of the heavy royal palanquin and the bearers almost cried off. But she assigned all but eight of them to take the royal palanquin in turns.

At 5 p.m. they set off by the short cut in the opposite direction from the assassins. The fields of tall grass and sugar cane could easily have concealed other assassins, or the fortress guard could have alerted the known assassination team to their different route. If they were accosted and asked whose cortege this was, the men were told only to say 'The Memsahib's', and Cornelia would do the talking in Urdu. She went in her palanquin first with four bearers at a time, then the Rani, with two of Cornelia's servants walking on either side, and finally the nurse and the Rani's woman servant in a cart surrounded by those bearers who were in between stints of carrying. Later, they were joined by two armed guards sent by the District Superintendent of Police. With nightfall they had a good moon. The Rani was hysterical. The exhausted bearers had to put the heavy palanquin down every few minutes and at every well restore strength with a smoke and a chat. As they travelled, the bearers chanted about Cornelia. In her rendering 'She spoke like the Viceroy to the guard, turning the men in,

---

ix Assassins.

shutting the gates on them and they obeyed. Who can she be?' (Chorus: 'Who can she be?'). 'She wears garments of silk, but eats only one piece of bread a day' (Chorus: 'half a piece').

Arrived safely at Orai, the Rani, still hysterical, had to be persuaded to travel by train with Cornelia, in a reserved lady's carriage, changing at Cawnpore for Allahabad, where her mother had gone to wait. She was safely delivered to her mother; the boy was made a ward of the British Court of Wards, and put under British protection, and a lunacy commission made arrangements for the care of the Raja. Cornelia had thus served the Court of Wards and the British administration, although it was to be many years before she was employed by them. She nonetheless had the story published as part of her campaign to gain employment.[62]

At this moment, however, Cornelia's hopes of impressing on the British the need for her services were very nearly sunk by a love affair with a senior English judge in Allahabad. We need to turn to her personal life.

CHAPTER 5

LOVE AND EXILE TO ENGLAND

In her personal life Cornelia's plan, carried out in Oxford and London, was to make friends only with older men, so as to avoid the unhappy romances experienced by her two oldest sisters, as described in Appendix 1. The plan seemed to be working in Allahabad in her friendship with Harrison Falkner Blair, who was 60 in 1898 as against her 32 in November of that year.

Eight days after he welcomed the new arrivals to Allahabad on March 19th 1897, Cornelia wrote, 'I am not sure of Blair. But he is most gentle: manlike and suave.' He had a moustache and beard and he smoked scented tobacco.[1] After Christmas, following a year of the most delightful family gatherings with Dick and Cornelia, he gave her his photograph and took her to be photographed. Then on January 2nd, he sat beside her in the boat on a river party and she was in love with him.[2]

For January 22nd 1898 he had arranged a most magnificent party.[3] There was to be a total eclipse of the sun viewable from a hill at Buxar, a five hour train journey away. He had booked a saloon carriage on a special train with a cooking carriage attached. Cornelia and Dick woke at 5, were at the station at 6.30, and breakfast was served for the party of 7 on the train. On arrival at Buxar, Dick unfortunately got separated and swept up into the Lieutenant Governor's party, and they went off to different camps, though his party looked for him everywhere. The eclipse was spectacular. Most birds went to bed, though one wheeled round their heads, and Cornelia was told that flowers closed their petals. Dick was reunited at the carriage to take them back, and they lunched, and made up nonsense verses on the way home. Cornelia called it one of the happiest days she had known.

Very soon, however, she was struggling. Falkner Blair was in love with her and saw her nearly every day and often twice. The relationship was never fully consummated, but by mid-January it involved physical contact and was delightful, yet caused her agonies, not only of waiting for the next meeting, but of thought about herself, about God and about Falkner Blair.[4] She spoke of the secluded well in the garden as handy, but the servants knew. The complications grew. On May 15th, with Dick away for a case, Mrs Falkner Blair asked Cornelia to stay for a few days and was very pleasant to her.[5] Dick only discovered the situation later that month, around April 28th, and his talk was not of God, but of how 'the devil looks out through your face'. Cornelia understood well enough, because she felt the need to ask God to 'forgive, cleanse and save her'. By June 30th, Dick was trying to get her away to the Poona home. He forbade writing to Falkner Blair and removed the ink. By August 3rd, Mrs Falkner Blair knew and came to see Dick, who at once had Cornelia summoned to Poona for over three months until October 8th 1898, while the Falkner Blairs went for a still longer restorative holiday to Kashmir.

The situation dragged on for two years. At first, Cornelia was not allowed to talk to Mrs Falkner Blair at all. As for Falkner Blair himself, after some painful clearing of the air, limited meetings resumed, supposedly chaperoned, and without unauthorised letter writing, but the restrictions did not hold and Dick appointed someone to shadow Cornelia when he had to be absent. Several times, he went to Poona and consulted, and for four months from May 30th to September 28th 1900, Cornelia was almost entirely removed from Allahabad, mostly to Poona, apart from a week of celebrations, which she was asked to conduct elsewhere, for Lord Roberts' occupation of Pretoria in the Boer War. On February 3rd 1901, Dick told her the final decision with the full weight of the family behind him: she was to be exiled via Poona to England. She left Allahabad on February 15th, helped in the Poona school and then sailed for England on April 26th 1901, for an exile that was to last three years. Blair was 63 and Cornelia 34.

From the family's perspective, Cornelia had fallen into a deeper moral hole than any she had complained about in connexion with Zuleika or Pheroze. Cornelia herself, in *India Calling*, runs together the period of exile with the student period of eight years earlier in London, so that the length of the exile does not have to be explained, and it is referred to only as an interlude due to ill health.[6] The family objected on moral grounds, but there were practical disadvantages too. The brother and sister team was finished. The cause of women lawyers would have been wrecked for a very long time, if its many opponents could say that the first woman lawyer to be let loose in India had stolen the affections of a judge from the wife who was entertaining her. There could have been no further campaign for a legal post. It would also have been very hard for Dick as a barrister and Falkner Blair as a judge to continue appearing in court before each other. As it was, people in Allahabad knew, and she referred subsequently to a conspiracy, evidently against Falkner Blair, and wrote to him, 'I can't help loving Dick for sticking by you.' The conspiracy seems to have deprived Falkner Blair of the expected succession to the post of Chief Justice.[7]

A LOVE AFFAIR THROUGH LETTERS

Cornelia refused to blame her beloved brother Dick for her exile, but she was very sad that he would not even correspond with her, unless she sent a letter of renunciation. She wanted Falkner Blair to tell her of the house she had shared with Dick, the garden, the friends, who was making tea, how Dick looked and his work.[8] It was only from Falkner Blair that she learnt that in January 1903 Dick was awarded a law lectureship in Allahabad, in addition to his work at the High Court,[9] and moved a few doors along from 10 to 19 Edmonstone Road. He would have been equidistant between the High Court and the University, and little more than a mile from either. She wrote to Falkner Blair:[10]

'you know how fond I was, am, of Dick, the only brother I've had and so much connected with Oxford and early Indian days . . . . It is not his fault. At a critical moment in our joint ménage, I widened my shoulders – understand? (was glad to) and then *folk* did their work completely. You see their object was a severance so complete that a return would be impossible for me. See? They were wise in their generation. And so it happens that I get no news of the dear little yellow house where I was so happy, and only an occasional statement that he is well and happy through my mother. But I am often wistful for news. Are things in their old places? The "altar" ' (probably in front of his father's picture, mentioned below) 'has it flowers? Does the sacred picture hang in its accustomed spot? Is the arrangement of the room the same? Who are his friends now? When folk tea with him, who makes tea? What of the garden? And my roses? . . . How does Dick look? Does his work prosper? . . . I am glad, so glad, whenever I hear of your being with Dick, or being good to him. I want him always to love and respect you. Love him and be good to him still for my sake, Titso. Remember two things – nothing is his fault, and I gladly pay my penalty. God takes toll from us when he blesses us beyond all thought. This is my toll. Who would not pay it?'

The first effect of the exile after a very short time was that the relationship between Cornelia and Falkner Blair became a very much happier one. Their love letters continued to 1907 – well after Cornelia had returned to India. During her years in England, the letters came by boat and were thus reduced to one or two a week. Not only were her tribulations calmed as soon as she could report them, but she looked at things with a view to telling him about them, her enjoyment was complete only when she did so and he replied, and she felt approved only if he endorsed the approval offered by others.[11] She sent him in 1903 the poem, 'I am not fair but thou hast thought me so,' which exactly expressed her feeling towards him.[12] 'I looked at everything', she writes from Alexandria en route to England, 'with a view to passing it on to you'.[13] The letters are informative about her life, moving and restrained. There are few explicit endearments in her letters to Falkner Blair, except for the word 'utterly'. Most of the others are expressed as 'take the things unsaid' or by minimal abbreviations, although a few are explained.[14]

Falkner Blair's letters have not survived. He had to write them in his dressing room, or on the rooftop.[15] None of Cornelia's family knew that she was still writing, although she did once have to ask Falkner Blair to conceal from Dick his knowledge of her doings. Nonetheless, in this altered situation she could focus on what she saw as the eternal character of their relationship, and she soon felt that she could talk to God, was getting free, and that their love would heal them.[16]

Cornelia wore as her favourite piece of jewellery a cloud-coloured moonstone which Blair sent her for her first Christmas in exile.[17] It is an intaglio showing the goddess of war, Bellona, but that goddess had been confused in the mythological tradition with the Persian moon goddess, which is no doubt why she was thought appropriate to a moonstone. Cornelia got a moonstone necklace for it and wore it with a flamingo saree, with pink carnations at her throat, and with an apricot saree with shimmering moonlight blouse.[18] 'Are you still interested in my clothes?' she asked Falkner Blair, before one of her many descriptions.

MEETINGS IN ENGLAND AT LONG LAST

In May 1903, Mrs Falkner Blair returned to England, an invalid, and so on August 31st Falkner Blair arrived on a visit to England lasting till October 9th, and spent the first ten days in London.[19] Cornelia wanted to introduce him to some of her most delightful new contacts. So after a first day walking in Green Park and visiting a club, she took him on the second to meet the sculptor G. F. Watts. Falkner Blair had sent her in exile a brown and grey engraving of Watts's picture 'Hope', and had on his own walls four similar engravings of Watts.[20] Next, on September 4th she took him, by arrangement with the owner who was abroad, to visit Great Tangley Manor, the eleventh century moated manor house with beautiful gardens and surrounding Surrey countryside, where she had stayed, the first time in Prince Rupert's four-poster bed in the Elizabethan state bedroom. Her host, the owner, 'ugly, but *nice* ugly', was Wickham Flower, an art collector, fat and white-whiskered. She had lovingly described everything to Falkner Blair: the stables, the cloisters, the rock garden, the bridge, the walled garden with arches, the bog garden and pond, the apple orchard, the narcissus field and the avenue up to the heather on Tangley Hill, the gables of the house, the leaded windows, the hall and log fire. Many of the treasures were in the tapestry room, where the star feature was a fifteenth century tapestry representing the marriage of Catherine of Medici, but which included not only tapestries, draperies and vestments from different eras and parts of the world, but books, furniture, lustre ware, Persian tiles, Botticellis, Rubens, Whistlers and Leightons.[21] Surrey, the Tudor poet, had once owned the house in the sixteenth century, and in 1641 John Evelyn had written his name on a window pane. She had wanted Falkner Blair to share everything in imagination, and now she could show him in reality.

With the ten days over, Blair left with his wife for Harrogate in Yorkshire, but there were visits to Yorkshire on the 19th and 22nd to Lady Ripon in Ripon Palace, with walks in the palace garden and an excursion to Fountains Abbey. For the final reunion with Falkner Blair on October 7th to 8th 1903, on his return through London for the boat back to India and Allahabad, Cornelia chose three people to meet him: her literary friend Una Taylor, her close companion Princess Louise, who was a granddaughter of Queen Victoria, and one of her favourite hostesses, Mary Cholomondley, who ran a salon.[22] Cornelia invited Mrs Falkner Blair to some of their meetings, but she got no reply.[23]

CORNELIA RETURNS TO INDIA, FALKNER BLAIR TO ENGLAND

When Cornelia finally got the job she wanted in 1904 and was able to return to India, her work was in Calcutta and all over Bengal, Bihar and Orissa, a good distance from Allahabad. Falkner Blair was already 66 and due to retire to England. He wrote offering to release her from any further obligation, but Cornelia was upset at the very suggestion and letters are missing for a period of months. But

14. Cornelia with the horse and trap left her by Falkner Blair 1905.

she saw him once more in Calcutta on December 27th to 30th 1904, 'beautiful as ever', and he sailed to retirement on March 25th 1905, re-joined his wife and settled in Hindhead in Surrey.[24] Cornelia inherited his horse, Grizzy, and buggy as a continuous reminder of him, and she showed the horse and buggy off more prominently than herself in a photograph. Dick inherited Falkner Blair's pots and pans and a photograph of him, which crowned his study.[25]

THE FINAL EMBRACE IN ENGLAND

Two years later, Falkner Blair was ill and in February 1907 nearly died,[26] but Cornelia planned a holiday in England, sailed on May 1st and arrived full of hope. She saw him briefly in London looking older, not 'beautiful' as last time, and she felt dampened. But they arranged an Oxford meeting for May 25th, with Cornelia staying in Somerville, her old college, once again her

15. Harrison Falkner Blair, photo owned by Cornelia.

source of support and object of gratitude. They went punting on the River Cherwell, still chaperoned with a Miss B and a Mr Collin making up the party. But in the boat Falkner Blair collapsed in agony. They struggled back to the boat house in the rain and Falkner Blair was soon moved to the Acland Hospital. When Mrs Falkner Blair was summoned from Surrey, Cornelia was apprehensive about how she would be received. But in the face of death the older lady sought Cornelia's help. Five days after the fatal expedition,

Falkner Blair died in Cornelia's arms. The end is best told in her own short-hand, slightly expanded, with the endearment 'Dads' used for Falkner Blair.[27]

May 25 'Punting with Dads with Miss B and Mr Collin. Suddenly Dads in ago-nies. Rain. Punt back. Send Dads home with Mrs Haddow. Miserable. Give the Lyons tea at Somerville. Dads moved to Acland. Still pouring. Very bad. Dine in Hall. Have a talk in Miss Penrose's room.[i] Fly round to inquire.'

May 26 'Up early to St Giles for Dads.[ii] Still pours. No better. Sit beside him through the day. Tell him about my book and stories from it and plans. Lunch at the West. Alice Bruce's room.[iii] Promise carpet for Common room.[iv] Tea with Alice M Bruce. Where is Pamela? With Dick[v] to Markby's.[vi] Dads is worse. Doctors think bad.'

May 27 'Spend day beside him after 9.30. Very feeble. Sick since 3. London spe-cialist called. To be operation. No one else whom Dads knows. After 9 p.m. may not sit beside him. Wire sent by matron to Grayshott, which may bring her.[vii] Mrs Blair arrived at midnight. Dads not so well.'

May 28 'Sit beside him all morning after getting handfuls of irises and tulips. Doubtful as to her reception,[viii] but it is alright, and as she is tired, I am allowed to sit with him all day. Godby arrives at 10.30 and consults with Symonds. Think may avoid operation. Dick and I stay with her.[ix] I am by him all day, read him the Princess' letter,[x] and he's pleased at her remembrance. Nurse turns her[xi] out at 8.30.'

May 29 'Night bad as ever. Mrs Blair has neuralgia and keeps her room. I stay with Dads. Doctors will cut him. They find acute peritonitis – no hope. Doctor says about midnight. Matron carries her[xii] off to bed. I stay with Dads. Has a tube. "It is a luxury to have you here, Babs". Asks for red roses and has at 1 o'clock. Asks for best one and gives it to me.'

---

i Principal of Somerville, formerly Cornelia's fellow-student in 1889.

ii The church nearest Somerville, much attended in her student days.

iii Her former fellow-student, since 1898 Vice-Principal.

iv The carpet promised in these circumstances dictated the Somerville Senior Common Room decor for many decades and was still there on my last visit.

v Her brother.

vi Her former teacher.

vii Mrs Falkner Blair.

viii Mrs Falkner Blair's reception of Cornelia.

ix Mrs Falkner Blair.

x Princess Louise.

xi Mrs Falkner Blair.

xii Mrs Falkner Blair.

May 30 'Face grey. Both arms around my neck at 12 noon. His last conscious act. Half a second looks at me at 3.05 straight in my eyes.'

May 31 'She[xiii] is so forlorn that I stay and we choose his grave with a lovely view over the fields to Oxford. Arrangement at Corpus.'[xiv]

June 1 'At 9.30 to the little cemetery. Rain'.

Cornelia returned to London. She felt in a way elevated. She says 'I was honoured standing by my friend as he passed,' not that this could prevent waves of sadness and wanting, including when she went over the Hindhead house from where he wrote her his love letters and she saw his paperknife in the book he last read.[28] But at least she knew once in her life a man's reciprocated love.

ANOTHER LOVE: W. R. GOURLAY

There was only one more time that Cornelia fell in love, and that did not go so deep and was not fully reciprocated. But it too had its tragic element, its noble renunciation and its surprising sequel, and should be told, even though it takes us further out of the chronological sequence.

She first mentions W. R. Gourlay to Falkner Blair in July 1905.[29] Gourlay was Private Secretary to the Lieutenant Governor of Bengal. She called him 'nice Mr Gourlay'. He was a tall Scot with a strong and clear Scots accent, 'clean-shaven and so reliable, you knew at once you would trust him with the life dearest to you'. He was excellent company and he was extremely helpful to Cornelia in her recently created Calcutta job. Because of the rapid expansion of her duties, he agreed that her salary and terms should be improved and he offered to take charge of that, while also urging her to keep a diary. She did indeed start a separate diary for her work in 1907, in addition to the personal diary.

Falkner Blair died in 1907. The catalyst for the new relationship was Alice, who told Cornelia on July 7th 1908 that she was engaged to be married to Theodore Pennell. This caused a struggle in Cornelia and she confides to her diary on July 11th, 'One must get past this sort of thing.' There was an interruption when Cornelia had to visit her mother in Nasik as she had had a stroke.

---

xiii Mrs Falkner Blair.
xiv For memorial.

But back at her work on tour in the Lugma district on September 3rd 1908, her thoughts were with Gourlay. One moment seemed to blot out all else and there was singing at her heart.

On her return from tour on September 20th 1908, Gourlay accepted a poem she wrote called 'Love's minting', and seemed to love it. The next day, asked, 'Is it true?', he replied, 'It is true, still true.' Though they were both on tour quite often, he would write when they were apart and would visit her regularly when they were in Calcutta and his duties allowed. When his mother, Adeline, and three sisters arrived from Scotland on November 7th 1908, Cornelia helped find them accommodation, put up at least one sister in her house and joined in giving them all dinner. His mother visited Cornelia and they met a number of times. A little after their arrival, Gourlay gave Cornelia a present, but her reaction led to one of their little setbacks. She said 'everything that should not be said', and he left, afterwards explaining that he was guarding his honour. Gourlay behaved absolutely properly by the standards of the time in refusing physical contact, but he was not exactly cautious. He clearly liked Cornelia a great deal. She was fascinating company, and he wanted to enjoy it, without committing himself, or perhaps not realising until later that he must make a decision.

On December 16th, there was a more decisive setback, when she asked him in person for a daily letter while he was on tour, which had been Falkner Blair's practice in the Allahabad days. He refused and after leaving, sent her instead a very off-putting letter (not preserved). Meetings became less regular after that, and a bigger change took place on February 22nd 1909. After much reflection, while the mother was still in Calcutta, she confessed to Gourlay by letter her earlier relationship with Falkner Blair. She was afraid that this might jeopardise any plans to propose to her. In fact, it had a quite different effect. Initially, the whole family was very nice to her. Gourlay called for an apparently understanding talk and insisted she came to dinner that day with the family: mother, brother and one sister. They could not have been kinder and the mother gave her a present. But after that, a little late in the day, Gourlay was even more cautious. He saw her less often and tended to hurry away. Of the 13 letters preserved from him, letters nearly all addressed to 'My Dear Lassie', those up to March 1909 still showed a certain intimacy, though he may latterly have trusted it was only spiritual.[30] He writes at that stage that he will never know how good she is and how much he owes her for having taught him about God. 'I, being near thee, cannot be so far from Him as I often fear.' He expressed himself thankful for further verses from her, though they were ones that brought peace by suggesting that there could be love on his terms. But from March he did see other women in the same non-committal way, which caused Cornelia agonies of jealousy, and her complaint to Gourlay provoked an ultimatum from him. He still watched out for her interests, but he, and even other friends, tended to keep the conversation to politics.

Much later, on November 16th 1910 in Darjeeling she was not allowed by Gourlay to speak with his mother, Adeline, and perhaps he was concealing something already. But Cornelia anxiously had him with his brother and sister to dinner in Calcutta on April 9th 1911. Moreover, Cornelia had accepted an invitation from his mother to visit her at the next opportunity in Scotland. Gourlay was due for leave back there, and Cornelia planned to follow him on her leave. In Cornelia's mind there was enough to allow the thought, on seeing him in Calcutta cathedral, that the two of them were wrapped together and that he felt that.

Gourlay sailed for Scotland on May 28th 1911. Cornelia followed on July 8th. But in between Gourlay wrote to her from board ship, confessing something that he had could not bring himself to tell her before. He was going to Scotland to get married to someone else. Cornelia was still committed to visiting his mother in Scotland and she arrived to stay on September 8th to 9th, just three days, as it proved, before the wedding. She acknowledged to her diary that God had prepared her for the letter from on board ship.[31]

She felt she could weep to see how well she, Cornelia, fitted into their household, and she felt that Adeline, the mother, knew about it all. She remembered what was happening with Blair on September 8th back in 1900. Nonetheless, she was determined to ask God to bless the couple. She read to herself the marriage service for them, and later thought about it being their first Sunday. She wrote letters both to Gourlay, though in the style of a mere acquaintance, and to Gourlay's mother. Cornelia's own mother had died on October 24th 1910, so her return to Calcutta was doubly lonely, apart from the reunion with her horse, Vanity.

This was not the end of the story. Gourlay wrote to her with relief and gratitude:[32]

'Dear Miss Sorabji,

Adeline has shown me the beautiful letter you have written her – a letter which has given her great happiness. The goodness and "forgivefulness" of what you have done fills me with a feeling I cannot describe: wonder and awe and amazement and thankfulness and humility – and all these together, and over all the great love of God as evident in the acts of his children. God bless you now and always,

Yours very sincerely,

W.R.Gourlay'.

When the Gourlays returned to Calcutta on November 6th, Cornelia found that they had taken a house a stone's throw from her own. He came to see her on November 9th. She was not prepared and they both showed too much emotion. He begged her to come to tea, but she was exhausted and declined.

Throughout 1912, she made every effort to love the new bride, looking for things to admire when she saw her around, or had her to tea, reassuring herself that it was best for Gourlay, thanking God when she managed, but checking how far she felt pain, feeling dissatisfied with herself when she did and elated when she did not. She wanted to show love unfeigned and tried to strengthen the feeling by sending the bride a little present of cohirs growing in a pot. A poem by Cornelia of May 22nd 1912, addressed to AG, presumably Gourlay's wife, describes the match as for the best and wishes them a happy life leading to heaven.[33] Gourlay had been promoted by March 17th to being Leader of the Governor of Bengal's Executive Council, and in September they were together in the Governor's summer town of retreat in the beautiful hills of Darjeeling, where Cornelia felt that her dissatisfaction with herself was even more self-considering. They entertained her, and Gourlay did all he could for her projects.

'WHAT AN ESCAPE I HAVE HAD': GOURLAY SIDES AGAINST CORNELIA

But by 1913, she felt that Mrs Gourlay seemed restless and not happy. Moreover, Gourlay's official position increasingly put him in opposition to Cornelia, who was remorseless with opposition, so far as her professional work was concerned. For his part, Gourlay saw himself as simply carrying out his duties. Cornelia had a long struggle about the terms of service she was offered.[34] The Governor, Lord Carmichael, was sympathetic to Cornelia's case. But she came to think that Gourlay, in his new role, had got the Governor to pass on unamended to the India Office in London an unfavourable view about those terms, which was that of the Governor's Council rather than of the Governor himself.[35] 'Such ill luck', she comments, 'that his should be the hand to strike'.[36] This was only the first of a series of cases in which it was Gourlay's job to side against Cornelia. In 1914, Cornelia had a serious quarrel with the wives of certain Civil Service officers, but Gourlay impeded Cornelia's complaining to the Governor or to his wife.[37] Gourlay also refused her an interview, while she was awaiting a reprimand in that year for the political content of one of her literary articles.[38]

In 1915, Gourlay was asked to head a commission to re-examine the evidence against a ward of Cornelia's, whom Cornelia had supported in his successful defence against a charge of terrorism. She regarded Gourlay as entirely unqualified for this legal job.[39] In 1916, she suspected that Gourlay was behind the refusal of the Governor's Council to let her see a certain report about her by a Commissioner. It was also up to Gourlay to make up the guest lists for the Governor's official parties, and it fell to Gourlay to strike her off the list for a number of occasions. She was struck off when the Viceroy came to visit two institutions where she worked, even though the Viceroy, Lord Chelmsford, was a personal friend from Oxford days and the Chelmsfords were very friendly to her when they saw her at two other evening parties. Gourlay explained that he felt required to exclude her because she now had quarrels on the Ladies' Committee of the Dufferin Hospital as well as in the National India Association.[40] Finally in 1917, she wrote in connexion with these same quarrels of a rude letter from Gourlay, and exclaimed, 'Thank God he has no power to hurt.' The next day she described how Gourlay engineered the election of an officer's wife, who was one of her opponents, to a post in the Dufferin Hospital Committee. And her comment was, 'What an escape I have had' – in other words from marrying Gourlay.[41]

Gourlay had told Cornelia in 1911 that his aim was to finish his service and return to his Scottish home at Linden Lodge.[42] In 1919, he took the opportunity of returning to England temporarily as the secretary of Cornelia's friend, Lord Sinha, who had just been appointed Parliamentary Under Secretary of State for India in London, and been made the first Indian member of the House of Lords.[43] Gourlay returned to India after a year, but when he finally retired, he was to write articles on antiquities in his beloved Scotland.

If Gourlay had ever intended to marry her, she would doubtless have had to give up her job as legal adviser. For Gourlay too, marriage to an Indian would at that time have been a most exceptional situation for an English member of the Indian Civil Service, and it is not clear that his career would have survived it. Cornelia described an English lady doctor being ostracised by the British in 1898 for marrying a Muslim.[44] But if it had been accepted, then as wife of the Private Secretary to the Governor, she might well have secured the Government premises she so often sought, Hastings House, as a venue for some of her social work for purdahnashins. She would then have been able to make some contribution to her chosen work. But in the event she carried it out on so much greater a scale.

CHAPTER 6

LIFE IN EXILE:
ARTISTS, WRITERS AND
LONDON SOCIETY 1901–1904

Cornelia's exile to London in 1901 did far more than restore her previous contacts in society from eight years earlier. She also met many new people and especially in the literary and artistic worlds, thanks to her new friend Una Taylor. Her reception in London society was not incidental to her future, because it eventually helped her push open the door to the career she wanted. During the London season, she would have from one to half a dozen invitations every day, though her neuralgia and rheumatism caused her to miss many occasions, especially in damp weather. When the season came to its abrupt end, she would be invited to stay in some of the most beautiful country houses in Britain. People would ask to meet her, or be brought up to be introduced. She was described (by the President of the Society of Women Artists) as being, in her yellow saree, the most beautiful bit of colouring in the room, and (by someone identified only as 'a man whose brains the world respects') as being one of the three brainiest women, along with George Eliot and the explorer Mary Kingsley.[1] She was good at all the things that were then fashionable in London salons. Like Margot Tennant and the circle of The Souls,[2] she was good at coining epigrams and she was very well read.

UNA TAYLOR AND ARTISTIC INTRODUCTIONS

Cornelia was introduced to the artistic world by a new friend, Una Taylor.[3] She was Irish, a writer, small, with an intelligent, rather than a pretty, face. Her father, Henry Taylor, had been a great friend of the writer Robert Louis Stevenson and the artist G. F. Watts, whom she had known all her childhood.

Watts had done portraits of her mother and father, as well making valentines for her mother. Una was to introduce Cornelia to Watts at his London studio in 1902. She had also made tapestries for her walls based on designs supplied to her by William Morris and Burne-Jones. She wrote poems and mystical stories and liked to pursue parallels between Irish and Indian folklore.

ARTISTS AND EXPERIMENTS IN THEATRE: *THE CLAY CART*

Cornelia also tried out her own writing on Una,[4] and one big project was to write an English version in four acts of a Sanskrit play, *The Clay Cart*, that would be acted over the course of a journey lasting a fortnight. The Sanskrit was about the self-sacrifice of a wife who, being childless, chose for her husband a young and lovely new bride to replace her. Cornelia admired the self-sacrifice of Indian women and was, from Christian motives, to practise it in a small way herself in her later efforts to like the bride of her beloved Gourlay.[5]

Cornelia first showed her version of the play to Una and Watts's daughter. They agreed about who should be shown it next in the hope of getting it performed. The choice fell upon another artist to whom Una had introduced Cornelia in 1902, Graham Forbes Robertson.[6] Robertson, the illustrator of Una's last book, was '*very* rich and quite young, rather like a rabbit in face and fair with tiny slits of eyes'. What mattered was that he had influence in the theatre, having painted the actresses Sarah Bernhardt, Ellen Terry and Mrs Patrick Campbell. Mrs Campbell trusted him as a critic, although her first critic was her very intimate friend, Bernard Shaw. The hope was that Mrs Patrick Campbell might be persuaded to play the role of the substituted bride. Robertson liked the play, but said that Cornelia should start again from the beginning and turn it all into blank verse (which she did), and should then negotiate with Mrs Patrick Campbell.[7]

MRS PATRICK CAMPBELL: 'AN ATTRACTIVELY REPELLENT SNAKE'

Cornelia had first met Mrs Patrick Campbell in another art studio, that of Mortimer Mempes, who had a phonograph, or gramophone – then a new invention – in his studio.[8] Initially Cornelia had liked Mrs Campbell, perhaps because they were discussing Cornelia's theories of art and of good and evil.⁹ They next met when they both happened to be visiting the art studios of G. F. Watts and Graham Forbes Robertson, which faced each other.¹⁰ Cornelia began to feel ambivalent about Mrs Campbell when she went to meet her at Robertson's studio, accompanied by Una Taylor:

> 'What a woman she is – every gesture is a pose. She is like some attractively repellent snake! I could imagine her *strangling* some man, coiling her beautiful self around his neck and holding him spellbound the while! She moved in *waves* too, as a snake does, and was exquisitely dressed.'¹¹

Cornelia and Una soon returned to Watts's studio, with its distinctly aesthetic ambience – his masterpieces all round him, and a Herr Zwinscher playing Bach, Mozart and Beethoven on his spinet. Mrs Campbell later entered Watts's studio rustling with her underskirt, prompting artist Philip Burne-Jones, son of the famous Edward Burne-Jones, to ask, 'Who is that hissing with her feet?' Herr Zwinscher took a dislike to Mrs Campbell and would play only vulgar dance music in her presence. When she begged for other things, he replied, 'I play to my audience.' When she left, he played to the rest of them, music from the date of the spinet, 1710. Cornelia's distaste for Mrs Campbell grew.

Mrs Campbell was greatly taken with the idea of the play and removed it to read. Robertson was ready to do the sketches for dresses etc, if it was performed. It was arranged that Cornelia and Mrs Patrick Campbell would stay Saturday to Monday at his house in the country and discuss the play. Meanwhile, Cornelia started to sit in her rose pink saree for a portrait by Robertson, a portrait that was later exhibited in the New Gallery in London.¹²

The trip to Robertson's country house in the pretty Surrey village of Witley was set for that very weekend, June 19th.¹³ Robertson drew in Cornelia's visiting book a black and white picture of Mrs Campbell with his large and fierce pet raven, Matthew.¹⁴ Although the visiting book survives, many of the best pictures, including this one, have unfortunately been removed.¹⁵ En route to Witley, most people were delayed at Waterloo station, because the King was also travelling. But Cornelia was, amusingly, taken to belong to the royal party and thus ushered forward, leaving Mrs Campbell for a while tearing her hair.

Robertson had a charming old house with roses at the window panes and William Morris hangings within, and a goose in the garden called 'Bernard Shaw'. He lived as a bachelor, but he shared grounds, including a dower house, along with meals and studios with his artist neighbour and wife, the Melvilles, and they joined in the weekend party. Cornelia wrote to Falkner Blair about how she sat next to the beautiful and serene Mrs Melville, while:

'vulgar Mrs Patrick Campbell rattled away. But she *is* vulgar, Dads – the things she says and *does*! Clever? Oh, yes, but impossible. Respectable? Certainly, and that is just it – you almost feel that what is so very wrong about her is her respectability!'[16]

Cornelia even disliked Mrs Campbell's dog, 'Pinkey', a 'monkey-griffen' given her by the King of Belgium.

Both nights, after dinner with the Melvilles, Cornelia read her play to the company, while Mrs Campbell lay full length on the hearth rug. Afterwards she played to them on the spinet, divinely, as Cornelia admitted. The Melvilles loved the play, and Mrs Campbell liked it, but she had some objections about her role. She could not endure being the young bride, with the self-sacrificing older wife being nice to her. Also, since she felt she must have the most important role, she pressed for the role of the Brahmin husband to be changed, to make him less important. Cornelia bridled at the idea of distorting the Sanskrit version. But Mrs Campbell pleaded:

'Do change it. I long to play in Indian draperies. Do I not remind you of an Indian dream?' . . .

'No'

'Of what do I remind you? You must say. It is something Indian, I am sure' . . .

'Of a snake – you move so sinuously do you not?' . . .

'I long to be a snake. I always try to imagine myself a snake'.[17]

Nonetheless, Cornelia refused to make the changes and did not think Mrs Patrick Campbell would take the play. Somehow she would not be sorry about that. However, Mrs Campbell was very nice to her, caressed her and begged Cornelia to be her secretary at a colossal salary. Cornelia felt she would rather starve, and on June 21st 1902 everyone dispersed.

BERNARD SHAW AND CORNELIA'S DISTASTE FOR ANACHRONISM

Mrs Campbell took her time and consulted her intimate friend Bernard Shaw, the playwright who was for a time so admired that people compared him with Shakespeare. Eventually Shaw came back with a very kind message:

'Excellent, now if you'd introduce the incident of the 9th Lancers and the Delhi Durbar, we'd put it on the stage for you.'[18] And he even sent a later message to ask if she had done it. The 9th Lancers regiment had been subjected to communal punishment by Lord Curzon as Viceroy, as a signal that he would insist on justice being shown to Indians.[19] But Cornelia was appalled that Shaw was proposing to mix a very recent event with a theme of the second century CE, not recognising, to her later regret, that this was his way of doing things. She thought he was mocking her and threw the play into a corner of the room.[20] It still exists, unperformed, in manuscript on my desk, under the title, '*The Clay-Cart*, Adapted from the Sanskrit of Sudraka, AD 190'.[21]

Cornelia only got to meet and like Shaw very much later in 1933 on a weekend at a beautiful country house of pink brick, with a twelfth century moat. This was Birtsmorton Court in Worcestershire,[22] reputedly home to two major political figures of the Tudor period, Thomas Cromwell and Cardinal Wolsey.[23]

16. Country house visits: Birtsmorton Court, Worcestershire, where Cornelia was reconciled with Bernard Shaw, 1933.

G. F. WATTS: CORNELIA GETS AN INSIGHT INTO ALLEGORY IN ART (AND LIFE)

Una's introduction of Cornelia to G. F. Watts and his wife led to many visits in which Watts explained to her the allegorical intentions of his works. Watts was then Britain's leading artist and was about to receive the highest honour available to an artist, the Order of Merit. Nowadays the English are not receptive to allegorical themes, but Hope, one of his favourite figures, was meaningful not only to Victorians anxious about the truth of the Christian story, but also to Cornelia in the midst of the campaign for her post. Her first visit was to Watts's London studio in the week of March 27th 1902.[24] He was a little old man, shrivelled with age, but with eyes that twinkled. He wore a black velvet cap and coat and looked the artist he was. One colossal sculpting of a man on a horse, on which he had been working for 14 years, represented Energy,[i] and he could only work on it with a step ladder in the summers, when it had been wheeled into the garden. He had just finished painting Peace with Goodwill in her lap. And Victory was painted at a distance from three figures, to show how remote she was from any of them. He loved Cornelia's yellow saree and said it was a joy to look on. He wanted to paint her in it, but also proposed the project to Wyke Bayliss, the President of the Royal Society of British Artists, who called while they were talking. In fact neither of them attempted a portrait, nor did another painter who wanted to, Holman Hunt, who later came up to Cornelia and said he had tried to catch her eight years earlier when she was in London, in the hope of painting her, but was now too blind.[ii]

This was the first of at least eight visits to Watts over two years. Some visits were to the London studio. But the Watts also had a house, Limnerslease, in the Surrey village of Compton, and often Cornelia used to stay there,

---

i This and the statue of Tennyson are still on display along with paintings in the galleries that Watts was building next to his house, as are the murals that Mrs Watts was designing further off in the temple which she showed Cornelia.

ii Letters to Blair, 165/22 and 23, May 2 1902; July 3 1903. Only the later reminiscence in *India Calling* says that Holman Hunt made a start of painting her in her presentation saree of 1893, but it is somewhat unreliable on this, and confuses two different aspirations to paint her, by suggesting that Watts put the choice to Hunt, not to Bayliss (London pp. 43–44, Delhi p. 39, Nottingham p. 32).

sometimes moving from Great Tangley Manor nearby, the house where the art collector Wickham Flower kept many of his treasures.[25] At Limnerslease she saw Watts's self-portrait and his nearly complete statue of Tennyson, intended for Lincoln, which is still on display, along with Energy, the horse. Watts also explained more of his allegories. In the series on Love, 'Love and Death' grew out of his painting of a loved and wealthy nobleman who was struck by consumption in the prime of life. But although Death pushes aside the little boy, Love, Death's face is meant to show pity, and the light on the victim is meant to suggest hope beyond the grave. Hope is more emphasised in the painting Watts liked best, 'Love and Life', where Love is presented as strong enough to lead to salvation. And in 'Love Triumphant' Time and Death lie hand in hand beneath the feet of Love. He was currently painting 'The flying hours', where one's thoughts are represented by a cascade of tumbling babies. And he had in his studio a series of pictures devoted to babies. These were what he now found it most enjoyable to paint. Mrs Watts also explained her allegories in the sundial she had sculpted representing his life and their marriage, and in her Art Nouveau murals representing all religions in the Byzantine temple a little further away.

Signor Watts, as Cornelia called him, signed Cornelia's visiting book,[26] using the motto which was carved on all the doors of a second new studio the Watts had built:

'G F Watts

The utmost for the highest

Signor'.

Below he drew a flaming cupid, and said to her, 'To mark the golden flying hours you spent with me'. He also gave her a set of photographs, of which only one survives in the visiting book, a photograph of Watts with the Hungarian violinist, Joseph Joachim. Missing are Watts's favourite picture of himself in robes and of himself beside the sundial.

On her last visit to Limnerslease in November 1903, Watts, she says, 'lay in his accustomed spot and I was allowed the seat of honour beside him'.[27] This was probably 'the niche', a seat for two under a sculpted metal arch, where Mrs Watts has been photographed reading to her husband, 32 years her senior. Watts wanted to hear Cornelia's stories twice, such as the Persian version of the 'Three Wise Men'. He confessed that sometimes he wished he had never been born, because he wanted to do so much and felt he did so little so badly, and she tried to tell him of his value to others.[28]

LITERARY HOSTESSES: ALICE MEYNELL AND OTTOLINE MORRELL

Another introduction offered by Una proved disappointing. Cornelia had sent Falkner Blair some of the poems of Alice Meynell, and they had discussed them. On June 27th 1902, Una took Cornelia to the Meynells' house to see the poetess and her husband. As Cornelia describes the visit:

> 'There are *broods* of children and they trail about the room. This is one's first impression. From out the mass and mess rises a tall, not ungraceful figure, who gives one greeting in the voice of one announcing that your *coffin* is at the door. This is the great A M! She has black hair, and great round, sad (but not beautiful, only stretched and startled) eyes. For the rest she is plain – high cheek bones, no nose or mouth, flabby cheeks. She talks in a rather precious way (if you know what I mean) and is clearly oppressed by domestic cares. The tea took an hour to make. Foreign guests were there mostly, Italian and French and American, all admirers. She talks French very easily and gets nervous at intervals and slips across to caress a child (ages 25 to 12). He jack-in-the-box-ed about, trailing a child on each arm or leg, or attached to some limb. Altogether, I was interested, if disappointed. She does not talk, but you can see that she loves her belongings. I am sure she feels all she writes'.[29]

Another literary hostess was the recently married Ottoline Morrell. But it was her husband, Phillip Morrell, to whom Cornelia was closest, having known his relatives at Oxford. She attended 'the swellest Oxford party of the season' in the grounds of their large Italianate house. It still stands on the crest of Headington Hill with views over Oxford. But the Morrells did not yet have Garsington Manor, where Ottoline was to entertain Bertrand Russell (who wrote her 2500 letters), Augustus John, D. H. Lawrence and others. Cornelia had a good talk with her and the only sign of her literary interests was that she and her husband were reading Jowett's translation of Plato together, but Cornelia felt that such a glamorous lady was very far from Platonic.[30]

THE SISTERS BRIEFLY REUNITED

During this period Cornelia's sister Alice was still in London, studying for her medical degree, and for some months (jealousy soothed for now) the sisters shared the Hobhouses' London flat, which the Hobhouses' daughter, Emily, had surrendered while she went out to South Africa to protest about British treatment of the Boers under Lord Kitchener. The sisters had to vacate, when

17. Ottoline and Philip Morrell's house overlooking Oxford, site of
the 'swellest' parties, 1901.

Emily was turned away from South Africa and returned, to bring a law suit
against Kitchener.[31] Cornelia was also allowed to make use of her future home,
Lincoln's Inn, where Dick had been called to the bar, and to use its law library
and chapel. She was admitted to use the library in order to research the history

of the law on secluded women in India. She also attended the opening of the law courts in Westminster Abbey.[32]

LITERARY SUCCESS FOR CORNELIA: LOVE AND LIFE BEHIND THE PURDAH

The years of exile in England were very good for Cornelia's writing. In the absence of a legal job, writing was her sole source of income. Her first article had been published ten years earlier when she was a student in 1891. It contained her plea for educating women before legislating for them and the journal had been *The Nineteenth Century*, which a decade later was still being edited by James Knowles. Cornelia had a very close admirer in the editorial office, identified only as 'Helen'. A note from her to Cornelia survives saying, 'Darling, This is only to say I love you.' When there was a change of editorial personnel a good many years later, Cornelia was worried that *The Nineteenth Century* would not remain one of her outlets, but she need not have worried.

Her first book, *Love and Life Behind the Purdah*, published in 1901, was, of course, a much bigger project than any article.[33] Moreover it was an important part of her campaign for a legal post, because it was a set of short stories illustrating the suffering, hardships and self-sacrifice of the secluded women whom she hoped to serve. It included a story, 'Greater Love', about the self-sacrificing disappearance of a childless wife that had parallels with Cornelia's abandoned 4-act play for Mrs Patrick Campbell. Lady Dufferin wrote an introductory note. There was only one hostile review in England. As we shall see in the Chapter 7, it was a letter to *The Times* written by a rival who wanted for the sake of his career to be regarded as the expert on India. The author of a literary history of India, R. W. Frazer, wrote to Cornelia that he had guessed the author of the letter immediately.[34] Otherwise the book had an overwhelming success. Within a year, Elliott and Fry photographed Cornelia in their series 'Distinguished people'[35] – they had earlier photographed Jowett. She wrote to Falkner Blair of one triumph after another, but said that her head was not swollen, because she was never fully pleased until he approved, and what she wanted was his opinion on every detail. In January Lady Dufferin wrote[36] that she was charmed and liked best 'Greater Love' and 'A Living Sacrifice' – the second being about the voluntary substitution of one sister for another in an act of suttee (widow-burning). Towards the end of January, Cornelia's favourite London hostess, Mary Cholomondeley, held a party of congratulation after her friends had asked to meet Cornelia. Cornelia described the events.[37]

'It seems Sir Julian Corbett, the historian, was at their house the other day and said, "There is one person whom above all others in the world I want to meet just now and that is the lady who wrote *Love and Life*, and they tell me she is in London". So Miss Cholomondeley wrote to ask if I would go and meet him. He said various other nice things about my book and – don't you know how when folk praise one, one wants to say one's prayers! The Cholomondeleys too are *so* kind and I appreciated their appreciation. So yesterday I went to their party. The historian is small and dark and distinguished and charming (of course charming, since he admired my firstling!), but I did not talk very much to him because Miss Cholomondeley brought up one after another. . . . Every one had read the little book and so strange it was to be valued as the author! Strange *and pleasing.* The ways the Cholomondeleys thank one for going makes of the smallest tea drinking a graciousness'.

On June 10th, Cornelia was celebrated at a grander event at The Criterion. She went, wearing the moonstone from Falkner Blair, as the literary guest of the Women Writers' Dinner. 'Everyone' (she meant every woman) 'whose name you've ever seen in print was there,' she told Blair.[38] 'There were over 300 of them and the arrangements were splendid. The committee received us all. (The Lady Mayoress and I were the only guests) and each person was given a plan of the tables, so that you knew who sat where. To our name cards were attached dear little crowns – coronation pins. The committee wore white badges with a tiny gold pen for pin.' At the top and bottom ends of the high table were Mrs W. K. Clifford – 'nice, ugly and substantial' – and Mary (Mrs Humphry) Ward, 'grey and softened by time – her face is full of quiet strength.' Cornelia had earlier met Mrs Humphry Ward at Jowett's. She was a sponsor of Somerville Hall and her influential novel, *Robert Elsmere*, described as the most successful since *Tom Sawyer*, portrayed the experience of losing religious faith in some of the story of Christ and of turning instead to social service under the influence of Jowett's philosopher-protégé, T. H. Green. The dinner concluded with the health of Cornelia and the Mayoress being proposed in a little speech.

By July, Cornelia was able to report that the sales were phenomenally good and by December that Mudie, the owner of one of the lending libraries of the time, was having to put four or five copies in each library.[39]

CORNELIA STUMBLES UPON TIPU SULTAN AND CLIVE – IN THE ENGLISH COUNTRYSIDE

Some of the country houses where Cornelia stayed during her exile contained major records of the history of British India. In one she became the first person since the time of Tipu Sultan to read that warrior's secret and confidential communications. Little did she know that in time she would be responsible for some of his descendants.[40] She read the papers at Christmas 1901 when she had one of her many stays at Escot in Devon,[41] the home of Sir John Kennaway of the famous beard, who a dozen years earlier had asked the Parliamentary question to bring her to England.[42] It was on this ten-day stay over Christmas and New Year that Sir John autographed the photos of the house in Cornelia's autograph book.[iii] His grandfather, the first Baronet, had been British Resident in Hyderabad from 1788–1794 and then aide-de-camp to Cornwallis, the first Governor General of India. Cornwallis was fighting against Tipu Sultan, his most formidable Indian opponent, as part of a larger struggle against the French for control of India. Cornwallis had made an alliance with the Nizam of Hyderabad against Tipu Sultan. Twice he took Tipu Sultan's sons away from him, the first time in 1792 as hostages, until Tipu complied with the conditions negotiated in the treaty of Seringapatam. The boys were returned when Tipu complied. But Tipu was not conquered and the war went on. Cornwallis received the sons a second time in 1799 when Tipu had been finally defeated and killed.

Tipu's humour and the beauty of his furnishings are well known in England from the museums which house the mechanical tiger eating a top-hatted European who groans, and from the beautiful fabric of his tent.[iv] In his capital at Seringapatam near Mysore there is a further display of his humour and of the victories which he and his father, Haidar Ali, won against the British. There in the pavilion his murals depict scenes of the British running away from his victorious troops. He was finally killed by a shot through the temple during the confused mêlée when Seringapatam was stormed.

When Cornelia was asked if she would like to look at an old box of Persian and Indian books, she found that some of Tipu's most important original state documents removed from Seringapatam were at that time in the house at Escot.[43]

---

iii Photo at p. 116.

iv Respectively at the Victoria and Albert Museum and Powys Castle.

18. Country house visits: Escot House, Devon, where Cornelia decoded Tipu
Sultan's secrets, 1901, photo autographed for Cornelia.

There were Tipu's instructions to spies in his own handwriting, his orders to the
engineer about fortifying Seringapatam, his unlawful correspondence with the
French commander-in-chief, Bussy, and his forecast of British rule. The grandfather's letters gave a picture of life in the Nizam of Hyderabad's dominions.
The grandfather had also written an account of the siege of Seringapatam day by
day and described the intrigue and treachery, along with the hookah-smoking,
leopard-hunting and laziness of the 'house of relaxation'.

The pictures in the house at Escot showed court life at Hyderabad, and at that time the Kennaways had a painting of Tipu's two boys being taken off for the first time as hostages in 1792. Tipu's letters showed that he had tried to trick the British about which son he would miss most. He urged that they could take one son, the second, instead of two, because the second son was Tipu's favourite. He claimed that he hated his first son, and that the youngest was an imbecile. But Cornwallis, replying courteously, insisted on taking two sons.[44]

Cornelia could not stop reading the box of papers until she had finished it, and she could not believe that the family seemed to have no interest. She wanted the son of the household, Jack, to edit the letters and, at her host's request, went through the papers with him.

Another house where Cornelia stayed had Indian connexions from just before Tipu's time. It was Sutton Court in Stowey, Somerset, the home of the Strachey family, with a part built by the redoubtable Bess of Hardwick in 1558, who had a Strachey for one of her successive husbands. The first Sir Henry Strachey had been secretary to Clive of India, who defeated the French in Bengal and was made its Governor after 1757. In the house were letters from Clive. There were pathetic accounts of his final illness which led to his suicide. There was correspondence about the accusation against Warren Hastings, Clive's successor as Governor of Bengal in 1772, that he had plundered Bengal, which led to Hastings's impeachment. Finally there was a story in manuscript of the imprisonment of a Strachey stepson, Mr Latham, by Tipu's father Haidar Ali for three years in Mysore, a narrative Cornelia found thrilling.[45]

PRINCESS LOUISE AND CORNELIA: AN INVALUABLE FRIENDSHIP

Cornelia's three-year stay in London was under a new sovereign. Queen Victoria had died on January 21st 1901. The Coronation of Edward VII, after a postponement for illness, was held on August 9th 1902. Cornelia had the privilege of a seat in the Royal Household stand at Hyde Park Gate,[46] and then on May 8th 1903, she was called for her second presentation at court.[47] She was dressed by Una's maid and wore a saree of shot silk, the pink-yellow of sunset as she described it, the blouse of crepe-de-chine, a shade paler, with shimmering opalescent French trimming at neck, wrist and waist, and she wore her moonstones. The occasion was particularly pleasant because, in addition to her presentation to the new King and Queen, one of the onlookers in the throne room was the other most intimate friend she made in this period besides Una. She was one of Queen Victoria's granddaughters, Princess Louise of Schleswig Holstein. Princess Louise wrote a letter afterwards to Cornelia saying she was proud that they understood each other's thoughts, and that her heart's true self went out and stood beside her when Cornelia came into the presence of the son (Edward) of what she liked to call 'our Queen' (Victoria). She felt she had been led across the stony path of sorrow, to hear the voice of sunrise (that was how she saw Cornelia) calling to the sunset, and that the East and West had found each other in true sympathy and friendship.

They had met on June 19th 1902 and immediately had a long talk. The two people the Princess loved best were her grandmother, Queen Victoria, and her brother killed in the Boer war. She told many stories of Queen Victoria and she found Cornelia a great comfort in her own sufferings. She felt that her marriage had been between a steady English cart horse and a wild colt (herself). Her husband had left, love was dead and she could never love another man. But her life was lonely and her stormy nature frustrated her when she had to perform royal duties.[48]

Princess Louise taught Cornelia how to make enamels and gave her one of her own enamel brooches.[49] Cornelia loved enamels and I remember her often wearing as a pendant from her neck a beautiful green enamel watch in Tiffany style with gold.[v] We will next turn to the story of how Louise played an invaluable role in Cornelia's campaign to have a legal post created.[50]

---

v Stolen in the 1990s from the repair shop of a reputable London jeweller.

CHAPTER 7

A DOOR OPENS: *THE TIMES* AND THE SECRETARY OF STATE AGAINST THE VICEROY AND THE REST 1904

The second part of Cornelia's ten-year search for a permanent legal job lasted for five years. It started with the reneging in 1899 on promises made by the Allahabad High Court[1] and it reached its final outcome in 1904 with the Viceroy being overridden. Her campaign during these five years was focused on creating a post of her own devising under British administration. She was to climb a tough uphill road with almost overwhelming obstacles. But she was to draw on a dazzling array of resources to overcome them. Her exile to London helped her in the end to find the resources.

THE POST PROPOSED

The post that Cornelia proposed was for a woman legal adviser to mediate between the British administration and the purdahnashins. She urged that such a post was necessary to help Hindu and Muslim women, normally widows, secluded behind the veil, or rather the curtain – curtain being the literal meaning of 'purdah'. Seclusion put a stop to education and made women dependent for legal advice on male relatives and estate managers, who often were the ones who cheated them. It was not even the custom for secluded women to see secluded women neighbours from outside the household. Such women could not see a lawyer face to face, because all lawyers were male, nor gain the education to question the unseen managers appointed by their male relatives. No member of the British Raj could interview them directly, for all British officials

were male. If such officials were skilful enough to get an interview, the inter-
viewee would be sitting behind a curtain and there was no way of ascertaining
to whom the officials were talking. The speaker might not even be female. Yet
these women were of the land-owning class and, as widows, responsible for
large estates either in their own right until death, or, as guardians, until the
heirs should come of age. There was intrigue, hidden from outsiders, about
whether their children or someone else's would inherit.

THE COURT OF WARDS

The British had a particular responsibility to these women in certain of the
non-Princely Provinces – those directly governed by the British. For in some
of these British Provinces a Court of Wards had been established and there, at
least, the British were responsible for the welfare of women like this who had
been brought under the Court.

The Court of Wards had been established in Bengal in 1791 to deal with the
estates of minors and women, and estates whose owners were incapacitated by
debts, quarrels, insanity or other problems. Some estates were accepted at the
request of the proprietress, others, after due investigation, at the request of the
reversioners, who stood next in line to the minor heir. Estates would be taken
over only until the minor came of age, or difficulties were resolved. The British
appointed local estate managers, improved revenues, saw to the education of
minor heirs and sought to deal with intrigues. The main beneficiaries were
the land-owners. The chief drawback for them was that their expenditures had
to be authorised by the relevant Indian Civil Service officers. Expenditures
included the upkeep of schools and roads belonging to the estate.[2] The British
did not take estate revenue for themselves. They ran the court for the benefit of wards, although they hoped to gain the loyalty of heirs who sometimes
became allies of the British and were sometimes anglicised. The improvement
of revenues could displace hangers-on, family members and middle men, and
had at one time proved hard on peasant tenants.[3] But by Cornelia's time the
British tried to ensure fairness in Bengal by paying peasants directly out of the
revenues of administered estates, instead of through the wards.[4]

Estates were often taken over because they were in debt. This made estate
revenue central to the enterprise. Hence the Court of Wards was overseen by
the Board of Revenue. The Board consisted of two members, a secretary and
the senior 'Honorary Member' who represented the Board on the Provincial

Governor's Council. The name 'Court of Wards' was not a name for an identifiable group of people. Rather it referred to the various officers of the Indian Civil Service in the Province in respect of a particular function of their work. Insofar as a piece of work was connected with the wards' estates, that work could be described as being done for the Court of Wards. Usually the work would come to the attention of the two Officers of the Board of Revenue only after it had been carried out.

COLLECTING OPINIONS ABOUT A POST OF LEGAL ADVISER

An early part of Cornelia's campaign was the process of collecting opinions about the need for such a post as she envisaged. In Cornelia's papers there is a whole folder with many of the replies to her inquiries about the need for a woman legal adviser,[5] and it makes depressing reading. The vast majority of replies are against the post, and of those few correspondents who support her, some record, like her opponents, that the people they consulted were unanimously against the idea. Some of her most prominent supporters were in any case old English friends whom she had made long ago: Falkner Blair himself and his fellow Allahabad judge, Knox, who had supported her inclusion on the rolls there, William Markby, her Oxford teacher, and Mountstuart Grant Duff, the former Governor of Bengal and one of her three favourite older men from her student days. The most significant new favourable opinions were from the nationalist Gokhale, later acknowledged by Gandhi as his guru, and from two High Court Judges in Calcutta, Mr Ameer Ali, whose opinion as a Muslim judge was important, and Mr Justice Stephen, who with his wife was to become a close friend for many years when Cornelia moved to Calcutta in 1904.[6]

Important people were against the scheme. One was Bhownagree, the Parsi Member of the British Parliament. Another was Cornelia's friend Sinha, later Lord Sinha and Parliamentary Undersecretary for India, and other leading Indians. The Lieutenant Governor of the Punjab consulted widely and reported the unanimous view that the scheme would not be useful there, and Mr Shah Din, speaking to the Punjab Law Society, though partly in favour, agreed. Cornelia was to hear a similar 'useful, but not here' argument elsewhere too.[i]

---

i In Madras in 1904.

Meanwhile *The Times of India*, and its editor, and nearly all the leading English language newspapers in India were against the scheme. In England the *Manchester Guardian* chimed in that regrettably the scheme would not succeed.[7]

Some people who were sympathetic specified difficulties nonetheless about such a scheme working anywhere. Thus one supporter, H. S. Cunningham, rather spoilt his support by saying that unfortunately there were not relays of Cornelia Sorabjis to do the job. Another supporter, Mr Landon, *The Times* correspondent, talked about the scheme with many people in India and had a different experience, that nobody denied the need, but they offered two principal objections: first, women (presumably, English) already had too much influence in India, and, secondly, there were not enough wards of court for a full-time job – a point made about the Punjab also by its Lieutenant Governor.[8]

One problem for Cornelia was deciding whether officials in India or in England should be asked to create the post. Because her old tutor in Oxford, Thomas Raleigh, out in India, was not very enthusiastic, she thought she would press the officials in England. But of respondents at the India Office in London one, Sir Alfred Lyall, whose lectures on India Cornelia had heard in Oxford at All Soul's, suggested that people in India would have to initiate. The other, Sir Charles Lyall, former Lieutenant Governor of the Punjab, said that people in England would nonetheless have to settle details such as salary.[9] In the end the first advice proved wholly wrong and the second partly so.

Thomas Raleigh, despite his doubts, did much more for Cornelia. He was one of three people who told her that she should write up her scheme, he did collect opinions and he did put the scheme to the Viceroy, Lord Curzon. For this Cornelia praised him as 'no coward'.[10] But he warned her that some enemy seemed to have been influencing Curzon against her. More than one person in fact alerted her that an enemy was at work. She spoke of a known enemy from her time in Allahabad called Tarly and wondered if he had got the ear of the former Lieutenant Governor, Sir Anthony ('Tony') Patrick Macdonnell, who was on the Viceroy's Council and whose farewell she had attended at Muir College in Allahabad.[11] It was fortunate for Cornelia, if that was so, that the Lieutenant Governor was shortly afterwards moved to a job in Ireland.

One enemy in London had been waging a continuous campaign against her – J. D. Rees, himself a former member of the Viceroy's Council in India. His motive was ambition. Bruce Richmond, assistant editor of *The Times*, told Cornelia that Rees was trying to succeed Cornelia's Oxford host, Sir William Hunter, at the India Office, and wanted to show himself knowledgeable enough to be able to contradict her, while Lady Galloway said that he had already tried to set against her Lord Percy, Under-secretary of State for India, when Lord Percy had up to then been favourable. Rees started his campaign in the *Times Literary Supplement* by being one of the very few to attack Cornelia's highly successful first book, *Love and Life Behind the Purdah*, in 1902, and she replied with a letter in *The Times*. He then moved on to attacking her scheme in a lecture at the Society of Arts, which she was attending. The Chairman Lord Harris stood up and begged her to reply, but although she spoke about other things that Rees said, she remarked that it was not the place to discuss her scheme, which would take care of itself. The secretary of the Society wrote to thank her for a charming speech.[12]

Cornelia went on to try another route to Curzon. Through Lady Galloway, the sister of Lord Salisbury, she got a meeting in early August 1902 at Lady Galloway's house with Curzon's private secretary, Mr Lawrence, having been encouraged by Lady Galloway to make notes on the scheme. Lawrence was very stiff at first as if he had heard something against Cornelia, but Cornelia was calm because she had decided not to put herself forward as one of the women to carry out the scheme, and as Lady Galloway remarked, he thawed moment by moment when he heard about it and admitted it was very good and there was a need. Lawrence warned Cornelia that Curzon disliked the idea of women doing business. Many English women already did so in connexion with the medical schemes of Lady Dufferin described above,[13] and the vernacular press complained that there were too many English women employed. Lawrence nonetheless promised to show the scheme to Curzon, if Cornelia would prepare a draft. She sent the draft to him at the beginning of September, and in November Lady Galloway herself sent Curzon all the papers.[14]

Another person with whom Cornelia had a meeting early in 1902 was Lord George Hamilton, Secretary of State for India until 1903. Una Taylor first took her to see Canon Wilberforce at Dean's Yard at Westminster Abbey, and he secured an interview with Hamilton for Cornelia. Hamilton was very interested in her account of the plight of the Kathiawar lady who had been denied her allowance for so many years, without as yet any redress.[15] Later in the year, Wilberforce took the supportive letters of Justices Knox and Ameer Ali about the scheme and arranged for them to be shown to Hamilton. This made a difference when Cornelia went to have an interview with Sir John Edge of the Viceroy's Council, who was on a visit from India at the India Office in London. He started by looking 'foxier than ever', cautious and discouraging, until he heard that Hamilton had called for the papers about her Kathiawar Rani and saw the letters in support of Cornelia. Then he veered round and said it was a splendid thing, and that of course Hamilton could make the post with a stroke of his pen, but that the salary would be decided by the

Viceroy's Council in India (the opposite of earlier advice given to Cornelia), and that on that she would have his (Edge's) own vote. Cornelia's comment showed her unconvinced. 'I thought, "Yes! if the influential votes are mine" '.[16]

LOBBYING PUBLIC OPINION: CORNELIA'S WRITING ON SECLUDED WOMEN

Cornelia's campaign was by no means confined to collecting opinions and see-ing officials. She also did a lot of writing, which elicited replies, some unfa-vourable, but some favourable. She was helped by the success of her book, *Love and life Behind the Purdah*, in 1901, and by the authority of one article in *The Nineteenth Century*, 'The legal status of women in India', 1898, as well as the vividness of another about the Tihur Rani whom Cornelia had rescued at such peril,[17] 'Concerning an imprisoned Rani', 1901.[18] Cornelia also made skilful use of the opinions she had newly collected. The favourable opinions were very powerful, and she circulated only those, and *not* the unfavourable ones. She also had her scheme ready to show as occasion arose.[19]

As a result of these efforts, a series of orchestrated events began to turn the corner against the opposition. Cornelia had met Valentine Chirol in May 1902, the foreign editor of *The Times*, Britain's leading newspaper. She described him as stoutish, middle-aged and red-haired. By arrangement with him she wrote a letter to *The Times*, explaining the predicament of secluded women and the case for the post of woman lawyer, and adding full statements by four main supporters, Justices Ameer Ali, Knox, Blair and Sir William Markby. The letter was published on September 26th 1902. By prearrangement the same day *The Times* had a leading article in Cornelia's favour.[20] She received many letters as a result, and Mountstuart Grant Duff and Mr Gerald Ritchie wrote further to *The Times* in her support, while another article in *The Times* cited a Poona adop-tion case as showing the need for the scheme. In less than a month, the scheme was being described in the Poona newspapers in India.[21]

Cornelia's writing did not stop there. She published a case history of the law on secluded women in India in *The Imperial and Asiatic Quarterly Review* for January 1903,[22] which also provoked plenty of discussion. On January 25th in London, the widely read *Evening Standard* gave a friendly account of its con-tents, and H. S. Cunningham wrote a favourable response and a further letter to *The Times*. She wrote many other articles, which provoked responses,[23] and there was further spontaneous support in the press.[24]

Just over a month after Cornelia's prearranged letter to *The Times*, her case moved to Parliament. On November 13th 1902, Mr Arthur Elliott, the husband of Madeleine Shaw-Lefevre,[ii] put a question in the House of Commons about her scheme to the Secretary of State for India, Lord George Hamilton, to whom Cornelia had already been talking. This repeated the tactic used by Sir John Kennaway back in 1888, when Cornelia was denied her scholarship to Oxford. Everything had been carefully prearranged. Elliott asked Lord George Hamilton whether his attention had been drawn to the disadvantages under which women behind the veil laboured in India and whether he would consider the advisability of steps being taken to protect them against injustice, by permitting competent women to qualify as their legal advisers. Lord Hamilton replied that, although the matter was not officially before him, the disabilities imposed on ladies in the greater part of India in the management of their affairs were well known, and he believed the Government had under consideration some proposals for allowing women to qualify as their legal advisers, though he had not been informed whether any conclusion had been arrived at.[25]

Right after this, a favourable article appeared in *The Pioneer* newspaper in India, and the *Manchester Guardian* changed its tune and offered, like *The Times*, to print a simultaneous letter from Cornelia and a leading article by themselves. In January 1903, Cornelia returned to the fray with a second letter in *The Times* about secluded women.[26]

THE NEW SECRETARY OF STATE FOR INDIA: A GLIMMER OF HOPE

Although Lord George Hamilton left the post of Secretary of State for India in 1903, his successor was even more significant. It was Brodrick, later Lord Midleton, the brother of her old supporter and host from Oxford days,[27] the Warden of Merton College. No doubt, Cornelia's close connexion with his brother helped her. Two people worked to secure a meeting for Cornelia with Brodrick. Princess Louise got Cornelia to write up a case for her to pass on to him and offered to put the scheme before him. She explained everything to

---

ii Madeleine Shaw-Lefevre was the earlier head of Somerville College who had helped to organise Cornelia's scholarship.

him at the State Ball, and he was really interested and angry that he had never been shown the scheme before. Cornelia wrote him a supplementary letter to ask if he would give his official endorsement to a tour at her own expense, to supplement her collection of opinions from India. Meanwhile Brodrick's cousin, Lady Encombe, said that Brodrick would come to tea at her house to talk to Cornelia. This was superseded when Mrs Brodrick herself invited Cornelia to tea in December 1903 to talk to her husband, and he could not have been more helpful and attentive. She described him as quite young, dark, with a stern face, but a smile that broke up the sternness. He made Cornelia tell him all about the scheme and the need for it, as if, he said, he had not read her papers. He asked many searching questions. Encouragingly, he identified himself with the scheme, saying, 'We must make it a success.' Then he asked her in which province she would like it tried and she said 'Bengal', because she thought the Lieutenant Governor there would be more favourable. He asked the Lieutenant Governor's name and said he would write to him. He asked if that would be a help and said he would write to the different officials there to ask them to give her a chance of talking things over. Princess Louise had told Brodrick that she and Cornelia planned a trip together to Ceylon (Sri Lanka), and he asked how soon she could be up North in Bengal. He invited her to tell him more and, when she had done so, gave her still more opportunity, saying, 'Now think: is there no single other fact which you would like me to know? There is no hurry. Take your time.'[28]

Brodrick did write to the Governor of Bengal who was obliged to reply that the scheme which Cornelia had sent could not be found in the office. Brodrick also wrote to Curzon.[29] Even so, Cornelia could not believe that Brodrick's intervention was the move that would work, and she remained unclear as to which exactly of the proposals canvassed was the one to hope for.

She herself had put proposals before Brodrick which presupposed that there was a considerable way still to go, and that she should return to England after her trip, to await the outcome. Her proposal was for a more extensive scheme run by three women in three provinces, preceded by a tour in one of those provinces – Madras in South India– to collect more opinions. Brodrick's proposal was different, that the scheme should first be tried by Cornelia in Bengal. Perhaps Cornelia still hankered after the bigger scheme, and she may have been daunted by the idea of Bengal. She acknowledged[30] that she then thought of Bengal as the uttermost part of the earth, because she was at that time unfamiliar with the language, customs and everything. Perhaps too, she did not recognise the weight that Brodrick's opinion carried, and thought that his Bengal suggestion would be subject to the unpredictable wishes of the Bengal officials. She could not know that Brodrick was shortly to side against the Viceroy, Lord Curzon, and with the Commander-in-Chief, Lord Kitchener, in a way that was to lead to Lord Curzon's resignation as Viceroy.

CORNELIA SETS OFF ON A VOYAGE WITH PRINCESS LOUISE

Cornelia sailed off almost immediately on December 4th 1903 on the long-awaited holiday with Princess Louise to Ceylon,[31] but she had built in a plan to continue on to South India to collect more opinions about her larger, three-province proposal. The Princess looked after the sea-sick Cornelia, wrapping her in her own chamois leather sheets which Queen Victoria had used. They had special receptions, because of the Princess, at Gibraltar and Naples, even though this was a private, not an official tour. On arrival at Colombo in Ceylon, Cornelia checked for messages from Brodrick and to confirm her later South India itinerary. She was enchanted by the train journey on to Kandy: 'the rhythm of the forms on the pines, the harmony of the delicate colouring down the hill slopes, with every here and there that arresting note of bright red in the Amherstia, ... the emerald green slopes of the paddy fields, the glisten of water. ... All nature seems like a series of wonderful gardens'.

The Princess had gone ahead with her companion, Mary Hughes, to stay in Government House, which was the magnificent King's Pavilion. Cornelia was met by the Government House carriage and taken to the Queen's Hotel at the pavilion gates. Then she embarked on a series of private talks with the Princess, drives round the lake and luncheons, teas, dinners and dances with their hosts in the pavilion, including its balcony in the moonlight. The Governor, Sir Henry Arthur Blake, had Irish charm and named the four ladies in the house, 'Beauty, Strength, Goodness and Purity', and sang to Cornelia, though she was also teased for wearing a saree the same yellow colour as the Buddhists' robes, having admitted an attraction to Buddhism.

She could afford the journey only because a legacy had just been left her by Mrs Darling, the sister-in-law of Cornelia's adoptive grandmother Lady Ford, who had taken her in student days to Mentone and other European resorts.[32] And she had bought a new wardrobe for Ceylon, as if-she said- she were getting married. On one occasion she wore white with red Amherstia at her breast and waist and Queen Victoria's diamonds, loaned by the Princess, at her throat; on another a primrose saree with a blouse made of a gold-spangled yashmak, the Princess' diamonds and a diamond brooch of Queen Victoria, which the Princess said she had left to Cornelia in her will.

Tours had been arranged by the Governor. They saw the Tooth in Kandy's Temple of the Tooth, and the whole temple filled with pilgrims and lit with 84,000 lamps for the 84,000 ways of righteousness at the Festival of the Tooth. They saw elephants bathing and disporting themselves in a wild garden; they visited moonstone pits, and at Lankatilaka, a temple procession of elephants with 'devil dancers'. On February 2nd, Cornelia left to see more of Ceylon on her way to collect opinions in South India, and she climbed the ancient rock fortress at Sigiriya, in 'draperies and heels', much of the way by iron ladder in mid-air. She was chagrined only that she could not in her clothes also manage a rope ladder over a 40-foot precipice.

AN INDEFINITE RETURN TO INDIA

At Colombo, she was told that, with the onset of war between Japan and Russia, Watson's bank – where she had placed her precious legacy from Mrs Darling– had failed. So she did not have enough money to return to England.[iii] But she went ahead with the search for opinions in Madras (Tamil Nadu), one of the provinces envisaged by her larger proposal, and elsewhere in the south of India.

In the city of Madras (now Chennai), she explained her scheme in the High Court, and then discussed it informally in the Lawyers Association Room with the officiating Chief Justice present, who was an Indian. She was put in touch with secluded Muslim women and asked to have dinner with them. She went on to meet with the Vakils Association for Indian lawyers of that rank, again with the officiating Chief Justice and Sir B. Iyengar, both highly orthodox Hindus who favoured the seclusion of women. The Chief

---

iii In her reminiscences in *India Calling*, she recalls this as coinciding with her stay in Kandy and with an invitation to work in Bengal, and as making her decide that she could not afford to return to England to discuss the larger proposal, and so should accept Bengal. But her reports at the time described the Bengal letter received in Kandy as the one that confessed it could not find a copy of her scheme, and no invitation from Bengal was forthcoming for some time yet. Personal diary, 165/65, Feb 10 1904; *India Calling* London pp. 121–123, Delhi pp. 93–94, Nottingham pp. 81–82; Letters to Blair, 1654/24, Feb 12, 28, Mar 3 and 14 1904.

Justice reluctantly acknowledged that only yesterday a woman had asked
for a woman to hear her evidence, and Iyengar guardedly admitted that
he had had to rely on a waiting-woman to identify the person speaking,
and that that speaker might have been under pressure. But neither of them
wanted encroachment on their own preserve, and they approved the need
up North, but denied it there in the South. In the Princely State of Arcot,
ruled by the Nawab elsewhere in the Province (or Presidency) of Madras,
the governess of the Nawab's daughters, Mrs Firth, openly said that Cornelia
would take away her job, and the British political agent tried to claim that
ladies in seclusion from males could use a male British solicitor.[33] The main
concessions were that Iyengar wrote an opinion in favour of Cornelia's
scheme, and the *Madras Mail* interviewed her for one and a half hours and
wrote two articles.

Cornelia also went to the Princely State of Hyderabad, where the Nawab
had employed a woman to take evidence from secluded women. Cornelia
had been urged to come and stay by Sarojini Naidu,[34] who was already a poet
and would become a leader in the Indian Independence Movement. She was
younger than Cornelia and very keen to see her, and remained very friendly,
until politics drew them apart. In Hyderabad, Cornelia heard, her scheme provoked an evenly matched debate.

The final stop was Poona, where Cornelia also wanted to sound out legal
opinion, because it was her home.[35] But the main reason for going was that
her mother's school was in crisis, because Lena, who had by now become the
mainstay, was due to go to England to recuperate from illness, and was to stay
away from 1904–1905. Cornelia arrived to take over on February 27th. This
released Lena who could now leave, and on February 30th Cornelia saw her off
to England. Cornelia was still hoping somehow to return to England herself to
pursue her three-province proposal.[36]

TO BENGAL – BRODRICK'S PLAN
BEGINS TO WORK

The family's relief at her arrival lasted little more than a week, because on
March 9th, Cornelia got a message from Calcutta that she should go up there
at the end of the month, to talk to the Government of Bengal.[37] Brodrick's
plan was working. Cornelia seems not to have explained to the family, perhaps
because she was so uncertain of the outcome, the hoops she was going through

and the difference between her aspiration of five years earlier – to be able to plead in court – and the campaign of the last five years to get a different kind of advisory legal post. At any rate, there would soon be family criticism about what she was doing up in Bengal with no clearly recognisable legal role.[38]

Cornelia left Poona on March 25th 1904, and the next day reached Allahabad. There at last she saw Dick, who had not communicated with her for over three years. In Calcutta, she was called to Government House for 8.30 a.m. on March 28th by the Lieutenant Governor, Sir Andrew Fraser. But first she talked with her old friend, his father Dr Fraser. In his study, Sir Andrew asked her for her proposal and her terms. She left the terms to them, which may have been to her permanent disadvantage, but the proposal he liked, especially her idea that she should work through the Bengal Court of Wards. The alternative was mentioned of working under the Lieutenant Governor's Legal Remembrancer whose job was to commission legal work required by the Government. But this would have produced a much less sympathetic outcome, judging from her later experience with holders of such posts.[39] Fraser was going to a meeting of his Council in one hour, where he would see Mr Hare and Mr Savage, senior officers of the Indian Civil Service, and he would ask them to see her next day. Meanwhile she was invited to join the family at breakfast and prayers.

At 10.30 at 4 Harrington Street, Savage and Hare were both frightening at first and then gradually thawed. Within an hour they were discussing terms. They admitted the need and thought that a woman might do much good, if she won the confidence of her client. They were right to appreciate the point about gaining confidence. Mr Hare, she later learned,[40] was at that stage against her appointment, but was converted later. It was Mr Savage who said, 'I don't see why we should not make the experiment, circumstances being favourable.' That was not a promise, but they asked for her papers, which were with Sir Andrew Fraser. Her ignorance of Bengali was raised, but she went on to get herself a teacher that very day, and was indescribably happy.

Thomas Raleigh, her old tutor, had called on her the previous night, as he was about to finish his term of duty and was to be knighted the following day in Calcutta for his work. He now told her of Curzon's objections, most of which were familiar from what Curzon's private secretary had already said. Indians would dislike women being allowed to share in the Government of the country, and women doctors had made mischief in the country. Everyone accepted that these objections did not apply to Cornelia, but that raised the other objection that there was only one Cornelia. It seemed that Brodrick had got agreement to the appointment despite Lord Curzon's views. In any case, there was no reason for Sir Andrew Fraser not to make a local experiment in Bengal. Even though that was also the location of Viceroy Curzon, it was at least not an all-India policy. As Raleigh was to go off with Fraser on a holiday on the waterways of the Sunderbans, she hoped that Raleigh would strengthen Fraser's resolve.[41]

For much of April, Cornelia stayed waiting in Calcutta for news, and nothing much happened, except that she was befriended by the young Justice Stephen (who had given her a supportive opinion) and his wife. But eventually she was summoned to Darjeeling, the beautiful summer hill station of the Bengal Government and of the Viceroy in those days before the capital was moved to Delhi. On April 27th she set off, taking the miniature railway up the mountain. The views where she stayed were of glorious sunlight and snow, when they were not of mist.[42] On May 6th she was made happy by a note saying that the Bengal Board of Revenue, her official employer, recommended her appointment.

Over the following twelve days, details became a little clearer. Cornelia would receive only a retaining fee of 200 or 250 rupees (about £15) a month, plus daily fees, travel costs and expense allowance while travelling on business. She would have to provide her own office. That meant that she would have to find additional private legal work, or do writing, to get enough to live on. Her work would cover Bengal, Bihar and Orissa.[43] More than half the wards spoke Urdu, as did Cornelia, a mixture of Persian and Hindi.[44] On May 12th, Cornelia received her official note and the terms were rather poorer than she had understood. But she visited Mr Savage, who recommended her to accept for now, for better or worse. The next day Mr Savage and the kindly bespectacled Mr Le Mesurier,[45] Secretary of the Board of Revenue, who was to be a long-term friend, briefed her on a case they wanted her to tackle. Her title was to be, 'Legal Adviser to Purdahnashins (women behind the curtain) in the Court of Wards'.[46]

Cornelia's campaign for a legal post was remarkable for the range of approaches tried, her persistence in the face of overwhelming opposition and, once she had the right backers, for the formidable orchestration of supporting events. One thing has not changed at all. Political appointments tend to be short-term, so in a long-term campaign officials can come and go, which may dramatically hinder or help the campaign. But something that may seem unfamiliar in the present day is the extent to which she fostered connexions in aristocratic society. However, at the time that was absolutely vital to her success. Her initial supporters were aristocratic, and the final breakthrough was due to Princess Louise gaining the interest of the aristocratic Brodrick, who had the highest relevant post, and whose brother Cornelia had known in the privileged context of Oxford. That is not the most likely route to success in more populist times, but then it would have been very foolish for her to try anything else. Another difference marking those times was that it was always men who had the posts and hence the ultimate authority. Women in England were more than two decades away from even having the vote. So Cornelia had less occasion to mention women. But she was often very close to them and more than half her confidants were women. Moreover, women played an extremely important role as persuaders of men, and in this connexion, they get mentioned a great deal.

CORNELIA'S WARDS: THE PURDAHNASHINS

The strictly secluded women for whom Cornelia was about to work, and to whom she became so devoted, were extremely orthodox in their religious beliefs and customs. The term 'orthodox' was used for Hindus with the strict-est observances and it included purdahnashin families among others.[47] The secluded purdahnashins were a million miles away from the progressive and sophisticated Indians whom most people in England were likely to meet. But that was going to be part of Cornelia's problem, because progressive Indians were likely to be even less sympathetic to the extremely orthodox than the British, who in the better cases did show understanding. And a further complexity was that one could never quite tell what little bits of orthodoxy were to be found in the most progressive, while there was also a spectrum of viewpoints in between.

Cornelia's wards included both Muslims and Hindus. She estimated that all Muslim women were secluded, whereas Hindus varied. In her area around Bengal only the land-owning and royal Hindus were secluded, but in the United Prov-inces and further North she thought that above the lowest class of servant most were secluded.[48] It was among the land-owning and royal classes that intrigue flourished most freely and Cornelia writes most about these, and more about Hindu purdahnashins than about Muslims. Cornelia herself, as a Parsee and a Christian, was impartial between Hindus and Muslims. The distraught Rani whose plight had inspired Cornelia's interest in the law at the age of nine had been a Hindu.[49] But Cornelia sought to help Muslims with their problems too.

The fact that seclusion, or 'purdah', was not in those days confined to Muslims is not widely known in modern India. But it was considered a matter of prestige to lead this costly way of life. How long did the practice continue among Hindus? Insofar as it continued, it did so in a much modified form. In Chapter 10 we shall come across a Hindu lady who remained voluntarily in purdah until 1992. Her mother, however, had resented having to adopt purdah upon her marriage at the beginning of the century, since it was not part of her own Kashmiri tradition. I have myself often stayed in the former women's quarters ('zenana') as guest of the granddaughter-in-law of one of the most sophisticated and effective Hindu leaders of India's Independence Movement, Sir Tej Bahadur Sapru. Here too the daughter was a Kashmiri Brahmin and adopted a modified purdah upon marriage only to conform with the customs of the region. Her daughter in turn repeatedly told me that in her early married days she could not go into the garden to play tennis, until it had been cleared of male gardeners. But there was the difference that she was perfectly free to play tennis with male members of the household. Cornelia herself thought it striking that purdah was practised in this particular family, when she stayed with them in 1937. She writes:

'Tej Bahadur Sapru's daughter, whom I'd known as a child.[iv] She has to keep purdah in Jaipur, which is very orthodox. Tent walls screen off the approach to the zenana in this very educated family. Her husband, Pandit Armanath Atal, is Finance Minister here, nice upstanding person, capable, broad-shouldered, and straight with nice frank face. English clothes beautifully groomed. She wears Kashmiri bobbles, sign of wifehood, over ears'.[50]

A good many of Cornelia's estate-owning clients had become utterly impoverished and their dwellings completely dilapidated. Others, like the descendants of Tipu Sultan, never had an estate. But at the other end of the scale, some women estate-owners, not all, had the title of Rani, or, higher, Maharani, being the wives or widows of Rajas or Maharajas. Maharajas and some Rajas were rulers who could pass laws and make legal judgements. They or their widows might have a Dewan, which I have rendered as 'Chief Minister'. Rulers could have other titles too, such as Thakur (female: Thakurani), or, in the case of Muslims, Nawab (male) and Begum (female), and some women ruled in their own right, a notable Muslim example being the Begum of Bhopal. When Cornelia worked for wealthy land-owners, it was only indirectly through them that she sought any benefits for their peasants. Direct help for other classes such as villagers, mill workers, or urban beggars was more a feature of her second career after 1922.[51]

---

iv In Allahabad.

134 OPENING DOORS

GENERAL SCOPE OF CORNELIA'S JOB

There could hardly be a fuller source of information about what was actually done in the Bengal Court of Wards from 1905 onwards than Cornelia's own records of her activities. She had responsibilities in two directions. She had to look after the welfare of the wards, but she was also responsible for persuading them, voluntarily if possible, to abide by British instructions, once she had done her best to shape those instructions. She shaped them, when she could, by persuading officers of the British-run Indian Civil Service at many different levels. Her relations to the wards will be the focus of Chapters 8–12. Relations to the officers will be described in Chapters 13–15.

During 1904–1906, her employment was on a probationary basis. In that period, she was assigned work with certain purdahnashin families by the Secretary of the Board of Revenue – at that time Mr Le Mesurier, and with the approval of the senior officer of the Board of Revenue, Mr Savage. Once her appointment was confirmed in 1906, she visited on her own initiative all wards of the Court throughout Bengal, Bihar, Orissa and Assam at least once a year if she could, more frequently if they lived in or near Calcutta, or were in crisis.

TYPICAL TASKS: ADMISSION TO THE COURT AND EDUCATION OF CHILDREN

Sometimes Cornelia was persuading women to become wards of Court in the first place, as she did in one of her first estates,[52] because the decision was normally a voluntary one. Once the status of ward had been given to a woman and her children, if any, Cornelia would advise the relevant officers on the suitability of governesses and tutors who might be appointed for the children, depending on what the estate could afford. This involved Cornelia in testing the tutors and governesses and re-testing the children at intervals. She wanted to involve herself in any case in the education of the children, and not only in that of the male heirs, who would eventually need to know how to run the estate. She expanded education to the girls as well, partly so that the next generation of women would be better equipped to protect family health, fend off rival claimants to the estate and understand the revenues. Cornelia's strong interest in the children not only cemented her friendships with many of the mothers, but also enabled her on her regular visits to inculcate in future land-owners her belief in the ideal of service to the less privileged. Her interest in education helped her to gain the confidence of the wards. Gaining their confidence also involved respect for their customs, even while she tried to modify some of them. Male children were not secluded and could be sent out to school when appropriate, although the agreement of mothers was sometimes hard to obtain. In one case Cornelia had to cope with a mother who came to school with a knife, threatening to kill her son and herself, if the boy was not brought home.[53] Girls could not be sent out to school after marriage, which for Hindu girls came early. Muslim girls might be sent to school as late as their teens, but then the pressure for marriage began to mount for them too.[54]

ESTATE MANAGERS

Ideally, the estate managers appointed by the British would not only improve estate revenues and stop intrigues, but would also appoint suitable tutors for heirs. But sometimes estate managers were themselves involved in intrigues, as Cornelia found on one of her earliest estates.[55] In these cases, Cornelia would, after investigation, alert the appropriate officers. Very occasionally she was able to recommend that a purdahnashin was capable of managing her own estate, without an estate manager. A bad estate manager could waste estate revenues and only a few purdahnashins had enough education to understand the revenue accounts which they were entitled to see. In more than one case Cornelia had to insist on accounts being shown. In the case of a wealthy Muslim ward, we shall see, Cornelia made a lasting enemy of a high-ranking officer by insisting on accounts being shown which revealed huge wastage of revenue by a manager supposedly under his supervision, while also revealing that the estate could support the ward's lavish life style to which the officer objected.[56]

HEALTH

If estates were to be protected by the Court of Wards, then the health of heirs and of their guardians, usually their mothers, needed to be protected too. Cornelia's first cases in 1905–1906 already supplied her with dramatic experience in the mismanagement of health.[57] But insensitive imposition of Western medicine had created implacable opposition to the Court of Wards on at least one estate.[58] Cornelia developed her own techniques of working instead with the grain of traditional custom, instead of against it, in persuading her wards to better health care.[59]

RULES OF INHERITANCE

When the mother of an heir was widowed, sometimes while still a child herself, the plots of rival claimants to the estate, and to the throne if there was one,
could include litigation, fraud and even murder. It was first necessary to be sure
who was the rightful heir. Here Cornelia's expertise on wills and on adoption
was an invaluable new asset to the Court. The law on adoption differed in different places. When Cornelia's view on the illegitimacy of a certain adoption
went unheeded by an officer who had become her enemy, this led to a massively
expensive legal defeat and humiliation for the Court.[60] Conversely, Cornelia's
unique knowledge of adoption law on her first estate was to enable her many
years later to protect the estate successfully from a takeover.[61] Cornelia loved
the varied customs surrounding adoption ceremonies, which she was invited
by her wards to witness personally.[62] The law on wills also varied as between
Muslims and Hindus. In a number of cases, Cornelia was asked to verify wills
on which rival claimants had been counting and found them to be invalid.[63]
Eventually, Cornelia became expert on different Muslim laws on divorce which
also affected property rights.[64]

FAMILY QUARRELS

Litigation arose not only from rival claims to an estate but also from family quarrels, which were particularly common between mother-in-law and
daughter-in-law. Litigation wasted estate revenues and the Court was pleased
that Cornelia healed two quarrels with mothers-in-law in the probationary
years of 1904–1906.[65] In each case, she made use of traditional custom in gaining reconciliation. The waste of estate revenue penalised both the widowed
guardian and the future heir.

RELIGIOUS NEEDS

The Court needed Cornelia's advice on what expenditures were legitimate. The
legitimacy of religious expenditures was particularly unclear to officers and
with some officers highly controversial. Cornelia determined the right amount
of expenditure for the soul of a deceased mother in one of her first estates.[66]
She also advised about legitimate expenditure on ceremonies for the soul of a

deceased husband and on pilgrimages for the future of a widow's soul.[67] Some
of the religious beliefs and practices that Cornelia encountered gained cur-
rency within a system of purdah that has now been swept away. Purdah upon
early marriage left female children short of education and in no position to
question ideas. Cornelia was sympathetic to the purdahnashins' ideas and customs so long as they were not harmful to the purdahnashins themselves. Her
descriptions of these ideas and customs preserve some of the history of India,
and her need to negotiate within their ambit reveals how much more challenging her job was than one might have expected. A number of examples will be
encountered in the description of her cases in Chapters 8 and 10, and others
will complete the picture in the resumptive account of custom in Chapter 12.

PARCELLING OF LAND

Estate revenues could be wasted in ways that were perfectly legal. After a husband's death female relatives might move in to a widow's property, or the estate
might be divided with co-sharers who stood to gain if anything befell the widow.
They could delay improvements in efficiency on the widow's land, withholding
permission if she needed to sell part of the land, or if she needed to re-parcel it
by exchanging isolated patches with them. Eventually, the widow, increasingly
impoverished, might have to sell her share to them at reduced price.

Dowries were an important subject in the households of wards. One type of
dowry, the *stridhan*, was not part of the estate but was a bride's own permanent
property, often in the form of jewellery. Purdahnashins were not allowed to
use banks, despite Cornelia's efforts, because male bankers could not identify
secluded women, so their valuables had normally to be kept in the house, with
all the insecurity that that implied.[68] An entirely different kind of dowry was
bestowed by the bride's family on her husband, and could make his family's
fortune, or imperil her family's.[69]

It is time to turn to the first four families for whom she worked, all of whom
were Hindu.

PART III

LEGAL ADVISER FOR WOMEN BEHIND THE CURTAIN

CHAPTER 8

FOUR EARLY ESTATES, 1904–1906: NARHAN, TAJHAT, CHURAMAON, KASIMBAZAR

Cornelia was uniquely qualified to carry out the job she had designed. But the job put her in a complex position serving both the British and the secluded women and children. The descriptions of Cornelia's role in official correspondence veer revealingly between 'Adviser *to* the purdahnashins' and 'Adviser *on* the purdahnashins'. She sought to befriend her wards, often having first to overcome their suspicions. She saw it as her role to ease problems by coaxing, educating and protecting mothers who were often much younger than herself and their children, while preserving their way of life. This could lead to genuine gratitude, and later to close friendships. Cornelia was assigned as her first case one where quarrels among wards had proved most intractable and where there was maximum suspicion of her. But even here suspicions were overcome. In the other estates to be described in this chapter, the mothers welcomed Cornelia into the nursery to play with the children. This often led to the appointment through Cornelia of a nurse or governess of their own religion. In several of these families we find Cornelia invited to attend and help with the major ceremonies in the child's life, which she felt to be a great privilege. As a result, friendship with the second generation was closer still, and when the invitations included ceremonies for the child's eventual marriage and subsequent motherhood, the friendship lasted into a third generation. Sometimes the ward's reaction was one of dependence and longing for Cornelia's visits. 'When you are here', one said, 'I forget I have troubles, I forget that I am lonely, I forget that I am ill'.[1] But dependency was not always in one direction. Cornelia finished completely depending on one ward (Peri Banu) for her work.[2]

Cornelia considered that two of the greatest dangers to secluded child widows were their relatives, who might want their estates, and their priests.[3]

141

In Chapters 14 and 15 we shall see that she thought a third great danger was bad administration by a minority of British civil servants, and she was outspoken about all three. Her comment on priests was not a criticism of the priesthood as such. It was rather that the girls' education had normally been stopped upon marriage, and with their husbands dead, their priests were among the very few educated males they could consult. The secluded widow had legal rights over the income from her estate. But as Cornelia said, 'She knows of few ways of spending money beyond its application to religious uses. Her priests see to it that her money is so applied.' This led Cornelia to many a tussle with both relatives and priests. It did not imply any quarrel with other types of religious person, not with her Sadhu and Sadhuin friends, to whom I shall come in a few moments.

In order to defend her wards, Cornelia had to know Hindu and Muslim law and local variations on it,[4] because the suits with which she was dealing in her households were civil, not criminal. In civil cases, although the British organised the law courts, it was local law that prevailed.

Cornelia was indignant with those individuals whom she took to be harming her wards, equally if they were British[5] or Indian.[6] She still believed by and large in the British, and regarded the individual cases of injustice that she encountered as letting down British standards.[7] It was more complicated when there were quarrels and manipulations within the family and among its retainers.[8] She would try to secure reconciliations, and her designs to that end could be manipulative, although she enjoyed that role too. Social workers and lawyers even in a non-colonial context tend to think they know best what their families should be doing, and it would be surprising if they did not.

Like her fellow Victorians, Cornelia was very interested in beliefs about the future of the soul after the present life. Her anti-missionary view that the differences of belief were to be cherished, not removed, led her into many conversations in which she found that the beliefs differed in ways she had not expected. She further used the beliefs about the soul successfully to persuade the British, against the opposition of some officers, that religious ceremonies were an absolutely legitimate expenditure. The British trusted her to ascertain the going rate, which she did partly because she accepted the view that some money should be left for the eventual heir, which was all the more urgent if the estate had started in debt.

Cornelia found customs as well as beliefs absorbing. She was to write a whole book on the ceremonies of purdahnashin women and children[9] and she translated or co-translated from Bengali sets of rules for ceremonies (*bratas*), which would otherwise by now have been lost.[10] Her descriptions tended to be exotic equally for ceremony among her wards and for British ceremony in Westminster Abbey or in the state visits of British Royalty.[11]

Cornelia might also write exotically, when her work with secluded women plunged her into startlingly unfamiliar situations. At least she might do if she was writing to a close friend who knew her seriousness of purpose. By the time she had to make official reports on the same situations, no exotic flavour remained. She would explain to the British the needs of her wards with great sympathy and an astonishing grasp of the complexities of their pre-dicaments.[12] Commenting on Cornelia's exoticism, one writer has compared British romanticism of the time about medieval England.[13] Another has con-trasted the voyeuristic exoticism of Europeans who gained one rare glimpse of secluded women's quarters with Cornelia's everyday attitude. Despite her taste for the fantastic, the author points out, Cornelia liked to present her-self, at least in her later recollections, as a professional getting down to the needs of her wards as individuals.[14] I would only add that at the first telling, which was sometimes the only telling, she had no need to remind her diary or her correspondent of her role as professional helper. Just occasionally,[15] Cornelia's description of ceremonies took on a critical slant if she suspected the motives of the participants. This could happen when rituals were an inte-gral part of quarrels and involved intimidation, or allegations of intimidation, but it was not the norm.

Cornelia's Hindu friendships extended far outside the circle of her secluded wards. She learnt much about religion from certain Sadhus and Sadhuins, holy men and women, whom she greatly admired. They were not secluded, but highly educated, and widely visited and consulted. Their genu-ine asceticism gave them authority, and one had more authority, Cornelia said, than the priests of the holy city of Benares. Their beliefs and attitudes were applied with flexibility and good humour to help people in their every-day troubles. Cornelia learnt some of her own techniques for giving help from three of them, Bawaji, Mathaji and Narayani, whom she described in her book *India Recalled*.[16] Their attitudes were not like those of her wards, who had been denied education by the purdah system, nor like those of the individuals who exploited her wards. Because the purdah system made her wards vulnerable, she encountered situations of great hardship. Her Sadhu and Sadhuin friends confirmed her belief in the possibility of alleviating hardship from within the system.

NARHAN

Cornelia was given her first cases in 1904–1906 on a probationary basis
and she was thrown in at the deep end into situations that the British had
found particularly difficult. Her very first case involved implacable quarrels
and deep suspicion. It took her by train on May 25th 1904, travelling with a
chaprassi (henchman) and a Nepalese ayah (nurse), from beautiful Darjeeling
to a palace in what she called the 'mud country' of Narhan in Bihar, not far
from Darbhanga.[17] The houses were made of mud and Cornelia described the
people as 'mud-coloured like detached pieces of their own houses', except in
the palace, where there were three separate courtyards housing three generations of women, all of them aggrieved. The women were the current Rani,[18]
her mother-in-law and the Rani's fourteen year old married daughter who
was heiress to the throne, and their quarrel was marked by suits and counter-
suits. Cornelia's instructions from the Secretary of the Board of Revenue had
been that peace was to be made at Narhan in the unlikely event of that being
possible. More realistically, he wanted her to try to get to the bottom of the
quarrel, and to try to get the suits and counter-suits withdrawn, since law
suits were wasting the estate. In fact, they had little hope of her doing more
than explain to the Rani face to face, so as to safeguard themselves, why the
family's lawsuits would fail and should be withdrawn. Generations of District
Collectors and Divisional Commissioners[19] had tried and failed to explain
this, and at the nearest railway stop the estate manager mocked the idea of her
even getting an interview.

Cornelia spent the first night in a smelly Dak Bungalow (rest house for
travellers), but was then moved with her servants to a Government guest
house. The Rani sent her Chief Minister and other officials to report on
Cornelia, while declaring that she was indisposed, so could not receive.
But the next day liveried servants came with trays of welcoming gifts to be
touched and returned with a silver coin, and an early meeting was requested
by the Rani.

At 5, the Rani's Chief Minister took Cornelia to the palace, accompanied by
retainers with crooked swords in hand, up a flight of stairs, through a courtyard and into a long room. Cornelia described the initial scene in her exotic
mode. The 'substantial' Rani, aged about 45, was in bed, wrapped in a white
saree with heavy gold ornaments, rows of maids fanning her and with retainers
behind a screen. The Rani's Treasurer and the Prime Minister hid behind the
curtain. After conversing about ordinary things, the Rani told her story and

her grievances. Whatever they were – and Cornelia does not say – they had led her to withhold her daughter's dowry in the form of jewellery. For years, the mother-in-law, and latterly the daughter's husband, who threatened litigation, had opposed the Rani's decision and taken the daughter's side.

Over the next days, everyone was worried as to what Cornelia wanted. Lesser members of the palace came to incriminate others, agreeing only on the wickedness of the Rani's beloved Treasurer, whom they accused of intrigues in his role as treasurer of revenues. Meanwhile Cornelia sounded people out on their willingness for peace and answered what was reported to her of the Rani's objections.

The day came when she was to see the Rani's mother-in-law and her grand-daughter, the Rani's 14 year old married daughter, at 4 o'clock, in the Rani's palace, which she described as 'a study in dilapidation and deshabillée'. She climbed some steep stairs into an upper chamber, where her first description of the mother-in-law was as a 'goitrous old dame', 'stern as irrevocable sin'. The Rani's daughter was robed in red, with hair unkempt and a crowd of dogs surrounding her. The Rani's daughter objected to visiting her mother – there was a rumour that her mother had tried to serve her a poisoned meal and had cursed her while having Colman's mustard powder scattered[i] to make her sneeze. When she sneezed, this was taken to prove that a devil had entered her.[20] But after two hours, the Rani's mother-in-law and daughter agreed to the proposal that the mother-in-law should take the girl to her mother.

Next day, Cornelia simply told the Chief Minister to arrange the interview between the three women. But she took the opportunity to meet the Rani's grandson, who was also a grandson of the Maharaja of Benares (Varanasi), which gave Benares a claim on the estate, a claim that Cornelia was to contest successfully many years later.[21] The Rani's grandson was 'a pretty boy of 14, well set up', and came accompanied by his uncle, 'all wrinkles', and by his tutor in a long black robe, who said to Cornelia, 'We look upon your com-ing as the coming of the Messiah.'[ii] The Rani's daughter was the heiress, but under local law it was difficult to discover who else might acquire rights of succession and Cornelia would soon set herself to study the law of succession

---

i In the original letters to Lady Hobhouse, the mustard allegation is ascribed not to the granddaughter explicitly but only to 'one little lady', and reports of attempted poisoning were certainly offered by others, 165/17, May 31, July 4 1900.

ii In the letter to Lady Hobhouse, of May 31 1900, it was the grandson who said this.

in Narhan.[22] This would stand her in good stead some 28 years later when her arguments as regards the claims of Benares were to succeed upon appeal.[23]

A visit to the Rani revealed her as genuinely pleased about the prospect of reconciliation, and she showed the magnificent jewels and clothes she had assembled and made for her daughter, but withheld, along with allowances, in the absence of peace.

When the day of reconciliation came, the whole proceedings took from 4 until 8 in a dark, stuffy room with all shutters closed, so that the men outside should not see. The Rani sat behind her curtain at the far end of the long room, lined with waiting women, each carrying ornaments on arms and forehead, and each silently flapping a huge peacock fan glittering with jewels planted in front of herself. At 4 o'clock the Rani was herself reluctant again. Cornelia had felt the importance of an outward sign of homage to the Rani's mother-in-law and urged the symbolism of falling at the senior person's feet. This was a ceremony that she thought particularly appropriate and was to use elsewhere again within a year, as we shall see. She had to stress to the Rani how much it added to her honour that the mother-in-law would come across from the neighbouring courtyard. The Rani's daughter had not come since she was five, nine years earlier. After many objections, Cornelia brought the Rani's mother-in-law and daughter. Cornelia seated the mother-in-law at the entrance, and then went to tell the Rani at the far end of the room, 'Your mother-in-law has come to see you. May I take you to her?' To give the Rani courage, she whispered to her, 'I want to see if your falling-at-the-feet is as pretty as ours in the West country'. 'Prettier', said the Rani, covered her face and went to fall at her mother-in-law's feet three times. Such subservience to a mother-in-law would have been the norm for many secluded widows, but this one had been protected by being a Rani in charge of the estate and its funds. As Cornelia described it, the mother-in-law stood stern and immovable. The daughter, still terrified by the stories about her mother, hung back clutching Cornelia's hand, but made the necessary gestures. Cornelia suggested that the mother-in-law should retire, so that the Rani need not continue standing, and then things went better with the daughter.

At 7, with the darkness eased by brass oil lamps, the Rani brought out the presents she had been withholding from her daughter. The Rani's Treasurer, accompanied by the Chief Minister, called out the inventory from behind a screen. The women called back that each item was present, while Cornelia attested to the transfer. There were six to eight rows of pearls with emeralds at each drop, white sapphires, diamonds, rubies, topaz, turquoise and gold.

When offered pearl and gold bracelets for herself, Cornelia refused, and the Rani called her her sister, protector and friend. Outside, crowds of tenants and peasants at the gates waited to see Cornelia, calling her the bringer of peace, and the whole palace was pleased.

The next day, Cornelia removed one source of quarrel and intrigue by getting the Rani to agree to a paper also restoring the allowance withheld from her daughter. But Cornelia thought that the Treasurer, who would reverse any reforms, must be removed, and to that end she told the Rani that Lord Curzon honoured people by sending them on leave. Should she not thus honour the Treasurer, once the reconciliation was over? He was reluctant to go and the Rani feigned illness, but Cornelia was inexorable and at midnight on her last day, she had him formally hand over his work, and made him leave before the morning train.

Back in Darjeeling, the result of this first experiment exceeded all expectation. Cornelia had achieved what had been considered the most difficult task, obtaining peace among the three women. Mr Le Mesurier, who had given Cornelia the assignment, was astonished. As Secretary of the Board of Revenue, he asked to call to take Cornelia to see Mr Savage, the 'Member', or senior officer, of the Board, who had been one of those who originally interviewed Cornelia for the probationary job. Mr Savage said nothing, but seemed pleased, since he immediately suggested another case. Moreover, unusually, the Lieutenant Governor himself wanted to see her report and see it the same day, so it had to be written by 6.30. Meanwhile, the Chief Minister of Narhan and the dismissed Treasurer with his brother arrived in Darjeeling, trying unsuccessfully to discover from Cornelia what was happening. The congratulatory annual report on the Court of Wards says, 'She was able to prevent litigation between the proprietrix of the Narhan estate and her son-in-law, and has devoted much attention to the health and education of the daughter of the proprietrix.'

ANOTHER VISIT TO NARHAN: SUPERNATURAL POWERS AND INTIMIDATION

The Board of Revenue asked Cornelia to visit Narhan again. One of the tasks she was set was to obtain dismissal of three further servants of the Rani believed to be involved in intrigue. The worst, in Cornelia's opinion, was her priest. Cornelia did not tell the Rani why she was recommending their departure.

She persuaded the Rani rather by her apparently supernatural knowledge. Though lacking eyes in the back of her head, she was aware that the brother of one of the suspects was listening behind the curtain, and she astonished the Rani by saying that he was free to stay. The next day, running on intuition, she told the Rani, 'I know you would not believe your confidant, when he told you that I wished you harm.' The Rani, astonished again, said, 'Who told you from inside things said at night in secret?'

Persuaded by Cornelia's uncanny knowledge, the Rani agreed to the three dismissals. The dismissed priest went to Calcutta to complain to the British Board of Revenue that Cornelia had bewitched the Rani, or so the complaint was translated to them. To counteract the bewitchment, he assembled in Narhan twenty of the holiest men, to try to send a devil into Cornelia.[24] They travelled over all the ground Cornelia had trodden, uttering what she called 'hideous incantations' from dawn till dusk, gathering dust from where she had stepped to make an image of her, to set it up in the temple garden and make passes over it. They also tried to curse the Rani's daughter, among other things throwing Colman's mustard powder at her.[25] The daughter believed in the priest's power and was thoroughly intimidated. Cornelia was determined to show the daughter that one need not be intimidated. In order to convince the terrified girl that the priest could cause no harm, she resorted to ridicule and asked the priest to perform the ceremony against herself again, when she could bring her Kodak camera from Calcutta.

Back in Calcutta a week later, Cornelia found the priest's emissary, one of the twenty skilled magicians, sitting against her gate post. She liked him and described him as 'the dearest old priest in the world, tatooed with sandalwood paste' and wearing 'becoming rosaries of brown seedlings punctuated with red beads'. But she still wanted to make sure that the inefficacy of his curses would be reported to the Narhan daughter. When he saw Cornelia, he 'chanted ominously to a wonderful Gregorian setting'. He told her that everyone was amazed that she was laughing at the devil, but that she had better take it seriously. She responded by getting him to live with her high-caste gardener in the gate house and accept meals from him, assuring him that he would see her more often there and be able to curse more effectively. The Rani's daughter was astonished that Cornelia could flourish under such powerful curses. When Cornelia explained that she believed in blessings, not curses, the daughter said she would learn to believe in blessings. After two weeks, the magician reported his failure and was told to return, but he made one last attempt and left a black kid with its throat cut on the lawn, the curse of Kali. Cornelia's servants were terrified, and she had to pay a carrier of the dead to clear it away.[26] But the convener of the twenty magicians appeared to be losing prestige.

POISON: THE NEED FOR PROTECTION FOR SECLUDED WOMEN

Cornelia had still further tasks at Narhan.[27] After reconciling the older ladies Cornelia separated them as soon as possible, which she describes as a strategy she used for preventing a recurrence.[28] The Board further agreed that the granddaughter, who was pregnant, should be sent away with her husband for her own safety. The Chief Minister opposed Cornelia on this, and she did not inform the absent Treasurer until later, but the Rani agreed at least to a temporary separation from her daughter.

Cornelia had the Rani's daughter housed six miles out of Calcutta, in an area of garden houses, tall palms, flowering trees and little temples. The dismissed priest had threatened the life of the Rani's daughter and her expected baby. So an armed guard was installed at the gate and Cornelia made the daughter promise to receive no food or gifts sent from the Narhan palace. The girl was at first lonely and hysterical. From Calcutta Cornelia brought her chow dog, Wanglo, every day,[29] as the girl loved dogs. But the girl objected to the visit of a doctor. Why should she show her tongue when the pain was in her stomach? Cornelia installed a nurse and also tested and appointed a governess and got lessons going in writing, arithmetic and sewing. The dismissed priest continued his measures against the Rani's daughter. As reported by Cornelia, he first tried to get the Narhan Rani to disinherit her. Finally, according to Cornelia, he succeeded in sending to the girl a basket of fruit with a loving message purporting to come from her Rani mother. It was poisoned and the girl died in agonies in 1907, shortly before her baby was to be born.[30]

The Rani at Narhan now exchanged visits with her mother-in-law, but according to Cornelia, she too fell victim to the priest. When the Rani fell ill, Cornelia summoned a doctor from the Dufferin hospital in Calcutta, who diagnosed arsenic poisoning and warned that the effects were very difficult to get rid of and might recur.[31] The Rani suspected a dismissed amla (household officer), but did not want him charged. Someone gave the cook a white substance to sprinkle on her food, which the cook did not recognise as arsenic. The illness recurred and the Rani died on July 5th 1912. Cornelia thought that fixing the blame would have been hopeless. She suspected the

priest, but before he could be questioned, he disappeared and was never
seen again.[32]

SUCCESSION OF THE BLIND MOTHER-IN-LAW

The mother-in-law applied for protection to the Court of Wards, and the
Board sided with her claim to succeed to the estate against the claims of her
own son, who was trying to get it. But claims to take over the estate were also
coming from the Maharaja of Benares, whose grandson on the Narhan estate
Cornelia had met on her first visit. Moreover, the mother-in-law agreed with
these claims. She was staying far away in Sultanpur and summoned one of
her clerks to witness a document assigning everything to Benares. She gave
the clerk a choice between a bribe of 175,000 rupees and the docking of his
allowance of 100 rupees a month. Even under this pressure, the clerk refused
to sign. Benares was also accusing the Narhan estate manager of mismanagement, even though he had substantially increased revenues. In November
1912, Cornelia consulted for two days at Narhan, and then set out at 3 a.m.
to see the mother-in-law at Sultanpur. It was an inaccessible retreat, reached
by horse and carriage along a rutted road and above a dangerous river bank.

Cornelia, having studied the local law of succession, told her that nobody
could be declared heir, while she was alive, and that included the Maharaja of
Benares.[33] The dangers of blindness for a secluded proprietress became all too
apparent. She kept her money in a locked palanquin, from which she handed
out payments herself, but could easily be deceived. The Court of Wards decided
to halt payments of her allowance until they could be safely delivered, through
her moving to somewhere safe other than Benares, where people went to die.
Under Cornelia's persuasion, she decided to return to Narhan for her residence, where she had been the previous year.[34] The Court of Wards appointed
a guardian to protect her, and in 1913 she became proprietress of Narhan.[35]

By 1916, she had erased the memory of her former quarrel, by completing
from her own money the expensive works in Narhan that her daughter-in-law
had intended. For the salvation of her soul she built two bridges for pilgrims,
one across the Ganges, which also strengthened trade and which was opened
with much fanfare. During the building she had camped for a month in great
discomfort at the site of the bridge, praying for the souls of everyone who might
use it. Cornelia's description of the Rani in her annual report to the Court of
Wards could hardly be in greater contrast with the initial description she had

allowed herself to her friend Falkner Blair eleven years earlier. Then the Rani had seemed an implacable party to a baffling family quarrel. Now Cornelia wrote:

'When we remember her condition (totally blind, leprous and disfigured by a goitre) and her great age, it adds to the pathos of the entire incident. She has allowed no one to see her save myself for over a year'.[36]

As a result of her good works, in May 1920 when the blind mother-in-law was 70 years old, Cornelia secured for her the title of 'Rani'. It was not automatic, but it was officially recognised for the ageing woman by the British Government. Royal titles were allowed in Narhan only to women. This was in memory of an earlier Rani who buried herself alive in shame at her husband's cowardice. At the bestowal of the much prized title, the band played 'Rule Britannia', the District Collector read out the grant of title, the Divisional Commissioner spoke of the new Rani's public works and Cornelia sat in the old lady's tent with her and translated.[37]

BACK TO NARHAN IN 1928

Cornelia was to perform a final service for Narhan, which was as dramatic as the first one. It came in the course of her second career back in India as a barrister in 1928. The claims of Benares upon the Narhan estate came to a head, and Cornelia was employed to defend the Narhan estate single-handed against a whole team led by one of the most prominent barristers in India, a major figure in the National Independence Movement and a family friend, but one who thought as much as anyone that the court room was not the place for ladies. If a lady dared to appear, she must be subjected to the merciless onslaught appropriate to male confrontations. Cornelia kept her head and had done her homework better than the opposing team. The case she prepared finally won on appeal, but as this was one of the few courtroom successes in her postponed attempt to get into the male preserve of the courtroom, it belongs to a later part of the story.[38]

THE SECOND ESTATE, TAJHAT

Immediately after the first Narhan visit, on July 20th, the Board of Revenue sent Cornelia for a new case to Calcutta and by August 12th she was studying the Tajhat estate. She started work in August 1904 and visited in September.[39] The Tajhat family had a house in Calcutta and a palace in East Bengal, five miles

19. Tajhat, Cornelia's second palace, 1905.

from Rangpur. The palace is still one of the sights to visit in Bangladesh. Cornelia described the approach as being through a flat green countryside relieved by
white flowering grasses, bamboo shoots being eaten by elephants, and houses
of plaited grass and split bamboo put together like card houses after an earthquake in 1899. The palace was still damaged by the earthquake. In a modern
photograph, taken in the mist with the mellowing of time, the leafy setting
of the garden with its Italian statuary looks most romantic, with the palace
reflected in the pond, and viewable from an elegant stone balustrade.[40] But at
that time, the palace was dilapidated, dirty and unfurnished after the earthquake. Cornelia thought it an odious structure in unplastered red brick with
green shutters rather than the present grey and white.

The Maharaja of Tajhat had died in the earthquake, and his Maharani widow
was now in charge. The Maharani, aged about 30, came down the steps to greet
Cornelia. Her dress was a white cotton saree, but sometimes she wore English
clothes, and she was a progressive person, compared with Cornelia's first
clients. She was also intelligent. Cornelia started by playing with the household's babies and putting them on their pots. Cornelia loved little children and

was practised in 'potting' them from the days of her childhood home. It was her enjoyment of playing with them that helped her to enter into the good graces of their mothers. In this case too it was partly through the children that Cornelia embarked on a growing friendship with the widowed Maharani. She started with a long talk about the Maharani's problems.

A FORGED WILL

These problems were connected with Cornelia's first task for Tajhat, which had been to investigate a will that appeared to be forged in favour of the current Maharani's son. It bequeathed him the throne when he should come of age.[41] The deceased Maharaja had had a first wife, and it is tempting to think that she had produced a rival heir, but if so, that heir was no longer in evidence. Cornelia had established several things to her own satisfaction. It was not the Chief Minister who was to blame for the forgery, nor yet the father of the current Maharani, although he may have played a subsidiary role, but the deceased Maharaja himself. Cornelia thought that it would be counter-productive to prosecute anybody now, even the Maharani's father.

Nonetheless, there was still litigation about the will from two sides. The British Government in Bengal wanted to expose the forgery. But against the Government those who supported the late Maharaja's choice of heir had filed suits in his support. They had also forbidden the peasants to pay rent or revenue to the Government of Bengal to be administered on behalf of the estate. It was not clear if the Court was exceeding its powers in trying to administer the estate informally. But in the absence of an effective administrator, many of the Maharani's ministers were benefiting from the estate's revenues through serving as co-guardians with the Maharani to the designated heir. Cornelia's first aim was to persuade everyone that there was not enough evidence to stand up in a court of law. British suits as well as the Indian counter-suits would therefore fail and should be withdrawn, and, until the designated heir came of age, the Maharani would herself benefit from handing the estate over formally for administration by the Court of Wards.

Eventually, the Maharani agreed to the terms for taking the estate into the Court of Wards. She accepted that estate expenditures would in future need British authorisation and she was reassured about her father not being prosecuted. But the Maharani's household still had to be convinced the next day, when two lawyers were assembled of vakil rank (below that of barrister). Every aspect of the transfer was thrashed out, and eventually everyone agreed, subject to a certain unwritten requirement that was expected of Cornelia in return: evidently dropping prosecution of the Maharani's father. About this Cornelia made no promise, although she held herself bound in honour rather than in writing. Cornelia put the case against prosecuting the father to the British prosecutors by comparing such a prosecution to a whipping, whose effects cannot be undone. The British and the late Maharaja's supporters met again for a third day and it was not until all the issues had been twice rehearsed again that Cornelia left late in the evening with the documents signed by all parties.

Mr Le Mesurier received the documents from Cornelia, and Government agreement to the terms of the Court takeover was forthcoming the next day, including agreement to the request not to prosecute the Maharani's father. Mr Savage was curt, but seemed to be pleased. In place of irresoluble law suits, Cornelia had secured a voluntary agreement. The Tajhat Prime Minister was sent to reassure the Maharani's vakils that all the terms, including non-prosecution of the Maharani's father, were agreed, and the Maharani's transfer of the estate to the Court of Wards was confirmed. The litigation was withdrawn on both sides and the tenants were told that rents should be redirected to the custody of the Court of Wards. The chief vakil on the late Maharaja's side, from having been Cornelia's opponent, now came to Cornelia to seek legal help with another case.

The next task, which took the whole of 1905, became urgent once the Court of Wards had official responsibility for the estate. It was to check how the Tajhat household had got into debt.[42] The men had run up a debt on the women's allowances at least partly by enrolling themselves as co-guardians of the designated heir. It became evident to Cornelia that the screen through which men and women spoke to each other resulted in a great deal of confusion and obfuscation. Even without a screen (as she was a woman), she found the involved and contradictory testimony of different generations of women so confusing that she had to put them all together on the opposite side of the room, to make any sense of it.

THE TAJHAT CHILDREN

Cornelia had been friends with the Tajhat children from the beginning and the women of the household did not resist her when she gave advice on infant welfare. The young heir had just been married, in 1904, and his child bride, aged 10, was the most beautiful girl Cornelia had seen, East or West. She was meant to keep her eyes downcast in her first year in her new women's quarters. Cornelia, to the delight of the women, used to tickle her under the chin to make her look up. Cornelia was allowed to appoint a governess for her and was invited to attend her ceremony of worshipping the aged family members with a feast. The ceremony ended with a formal exchange. 'Have we leave to depart, little mothers?', the aged asked. 'Come again,' replied the children. Later Cornelia would attend the rice-in-the mouth ceremony for the little Rani's own baby, when it celebrated the passage from a purely milk diet.[43] The little unmarried daughter of the family had to choose a bridegroom in April 1905, and after peeping through the door at candidates, she would ask Cornelia quite sensible questions. Was he sickly, and did he look good and kind? Cornelia had to budget for the wedding, and 12 days before that event she was pleased to be invited to the tikka ceremony, where the bride was blessed and had presents of sweets, toys and little pots and pans of dolls house size, such as she would learn to use in her new household.

The heir to the Tajhat throne was in very great danger from contestants of the will so long as he stayed in Tajhat. Cornelia later persuaded the family to let him be taken away urgently in January 1905, though they required two days to prepare. He was first taken to Raipur with his mother (the Maharani), which he did not like, and then to Calcutta, where he waited for a house to be got ready for him and a tutor appointed.[44]

A MURDER

On August 10th of the same year, 1905,[45] Cornelia received a call to the Tajhat's Calcutta house, as the 30 year old Maharani was ill. Cornelia went at once and it seemed to her that she was not very unwell, but chiefly worried about a quarrel with a male relative. This relative owed a debt so long as she remained alive. Cornelia stayed two hours and recommended a second opinion on her health. Between 11 and 12 at night, Cornelia was roused to go to the Maharani again, as her young friend was dying. Cornelia found her alive, but in a diabetic coma, with a Bengali doctor already anointing her legs with sandalwood for the funeral pyre. The priests carried her down two of the three flights of stairs, so that she should die close to mother earth instead of aloft, the territory of demons. But they bumped her on each step and shouted at her to call on Kali, the goddess of destruction. Cornelia felt sure that they were trying to revive the dying woman long enough to bestow a gift on the priesthood. She got the bumping postponed a little, but the doctor arrived from the Dufferin Hospital by 2 a.m. and said it would make no difference. The priests had got her only as far as the landing of the women's quarters, before she died at 2.45 a.m. The children, who had been present throughout, clung, sobbing, to Cornelia and calling her 'Aunt-Mother' (*mashima*).[46]

It turned out that before Cornelia's arrival in Calcutta, the debtor-relative had discovered from the Maharani's doctor what food was forbidden her as a diabetic. Having discovered the answer, he came purporting to offer apologies for the quarrel. Would she show forgiveness by eating his offering instead of her midday meal? Having thus put an end to her life, he no longer owed his debt.

A CEREMONY FOR THE SOUL OF THE MAHARANI

The estate now had to provide the same priests with a budget for the death ceremonies. Cornelia was determined to support what the Maharani would have wished. One of the ceremonies, held at least a week after the cremation, was described as making the Maharani's soul sinless through the next thousand incarnations. Cornelia took the Maharani's beliefs about the future of her soul to be literal and not a dead metaphor, just as her own beliefs were literal. From the British she wanted an expenditure authorised adequate for the ceremony. At the same time, as protector of the estate for the designated heir, she did not want the British to be deceived about the normal sums required. She saw the priests as trying to recoup the loss they made when the Maharani died before she could offer a donation,[47] Three thousand Brahmins were to be fed at the ceremony, and the priests asked for 60,000 rupees or £4,500. But Cornelia examined precedents which showed that a third of that was the norm. That was all she would recommend the Court of Wards to sanction out of the estate.

At the ceremony Cornelia liked the thirteen priests in the morning reciting from the *Bhagavad Gita*, and offering to the deceased flowers, fruit and a lighted wick in a saucer. Over the altars there were awnings and an arrangement of four gates with mirrors to catch the late Maharani's passing spirit. Cornelia also liked the setting in the afternoon. There was a huge image of the Maharani with a cow tethered to it. On the verandahs sat the Brahmin cooks busy with vegetables and spices, while the women peeped from the third-floor balcony. When the Brahmins crowded into the house itself, to eat from cups of dry leaves the food fetched from steaming cauldrons in the courtyard and drink a curd poured into earthenware pots, she allowed herself a little asperity about their gusto, and since the numbers already exceeded the agreed figure of 3,000, she finally shut the gates. Gifts were then distributed to the Brahmins of gold, silver and brass vessels, some of beautiful design, but broken into pieces for the value of the metal.[48]

CREDITORS

After the ceremonies were over, the Maharani's debts had to be seen to.[49] The custom for creditors was to ask for three times what was owed, but Cornelia explained that that was because the recovery of debts was doubtful. She announced that she would pay immediately the sums actually due, and if claimants did not agree, they should sue in the courts. Almost all accepted. Then a figure appeared whom she described as shrivelled and desiccated with a claim, wholly unsupported, for a sum as great as had been spent on the Maharani's funeral – 20,000 rupees. Cornelia's job was to protect the estate for the heir from fraudulent claims and she refused, whereupon he said he would sit 'dharna' on her doorstep. In other words, he would fast there until he died, and his blood would be on the heads of Cornelia and her descendants for 100 generations.[iii] Faced with this demand, she freely offered the claimant her doorstep, but he did better, and sat under a statue of Ganesh, thus announcing the god's support. The women of the household were terrified and took off all their personal jewellery for Cornelia to buy him off. But she preferred another approach and tried, without success, to have savoury dishes set beside him, and installed a doctor with instructions that she was to be called if he was in danger. Finally she was summoned: he was dying. The women had poured their jewels at his feet, but he showed no reaction. Priests, doctors and the heir shouted at him, with no result. Cornelia knew that fraud must be stamped out then or never. She ordered rupees to be chinked against a stone, at which his eyelids fluttered and a Brahmin gave him water. Cornelia then promised to pay him the amount she decided, if he returned to life, but it would not be the £1,500 he wanted. As Cornelia tells it, he smiled, having won his point, and eventually walked away with £7 and a half, seemingly content.

---

iii This was a curse she received on another occasion from an engaging seven -year old: See 'A Bengali woman revolutionary', *The Nineteenth Century* 1933, pp. 604–611.

ANOTHER TAJHAT RECONCILIATION

Cornelia had dealings with another Tajhat relative, the daughter of the late Maharaja of Tajhat's first wife. She had had a daughter and this daughter ran away in December 1906 from a drunken husband in Tajhat who beat her.[50] This gave Cornelia a further task. According to Cornelia's account, a wife belonged to her husband, and to run away was a disgrace to family and to religion. None of the family could seek her, because that would be to suggest that her running away was acceptable. A woman servant had heard her conversation at the railway ticket office and knew she had gone to Sheraphuli. The heir to the lady's estate, no longer a ward, came to ask Cornelia to seek the lady and bring her back to her husband. But Cornelia agreed to seek her only on a condition very difficult for them, that they agreed to take her back into the women's quarters as Cornelia's own guest there, not forcing her to go to her husband, but sending the husband to Cornelia.

Having got agreement, Cornelia took a train at dawn to Sheraphuli, and found the lady in a 'dank and dismal' swamp by a drain, hugging her son to her, and both chilled to the bone. There was a green water tank, and she was squatting on a mat, with her back against the wall of an empty brick hut she had found, that was falling to pieces, with overgrown bamboos and crooked palm trees – 'decay writ large'. She had chosen Sheraphuli because that was as far as her money would take her, and she had no further plan.

Somehow Cornelia found a chair and said she had come to take her home. But that would be impossible, the lady protested. She had run away, and they would not let her back. Moreover, 'he' would find her (a purdahnashin lady might not speak her husband's name). But Cornelia persuaded her it was all agreed otherwise, tucked her, with bag and baggage, under her arm, and brought her to Calcutta and on to Tajhat, where the women took her in. To the husband Cornelia said that he needed to overcome his drinking, which was in any case contrary to his religion, and she would have to assess whether he had done so. If he had, she would still only arrange for his wife to return, if she was well enough and consented. Meanwhile she looked for a separate residence in Rangpur, in case the wife wanted it, and advised her on the relevant law about her son as heir. Even though the husband cured his drinking, the wife kept changing her mind about going back. Eventually on April 7th 1907, the husband and wife met in a private room in Cornelia's house. The wife had insisted that her brother and Cornelia stayed close outside in case he tried to murder her. In about an hour, a beaming husband and shy wife emerged. She was to return to her husband's house that evening, and then return to him for good in 5 days.

CHURAMAON: THE PLEASURES OF TRAVEL

A new estate for Cornelia in the same year, 1907, was Churamaon (Chooramun) then in Bihar.[iv] Cornelia loved her repeated journeys there, usually by elephant, and she described them more than once.[51] As she tells in one account, one elephant was called 'Speedy Beloved', to encourage him to move faster. One, 'Beloved of Ganda', was the widow of the deceased 'Ganda'. A third, 'The Perfection of Beauty', was not full grown at 3 years, so that Cornelia kept slipping off his back, but he was faster than the others. A one year old 'gurgling baby elephant', 'The Warrior Emperor', ran alongside, impeding the progress of 'The Perfection of Beauty'. They had to cross three rivers and in the rainy season, they would take a detour, because the bridges would be washed away. Cornelia would be carried safely across the floods, but her baggage would be ritually dunked and rescued, because this was always rewarded with extra tips. The villagers on the way, dressed in mat hats and loin cloths, would be ploughing, or 'planting out the bright green rice', or fishing, which they did by damning off an area of water, and emptying it out with mat baskets, until the fish were revealed. It was usually 4 in the morning when Cornelia mounted her elephant, and all the world was 'grey mist, or silver-grey' if the moon had stayed up late. 'Emerald green fields stretched away to a blur where there would be the palms and huddled mat huts of a village, and beyond the village was a dark blue-purple line of hills.' Outriders from the house would join the party part way, until they reached Churamaon, and the narrow street of weavers sitting in their low huts.[52] At Churamaon Cornelia could watch the elephants[53] resting in their playing field and breaking off trees for food.

On Cornelia's first visit to Churamaon, there was a less comfortable cart drawn by white bulls instead of the elephants. But in spite of the discomfort, Cornelia was charmed by the birds.[54]

> 'Spite of it, however, I much enjoyed the journey. The trees are very fine in that part of Bengal, pretty bamboos, feathery tamarinds, mango groves, *neem* avenues, and many other trees whose names are hid from me. Then the birds are nicer than any I've seen outside Ceylon – sunbirds, little darlings, dressed in yellow and green with blue linings to their wings, kingfishers in gorgeous blues and red-browns, of whom I loved best the babies – the blue of their coats was true china blue and their breasts were a red-gold – parrots and parakeets and quaint black birds, jet black, something the size of *minas* (mina birds), but wearing long *trains* forked at the end. It was curious, but they suggested Dowagers in velvet dresses and long trains.'

---

iv Now across the border in West Bengal.

At Churamaon, as at Narhan, there was a quarrel between the widowed
Rani and her widowed mother-in-law. The mother-in-law wanted a joint
residence with her daughter-in-law in Churamaon, until she could go to
Benares to end her days. But, given the quarrels, the Court of Wards preferred a safer distance and refused.[55] They offered a residence at Benares
once the ladies were reconciled. The reconciliation was carried out in the
same way as at Narhan, in that Cornelia required a falling-at-the-feet of the
older lady.

The wealth of the Churamaon estate, however, involved Cornelia in an
entirely different range of activities. Cornelia accompanied the Rani when she
asked the British Collector to authorise out of estate revenues the construction
of a number of buildings.[56] This showed the British Raj's Court of Wards at its
most ambitious.[57] A river had earlier been diverted for the Churamaon family,
but there was a lot of repair work that remained undone. Now the Collector
brought an engineer, who went over the house with the ladies and Cornelia
over a period of three days. Parts were unsafe, including a well and some steps,
parts were incomplete and a verandah needed roofing. Space was wasted,
courtyards cluttered with lumber needed turning into gardens for the ladies,
and places used for storage turned into rooms for them, the children needed
a bathroom where the schoolroom was and their bedroom was to become the
schoolroom. Extra sweepers were needed to keep the water tank hygienic.
Three kitchens were needed, because, as Cornelia explained, people of different castes could not share kitchens, and they were all, as a fire precaution, to
be clear of the house.

The Collector agreed with Cornelia's proposal to replace the manager, who,
she believed, had stirred up the quarrels and was corrupt. Cornelia examined
the wards over their lessons and had the tutor rewarded with a pay rise. The
mother was unusual in that, after talking with Cornelia, she wanted her private
endowment of jewellery taken care of by the Court of Wards treasury, not
kept in the house, as it normally would be. How much of the rebuilding was
completed is unclear, because the family soon had to move,[58] taking their pet
leopards with them, to the nearest British town for the education of the boy,
Bhopal, and then on to Calcutta. Also, the river was still encroaching on the
property. But the scale of the planning was exceptional because of the wealth of
the estate. This work by the Court of Wards on a wealthy estate in 1905–1906
contrasts with provisions on a poor estate such as one that Cornelia liked visiting in the watery districts of East Bengal (now Bangladesh) in 1912–1915,
where even minimal repairs did not get done.[59]

BHOPAL, THE CHURAMAON HEIR

The children at Churamaon were Kalidasi, the girl, and her elder brother, Bhopal,[60] heir to the throne of Churamaon. But Cornelia called Kalidasi 'Shubala', to protect confidentiality, and evidently used the name 'Madan Mohun' as a disguise for Bhopal.[v] Bhopal's mother was designated his official guardian, and a Bhopali pony and groom and stables were arranged for him at Churamaon.[61] Cornelia recommended all the equestrian purchases to the Court of Wards and, as usual, made friends with the children as much as with their mother. After the move to Calcutta, Bhopal went to the Scottish Church Collegiate School and visited Cornelia on Sundays and in holidays. She was pleased that he gave up his wish for a motor car, when he heard that the Churamaon peasants had lost their homes in floods, while he made light of it by announcing that he was delaying the purchase until his matriculation.[62] Cornelia's only regret was that he did not study agriculture against the time when he would return to rule in Churamaon.

The eventual return and ascent to the throne was celebrated with food for 10,000 people, but that happened only in 1920, when they were all grown up. Bhopal's sister, Kalidasi, was at the enthronement celebrations cutting up vegetables. After the long absence in Calcutta, Cornelia advised Bhopal to say to his people that he had been preparing himself for them while he was away on his studies. The enthronement was magnificent. Cornelia went by car, which was good exercise on bumpy roads that kept throwing her in the air and catching her again. Elephants and people fled before the motor and the elephants finished up seven miles behind. Bhopal on his regal throne with umbrella was shy and grinned at Cornelia. After the ceremony, he drove her back to her bungalow and talked while she dined. He still treated her as a special confidant, and she in turn stayed until the very end of his celebrations, when the elephants were eating the decorations.[63] By the next year, 1921, Bhopal was building a hospital with a woman's block and had employed district maternity nurses. This was the kind of transformation in social attitude that Cornelia had hoped for.[64]

---

v 'Madan Mohun' was actually the name of an old man she had met in Allahabad, Letters to Lady Hobhouse, 165/17, Nov 21 1900. Admittedly, in the original reports Bhopal is said to have been only five when Cornelia first visited, whereas Madan Mohun is later said to have been eight, but a small slip of memory about the boy's age does not mean that she was talking about two different boys.

Cornelia's greater anxiety was for the sister, Kalidasi, the one she calls
'Shubala' in published sketches of her.[65] When Cornelia first visited, the Rani
(Kalidasi's mother) was seeking sewing lessons for her. Kalidasi was very happy
at least up to her marriage, at ten and a half, but after that she had to remain
secluded 'on the inside', and could not be seen outside again. Out of deference
to Cornelia, the marriage[66] had been delayed from the earlier age of four at
which Kalidasi's mother had been married.

KALIDASI, HIS SISTER: MARRIAGE, MOVE
TO KASIMBAZAR (COSSIMBAZAR)
AND MEDICAL HAZARDS

Kalidasi's marriage was arranged with a young nephew of the Maharajah of
Kasimbazar (Cossimbazar). When the various candidates were interviewed,
custom had allowed Kalidasi no more than peeping through a hole in the door.
Although she had choice in a sense and could subsequently ask Cornelia questions,
these questions were narrower than the ones Cornelia answered at Tajhat, and were
confined to the suitor's womenfolk with whom Kalidasi would have to live, and
the suitor's qualifications, if any, from Calcutta University. But the prospect, ever
postponed as it turned out, of her husband getting an allowance from his uncle, the
Maharaja of Kasimbazar, persuaded her to choose the Maharaja's nephew.

The only untraditional event in a gorgeous traditional wedding on May 2nd
1908 was that the bridegroom fetched her in a Rolls Royce car decorated with
strings of pink roses and yellow marigolds. The day after the wedding, at the
ceremony which Cornelia rendered as 'Blessing of the Women', the couple
stood hand in hand, tied together, while the women one by one blessed them
with paan leaves and offerings, hands travelling from head to feet. Afterwards
the couple drove off in the Rolls, her saree tied to his dhoti.

By July 30th 1910, Kalidasi, aged 12, was pregnant.[67] 'The air of hushed
expectancy in the house is wonderful,' wrote Cornelia. Kalidasi went back to her
mother's house in Calcutta for the baby's birth, with her father-in-law arriving
to sit outside the door reading out instructions for the midwife from an ancient
vernacular text. On February 3rd 1911, Kalidasi was having convulsions and
Cornelia got a message at midnight that Kalidasi was dying and she was to come
with whatever doctors and nurses she thought necessary. A qualified doctor and
nurse rescued Kalidasi and delivered the baby successfully. When the doctor

left, the father-in-law read out the instruction, 'Now it is time to light a fire on top of the mother.' The idea was to place lighted coals in a tin dish on Kalidasi's stomach, so as to leave a burn. Cornelia did not contest the power of fire, but she urged that they should not neglect the power of holy Ganges water, and she persuaded them to use the fire not directly on the stomach, but to heat the Ganges water and put it in hot water bottles. That would be a *double* source of protection. The naked coals still had to be used separately, but it was accepted that they be placed on a window to burn.[vi] This was one of Cornelia's appeals to custom to modify custom.[68] Another part of tradition was that the baby and mother could not be touched for 40 days by the grandmother, or great-grandmother, because birth was considered unclean, and that the servants had to use lamp black under its eyes, to avert the evil eye.

Kalidasi returned quite often with her children to the Calcutta house, and she adopted some modern practices, sending a daughter and a granddaughter to school at the Diocesan School in Calcutta.[69] But Cornelia describes her as continuing to suffer from mistaken remedies for sickness. At a sick bed of 1912, she sought to protect Kalidasi from the priest shouting mantras at her and, as she put it, from women attendants 'pawing' her. And in 1913, Kalidasi had measles, but she herself refused a nurse, saying that the goddess inhabiting her might not like it. By the age of 18, Kalidasi had had 6 children and her health was ruined. She died after her 15th child in 1930.[70]

A HAPPIER BROTHER AND SISTER IN KASIMBAZAR: CHUNDI A HOPE FOR THE FUTURE OF SECLUDED WOMEN

A much happier life was led by another brother and sister in Kasimbazar. Kamala Ranjan Roy, the brother, and Chundi, the sister, grew up there. The boy was a ward of Cornelia. They were looked after by two widowed Ranis, their mother[71] and grandmother. The grandmother, Arnakali Devi, particularly impressed Cornelia. She showed Cornelia the shrivelled little finger with which she was taught at the age of three to stir the rice, to prepare her for living death on the funeral pyre (suttee), if her husband died before her.[72] Chundi and

---

vi In some versions of the story, Cornelia recommended only that fire should burn on the windowsill, and did not refer to its use in heating the water, which may be a literary improvement.

Kalidasi were not only relatives by marriage, but friends. Cornelia described Chundi as 'living in the second and the twentieth centuries at the same time'. She thought that her mixture of traditionalism and rebellious modernism represented 'the high water mark of possibility for keepers of the law of Hinduism' and 'the best solution of our problems'. In *India Recalled*, Chundi is the central character, but her name and identity are disguised to protect her privacy.[73]

Cornelia knew Chundi from the age of three and gave her an English doll, which she called 'Mees' and to which she was devoted.[74] She went on to marry the Maharaja of Nadia not far away.[75] Cornelia was called as soon as Chundi's first baby was born. But that was when Chundi was fifteen, not ten and a half. Even then Chundi was very disgusted by the prospect of having to have a baby, since she already had Mees. The official name of the baby girl had to appear miraculously on a writing tablet beside Chundi's mother's bed, and then be approved by priests from the holy sites of Benares, Puri and Rishikesh. But Chundi gave the baby the private name of 'little Mees'. Chundi felt rebellious when her mother and grandmother were not allowed to touch the baby for 30 days, although the grandmother did sit up for 40 nights beside the baby to ward off evil spirits. Cornelia attended all the traditional ceremonies for Chundi's baby, the naming ceremony, the day of dressing her in leaves pinned with thorns to make her at one with the kingdom of nature, the day of shaving her head so that her father could safely go hunting, the annual day of worshipping the cow with Sanskrit words, food, flowers and ointment. Chundi eventually gave her Maharaja husband a second daughter and a son. Cornelia was allowed to appoint a governess and she personally checked the children's lessons. Meanwhile Chundi's mother was taken ill and was unwilling to be treated by a nurse. So Chundi, at her husband's suggestion, learnt the nursing techniques at great speed and restored her mother to health.

Chundi, like Kalidasi, had herself had a dramatic illness that called on Cornelia's resources. When Chundi was newly married, Cornelia was summoned because she had gastro-enteritis with a temperature of 105 F. A priest and disciple were burning melted butter under her nose, shouting at her to call on Kali, ringing bells and snapping their fingers at her body, to cast out the devil, while the waiting women blew conch shells, and the young girl moaned and turned her face away. With the grandmother's permission, Cornelia spoke to the priest, appealing to his beliefs in order to save her ward. 'So highly paid a magician as you could work your cure, I suppose, from Cape Comorin or the Himalayas.' He had not thought of this, but agreed it was true. 'Then I must apologise that they have brought you so close to your patient. This is a zenana in my charge and I have had them prepare a room for you in the "Outside", and when the Maharani is well, I will myself bear witness that you were indeed as far removed as possible from the patient.' He left without a word, and when Chundi pulled through, he took full credit for the cure.[76]

Chundi seemed to have complete control over her husband. Though devoted to him, she led him a dance, and played the coquette with him. She even 'lorded it' over her mother-in-law. She was one of the first purdahnashins to join Cornelia in performing social work,[77] and she plucked up courage to hold her first party for women in purdah and invite Lord Carmichael, the Governor of Bengal, and Lady Carmichael to stay. When planning the party, she leaned over the banisters, which was forbidden, calling to Cornelia that she was to come when the party took place. When Cornelia could not come because of illness, she visited Cornelia's hospital with her husband, saying that she had come to 'scold' Cornelia for not coming, but also telling her husband that he should go home, because she was going to stay always and always with 'Aunt-Mother'. He in turn wanted his wife to learn English and how to pour tea.[78] When he got into debt in 1920, she took his finances over completely, allowed him only two rooms and 10 rupees out of the 3000 a month that he earned from his membership of the Bengal legislature, and made him account for every fraction of a rupee. But she still fed him in private in the traditional fashion, and she had to keep the money in a tin box, because the banks refused to open an account for a secluded woman.[79]

Chundi displayed the same mixture of tradition and unconventionality during her pregnancies. On the one hand, she followed traditional practices which Cornelia wanted to modify as insanitary, gulping Ganges water and eating food offered to Kali and carried in a waiting-woman's bare hands. On the other hand, she was quite willing to sew things for the expected baby, in contravention of tradition, which forbade expectant mothers to close anything, even by stitching.[80]

Eventually Chundi's husband died unexpectedly in a single night. Chundi's priests criticised her, arguing that her husband's early death was partly due to her adoption of new ways, including the holding of tea parties, and this would need to be expiated by extra payments. Meanwhile the estate was liable to fall under the Court of Wards until the heir reached maturity. But Cornelia argued successfully that Chundi was perfectly capable of managing the estate herself. This was a model of what Cornelia hoped could happen elsewhere.

Chundi went on to postpone marriage for her daughter, Little Mees, beyond the age of eleven, and did not even rush to get her married, when it was announced in 1929 that the Sarda Act would come into force, making early marriage illegal. Little Mees saw the prospective bridegrooms chosen by the priests in the traditional way through a hole in the curtain. But Chundi had already chosen the bridegroom herself, a future Maharaja from a neigh-bouring state. Cornelia attended the wedding, and Chundi insisted that her daughter would remain with her husband in a dower house built on her own property until the son-in-law succeeded to the throne of his kingdom.

Cornelia wrote the story of Kalidasi's and Chundi's illnesses, disguised for confidentiality by amalgamation with other stories, for the Infant Welfare Exhibition of 1920, at the request of the Viceroy's wife, Lady Chelmsford, to whom Cornelia had proposed the exhibition.[81] Cornelia had earlier, in 1917, included the story of Kalidasi's pregnancy, but without names attached, in her most thoroughgoing analysis of what was needed for Hindu orthodox women: *The Purdahnashin*. She believed that with loving care and education, secluded women could keep most of their way of life, but could steadily gain, as Chundi had to some extent gained, more freedom from its dis-advantages.

CHUNDI'S BROTHER KAMALA RANJAN: EDUCATION OF A BOY PRINCELING

Chundi's brother, Kamala Ranjan, had been subject in his infancy to an attempt at poisoning, so his grandmother got up at 5 every morning to prepare his food herself.[82] In 1906, when he was ten years old, the Prince and Princess of Wales, the future King George V and Queen Mary, were coming on an official visit to Calcutta, amid much splendour, and Kamala Ranjan wore a tin sword, even in bed, to protect the future Queen. Cornelia arranged through Lady Minto, the wife of the new Viceroy, that he should be presented to the Prince and Princess. He wore a jewelled dress of gold and ruby-coloured velvet, with a diamond spray in his turban, a necklet of emeralds and pearls, and his toy sword, and Cornelia gave him a rehearsal. On the day, he made a beautiful bow, and the Prince of Wales touched the sword.[83]

Kamala Ranjan's Rani mother was very orthodox. Cornelia was pleased that Kamala Ranjan tried to dissuade her from taking over-long fasts which her priest prescribed.[84] She in turn complained that her son was of a higher caste than his brother-in-law, the Maharaja of Nadia. Why, then, she asked, were the British giving all the honours to the Maharaja, and ignoring the higher caste of Kamala Ranjan?[85] She was orthodox enough to have Kamala Ranjan married to a child bride, which resulted in a younger and even more dangerous pregnancy than Kalidasi's.[86]

Cornelia continued visiting Kamala Ranjan and his mother on her regular visits to Kasimbazar and watched over his education and outlook. Many years, later in 1933, aged 25 and still living with his mother, he had long since taken his Kasimbazar estate from the Court of Wards into his own hands and Cornelia thought that he was running it beautifully. He was studying the conditions of his peasants there. To Cornelia's pleasure, he wanted welfare work for the village and was replacing money lenders with banks. Chundi had also taken over her own estate as Maharani of Nadia.[87]

Cornelia's first four estates prepared her for the enormous expansion in numbers and variety of estate that were to follow.[88] Meanwhile she thought that Chundi and Kamala Ranjan represented a success for her educational methods, which will be further described.[89]

CHAPTER 9

SETTLING DOWN IN CALCUTTA: EARLY YEARS FROM 1904

Before we move from the successes of 1904–6 to Cornelia's later cases, we need to catch up on her domestic and social life in Calcutta. When her job was offered her, Cornelia was in the hills in Darjeeling, where Calcutta officialdom spent the hot season. Just as she went off to Narhan in May 1904, Francis Younghusband was mounting his controversial expedition into Tibet, which had originally been planned as a 'mission', not an invasion. He had made his name originally through daring reconnaissance in the Hima-layas in opposition to Russian military adventurers, but the present expedi-tion gave rise to dispute. As Cornelia reports, the war was being described by Mr Candler, the wounded correspondent of the *Daily Mail,* as the biggest blunder yet made by the British. Candler had been injured in the scuffle which led to the massacre with machine guns of retreating Tibetans who walked instead of running away. Younghusband's official role was diplomatic, not mili-tary, but it has been argued that he was more committed to invasion than the commander of his military escort.[1] Back in Darjeeling, Cornelia called on Mrs Younghusband, as she was then, and found her already sad about the invasion of Tibet.[2]

It was in Calcutta, not Darjeeling, however, that Cornelia needed to make her main home, and there was a season there too. Cornelia was invited to parties every day after Christmas through to February, but these stopped in March for the Christian season of Lent. Moreover, from May to Novem-ber many would have retreated to the Darjeeling hills. She was at that time the only Indian woman invited to English dinner parties.[3] In 1907, she was wearing a new party saree made of beetles-wing material,[4] a fashion surely inspired by the dress of her favourite actress Ellen Terry, made of opalescent

168

20. Cornelia established in Bengal, 1909.

green beetles' wings and still on display at the actress's former home in Smallhythe.

Some of Cornelia's wards had their houses or their second houses in Calcutta, so that she could visit them, or they visit her, and she could help the children with lessons. She saw it as already a sign of progress when they were ready to leave the seclusion of their houses in order to visit her.[5]

CORNELIA'S HOMES, GARDENS AND OFFICE IN CALCUTTA

Cornelia had many different homes over her first 18 years in Calcutta, but from 1909 just one office, which was with the Civil Service Secretariat in Writers' Buildings.[6] It was here that her beloved Gourlay had an office and on some days she would see him there. Writers' Buildings was next to the High Court of Calcutta, but to the High Court she would not gain entry until after retirement.

The most spectacular of her Calcutta residences was in the grand promenade of Chowringee. From 1914–1921, she had a flat three flights up at 41

21. In darkest Writers' Buildings, Calcutta, 1906–1922.

22. Calcutta High Court's splendour: Cornelia received as
first woman, 1924.

Chowringee, with a 'gorgeous' view over the spacious grass acres of the Maidan
towards the outworks of the fort, the shipping and the sunset. From this she
would look across the grass to the pre-dawn light on the domed Victoria

memorial building, and in 1921 she watched the fireworks on the Maidan for
the Prince of Wales' visit.[7]

One of her greatest pleasures came from the gardens and from the gardeners (malis) for the special devotion they expressed to plants. In Allahabad
she had overridden the landlord's guru, when he refused to cut the mango
trees clear of the driveway, on the ground that they might be reincarnations
of friends from a former birth.[8] But now in Calcutta she was keen to listen
and learn. Almost her first residence in Calcutta was at 6 Camac Street, parallel to Chowringee, but further from the Maidan. There she replanted the
garden, but her gardener balked, when asked to move the tulsi tree two yards
along, to protect it from carriages in the driveway. The tulsi tree is a sacred
plant and it was moved only after a ceremony of apology to the tree held in
her presence with the aid of a holy man. She was charmed, described it in
detail and later consulted her wards about it. As seen through her eyes, it
required, in brief, full explanations to the tree, prayers and obeisance to the
earth.[9] Among the implements were holy water and lights, white lilies, rice
and sugar cakes.

In her last Calcutta period in 1925–1926, there was a gardener at 28
Chowringee ready to sacrifice his comfort to his plants, as she describes.[10]

'The old mali at Number 28. He's a *dear.* I must get a photograph of his honest –
gentle – humorous old face. He is *devoted* to the garden and potters about all
day. The plants are his children. This is the difficult time of year for seedlings in
Calcutta gardens, as you will guess. All the cold weather annuals get sown and
yet rain threatens sometimes. A little sprinkling is good, but the floods we had
last week would of course be disastrous. The bother is that you can't keep the
nearly-sown garden people *entirely* under shelter. The dew at night is good for
them.

'The old mali takes this course. He keeps them safely during the heat time in
pots and seed pans (the earth at large is too risky) and covers their defenceless
heads with mat shelters, or lines them up under the shelter of the verandah.
At night he carries them out and places them huddled together just outside his
hut. Then he goes to sleep, *but he sleeps with his toes out in the open*, so that if it
should begin to rain in the night, he may be warned and can bustle up in time
and carry his seedling children into his hut! There won't be room for both him
(to lie a-stretch) in the hut and for the children to crowd together. So of course
he disposes them securely, and sits up the rest of the night – sits on his haunches
dozing as best he can'.

THE VICEREINE AND ROYALTY: LADY MINTO'S SUPPORT OF CORNELIA'S WORK

In 1905, Lord Curzon was still Viceroy and Cornelia was repeatedly invited to entertainments, including one on his launch to Barrackpore for tea and a moonlit evening.[11] But she got to know much better the next Viceroy and his wife, Lord and Lady Minto. Curzon had been opposed by Lord Kitchener (KK), who had been appointed Commander-in-chief in India, and by August 1905, Curzon had had to resign as Viceroy.[12] As Cornelia reported, his parody of the well-known hymn was, 'Change and KK in all around I see'.[13]

Cornelia's close links with the Mintos started in January 1906 soon after their arrival, when the future King George and Queen Mary paid a State visit to Calcutta.[14] The Mintos came in to replace Curzon just in time for the State visit, and they started by supporting Cornelia's work, when, as described in Chapter 8, they arranged that her ten year old ward, Kamala Ranjan, should be presented to the Prince. It was Kitchener who flanked the future King George V at the military part of the State visit on December 30th 1905,[15] and Lord Minto made him a member of the Viceroy's Council.[16]

In her early years in Calcutta, Cornelia had long talks with Lady Minto, and we shall see how supportive Lady Minto was to Cornelia at many stages. In 1905–1906, Cornelia had made the experiment of giving a party for women in purdah.[17] By 1906, this example had been taken up by the wife of the Lieutenant Governor of Bengal, Lady Fraser, and Lady Minto as Vicereine was also planning a purdah party.[18] Lady Minto further commissioned from Cornelia a proposal on what should be done for women in purdah, and obtained a letter from the Queen addressed to such women.[19] Cornelia was thrilled that England's leading composer, Elgar, had written sea songs for her, which she heard at a concert in 1909.[20] By 1910, at Lady Minto's suggestion Cornelia started taking her on sightseeing trips in Calcutta.[21]

At the time of the State visit, Cornelia saw from Writers' Buildings the initial arrival procession of Prince George and Princess Mary on November 22nd 1905.[22] She was next given prime seats for the official visit a month later. The streets were adorned with banners and lanterns. She had a seat overlooking the gold and red dais at the ghat where they landed, with glittering Rajas and gold-laced officials awaiting them. The next day, her seat was in the green ground of the fort for the Prince's presentation of new colours to the King's Own Light Infantry. The Prince himself was given a necklace from the collection of the

Maharaja of Dholpur. Cornelia was later to defend his widowed Maharani from a charge about missing jewellery.[23]

On a third day, she sat with the Rajas' families to watch the ethnic dances in the gold, white and blue amphitheatre. This is where Kamala Ranjan,[24] aged ten, made his first bow, and she stayed on to watch the fireworks with him and other children. The following day, at the Mintos' garden party, she was invited by them to present Kamala Ranjan to the Prince, and she joined the royal procession to see the illuminations which covered every tree, the masts of the ships in the Strand, the fort, Writers' Buildings, the High Court and all other buildings. She was asked for every dance at the State ball in Government House the next day, to sit it out and talk, and was taken in to supper by the Mintos' private secretary. Although she stayed only until half time, she had never enjoyed a ball better, at least 'I mean', she told Falkner Blair, 'never of late'.[25]

Government House and its gardens had been built in 1803, and its ballroom on the third storey still has ample space for sitting out on either side of the extensive dance floor. It was the Viceroy's residence until 1912 and thereafter the Governor of Bengal's. As the only Indian woman regularly invited by the Governor to parties in the upper rooms and to interviews in the sitting room below, the building had great significance for Cornelia, not least when a quarrel led to her being temporarily excluded.[26]

Princess Louise, Cornelia's companion in Ceylon, was in the royal party, and arranged for Cornelia to join her in the party as it continued on to Burma, a three-day voyage from the River Hooghly to the River Irrawaddy.[27] Government House at Mandalay, where they stayed, was a former monastery with roof on roof of red wood in pagoda style, ornamented with red lacquer and gold, all within a fort. Cornelia liked the cheerful atmosphere she found in Buddhist worship in Burma, and she was struck that the women were not in purdah and could choose their own husbands. Yet for all these advantages, they still wanted to be reborn as men.[28] As well as seeing and enjoying Burma, she had long conversations with her sad and turbulent Princess friend. But Cornelia had to return to work in two weeks and so after a final happy afternoon by the river, she saw the Princess off on her boat.

OTHER FRIENDS

1905 was the year in which not only was Cornelia congratulated all round on her work by her seniors,[29] but Mr Le Mesurier wrote to say that one gain for his wife and himself was her friendship.[30] He was Secretary of the Board of Revenue, and the person to whom she first reported on her early cases. Although he would move in 1906 to become the Commissioner in Dacca (Dhaka), and later to other posts, he was the one who secured the job as Head-mistress of a school in Dacca for Lena, Cornelia's sister, and he remained a staunch supporter and consultant to the end of Cornelia's first career.

Another very close pair of friends in Calcutta were Harry and Barbara Stephen. The judge had given positive evidence when she was making the case for her post. His wife, a niece of Florence Nightingale, had once been secretary to Girton College, Cambridge,[31] and she accompanied Cornelia on one of the elephant rides to Churamaon, as described in Chapter 11. Cornelia was sad that they were going on leave to England in mid-1906, and she felt she would miss them badly. Unhappily, a serious misunderstanding was to arise in 1914, but that is part of the story of later troubles.[32]

A NATIONALIST LEADER: GOKHALE

A still earlier supporter and friend of Cornelia was Gokhale, a nationalist leader who was recognised both by Indians and by the British. The British appointed him to the Imperial Legislative Council in 1902 and again in 1910. In 1905, he founded the Servants of India Society to promote social reform, and was elected President of the Indian National Congress, which evolved into the Congress Party later dominated by Gandhi. He had originally been prominent as a resident of Poona.[33] Cornelia was thus his fellow townswoman as well as his exact contemporary. In 1897, Gokhale had been caught up in the aftermath of the outbreak in Poona of bubonic plague for whose victims Cornelia's mother had been caring. The use of uninstructed British soldiers for compulsory dis-infecting of houses had caused deep indignation, which Cornelia's mother did her best to calm. But in the ensuing uproar, the British head of the Plague Commission and an aide had been shot dead in Poona. Gokhale had been in London at the time, where he was giving evidence to the Royal Commission on Indian Expenditure, which was considering, among other things, complaints about the lack of benefits to Indians. Gokhale was asked to explain events in Poona, and his comments on the role of British soldiers had got him into trouble.

Gokhale was also closely associated with Florence Nightingale. He had been secretary of the Poona Sarvajanik Sabha and editor of its *Quarterly Journal*, with which Florence Nightingale had corresponded. When he was in London in 1897, she summoned him to come and see her. Later, in 1910, Gokhale and others honoured a friend of Florence Nightingale by raising funds which were largely given to the Nightingale Fund for Village Sanitation in India. The fund was later renamed the Gokhale Fund, and used for scholarships for Indian girls to study sanitation.

Cornelia's first direct exchange with Gokhale came after they had both moved to Calcutta. He had given evidence in favour of creating her post, and immediately after her interview in 1904, wanted to take her to a debate in Government House, but she declined, so he came to tea instead and stayed until nearly supper.[34] Before she went off to Burma for two weeks in January 1906, he called after ten o'clock at night to say goodbye.[35] He had been appointed to the Viceroy's Council and had tried to defend Curzon from critics, but told Cornelia that he had become disillusioned with petty animosities between London and Calcutta.[36] Cornelia, as a conservative, always argued with him about politics,[37] and said he would never be content.[38] But she praised his speeches more than once, especially a speech in 1909 in which he told Bengali students to study politics, but not to clamour for rebellion.[39] His was the kind of law-abiding nationalism that she approved. Although his disciple, Gandhi was only three years younger, his was a nationalism belonging to a later period, very different from Gokhale's. 'Gokhale', she said, 'that level-headed and sincere reformer, realized Gandhi's danger and put him under promise not to interfere in politics'.[40] Gokhale died prematurely in 1915, but when a school was built in his memory 14 years later, Cornelia wrote a memorial notice in *The Statesman*. She drew attention to his bequest of a library of political history and, as she claimed, British statesmanship.[41] Still later she recalled that Gokhale had wanted education to be compulsory. She praised him for having sought political protection for Muslims as early as 1907,[42] and she thought of him as a true patriot without ulterior motives.[43]

THE BENGALI LEADER RABINDRANATH TAGORE

I shall take out of sequence Cornelia's encounters with another nationalist leader, Rabindranath Tagore, because they formed part of her life in Calcutta, although not until much later from 1914 onwards. It was then that she saw him receive in Calcutta his Nobel Prize for literature.[44] He too belonged to the older generation of nationalist leaders, being five years older than Cornelia. Cornelia gave three accounts of Tagore in 1921, 1925 and 1928.[45] She also wrote in 1919 and 1924 unpublished reviews concerned with the politics in two of his novels, *Home and the World* and *Gora* (*Fair-Faced*).[46]

On the occasion in 1921, Tagore was dressed in Tussore silk, and lectured on education against Gandhi's Non-cooperation Movement before a rapt student audience. The students followed Gandhi's Nationalist Movement in wearing swadeshi (home spun) clothes, a pointed contrast with Tagore's silk. Cornelia liked his advocating to students cooperation with the West, education and the acceptance of machinery, however much she disliked his criticisms of England.[47]

> 'I was glad to be back on Monday. Tagore was lecturing on national education to Indian students. I went to hear him, taking two English friends with me (who happened to be the only English folk there). It was a pouring wet day, yet the Hall was packed and had been almost an hour before the lecture, although admission was by card. We got half an hour before the time fixed and there was a riot going on at one gate, students trying to force a way in. Luckily, there was another gate and we got in the wake of the "Chair" just arriving, Sir A. Chowduri, whom I knew, and got very good seats. You've seen Tagore, have you not? He wears Indian-y robes – was dressed in tussore silk with a white dhoti, folded as if it were a stole, round his shoulders. He has a long beard and very bushy eyebrows – very grey now. He made a fine picture and he speaks wonderfully – beautiful limpid Bengali. He read his paper, gesticulating much and very characteristically with a very shapely right hand and arm. He has the eyes of a mystic and as he spoke, his intense earnestness pierced through, changing him from a dreamer to a fighter and anon to a cynical *jester*. Everyone was in swadeshi clothes.[i] The aim of the meeting was evident – *anti-Gandhi.* He urged education on the students, showed them the advantages of education, of machinery, of co-operation,[ii] even between the East and the West. But he was not for the West. He poured scorn on the West, on England in particular, while applauding her use of learning and of things material. It seems England is without peace and joy and ideals – all which things India can give her. He also spoke against caste[iii] – divisions were bad. England, it seems, maintains these, although Jesus Christ said, "I and my Father are one"! None of his jibes appear in the English summary sent to him by the Press – of course not. But why does he hate England so, I wonder, even when for political purposes (for he was lecturing for the moderates against Gandhi and the Extremists) he approves her'.

In 1925, Cornelia saw Tagore looking even more romantic at a philosophical conference in Calcutta University.[48]

---

i An anti-British gesture.
ii The opposite of Gandhi's Non-cooperation.
iii Katherine Mayo (Chapter 18) was to misrepresent Tagore on this.

'The Philosophical Congress was held here for the first time. I went to the opening and was glad I did, if only to see Rabindranath Tagore. He looked wonderful.
He has aged, and his beard is longer and thicker and whiter. He sat cross-legged
on a table between purple bolster cushions. He was draped in a white shawl
and the purple blue light fell on his head and face – the sun shining through a
stained glass window in the Senate House.[iv] It made him look like some wonderful, mystic divine being. I expect he staged and rehearsed that effect, but it was
nonetheless wonderful. For that dear old Mr Justice Greaves, Vice-Chancellor,
sat on a chair close by and in due time the light reached him, but only made his
rubicund and beef-y countenance look an awful colour. Most unfair, I call it.
Lord Lytton, Chancellor, spoke first – excellent address, idealistic – urging the
service of others as a joy, not a "sacrifice". In Tagore I was disappointed, both as
to delivery and matter. He spoke in the nasal whine that he keeps for the English
tongue and he ended on a note of defeat and illusion'.

Cornelia's final encounter was in 1928, when she took the singer Dame Clara Butt
and her biographer to see Tagore at Santiniketan, where he had his library, art gallery,
school and Viswa Bharati University, in which you come across open-air classrooms
with blackboards amid the gardens. C. F. Andrews, Gandhi's and Tagore's Christian
disciple, wearing a dhoti, was protecting the poet, but thawed sufficiently over tea
to say that they might all meet him. So they went in a body to Tagore's house.[49]

'Well, there was the poet dressed in brown silk robes in a modern house, though
furnished with specifically designed teak furniture. He looked very fine. His hair
is snow white…and he is rather, to look at, like Tennyson in his last days. He
talked in a weak little thin voice about poetry and music, nothing memorable.
Then we went to his old house, where most of his poems had been written. This
is beautiful. An elongated portico, pillared and giving views straight through, as
it were through a tunnel, views of the far set horizon, at that moment misty and
like a smoking fire. The sun had just set. The garden side was sweet with fluffy
yellow balls of mimosa and with…the white cup champa with the buttercup-
coloured dregs inside,…and an occasional bougainvillea. We climbed onto the
roof, and that was a perfect moment indeed. The sunset fire banked up high,
almost overhead, blazed forth flame-red and gold, slashed with purple and
aquamarine.'

They went on to the house of a Dutchman and his saree-clad wife who had
been with Tagore for two years, while he put Tagore's music for his songs into
English notation. There were others at work, in the library a Tibetan lama
engaged on Buddhist manuscripts and a Bengali girl translating a manuscript
into modern Bengali, and in the art gallery another Bengali copying an ancient

---

iv I am told that this building no longer exists.

fresco. The school's agricultural, horticultural and industrial training matched Cornelia's own aspirations for India, and she found it very hopeful, and Tagore himself was the legend that made all this possible.

On the second day, Tagore sang his songs to Clara Butt, sitting beside her, his back to the audience, his voice very thin, old and weak, contrasting with her strong voice and her accompaniment. Cornelia felt the pathos of Tagore's age, but when Clara Butt rendered the songs, she thought the concert wonderful.

FAMILY

Back in Cornelia's early days from 1906, only two of her family were in easy reach of Calcutta, Dick and later Lena, although the question arose of Alice coming. Two others were down South, Susie in Poona and her mother, to whom she wrote every day,[50] in Nasik. In August 1907, Alice applied for a job at the Dufferin Hospital in Calcutta, the hospital where Cornelia was on the committee. Cornelia had possessively told Alice that her application would create 'awkwardnesses'. Not only had Cornelia known Lady Dufferin, but she probably saw herself as in some ways carrying on Lady Dufferin's work. Cornelia's fallible sister might either have let down the standards, or shared the limelight. Cornelia spoke to someone in the know. That someone was able to report back a month later that Alice had been ruled out in the first round as not sufficiently experienced.[51]

Lena arrived to become headmistress of Eden College, a residential girls school in Dacca in East Bengal (now Bangladesh), in January 1910. The school was for nonpurdahed Hindu girls, Muslims and Christians, with Hindus predominating.[52] Cornelia steered a number of Muslim girls towards the school and she and Lena became allies in encouraging lengthened female education. For them she was able to arrange strict purdah when required.[53] Cornelia tended to spend Christmas day alone, but Dick and Lena would come to stay in Calcutta immediately afterwards. Cornelia saw Lena on her working trips to Dacca, but she saw Dick most regularly, visiting him once a month in Allahabad. This continued most of the time until they left for England together in 1922, and she found it very restorative.[54] When they went to important functions together, she loved him, as a mark of being a Parsee, to wear his Persian costume,[55] in which she thought him most handsome.

Dick's life had changed since Cornelia left their joint home in 1901. On January 10th 1903, Cornelia heard from Falkner Blair that Dick had got the

23. Dick in Cornelia's favourite Persian costume.

law lectureship in Allahabad, and in January 1904 that he had moved house,[56] although only further along Edmonstone road. He would have had an easy journey 2 kilometres in one direction to the High Court in the mornings and 4 kilometres in the other direction to Muir Central College in the afternoons.[57] The courthouse is forbidding, a massive succession of courtyards relieved by lattice stonework. Muir Central College by contrast has already been described above.[58] It is a very handsome building in which Sicilian capitals are happily combined with a Moghul-style tiled dome and stone lattices. There are sand-coloured colonnades of stonework, a magnificent marble hall, and ornate shuttered lecture rooms. Dick had given up the bicycle of their time together in 1899–1901, and had a pretty cart in 1904 and a new brougham in 1905.[59]

His next promotion was to be Principal of the law college. The Allahabad Golden Jubilee book described him as 'a man of irrepressible buoyancy with 150 students',[60] and in 1909 a local newspaper reported a speech by his younger colleague, Tej Bahadhur Sapru, made about him at the anniversary of the University's School of Law.[61] Why should the law students, the writer asked, evince more esprit de corps than the students of older and more fortunately situated institutions? The reason, as Dr Sapru so well put it, was that they

> 'have the peculiar good luck of having a Principal who is thoroughly identified with them.'

The writer goes on 'His genial personality is the force that has conquered all the disintegrating elements which are working at present in his institution', and he is very keen to stress the unusual fact that this Principal, who had inspired so much affection and confidence in his students and who had absolute control over them, was an *Indian*.

One more episode is recorded from Dick's legal career in a book[62] about an apparently open and shut case of double murder in Agra in 1911. It was heard in a packed court before the Chief Justice who called it one of the cruellest murders that had ever been investigated. A pair of lovers murdered their spouses after a series of bungled attempts involving poison and bludgeoning, and they had kept a full record of what they were doing. Dick, who is credited with the best forensic performance of the trials, defended the woman, arguing that at first she thought her lover was supplying medicine, and then that at least the reduced dose of poison she administered would do no more than keep her husband in hospital. In the event, the woman was spared the death penalty only on the grounds that she was pregnant, and sentenced to penal servitude for life. *The Times* of June 1st 1914 records that she died of heat stroke in Naini jail ten months after a son was born to her there.

Dick was against the death penalty, but on the other hand, he felt free to advocate divorce in some cases, despite the marriage service injunction, 'Those whom God hath joined together let no man put asunder', on the grounds that God could certainly have had no hand in joining some of his clients with their partners.

CHAPTER 10

THE RAMGARH RESCUE AND THE EXPANSION OF TASKS, 1906–1922

Narhan and Tajhat were Cornelia's first two estates, with Churamaon and its associate, Kasimbazaar, soon afterwards. Cornelia started work on all four estates in her first three years, 1904–1906. But, amazingly, by 1917 her work had grown to the point where she personally visited 111 estates, with 569 women and children as wards, 259 days on tour and 20,500 miles travelled.[1] In 1919 she had no fewer than 126 estates with 600 women and children and she travelled 26,313 miles.[2] Increasingly Cornelia found that most of her legal work and most of her visits were at the request of the wards themselves, and that few of them, however distant, were content with only one visit a year.[3] Instead of being suspicious about education, she found that they were clamouring for it.[4] Without education, moreover, she considered that they would never be able to enforce their legal rights for themselves.

In the next three chapters, I shall look to see how her work with secluded women developed over its 18 year term up to 1922. Nearly all the stories in this chapter involve bringing protection to wards. Some reveal their gratitude or the sympathy that developed with them.

By 1905, Cornelia was gaining success on two fronts. First, she found that vakils, the sub-barrister pleaders, were bringing private legal work to her, because, whether the vakils liked it or not, women were calling her 'Shosti Devi', the goddess who protects children and the defenceless. Thus Indian religious belief was achieving for her what was so long resisted by the British during the long years of her campaign for a post.[5]

By 1906, the British too regarded Cornelia's work as such a success that all the officials she dealt with were converted to the scheme. She received compliments all round, and her private legal practice was stopped, so that she could work full time.[6] Mr Le Mesurier wrote:[7]

'Dear Miss Sorabji,

It was very pleasant to see in the "Pioneer" that the Board of Revenue were so thoroughly satisfied with the experience of having a lady legal officer (would this not be a good "portmanteau" for the much discussed title?) and the actual results of the first year's work. ...May. I congratulate you most warmly on the success of your first year and associate myself with you in it, as it was my good fortune to be associated in the beginnings?...'

Cornelia was employed by the Board of Revenue in the Government of Bengal, with many of the privileges of the India-wide élite, the Indian Civil Service, but with an anomalous relationship to their ranking system. Entry to the Indian Civil Service was by a most prestigious examination in England, and those who were successful would be sent to work in a particular province. There were at least four standard grades in the districts administered by the Indian Civil Service,[8] but she was not given one of these, nor paid or pensioned at those rates, although her travel expenses were at the lofty level of a Commissioner's. In the lowest of the grades, a new man would work as a sub-Divisional Officer. The Collector was the District Officer and had jurisdiction over the estates in his district, which might cover an enormous area. This was a huge responsibility and an opportunity for the ambitious on a scale which nowadays does not exist. But appeals would be sent higher to the Divisional Commissioner, thence to Headquarters, which meant in Cornelia's case to the 'Member' of the Board of Revenue, a still higher officer in the chain, as explained in Chapter 7. Cornelia herself was given the office in Writers' Buildings with clerks provided, because the Board of Revenue was part of the secretariat. The Board Member would refer to the chief official of the province in case of need. The chief official in Bengal was called Lieutenant Governor up to 1912, and after that Governor. From 1912, the Governor would be appointed from outside the Indian Civil Service. Not only the Provincial Governor's view, but the collective view of members of his Council, could be forwarded to the Viceroy of India, who had his own Council, and thence to the Secretary of State for India back in London, who was a cabinet member of the Government in office in England.

Cornelia remained on a retaining fee, with each activity separately paid for. In return for not having a grade, she negotiated that she must be free to put her case immediately to officials of any grade without her request being passed up through the levels. This gave her freedom, but would also eventually cause resentment, especially given that she had not taken the prized examination and climbed through the ranks.[9] After 1905, with Curzon's experimental division and enlargement of Bengal, she gained Assam and bits of central India, while also keeping Bihar, Orissa and the original Bengal.[10] On June 25th 1909, Cornelia recorded receiving telegrams all day. She was awakened by one from the Lieutenant Governor at 1 a.m. Gourlay and others came to congratulate her and the telegrams came also from England.[11] This was the first of two awards of the Kaiser-i-Hind medal in recognition of her work, the medal introduced by Queen Victoria for signal civilian work in India.

RAMGARH SCENERY AND TRAVEL

I now move to 1920–1921, close to the end of Cornelia's employment in 1922. Despite mounting opposition from some British officials, Cornelia was still successful in her late activities in the eyes both of her wards and of most of the British. A particularly dramatic case was the rescue in 1922 of a Rani and her children from Ramgarh. The palace of the Ramgarh estate was at Padma in Bihar on the Hazaribagh–Barhi road, where it still stands South of Hazaribagh and North of Ranchi, and Cornelia's journeys there were among her most exotic.[12] On the Hazaribagh route she saw a bear coming out of the jungle, and a panther lying one foot from the car as she was driven through the jungle. The journey of 42 miles to Hazaribagh took six hours and was usually by night. One time, the tyres were punctured twice and stuffed with hay, which was the standard remedy. They drove on by night with no moon, and she heard roaring beasts. If they broke down again, they could only wait for the postal lorry to catch them up. On the Ranchi route, with jungle and wavy grey hills, she saw not only a hyaena and a wild cat, but also two tigers, an hour apart, one of them lame. An extra hazard in 1921 was that the followers of Gandhi, as she identified them, were stoning the official car both at Hazaribagh and at Ranchi, and at Ranchi they hit the driver.[13]

   To reach the palace at Padma from Hazaribagh, there were another 18–20 miles of driving through the uplands of the Chota Nagpur forest. The palace was in a lovely spot beside a river, stony and picturesque. She described a sal tree rather like a birch as 'standing sentinel' on a bank opposite the windows of the women's quarters. The estate comprised 5000 square miles of mineral land, including coal, and this created dangers for the safety of any potential heir, since he could expect to be a multi-millionaire.

RESCUE FROM RAMGARH PALACE AT PADMA

Trouble started with a cholera outbreak in April 1918 that had killed the father, and then the heir to the estate within five days of his coming of age.[14] The deceased heir and his little Rani widow had two sons, but the oldest was not yet two years old, so the estate was to be in the administration of the Court of Wards for a further 18 years. The widowed grandmother had at first forbidden cholera injections for her husband, and then her son was injected too late. As Cornelia told the story, the heir by local law was the Rani's elder son. But the grandmother did not want the Rani's child to succeed to the estate. Instead, she wanted her own younger son to succeed, and that younger son was the *Reversioner*, in other words, the person to whom the estate would revert if the baby heirs died. The Reversioner's men were reported not to be using legal means. They had been found crawling on the roof of the palace, so the children were in great danger. The manager of the estate did not want Cornelia to succeed, because he was a friend of the Reversioner and had once been manager for him. Moreover, the servants in the Reversioner's house were related to the servants of the Rani, so there was intrigue. Later the Rani was to say to Cornelia that the grandmother had attempted poisoning. When violence was threatened instead of litigation, the Court of Wards considered the possibility of rescue, but had to avoid itself authorising the use of force.

At the first meeting in February 1920, Cornelia sat with the old grandmother, whom she described as heart-broken about the injections. She was still full of remorse, worry and vain longing. She believed it was the cholera injection that had killed her elder son, and that the doctor had acted out of anger at her using the wrong doctors. The little Rani, as required, sat silent in the presence of her mother-in-law, the grandmother. Cornelia described the two women as huddled together and peeping through a slit in the door. She came and sat with the grandmother, and asked her whether a man would not die or live according to whether or not *karma* had brought his time around, independently of whether he got the right medicine or not.

Cornelia urged that they should all come and live in the town of Hazaribagh for safety. The little Rani spoke once – and Cornelia admired her bravery – to say that she was willing to take her children from Padma to Hazaribagh. At first they both seemed to be willing, but the little Rani changed her mind after her enemy, the manager, put that idea in writing as his own. The Reversioner would have been only a stone's throw away there. Furthermore, one of Cornelia's bêtes noires, Morshead, the Commissioner of a division in Bihar from 1914 and the Member of the Board of Revenue from 1919, insisted, without telling Cornelia, that he would install a Western lady doctor in the palace at Padma. This was despite all the grandmother's anxieties concerning the earlier Western-style injections. After that, the grandmother would not hear of moving, and became an implacable opponent, although Morshead was overridden by Mr Lyall, the next Commissioner, about the idea of a Western doctor at Padma.

Cornelia suggested to the Commissioner and Collector the town of Ranchi in the opposite direction as an alternative safe place for the little Rani and her children. At a meeting in June 1920, the grandmother refused, but the little Rani, who was forbidden to talk, was in the plot and used eyes, smiles, nods, soundless lips and shakes of her head, while nonetheless seeming to confirm what her mother-in-law said. She was shaking with laughter, which the mother-in-law put down to fever.

People identified by the little Rani as followers of Gandhi had meanwhile picked up an entirely different issue, that the estate's coal mining leases had been given to an English mining company, not to Indians, and the only Indians to benefit were the landowners. Gandhi's followers regarded Cornelia and the Court of Wards as enemies, since they protected the landowners. That was why they were throwing stones at the car that fetched Cornelia, and in April 1921 managed to hit the driver. By May, Cornelia was convinced that they had got control of the grandmother, so that, when Cornelia's party called at Padma, the ladies were not in the palace, though polite and uninformative messages were exchanged with the staff. The non-cooperator followers of Gandhi, Cornelia thought, were using the case as a test of 'whether the British Raj was at an end'.[15] A little later she wrote, 'Gandhi is controlling the situation'.

Cornelia insisted that force must not be authorised by themselves, although it might be needed if the lives of the Rani and her children were to be saved. She suggested enlisting the father of the little Rani, the Raja of Porahat. He reported that the grandmother, would not let him see the children, who were now aged 3 and 5. So a first plan was made to go with the father to see the little Rani at Padma, and to take her with her children to Ranchi. The Deputy Commissioner would be waiting outside in case of refusal, and would then make an order, which they would all execute. Cornelia begged the father to be the children's guardian temporarily, since he would then be entitled to authorise the use of force. He was officially made guardian and Cornelia took him to the palace and got him a few minutes' conversation with his daughter through the purdah screen, while Cornelia saw the implacable grandmother and the children.

The first attempt at rescue was set for June 16th 1921. It failed. 'We failed', wrote Cornelia, 'with all the majesty of the Government at our backs'. There were two red lorries and five cars outside the palace, the Deputy Commissioner, the sub-Divisional Officer, magistrates, a posse of police and the Rani's Father. The problem was partly the timidity of the sub-Divisional Officer who was to issue the warrant and the timidity and toothache of the substitute for the Deputy Commissioner who was ill. Instead of effecting surprise, they started negotiating through the estate's Chief Minister. Cornelia wanted the father to have the warrant merely as a matter of form, with herself inside the door acting with self-assurance. The Chief Minister she described as 'an oily creature in a white embroidered cap and a long white muslin *kurtha*,[i] who came boring and arguing with hands joined – *insolent*, yet with a show of humility, the worst kind of insolence. He barred the door to the zenana, and finally at 4.30 he said, "Take the *children*. You take the *Rani* only across dead bodies". 'They could not at that late hour separate the 3 and 5 year old from their mother for a 78 mile car ride to Ranchi.

A second rescue visit in August by Cornelia with the Deputy Commissioner and the manager was also aborted. The plan was to take the mother and children to Ranchi, but it turned out that the grandmother had appealed to the Viceroy. The mother of the children was in law the one to have them, but she wanted to await the Viceroy's answer and then obey. Back at Ranchi, Cornelia again persuaded the Commissioner, Mr Lyall, not to use force.

The final rescue was staged in September with Cornelia, Mr Lyall the Commissioner, the Deputy Commissioner, the Civil Surgeon, the little Rani's father and others, and the 'big red motor bus of the armed police'. There had been a delay because the distinguished Indian lawyer Lord Sinha had been consulted about the appeal to the Viceroy and had taken time to decide. The rules of engagement were that the Rani was to go only if willing, the children only with the Rani. The Rani could return any time, but she would not be rescued again. Force was available to be used only if the Rani was detained against her will. Cornelia was to engage the grandmother, while the surgeon examined the children and the father took charge of his Rani daughter. There was to be no deception. Cornelia was to tell the grandmother what they were doing.

---

i Tunic-shirt.

Cornelia's plan was to have the father's car at the door of the annexe, with the flight to take place from there.

They were not expected. They all sat in the upper room of the annexe, while the Raja father negotiated with his daughter, or rather sought access to her, and Cornelia to the grandmother. The grandmother refused access, but the children came in and recognised Cornelia, and she invented ever new games for over an hour, to stop the servants taking them away. The children were dressed in pale turquoise blue silk coats with little dhotis (male draperies over legs and shoulders) and emerald green velvet and gold caps. One of the children sat on Cornelia's knee and the other beside her. A lawyer appeared for the grandmother, and Cornelia's side had the registrar. The Rani was timid and undecided. The father was still delayed and Mr Lyall let Cornelia go and see what was happening. The Rani wanted her mother-in-law (the grandmother) to be told, but the grand-mother still refused to be seen. So the Commissioner made an announcement to the priests, household officers, guards and servants to say what they were going to do, and on what terms, about ascertaining the Rani's consent. He declared, to a general gasp, 'And now the children will go to the motor'.

Cornelia and the sub-Divisional Officer held the two children, but the ser-vants grabbed one from the sub-Divisional Officer and made him cry. The baby sat with Cornelia in the car at the door of the annexe, while the servants complained at the tops of their voices in the compound and on the verandah. Cornelia was sent with the little Rani's uncle to see her.

There were women and priests on the verandah of the 'Inside'. Mr Lyall was at the door and the sub-Divisional Officer on steps further in. The father said, 'She wants to come, but has fears in case she has to return', and she also did not want to declare her willingness to Mr Lyall.

All the grandmother's men were now at the door, so the Rani needed to say if she was willing in front of them. The Commissioner agreed with Cornelia that she need not violate purdah by letting her voice be heard by men. So she said 'Yes' to Cornelia, and Cornelia said, 'Please clear the passages, as purdah must be kept. I will bring her with Rajah Sahib and her uncle to the car. She shall walk freely, no hand laid on her. The father and uncle will hold the purdah net (a kind of mosquito net of opaque stuff). I will walk before. She can turn back at any point'.

Mr Lyall cleared all men out of the way. A few waiting-women cried, but the party was not molested and got through the courtyard and down the stairs by the annexe. Near the exit an old man tried to intervene, but the sub-Divisional Officer was tactful and said, 'Stand here and look if you wish, but you see she is going of her own accord, her purdah alone protected'. The car was purdahed with screens and the crowd at the doors was removed to a distance by the doctor and the sub-Divisional Officer. The baby boy was in the car where Cornelia had left him, and she soon recovered the bigger boy for the mother from the servants. Two maidservants were allowed to go with them.

The woman servants complained that Cornelia's party had stopped their bread and water, a huge meal due to them. The men and priests left muttering and threatening. But the father fulfilled every expectation. His brother, the uncle, drove the car. Mr Lyall followed to Ranchi, 78 miles away. Cornelia went with him only as far as the Circuit House 20 miles away for a snack before returning to Calcutta. There were armed police in a big red motor bus at the Circuit House, but they were never called.

It turned out that the rescue had not gone quite as smoothly as Cornelia thought. Mr Lyall confessed that he had himself entered the women's quarters, while Cornelia was occupied elsewhere, and this had provoked a free fight over the young Rani's person between the household servants and the Rani's father. Mr Lyall asked Cornelia to prepare a defence in case a complaint should be lodged.

By November, Cornelia visited the Rani, who was happy, and she and the children were different beings. Fifteen years later in 1936, on Cornelia's visit to the boys, the Rani told the story of the rescue and also alleged the grandmother's attempted poisoning. By 1941, the older of the two boys had married the daughter of the then ambassador from Nepal.

The Ramgarh incident of 1920-1921 shows Cornelia still at the height of her powers a year before her retirement in 1922. The heir sanctioned by local law and his mother and brother had been rescued with family support, and Cornelia had enjoyed the cooperation of senior British Civil Service officers on the ground, whatever the attitude of certain other British officers to her.

I have looked at Cornelia's first estates of 1904-1906, and at one of the last from 1920-1921. It remains to get a sense of the huge range of her tasks. I shall select half a dozen illustrations from the period in between. Starting from 1907, I shall work forwards, finishing with a ward who died only in 2007.

A CASE OF SUCCESSION: BONES, MINES AND PARROTS

In 1907 at Pandra (Podardiki), a palki ride distant from Mugma, a mother-in-law and daughter-in-law were quarrelling. The older Rani wanted a different grandson to succeed to the throne of an impoverished estate in Bihar, not the disliked daughter-in-law's 7-year-old son, Ratan Singh (disguised by Cornelia as Kalidas), who was the heir by local law and a ward of court.[16] Family members feared that she might poison the boy and claimed that she had cursed him with a human thigh bone under the bed. Cornelia had it demonstrated that there was only a mutton bone there. The older Rani for her part made a common accusation that the boy had been bought in the bazaar, not born to the daughter-in-law. Cornelia achieved a reluctant reconciliation between the two Ranis, to the point where the mother-in-law insisted on the boy's genuine lineage. But Cornelia prolonged the reconciliation, with the District Collector's support, by having a journey authorised for the older Rani out of estate funds to the most distant possible place of pilgrimage.

The boy's life was now safer, but the question remained of his future livelihood. This was addressed by marrying him, at the age of ten, to the child heiress of a very wealthy coal estate. The question of a dowry for the bridegroom arose, a question that can penalise the bride's family. But in the present case it was the bride's family that prevailed. The Court of Wards sought to restore the estate's fortunes by asking that the dowry, which could easily be afforded, should include one of the villages which had coal, but no land was forthcoming. Cornelia's adviser said there was one last chance. The wealthy father-in-law would have to offer the boy whatever he asked for before the first meal during the wedding. This was held in the father-in-law's house, since Cornelia, as often, had got the transfer of the bride to her new house delayed while the husband grew up. The meal was announced and the boy was asked what he wanted. As pre-planned, he replied, 'a village with a coal mine'. The father-in-law was aghast and dropped the emeralds and rubies he had thought to offer. But his astute Chief Minister stepped forward, overrode the announcement of the meal, and had the boy shown a collection of birds. He was only ten, and quickly changed his mind to ask for a blue-green parrot. The meal was instantly served.

WILLS INSIDE CASKETS

It was also in 1907 that Cornelia encountered her first case of a will kept inside caskets. Wills were often kept as treasures, but they did not always establish what was expected. In one case, many neighbouring states were seeking to prove their entitlement to the estate of the widowed Maharani of Bettiah because she had no heir. In fact, Cornelia had ascertained that no decision could legally be made while she lived and she was still very much alive, as will emerge later.[17] Cornelia thought the estate was likely to revert to the British in the absence of an heir, because it had been given to her husband's forbears by the British as a reward for loyalty in the 1857 Uprising. Nonetheless, a royal claimant – the Maharaja of Benares – asked Cornelia to come and see the evidence of his entitlement, and the Maharani and the Government agreed that this might be informative. So Cornelia was regally received and taken by boat to the water gate of the women's quarters, then through tunnels guarded by sentries and up many stairs, into the daylight of a magnificent portrait gallery. When the Maharaja appeared, Cornelia explained the true position. But he wanted her to see his document.[18] The story can be told in Cornelia's words.

> 'There followed a scene which was wasted on an audience of one. A jewelled casket was produced, and, in silence, the officer in charge of the key stepped forward and opened it. But the document was not inside; there was only a smaller casket, opened by yet another officer, and so on through a nest of six caskets, a separate man in charge of each, and each man, producing his key with a flourish, added his own interpretation of secrecy. It was a symphony in secrecy: bold ("what d'you think of that!"); obstinate ("Death would not drag it out of me!"); tight and misleading ("There isn't really a secret"); arch, sly, even coy. Last of all His Highness, the key on his chain – "Victory! Now you'll see!" – as from the inmost and most jewel-bespattered box he produced a document. The Maharajah handed it to me, and the entire company sat back on its haunches watching me read, letting me feel the while that there was plenty of time, I need not hurry.

> 'So I read – not without an expectant thrill. But when I had finished I could have laughed aloud. The document was the will of a lady in no way entitled to deal with the contested property. It was she who had left it to his Highness! As I folded up the paper, they sprang at me.

> ' "Well?" said His Highness. "It is of as little use to your Highness as would be a like bequest in my own will", was what I said. They took it very well'.... 'Their courtesy did not fail, and I was as magnificently conducted out of my strange experience as I had been ushered into it'.

In another case in 1921 at Paschimgaon in East Bengal,[ii] the widow of a Muslim Raja asked Cornelia to offer care under the Court of Wards to two of his concubines and the son of one of them. But downstairs in the same house, the

---

ii 12 miles South-west of Dacca in East Bengal (now Bangladesh).

husbands of the Raja's four daughters contested the arrangement. Cornelia described her visit partly in exotic mode.[19]

> 'I went into the zenana to see the Begum and found her charming. She commended her husband's concubines and an unrecognisable son of one of them, saying, "My husband held them dear. Please provide for them".

> 'We then went upstairs and did her business – the property is not to be divided and other details. She told me also of a wakf[iii] which she knew her husband had made and of her own claim under Kabin[iv] to 5000/-[v] and a loan of 20,000/-, etc.

> 'When I went downstairs to the outside,[vi] I found the four sons-in-law assembled to contest the shares under the Mohammedan law which their wives would get, and to claim division, etc. Collector and Commissioner were there – the sons-in-law looking like Delhi miniatures, one with black hair curling round his ears, one with a Moghul Emperor's face, etc.'

To them so assembled it was Cornelia Sorabji's duty to say, 'The Begum says there is a wakf in existence. May we search for it before going further?'

> 'Enquiry revealed an unopened deed box. The Commissioner commanded it to be broken open, keys not forthcoming. Imagine the excitement as paper after paper was produced – old deeds, lists of property, collections, etc. Finally – the wakf. The sons-in-law craned forward. Someone said, "only a draft" in the tense silence. "Yes, but here is the deed, sealed and duly executed," said the Commissioner, lifting out the paper. Then we read it. *Nothing to the daughters*, "because I have married them well to men who can afford to look after them". (Imagine the falling back of now this one and now that, and the varying expressions on their faces – they who had come to contest a share now had no right to contest at all). The Begum gets only 100/- per month, far less than her share had there been no document. The concubines are provided for, "because in the sight of God I am responsible for them and the son of one of them".

> 'His two legitimate sons will be joint Mutwalis, administrators of the religious trust on majority, Court of Wards retaining property till then. The whole thing was most dramatic. We found also the Kabin for 5000/-, but not the bonds for 20,000/-. Poor Begum'.

---

iii Muslim grant for religious purposes.

iv A Muslim legal undertaking.

v Rupees.

vi 'Outside' means outside the zenana, or women's quarters, where the Collector and Commissioner would not have been allowed.

ADOPTION AND PEACOCKS

Adoption was very important for a sonless widow. The right adoptee could successfully pray for the soul of her departed husband and take the place of the son she had lost or failed to provide. The family who gave their son away to the royal household would at the same time gain in importance. In 1913, Cornelia was pleased to be invited to the most beautiful adoption ceremony she ever witnessed. She was an expert on adoption law, which was central to the cases described in Chapters 12 and 17 of 'once a corpse, always a corpse' and of Cornelia's contest with Sapru. But she also very much enjoyed the adoption ceremonies themselves, with the questions, 'Do you give?', 'Do you take?'. The adoption ceremony that she attended on June 10th, 1913, was of a Kashmiri boy[20] on the Madhupur estate[vii] in Orissa. The women's quarters there were guarded by peacocks that were trained to peck the eyes of any unrecognised male who approached. For the adoption ceremony Cornelia accompanied the adopting Rani to a distant temple.[21]

> 'To my right gleamed the sluggish canal, slimy and shiny as a snake, drowsing between mud and banks. This is the chief water-way for country boats laden with hay, or for the "green" boat, the local house-boat, perilous as to kitchen and stuffy as to cabin.... Beyond the canal, the horizon had been pushed away and away, and it was some time before I realised that the gigantic "love-in-a-mist" plant-like trees were dying bamboos. To my left the low shrub was full of things to see: birds and lizards, jackals and kharghosh,[viii] a million butterflies. To the Rani...pilgrims brought a cow apiece. In a minute we had come upon their grazing ground – the loveliest sight, for the dainty little creatures had to be milk-white, and were stalled in the temple fields – a pleasing harmony in white and green.

> 'Straight from the grazing-ground began the ascent of the hills to the great temple itself. When I came to travel this bit, I had already long since changed into my "conveyance of the country". It was a red-enamelled carrying chair, most comfortable, but oh, so noisy! For my lusty Ooriya carriers shouted at the top of their voices "hum-hum, hum-hum, hum-hum" '.

On arrival, the Rani first bathed in the temple pond. The adoption ceremony itself – 'Do you give?' 'Do you take?' – was very simple, with the boy's mother

---

vii This is adjacent to the pan estate to be mentioned below. Both have their southern boundaries some 15 miles north of Cuttack in Orissa.

viii Rabbit.

and father and the adopting Rani standing either side of the boy. The ceremony completed, the adopted boy sat on the temple plinth, and Cornelia asked him about the transformation he had undergone. His reply was simple. 'My mother cannot love me any more. It would be a sin.'

The gigantic return procession of the entire populace was led by

'the dancers and the pike-bearers, a gorgeous company in bright red uniforms, their arms bound with peacocks' feathers. They were followed by crowds and crowds of people – zenana folk in palkis[ix] and hooded carrying-chairs, men on elephants, on horses, on foot, or sitting under umbrellas on wheels drawn by atoms of ponies.... The great open cauldron of the sky, and the hot-coal colour of the wild men's uniform, then the patchwork of the crowd and the cool green of the forest for background. Then suddenly it was dark, and as suddenly a hundred torches leapt into life, and all that was gorgeous or garish was now lurid and sinister and creepy.... And across the drums and conch shells the wild peacocks called to the evening dance in the scrub below the foothills'.

But when they got back, the *trained* peacocks had been released for ever, for the adopted boy to choose a new guardian bird or beast. There were still the *wild* peacocks, which Cornelia saw on her next visit in July, dancing in the moonlight and the dawn.[22]

EDUCATION SUBSTITUTED FOR UNSUITABLE DANCING AND THEATRE

In 1919, Cornelia attempted to protect the children of another family. She was sent to a remote tea plantation in Sylhet in the eastern part of Bengal (now Bangladesh).[23]

'At one place we crossed a river – motor on a raft, we on a tiny paddle boat. The country was lovely and green. We got lots of exercise in the bumps provided by the state of the road, but not more than we could bear, and the outlook – blue hills, straight for which we were heading, across swamped rice fields and through the heart of wooded lower hills (wooded with bamboo and tall sugar cane crops) past little hamlets of neatly plaited split bamboo huts among the wavy plumes of the bamboo and supari-tufted palm trees – was really lovely'.

The father of Cornelia's wards had gone against orthodox custom by having a pet servant, who was a theatre boy. Theatre and dancing were considered

---

ix Palanquins, stretcher-carriers with a lid.

unsuitable, especially for purdahnashins. According to Cornelia, the father also made away with the children's money, and his daughter was prepared to testify that she had seen him poison their mother. The Court of Wards had obtained control of the children, and had promised the grandfather not to let them back to the father's house. But while Cornelia was away, the Commissioner (Mr Beatson-Bell, a bête noire of Cornelia's) 'forgot', and the father regained control of the children and married his child daughter off to the pet theatre boy in this remote spot. The orthodox governess begged the Government to interfere. She and Cornelia regarded the theatre types as the lowest. There were shows almost daily and stage properties in the household. The dancing women were housed in a compound, and the daughter spent all her time in their huts. Her education had been stopped and she was dancing suggestive dances. Cornelia sent the son off to the American agricultural college in Allahabad, and set about finding a new governess for the daughter, until she could send her to a Diocesan school.

RELICS OF PAST CONQUESTS PENSIONED

From 1918, Cornelia had to deal with certain pathetic cases arising out of past British conquests. Her first such case concerned the former kingdom of Oudh to the East of Delhi. In 1856, the year before the 1857 Uprising, the British provoked hostility by annexing and plundering the kingdom of Oudh to the East of Delhi, which had been a faithful ally. The Nawab or Muslim King was given by way of compensation a grand estate at Garden Reach on the river in Calcutta opposite to the present Botanical Gardens. In 1918–1919, Cornelia was summoned there by his princely grandson, first to advise his Shia wife about the sale of her share of some inherited property, the second time to give the Prince free advice about mortgages.[24] The Prince used to come to tea sometimes with Cornelia. He was elderly and looked like Akbar, the Moghul Emperor, 'a delightfully archaic figure in his Persian hat and long coat, and his perfect manners'. She describes the first visit to him.[25]

> 'Ruins of little cell-like single-eyed houses amble down the road that leads to St. George's Docks. "The 500 houses of the king's 500 concubines", said my friend Prince Mirza showing them to me. The late asylum of the concubines was then of no marketable value. We drove on to the Palace. There was a gateway which would do honour to a reigning sovereign with a Naubat Khana

(house of music) sitting astride the archway – the brave "side to face the world with". A single custodian in tatters, albeit tatters of red cloth and gold lace, threw the gates open with a flourish. I could have cried: desolation upon desolation was what the Gateway had hidden. That ghostly army of pillars standing in nettles must have been the Durbar Hall, and there, where a broken window frame looked out onto a marble platform near a fountain, was the King's House of Dreams. There was nothing of masonry that could give shelter even to straying cattle. One passed on along a broken pathway to "the Inside", or women's apartments. Here the roses and jasmines were rioting in a wild tangle, and there were just a few liveable rooms clutching on to one another inside the Zenana courtyard. The long inner room was the Zenana and had to serve four generations: the Prince and his sons lived in an annexe close by'.

The Government was buying some of the land back from the Prince to expand the Calcutta docks. The Prince's wife lived with relics of a visit the ousted King had paid to seek justice from Queen Victoria in London, travelling with his mother, who died in Turkey on the way. The Prince described the ousted King not as a debauchee as British apologists had characterised him, but as working hard from 6 to 9 and 11 to 3 writing bad Persian couplets, before exercising his kingly function of driving to receive petitions. These could be placed by anyone, even a beggar, in a big box on the back of his carriage with a slit in it. If the petition was written in good couplets the petitioner might become a courtier overnight, although if he then failed to appreciate the King's couplets, he might have his head cut off. The Prince said the King was, however, drugged by enemies and went mad.[26]

Another relic of conquest were the descendants of Britain's powerful adversary the Muslim Tipu Sultan. Cornelia had to help some of these in later years, 1920 and 1930. Original records of the British taking into care his sons in 1799 had been read in manuscript by Cornelia at a country house during her exile in England.[27] The princes were at first housed quite grandly in what became the Tollygunge House in Calcutta. The first time that Cornelia had to do with Tipu's descendants, in 1920, she was asked to check the bruises on a secluded Muslim girl 'practically enslaved by her uncle'. Her Mysore family was descended from Tipu Sultan, and the Court of Wards thought that it might be able to take her property in trust. Later in 1930, a great granddaughter of Tipu Sultan was living in poverty near the Calcutta tanneries and wanted a pension from the Government of India. The Government had made a treaty concerning Tipu Sultan in 1799, to maintain his descendants, and a sum was capitalised to yield the pension once and for all, so that it would not have to be raised anew.

Lord Minto had ruled that the pensions should be paid as of right down to the fourth generation, and thereafter on the merits of the case. Cornelia's client came within the time period and secured her pension.[28]

A final relic of conquest, befriended by Cornelia in 1913, was a Burmese Princess Myngandine Mithami, or Myngandine Hbati Tui Mah Gyee (disguised by Cornelia as 'Tum-Ta'). She had a pension from the British, because in the conquest of Burma they had ousted her father from his kingdom. Under pressure, she had insouciantly agreed to marriage, although her own customs did not require that, and the British-style experiment of a honeymoon was not successful. Cornelia admired her selflessness in caring for the second lady her husband took and using her pension to educate the children of that partnership as well as of her own. According to Cornelia, her selflessness continued even after her own children were removed by her husband and she was left with a cross-eyed and an epileptic child, neither of whom were her own.[29]

A FORGED WILL AND INSANITY CONCEALED

In 1921, Cornelia had an unusual case of insanity. She often had to deal with genuine insanity. The case of Tihur, described above, and that of the Maharani of Bettiah, described below, were not the only ones.[30] Sometimes the insanity of a proprietress was *falsely* alleged by claimants to an estate.[31] But in 1921 at the Banailli estate, near Bhagalpur, insanity was *concealed*.[32] According to Cornelia, the insane widow in charge of her husband's share of an estate was pushed by three conspiring sons-in-law into pretending sanity, in order to attest a forged will which made them eventual heirs, instead of the boy nephew, who by custom would inherit when the widow died in the absence of any will made by her husband. The estate did not fall under the Court of Wards, but the question was whether, because of the insanity, or provided the custom could be proved in court, the estate could be taken over without voluntary agreement to protect the nephew. The old Chief Minister had been dismissed and replaced by the forger, who worked for a son-in-law. A government lawyer, instead of helping the Court of Wards, had persuaded the young Collector to side with the sons-in-law.

On Cornelia's first visit, with the three sons-in-law and their supporting servants present, the lady had been told to pretend a trance, which she was said to have been in for three days. The boy's grandmother told Cornelia that this was to conceal her insanity. The lady was in bed, a priest was shouting mantras, and one son-in-law was whispering to her what to do. Cornelia cleared the room of all but the whisperer. The lady would not speak, and shut her eyes, but forgot the trance when Cornelia was going, opened her eyes and out of habit salaamed her.

Cornelia planned to return unannounced, but the lady got wind of this and had left for Bhagalpur, where Cornelia tracked her down. She admitted to Cornelia that she had peeped. She had been coached to memorise a stock answer to two anticipated questions, but she gave the answers at inappropriate moments. She was also incompetent to be the proprietress, because she could not write or recognise figures, did not know measures, nor the day or date.

A HAPPY ENDING

I shall finish with a ward of Cornelia's who died in 2007 at the age of 100, and a hundred years after Cornelia's first visit to her mother. The centenarian was the daughter of Laxmi Rani of Cuttack in Orissa. The family were landowners with a grand house in Cuttack and the estate of Darpan extending over 100 square miles, starting 15 miles to the north. It was adjacent to the Madhupur estate with its male-attacking peacocks. Laxmi Rani was widowed at the age of 13, and other family members would have taken over her house and estate if it had not been brought under the Court of Wards.

Cornelia first visited in 1907. The young widow, Laxmi Rani, of Kashmiri stock, had come from the United Provinces to marry, and resented the system of purdahed seclusion, which was alien to her own tradition. She was determined at least to take over the running of her stables, and Cornelia had to explain that the brandy for which the grooms were charging was not a drink taken by horses.[33]

She went on to adopt an heir when she was 18 and subsequently chose a child bride for him. This bride was the one who lived until 2007. She was also the one who voluntarily remained in purdah until 1992.[34] She knew Cornelia well and often talked about Cornelia to her son. The son, Ramesh Suthoo, still spends some of each year in the Cuttack house. He has expressed his appreciation of the Court of Wards as follows.[35]

'When he [my grandfather] died, my grandmother was all of 13 years old and as there was no issue, the entire estate was taken over by the British (who were ruling India at that time) to administer under their Court of Wards. This was a system of the British to ensure estates, or rajwadas, or zemindaris were not usurped and that proper succession was given to the true descendants. Whatever may be said about the British, one thing is clear, that despite their interest in India for their own reasons, they at least believed in justice and good administration and it is on account of this Court of Wards that our family exists as it does today.

He was afraid his family would otherwise have been 'consigned to oblivion'. I would only add one thing, that however sincere the British Court of Wards may have been in seeking to secure succession of the right heirs, it was in many cases possible for them to discover who should be inheriting only after they had appointed Cornelia as their investigator.

CORNELIA'S FINAL CONCLUSIONS ON WHAT THE COURT OF WARDS SHOULD BE DOING

As Cornelia's career approached its end, she got more and more expansive ideas about what she would like to see the Court of Wards doing. She kept urging the British to give agricultural education to male heirs, with a training estate set aside and with scholarships where necessary, because their own estates would run better, and they would be more respected by the peasants, if they understood how their land should be worked.[36] She thought that arrangements for tutoring should be replaced, because local tutors appointed by local managers did not dare discipline the boys who would later be their masters. One boy felt free to say that because he was a Raja, only he was allowed to cry for things he saw in shop windows, and only he could be skilful at telling lies.[37]

Cornelia acknowledged in response to criticism that the education, health, domestic comfort and contentment of her wards 'was not in the original programme of this post'.[38] But this did not stop her proposing ever more extensive reforms. She insisted in her annual reports that the education of heirs was specified in the Court of Wards Act. By the time of her annual report of August 1920 she was in vain urging on the Court of Wards a vastly expanded conception of what it could be doing. She acknowledged the movement in the direction of Home Rule for India, and argued it to be all the more important to train the wards in a sense of service to district and nation. She contrasted that picture with the limited ambitions of the Court of Wards as it was. And she called for an enlarged Court making use of more experts, in order to meet more effectively the needs of its wards.[39]

'In these wards who own a stake in the soil and are mostly representative of that slow-moving India of the district places (which *is* India if numbers are to count for anything), we have our best hostages for the future. If we can make them aware of their responsibility, if we can awake in them civic and national consciousness, if we can educate them to the service of their dependants, their district, their country – the Government will be leaving safeguards in the wake of its new liberties and charters of self-rule.

'I should like to see it,' (the Court of Wards) 'a Department complete in itself under an Inspector General with Deputy Inspectors – a Department of Experts and Enthusiasts, interested not in sections of a Code and in the reduction of debt, so much as in human beings and in the forces which make for the economic, social and moral progress of the country....

'As now run, it [The Court of Wards] is an organisation of functions rather than of faculties.... it wants "making over" in the light of modern demand and up-to-date knowledge. It really needs the service of Experts – Experts in Hindu custom, in Law, in Agriculture, in Forestry, in Mining contracts, in the right development of whatever property is entrusted to us – in fact in the management of property generally....

We shall see in Chapter 14 how Cornelia's final vision was greeted.

CHAPTER 11

THE JOYS AND DANGERS OF TRAVEL

O ne of the things that Cornelia enjoyed most about her job was the hazards and joys of travel. She described the different experiences very colourfully, and I shall in this chapter quote her own descriptions more than usual. She described her journeys as involving working days of 24 hours, with night time travel, work between trains and few halts.[1] In 1917, she drew up a list of qualifications that would be needed by any assistant and successor and the very first qualification was the capacity for arduous travel.[2] She warned of fierce heat, early dawn arrivals, and elephants swimming streams with you on their backs, your luggage in the water and you sore all over. Her illustration for the assistant and successor was based on her most recent trip and it will be no surprise that it described a journey by her favourite form of transport, the elephant.[3] This is how she chose to prepare the mind of any appointee.[4]

'I rode The Rose Lady and when she lifted up one foot to scratch another (I sympathised; it must have been a mosquito), I nearly dropped off her back. And when she felt affectionate, I had to cleave to the ropes of the pads! She was carrying me; her mother, the Wisdom Lady, carried my servants; her grandmother, the Dancer (a creature as huge as a house with feet!), had preceded me and was about two miles ahead on the road. Rose Lady sniffed her in the air, said the mahout,[i] the air being moist, and felt affectionate, so she trumpeted. I can't tell you what it was like. You really must ride her and see and *feel*—a rumble under you like trains rushing through your *own* inside, then the awful noise, the Wisdom Lady behind joining in, while you are rocked about, and the mahout says, 'Beloved Rose Lady, you are feeling affectionate.'

I have tended to concentrate on the pleasures of travel, but Cornelia also revelled in the dangers.

---

i Driver.

THE DANGERS OF TRAVEL

The hazards of visiting Ramgarh have already been described,[5] with bear, panther and tiger in the jungle, punctured tyres repaired with hay on the same route, and stone-throwing assailants added in. Punctured tyres were stuffed with hay on another occasion too and a palanquin broke on the same journey and had to be taken to a blacksmith. The poles broke on more than one excursion and could drop you suddenly.[6] Nor were the palanquin bearers always reliable. One lot ran away and she had to walk six miles back partly through jungle.[7]

Sometimes her base was a railway carriage in a siding that was to be re-attached to the main train at the railway station, but once the carriage was overturned by the wind while she was at the Collector's house for dinner, and after dinner there were fresh hazards on the way to the station. The horses failed and they had to walk in the dark. The Collector slipped down a bank, they were nearly dropped in a water tank and Cornelia found herself half an inch from a huge snake rearing its head at her. But she got away in the still swaying railway carriages.[8]

Sometimes she would drive the horse and trap herself through the dark, once a palace trap put together with string through a leopard-infested forest, and once because floods made it impossible for a car. It was a sopping 4-hour and 13-mile ride through the dark to the station, struggling against sleep. There was no light except for a boy running ahead with a smoky lantern, his bare legs swishing in the water. A groom crouched in the back holding an umbrella for Cornelia, and calling 'to the right', 'no, *no*, to the left' as he saw holes in the road, which was under water with drops to the side down to the river.[9]

CALCUTTA TO CHURAMAON

Cornelia's journeys to the white palace at Churamaon in 1905–1906 were briefly described in Chapter 8. But her visits were regular and her fullest description came from 1907, when she went with her Calcutta friend Barbara Stephen, the wife of Harry Stephen, the Calcutta judge. She included the return train journey from Calcutta in her account of the splendours of travel and arrival.[10]

> 'Mrs Stephen came with me. . . . We left by the Darjeeling mail on Friday and the first part of the journey is as you know it – train and boat – the picturesque boat, when the lights are on the water – flashlights – making the bits of shore . . . look

like a panorama or a stage. It is all so unreal – the dark blackness and then the little pictures leaping forth. Now a bit of basti,[ii] now a steamer, now a dug-out moored to a sandbank, now a group of bronze fishermen standing rope in hand . . . unreal all of it – and deliciously real. Our carriage slipped itself in the middle of the night across the river and we found ourselves at our terminus at 5 a.m. Here was a great cavalcade awaiting us – three elephants, one with a howdah,[iii] one with a pad and lovely red draperies, one less magnificent, but carrying the steps wherewith to mount the howdah, a shampini (or cart with springs drawn by great bulls) and a collection of ox carts with covers for our servants and luggage, a whole line of policemen and every District Officer in the station. . . .

'We started, Mrs Stephen and I on The Noble Prasad with The Speedy Beloved and The Happy Stepper following us, and after them the shampini and ox carts. A policeman, Circle Officer, rode beside us on an ambling white palfry, and at each village there was a policeman to greet us, a policeman armed with a spear to stick any venturesome dacoit lurking to hurt our noble presences. . . . The air was crisp and the country pretty, a succession of fields and mango groves and bamboo clumps and of quaint villagers sitting down here and there in their mat roofings and mud walls, with the babies and pigs and goats and godlings playing about promiscuous.

'The palace, a white, imposing structure on the river bank, came in sight after 14 miles of road. . . . White dog roses abound in the desert and I've told you before how one crosses the river on a raft, carts, bulls and all, and the Rani had salutes fired for me, as if I were the Amir or the Viceroy. My camp was pitched in the mango grove beside the Commissioner's and they had given me an extra tent for my friend. The Commissioner had arranged everything most luxuri-ously: each of us had a 3-roomed tent fully furnished. . . .

(After business with the Commissioner, Collector, Ranis and Palace) 'I was dead-tired by night, but you know how the life under canvas restores one. I love all the earth sounds and the earth silences and the wonder of the stars and the freshness of the early mornings. . . .

(After another day's business) 'Early next morning, we woke before it was day and were on our elephant, a pad this time, far more comfy than a howdah and off by 7 a.m. We rode The Goddess of Luck, who is attended everywhere by her son, The Beautiful Warrior, a great baby of 12 years standing as high as an English hill. He will not go anywhere without her, or let her go unattended, and he is a great, *great* baby, for even at sight of a pony on the road, a thing so small that he could eat it at one mouthful, he put up his trunk and snorted, and the Lucky one

---

ii Village.
iii Roofed seat.

would veer round promptly, to see what ailed her baby-ling. This to our no small
discomfort who were nearly unseated for his cowardice (not nearly unseated,
for the back of Luck is broad, but unseated in our imagination and apprehen-
sion).... We crossed the river on our elephant and the swish of her toes in the
water was most enjoyable. So gently she went too, wading carefully not to get
me into deep places.

(Back by train and boat) 'Our last nice happening was dawn on the Ganges.
Think of bands of dark blue and purple, and then bands of burnt yellow and
gold, and later a golden fleece of wavelets in the wake of our boat, and across the
wavelets suddenly a devil ship, dark as night, with mysterious clouds of smoke
from a funnel dark as night, all wandering across the colour in the sky and getting transformed into wonderful clouds of rosiness.'

TRAVEL TO LUGMA: DESERT, LOTUS-BEDS AND FLOOD

Another very early assignment was to the estate of Lugma starting in 1906,
although it was not until 1919 that the estate called on her full legal resources.
The journey started in June 1906 with a slow train ride from Bhagalpur up a
branch line to Mansi,[iv] passing through desert and Cornelia described a scene
amidst the patterned sand dunes.

'Suddenly we had come upon rivers of sand – no, *seas* of sand. It took my breath
away, waves and *waves* of ups and downs, all beautifully patterned, as inspec-
tion showed, by some sand insect or other – all a-shimmer (it was full of mica)
under that fierce light. Under a tree, a tree of white great thorns, bare of leaves,
lay a child shock-headed. She lay quite still, almost stiff, on her back, the bright
pink of her little chudder[v] making the one spot of colour in that desert. In the
distance walked a woman with a water pot on her head, away and away over
the sand, looking back every now and then to that white-thorn mock-sheltering
tree. You knew what she went to seek. Would she be in time? And the train
curved out of sight, and the little pink bundle lay still, so still'

At Mansi, there was only a shelter for a booking office, and neither the road
transport for a cool night ride nor the first meal for 3 days were ready, so she
spent the night without a meal and had a ride next day by railway trolley, lent
by the railway's resident engineer, which had its compensations.[11]

iv The railway now goes on to Khagaria.
v Head to foot veil.

'Off by trolly, then, ... 6 a.m., 18 miles of trolly, passing between hot chalk embankments, but once past a *glorious* bed of pale pink lotuses, a bed as far as the eye could reach. The trolly men stopped and gathered me armsful of the lovely flowers. They grew waist-high with leaves as big as plates, and a kind of fruit shaped so. At the base of the cup, you find little nuts hidden away in the pulp, nuts like monkey nuts in taste great favourites I find in Bengal. ... I put the big leaves over my feet to keep them cool, and wore them on my head, while in my lap were sheaves of the beauteous blossom. ...'

Unfortunately, on arrival at 10 the onward road transport had again not been assembled and there was no shelter from the scorching sun, nor anything to drink but the rose water in her toilet bag, so she had to abandon the journey to Lugma, take the trolley back to Mansi and go back all the way to Calcutta.

She returned later in the month to Lugma. This time the 18 mile trolley ride to the terminal was by night, as she had intended, and it was exhilarating:[12]

'It was a *glorious* run. Think of it, a dark night of stars, absolute silence and aloneness, i.e. absolute harmony, and that whizz through the air. There was nothing almost to see. One just sat still and felt the winds of God blowing through, and every now and then you half-waked from your delicious other-consciousness to see a stack of light – a brick kiln, or a river and the quaint ferry boats at anchor. It was a world curiously rid of humans.'

Her bungalow for the night, however, was not to be found after two miles of walking, and checking an encampment and more than one wrong house. Once identified, it turned out to be infested by whirling and dropping bats. Still, after an hour or two of sleep, she was off on a palanquin ride for the ten miles to Lugma at 6 the next morning, and it was as good as the trolley ride the night before.

'The palki-men[vi] ran beautifully, smoothly and always across country, and the air was fresh, and we forded the loveliest lotus beds – the men thigh deep in water – I secure and dry with both hands free to pluck the beautiful blossom.'

The main problem on the Lugma estate was already apparent in 1906. According to Cornelia, the priest of the proprietress was pressing her to erect a temple that would continue after her death. Cornelia explained that after her death the proprietress would lose all rights over expenditure from the estate. By 1919, when the proprietress was nearly 80, the problem was still there, but Cornelia had found a legal solution, to be described in Chapter 12.[13] The journey to Lugma involved more than one river crossing and in December of 1919 Cornelia had travelled 14 miles by

---

vi Palanquin bearers.

steamer instead of 2, because the river had changed course.[14] Near Lugma her palki-bearers lost their way and took her to the wrong river crossing. Although she got a ferryman to take her across and to go back for the bearers, the ferryman dumped her by mistake up to her ankles in a bog, and she had to climb out over planks and paddles taken from a wreck. When the bearers caught up and carried her with one leg hanging out to dry, they nearly walked into an unprotected well, and recoiling from that, banged her extended leg and came close to breaking it.[15]

FLOODS

On many other occasions Cornelia's journeys had taken her through scenes of flooding. The diaries of 1906 and 1907 describe this already.

> 1906 (East Bengal) 'Floods. Trollied[vii] across the worst bits. Seas of fields with quaint little mud huts floating in them.'[16]

> 1907 'Floods. Bad in Orissa. The earth a great waterway with thatches of houses and tips of plantain trees showing where once there were streets. The Collector manages in his boat. Wretched families clinging to thatches and tops of trees– one woman with three babies. Nothing to eat but plantain leaves. Relief difficult to carry. How shall they cook? Pitiable.'[17]

In another mood, Cornelia found floods picturesque.

> 'The masses of red cotton tree blossom and the floating vegetables suggest a water garden, and the earthware pots and pans dance like water nymphs with swollen heads. You must turn your eyes away when the goats or poultry come along.'[18]

In 1919 there were floods not only on the route to Lugma, but in the further East, where Assam had endured a cyclone. There Cornelia found the river rising 9 feet in some places and swallowing land, while in other places the silt made new banks. The grass was ruined, huts unroofed, trees uprooted, though the people had resumed fishing the small fish they used in their curries.[19]

BARISAL: WATER JOURNEYS AND DILAPIDATION

East Bengal, roughly the present Bangladesh, was very watery. One of Cornelia's favourite journeys from 1912 onwards was 116 miles through tidal waters by steamer to Barisal and then from Barisal towards the sea to Dasmina by the

---

vii Travelled by railway trolley.

Collector's white launch and finally by 'jolly boat'. The tides were very vari-able, there were storms and heavy seas, the jolly boat could get off course, and once it had a two foot hole knocked in it. But despite the dangers, she found it calming.[20]

> 1912 Feb 18th. 'I sit in the dark at the ghat, as it[viii] has gone away to coal. Very misty at first, then flat banks with banana, palm and bamboo showing, and great red burrs of the cotton tree. 8.45 Barisal.... Darling white launch. 19th. Gorgeous glimmer of dawn and hasten...to catch the tide. Very low water. Soundings have to be taken. Storm, so not arrive till 3.30. Anchor and I go off in the jolly boat.'[21]

> 1915 Apr 14th.[22] 'It has been so lovely and quiet. I was very much to pieces, though I knew it not, after the hard work of the case and my ordinary work as well, and I have loved this quiet time.... Yesterday we got as near as I could to my Raj estate, so we launched the little jolly boat, and despite the sun (mid-day) rowed along the tidal waterways to within walking distance of my bari.[ix] You would have loved that boat journey. The two ship's men I took rowed or punted or towed as was most convenient. The banks were lovely – tree ferns and bamboo and delicious grasses and again fields and basti. Once we got the villagers to lift our boat over a neck of land, and more than once we had to lie flat as we slipped under the bamboo bridges. When we were within about a mile (they called it that; I know it was shorter) of my bari, I walked across the fields to the ruins of what must once have been a very fine Raj house. There was an earthen pot tied over the door, to keep away cholera.'

At Barisal the palace was in ruins because of poverty, and the repair programme was a failure in contrast with the lavish plans described above[23] at Churamaon. Cornelia brought along the Collector on one occasion, because he had not been to inspect for a year, but next year the repairs were still not done, because the local workman was being paid by the day until he completed them and other people were sharing his profits.[24]

BUDDHIST TEMPLE OF BODH GAYA

A favourite place that Cornelia visited as early as 1906 was the holy city of Bodh Gaya (Gaya),[25] where Hindu and Buddhist shrines are intermingled, the Buddhist origins having been rediscovered only in recent times. She had ward

---

viii The steamboat.
ix Rajbari, royal palace.

business not only in Bodh Gaya, but also two days' further trek by horse and on foot into hill country at Chatra, which she found lovely. She passed great gorges and mountain streams, a panther crossed their path, and the horses got stuck in river beds, for as much as three hours in the Sherghati sand beds.

On approaching Bodh Gaya, she was enthralled by the sight of the monastery with old battlements and green parrots hiding in holes. She visited the Buddhist temple of 243 BCE with its ancient stone railings and the monastery next to it. She was startled that in the Buddhist precincts the temple preacher and the Abbot were both Hindus, but the Abbot received her kindly and talked Buddhism. In Bodh Gaya she found:

> 'The sunlight slanting on a street that looked part early Italian, but for the little templets squatting at the corner, the sellers of brass and soapstone, of Bishu pads (Vishnu's Foot), and caste mark seals,[x] the oddments of laziness twanging zithars, the unexpected flights of steps round unexpected corners, here and there the face of a really holy ascetic, seen through a clean courtyard doorway praying in silence and aloofness. . . .'

In the Hindu temple of Vishnu's Foot, she found a roofed over collection of pillars and empty spaces which suggested to her Buddhism rather than Hinduism.

> 'The darkness gradually grows lighter to your eye, and you see a priest and his disciple doing pooja[xi] to the Foot for a poor woman, a leper, who stands by in an agony of entreaty and faith. . . . Every now and then the disciple lights a farthing[xii] dip, and makes circles of blessing over his head and the Foot. The light falls fitfully on the leper's progress to decay, and she stands still, so still, her eyes shut, her face a prayer, poor distorted leprous face.'

I turn now to what Cornelia learnt over her career about the attitudes of her wards and to her responses in methods of education and social work.

---

x Worn by Hindus.

xi Prayer.

xii One quarter of a penny.

CHAPTER 12

PURDAHNASHIN ATTITUDES: CORNELIA'S LEARNING BEFORE TEACHING

Cornelia had first to learn about the attitudes of her purdahnashin wards, which sometimes startled and often impressed her. Her methods of education and social work grew along with her understanding of their attitudes. In her first two years of probation, 1905–1906, she had been assigned to work with families whose disputes the male British officers had found beyond their comprehension.[1] Her ideas were first developed in that crucible. But by the time of her retirement in 1922, she had had eighteen years of work with her wards, and she had a wider canvas on which to base her interpretation of the purdahnashins' ideas and her own methods. Those methods were designed to respect her wards' attitudes, but to win agreement to modifications of custom when it caused them unnecessary hardship.

It was explained in Chapter 8 that Cornelia took seriously the literal meaning of what her Hindu wards said about death, and in particular about the soul's future after the present life. She used her understanding of what her wards believed to secure British authorisation of expenditure on religion, despite the opposition of some British officers. Indeed, her sympathetic accounts of her wards' beliefs ought to have persuaded any British officer with the slightest imagination and humanity, and she evidently succeeded in securing payments. We need to see how Cornelia understood their attitudes and beliefs, especially as regards the soul before and after the present life.

THE SOUL BEFORE AND AFTER THE PRESENT LIFE

The subject became imperative for Cornelia as early as 1905–1906.[2] But it engaged her emotions even more in the First World War of 1914–1918 when her two closest British supporters, Lady Minto, the former Vicereine, and Mr Le Mesurier, who had given her her first assignments, both lost children in the war. Cornelia was pleased that the two constituencies she loved most, the British and her wards, seemed to be drawn together by the war and its tragedy. In her purdah parties she showed her wards lantern slides of the war. The pictures projected on screen took her wards outside the purdah curtain to things they had never seen and won their immediate sympathy for the British cause. As the mothers were widows, they were sympathetic to a mother's loss, and Cornelia at first imagined that their reactions would therefore be the same in other respects. She was fascinated to learn that she was wrong. One widow, Arnakali Devi the Kasimbazar grandmother,[3] was horrified at Cornelia's inquiry whether she expected ever to be reunited with her late husband. She would not wish him again to be associated with such an unlucky person as herself. Rather, she prayed for his highest good.[4] Another woman friend, probably the Sadhuin Narayani, was against remembering the dead. That was 'to keep in your hand the kite that would otherwise fly beyond the hold of things of this world'.[5] As explained in Chapter 8, Cornelia gained knowledge from her unsecluded Sadhu and Sadhuin friends as well as from her wards.

Cornelia was touched that some wards expressed their affection for her through their beliefs. One said to the childless Cornelia,

> 'You always know, Miss Sahiba — you know how it feels when the little ones come, and how when they are grown, and how when the soundless rod of God falls upon them and we are desolate. Sons and sons you have had, and some have lived, but many have gone away'.

When the childless Cornelia asked for an explanation, she replied,

> 'But it is true nonetheless. Many sons has the Miss Sahiba had in previous births. How else should she know?'[6]

Similarly touching to Cornelia was the reaction of the forgiving Rani ('God resents it for us') from Cornelia's period in the Princely States before she started her work for the Court of Wards.[7] Asked 'why do the squirrels love you so?', she replied, 'They know that I remember the time when I too was a squirrel and played with them.'[8]

RELIGIOUS EXPENDITURE

It was not only particular conversations, but also her official work that required Cornelia to learn about attitudes and beliefs she had not known before. The importance of religious expenditure was illustrated above by the case of ceremonies to secure the future of a Maharani's soul.[9] But it involved Cornelia in many other contexts. Rani Murat of Bharatpura, living at Benares, wanted four pilgrimages to be authorised out of her estate which the Court of Wards held in trust, since this would give her liberation from rebirth.[10] Faced with such momentous rewards, what value could one possibly attach to the perspective of a British officer who had been on a religious expenses committee and who fined a ward without warning for asking to borrow against her future allowance rather than from a money-lender, so as to complete the 14th and last of her vowed annual ceremonies, or of an officer who thought that keeping the estate in surplus was more important than ceremonies?[11] Cornelia made a list of religious expenses upheld in court under Hindu law,[12] so that she had legal as well as moral backing for her recommendations on expenditure.

I have mentioned only briefly the desire of one widow in Lugma to create a temple to continue after her death, when Hindu law gave her no further right of expenditure from the estate.[13] Cornelia devised a trust fund to continue after the widow's death. Later she described how creating such a trust can take five years of theological deliberation.[14] In the present case she was able to get the trust registered in 1920 and to write to the widow just in time before she died the next year with news of the trust and of the completion of the temple building. 'For this alone I waited,' said the grateful widow, one of many expressions of gratitude Cornelia received. As Cornelia relates it, she was carried to her temple to give thanks for the fulfilment of her earthly dreams and died while performing the ceremony.[15]

INHERITANCE AND ADOPTION

Cornelia was involved in many legal cases of inheritance and adoption, and she maintained that this subject was equally bound up with beliefs about death. She spoke with exaggeration in order to explain her point to the British. Inheritance, she said, and adoption were sought for the sake of ancestors, not descendants.[16] Only the right heir could do the ceremonies for the deceased male and affect his next rebirth. Among other things, the heir needed to have worshipped the same gods as the deceased, so that his prayers would be heard. The British Collector who was ready to allow a disputed claimant to perform the ceremonies instead was threatening the after-life and rebirth of the deceased.[17] Not even a direct descendant could pray for the deceased, if he had changed the gods he worshipped.[18] Nor could a daughter do it, so there was consternation among Cornelia's wards in 1923, when a new law allowed daughters or sisters to inherit, even though they could not pray for the deceased male.[19] This would have made no difference in places where property passed down the female line – which was not unknown in India. But in Cornelia's households, the whole question of who could inherit depended on prospects for rebirth of the deceased male.

HEAVENS AND HELLS FOR PARENTS

It was seen in Chapter 8 that the marriage of one girl, Kalidasi from Churamaon, was postponed to the age of 10 at Cornelia's urging. In 1907, another widow, Gauribala Dasi, conceded Cornelia's requests for delaying a girl's marriage, but explained that the parents would go to the best heaven if their daughter was married between 4 and 7, the next best if between 7 and 9, worse if between 9 and 11, and after that to hell. Cornelia interpreted these heavens and hells as the next rebirth, but they may rather have covered an intermediate period before the next rebirth.[20] She took the explanation very seriously and it confirmed her view that legislation would not on its own be enough to change things without changes of attitude. She hoped that help might come from closer study of Scripture by authenticated religious authorities.

ONCE A CORPSE, ALWAYS A CORPSE

One case involving Cornelia concerned a Raja supposedly dead and cremated, who returned after twelve years to the acclaim of his tenants and the consternation of most of his family. The case illustrates the very wide range of practices and beliefs concerning death that Cornelia's work called on her to understand. She certainly did understand more than the British officers, as many were graceful enough to recognise. She needed to know about sannyasis, pollution, the laws of adoption and the austerities owed by a purdahnashin widow. The case was so dramatic that it has been the subject of a whole book, *A Princely Impostor?*, but Cornelia offers some insights that the book does not record.[21] Through one British officer's refusal to consult Cornelia, the Court of Wards was brought into disgrace and lost the resulting litigation in 1946 at enormous cost after thirty six years. The supposed widow's refusal to accept the financial rewards of the litigation would have impressed Cornelia by its integrity, if she had learnt the final outcome.

Three brothers were Rajas with equal shares in an estate at Bhawal near Dacca. The second brother, who became the subject of controversy, reportedly died in Darjeeling on May 7th 1909, and his elder brother the next year. The youngest was judged incompetent to administer his own share, so that by 1912, all three shares were administered by the Court of Wards.

But a question arose as to whether the second brother had really died, as had been accepted by the Court of Wards and by the supposed widow, who lived in Calcutta. Cornelia heard rumours from the start in the women's quarters of the palace (today government offices) that he was alive. The story was that he had been taken for cremation in the evening, but a rain storm (or in Cornelia's report, a rain and hail storm) had scattered the officiators, and when they returned, he had disappeared. Cornelia heard from the women's quarters and from many other sources that the hail had revived the prince. It turned out that he had woken up on the pyre and said, 'I am a corpse. Once a corpse, always a corpse.' Behind him a voice repeated, 'Once a corpse, always a corpse,' and a passing Bhutan lama encouraged him to leave, before the rain stopped, and go off with him to learn how to become a lama. In fact he remained a Hindu, but became a Hindu ascetic (a Sannyasi). By having been carried to the burning ghat the supposedly dead Raja had incurred pollution, which would normally preclude his returning from the ghat, even if he lived. Hence his declaration, 'Once a corpse, always a corpse.' But, Cornelia points out, it is permissible, if one ignores the complication of having been taken to the burning ghat, for a Sannyasi who has exchanged life with his family for retreat to the forest and an adopted life of meditation, to return home incognito after twelve years, to see how people are getting along. Twelve years later, to the day, the Raja-turned-Sannyasi returned for a quick look, but some people recognised him.

In the interim, however, in 1919 the Rani widow of the third brother had improved her position by getting permission to adopt an heir, who, as the only heir, became beneficiary of all three shares in the estate. Cornelia considered the adoption 'shady', but was shut out of the decision by one of her bêtes noirs, Mr Stevenson-Moore. The widow had adopted the son of her brother, which was unconventional in Hindu law. The Court of Wards should have checked that the adoption was valid. It would also be invalid, if the missing Raja was still alive. Moreover, rents would in that case be owed directly to the missing Raja, and should not have been collected by the Court of Wards for the adopted heir, without testing the rumours in a court of law. When the Raja's return was rumoured, Cornelia was asked to try to discover the truth. One thing she found was that a forged death certificate had secured an insurance payment. But, more remarkably, when she asked the supposed widow of the Raja who had disappeared to see if she could identify him, at least by peeping from behind a curtain, she refused. The widow, who had been very young when married, refused even to look, on the grounds that she had undergone twelve years of prayer and fasting for her husband's soul, whereas whoever it was who had now returned was a casteless outcaste, with whom one could not eat and whose home was the burning ghat.

It suited the supposed widow's brother, who benefited from her allowance, also to disown the returnee, and naturally it suited the adoptive mother, and in no time the returnee was declared an impostor. But his tenants and, bravely enough, his sister accepted him. The tenants, mostly Muslim, supplied 100,000 rupees to help him resume his kingdom and his sister financed the trial, which the Court of Wards was avoiding. Cornelia commented in 1923 that the Court of Wards' case against the claimant looked 'fishy'. Later in 1934, she recorded that the Raja was going to court against the British Collector who called him an impostor, but the beneficiaries of his exclusion were threatening the lives of those who gave evidence for him. According to *A Princely Impostor?*, the Court of Wards pressured witnesses, withheld documents and used a false photograph, and in the first trial the judge found against the Raja, but his sister financed an appeal.

There were witnesses that back in 1909 a second cremation party had been organised in Darjeeling the following morning, which took a body said to be the Raja's from Step Away, the house in Darjeeling where the Raja had been staying. But whose was the body? Could another body have been introduced? There was no one who had witnessed both the evening and the subsequent morning cremation parties. Several witnesses recognised the scaly ankles of the returnee, but there were rival questions about marks on his body. With Indian judges, the returnee won on appeal and was awarded his one third share by the High Court in May 1941. But now the horrified 'widow' insisted on an appeal to the Privy Council in London, dragging the Court of Wards into further litigation. In July 1946, the returnee won again, but two days later died in London. The 'widow', true to her beliefs, refused her one third share of more than 800,000 rupees, which the Court of Wards was now required to offer. Given the complexities of pollution and adoption, and the humiliation and expense they now suffered, the Court of Wards would have done better to make fuller use of Cornelia's familiarity with adoption practice from the start.

LEGISLATION AGAINST SUTTEE INEFFECTIVE

A final issue about life and death reinforced Cornelia's belief about the ineffectiveness of social legislation unaccompanied by a change of attitude. As early as 1829, the British outlawed suttee (Sati), the practice whereby Hindu widows had to mount their husband's funeral pyre to be burnt alive. But Cornelia found cases of voluntary suttee nearly a century later. In her first week working in Calcutta in 1904, a bier passed her in the opposite direction as she was being driven, and the wind exposed the face of the supposedly dead woman, who opened her eyes and looked at Cornelia. She could not get her driver to follow the bier.

When Cornelia asked about what she had seen, a Hindu friend said his own grandmother had been taken alive to be burnt, but had leapt off the pyre. But since one is polluted once taken to be burnt, she could never return, and the grandson had his grandmother pointed out when his father died and was burnt at the same place. She was an old woman bent in two, living there off offerings to the dead.[22] We have already encountered another friend, Arnakali Devi, who showed Cornelia the shrivelled little finger with which she had been made to stir rice, to prepare her for suttee.[23] She died a widow in 1914 not by suttee.

In 1921, however, Cornelia was involved in the voluntary suttee of another widow, Lakhsmi Devi.[24] She was widowed and was still prepared and wait-ing. Her preparedness was seconded by her son, a ward of court, who for seven years had been asking the local authority, at the slightest sign of illness, for funeral expenses for his mother's death. The authority would telegraph Cornelia, who would report back that the mother was alive and kicking. But in 1921, the son waited until Cornelia was out of town and took her alive down to the burning ghat. Cornelia got the message on return and drove straight to the ghat, where the widow, with her feet already in the river, was surrounded by priests, four deep as Cornelia described them. Cornelia mistrusted them as standing to get the money for death ceremonies. The ward had been in the burning sun from 1 until 7, and after that there was heavy dew. The priests claimed she was dead, or at least out of her senses, but they made way for Cornelia, who took her hand and asked her what she was doing there. She replied that it was good to have one's feet in the river and she astutely asked not for her son, but for her grandson. She too could never leave the burning ghats again. But Cornelia thinned the crowd and had her given air and taken to the shelter of a dressing station for corpses, where she appointed a woman doc-tor keep watch. Cornelia got telephone reports every hour, though more than once the priests claimed that she was dead. The woman doctor reported her swallowing milk without difficulty the next day at 10 a.m. But the son brought a Hindu doctor, who pronounced her dead at 11, and forbade the non-Hindu woman doctor to touch the 'dead'. By the time Cornelia got there, she looked alive, but was on the funeral pyre, anointed with butter for burning, with earth of the tulsi plant on her forehead and looking happy in her prayer shawl of gold and crimson. Cornelia saw the grandson put the live coal to her feet and lips and turned away when the pyre was lit. The lady was 85 and had been widowed for at least 30 years. She had been born in 1836, seven years after suttee was outlawed, but the legislation still failed to hold after 92 years.

SELFLESSNESS AND FORGIVENESS ADMIRED

These were some of the beliefs about death that Cornelia reported herself as encountering. In her female wards they called for an attitude of selflessness that she greatly admired. Selflessness was supposed to be a Christian value, but Cornelia thought that her female wards exemplified it more fully than Christians. Selflessness was shown by the widow who prayed for her husband to receive a better fate than reunion with someone as unlucky as herself. It was shown by every widow who for the rest of her life underwent austerities for the soul of her husband.

Selflessness was shown also in contexts other than death. Some wives forgave injustice without resentment, and forgiveness too was an imperfectly realised Christian ideal. One forgiving wife was the one in Kathiawar who was denied her allowance for decades in Cornelia's early days. She was the one who said, 'God will resent it for us.'[25] There were other forgiving wives too. I have spoken of the Burmese Princess who came to Cornelia in 1913, and who continued caring for the children of her husband's second woman after her husband had removed her own.[26] In the same year, 1913, Cornelia met another forgiving wife on the Banailli estate at Bhagalpur. Although Cornelia claimed that the husband took cocaine and had another woman, the wife used her private funds to house and support him and his lady and eventually to commemorate him. In the last two cases Cornelia was not able properly to reward the selflessness, as she had in Kathiawar. She stopped the British using the Banailli lady's revenue to pay for her husband's debts. But the lady's son proved to be insane and died, and Cornelia only just persuaded her not to hurl herself off the roof.[27]

A STERNER VIEW OF THESE ATTITUDES: PROGRESSIVES AGAINST CORNELIA

Certain progressive Indians, according to Cornelia, regarded both the religious customs and the particular forms taken by the belief in reincarnation as mere superstition, and they said that it would be swept away in the new India, freed from the British. It was the British in the person of Queen Victoria who had under-taken, after the Uprising of 1857, not to interfere with religion. But Cornelia had an objection to these progressives. In her view, they were a tiny minority amidst India's then 149 million Hindus. Those progressives most prominent in Bengal, the Brahmos (not Brahmins), she estimated at 1000, although the later census of 1921 put them at over 5000. They were a socially progressive group of Hindus reformed by Ram Mohun Roy in 1828 to believe in only one God and to adopt a strict moral-ity, which one of their number has described as influenced by Christian Puritan-ism and Non-conformism.[28] Jowett had written admiringly to Cornelia of their founder,[29] and Cornelia spoke well of them in some ways, but not of their ability to deal with the orthodox, who, she thought, would not regard them as Hindu at all. Given that the Brahmos were such a small minority, why, she asked, was the British Government catering to them in Bengal? When the Montagu-Chelmsford Reforms gave more administrative posts to Indians in 1919, she wrote to Lord Montagu, following up a conversation with him, and sent a 40-page typewritten memorandum about the need for safeguards to protect her wards.[30] The Brahmos were outcastes from the point of view of her orthodox wards, and unwelcome, and certainly did not understand religion. How could they enter orthodox households and deal with questions related to religion? And how would the Brahmos take to being told by people who lacked their education that they did not understand?

As Cornelia characterised the Brahmos, they wanted what they saw as superstition to be swept away. Cornelia, by contrast, aspired simply to coax away those of the beliefs that were causing her wards harm, but only at a pace acceptable to them.

THE DISADVANTAGES OF PURDAHNASHINS

Cornelia thought that a long educational process would be required to modify the disadvantages suffered by women and children in purdah. We need to see what she thought of as the principal disadvantages that could not quickly be removed. Child marriage was one with its consequences for health. Coupled with the purdah system, child marriage was worse, because it curtailed girls' education, and that meant that even sons were first reared by uneducated moth-ers. Many practices among Cornelia's wards disfavoured females. Divorce was not then allowed to the Hindu women, nor until 1921 was remarriage. Even after that, Cornelia encountered no case of widow remarriage, except after 1926 in the Princely State of Bharatpur, as described below.[31] Hindu males in the purdah system were allowed not only remarriage, but in special circumstances more than one wife at a time, for example if no male heir was forthcoming. Cornelia admired the austerities voluntarily undertaken by widows, which included shaving the head and never again wearing ornaments, or taking more than one meal a day. But they were based on the belief, which her wards appeared to her to take literally, that the husband's death was due to the widow's wrong conduct in a past incarnation, not to the husband's. A proprietress at Sombassa who had lost three family members said, in Cornelia's translation, that she must have been sinful for aeon upon aeon. Lakhsmi Devi, the widow who accepted suttee, nonetheless told Cornelia that she could not remember the sin in her previous life which had caused her to lose her husband,[32] and there were other similar cases.[33] A hostile mother-in-law could exploit the belief in past fault and blame the widow, who might have to live with her, for the loss of her son. On infanticide, we shall see, Cornelia was to make a major legal contribution.[34] Without female remarriage, a widow who became pregnant might be forced into infanticide, to spare her family disgrace. Other reasons favoured female infanticide. Females were undervalued in the system, since they could not effectively pray for the soul of a departed husband, and since they required expensive dowries. A particular sorrow of Cornelia's was the belief in pollution at birth, which prevented a grandmother handling a newborn baby or its mother.

Some disadvantages flowed directly from the seclusion of purdah itself. It fostered intrigue, separated the women from education about health, or the management of estates and from reliable legal advice. As already explained, there were no banking facilities for purdahnashins, and so their private possessions, often in the form of jewellery which represented all they had of their own against hard times, normally had to be kept in the house.[35] Purdah had implications for Cornelia's Muslim households too, concerning marriage before the completion of education, inheritance and various Muslim systems of divorce. In general, seclusion prevented the world looking in and the women looking out

CHILD MARRIAGE AND HINDU PURDAH SWEPT AWAY

In modern India child marriage and Hindu purdah have been swept away so completely that it is hard to imagine what the original combination was like in its consequences. Even before the departure of the British, who were hesitant to interfere in religion, facets of the system were beginning to be modified, as Cornelia was to find in the Princely States of Bharatpur and Gwalior as early as 1921.[36] By 1928 Cornelia was recording nationalists, both Hindu and Muslim, mounting a 'purdah must go' campaign, which was incompatible with the idea that Cornelia shared with her friends in the Princely States of retaining but modifying purdah. The case I have mentioned above of purdah lasting until 1992 will have involved purdah of a modified kind.[37] We shall see below that Cornelia thought the 'purdah must go' campaign did not yet correspond to what was actually happening either among her wards, or in the more enlightened Princely States.

Cornelia's aspiration to retain purdah, but modify it, was particularly difficult to achieve and her sister, Alice, did not agree with her about it. Given the hardships, it is not surprising that Alice shared the Progressives' view that seclusion in such estates should be swept away. Alice was not speaking of purdah among her Afghan frontier tribesmen, nor among the citizens of her frontier town, Bannu, who at least had access to her medical treatment, if they chose, and whose intrigues were not palace intrigues. What she pictured instead, in one of her novels,[38] was seclusion for the womenfolk of a Northern Muslim estate owner. Her objections were to the intrigue, the ignorance about health and to their being kept from knowledge of other models, not the model of the West, which Alice regarded as of uncertain benefit, but knowledge of better models of Islam in other parts of India. Not for the last time, Alice's different experience led her to a different conclusion from Cornelia's and she reminded Cornelia that different parts of India were not the same. Cornelia's path was not easy: the retention of seclusion in her estates coupled with its amelioration. We can now see, however, why Cornelia advocated the educational remedy that she did, and what was correct and what incorrect in her thinking about policy.

CORNELIA'S IDEAS ON REMEDY: LEGISLATION INEFFECTIVE WITHOUT EDUCATION

Very early on, in a letter of April 1891 to her family at 80 Civil Lines, Poona (she calls them 'Number 80'), Cornelia announced the policy which she would continue to follow, which was that education, not legislation, was what was needed to protect purdahnashin women from the disadvantages of their situation.

> 'I am, I fear, very unorthodox, for I do not see how any legislation can meet the difficulty. India lacks the moral courage' (Sir William Hunter turned this phrase against her when he asked if she had the moral courage to get married)

'to make her own social reforms, and I think legislation would only be giving her a crutch, which, moreover, I doubt whether she will use. The fault of our country has always been. the talking and agitating too much and acting too little. However, I will refrain from corrupting your respectable ideas on the subject, dear Number 80. It is sufficient if one of the family is heterodox.'

She repeated her preference for education over legislation in October 1891 in an article in *The Nineteenth Century*. The article raised a storm and her sister Mary defended her in *The Christian Patriot* in 1891. As was pointed out in Chapter 2, her preference was opposite to that of her contemporary, the pioneer Rukhmabai, but in line with that of Florence Nightingale.

Cornelia admired the Bombay reformers Malabari, who helped secure the Age of Consent Act of 1891 with strong support from his friend Florence Nightingale,[39] and Ranade who campaigned against child marriage and the shaving of widows' heads and for female education and widow remarriage. In 1894, Ranade had chaired her lecture on the need for women lawyers, and in 1895, Malabari had come to see her and spoken of being rejected by his fellow-Parsis and by Hindus.[40] What she felt was that, like earlier legislation (the Hindu Widows' Remarriage Act of 1856, and the consent to introduce an Age of Marriage Bill in 1873), the legislation did not work. She thought that more was achieved by women such as Ranade's wife and Pandita Ramabai, both of whom she knew in Poona.[41] The first had founded an Industrial Home of Service for women and Pandita Ramabai had created a Widows' Home with schools and training centres attached.[42] But Cornelia gave a special place to her aged sadhuin friend, Mathaji, who had moved from her Himalayan cave to Calcutta, where she founded schools for orthodox Hindus.[43]

Cornelia not only favoured education as a remedy for disadvantages, but devised her own approach to education in purdahnashin households. Her ideas on education were informed by the flexible use that her sadhu and sadhuin friends made of religious beliefs in order to lighten the hardships in individual lives.[44]

EDUCATION THROUGH CUSTOM
AGAINST CUSTOM

The type of education that Cornelia was to work out was something unique, an education, based on house to house visiting and gaining confidence through loving support in relation to expressed needs. For her 600 women and children it often worked. In 1917, she published a booklet, *The Purdahnashin* (literally, the one who sits behind a curtain), developing her views more fully, as well as telling them in a letter to Elena. The cover, used again in another booklet, shows a secluded lady watering the tulsi or sacred basil plant in her garden.[45] A former Vicereine, Lady Minto wrote a foreword, and the current Vicereine, Lady Chelmsford, expressed her appreciation.[46]

Cornelia called the first part of the booklet 'Back to the woman' because she was arguing that the education of women was crucial, since, however much power men wielded outside the home, they did not contradict the women on how children were to be reared in the women's quarters 'inside'. The women should not be confined indoors, like her ward who thought that flowers were picked off the ground like stones,[47] but should have their own gardens. House to house education in the vernacular languages for secluded women should be followed by securely screened meetings in parks where they could actually meet each other, with play arranged for children and advice on rearing them.

At the same time Cornelia went to see Lord Montagu, the Secretary of State for India, who was preparing with the Viceroy, Lord Chelmsford, the Montagu-Chelmsford Report of 1918 on administrative authority for Indians. She now expressed a belief with which Gandhi would later concur in village councils. They, she suggested, could be the site of education in corporate life and responsibility, encouraging a look beyond one's own household. Villages in turn could send representatives to divisional meetings. But Lord Montagu thought the use of village councils too slow a method.[48]

Cornelia was also in close touch with her friend Elena in England and in 1919 Elena established a supportive forum of English women, the Purdahnashin Study Group, to study Cornelia's reports on the needs of purdahnashins.

Cornelia's method of education in households, advocated in *The Purdahnashin*, was to appeal to custom to alter custom, and it has been much illustrated already. Kalidasi in sickness was saved from the application of hot coals by appeal to the alternative power of Ganges water. Chundi, in like case, was saved from noise and smoking butter by appeal to the power of a magician to act at a distance.[49] Cornelia persuaded an orthodox lady that the flies which were fouling her kitchen were breaking her caste, since they touched her food after alighting on the refuse of people of a different caste.[50] She persuaded a village to accept vaccination against the Kali sickness, or smallpox, by urging that although the goddess Kali wanted blood, in this case she would be satisfied with one prick.[51] She argued that an agricultural training was suitable for Brahmins not only because many of them would become owners of agricultural estates, but also because the goddess Sita was found in a furrow.

She wanted to persuade the land-owning families that agricultural training was far more important than the Bachelor of Arts considered appropriate to Brahmins.[52] She thought that the cow ceremony and the rain ceremony could have been exploited to teach children about the care of cows and the alleviation of drought, and she thought that witnesses in court could usefully be made to take a familiar oath by touching 'the five sacred things', or announcing, 'may I be a leper if I lie'.[53]

Cornelia may surely have been right that legislation would not work without a change of attitude. What she did not foresee was that changes of attitude might come not only from her slow and gentle educational method, but on a big scale from startlingly sudden and often uncomfortable changes in society. The nationalists of 1928 were right in the long run that purdah would be swept away. But in 1905–1922, the period of Cornelia's appointment, it would have been difficult for anyone to foresee how that would be possible. Even nowadays, I shall suggest below,[54] Cornelia's gentle method of changing custom through custom would be helpful in the context of gaining acceptance for birth control. When birth control by compulsory sterilisation was tried, it proved entirely counter-productive. If birth control is thought to go against religious requirements, it can only be promoted through a sympathetic understanding of religion, and in a case like that, Cornelia's methods of reform would still, in my view, be the best.

SOCIAL SERVICE MEASURES: PURDAH PARTIES

Cornelia took many further social service measures outside her employment and one was the introduction of purdah events. For one thing, she held regular purdah parties in her own Calcutta house, and this innovation was singled out in the annual report on the work of the Court of Wards in 1906–1907.[55] She persuaded the Vicereine, Lady Minto, to do the same, since the Viceroys did not move from Calcutta to Delhi until 1912. Lady Minto was planning a purdah party as early as 1906, when the Lieutenant Governor's wife, Lady Fraser, also gave one,[56] presumably under Cornelia's influence. Lady Minto gave one in 1909, and the new Governor's wife, Lady Carmichael, in 1911.[57] At a purdah party, women behind the veil could meet each other, with strict seclusion arranged, so that no male could see them arrive or leave between the awnings. In these parties, they were introduced to things they had never seen in their lives, such as lantern slides of the outside world. In 1907, a purdah bazaar was arranged, and a purdah day at Lady Minto's exhibition. By 1919, there were purdah boxes in cinemas.[58]

SCHEMES AND PROPOSALS

Cornelia's furtherance of social work was only partly through the organisations in which she played a prominent part, starting in 1897 soon after her return from student days in England.[59] In addition, she formulated a number of schemes and proposals. In 1906, she drafted an account at Lady Minto's request of what could be done for Indian women,[60] which Lady Minto used in her work in India, and in 1910, Cornelia secured through her a personal letter from the Queen to selected women in seclusion.[61] *The Purdahnashin*, the booklet written in 1917, at the instigation of the Vicereine, Lady Chelmsford, was the best of all her explanations of what needed doing for Indian women, and how it should be done, and an appeal for help. Lady Chelmsford went on to commission a second booklet on child health in 1920.[62]

A NEW METHOD: PURDAHNASHINS TRAINED TO NURSE PURDAHNASHINS

In 1919, Cornelia created a successful scheme for training orthodox Hindu women as nurses, in conditions of purdah, at the Dufferin Hospital in Calcutta. Cornelia's scheme went beyond Lady Dufferin's project of bringing medical help to secluded women. Cornelia, not for the last time,[63] was using secluded women to bring help to secluded women. She thought that the cottages in the grounds of the Dufferin Hospital would provide sufficient seclusion for the trainees, and she already had candidates as early as 1913, but she took leave in England that year and the momentum for agreement was lost. By 1919 she had assembled five candidates for training, but in 1920, the Dufferin Hospital turned away the first candidate, because they wanted use of the cottage. Cornelia, who was on the Dufferin Committee, threatened that the fund set up for the purpose should be moved elsewhere, if they would not carry out the scheme, so they allowed the first candidate, Haridasi, but then tried to dissuade her from the nursing course, so Cornelia raised her threat again. The Dufferin Hospital then offered a two month trial if Cornelia would find three candidates. She found six of whom they took three, and they, as well as Haridasi, were doing very well by the end of the

24. Warren Hastings's house, Calcutta: the secluded haven denied
to Cornelia's Purdahnashins, 1914.

year, with one student proposing to learn English. But Cornelia had all along asked for lectures in the vernacular. That may have been granted by the end of the year, and by 1921, *The Purdahnashin* had an effect, because the Government was adopting its recommendation that doctors should learn a vernacular language.[64]

WARREN HASTINGS'S HOUSE

Not every proposal was equally rewarded with success. Cornelia had three further schemes which from 1912 she tried to install in a house in Calcutta that had once been the country house of Warren Hastings.[65] He had been the first Governor of Bengal in 1772 and Governor General of India in 1773. He had built the house in 1776 and it is still standing, well within the modern city, capacious with a ballroom and extensive grounds. The value for Cornelia's first project was that a secluded approach could easily have been made for women in purdah to an entrance at the side. There they could have met each other and received all sorts of training in complete seclusion. In 1901, the house had been sold to the Secretary of State for India, and in 1906, Curzon as Viceroy used it for Government, but it was now unused. Meanwhile Lady Minto had ceased to be Vicereine and had become Lady-in-Waiting to the Queen, so Cornelia sent her a copy of her proposal and asked if Queen Mary's support could be obtained again.[66] Unfortunately, some British wives, including Cornelia's friend Lady Stephen, had secured a much smaller house for the National India Association, which offered less complete seclusion for women, and consequently Cornelia's bid was turned down in January 1914.[67] Hastings House itself was used rather unimaginatively as a school for well-to-do boys.

When the continuation of the boys' school came into question in 1919, Cornelia campaigned again to have it used for her second scheme, to teach agriculture to the heirs of agricultural estates. Cornelia had had to arrange agricultural training individually at the few places which offered it. Because of its extensive grounds, Hastings House would have been very appropriate for a Government training scheme. However, the school staggered on for a while, and stopped only in 1921, when Cornelia renewed her original hopes for the house's use for women in purdah.[68]

When this second scheme failed, there was an almost final vacancy in 1927, and by that time Cornelia was running a third scheme in which her more progressive secluded women were helping her with many different kinds of social service for others.[69] She wrote to the wife of the Governor, Lady Jackson, about using Hastings House for her new League of Social Service for Women. This too was imaginative, and the house was being used only for flats for officials,[70] but there was a rival bid for teacher training, and her campaign lasted until 1930, when she was again turned down.[71] Finally, in her last year in India in 1937, the building was shut up and unused,[72] although it was again a teacher training college when I visited in 2006. Cornelia's failure to secure Hastings House was deeply frustrating to her, but it was the exception rather than the rule.

ASSESSMENT

I have described from Chapter 8 onwards the friendships that grew up between Cornelia and many of her 600 wards, the longing for her visits, the special links with the children of the second generation and the directions in which she tried to educate them. At the level of the individual wards, Cornelia transformed their welfare and made provisions for their future, and, when she could, for that of their tenants or subjects. In the present chapter I have described her learning about her wards' attitudes, her educational methods and her social work.

Cornelia's knowledge of the customs, beliefs and attitudes prevailing in her isolated households was unique, because no other educated person had the opportunity of getting to know so many households. Also unique were her views about how to reform these practices and her techniques for doing so. In her social work she had influence at Government level, establishing the institution of purdah parties in the households of Lieutenant Governor and Viceroy. From the beginning she was included in organisations that offered help, and she went on to create new organisations. Her proposals, some in booklet form, were put to use by two Vicereines and her recommendations on training became official Government policy.

We shall see[73] that it was the needs of her former wards that brought her back to India from retirement in 1924 in the new role of woman barrister. And we shall see that her expertise in social work was immediately recognised at Government level, more readily than her expertise in law. So her retirement in 1922 was by no means the end of her social practice. But the political context was changing in the 1920s and, partly through her own misjudgement, the new politics was first to impede and then to wreck her most innovative social experiment of all, The Bengal League of Social Service for Women.[74] But all this lay in the future. I must first describe the other side of her liaison work in 1904–1922 between the purdahnashins and the British Administration: her relations with British officers.

PART IV

FRIENDS AND FOES: THE COST OF OVERRIDING BRITISH OFFICERS AND RETIREMENT TO ENGLAND

CHAPTER 13

TWO SELF-CONFESSED TERRORISTS REWARDED, 1908 AND 1914

There were two sides to Cornelia's career in the Court of Wards. The one so far discussed related to the wards themselves. The other related to the British officers who ran the Civil Service, and to these I shall turn in the next three chapters. In 1913–1914, half way through Cornelia's career, mutual objections were raised by Cornelia and a small number of British officers. The failings she alleged suggest weaknesses, rather than Machiavellian strength, and cast rather a different light on the Raj. She stood up to these officers and she defended her wards against them, but in some of the quarrels, she was not entirely blameless. In Chapter 16, I shall describe what was happening to the family in these years from 1913 up to 1922.

A BENGALI WOMAN BOMB MAKER

Cornelia was involved in two very strange cases of terrorism against the British. The word 'terrorism' has been much misused, but I use it here because the context of each case was a British charge of terrorism, or rather 'anarchism', as it was then called. Both cases required extensive work with British officers. The second led directly to one of the quarrels of 1914. In the first incident, however, Cornelia was still at the height of her popularity with the Bengal Government. In 1908, she was asked to accommodate a terrorist in her flat. There had been an attempt in Bengal to celebrate the 50th anniversary of the Indian Uprising of 1857 with terrorist activity. A Bengali woman revolutionary, aged about 30, had interrupted a terrorist trial in 1908, saying that she was the guilty one and should replace the political leader who was under trial.

When she was dismissed, she threatened to commit suicide in a police station, and when prevented, would not answer any questions. The Commissioner of Police asked Cornelia to assess her. Cornelia noticed that although she claimed to be a secluded orthodox Hindu, her nails had been painted with henna in the Muslim style. When Cornelia looked, she hid her hands. It later turned out that she had adopted the Muslim style in an unsuccessful attempt to get into a wealthy Muslim household, to raise funds for terrorism. Cornelia decided to exploit the deception, whatever it was, and place her in an exaggerated version of Hindu seclusion. So she offered the woman the entire lower floor where she was living, which happened to be empty. The kitchen had just been washed with lime, so the lady's food could not be contaminated, and she would have an orthodox Hindu of the highest caste to cook her meals. She accepted the offer, in the hope that she would get to know Cornelia's wealthy clients and raise funds, after which, as Cornelia tells it, she would blow Cornelia up. She was brought to the house in a screened carriage, and Cornelia kept her in exaggeratedly strict seclusion, never inviting her to join in her own eating or friendships or life, which would have broken the caste of a secluded orthodox Hindu woman, and speaking to her only in Bengali, since seclusion would have kept her from learning English. In frustration, the lady borrowed Cornelia's English-language newspaper, *The Statesman*, one day, and after that the one concession allowed was a daily English-language newspaper. Cornelia was sure that she was a progressive Brahmo, and that she had never practised the ways of seclusion. Indeed, it was reported that in her frustration she would look out of the window and stamp her feet.

The pretence became too much for her on the day that Cornelia gave a party at her house for genuinely secluded orthodox women, with tenting in place, so that nobody should see them on arrival or departure. The revolutionary was not invited, so was missing any chance of lucrative contacts with these wealthy women. When the party was over, she sent a message to say that Cornelia must see her at once, so that she could say who she really was. Cornelia offered to listen only on the condition that every word would be written down, the lady would sign the transcript, and it would be sent to the Commissioner of Police, conditions which she accepted.

Her story was that she had been making bombs, but the picric acid burnt her fingers, so she was taken off that work and sent to women's quarters all over India to raise sympathy and money for the cause. She was an important person who was due to go to Afghanistan to raise reinforcements for a new uprising. She showed her importance by naming the inner council members, and by telling where Japanese guns, acquired in sections, had been buried for future use. But she had lost the list of supporters and her confederates had accused her of selling it to the police. To prove her loyalty, she had sought her own death, but she could not stand being smothered with kindness and secluded by Cornelia, when every day she had seen English people she would like to assassinate come to the house. The last straw was being kept away from the real purdah party, which lost her the chance of restoring her reputation by raising funds. She now believed that by telling the whole story, she would make her confederates proud of her again.

When the Police Commissioner received her full story, the British reacted with some canniness. They gave her a carriage and some money and told her she was free to go wherever she liked. She had already given away her confederates' secrets. Being helped by the British ensured even further that she would never be accepted by the revolutionaries again, although for good measure her movements were checked every day thereafter. Cornelia heard of her only once again, when she applied to work as a governess for households under the Court of Wards.[1]

A WARD ACCUSED: NOGEN

In the second case in 1914, Cornelia defended one of her wards from a charge of terrorism, and this was the case that led to one of her quarrels. On November 29th 1914, she went to see her ward in hospital under police custody, charged with throwing a bomb at a policeman's house and carrying a revolver. He had been injured in the bomb blast and would not give his name. Cornelia knew him as Nogen, short for Nogendra Nath Sen Gupta. He told her that he had taken a wrong turn and been blown unconscious when the bomb went off, and that he had never handled a revolver. His other great supporter besides Cornelia was Mr Holmes of the Oxford Mission to Calcutta, and he established that Nogen had been playing tennis at some point that same day. Many people were sure of his guilt and they started flocking to see Cornelia and demanding to see her files. P. C. Lyon, who had been a friend since before 1906, when he entertained Cornelia in a beautiful setting at Shillong,[i] was among the first to be convinced of Nogen's guilt, and treated Cornelia's

---

i A photograph of the Lyons' Indian house is in Cornelia's visiting book of the period, 1901–1904, Richard Sorabji collection.

defence of Nogen accordingly. But Cornelia countered the first accusation. She conceded that at the age of 11 Nogen had been subjected to propaganda while at a school run by the National School Movement, a group seen as seditious. But he had told Cornelia at the time what they were teaching him and she had had him moved to another school. She had his records since 1908 and there was nothing against him.

He was moved to Alipore jail in December and asked to see her again in January. In detention, he looked splendid, carefree and frank and seemed a favourite with everyone. His win would be the greater in that S. P. (later Lord) Sinha was to be the prosecutor. The same day Cornelia spent 18 minutes with the Governor of Bengal, gaining sympathy for Nogen's case. At a conference in her office, Mr R. M. Chatterjee and Mr Langford-James were invited to undertake the defence. An advantage of the choice was that neither had a history of defending terrorists.[2] Terrorism was to be against Gandhi's beliefs, when he came on the scene, but it already attracted a following.

At the end of January, Nogen's brother did not want to help their defence lawyer, and his mother tried to cancel the lawyer's appointment, but the lawyer was employed by the Court of Wards, not by her. Cornelia visited Nogen again and was impressed that he had refused attempts to secure a confession, and the next day she again visited the Governor of Bengal to request sufficient money for the defence. The Governor asked her to write up Nogen's case and the plea for money, and took her view that all the money wanted should be allowed, and that Nogen should not be in a worse position for being their ward than if he had had an ordinary guardian or father.[3]

She drafted the case at the beginning of February. Mr Stevenson-Moore, 'Member' of the Board of Revenue of Bengal, wanted a limit on the defence fund, but Cornelia went into the figures with him and two days later was pleased that the Government was allowing legal costs at the daily rate. Although she had been excluded from the initial inquiry, she was now allowed to read the evidence against Nogen, which had been supplied to him and passed by him on to the defence, and she considered it absurd to think he would be convicted on that basis. Later in the month, she read the case prepared for him and went to see him in jail the next day.[4]

She saw him again the day before the trial and noted, 'Demeanour excellent–neither defiant, nor cowed'. The prosecutor's opening on 8 March was 'not very grand', and the next day she recorded, 'Chief prosecutor's witness entirely breaks down – a great crowd in court and the atmosphere deadly'. The prosecution case continued for 11 days, but an expert on bombs was helpful about the distance from which the bomb was thrown and a prosecution witness retracted all he had said before and admitted picking up the pistol or revolver and carrying it away some distance. Cornelia considered that Langford-James spoke very well during his two days of defence. On March 22nd, Nogen was acquitted by all three judges, who delivered three separate judgements to emphasise his innocence. Two of them said that the prosecution was vindictive.[5]

Later Cornelia recorded Nogen's claim that the head of the police had said in his hearing in hospital, 'You must make him live. We have got to hang him,' and that another policeman had said in his hearing, 'You can't promise pardon if he tells on his confederates. Fred is determined to hang him.'[6]

Cornelia thought it important that Nogen should go abroad with a scholarship, partly for his own sake and also in case 'anarchists' should make use of him. She formed a plan with Mr Holmes, which she then put to the Governor's private secretary, Mr Gourlay, and to Mr Stevenson-Moore. She felt there was no time to lose with days slipping by after the acquittal and asked for an interview with the Governor, Lord Carmichael. Mr Lyon was very antagonistic to Nogen, although his wife did everything to keep relations with Cornelia pleasant. Lyon now came to oppose her idea of any posting abroad. Further, the Chief Justice warned Cornelia that the prosecutor was still saying that Nogen's guilt was convincing, and when Cornelia saw the Governor on April 4th, he said that the suspicions were his chief difficulty in arranging the scholarship she had proposed. Two days later, he asked Cornelia to prove that his own rules allowed him to override his Board, which she did, and on April 7th, Gourlay took her to see the Governor again, for a final decision. Mr Lyon proposed sending Nogen close by to Agra, but Mr Monahan, the Honorary Member of the Board of Revenue who was present, backed Cornelia's plan. She and Mr Holmes heard at 7 p.m. that night that they had won, that the Government would advance 2500 rupees and that, despite the difficulties of wartime shipping in the First World War, Nogen would sail for England with Mr Holmes on April 12th aboard the City of Cairo from Bombay.[7]

In the two days remaining, Cornelia had to estimate costs for Nogen's time in England, check them with Mr Stevenson-Moore, get his agreement to find Nogen a job when qualified, take Nogen shopping to buy clothes, settle about applying to Aberystwyth to study agriculture, get him a passage and passport, check all this with other members of the Board and see him off on the train.[8]

But already a bigger storm was being raised by Nogen's opponents who believed him guilty. A Commission of Inquiry was set up with Mr Monahan,

Mr Duval, whose wife was an opponent of Cornelia on another matter,[9] and Mr B. L. Gupta, brother-in-law of one of Nogen's unsuccessful prosecutors, a choice criticised by others as not impartial.[10] Cornelia was particularly outraged that the Chairman was her one time intimate Mr Gourlay, since he knew neither law nor Bengali. Of course, the Commission could not examine the acquittal. Instead it examined the police handling of the case. A dossier was compiled by a police officer which started with Cornelia's commandeered records of Nogen as a ward, and continued with leaflets distributed in 1909 while he was a ward. The commission interrogated her on these records and demanded to see her letters to Nogen's mother and the replies in translation. She was never allowed to see the police dossier, despite the Governor's request that it be shown. Nor was she told the Commission's terms of reference, although the terms came to be published in the newspapers anyhow and the Governor also sent them to her. She wrote to the defence barrister, Langford-James, and asked whether the prosecutor had not conceded that there was nothing against Nogen throughout the time of his wardship and Langford-James asked permission to forward her letter to the Governor. On the other side the police planned to retire in a body, if the commission report went against them, saying that they had followed advice from the prosecutor, Sinha, every step of the way. After the report was written up, orders for Nogen to be paid were reversed, but Cornelia was never allowed to see the report.[11]

In May, the Governor asked Cornelia to help, saying that only she was brave enough to tell him things or to stand by what she said. So she sent him a note on the Inquiry and he wired back asking if he could use it, to which she agreed. Even at the time, she thought she was being thrown to the dogs, but did not mind, so long as it helped. Things did indeed go wrong. She found the next interview with the Governor too painful to record in her work diary, although it included discussion of his asking for her note, but she says to Elena and in her personal diary that she was put on the defensive by him, asking her if she had done this and that, as if it were 'a school girl's quarrel', and that he accused her of making mischief among officials. In fact, before the painful interview, other things had been happening. Mr Monahan asked for an explanation of her note being sent to the Governor and by replying openly she may have implicated the Governor. Further, Langford-James came and pumped her for all she had to tell, and reported that the Governor had said that she had only herself to blame for the Inquiry being set up. She nonetheless sent a further note about the case to the Governor's private secretary, and this was followed by the Governor sending her a letter of undisclosed content that she found 'astounding'.[12]

Cornelia's defence of Nogen had made her unpopular, but at least he was now safely in England and he made a tremendous success of his studies. In July 1916, he got first class marks in Physics and Chemistry at Aberystwyth, was the top student in Zoology[13] and won the Earl Grey Fellowship to continue.[14] In 1919, the Government of India was willing to pay for a postgraduate year, if needed, but he won first class honours at Aberystwyth and got a fellowship of his own, beating even some postgraduate applicants,[15] and went on to study agricultural chemistry.[16] In December that year, Cornelia was in England taking a health treatment in Bath, and he came to see her most devotedly, and showed her his writing.[17]

Nogen was now not only cleared by three judges, but exceptionally qualified in a subject that India needed. But the British authorities in India started acting with strange indecision. From 1919, they oscillated on whether to refuse payment for his return to India or whether to insist on return and whether to deny him a government job when he got there. In 1920, the India Office in London advised his return, but only because the funds set aside were running out and meanwhile they turned down a grant application from him. Cornelia objected that this could leave him with no funds except from extremist movements. She had a meeting with Tata to ask for a job for him in the private sector. Next, she found that for a long time he had been denied money from his own estate, which was under the Court of Wards, because it was a shared estate and they were using his share to pay off the debts of his sharer. Cornelia pointed out that he could ask to see the accounts and she got the shares separated, after which the District Collector was able to say that £50 was available. The Government of India instructed the Government of Bengal that Cornelia should be urged to tell him to return, but she had instead offered to support him in England until he was given a job. The £50 was next refused to Nogen if used for anything other than his passage back, but Cornelia said that he could use her own £50 for a passage. Finally, the Commissioner advanced him £40, but the Government of India reverted to saying that he could not have government work.[18]

The next person to act unpredictably was Nogen himself. Over the next three years, though from a very orthodox family, he first was baptised as a Christian in England, and then, on return to India was confirmed as a Christian by Father Douglas at Behala in Calcutta, although Cornelia was not invited. He then got engaged and married to a Christian girl, a Presbyterian, in 1924. Cornelia had met her and, unaware of the strain she might be under, found her artificial. Moreover, Nogen shed his usual frankness and stopped sharing his joys with Cornelia. Instead, he started writing cagily to Cornelia, with no description of the wedding. He said that he was giving up his past, and finally sent her a self-defensive letter.[19]

The truth emerged suddenly for Cornelia in December 1925. Nogen had confessed to the Viceroy, Lord Reading, that he *had* thrown the bomb, and it was agreed that he would make a negotiated public statement. Moreover, he was rewarded within a week by the Governor of Bengal, Lord Lytton, with a job such as he had been denied since 1919, so keen were the British to avoid his becoming a rallying point in the anti-British cause. The promised (and delayed) statement was part of the deal, but it was entirely unlike the letter he had written to Cornelia, in which he stressed all the occasions on which he had sided with the British. The statement, on the contrary, sided against the British, except that he now eschewed terrorism, which was evidently what he had meant by 'giving up the past'. He was in a contradictory relationship with Cornelia, who had fearlessly opposed the British authorities on his behalf for 11 years, and made herself thoroughly unpopular. It turned out that Lord Lytton had told Father Douglas that Nogen ought to confess to him as priest before being confirmed in the Christian faith in 1922. The Viceroy already knew about him before Nogen's later confession to him, because an accomplice in China had confessed and implicated Nogen, although Nogen's statement said that he acted alone.[20]

This was not the end of the story. When he reluctantly agreed to come and see Cornelia, she found him haughty and dishonest,[21] and seven years later she heard him described as a fierce nationalist.[22] His wife would have nothing to do with Cornelia. But there were several further twists of fortune. In 1933, she was visiting political detainees and prisoners in Midnapur jail and talking to them. The women had shot at or shot dead various British officials. They were defiant when she arrived, but with a kind word about what good they might still do for India, were crying when she left. One meeting was with the police-man who had wanted Nogen convicted, and his hostility to her ended when he discovered that she had really believed Nogen. But even more surprisingly, Cornelia was confronted by the men detainees, but was safe because one of them, Lahiri, recognised her as the one who saved Nogen from the hangman. 'You are Nogen's guardian,' he said. 'He was my class fellow. He often spoke of you, and he owed his life to you, we all heard.' She told the man that Nogen had deceived her, and said how hard it was to find the truth. The old Indian prison commandant said to her, 'You do not know how you have helped me today. Give me your blessing before you go, that we might carry through with this to the end.' Briefly she was acceptable to both sides instead of to neither.

Finally, at Christmas 1940, when Cornelia's life was in daily danger from German bombing in the middle of London, Nogen broke his silence. He was then a Deputy Director of Scientific and Industrial Research, and he showed his concern by writing to her about his gratitude.[23]

The British of the time had thus rewarded two self-proclaimed terrorists, in the case both of Nogen and of the Bengali, with the pragmatic aim of reducing their influence, rather than engaging in the rhetoric of victory over them.

Cornelia's misjudgement about Nogen was not necessarily her fault. All three judges were on her side, and it is known that 'terrorism' in a situation seen as unjust can attract the most educated and accomplished, and therefore the most unexpected, young people. But she was left in a very awkward position. She had gone out on a limb in defence of Nogen and had made herself unpopular in some quarters. But Nogen had shown her to be entirely wrong.

We will now turn to the strange contrast between the British acclaim for Cornelia in the first half of her service and the sudden cooling off around the time of the Nogen episode. It will turn out that there were other episodes in mid-career which led to a series of quarrels.

CHAPTER 14

FROM GLOWING REPORTS TO QUARRELS BEHIND THE CURTAIN OF THE BRITISH RAJ, 1913–1917

C ornelia's clients were hidden behind a veil, or rather a curtain, but so also were internal battles within the British Raj. The Indian Civil Service was an élite. Entry to it was by some of the most difficult examinations that England could devise. It led quickly to responsibility for huge tracts of India and often culminated in a knighthood. Such was the prestige of the service that its members were credited in Britain with the highest standards of conduct. A hundred years later the wrongs of colonialism and of its entire structure are so well known that there is a danger of sweeping all members into the opposite broad category of colonialists. But if we ask a different question, whether they lived up to their own standards, much more interesting differences begin to appear. By 1913, the civil service élite had for nine years shown admirable open-mindedness in supporting the thoroughly unconventional appointment of one single Indian woman adviser. But neither Cornelia nor the Civil Service was perfect. Around the middle of her career, quarrels began to arise. Cornelia entirely accepted that one did not tell the public about these, and so they are not to be found clearly enunciated in her public writings. They have to be ferreted out from her diaries and letters to confidants. But these reveal the agony that she began to suffer from 1914, and they show a side of the Indian Civil Service which is not normally open to view.

ANNUAL REPORTS ON CORNELIA

From 1904–1905 until 1912–1913, the situation had been entirely different. Cornelia had received glowing mention in the annual reports on the Court of Wards published by her employers, the Board of Revenue in the Government of Bengal.[1] These were quite different from the annual reports which Cornelia herself wrote and presented to the Court of Wards, and of which only three years survive. The Board's own annual reports were on the Court of Wards in general and were not obliged to single out, as they did, a report on Cornelia's achievements. For some years, after Curzon had split the province, she received equally enthusiastic praise in a second lot of annual reports from the adjacent Board of Revenue in the Government of Assam and Eastern Bengal.[2] The praise was repeated and endorsed at the end of the report by the Lieutenant Governor of the Province first in Assam and then in Bengal in 1909–1910. The secretary to the Bengal Government who drafted the endorsement was then her beloved Gourlay,[3] and Gourlay was thus able in a small way to repay her friendship.

Some reports explicitly praised her *legal*, and some her *financial,* work. Her tact and judgement are often mentioned in resolving quarrels, and thereby saving the estates huge fees in litigation. She was seen as a sympathetic two-way conduit for representing to the wards the wishes of the Court when they might seem unpalatable and for representing to the Court legitimate grievances of the wards. By 1906, they wanted her not only to resolve quarrels that had already arisen, but also to forestall quarrels by visiting all wards over this huge segment of India and gaining their confidence in advance. In this connexion, it was important that she was 'signally successful' in helping with the health, education, physical comfort and companionship of the wards, although this was only one of many factors mentioned. It was noticed that the wards freely sought her advice. Her indefatigable energy is commented on. By 1908–1909, they wanted to give her a definite place in the chain of officers, and to get all Managers and Collectors to cooperate with her, so that the Court could obtain the full benefit of her visits. Further, proposals were under consideration to get her services full time, and to 'provide her with an *assistant* to be trained by her and *eventually to carry on the work* which she ha[d] so ably begun'. The next year, the Secretary of State had made her post permanent and pensionable. Meanwhile, there had been another glowing citation, because in 1909, at the age of 42, she had been awarded the gold first class medal of the Kaiser-i-Hind. The award was to be repeated on her retirement in 1922, in the form of a bar to the medal, on the recommendation of the Secretary of State for India, her friend, Lord Montagu.[4] This citation and some specimen annual reports are included in Appendix 2.

This acclaim needs to be emphasised because of the curious contrast with what started happening from 1913. The reports suddenly confine themselves, with a revealing exception to be mentioned, to what had previously been only one item: her contribution to the health, education, physical comfort and companionship of the wards. We shall see that a change in her title from 'Legal Adviser' to 'Lady Adviser', originally intended to reflect the breadth of her services, was now fiercely insisted on, in order to conceal her legal role altogether. We shall further see that the story was put about that she was just doing charitable work, so that it was questionable why a paid and pensionable post should be needed. Yet it was not Cornelia's role that had changed, as can be seen from her diaries, her letters and her own surviving annual reports. In these reports she continues to praise and thank Collectors and Commissioners for being almost invariably helpful on the ground. The change was in the Board's reports. What had happened?

A TERROR SUSPECT DEFENDED AND FOUR OTHER BATTLES

The trouble was that Cornelia had begun trying to override senior members of the Indian Civil Service and their wives. The battle over the terror suspect, Nogen, has been described already.[5] Earlier that year, there was a battle over financial accounts and another over Cornelia's alleged political activity. Before that, in 1911, a battle began over the treatment of an insane ward, the Maharani of Bettiah, and another started in 1913 with the wives of British officials. From 1914 several battles were going on simultaneously and fed on each other, often involving the same individuals. Cornelia wrote to Elena in a much later context that she was telling her things on the principle of the ancient Greek story about the tyrant Midas. 'I use you as my reeds and bulrushes,' she wrote.[6] Midas was punished by the god Apollo by being given ass's ears. Only his barber knew the secret, and longing to tell someone, whispered the secret down a hole. But reeds sprang up in the hole, and, when blown by the wind, whispered, 'Midas has ass's ears.' Cornelia wanted no such repetition. She merely felt that it relieved her, like the barber, to be able to tell someone, and she saw that as one of the values of friendship. Her first whisperings were to Valentine

Chirol,[7] her later ones to Elena Richmond (née Rathbone), and she always whispered to her diaries.

THE CORRECTION OF NEGLECTED FINANCIAL IRREGULARITIES

Among the British, she thought that some of the objections to her had been started by Beatson-Bell, then Divisional Commissioner of Dacca in East Bengal.[8] He opposed Cornelia in 1914 both in connexion with Nogen and in connexion with Cornelia's alleged political activity. But Cornelia thought that his opposition stemmed from a dispute over a third matter that year, a case of financial irregularity. Beatson-Bell was at the time substituting for her old friend P. C. Lyon on the Executive Council of the Governor of Bengal. From 1914–1918, he became a member of the Council. He was angry with Cornelia for making him supply accounts to two of her wards, Khodija Begum, widow of the Nawab of Dacca whose husband had died in 1901, and her step-daughter Peri Banu.[9] The accounts showed that under his supervision their estate manager had lost the estate 400,000 rupees by ignoring legal requirements. Cornelia had received a 'wigging' (informal reprimand) for her investigation.[10] She commented at the time how important it was to know the law.[11] But it was her legal knowledge, as will be seen in the next chapter, that embarrassed officials sought to challenge as an unwanted irrelevance.

Cornelia commented also that her opponents in the Civil Service objected to the lavish life style of the wards to whom she got the accounts shown. Certainly, the two ladies celebrated Cornelia's success in 1920 over their financial accounts by giving her a flight in a Handley Page aeroplane that was fully screened or 'purdahed', and bringing her back to tea.[12] Peri Banu was the most progressive of Cornelia's secluded friends, and in Cornelia's second career, some years later, Peri Banu was to repay her more fully by taking the lead in Cornelia's new social experiments.[13]

There is striking confirmation of Cornelia's suspicion about the hostility to her in the report of 1919–1920 by the Bengal Board of Revenue on the Court of Wards. The Secretary to that board regarded Cornelia's investigation of the finances of the estate already mentioned, the family estate of the Nawab of Dacca, as being (apart from the rehabilitation of Nogen) 'the most important feature' of her work. He also approved Cornelia's looking into the competence of the estate's *managers* and revealed that management had been *ordered* to align itself with proper practice elsewhere. This was presumably felt as a slap in the face by Beatson-Bell. The report, with my italics, reads as follows:

> 'Miss Cornelia Sorabji, Lady Advisor to the Court of Wards, has, as usual, been indefatigable in the discharge of the strenuous duties which her office involves. Apart from subjects referred to in this report' (which included the educational success of the accused terrorist, Nogen), 'the *most important feature* has been a thorough examination of the system of *administration in the Nawab of Dacca's family estate. . . . Orders* have been issued *bringing the estate into line with the general system of management in force.* A question of *considerable importance* has been raised regarding the *capacity and qualifications of the existing type of managers*: the question will receive full consideration of the Board'.

This report had to be commented on in a resolution by the 'Governor in Council', which, as we shall see, did not have to mean Cornelia's friend, the Governor, but could mean any relevant members of the Governor's Council. Beatson-Bell had been on the Council from 1914 up to March 1918.[14] He could very well have left behind, not with the Governor, but with other members of Council, his own impressions of Cornelia. At any rate, the feature called '*most important*' in Cornelia's work is conspicuous by its absence from the resolution of the 'Governor in Council'. All that is mentioned is Cornelia's education of female wards, along with the educational success of Nogen, whose connexion with Cornelia is not, however, mentioned in the original report or in the resolution on it.

BATTLE ABOUT A MAHARANI'S HEALTH

The next quarrel revolved around the Maharani of Bettiah, or Bettiah as Cornelia called her for short. Bettiah's story was extremely sad.[15] For a long time, she told Cornelia, she could not get married because her horoscope said that any husband would die within a month of marriage. The parents' chance of avoiding hell by getting her married in time had long since passed. But eventually a certain Maharaja needed a third wife, because the first two were old and childless. So her parents' priest had her horoscope faked and the marriage took place. Her husband died within one month of the marriage through accidentally falling between the royal saloon carriage on his train and the station platform. She remembered seeing him only once briefly, when he sat on her bed and she at his feet and she talked to him from 1 till 4 a.m., after he returned from the theatre.[16]

The other two wives died very soon and she then owned a very large and fertile property with no heir. She herself was subject to violent rages, and the property was managed by the Court of Wards. In the absence of an heir, all the neighbouring estate-owners with a similar pedigree were trying to gain succession to the property. The Maharaja of Benares was among the claimants, as he was also for the estate of Narhan, and it was for this reason that Cornelia was invited to Benares to inspect the legal document contained within the sixth of six caskets, as described earlier.[17]

Cornelia met Bettiah as a ward in 1905[18] and went on to persuade her to take a house in Calcutta, so that they could see each other more often. She took a place opposite the Tollygunge Club and insisted on Cornelia's presence frequently. She would not even take pills unless Cornelia swallowed some first.[19] During this period, Bettiah founded schools and hospitals in her territory.[20]

In 1911, Bettiah succumbed to a violent type of madness. Her servants thought that her priest had poisoned her with dhatura, but Cornelia believed that, whatever the other causes, the loss of any love in her life must have contributed. After a week or so, a Commission in Lunacy had to be held in Bettiah's house with a High Court Judge to assess her condition. The first time Cornelia knew of things was on return from one of her tours.[21] English nurses were in charge, which was against the rules for orthodox Hindus without their permission, and she was being force-fed by four of them who held her down. Her nose was bleeding, but the ring had not been taken out. Her mouth was swollen, she screamed and raved and tried to strike Cornelia. Her purdah was being broken by the doctor, who was not screened from her, and by the English women holding her down. She was quite right, Cornelia insisted, that water had to be rejected as defiled, so long as it had to be brought past a sweeper and his broom on the stairs, although one of the nurses was complaining that the place was filthy. She could not eat without having bathed, and she could not bathe while the nurses remained in the house, although Cornelia persuaded her to change her clothes. They dragged her along the floor in trying to feed her, but after Cornelia saw that, she was forbidden to witness the feeding again. Still, she knew that they gagged her in the course of it, tied her hands and gave her a drug, hyacide, which made her even less sensible. The Maharani thought that they were trying to kill her. The District Collector had ordered soldiers from the fort to do the force-feeding instead of nurses. But Cornelia got the priest and private secretary to say what religion would allow. Under pressure, policemen were proposed instead of soldiers, and Cornelia arranged that they should be allowed to pitch a tent in the grounds, as it would offend the household to have them under the roof, and she requested that they should not wear uniform, as policemen were one of the lady's aversions. Her father was brought to see her, and it was arranged that he would take her to Allahabad.

All this caused a battle with the authorities, although the father took Cornelia's side. Cornelia felt that Dr Lester, the doctor, replied to her interventions as if she were an enemy, and the Honorary Member of the Bihar Board of Revenue took the doctor's side. He asked Cornelia what good she was doing by visiting and told her that she would not be needed now. But the father begged her to accompany the Maharani and put her in the car for the journey to Allahabad, as she had never been in one before. This was not allowed and on the day of travel, since nobody had explained, Bettiah thought she was being taken to prison.

For some years, Cornelia was able to see her regularly in Allahabad, when visiting her brother Dick. But the doctor appointed for her, Col. MacLaren, had Cornelia's soothing visits stopped,[22] although he allowed distressing visits from emissaries of the royal Benares claimant to continue.[23] Cornelia's letters to Bettiah were being opened. Cornelia complained that the doctor himself stopped visiting the Maharani, because she could not stand him, especially as he used to walk in while she was bathing, a practice he defended as stimulating her. Her house had no electric lights or fans, and when her father died, she finished up being denied all company.[24] Cornelia pressed the Court of Wards to provide a woman companion, a daily female nurse, or a visit from a female doctor as an independent observer. When that was refused, she eventually forced them in 1917 to let the Maharani see a specialist, Dr Peebles. Cornelia was then told a lie, that the specialist also opposed her visits. But in fact the specialist had never been told about Cornelia or about her knowledge of the Maharani since 1905.

Cornelia got one more visit allowed by sheer insistence in 1917, and she was allowed to visit again in 1919 under a new Honorary Member of the Board. But in 1921, she was told by Bihar that she could not visit because a new treatment was starting. When she demanded to know what the new treatment was, it turned out to be simply the absence of Cornelia. For these decisions she blamed Morshead, Divisional Commissioner from 1914, and 'Member' of the Board of Revenue from 1919. That would have put him in a position to override Cornelia, if persuaded by the doctors. Their deception was a sign of the trouble they knew the now formidable Cornelia would cause. She never learnt the end of the story, but, with the Maharani still alive in 1944, the Bettiah estate still then remained in the Court of Wards and Cornelia was corresponding with the Vicereine about using the property for her project of providing wards with agricultural training.[25]

REPRIMAND ON POLITICAL ACTIVITY

The two battles about Nogen and Bettiah were each about an individual ward, but two others were about policy. When Cornelia was returning from her brief trip to England in 1914, just as war was breaking out, a bombshell was awaiting her in the mail at the port of Aden.[26] It was from the Governor in Council, in other words apparently from her supporter, Lord Carmichael, although it turned out that the charge had actually been made by her enemy, Beatson-Bell.[27] It complained that she had violated her rules of employment (which had not been shown her) by writing a political article in *The Nineteenth Century* for July 1914. The article was said to describe all Bengalis as 'windbags' and to have caused ill feeling in the vernacular press.[28] In fact, there was little to complain about in the article. It was a humorous Kiplingesque piece in a literary journal, portraying her idiosyncratic Sadhu friend, Bawaji. The Sadhu was caricaturing not Bengalis in general, but a hot headed Bengali student, who did nothing himself (hence 'windbag'), but rejoiced that the revolutionary assassin of two English women had not yet been punished. But Cornelia was also affectionately caricaturing the Sadhu, in a way that she never used on her women Sadhuin friends. She portrayed him as nostalgic for the mispronounced 'John Nickensen' (Nicholson) as someone who ruthlessly put down the Indian Uprising of 1857, and as recommending such alternatives as using priestly curses on revolutionaries, or making them curse themselves if they lied. There was no suggestion that the guru's views were Cornelia's. The article was clearly entitled, 'A Hindu guru's views of the political situation in India', and the only idea to which she elsewhere ascribed any merit was the last one of substituting self-cursing for oaths to promote veracity in Court.[29] This fitted with her belief in using local custom, not alien custom, to produce improvements. For the rest, she was revealing not her own views, but the support of at least one Hindu for British rule and his contempt for support of terrorism. But Bawaji's real name was Sat-Nam-Singh, which Cornelia had translated literally as 'truthnamed Singh'. From this translation her accuser had inferred that she was endorsing the truth of what he said.

Cornelia cried out to her friend Valentine Chirol:[30]

'To ignore the fact that for ten years I have lived absolutely at peace with every
community in these provinces; and that my published writings – so far from
sneering at Bengalis – show a real admiration and love for them: and that I have
given all my spare time to making English folk appreciate and like them – to
ignore all this and put – what is put on record against me in this letter: this
seems to me most unjust and unfair. . . . All the heart is taken out of one and oh!
one is so terribly alone and friendless'.

She learnt from her eventual interview with the Governor of Bengal that
Beatson-Bell had added much more, that Cornelia was very unpopular among
her wards and among Bengalis generally and was causing great trouble to
Government, and that officers all over the districts were saying this. When she
questioned the Governor, she was told that the Bengalis referred to were not
her wards at all, but belonged to the socially progressive Brahmo community,
which often despised her wards.[31]

The official complaint also mentioned a letter which Cornelia had written to *The Times* in which she had replied to a prominent English supporter of
India, Dr Annie Besant. Besant had complained in *The Times* of unfair treatment
of Indians, and Cornelia saw Besant, not herself, as making trouble for the
Government.[32] Cornelia did not admit that her reply in *The Times* was highly
political, but it was, and it will feature again in Cornelia's story.[33] But the tale
told to the Governor that her letter incited enmity between different races in
India must have come from an enemy.

Cornelia was instructed to travel, on arrival back in India, to Darjeeling,
where the Government of Bengal had repaired for the hot season, and she
waited very close to the residence of the Governor, Lord Carmichael, to be
summoned to hear his displeasure. But the shutters came down on communication with the Governor and other administrators, and she could not even
hear the charge against her. During her wait, she was asked if she had seen the
rules of her employment. These turned out to have remained with a clerk since
1910, and the covering letter, not in her possession, took still longer to find.
But when she saw the rules, she believed they allowed her to write while on
unpaid leave, provided that she did not use the Government's address.

The Governor's private secretary, her once beloved Gourlay, refused to
see Cornelia during her wait. But her brother Dick came and arranged through
Gourlay to see the Governor himself. After that, Cornelia was summoned to
see him too. It turned out that the Governor did not know she had been written to and had not investigated the matter. The expression 'The Governor in
Council' meant that the Governor's Council had heard Beatson-Bell's report

and agreed to an investigation, not that the Governor himself had made any decision. It was at this interview that Cornelia learnt of Beatson-Bell's role. The continuing delay was due to the fact that Cornelia's friend, P. C. Lyon, had taken back the case from his deputy, Beatson-Bell, but did not want it discussed until he got back from Simla to Darjeeling, where Cornelia was waiting.

Any relief Cornelia might have felt was soon dashed. When Lyon eventually arrived, he gave Cornelia an interview which she found shattering and returned the next day to extract more information. She asked Lyon to say which Bengalis had taken offence and to let her see the newspapers which had accused her. But he said that was not the cause and she was not to probe. He then wrote an official censure, and Cornelia said, 'it could not be more severe if I planned a felony.'[34] The Governor and his wife immediately afterwards gave her a very nice tea, but when she asked for an interview, he said, 'we must see it with Lyon's eyes.'[35]

Cornelia thought that none of the British officials involved had read the article, but official papers show that it had been read by one of her main supporters, J. H. Kerr, Secretary, not to the Governor, but to his Council and the Government of Bengal. He and the Governor both thought that there had been some misjudgement on Cornelia's part.[36] The preserved order from Marr, the Secretary to the Board of Revenue of Bengal, was perfectly straightforward and appropriate, merely telling her what rules about publication she must in future obey.[37] Lyon did not feel any personal animosity and he and his wife were still coming to tea and dinner as friends in 1916 and were friends for years after that when they had retired to Oxford.[38] It is possible that Beatson-Bell had been the only enemy.

BATTLE ABOUT QUALIFICATIONS FOR HELPING PURDAHNASHINS

A final battle started in 1913 and was abruptly terminated in 1917. It became uncomfortably personal and was probably the more damaging for Cornelia for being with the wives of British officials at the moment when their husbands were considering Cornelia's terms of employment. The dispute might have been handled better on both sides. In 1912, we have seen,[39] Cornelia was refused her imaginative project for using Hastings House to educate substantial numbers of her secluded women. The house of Warren Hastings was an eighteenth century house, cool, breezy, and spacious, with a large garden and ample grounds and easy to provide with secluded access. So Cornelia had been very disappointed and in 1913, she was pressing an alternative scheme of providing training for nurses in secluded cottages in the Dufferin Hospital. The reason for the loss of Hastings House, we saw, was that some British wives, wanting to be useful, had secured a much smaller house in 1912 at 17 Store Road, in the hope of doing some of the same things on a smaller scale. They were working under the flag of the National India Association, whose local branch had been started by Cornelia herself back in 1907. The Governor and his wife, Lord and Lady Carmichael, had been very supportive to Cornelia about Hastings House and, now that this proved unavailable, Lady Carmichael planned that Cornelia should carry out some of her work in Store Road instead. The committees of both the National India Association and the Dufferin Hospital were hosted by Lady Carmichael in Government House.

The house in Store Road was opened on December 2nd 1912. Two weeks later, Lady Carmichael discussed with Cornelia what its rules should be, and Cornelia typed up a draft.[40] This immediately caused friction with the British wives. Cornelia appeared to them to be overriding their activities in secret behind their backs. A Mrs Duval demanded to know what authority Lady Carmichael had and why Cornelia was advising her. From that moment Cornelia found Mrs Duval, but not yet the others, openly rude and hostile. Nonetheless, Cornelia used the Store Road facilities for various activities and had the disgruntled members to tea, which might have calmed things, but for an ambitious and vivid evening of tableaux that Mrs Duval arranged for secluded women on August 4th 1913. Cornelia warned in advance that, for secluded Hindu women, painted faces implied loose morals and statues of the gods were holy and could not be treated as stage properties. But plans for the entertainment were already settled and Cornelia's warning was taken as criticism. By now Cornelia had offended more members of the group, and the next development was worse.

Her old friend Barbara Stephen had travelled with her to Churamaon and to the Tajhat saving-of-the-soul ceremony.[41] She was now Lady Stephen, since her husband had just been knighted, and she had been one of those who secured the house in Store Road. She was upset because the rules for the house were still under discussion at the beginning of 1914, and she thought that Cornelia had agreed secret conditions with Lady Carmichael and another senior figure, identified only as Lady J. A meeting and letters did not help. So her husband, who had supported Cornelia more than ten years earlier when she sought backing for the initial creation of her post, came to see Cornelia for three and a half hours. Friendship alone might have made Cornelia rethink her tactics, quite apart from the advantage of having at the centre a friend who knew intimately the kind of work Cornelia did. But Cornelia had very strong views on the extensive training in language and custom needed for helping purdahnashins. Without this the British wives could not offer them training and needed guidance, she thought, even on providing entertainment. Store Road was a very different sort of project from her proposal for Hastings House. But she was trying to make the best of it. She also had at that time the commitment of Government House and of the most senior ladies in Calcutta who agreed with her, and under the next administration her views on training would become British Government policy. Moreover, the long struggle had closed her mind to a change of tactic, and she thought in any case that Sir Harry Stephen had persuaded his wife to relent. In fact, Barbara Stephen sent in her resignation. The Governor backed Cornelia and so did all the senior ladies, who turned up in a body. A resignation had to be noted without discussion. Afterwards Lady Carmichael brought Cornelia home and Lady J sent her flowers. Shortly afterwards the rules were agreed, against opposition, but with the backing of Lady Carmichael.

There was a price for this lack of compromise. Quarrels expanded, and women were directly rude to Cornelia not only on the committee of the National India Association,[42] but also on the committees of the Dufferin Hospital Committee,[43] the University Association of Women in Calcutta[44] of which she was President, and elsewhere.[45]

Lady Carmichael had so far been completely supportive. But during Cornelia's trip to England from March to September 1914, her opponents got Lady Carmichael's ear,[46] and Lady Carmichael seemed to lack the skill to bring the quarrel to an end. On Cornelia's return, she started talking of finding another centre for Cornelia's work separate from the others, and she never mentioned the wives' forum at the National India Association again.[47] Moreover, Cornelia found herself ostracised from activities organised by Government House. She had come back from the outbreak in England of the First World War, full of ideas about support for Britain's war effort. But she was kept off Lady Carmichael's war committee.[48] Only Bihar, not Bengal, would pay for her important idea of having vernacular reports printed for purdahnashins about the war, to counteract the widespread impression that Germany had already won and would take over the Indian Empire,[49] and she was snubbed in her suggestions about war time food control.[50]

More woundingly, she was kept out of social events by Government House too, with Gourlay making up the guest lists. She was not invited to the wedding of the Carmichaels' daughter,[51] and much more remarkable was the attempted exclusion of Cornelia when the new Viceroy, Lord Chelmsford, a friend of hers from Oxford days, made his first official visit to Calcutta from Delhi, where the Viceroy's seat now was. When Lady Chelmsford visited the Dufferin Hospital and the National India Association, on whose committees Cornelia served, she was not invited at all, and when the Governor of Bengal held two evening parties for the new Viceroy, she was not sent tickets and had to ask Gourlay for them. The Viceroy and his wife knew nothing of the local attempts at ostracism, and at the evening parties, Lady Chelmsford sent an aide to find Cornelia, and the Viceroy came across to thank her for the note about women he had commissioned from her. He said, 'you know most and we should take your suggestions.' He had given her note to the Member of the Bengal Board of Revenue for a report.[52] The tide was about to turn.

It was at this point that Cornelia finally changed her opinion about Gourlay and wrote, 'Thank God he has no power to hurt. What an escape I have had.'[53] In 1918, she still felt that the Carmichaels had forsaken her, and meeting them in England at the wedding of Margot Asquith's daughter, she did not take up their request that she go and visit them.[54] All the same, to his credit, Lord Carmichael continued to support her to the end of his Governorship as regards her terms of employment.[55] But what made a bigger difference was the arrival of the new Viceroy in 1916 and shortly afterwards of a new Governor in 1917. With new leadership, the wives changed completely, at least in their outward relations to Cornelia.

THE TIDE TURNS

Lord Chelmsford of the Montagu-Chelmsford reforms was Cornelia's fourth Viceroy after Curzon, Minto and Hardinge. She met Lord Chelmsford and his wife early in 1916 shortly before he took office, and he reminded her that they had been to the same lectures at Oxford.[56] Cornelia now started being consulted extensively as President of the University Association of Women, and the Governor, Lord Carmichael, asked her officially to advise on behalf of the Chelmsfords on their question what qualifications English wives would need in order to be useful to Indian women.[57] Lord Chelmsford had her over to talk to the 'Member' in charge of the Board of Revenue, her employer. She spent the afternoon there and was asked to write Lord Chelmsford a note and another note for Lady Chelmsford on etiquette and caste rules in hospitals.[58] This was the note for which the Viceroy Lord Chelmsford thanked her at the party. The note developed her initial response that the necessary training would include one vernacular language, an existing examination in writing and reading, and understanding of etiquette, custom and religion.[59] After that, Lady Chelmsford had Cornelia write two booklets for her. One, *The Purdahnashin* of 1917, was designed to instruct women on how to help the secluded,[60] and one, *Shubala, A Child-Mother*, 1920, was for Lady Chelmsford's infant welfare exhibition, attended also by Cornelia's sister Alice, in 1920.[61]

In 1917, the Governor of Bengal, Lord Carmichael, was also replaced. His successor was Lord Ronaldshay, later the Marquess of Zetland. The new Governor and his wife did decide, it seems, to put an end to the quarrelling. Suddenly, everyone was very pleasant at the National India Association, and at the Dufferin Hospital Committee, which was chaired by Lady Ronaldshay.[62] The cessation of hostilities was all the more surprising, in that Cornelia had already lit the fuse of one more bomb. *The Purdahnashin* was her most informative discussion of the way to help purdahnashins. But in it Cornelia illustrated wrong methods by taking examples such as Mrs Duval's tableaux party. Her aim was to prevent a recurrence and make sure that British women helpers were properly trained. She intended to get the booklet printed in England for the training of women in England who, she hoped, would come out to India from there to help. That way, she thought, her Calcutta associates would never read it.[63] But paper for print was strictly rationed in England during the First World War,[64] and in any case, Lady Carmichael wanted English women to get their training not in England, but at Mission Hospitals in India.[65] The effect of Cornelia's booklet on her associates was surprisingly muted. She was told that at a party given by Mrs Duval and another lady everyone was talking about Cornelia having become anti-British. Cornelia tried to make amends much later by writing an article in *The Queen*, 'What English women have done in India.'[66] But before that in 1920, she reported that the Calcutta branch of the National India Association was moribund.[67] *The Purdahnashin* was important because[68] for a while the need for training which it advocated became official Government policy, and, as already mentioned, by 1921, the Government was adopting the recommendation that doctors too should learn a vernacular language.[69] The effect was not as great as it should have been, however, for during the First World War, women could not be sent out from England, and after the war in 1921 and 1922 the Chelmsfords and then Cornelia left their posts.

THE RESPONSE TO CORNELIA'S VISION
FOR THE COURT OF WARDS

Although Lord Chelmsford and Lord Ronaldshay put an end to the quarrel with the wives, some conflict arose as late as 1920, because of Cornelia's criticism of a senior Civil Servant in Bihar. In Chapter 10, it was seen that Cornelia's annual report of 1920 offered a new vision of what an expanded and more expert Court of Wards could do to prepare agricultural land-owners for a greater measure of home rule. But her proposals included criticisms of a lack of expertise in the existing Court of Wards. She wrote:[70]

> 'I have submitted to the Authorities a note on my dream of what the Court of Wards might become. It still seems to me desirable and worth consideration. I heard that it was dismissed with a remark that the allegations made were not admitted.... The officials for the moment at the Board had not the experience on which I based my statements, and rejected what was outside their personal observation'.

We can see what the offending criticism must have been. In January 1921, Cornelia was told by Morshead, who was later supported by Monahan as the 'Member' since 1914 of the Bengal Board of Revenue, to re-write her annual report on Bihar, omitting her criticisms, or the report would not be published.[71] This must be the report of August 1920, and its original version will have been more explicit in criticising Morshead for the treatment of Bettiah and for exacerbating the dangerous situation at Ramgarh,[72] both in Bihar and both involving decisions on medical treatment. Cornelia at first refused to re-write her report, but in the end was forced to give in. Her larger vision was not addressed.

After her retirement and subsequent return to India in 1924, Cornelia was to try a new tack, using the most progressive of her purdahnashins to carry out social work, with financial support from a later Vicereine, Lady Irwin. But for the time being, her standing up for lost causes, as she put it,[73] was to exact a price in the long-standing negotiations on her terms of employment in the Court of Wards, to which I shall now turn.

CHAPTER 15

SKULDUGGERY OVER TERMS OF EMPLOYMENT FOR AN INDIAN WOMAN, 1914–1922

The year 1914 was not only the year when quarrels came to a head with certain British officers. It was also the year in which Cornelia came to realise that she was facing serious opposition about her terms of service. The opposition had started quietly as far back as 1911, but after the quarrels of 1914 it offered a way for hostile British officers to retaliate against Cornelia. There had been a certain unclarity when her post was confirmed in 1906 concerning her salary, pension, leave, title, need for transport and training of an assistant as an eventual successor. The uncertainties came to light only in 1909. Virtually all the senior officials in Bengal were extremely supportive of Cornelia and the Viceroy's Council accepted their view. Insofar as there were problems, that was because her role was unique, and did not fit with Civil Service Regulations, which officers had to follow, while she was unaware of them and relied simply on informal assurances.[1]

The first serious setback occurred when in 1911, back in London, the Secretary of State for India, Lord Crewe, rejected unanimous recommendations from the Government of Bengal for favourable terms of service. The Viceroy who forwarded the recommendations, Lord Hardinge, also had reduced knowledge of Bengal conditions, because he was away transferring the capital from Calcutta to Delhi, leaving the Lieutenant Governor of Bengal in sole charge. The Lieutenant Governor wholly supported Cornelia and had in 1909 set aside as 'astonishing' a mention made to him of discontent about the extent of Cornelia's powers.[2] London might have been listening to similar unauthorised complaints. At any rate, one of the few Indian officers in the Bengal Government, S. S. Huda, opposed Cornelia's requests on every point, and some members of the Finance

Department opposed her on some.[3] But their objections were not accepted by the Lieutenant Governor and should not have prevailed.

Huda's opposition, like that of many other opponents, seems to have arisen from Cornelia getting him overridden, which happened in the same year, 1912.[4] Huda claimed to be representing a Muslim group and asked for a Muslim girl of 14, Khatun, to be transferred closer to home from the school run in Dacca by Cornelia's sister, Lena. In fact the school gave the girl practice in three languages, English, Bengali and Urdu, a language favoured by Muslims, and she was being taught the Koran in Arabic by a Muslim teacher. She was protected by strict purdah, and in the company of other Muslim girls of the same social standing. She was very successful in music with piano and violin. All these facilities would have been unavailable at the school proposed, which was in any case for infants, and had no suitable lodging for someone of her class. The Commissioner agreed to override Huda, with whom not even the girl's mother agreed. The mother, a widowed Muslim convert, attended with Cornelia her daughter's betrothal two years later at the school, and said that her daughter was getting a better understanding of Islam by staying there.[5]

Cornelia did not know that the opposition to her was dangerous until 1914, and by 1916 or earlier, there was, if we can judge from Cornelia's descriptions, a new element: an ongoing campaign against her by one senior official in Bengal. In a less senior role he had previously co-operated with her over sending the terrorist suspect Nogen to study in England. Now she represents Mr (later Sir C. J.) Stevenson-Moore as seeking to damage her career in every possible way. Once again there was a contrast with the first half of her career in which she had been entirely free of harassment and had received nothing but support.

SUPPORT IN BENGAL AND ASSAM ON CORNELIA'S TERMS OF EMPLOYMENT

A major problem about salary, pension and leave was the huge difference between the rates of pay for officers appointed from England and for those appointed from India. Because her offer came in 1904 and 1906 from the Government of Bengal to her in India, she turned out to be at the lower rate offered at that time to Indians.[6] Cornelia intended to take her leaves and retirement in England, and the far higher cost of living there made it particularly important that at least pension and leave should be at the higher rate. The Lieutenant Governors of Bengal and Assam, Sir Edward Baker and Sir Francis Slacke, entirely supported Cornelia,

SKULDUGGERY OVER TERMS 1914–22

and Baker wrote a strong official recommendation in 1909.[7] A handsome salary was proposed, with leave on the European scale, and it was recommended that the post should be permanent and pensionable.[8]

As regards her choosing and training an assistant as an eventual successor, Baker and Slacke agreed, except that Baker thought it would be politically necessary to appoint an Indian, not an English trainee.[9] As regards Cornelia's title, another supporter in Assam, Mr Savage, persuaded Baker that her title be 'Lady Adviser' instead of 'Legal Adviser'. The motive was not to deny her use of legal expertise, but to reflect how many different things she was doing for her women.[10] The proposal was forwarded through the Viceroy's Council to the Secretary of State in London.

SECRETARY OF STATE REJECTS RECOMMENDED SALARY, PENSION AND LEAVE

The Viceroy's Council approved, but in London in 1911 the Secretary of State asked for more information, and then, without waiting for it, suggested a lowered salary and said that Cornelia had no pension or leave privileges.[11] This made her supporters in Bengal and Assam put their thinking caps on, and official papers show that they could not have done more for her. All along they had circulated information favourable to her case: the grounds for the original post, the glowing annual reports, their own favourable comments and any evidence that Cornelia herself added. Now they brought in the Lieutenant Governor of her third province, Bihar and Orissa, deliberated what approach had the most chance of success and added new considerations: Cornelia had had an expensive training in England, she had given up a private practice to work for them, she contributed the use of her own house by receiving wards there and she would retire to England. The resulting proposal, agreed by all three of her provinces, was sent to the Secretary of State in London by the new Governor of Bengal (as the post was now styled), Lord Carmichael, in November 1912.[12]

To cut a long story short, in April 1912 Lord Crewe allowed only a small compromise on salary, not on leave or pension. Moreover, he opened up a new question about the whole nature of the post by adding casually that the appointment might not necessarily be continued after Cornelia. Powerful supporters continued to consult with Cornelia about how to make the case for the pension,[13] including Mr Montagu, later known for the Montagu-Chelmsford reforms,[14] and Lord Carmichael once he became Governor of Bengal in 1912.[15]

It was on a trip to London in 1914 that Cornelia visited the India Office and learnt how serious the opposition was. She was told that Lord Hardinge, the Viceroy, who had forwarded the original request for better terms, was now against her.[16] Sir Thomas Holderness, Permanent Undersecretary at the India Office, asked, 'Are you just an interpreter for groups of women?' and said she could relinquish her post if she wished,[17] a suggestion that was officially repeated in 1915.[18] Cornelia seriously considered whether to accept the suggestion and retire early, but decided against it.[19] She accepted Lord Crewe's terms in principle in March 1915.

There is no doubt that Cornelia's final long illness in England could have been less uncomfortable, but for the decision on her pension. Another effect, more fortunate for us, of the reduced pay and pension was that all her life she had to write literary articles and books, in order to make enough to live on, even in old age when she was making contributions to the incomes of one or two of her sisters and to the education of Dick's children.

A SECRET FILE AND STEVENSON-MOORE'S DISINFORMATION

So far, support in her three provinces had been very strong, and it looked as if it was people elsewhere who were against her. But she got a shock in 1916 when by accident she saw the pay and pension file sent to her for another purpose. It contained rude notes about her from clerks and under-officers, and from Mr Stevenson-Moore, who was in a position to harm her. By 1910, he was Chief Secretary to the Government of Bengal, and by 1914 he had even more direct influence over her, being the 'Member' of the Board of Revenue, her official employer. This made him Cornelia's manager, since the only other official on the Board was its Secretary. Stevenson-Moore said that her post did not warrant mental abilities and any missionary could do it, since it required only sympathy and intelligence, if one set aside knowledge of language and of secluded women's quarters. A legal education was wholly unnecessary. Moreover, a reduced pension would be quite enough for an unmarried woman, and Cornelia's case records had been highly coloured by her.[20]

He had evidently spread his view around, because when Cornelia was a guest of her friend J. du Boulay in 1916, he used, with kindly intent, the same wording about missionaries, particularly galling for Cornelia whose aim was the opposite of conversion. But as a guest, she felt unable to protest. What du Boulay

said was, 'You cannot expect the Government of India to pay for the philanthropic work of a missionary.'[21] She recalled the description of her in London in
1914, as 'just an interpreter for groups of women'. Still earlier in 1913, she had
been handed another confidential file by mistake, which quoted 'letters' which
did not exist, and 'statements' of hers which had never been made.[22] So what
information was being given to London and for how long had it been given? It
evidently went back at least to 1914 when she visited London. That was also the
year in which all five of the disputes described in the last chapter were raging
and Cornelia had made many enemies. Misinformation continued: In 1921, the
Council was to vote against an assistant for Cornelia on the sole basis of a note
from the then Secretary of the Board of Revenue, apparently Stevenson-Moore
again, that Cornelia looked after the education of a few minor wards.[23]

Cornelia wrote to Elena in agony:[24]

'All this were done behind my back. I can't tell you how I felt. It was as if blud-
geons had been used on my body. I was sore all over and aching physically. The
man who wrote this was apparently such a nice frank *English* Englishman, stupid
and reported stupid, but one had believed him honest and a gentleman. A secret
file to damn a person. It ought not to be possible. For about three days I was
dazed and went about my work with an awful feeling in my heart. We have not,
then, one standard of honour in regard to co-officials in one's department. Of
course there was nothing to be done, no one to whom one could even talk out
the trouble that was hurting'.

CORNELIA'S TITLE

When Cornelia felt so unappreciated, she became anxious about having lost
the title 'legal adviser'. The change, originally intended to support Cornelia,
was being taken, absurdly, to mean that she did not do legal work. It was seen
in earlier chapters just how extensive her legal knowledge needed to be[25] and
how fully it featured in her own annual reports and had been acknowledged
in the Board's annual reports.[26] Even from the point of view of her duties as
a lawyer, any idea that she could confine herself to legal matters would have
involved a misunderstanding. For one thing, she had actually been asked to get
the confidence of her wards and that involved appreciating their problems as a
whole. Further, legal problems do not crop up in people's lives ready labelled
as such, and especially not in the case of her clients who had been denied any
knowledge of the law. It was part of her task to discover where the law might

and might not be used for them. Where possible, she needed to ensure that they, and the next generation, were better educated, so that they could enforce their legal rights. And another part of her task was to secure reconciliations, precisely so that the funds of the estates would not be diverted into needless litigation. She commented in 1918 that she had had four legal problems simply *sprung* on her on a single trip from which she had just returned.[27]

1. How far a widow may divest herself of a widow's estate to 'make her soul'.
2. How far a court is obliged to give effect to spiritual obligations imposed on an estate by a widow.
3. The difference between savings and accumulations on a widow's estate.
4. The question of succession in opposition to the devolution of property under a will.

When in 1916 Cornelia had asked Stevenson-Moore for restoration of the title 'legal adviser', he refused. He would not agree either, if the description 'legal' was forbidden, to switch to 'Zenana officer'. That, he said, made the character of her work, its philanthropic character in his view, all too obvious. Against objections his reply was, 'My opinion is otherwise. You and I do not agree, you see.'[28] Lord Carmichael as Governor was on her side and asked in June 1916 for the title 'legal' to be restored.[29] But in January 1917 Cornelia said goodbye to the Carmichaels[30] before the arrival of the next Governor, and the decision to refuse restoration of the 'legal' title was taken in the interim between Governors by the so-called 'Governor in Council', so that Stevenson-Moore's view could not be questioned.[31]

LEGAL SUCCESSOR REFUSED

Stevenson-Moore's attack on the 'legal' title was connected with his refusal of a legal successor or of an assistant who would be capable of any demanding work, legal or not. His opening may have been provided by Lord Crewe's casual remark that the appointment would not necessarily be continued after Cornelia. If the assistant did not have to be trained as a successor, then, he may have thought, only routine help would be required.

This was a particular disappointment to Cornelia, because of her ambition to open doors closed to women. She had deliberately connected the roles of assistant and successor by negotiating as one of two conditions in 1906 that, in compensation for not being given a civil service rank with its perquisites, she would have an assistant whom she would train as successor.[32] The proposal for the connected roles of assistant and successor was further recorded in the annual report on the Court of Wards for Eastern Bengal and Assam in 1908–1909 quoted in Appendix 2.[33] We have seen that the idea was accepted by the Lieutenant Governors in her provinces in 1909, who thought she should choose the assistant-successor. And a later Governor, Lord Carmichael, also wanted Cornelia to be on the search committee.[34] The only qualification was Baker's, that the assistant should be Indian, but he relaxed that, saying that she should look first for an Indian and if that failed, could have the woman she wanted.[35] Cornelia had found an ideal trainee-successor from England in 1910 in Josephine Stuart,[36] the daughter of friends. She had had them to breakfast in Calcutta to discuss the matter in March of that year. Gourlay had supported Cornelia's interest, and the Lieutenant Governor of Bengal, Sir Edward Baker, had been happy to allow it, if a suitable Bengali could not be found. Cornelia argued the case all over again to Baker's successor, Lord Carmichael, and to the then Honorary Member of the Board of Revenue, that she needed an English assistant who knew the law.[37] The First World War of 1914–1918 caused a delay, because it was too dangerous to send anyone out from England then. But, still full of hope, in 1917 Cornelia outlined the qualities that would be needed in an assistant.[38] The post required

1. Very arduous travelling.
2. Knowledge of at least three Indian languages.
3. Knowledge of office work and accounts.
4. Knowledge of law.
5. Knowledge of Hindu custom and customary law.
6. Knowledge of Muslim law and custom relating to personal matters and ceremonies.
7. Ability to deal on the spot without consultation.

However, in 1916 Stevenson-Moore had altered the terms of the search completely. He said that any successor could perfectly well be a doctor or an educationalist. He did agree that after the war an assistant might be got from England, but, he said, she could be a doctor.[39] As for an assistant, he treated that as a separate question, refused anyone from England and, in line with his views about the triviality of Cornelia's work, sent her a series of women who were at best completely unqualified,[40] one of them a progressive from the Brahmo community which, Cornelia complained, regarded Hindu orthodoxy as positively superstition.[41]

OFFICE ACCOMMODATION: EYE FAILURE IN THE DARK

In 1918, Cornelia was told she had to have an operation on her eyes, which had agonising attacks of pain and were failing. After the operation, the eye operated on went blind and the eyes did not stop being painful.[42] She was deliberately confined for years to the worst lit office in Writers' Buildings at this time of frightening eye problems. The chambers are still dark today and their doors still have frosted glass.[43] Among the crumpled, yellowing documents still stacked in the corridors, it would not be surprising if some went back to Cornelia's time. Her relegation to the worst room added pressure to the suggestion that she might take early retirement. This would now in English law be called 'constructive dismissal', an illegal attempt to dismiss someone without due process. The room was also very hot, and the last days before the monsoon that comes in summer are a great burden, with the clouds building up, but as yet shedding no rain.[44] At the time of her operation, it was winter, but Cornelia was working 18–19 hours a day. She wrote to her friend Elena about Stevenson-Moore's reactions when she told him about her eye problem.[45]

'I must send you one little line, even tho' I've been forbidden to use my eyes. Mails go so seldom now. My eyes have been v. bad. Overstrain, our eye specialist says. The agony in the eye balls is terrible while the attacks of pain last. Thank God there are drops, which help – and in from 24 to 48 hours the worst pain is got under. I am being wise and doing less; but one is alone in house and office and it is not possible to obey the doctor entirely. In office I get no sympathy from the member of the Board. He just laughed when I told him the doctor's verdict and said he did not believe it! It's the civilian attitude. And they won't change my *dark* office room for me. I work by electric light here on the glariest day and the doctor has often told me how bad it is for me. They can be inhuman. But I don't really mind now.

'Mr Stevenson-Moore, the Member, sent for me the day I made the confidence about my eyes, to scold me because I'd not put that stupid Assistant business through' (interviewing one of his unsuited candidates for assistant). 'I thought he was going to be rather pleased wi' me that, 'spite of all the extra F. P. examination work, I had not let my office work get even one letter in arrears. – Everything up to date. It had not been easy to secure that. I'd worked for 18 to 19 hours a day the last few months. But – I had not pushed on that unfit creature's desires – so all else was nought. It's v. typical of the modern kind of Bengal civilian. However, I wrote at once to arrange for the old, unfit woman of whom I've told you to come and see me'.

Cornelia started asking, year in year out, but with no effect, for a less dark room, repeating that she had to work by electric light even on glaring days.[46] Gradually a rainbow-coloured halo began to form around the vision in her other eye, until it became a complete circle and extended to the operated eye.[47] The new Secretary of the Board of Revenue, Mr Spry, was nice, and though nobody would give up his office to the only woman in the building, after a year a young man came to inspect and proposed white-washing the wall, substituting plain glass for cloudy, frosted glass for wooden partitions and a more powerful electric light. He also suggested that she ask a young military officer to change rooms with her. But in the end it was deemed too expensive to substitute glass for wood. After more than two years a lighter room was promised, but Stevenson-Moore took it after all for a Mr Lethbridge. It was only in her last year, 1921, that somebody was asked to make room for her.[48]

NO MOTOR CAR – EXCEPT FOR MISS BROOK

Stevenson-Moore played a role also in the saga of the motor car. When first appointed, Cornelia realised that she would have to supply her own trap for transport in Calcutta as well as her own office.[49] But by 1910, the Lieutenant Governor of Bengal, Sir Edward Baker, thought that she should have a motor car. The Bengal Board of Revenue asked her annual mileage, but she received no answer for three years until 1913 when her road mileage was used as a basis for refusal.[50] In 1916 her mileage in Calcutta was 541 miles,[51] but they wanted her total mileage in the provinces. In 1917 that was 20,500 miles, and she claimed a car again, citing Government rules. But Stevenson-Moore was by then on the scene and refused the car along with everything else.[52]

The refusal now turned out to discriminate between a European woman and Cornelia. There was a European school inspectress, Miss Brook, who was being considered for a vehicle allowance ahead of Cornelia, although she served only one province as against Cornelia's three. When Cornelia was shown the motor file in 1919, it became clear why Miss Brook was considered ahead. They thought her case might serve as a precedent for Cornelia's. But when Miss Brook got her car allowance, they decided not to use that as a precedent for Cornelia after all.[53] In 1919, the car was refused, both in Bengal and in Bihar.[54] She was still driving a two-wheeled trap in Calcutta with her old horse Vanity, and said she was about the only woman to be driving a trap. When she protested, a trick was played. Bengal asked for her mileage during a year when her sight had some of the time been too bad for her to drive.[55] Nonetheless, ten years after it had been recommended, Bengal consented in 1920 to an allowance of 75 rupees a mile for motor upkeep. She had to buy the car, garage and petrol, but this paid for the driver. She asked the province of Bihar for a further 25 rupees a mile for upkeep, but that simply led to Bengal cutting 25 rupees off their allowance.[56] Nonetheless she celebrated by buying an Overland 4. She took driving lessons and got her licence in the final year of her employment.[57]

PERMISSION REQUIRED FOR VISITING WARDS

Another restriction in 1916 was imposed by a former supporter, Mr Monahan, writing as the 'Member' of the Bengal Board of Revenue since 1914. Suddenly, Cornelia was not to visit her wards without the leave of the local District Collector.[58] Not only was this impractical, since Collectors, who could not see the ladies themselves, could be up to two or three days' journey away, and could not deal with emergencies. In any case, it violated one of the two conditions that Cornelia negotiated in 1906, as compensation for her not being given a rank and its perquisites within the Civil Service hierarchy. The condition was that she must be free, according to the needs of the case, to appeal directly over their heads to the Divisional Commissioner, the Governor or the Viceroy.[59] When in 1912 an earlier District Collector had sought to make Cornelia seek his leave for visits, Mr Lyon had made him withdraw his letter.[60] Cornelia challenged the new order as politely as she could, and its impracticality was illustrated almost immediately.[61] A boy ward needed an operation for what turned out to be an abdominal fistula. He needed it operated on as soon as possible according to the doctor at the Dufferin Hospital. But Cornelia now had to get the agreement of the Commissioner, which took ten days, and everything had to be done in writing. By the time the father and family lawyers had been consulted, the urgent operation was postponed for nearly three months. Mr Monahan, however, though particularly liable to mistakes in Cornelia's view, was not uniformly hostile. He had supported Cornelia over the scholarship for her ward, the terrorist suspect Nogen, and she found his unexpected sympathy over her terms of employment 'miraculous'.[62]

LEAVE

A final irritation was over the terms of leave. Already half her salary was held back during her leaves, because of the fiction that they might need that ever-elusive assistant to replace her while she was absent.[63] But when she was finally due to retire in 1922, she was encouraged to arrange unused furlough which carried a pension, only to be told too late that it would reclassified as leave and payment reduced. The refusal to rectify this dragged nearly two years into her retirement, and all allowances were stopped until it was settled – in her disfavour.[64]

Cornelia's enemies in the Civil Service may have been few, and in the over-whelming majority of cases the enmities seem to have arisen from her getting people who considered themselves élite overridden (Huda, Beatson-Bell, Mor-shead, the opponents of Nogen, and the memsahibs), or *attempting* to get them overridden (the doctors appointed for Bettiah under Morshead). The British officers had all started their careers by the time Cornelia went as a student to Oxford.[65] It was to the credit of the service that so few complained about her freedom to go above the heads of District Collectors, but it was a policy that was bound to lead to some resentment. Cornelia confined herself to a few comments: some officials 'could not bear anyone who could contradict their own legal opinions'. 'The present generation of English folk have no use in this Province for you, unless they are exercising a patronage which gives them a feeling of superiority.' Elsewhere, she simply said that she was unpopular for defending lost causes.[66]

EFFECTS OF IGNORING CORNELIA'S EXPERTISE

It was inevitable that without her expertise, officials were likely to make mis-takes, and the great majority were gracious enough to recognise this. But she did find that those who disvalued her expertise were particularly liable to mis-takes, unless it was that those whom she found particularly prone to mistakes were motivated to discount her expertise. Examples have been given already,[67] but the worst mistake was that of Stevenson-Moore. By shutting Cornelia out of a shady decision to allow an adoption in 1919, he got the Court of Wards dragged for 14 years into the publicity of a major law suit concerning the prince they wrongly regarded as an impostor. As seen in an earlier chapter,[68] they finally lost the case at colossal expense in 1946.

Education was sometimes needlessly curtailed by the authorisation of a child marriage. When Stevenson-Moore authorised such a marriage in 1920, his colleague, the Board Secretary, said to Cornelia timidly, 'I was afraid to come and tell you that the Honorary Member (of the Board) had permitted it.'[69]

It had been the Provincial Governors and the senior Indian Civil Service officers under them who supported Cornelia so enthusiastically for nine years up to 1913. It was now only two senior members of the Indian Civil Service who tried to obstruct her. There was a safeguard in that the Governor of Bengal after 1912 and the Viceroy of India were appointed from outside the Indian Civil Service and nearly always supported her. But they could not override officials all the time on everyday business. The great majority of officers on the ground also continued to collaborate with Cornelia to the end of her career, despite her anomalous position. This was best illustrated by the rescue of the young Rani and her children from the palace of Ramgarh in 1921.[70] It required the total confidence in her of the Divisional Commissioner, the Deputy Commissioner, the Collector and the Sub-Divisional Officer.

Jowett's prediction had come abundantly true that Cornelia would have many phases both of exaltation and depression.[71] Besides the opposition to her and the worry about her eyes, all her life she had severe pains in her limbs which she called neuralgia. It was in the midst of the worst opposition that Cornelia went in 1917 to visit her successful sister Alice at her hospital in Bannu on the Afghan frontier. Her first thought was, 'It is lovely seeing her so loved and so efficient.' Alice had run the hospital in this dangerous spot, sometimes without another doctor, since her husband died in 1912, and she was surrounded by love when Cornelia felt surrounded by hostility. It is not surprising that Cornelia also thought, 'It's dreadful feeling a failure and *despicable*, as Alice somehow makes one feel.'[72]

In 1916, she wrote to Elena, 'I am happier than in 1907.'[73] But 1907 was the year that Harrison Falkner Blair died. Nonetheless, her situation was much better than it would be when she sought to return to India as a barrister in 1924 after retiring from the Civil Service. Then trickery and solitude would prove to be the rule rather than the exception,[74] whereas now at least her closest purdahnashins were full of gratitude and appreciation.

CHAPTER 16

DICK, CORNELIA AND FAMILY, ENGLAND CALLING 1913–1922

What was happening to Cornelia's family during the years in which she met opposition, 1913–1922? Dick and she each made two visits to England between 1913 and 1919. Three were wartime visits in the First World War when the sea voyage was dangerous. Cornelia's visits gave her solace. By the time she returned from the last visit in 1919, Lena was leaving her job as headmistress in Dacca and returning permanently to join the three sisters already in England. Dick and Cornelia had only three years left of their work in India. In 1922, Dick and Cornelia retired to England on the same day and Alice exchanged her job on the Afghan frontier for one in Europe. Only Cornelia and Alice would eventually return to new work in India. In 1924 Cornelia found that India called more strongly than England, but only after she had taken advantage of the new opportunities for women in England and studied in London to qualify as a barrister.

DICK'S TWO VISITS TO ENGLAND

Dick and Cornelia had last been in England in 1907, when Harrison Falkner Blair died. But now in 1913, Dick, to Cornelia's surprise, went to England again. His oldest sister Zuleika had persuaded a young lady in England, Joan Butler, that Dick, who was 40, should come over to England with a view to their marrying and returning to India. Dick moved to a larger house in Allahabad, along Edmonstone Road at number 19, and sailed on June 28th. Joan was beautiful and fell very much in love with Dick when he arrived to stay in Zuleika's London house. Dick saw the girl's parents, who liked him, and by

August 14th the wedding was arranged for September 23rd. But Dick was not equally enthusiastic. Playing things down for Cornelia, he had originally said he might be bringing a secretary home, and he did not seem to have changed his outlook very much. Joan Butler's parents reversed their agreement and by August 24th he cabled that he had decided to remain single. Cornelia helped get his new house ready and welcome him home. He seemed relieved, but he now expected he would never have the chance of getting married.[1] Whether this thought, along with physical ill health, contributed to his subsequent depression is not clear. But his second visit to England in 1916 was to recuperate from ill health.

In 1916 it was Cornelia who sent Dick to England. His much remarked ebullience[2] had disappeared the previous year. He was not eating and was both physically ill and depressed.[3] He still drove Cornelia on her visit to see her ward Bettiah, went to court, settled a quarrel between a Muslim professor and Hindus and visited the sick, but he had no cheer. He had to come to Calcutta for an operation for piles, and his sister Susie came up from Poona, so that she as well as Cornelia could see him. But after the operation, he was still unwell and depressed, and a year later the depression was worse. He went with his sister Lena in 1916 for 'electric' treatment, probably involving shocks, at Mussoorie in the Himalayan foothills and came back worse, unable to get out of the car in case his friends saw him. In a letter of August 1916 Cornelia wrote to Dick's old Oxford friend Richard Burn in Allahabad,[4] explaining that, as Dick could not make decisions, she had booked a boat from Bombay for ten days later, for him to sail to England. She would be coming in four days to pack his things, but she asked Burn to get Dick sick leave and a passport. It was wartime, and Dick was to spend time in England, but also go to help with war work at the YMCA (Young Men's Christian Association) near the front in Paris, while he recuperated. Six months later he returned through dangerous war time seas and reached Bombay in March 1917, very much better for his time in England and Paris,[5] although well into 1918 his spirits continued fluctuating, sometimes, as Lena reported, by the day.

CORNELIA'S TWO WARTIME VISITS TO ENGLAND

In 1914, Cornelia made her own visit to England for six months. She sailed on March 22nd.[6] Much of her attention at first was given to the interviews already described[7] at the India Office about her terms of employment, but there were new developments too. She saw Edmund Dulac in his studio, surely the most exotic illustrator of folk tales of the period, and he discussed with her doing illustrations of the children in her *Sun Babies* book (Second Series).[i] She described Dulac as a 'naturalised Frenchman, simple and straight. He has a nice partly Italian wife, a chow dog, a lovely garden and a Gobelin tapestry of his Circe, his one picture'.[8] Cornelia's new and newly married confidant, Elena Richmond (née Rathbone), was meanwhile being sketched in her house by the great portraitist John Sargent.[9]

While Cornelia was in England, her letter appeared in *The Times* of June 1914 alongside one by Jinnah. The two letters were presented by *The Times* as opposite responses to Mrs Besant's letter. The letters concerned the Council of India Bill, which considered the representation of Indians on the Viceroy's Council in India. Mrs Besant had accepted the bill's tenor, but complained of many other injustices to Indians that were not addressed. Jinnah did not accept its tenor, but objected that it fell far short of what was required. Cornelia, took a third position, denying at least some of the injustices of which Mrs Besant complained,[10] and it was this letter that, among other things, led to her reprimand, already described, for political activity.[11]

Cornelia heard the debate in the House of Lords on the Council of India Bill. She saw Lord Curzon there and found him delightful. On her second visit to the Lords she met Lord Roberts, who took her to tea. He was a friend of her sister Alice and her husband from Afghan frontier days. Field Marshall Lord Roberts had gained distinction in the Indian Uprising of 1857. After winning two victories in Afghanistan, he had become Commander-in-Chief in India in 1885. In the Boer War, Cornelia had celebrated his occupation of Pretoria. When the debates on the Council of India Bill were over, Lord Roberts had Cornelia to stay several days in his house, Englemere, at Ascot. At that time he had in the house well known portraits of Tipu Sultan, a tracing from Tipu's palace of one of his pictures of victorious battles against the British and a statue of him. Within two months Lord Roberts would be dead of pneumonia after visiting Indian soldiers at the front. The First World War had started.[12]

The Archduke, heir to the Austrian throne, was assassinated on June 28th 1914, and the talk of war was immediate, although it was not declared until August 3rd. Cornelia described Prime Minister Asquith's speech on the occasion as splendid. She had meanwhile had lunch with her old friend Margot

---

i The commission went in the end to Miss G. Hadenfeldt – not world-famous like Dulac, but her illustrations helped to win plaudits for the book.

Asquith, who was to keep up her reputation for wit by saying in 1915, alleg-
edly, that she found the first German zeppelin raid on England disappointing.
Luxembourg and Belgium were invaded by Germany and Liège besieged. There
were services of intercession at St Paul's Cathedral and Westminster Abbey,
with Archdeacon Wilberforce preaching on the meaning of intercession.[13] Lord
Kitchener became War Minister on 'all or nothing' terms, having once again (as
with Curzon)[14] refused to share responsibility with anyone else.[15]

Cornelia attended the State Ball, postponed from June 29th to July 16th,
wearing a red and gold saree. She was given a very good seat to see the pageant
of the uniformed Beefeaters, and the chamberlains with their wands walking
backwards in front of the King and Queen, both of whom recognised her.[16] In
a further letter to The Times, on which she received many congratulations, she
contrasted the State Ball with the new war situation, praised English calm and
cited examples from the Ramayana and Mahabharata of people and gods rejecting the idea that one should shrink from war.[17]

From the day after the declaration of war, passages back to India were very
difficult to obtain. At Cornelia's first attempt on August 8th, she could not get
on the train at the station because the boat on which she meant to sail had been
commandeered by the Admiralty for military and civilian officers. Princess
Louise asked her for help with her hospital, and Cornelia started on Red Cross
work, sewing red jackets and pyjamas. She dined at Kensington Palace with
the Princesses Louise and Beatrice and they began knitting a sock for her, to
show her how to do it. She hated leaving England in its adversity and there was
pandemonium at the station when she finally got off on 29 August. She sailed,
knitting socks, through guarded waters to Plymouth, saw captured German
boats at Gibraltar, passed many troop ships at Suez and after that the Admiralty
warned they must go slow and warily.[18] It was at Aden that she found waiting
for her the accusation about her political writing, including her letter to The
Times on Mrs Besant described earlier.[19]

The war reached India at once. A German cruiser destroyed six merchant
ships and the Linden fired 25 shells into Madras (Chennai). Many of Cornelia's
wards thought that Germany was somewhere near Madras.[20] On reaching India,
Cornelia started composing letters to explain the war to her wards and translated them into vernacular languages.[21] The need was clear. The wards could
not distinguish in vernacular newspapers between English and Germans, since
both were called 'Ingrez'. The same papers reproduced German claims that
the Germans were only defending themselves from Russia. Wards also quite
reasonably wanted to know why the British were fighting against Muslims in

Turkey. Later the wards read that the Germans were winning, and that Indian troops had mutinied.[22] The province of Bihar printed Cornelia's letters, but the Bengal Board of Revenue decided that they should not be printed in Bengal. Mr Lyon's explanation, that printing them would suggest an undue importance for her, sounds like the view of her detractors. He told her it had been suggested that the wives of Collectors could explain things to orthodox women, but they lacked the languages to talk to them. Lyon allowed only that in Bengal the letters, hundreds of them, could be handwritten. Cornelia appealed to Lord Carmichael, the Governor of Bengal, but printed letters for Bengal were refused.[23] There were in the end some funds set aside for the war letters, although they were docked in 1917.[24]

Other contributions to the war effort were allowed. She had found herself the only person in Darjeeling knitting socks, but she soon had her wards knitting socks, and even a husband, the Maharaja of Nadia, was knitting mufflers.[25] This was when she showed lantern slides about the war to her wards who had never seen anything like lantern slides before. They were fascinated and became wholly supportive of the British war effort.[26] Moreover, as part of that effort, Cornelia took a course in casualty nursing. She came out top.[27]

The effects of the war were very noticeable. In rapid succession, the *Lusitania* and a hospital ship were sunk.[28] Increased raiding in Afghanistan made Cornelia worry about Alice.[29] Mails were lost at sea in the *Arabia*, but salvaged from the *Mongolia*. Mails were slowed, eventually to once a fortnight, and all mail was censored.[30] Finally, all sailing to England was stopped.[31] Everybody lost, or knew someone who had lost, a close relative. From among her supporters in India, the Le Mesuriers lost two sons and a bullet-ridden letter was recovered from the body of one of them. The Mintos lost a son. From the mentors on Indian matters of her student days, Sir Alfred Lyall, whom she had known as an Indian expert, lost a son, as did one of Cornelia's closest Somerville friends, Nell Holland, and her sister Pheroze lost her husband, as did Pheroze's daughter.[32]

In November 1917, Cornelia's sister Alice was moved by the government for some months from the Afghan frontier to a war hospital for the wounded in Bombay, and Cornelia visited her there and saw where the wounded were taught trades. The frontier men's faces shone when Alice spoke to them in Pushtu. Some had known her husband Theodore. Cornelia thought Alice's hospital wonderful and her sister very talented.[33] The following year, like Cornelia, Alice was awarded the gold medal of the Kaiser-i-Hind.[34]

Having seen the first day of the World War in England, Cornelia also saw the last, when in 1918, she made her second wartime visit to England. She had

had an unsuccessful operation on her eye,[35] and she needed to go to England to get better treatment. She was offered a passage on a ship to England for women and children, diverted for safety by the long route round the African Cape. She declined it and was then offered by General St John a transport ship, but only as far as Egypt. As her doctor thought that a long journey would endanger her sight further, the Viceroy, Lord Chelmsford, allowed her to go through Suez, which was then closed to women. She also needed to get approval for a passport both from him in Simla and from London. Eventually a passage was booked on a camouflaged troop carrier, the *Nore*, for October 5th, though dates of sailing could not be wired to England.[36]

By this time, Germany was negotiating, and the Kaiser, the Emperor of Germany, had fled, but the voyage was still very dangerous. The ship was required to zig-zag and the passengers to wear their life jackets at all times. There were three summons to the life boats en route. 'Aeroplanes flew quite low,' she wrote. 'We can see inside the big brown birds.' Progress was repeatedly halted. At Suez they were stuck in the Bitter Lakes and could see the soldiers' trenches and later they passed the hulk of a ship burnt out by explosions. They were in the middle of a convoy of 14 merchant ships with protective cruisers and with two aeroplanes overhead. The lights were out on deck and it was very dark. Gradually more news came in. Austria had surrendered unconditionally, Turkey and Belgium 'had come in' and the German Navy had mutinied. Finally, on November 10th 1918, as they approached London, a boat came alongside and announced that the Kaiser had abdicated. There was revolution in Germany, with everywhere except Berlin in a state of rebellion. The convoy left them and lights were allowed on deck. Cornelia wrote in her personal diary: 'I can think of nothing else. "God save the King", my little Princess and the darling Queen and all one's friends.'

All flags were flying. Their own ship was flying 70 of them and had hoisted a broom on the mast – a reference to the song, 'A broom to sweep the seas with'. Cornelia got a train to London at 1. 30 p.m. on November 11th, and 24 soldiers and munitions girls crowded into the first class carriage. The girls said, 'We've won the war,' but the soldiers said, 'I thought we had something to do with it.' Cornelia was met at Liverpool Street in London by her Somerville friend, Nell Holland, who had lost her son, and by her old hostess, Lady Cholomondley. There was only one taxi available, but she got it. The streets were crowded with masses of people waiting to see the King and Queen drive past.

The next day, there was a packed service at St Paul's Cathedral. A kind woman lifted Cornelia onto a bench, and she saw her friend the Princess and the King and Queen in procession. She stood by a banner and joined in singing hymns of praise that she found particularly stirring. Wilson, President of the United States, was to come to London a little later and make a triumphant progress through England.[37] Cornelia had seen the beginning of the war and its end, and been absorbed by everything in between.

Her eye trouble turned out to have been wrongly diagnosed in Calcutta. It was not glaucoma and the doctor should not have bored a hole in the lens. The specialist diagnosed the problem as rheumatoid arthritis of the eye cartilage, and he did improve her sight.[38] This was when she went at Christmas for water treatment at Bath.[39]

After eight months she was able to return to India, and arrived on July 2nd 1919. That was the day after her sister Lena retired from the school in Dacca and prepared to return to join the other three sisters in England.[40] So now, with Susie down in Poona and Alice back on the Afghan frontier, only Dick was within easy reach of Cornelia. Moreover, he was beginning to do well again, and she wrote, 'I never knew how much I counted on the monthly visits.'[41] He did indeed, when well, meet her at the station, feed her up, give her parties, drive her and leave her with huge picnic hampers for the journey back.

DICK'S NEW ACTIVITIES AND CORNELIA'S HOPES FOR HIS FUTURE ROLE

His health recovered, Dick plunged into new activities for his last three years in India. In 1919 and 1921, he was sought as arbitrator in railway disputes.[42] But his most lasting interest lay in the call in 1921 of his colleague, Tej Bahadur Sapru, to discuss India's future constitution with him. Sapru had agreed to join the Viceroy's Council and Cornelia entertained hopes for Dick's future role in India, hopes that were misplaced since they did not correspond to Dick's wishes. Sapru was his younger colleague at the Allahabad bar who had praised Dick in 1909 when Dick was Principal of the Law College.[43] He was also a Nationalist leader who retained his belief in constitutionalism, even after the new methods of Gandhi prevailed.[44] That meant that he had now left the Congress Party and was currently serving from 1920–1923 as the Law Member on the Executive Council of the Viceroy Lord Reading, until he resigned at Gandhi's arrest. But even then he served out his term, while at the same time remaining on good terms with Gandhi and the Nehrus, father and son.[45] According to D. A. Low, Sapru played a major role in Indian Independence by outwitting Churchill in 1942.[46] But an earlier activity was the three Round Table Conferences in 1931–1932 in London about India's future independent status. Because both Dick and Cornelia were involved in the last conference, it will be discussed below.[47] The common interest of Sapru and Dick was in accommodating the Princely States in a future Indian Constitution.

Dick went to stay with Sapru in Delhi and Simla during his period on the Viceroy's Council. It was then that Cornelia first revealed that she longed for him to 'get his chance' and in 1922 she saw Sapru at her request and had a talk about this. Sapru said he would sound Dick out and see if there was anything he could get for him in India. But Dick did not in any way share Cornelia's ambitions. He merely continued to support Sapru's activities over the coming years, though with an enthusiasm that Cornelia did not share.[48]

THE MAHARAJA OF BHARATPUR'S FESTIVITIES, 1919–1922

Dick was useful to Sapru not merely because of his legal knowledge, but because of his familiarity with a number of Princes. Dick's most colourful Princely activity involved Cornelia too. Two or three years running, Dick was master of ceremonies and deputy host at the Maharaja of Bharatpur's week-long celebration.[49] In the second year, Cornelia was invited and came to know the Bharatpur family. The celebrations were on a scale not likely to be found in more democratic times, even though India, like Britain, still excels in pageantry. Both Dick and Cornelia liked the pageantry, quite possibly more than Alice, who favoured her hardy Afghans.

In 1919, the Maharaja of Bharatpur was 22 years old. As Dick describes his camp of Christmas 1919, there was a canvas city of white and gold with red-coated sentries. There were two streets of dwelling tents, and guests could be driven in carriages drawn by royal bulls, in brakes with trotting camels, in carriages with matched pairs of horses, or in motor cars, or they could ride elephants or horses. What Dick liked best in the whole week was the horseman who could call a wild black buck to within a few yards of the spectators, charmed, but torn all the time between the irresistible call and the desire to run back into the forest.

In the second year, at Christmas 1920, Cornelia was present at Dick's instigation, along with 80 guests. The Maharaja met Cornelia and her friend with a Rolls Royce at midnight and gave them supper in the camp. The next day he carried Dick and Cornelia off to meet his mother in the palace.

Dick saw the famous annual duck shoot, a year before the Prince of Wales attended, where record numbers of birds were shot. The shoot included a picnic in the wetlands, which are still a park today, but for bird-watching, not shooting. They were both involved in the Christmas celebrations. There was a beehive-shaped church for the Christmas day service and a Christmas tree with gifts in the ballroom, which Dick and Cornelia decorated. To play the role of Father Christmas they made up a bearded Sikh. Dick conducted charades and with others made up nonsense rhymes about the guests which were written in a silver-bound book and presented to the Maharajah.[ii]

The third camp was held in October 1921 and Cornelia was again met at midnight by the Maharaja, this time in his Fiat. This third camp culminated in the grandest pageantry of all. The last two days were devoted to the festival of *Dashera*. Cornelia wrote a series of descriptions,[50] starting with the first evening, when she watched from marbled balconies the Maharaja accepting the homage first of his elephants and then of his horses. She felt it as 'an Arabian Nights romance', watching in the still night air the ceremonies half-lit by moonlight and torches, as firework squibs were put to the foreheads of the imperturbable elephants – a relic of their training for battle.[iii]

On the final day, Cornelia herself joined the procession, riding through the city streets past the coloured mosaic of citizens on the third elephant in a silver and gold howdah with the white-moustached Chief Minister of Council.

THE MAHARANI OF BHARATPUR AND THE BEGINNINGS OF SOCIAL REFORM

More important to Cornelia than the Maharaja was his Maharani mother. She had taken over the education of her son, when her husband had been forced to abdicate in humiliating circumstances. She persuaded her people that she should be allowed to take her only son 'across the black waters' to England. There she visited iron and steel factories and the poorest pickers of hops in the fields, whom she joined with her attendants and her son. She studied the conditions of workers, and when she returned to India she built schools and hospitals which Cornelia visited in her kingdom. She wrote her own publicity for these facilities and she had the milk and water supplies sterilised. While respecting custom, she modified

---

ii Verses about guests and the presentation to the host of a book composed by guests had been features of Curzon's parties given to the Souls: Jane Abdy, Charlotte Gere, *The Souls*, London 1984, Ch. 1. See Chapter 2.

iii This tradition is illustrated in Indian miniatures.

her purdah by travelling in an open car, shielded only by an open umbrella.[51] After a talk with Cornelia, she responded by arranging remarriage, previously unthinkable, for a widowed Brahmin and giving her a dowry. Her daughter-in-law, the younger Maharani of Bharatpur, was also to break down the barriers between women in purdah by receiving a visit from the Maharani of Gwalior, a neighbouring state, who was herself an innovator. The Gwalior lady did not shave her head when her husband died and she wanted her daughter to have a profession. The Bharatpur son, the current Maharaja, also engaged in 1926 in progressive legislation for women, since he was free as ruler of a Princely State to introduce his own. He allowed widows to remarry, and their children to inherit, and he disallowed child marriage below the ages of 16 for males and 14 for females.[52] Cornelia felt that this gradualist reform was where hope for the future lay.

When the Maharaja's mother died in 1922,[53] Cornelia paid a nostalgic visit to the chattri (domed pavilion) where her ashes were buried. Each of the former Bharatpur Maharajas was commemorated in a quiet spot contrasting with the grandeur of their palaces. For each there was a chattri with a separate garden and tank. The mother's chattri was simple and separate, of white marble pierced with patterns, bare inside, except for the memorial stone with two feet facing North, to mark the direction of heaven. There were symbols round the outside in coloured marble, a conch shell blown at ceremonies, the sun, the moon and medallions. Scattered on the slab were jasmine flowers and scented white honey flowers with yellow hearts. A priest sat at appointed times and read from the *Mahabharata* and *Ramayana* and pilgrims came to meditate. The priest felt that the mother came to visit and he gave Cornelia dates and nuts, which he described as a parting present from her.[54]

By 1926 when Cornelia took part in another of the Maharaja's celebrations, her high expectations for the future were dashed. By that time the Maharaja had 150 cars and was in debt. His debts and early death led to her receiving no payment when, later again, she took on for him a criminal case involving stolen state jewels.[55]

FAREWELLS: VICEREGAL LODGE, NEW DELHI

As the time to retire approached in 1921, Cornelia found it more of a wrench than she expected. 'My heart' she wrote, 'is like a banyan tree with roots in the zenanas. The great uprooting is painful'. But in the same letter to Elena, written while in Delhi, she was very pleased to find the staff of the Viceroy, Lord

Reading, so good to her. She thought it was on account of Dick, whom they liked very much, and was pleased again when she heard renewed appreciations of him. She again expressed a wish that they would find him a role in India.

The next month she was staying in Viceregal Lodge in Delhi and attended discussion in the Viceroy's Council all day, on whether current measures were too severe. She then heard for the first time of proposals for a round table conference, and of its possibly being used as a context for releasing political prisoners. Gandhi's non-committal response was read out. Lady Reading asked Dick to come for the weekend, and Lord Reading had them back for a final stay, to give Dick a leaving present.[56]

Cornelia received a bar to her Kaiser-i-Hind, in other words a second award of it, in January 1922. She was pleased by a 'beautiful' letter about her work written by Le Mesurier, who had supervised her first task eighteen years earlier in 1904. At the final meeting of the University Association, it was said by an American that she had the idealism of India, the training and administrative power of Great Britain and the energy of America. Lady Reading proposed a vote of thanks for her at the Woman's Council.[57]

FAREWELLS: ALICE ON THE AFGHAN FRONTIER

Cornelia made her second and farewell visit to see Alice on the Afghan frontier in 1922.[58] On the way, she went to the scene of the notorious massacre of 1919 by General Dyer in Amritsar. She was shown where Dyer stood and went on firing and firing, and was told what happened in factual and unrhetorical terms – at the time, news had been blacked out. A live child had been found in the morning, sitting on the body of its long dead mother, trying to find her breasts, and a dead child was hanging out of a window, where it was shot when looking out to see what was happening. The Civil Surgeon at the hospital was alleged to have said, 'Go to Gandhi to dress your wounds.' Because a curfew had been imposed for eight to nine days, the dead could not be collected until the morning, and, because of being made by Dyer after the massacre to crawl, some were caught unable to get their well water or their purchases back in time before the curfew. Cornelia said she had never understood about Dyer before.[59] She went straight on to see Alice, driving with Lord Montagu, the Secretary of State for India, who had favoured Gandhi as peace-maker and who had insisted, against opposition, on an investigation by Lord Hunter into the massacre.

25. Alice, cheerfully informal, with Theodore outside the Afghan
frontier house he built.

Cornelia met Alice at Peshawar station. They were driven up the Khyber Pass by
Lord Montagu[60] and were taken further than normally allowed in his Rolls Royce,
until they could see the snow line of the Hindu Kush Mountains. Back via the Kohat
Pass, everywhere fortified against Afghan attack, to Bannu, they had to stay for safety
in the original house of Theodore and Alice. It had been designed by Theodore and

26. Alice with Theodore and domestics outside the same house.

was circular with rooms radiating off a central hall. They called at the new house which Alice had built for herself, but it was surrounded by barbed wire, and it could not be made safe until she could get the land to have a road through to the original bungalow. There had been an attempt to kidnap Alice for ransom in 1916, and both the hospital outposts created by Theodore had been overrun by hundreds of Afghan soldiers in 1919 and 1920.[61] The situation now was still more dangerous.

Cornelia watched Alice do eye operations. 'It is delightful being with my Pennell sister and seeing her operate and realising how she is loved and adored by these people. Her great skill and her great charm and her great courage, in what must be a continually renewed loneliness, fill me with pride and admiration.'[62] Cornelia felt for Alice, not seeing how she could bear to live surrounded by reminders of her late husband's life and death. But she nonetheless always describes Alice as 'cheery'.

That year, 1922, with both Dick and Cornelia retiring to new occupations in England, and in the strained conditions, Alice too offered her resignation.[63] Cornelia could not help noticing that, when the time came, Alice too received a series of fond farewells from the Viceroy and Vicereine, Lord and Lady Reading.[64] Cornelia was not the only star in the family.

Cornelia and Dick left India on the same day, April 1st, but on different boats. They failed to coordinate probably because she had not wanted to believe that Dick really wanted to retire when she did, and continued to hope he would get important work in India. She wrote, 'My last day in India. There is a lovely dawn out of the window over the sea. We go at 9.45 to the Cathedral. I think of all the ways by which God has led me.'

ARRIVAL IN ENGLAND

There was no problem in England, as there might have been in America or Canada, for Indians coming to visit or settle in England. It was a matter of pride that there was a single British Empire. The family simply got their passports from India. There were to be problems for all members of the family about money, except for Alice for whom her late husband had sufficiently provided. But Cornelia, with her small legacies long since exhausted early in her career, and penalised by her reduced pension, made ends meet in her usual way by writing for literary publication.[65] By this means she also helped those sisters who were even poorer than herself, and later helped with the education of Dick's children, her nephew and niece. Her small income never prevented her dressing beautifully, but as she reveals, her beautiful sarees of silk, which was the normal Parsee material, could still be worn to effect nine years after purchase.[66]

After arriving in England, Cornelia still had ambitions for Dick. To these he paid no attention. She wished he would apply to become the High Commissioner for India, when the first incumbent, Sir William Meyer, died. Then the India Office asked him to speak for the Empire at the British–Indian Union, but he refused, although he later hosted a party she thought extremely successful for the Union. The only work of this kind that interested him was continuing to support Sapru when he was over in London. Cornelia met Sapru at Dick's flat, then at a British–Indian Union lunch with Dick, and then at Sapru's party in the Carlton Club, where Dick wore the Persian costume she liked best and made a speech.[67]

Cornelia's picture of herself suffered a shock. She was invited to join a committee for the Wembley Exhibition, but declined, because, from her point of view, the other Indians invited were extremists. She then felt herself isolated when she was told that these 'extremists' would be the only Indians invited onto the committee, because people like herself with different views were not representative of India. Her pro-Britishness was beginning to embarrass some Britons, and this made her feel that she belonged nowhere.[68] On the other hand, the King appeared to be more on Cornelia's side. At the Braemar Games in Scotland, the King and Queen sent for her and the King had a long talk about India. He told her that he had refused Prime Minister Ramsay MacDonald's request that he see C. R. Das, a member of the Viceroy's Council, because he (the King) believed him to be an extremist.[69]

Dick's main activity after reaching England was giving talks, and some of these were important for the very different future that he was going to choose. Notably he was asked to speak at the Church of St Martin-in-the-Fields in Trafalgar Square on education as the link that had 'given way' in India. After that, he was asked by Dick Sheppard, Vicar of St Martin, to give all the Friday lunchtime talks there in November, and he also organised tableaux in the crypt which Cornelia found most effective.[70]

CORNELIA CALLED TO THE BAR IN LONDON

Cornelia's main ambition lay in a new direction. In India, no woman had been called to the bar, that is, admitted to appear in court as a barrister, the highest rank of pleader. But the first woman in England, Ivy Williams, had passed the examinations in 1921 and was called on May 10th of the year Cornelia returned, 1922, although she would not go on to practise. Cornelia had recently been admitted to the rolls in Allahabad as a pleader with the lower rank of vakil, reserved for Indians, but now she saw her chance to become a barrister. Under the British system, barristers and Indian vakils were both distinguished from solicitors who could prepare cases, but not plead in court. The training for barristers was supplied at the medieval Inns of Court in London, and, like Dick before her, she decided to study at Lincoln's Inn. It was there that she had been allowed to use the library in 1891. A Mr Burns and a Mr Blake Odyers were willing to take her as pupil. The day after Ivy Williams was called, Cornelia ate the first of the three dinners required in addition to the examinations, and she got first class marks in Civil Law in her first examination. In the autumn term she had to attend lectures and the examination results were not so good with second and third class marks.[71] The family did not understand why she should now be working as hard as ever and shutting herself away, and they made ribald comments on her performance, though Odyers cheered her up by saying she had told him of an Act of which he did not know. At the Lincoln's Inn commemoration ceremony, the Queen caused a great sensation among the senior justices by insisting on returning to the hall when she sighted Cornelia, so as to go and speak to

27. Cornelia, future conqueror of Sapru, 1924.

her. Cornelia had modestly placed herself among the students, and everyone thought she should have had a special place at the banquet.[72] The next year, 1923, in her finals she got second-class marks and a call to the bar with papers signed by her old teacher, Sir Frederick Pollock. On the night, the call was worded, 'By the authority and on behalf of the Masters of the Bench, I pro-claim you a Barrister of the Society.' She could now wear a barrister's wig, which she kept in a special black metal wig box with her name in gold letters. She dined with the Benchers, and at dinner was asked to speak second after Mr Denning (later as Lord Denning called the most celebrated English judge of the twentieth century), who was called to the bar the same year. On the opening of the Law Courts the following autumn, there were for the first time seven women in the procession at Westminster Abbey, and the dining rules were changed in Lincoln's Inn to accommodate women guests. Cornelia was admitted into the chambers of Mr Morle and given legal work there. She was still very uncertain what work might open up for her, and therefore continued working as hard as ever at what she had got, but felt a certain self-disgust at neglecting the family.[73]

The other recognition closed to women until 1920 was the bestowal of Oxford degrees. Although Cornelia had passed the Bachelor of Civil Law examination thirty years earlier in 1892, she had not been able to claim the degree. In 1922 she arranged with Emily Penrose, the Principal, to join the Somerville party in Oxford for the ceremony of matriculation (admission to candidacy), where some of her Somerville friends joined her. She then paid a second visit to be awarded the degree itself in the examination schools. On this occasion she was written up in the *Oxford Magazine*. The Regius Professor of Law presented her to the Vice-Chancellor, and she was sent out to don her blue hood and return a Bachelor of Civil Law. Her old friend and admonisher P. C. Lyon now lived in a large house called Wester Ogil on the crest of Headington Hill, near where Lady Markby was still living. He took her to watch the student racing crews rowing on the river from the then preferred viewing platform of a college barge.[74] The rococo barges, which then lined the Oxford river bank, were for a whole week the venue to bring ladies in their best summer dresses and hats – Cornelia, of course in her saree – and to consume strawberries and cream, while turning at intervals to cheer, as the rowing 'eights' raced by.

DICK'S WEDDING

The most unexpected event in these years was Dick's marriage. Its postponement until he was 52 illustrates the family's difficulty in finding spouses, a difficulty that Cornelia never overcame. It meant that in future Cornelia's descents on Dick were to be on a whole family, no longer on a bachelor brother. When Dick's proposed engagement of 1913 did not work out, he had given up expecting to marry. He was now living in Piccadilly in the centre of London and not anticipating expenses other than those of a bachelor. But his work in the church of St Martin-in-the-Fields was to have an unexpected outcome. Mary Monkhouse was an English girl, thirty years younger, and they met through his talks at the church. May Monkhouse, Mary's mother, had no objection to the difference of age or race, and she came up to London to meet Cornelia and Dick's other sisters. She was a thoughtful and stoical person, whose early married life had involved supporting a bush-clearing family in New Zealand as the only woman in a 20-mile radius, with a single cooking pot and an axe in her kitchen. Back in England her husband had died and she had brought up Mary as a country girl with a smattering of polish from a brief spell at Cheltenham Ladies College, and a strong sense of romance. When Mary met Dick, she was transported to a world of unimaginable fascination with Indians and English people in the heart of London. At about this time, Dick hired her as a secretary for the Zenana Mission, which in the days of Dick's mother had been co-owners of the Poona family school and home.[iv]

Cornelia first met Mary Monkhouse with Dick in January 1924. By mid-March, she was calling her 'the eternal Mollie Monkhouse'. On May 8th Dick and Mary were engaged, and Cornelia met Mary Monkhouse's mother on May 29th and found her charming. The sisters gave Mary a party, and Cornelia was allowed to take her shopping.

The wedding took place on July 28th, nine months after the engagement and 101 years after the birth of Dick's father. The tiny village of Willersey, where Mary had lived with her mother, was a cluster of little old cottages round the green of the church. All the village was there, spilling onto the pathway and round the church and house. They never forgot the sight of so many Indian sisters in their brilliant sarees. Mary herself wore a tabard, a medieval style of dress. It was of silver and blue saree material, made up with a train, a wedding dress distinctive enough to be now in the Cheltenham Museum. Mary said the responses firmly, but Dick, not having expected he would have the opportunity to marry, broke down when asked, 'Do you take this woman to be your wife?', which Cornelia found touching in so self-assured a person.[75]

The wedding was a surprise not only to the villagers of Willersey. The Vicereine Lady Reading commented on the marriage in her published diaries and wrote that she had nothing against a marriage between the races in itself, but she was afraid that the children would suffer discrimination.[76]

---

iv The Mission's rooms in London were the very ones where almost 50 years later Dick's son was to give his first London University lecture.

28. Dick and his bride, 1924, with sisters (from left, back row: Alice, Cornelia; front row: Pheroze, Mary, Lena).

29. Dick's wedding in a country village, Willersey, 1924.

CORNELIA'S DECISION: RETURN TO INDIA

Cornelia now had to decide her own future and it was going to diverge from Dick's. At one point she felt almost persuaded to stay in England.[77] She decided to return to India. What decided her was the needs of her purdhanashins, and the fact that she had been allowed no successor who could help them. One purdahnashin was worried in 1923, when a new law allowed daughters or sisters to inherit, even though they could not pray for the deceased male.[78] Cornelia thought that now she was a qualified barrister, she would have a new way of helping them by taking up a second career. She did not foresee that the obstacles would be even greater than before.

PART V

RETURN TO INDIA: THE BAR, SOCIAL WORK AND POLITICS

CHAPTER 17

BARRISTER IN CALCUTTA, 1924–1929: MISOGYNY, SABOTAGE, FAILURE AND SUCCESS

O n Cornelia's return to India in 1924, she enjoyed some important successes and a triumph, but only after encountering opposition to a woman even stronger than before and political sabotage. On the journey back to India, she learnt of a new regulation, that the second rank of pleader, the vakils, could become barristers after ten years. There would clearly be a rush of applicants to the bar in Calcutta.[1] Despite the Registrar's strong opposition to Cornelia's enrolment, the leader of the Calcutta bar, Mr Pugh, supported her and she was enrolled in the High Court of Calcutta in November, and found herself chambers with a clerk in Hastrup Street and lodgings at 28 Chowringee.[2]

THE CALCUTTA HIGH COURT

Everything seemed to start well. Her first case came within a week, and her clerk said that 20 vakils wanted her address. The barristers were charming to her on arrival, the Administrator General of Bengal asked her opinion on some legacies and a Rani telegraphed that she was sending her agent on a private matter. The supporters of one of her clients squatted on the edge of her carpet, saying, 'Huzoor. Your name will become a word of the world, if you save the poor Brahmin.' She persuaded the leader of the bar to change his opinion on a case and he said her opinion was worth five gold mohurs (or guineas).[3] This was progress because as a junior, she had received only three from the Administrator General.[4]

In November, a year after enrolment, such was Cornelia's reputation that she got the first case in which she was asked to lead. Her client's priest said, wagging his head, 'Did I not report truly? Now your opponent is a dead man.' In a case shortly after, it was cabled to the English newspapers that a woman had appeared for the Crown for the first time in a High Court in India. But she was there as a junior and her senior failed to use her arguments, or objections, except for one that he took without acknowledgement, and he slept for half an hour during the trial. Despite the judge's support of Cornelia, the jury would not convict. Cornelia was to have some successes and triumphs at the bar, but on the whole the atmosphere turned out to be more hostile than any she had experienced in her earlier work for the Government of Bengal, and she had to pass through many obstacles before winning the successes.

THREE EARLY SIGNS OF OPPOSITION: EXCLUSION FROM THE BAR LIBRARY, DENIAL OF GOVERNMENT WORK AND A VAKIL'S MISOGYNY

A first obstacle concerned the all-important membership of the bar library.[5] Solicitors went to the bar library to find barristers to undertake briefs. But a new rule, designed to prevent a rush of vakils into the bar library, stated that there would be no new admissions until there was room. This cut Cornelia off from briefs and from books for preparing cases, unlike the vakils, who had their own library. In addition, some hostile Bengalis inferred that she must be incompetent when they did not see her in the library. The Viceroy's wife, Lady Reading, sought redress. But although Cornelia was elected to the bar library, it was with restrictions. Except in the vacations, she was allowed only to use a room three stories above the library and to ask for books to be brought. It would have taken several minutes to carry them up when found. Even in the vacations, though downstairs and able to look at the books, she was required to use an inner room, so as not to compete for briefs with seniors. All the same, she was given the job of summoning bar library meetings and taking the minutes.[6] Excluded from the library proper, she got little more than paper work and some cases from the British and cases without fee for paupers.[7] She was also not able to see newspapers, being unable as a woman to belong to any club in Calcutta, although during summer visits to Darjeeling, she joined the Darjeeling Gymkhana Club.[8]

Cornelia could have expected legal work for the Government. It was the role of the so-called Legal Remembrancer's to commission this. But the Legal Remembrancer refused to pay Cornelia the three guineas promised for her first Government case, because that would commit him to giving her several briefs a year.[9] In fact, he never put her on the panel to compete with others for briefs, but preferred junior vakils with imperfect English,[10] whereas junior barristers were normally put on a roster as a matter of course for prosecution work for the Government.[11] It was a considerable time before she got any paid Government work for the Crown.

Hostility to women was clearly manifested in January 1926 during a summing up in a crowded court of the High Court. A vakil demanded Cornelia's chair because he was standing. There were barristers as well as vakils standing, and he would not have dared speak to a male barrister that way. Cornelia was seated at Counsel's table, and she refused, though when he would not get someone to bring him a chair, she had someone fetch one for him from another court.[12]

THEFT OF ARGUMENTS, CASES AND PAY

Another problem for Cornelia was that her arguments or cases were stolen from her by male lawyers, even when clients wanted her. The motive with pleaders was often to get the case for themselves. But in one case the solicitor was also a money lender who offered cases only to barristers who would borrow from him.[13] Again, a purdahnashin's attorneys assured their client that a woman – Cornelia – could not possibly know the law.[14] The methods of theft were various. Sometimes the client was told that Cornelia's arguments were no good,[15] or the magistrate was told that she had agreed or asked to withdraw.[16] Not only vakils and barristers junior to her were involved,[17] but senior barristers too might just take a case off her, in one case, she thought, because she was disliked as a woman.[18] One, when confronted, was ashamed and abandoned the case, but it was still he who collected the fee.[19] Another senior barrister offered a case to Cornelia, so that she declined appearing for the other side, but he then gave the role to someone else, pretending it had been stolen out of his briefcase. She believed he was drinking.[20] All this made it very hard to discuss with junior barristers how to conduct a case. They might think it was not worth fighting or have an approach she thought wrong, and to persuade them, she would need to reveal her own insight. But then they might switch and try to get the case and the arguments for themselves.[21]

A particularly blatant case involved an acting Public Prosecutor, a vakil, in the police courts. It concerned a jewel robbery from her friend the Maharaja of Bharatpur. Cornelia was thrilled that she was briefed to act for the Crown. The Public Prosecutor had not studied the case, so she slipped him notes on what question to ask the witnesses next. He would say aloud in the Court, 'No, I can't ask that,' and then would ask it as if it were his idea. She also wrote his speech for him. At the next sitting, the Commissioner of Police, whose decision it was, asked Cornelia herself to take over the pleading, but the Public Prosecutor wanted the case for himself and told the magistrate wrongly that the case fell under a different regulation, so that it was up to him who should do the pleading. The Commissioner of Police nonetheless wrote Cornelia a letter telling her to continue, but the Public Prosecutor intercepted the letter and did not show it to her. Cornelia thought that he had 'probably' told the magistrate that Cornelia had agreed to his taking over, and meanwhile he had taken her notes. He went on to lose the case by ignoring the two crucial points on which Cornelia had warned him.[22] This was the case in which the Maharaja had asked Cornelia to do some preliminary detective work for him and then ran into debt and asked to be excused from paying. When he died shortly after and she forgave the debt, his administrators nonetheless wrote and accused Cornelia of asking for something that had already been paid.[23]

This trial was conducted not in the High Court, but in a police court, where Cornelia normally fared better than in the High Court. She appeared in a number of other courts too, and at least she found a completely different attitude when she took cases across the river at Howrah District Court. The vakils and pleaders asked her to go often. The Bengali judge seemed afraid of keeping a woman barrister waiting and confided afterwards that his wife was a purdah-nashin, that he had read Cornelia's work, was proud to have her plead and that she should have costs, as she was taking no fee.[24]

Even when Cornelia did get to plead, a further problem was the withholding of her fees, first and foremost because she was a woman. In 1926, the wife of a barrister had burst out with the remark that Cornelia did not want fees, only the glamour of wearing a wig. Her clerk had then told her that barristers in the bar library were putting that rumour about and he appeared to be furious.[25] In fact, the rumour suited him very well since it could be used to explain his failure to hand her fees over.

The solicitors also seemed to exercise what she called a boycott against her.[26] She learnt that when solicitors did not pay, the only redress was to report them to the relevant board. When she did finally go to the board, one of the five members himself was reluctant to press the solicitors for the full amount owed her.[27]

Her willingness to work without fee was partly due to her concern to act for paupers, which carried no fee, and partly connected with her wish to gain enough experience to convince those who would not give her work. Others could refuse to take briefs until paid in advance, but as a woman trying to break into the profession, she dared not do that. She also did not wish to be seen outside the court claiming unpaid fees, as that would have been very bad publicity.[28] So she had to scribble pot-boilers for literary magazines in order to make ends meet.[29] But the very reputation for acting without fee further encouraged non-payment.

Other reasons for her getting no fees included her initial isolation from the bar library, her belief that her first duty was to secure justice regardless of fee, as in the Princely States of Narhan, Dholpur and Janjira to be described in Chapter 22, and her entanglement in the political controversy over Mayo, in which her clerk turned out to be involved. By September 1926, she was owed for eight cases,[30] and by January 1929, she had had no paid briefs for five months since August of the previous year. In November of that year, when she reached the age of 63, she decided to give priority to social service over pleading, although that also paid no money.[31]

ANOTHER KIND OF THEFT: UNACKNOWLEDGED AND UNREWARDED 'DEVILLING'

There was another kind of theft. Some senior barristers used Cornelia for 'devilling'. That was like getting an apprentice to do the work, find the arguments and the precedents, without having to pay them at all, and it was only occasionally and to random listeners that the senior barrister would acknowledge this help. One senior barrister got Cornelia to do this again and again with promises that he would later want her as a junior, which he never did, although he told those who happened to be listening that he had won through her suggestions.[32] Another never acknowledged her devilling, and Cornelia commented that Indian men could not bear to be beholden to a woman, and older barristers were even twitted for using her. Some used her for mere devilling, she thought, because neither Indian nor English seniors wanted to have a woman as their junior.[33]

Not everyone refused to acknowledge her help. A Bengali counsel for the Crown asked to postpone his summing up because he wanted to base it on Cornelia's brilliant suggestion and thank her. He was not in fact allowed to do that, because she was not officially his junior.[34]

POSTPONEMENTS: WAITING FOR A SLEEPY JUDGE AGAINST A TIME LIMIT

There were problems of other kinds too. Some judges were better than others. One would go to sleep during trials.[35] Among magistrates, some were former barristers, but those from the Indian Civil Service had learnt only the abbreviated law codes.[36] It was a trick of opposing Counsel, if they had a weak case, to have the case postponed, so that it could be moved to a bad judge. On the other hand, if one responded by waiting for a good judge, one might fall foul of a time limit.[37]

LACK OF SOCIAL LIFE

In all these troubles, the bar did not give Cornelia the supporting social life which she had enjoyed in her career with the Government of Bengal. The judges were always very pleasant to her at the ceremonial re-opening of the courts after the summer recess,[38] but her only close legal friends were Justice and Mrs Page.[39] She saw more, as in the old days, of the Governor of Bengal and his wife and the circles of Government House than she did of her fellow barristers.

A NEW PROBLEM: POLITICAL ATTACK BY DISHONEST CLERK

The preceding problems she would have encountered as a woman, even without political interference. But the most serious attack on her was by a dishonest clerk supported, as she thought, by political funding. Her clerk turned out to be 'borrowing' (she does not say 'embezzling') the fees handed over by clients for his own use, and promising to repay the clients at 6 per cent interest. The etiquette should have been for the clerk to collect the fee from the client and pass it to her. He had also apparently been selling to vakils briefs offered to Cornelia in return for a commission. The clerk eventually confessed, but had meanwhile gained the solidarity of other clerks, so that they refused to take his place when he was sacked. He got the financial support, Cornelia felt sure, of Gandhi's Swarajists to sue Cornelia and boasted that hundreds of rupees would not make him desist. As a result she was actually sued in her own court. It was the time that Cornelia was being attacked as the accomplice of Mayo in Mayo's denigration of India, as will be described in the next chapter. The clerk made use of that controversy. He had copied her letters about India and Bengal to portray her as a friend of Mayo, and that helped him to get the support of the Swarajists. He was also telling barristers that she was a bad employer, engaged in malpractice and was anti-Indian and anti-Bengali. He demanded to see her accounts, claiming that there was an irregularity. The court examined Cornelia for six hours. Her clerk had changed the date on his dismissal notice, pretended he was owed fees from the time before he was employed and had stolen receipts acknowledging his payments from the filing cabinet, but Cornelia had records of all payments to him. It turned out that she was not underpaying, but overpaying him, because during her isolation three stories up from the bar library, she could not find out what the etiquette was. But even then he tried to present the overpayment as if it were malpractice, paying for illicit briefs from touts. The judge was very angry with him and said that it was a speculative suit to harass a respectable member of the bar. Nonetheless, the day after the trial, *The Statesman* put its report in big headlines, 'Woman barrister sued,' then put his side of the case in full and Cornelia's briefly, without reference to the reason for the clerk's dismissal, the judge's description of the suit as vexatious, or the fact that she had paid the clerk all his dues. The editor, Fraser Blair, was someone whom Cornelia had known for a very long time. But his only explanation was that anything about her was news.[40]

The clerk sought leave to appeal. He hung around the corridors, following Cornelia up and down stairs and turned clients away. Cornelia did not take the bar library's advice to call the police. The next clerk, when she finally got one, did no work and turned out not to have passed on to her a client's papers, so that she would not get the job. She finished up with no help but a private offer of typing.[41]

Cornelia spoke of her loneliness and said that she was kept going only by her mail from Elena, and her religion.[42] Her religion enabled her repeatedly to say to herself, 'God removes mountains,' 'I must have faith in the outcome,' 'must learn trust in God'. She also repeated the words of her deceased Kathiawari

Rani, described in Chapter 4, who said, when Cornelia got her 30 years of withheld allowance, that she did not resent the withholding because 'God will resent it for me.' The fullest statement of her reasons for staying on was given in a letter of 1927 to Elena, whom she called her 'Partner'.[43]

> 'You can't think how lovely it felt to know that the "Partner" thought there was something which Cornelia could do: and that she cared about the weariness and the frustrations out here, and that she *understood*. . . . That's perhaps the biggest thing of all – someone who understands, just what giving up (in) here and now would mean'. . . . 'I must make of the job must I not? a success – must make money at it, to show that it can be done: must plead as I would like to plead to prove that women can do this thing also: and to encourage those who come after to stick to their attempt and not lose heart'. . . . 'I feel that God would not have made it possible for me to get my call and come out again, unless I was meant to try and struggle on a while at this job here'.

SUCCESS IN LEGAL OPINIONS OPENS UP THE BAR LIBRARY

So much for the obstacles to Cornelia's work at the bar. But she had her successes too. About one thing in the Calcutta bar, there was no quarrel. The Government of India in Delhi asked the bar library for an opinion on changing the law of infanticide, and Cornelia was asked in 1926 to write the entire reply for the committee consisting of the Advocate General and the senior Barrister. Cornelia wrote a magisterial opinion, outlining the latest state of the law in England and Europe, and contrasting the motivations for infanticide in India. These included not only the cost of the bride price for daughters, but also family disgrace over pregnancies of women widowed in childhood and forbidden remarriage, where the family might order the mother to commit infanticide at a time when she might in addition be suffering from post-natal depression. The current Indian law allowed only the penalties of death or penal servitude for life.

Not only did the bar library pay Cornelia at once, but the Advocate General said, 'We have never had an opinion like this. I congratulate you,' and to the bar library he added, 'I want you to know that Miss Sorabji wrote a most valuable and illuminating note going into the history of the subject, so that the committee was able at once to adopt an opinion.' The men shouted, 'Hear Hear'.[44]

As a result of the opinion, after more than a year at the Calcutta bar she received 50 votes more than necessary to become a permanent member of the bar library, more than any man, and with no black ball, a single one of which would have excluded her. So she could use the library downstairs. The first three months were probationary and as a junior she would have to give up her seat to any senior.[45] But by June she was being congratulated in the bar library for having made such a good start, and she received courtesies of being allowed to go in to plead ahead of the men.[46]

Cornelia was to write a series of further opinions for the bar library by request, and this was a major success at the Calcutta bar. There was no opposition to a woman writing learned opinions. The opposition she met was to a woman appearing in court to plead. Two further opinions were on a politically controversial subject central to her concerns – the age of consent both in marriage and in prostitution. She discovered that the law protected married and unmarried girl babies, but had forgotten to offer protection to widowed girl babies.[47] Other subjects included the slander of women, and their abduction,[48] and redress for women in Princely States.[49] The last will be discussed in Chapter 22.

SUCCESS WITH COURT OF WARDS ESTATES

In a second area of the law Cornelia was successful again. There were cases for estates in British India connected with her old employers, the Board of Revenue and the Court of Wards. She admitted that she would have preferred work at the Calcutta High Court to work from the Board of Revenue.[50] But in this work she was successful, and in one case triumphant. As with the legal opinions for the bar library, this was an area where there were not the same objections to her working. It was the area of her purdahnashin expertise. Early on a judge asked her to act as interpreter for a purdahnashin and even the opposition congratulated her on the speed with which that enabled them to work.[51]

The appeal that decided her to return to India had been by a purdahnashin against inheritance by a sister's son. According to orthodox belief, only those could inherit who would on religious grounds be qualified to pray for the soul of a late husband. The protest against the new British proposal for inheritance by a sister's son was settled initially, when Cornelia persuaded the District Collector at Banailli that he should not anticipate the new legislation on inheritance which had not yet been passed. The case had also to be settled in the law courts, but she won there too.[52]

Sometimes in these cases, a vicious circle arose in which the Board of Revenue would not reopen a case unless the District Commissioner showed cause and the District Commissioner would not show cause until the Board reopened the case.

This happened in a dispute involving the very same district at Banailli. A Rani was in debt but all she needed to do was to clear the debt by selling off to her co-sharers some of her scattered property. The sale was opposed by her reversioners, the people who would inherit if anything adverse happened to her, because they benefited from her being in debt. Cornelia explained the situation, and in 1927, the leading legal authority on such problems said that he could not add one dot to Cornelia's written opinion, and she received seven gold mohurs. The Board then agreed to the debt-clearing sale, though the Bengali Commissioner still stalled. Cornelia thought that as manager of the estate he benefited from the status quo. But he too gave in to the sale when Cornelia succeeded in getting the accounts for the last 12 years. No accounts had been shown to the ward for 24 years.[53]

Cornelia was also invited to arbitrate and seek reconciliation in a dispute in Dacca between her former ward and later staunch collaborator in social service, the wealthy Peri Banu,[54] and her equally wealthy older relative Khodija Begum, who had made an invalid attempt to revoke Peri Banu's trust funds. The Board of Revenue was using strong-arm tactics to take over the trust estate from Khodija Begum and give it to Peri Banu, but Cornelia pointed out that this exceeded the Board's powers. The Legal Remembrancer of the Board of Revenue said, 'We find it difficult to answer your argument, Miss Sorabji,' and it was agreed that Khodija Begum should keep the trust estate for the time being, while Cornelia acted as a messenger of peace to get a voluntary agreement, which she did. But Cornelia had also to persuade the Board to admit that they were (illicitly) trying to take over the estate, so that she could take the matter to court and get the take-over officially withdrawn. She further wanted, with the agreement of the Governor of the Province, a series of legal actions between Peri Banu and her opponents withdrawn before the estate was released. Despite reluctance from the opponents, she secured this objective too, and Peri Banu wept and said that God had sent Cornelia to her aid.[55] Her gratitude was to be translated into the most wonderful help with Cornelia's projects, although, with her wealth confirmed, Peri Banu was also to be a victim of demands for money with menaces from political activists.[56]

TRIUMPH AGAINST SAPRU ON THE SUCCESSION AT NARHAN

The most important case, however, involving Government employment under the Board of Revenue concerned the estate of Narhan in Bihar, the very first estate Cornelia had ever handled when appointed as legal adviser 22 years earlier in 1904. We have only Cornelia's account of what happened plus the fact that her arguments won on appeal. The Maharaja of Benares (Varanasi) was claiming the State. The Narhan Rani thought the take-over inevitable, but Cornelia felt obliged to oppose it, although she regretted being against the Maharaja.[57] She had already studied the legal history of the Narhan throne back to 1773. The Maharaja's agents, according to Cornelia, had first attempted to bribe the Narhan side to drop the case and had then had the case put on at a distance from Narhan, on the grounds that Narhan had an outlying property under the jurisdiction of Allahabad in Muzapur. Narhan asked Cornelia to cross-examine the Maharaja's witnesses for them in preliminary hearings already under way in Muzapur, because they could not afford to send their own witnesses that far. Narhan could also only afford ineffective local lawyers and had so far been blocked in everything they did. They could offer Cornelia only a pittance, but she accepted the brief provided she was paid in advance. The brief was 'a stack as high as her arm'. One question was whether a Maharaja in a Princely State (Benares) could take over a part of British India (Narhan). Cornelia found a letter from the Court of Wards telling Benares that a ruler would have to choose between his Princely estate and a British India estate, but could not have both.

Cornelia's opponent in Muzapur turned out to be the most famous barrister in the North of India, and a Nationalist leader, Dick's friend and colleague, now leader of the bar in Allahabad, Sir Tej Bahadur Sapru K. C. (King's Counsel). He was a giant and a specialist in succession cases. Cornelia regarded him at the time as one with Gandhi, although in fact he was a constitutionalist supporter of Home Rule.[58]

The claim of Benares to own Narhan depended on the adoption into the Benares family in the distant past of an alleged heir to Narhan. Cornelia once again used her knowledge that the validity of an adoption depends on the qualifications of the adoptee to pray for the soul of the deceased male owner. But the qualification to pray depends in turn on the gods worshipped by the adoptee, because he needs to be heard by the right gods. In the case in question, Cornelia found, the adoptee had been required to change the gods he worshipped as a condition of being adopted by the Benares line. Consequently there had been no religious connexion with Narhan for 150 years, although Cornelia would need witnesses to support these points about Bihar custom and religious implications.

Cornelia also found that everyone had been mistaken about the identity of the adoptee. The adoptee was not the clerk from Narhan who had married the daughter of a Benares Maharaja in the eighteenth century. A document of

1773 showed that it was rather the son of that clerk. Moreover, there was a document of 1808 showing the adoptee's younger brother declaring that their father was excluded from Narhan for ever.

When Cornelia arrived at Muzapur, neither the Narhan clients nor the pleader they had engaged to act as junior met her, and there were only primitive carriages called ekkas for transport. She spotted a decrepit Ford taxi and drove with her travelling boy to a primitive Dak bungalow, or rest house, which smelt of bats. It was very hot and had not rained. There were no lights except a smoking lantern, so she could not work after dark and sometimes had to get up at 4.30 a.m. The pleader with whom she was meant to be preparing the case was angry that Cornelia had been asked to lead and wrote that he could not see her at all. Even when she got the Ford taxi, accompanied now at least by her clients, and found him in court, he said he was not free all day and could not come to her because he had a grandchild at home with sore eyes. She said she understood and would instead come to his house at 4.30. He had then collected a crowd to show off and rejected her opinions. But when she asked his, he repeated what she had said, except that she made him add two extra issues which were important.

Sapru in Court the next day wore his King's Counsel gown. He had three juniors, one his son, and any number of vakils. Sapru had to confront the adoption issue which Cornelia had just got added to the case. He produced a huge pile of historical books and argued that since W. Haskeys did not list the ancestor as adopted, he was not. Cornelia felt that Sapru was relying on bluff. He also tried to argue against Cornelia's further submissions that the ancestor had retained both sets of religious affiliations, but that is not allowed by custom. Cornelia's years of religious knowledge were coming into play.

The next session was to be in July. But a new problem was that during the interval all but three of her Narhan clients were bought off, according to Cornelia, and had dropped their suit. So evidently was the pleader, who was supposed to be helping Cornelia. He started behaving suspiciously, refusing to work without a superfluous second copy of the briefs, and failing to call or even list her witnesses. Instead he wrote to Cornelia that she was superseded and that she should not come back. However, the three surviving clients cabled that she should.

While waiting for her turn at defence Cornelia combed the digests from 1837–1927 and found two rulings which killed the Benares case dead, but also two rulings on the other side which overrode Indian rulings. When she arrived for her defence, her pleader was hob-nobbing with the other side and appeared to have told them all he knew about her arguments and weak places. Sapru 'lauded him to the skies' and Cornelia carried on alone, though a junior pleader joined her for the sake of appearances half way through. She felt that with the right judge they could win on technical questions such as time limitation, and on the question of the adoption. The battle now hotted up, and Cornelia gave her version of the dialogue:[59]

> 'Sapru was *horrid* to me and most unfair professionally. Trying to make the judge, a poor little Muslim Munsiff[i] converted into a sub-judge to try the case, accept his repeated statements that I was accusing the court of partiality, etc. I used the words, "Plaintiff's Counsel has obtained many privileges, (1) the right to begin...."

> ' "The Defendant's Counsel says you show me *favour*", he roared and shouted. "I beg that it be noticed that the Court has been accused...." Or again, when he got his right of reply (wrongly under order XVIII.3, as I showed), and I asked the Court to notice that he was exceeding their permission to introduce fresh evidence, he yelled again:

> "would I withdraw?"

> '*Cornelia*. "No – that is my submission".

> '*He*. "That is Contempt of Court."

> '*Cornelia* (to the judge). "I submit, your Honour, that my remarks about Plaintiff's Counsel are within my rights and cannot be Contempt of Court. But if your Honour believes for any reason that they are so, I beg you will take the necessary action against me and not allow Plaintiff's Counsel's suggestions to prejudice my case. I cannot withdraw the remarks I have made and I can substantiate them" (which I did as the case proceeded, moving to point to each infringement of the law of evidence).

> 'Sapru would yell at me: "Madam, when you know a little more law, you will realise..., etc". He called the Court of Wards "liars" and alleged a deep plot between the Defendants and the Court of Wards. He poured scorn on me personally: "My learned friend does not realise that not poetical fancies but the law prevails in these courts. Her case may be all very well written as the story of an imaginary Prince for a magazine of fiction. I will grant she knows English, She knows nothing else."

---

i A Munsiff was the most junior kind of judge in the Subordinate Civil Service, which was below the Provincial Civil Service and below the prestigious Indian Civil Service. A Munsiff was normally restricted to hearing cases involving a few hundred rupees.

'I had to sit quite still through these tirades. Once I said: could he not observe the professional courtesies, to which we both should have been used? He *roared*, "If you come into the profession, Madam, realise the Court is not a drawing room, and do not whine for courtesy." I felt I must ignore personal insult, since the judge could not or would not control him, and devote my whole being to watching my case while he spoke. So I let him abuse, only rising to correct mis-statements of fact or law.

'He was *bare-faced*, denying one moment what he had said the moment before, and there is no short-hand writer in these courts. When he lied about any *written* word of mine, in written applications mostly, I intervened and just read out the actual words. This made him very angry.

'He was *furious* that I knew about Hindu law and religion. And could check his statements. He said that the Privy Council had decided that a man might eat with English folk and even marry an English woman and *yet be a Hindu* (case of Baroda 1923). I had to rise then to ask whether he was not referring to the Probate and Administration Act, and the decision of the Privy Council that *for purposes of that Act*, not of religion, a man's *race* remained Hindu. You will guess how he stormed. "Miss Sorabji cannot understand these questions about Hindu race and religion". – Abuse his only response.

'Oh dear, there is so much to tell you and to laugh over with you. Wait till I come. Won't we talk! Do keep time for me, Elena. I feel *starved* for a talk with you and your all-the-way comprehension, my partner – bless you! And oh, I did so want you beside me all the time. I was terribly alone. All six juniors would jump up and roar and answer questions I addressed to the Bench.

'Once when Sapru was reading out the documentary evidence, he *stressed* by mistake a point dead against himself, and in my favour. I said, "Ha! ha!" He almost leapt into the air. "Defendant's Counsel says 'Ha! ha!'. This is Con-tempt of Court" (to the Bench). To me: "Will you withdraw those words, Madam?"

'*Cornelia.* "No. They were a remark on what you were reading addressed to you, not to the Court. I still feel like that – Ha! ha!". He raved a while longer. The judge sat still, and then he had to desist and go on. But when the clients came to see me "for comfort", as they did daily at 8 o'clock after court, to be told all about the legal portents, etc., etc. (they know no English or very little), we all said, or at least I did and I taught them how to say it, "Ha! ha!", and had a good laugh, which took the sting out of a trying day of Sapru's nastiness.

'He would walk up to the Bench and lean over and address the judge, show-ing him books, back to the Court, and I could not hear what he said. When I objected he roared, "All the High Court judges in Allahabad respect me. No one has dared to say that I am doing what is irregular".

'The judge came to Court in the Benares car. Surely that was wrong. There were other things too. I could swear that Sapru drafted two of the most important issues, getting them his way. I objected to them and even the judge said, "Issue 8" (it is not in your copy – it was reversed) "is useless. The Defendant has never said it was an A. valid under the Hindu law". Plaintiff's Counsel said, "the meaning of that issue is . . .", and the judge let it stand. If the *judge* had drafted it, the scene was incomprehensible.

'The last day Sapru made a speech saying he had abused me, but he must pay tribute to the eloquence and the research I had used for my clients. And we shook hands all round. All very well, but he had got unfair things down to prejudice the judge and he looked ashamed at the end. I've lost all respect for him. As an advocate he is nowhere. He is a political speaker, not a lawyer.'

Cornelia was able to spring other surprises on Sapru, including the Maharaja's admitting that his ancestor was adopted. Sapru's juniors were paid 6000 rupees just to look through books, whereas Cornelia had to do all the looking up for herself. Sapru charged 200 rupees an hour for reading his brief and 2800 a day during the 20-day case, his six juniors 200 a day each. The Narhan estate was worth only 300,000 rupees. Cornelia thought that the interest of Benares might be that if they won on the adoption question over Narhan, they would also be able to claim another estate which they wanted, that of Cornelia's old friend and ward, the Maharani of Bettiah.[60]

Cornelia's clients said that all the village folk and local landowners who watched the case said, 'Why does Sapru shout and scream and wave his hands? He does this. Then the Miss Sahib barrister Sahabji stands up and says a few firm words quietly to the judge, and then only can the case proceed.' The judge at the end said that it was the first time a woman barrister had appeared in the United Provinces, and in a case of that magnitude anywhere in the Empire.

The judge decided against Cornelia. She believed that Sapru had succeeded in terrifying him. But she wrote the arguments to be used in the appeal to the High Court, which was sent in four months later, and in 1933, she heard that the appeal had succeeded and was congratulated as she passed through Muzapur.[61] Although a final stage was expected of appeal to the Privy Council,[62] the part that Cornelia worked on ended in success, not to say triumph, satisfactorily rounding off the work for her very first estate of Narhan.

How could a family friend very close indeed to Dick, whose photographs and public conduct reveal such gravity, have behaved in this way? It looks as if he was taken by surprise to realise that he might be defeated by a woman, herself a junior, in front of his son and other juniors. Sapru was a great man, and some of his greatness will emerge from the account of the Round Table Conferences in Chapter 21. It shows what Cornelia was up against that even a great man could not bear to be defeated by a woman.

LUCRATIVE LEGAL PRACTICE DECLINED

People now brought Cornelia fresh briefs to plead in Muzapur and also asked if she would oppose Sapru in Allahabad. One case against him there was worth 1,700,000 rupees. This might have been her chance to show that a woman could succeed at the bar. But she was committed back in Calcutta to some paupers in a philanthropic case with no fee, and declined. It turned out that she had not been told that her philanthropic case in Calcutta was postponed. Her only comment: 'these are the sorrowful chances of the profession.'[63]

It was appropriate that Cornelia's successes in her career as a barrister should have been connected with the estates of wards and former wards, giving continuity to her career.

CHAPTER 18

THE MAYO DEBACLE, 1927

Almost the greatest damage to Cornelia's career was inflicted by Katherine Mayo. Mayo was an American with a powerful record of supporting right wing causes in the USA. In connexion with India she had at least two agendas. She wanted to support British rule in India, as she had supported American rule in the Philippines, by presenting the population as unfit to govern itself. She also supported the movement in America which in 1923 and 1924 had revoked US citizenship for a good proportion of Indians on the grounds that, though Caucasian, they were not white, and had denied Indians further immigration. At the time of meeting her, Cornelia knew only of her support for American rule in the Philippines in her book, *The Isles of Fear*, and she seems never to have known of Mayo's campaigns against allowing Indians to live in America.

THREE DAYS OF SEMINAR IN CORNELIA'S GARDEN, 1926

She was a clever woman and Cornelia fell under her spell. In order to see why, one needs to know of the three days of seminar and discussion that Cornelia arranged for her with Indians of different persuasions in her Calcutta house and garden in February 1926.[1]

> 'My great excitement has been seeing Miss Mayo, the Philippines lady. She is charming. They sent her on to me from Delhi, and while the Lyttons[i] were still away, I saw her Thursday, Saturday, Sunday, her and Miss Newell, her companion, and Captain Field. They came to tea in the garden and we talked and talked. I tried to answer her questions. She is a good extractor of information. I admire her and her questions give one to think. And as a cross-examiner she is A1.

---

i Governor of Bengal and his wife.

'I got her an interview with Sinha and arranged for the other men on her list to meet her here. Lord Sinha, for all his late, and earlier, support of the Government, *had* a case against Britain. And his list included neglect of villages, poverty, malaria. Miss Mayo very cleverly got out of him that he had not visited his own village people[ii] for 17 years. It's useful comment on his charges. Apparently, they let themselves go[iii] to Americans, even the Sinhas amongst them.

'Among the others she interviewed here were the Deputy President of the Council (Muslim), a Swarajist[iv] old style and new (Hindu), and a so-called liberal - Brahmo. They came on Sunday and we sat in the garden. I suggested that she should throw a question into the ring and that each of us should answer it. She did this. I can't tell you how interesting it was. At first, the men were at each other's throats. Then her unifying influence told.

'One question was, "What would unite us?" They made me answer first. I said: the caring for something outside ourselves, more than ourselves, country, religion, work for the less fortunate. The young Swarajist said: intermarriage. The older Swarajist said, practically, that nothing would. The Muslim said Hindus and Muslims never would unite. The Brahmo talked at large. She then asked them about the case against the British, and about what Tagore meant to India. She is writing this all up, so you will hear what they said.

'Then, as it was growing dark, she spoke movingly, beautifully. She told us a story of how she was once lost in a New Guinea forest and saved by an East Indian. And then she told them her vision for India, of these young men going out into the villages and working, forsaking personal ambition to give to the poor and the ignorant. It was beautifully told. We were all moved deeply, I am sure. The nice young Swarajist boy broke the silence. "Do you remember", he said, "the story in the Talmud? One saw in the distance a form approach him, a terrifying being. 'It is a giant', he said. He came nearer. 'Oh no, it is a man.' He came nearer. 'Oh no, it is my brother'." The older Swarajist said, "if only that were true. If only he could be a brother", and broke the spell, for we all laughed and chaffed him.'

What a different Mayo that was from the one who was to be revealed. But Cornelia never lost her feeling that that was the true Mayo, a person of sharp intelligence who understood the need to help the oppressed and could inspire others to do so. Without that initial self-presentation, it would be hard to understand Cornelia's attachment to her. Indeed, Cornelia loved her at once. She took her to the High Court and introduced her to more people at the

---

ii Cornelia's review of Mayo calls him the head of the village.

iii Speak unguardedly.

iv Campaigner for Home Rule.

Government House garden party. The Governor then took over and arranged for Mayo to go to the villages. In July, Cornelia arranged another seminar of Indians at her house to answer questions sent by Mayo about the place of the village in schemes for Home Rule. But in Mayo's absence, this seminar was not a success. Mayo returned to see Cornelia in March and said, 'You are the best thing that has happened to me in India.' When Mayo's controversial book finally came out, Cornelia still recalled both in conversation and in her book review how Mayo had united everybody in her garden.[2]

MAYO'S BOOK SPRINGS A SURPRISE, 1927

When the book appeared in 1927, it was totally different from the spirit of their discussion. It was an attack on Hinduism completely contrary to Cornelia's own attitude, but Mayo had implicated Cornelia. Mayo also knew that she had deceived Cornelia about the content of the book, since she did not at first send Cornelia a copy as promised and was uncertain how Cornelia would take it, saying 'if you will have it now'.[3] At the beginning of the book, she said she could not make the acknowledgements she would like, because her informants did not know how she would use their material. But unfortunately she said enough to identify Cornelia, not only three times quoting her stories from *Between the Twilights* by name, but also referring to her sister Lena by name and telling at length the story of the fire on Kalidasi's stomach as being given by 'an Indian Christian lady of distinguished position and attainment whose character has opened to her many doors that remain to others fast closed'.[4] But while Cornelia was thus implicated, she noticed at once that Mayo had changed the original plan of the book as she knew it, and that Bengalis would be angry. She commented that what Mayo did wrong was not to tell her friends what she would write,[5] and this was not the only time that Mayo deceived people whose help she wanted about the character of what she was about to publish.[6] The book purported through its title, *Mother India*, to apply to the whole of India. It was recognised as an attack on Hinduism by almost everyone except Cornelia. But Cornelia made things worse for herself by trying to reinterpret it in the light of Mayo's speech in her garden.

The opening theme of the book was that it was obsessive Hindu pandering to male sexual indulgence, what she called 'the phallic symbol', which caused the ill health and degeneracy of their women and children, sons included. Mayo attributed this theme to a distinguished Bombay physician.[7] But a month after

Cornelia had got the book, a pleader across the river at Howrah was saying that the India Office had sent Mayo to the British Central Intelligence Division to get material against India.[8] Recent research by Mrinalini Sinha has amply confirmed this,[9] although Cornelia did not have reason to believe it. Mayo's theme had already been suggested to her when she sailed for India from England by a British agent of the Central Intelligence Division, J. H. Adams, and Mayo even admitted British Government help to the embarrassment of the British. Cornelia was to tread on the same dangerous ground in 1933–1934, when she too was given information on anti-British terrorism by the Criminal Investigation Department. But fortunately in that case the British authorities themselves discounted the scare stories and took pains to conceal them from Churchill.[10]

The first two parts of Mayo's book were properly researched and included statistics from hospitals on bad health as well as the kind of information given by Cornelia. In the remaining three parts, a little was researched, such as the information on lack of education and mistreatment of the sacred cow. But much read like stuffing packed in by an elementary student who had not finished her homework: a miscellany of criticisms of India, including travellers' tales randomly culled from different centuries, coupled with indiscriminate praise of the British. The randomness of the criticisms discredited Cornelia's belief in Mayo's benign purpose.

REACTIONS TO THE BOOK

Cornelia worsened her own position further by writing a review in which, despite some criticisms, her main message was that no time should be wasted on resenting Mayo, that Indians had already begun the task of reform. Cornelia cited not a modern woman, but her aged friend, the Sadhuin or holy woman Mathaji Maharani Tapaswami, who had founded schools for the orthodox in Calcutta.[11] Now, Cornelia said, people should be trained everywhere to go out and help those women who really were disadvantaged. She sought to claim that this was also the main intention of Mayo.[12]

Cornelia sought to defend Mayo, not only in the review, but in letters to Elena. Against the charge that she only noticed what was bad, Cornelia had to scrape the barrel, mentioning one appreciation of a certain landscape and her support for Gandhi's call for social reform. She also cited a meeting that Mayo intended to hold in New York, to discuss help for India, but no programme of help is reported.[13] Otherwise, the defence consisted largely in protestations about her good motives.[14] But the most important line of defence was the claim to which I will return, that Mayo had inspired some of the necessary social reform.

Cornelia had criticisms as she read the book. She wished that Mayo had had people check the manuscript, as her remarks on purdah and education were less well researched and needed qualifying. She did not sufficiently distinguish (although she did briefly) the martial races of India, she should have omitted the politics of British rule, including the gushing treatment of the Prince of Wales' visit, which the Congress boycotted and which, as Princess Louise later told Cornelia, the Royal family itself regarded as a failure. After the hostile reaction to her book, Mayo, she thought, should not try to justify and explain. As for Mayo's next book, a second volume in 1931, Cornelia thought she did not realise that the pace of reform could not be forced.[15]

By far the best description of the book was written by Gandhi. He hit the right note by saying that it was a drain inspector's report. He nonetheless added that every Indian should read it. The charge as framed by Mayo might be repudiated, he said, but not the substance underlying her many allegations. In the outcry after publication, nearly all the book reviews in India, except for Cornelia's and, in a way, Gandhi's, were hostile. The only exception she saw was in *The Statesman*, although even there a reader reasonably objected to Mayo's tone.[16] There were lectures and plays about Mayo. There were two student protest meetings in Calcutta. The first was packed out and reported by C.R. Das' paper *Forward*, which added an interview with Sarojini Naidu. To the second meeting Cornelia was begged to come.[17]

Cornelia's sister, Alice, in Delhi completely rejected Mayo's medical findings and statistics as inapplicable to any women patients she had known and as ignorant about how hospital data are compiled. Dick also lectured in London against Mayo's book.[18] Another woman doctor, Dr Balfour, like Alice, said that the medical statistics would not fit the towns of the Province or Presidency of Madras.[19]

MAYO'S MOTIVES

The book was intended to serve the two purposes mentioned above: perpetuating both British rule and the exclusion of Indians from America. In pursuit of the first purpose, it drew a parallel between British rule in India and American rule in the Philippines. As regards the second purpose, the exclusion of Indian workers from America and Canada had been going on for some time, even though Canada was part of the British Empire and Great Britain had no policy of exclusion at that time. In 1914, when Cornelia was reprimanded for writing a political letter in *The Times*, Annie Besant had been complaining that Indians were not admitted as immigrants into other countries of the Empire. On the day of Cornelia's letter, the paper carried a report of a shipload of Indians being kept out of Canada.[20] Mayo objected that her countrymen were being asked to admit Indians as citizens, as well as guests. She wrote a paper, 'When Asia knocks at the door', against admitting Indians as neighbours in the USA.[21] Her campaign to exclude Indians from America was already well started when she wrote to Eleanor Rathbone that only the sewage matters, if you are buying the house next door.[22] 'If the cellar is full of sewage, if its water supply is poison-ous, if the residents are magazines of infection, and if their common habits or domestic relations scandalise me, I am but little affected by whatever virtues may offset these points or whatever beauty the face may show, when I think of acquiring that house as a next door neighbour.'

Mrinalini Sinha details that Mayo actually distorted in later writings, to focus her attack more on Hinduism.[23] In her *Slaves of the Gods* of 1929, Mayo retold stories with Muslim and Christian names changed to Hindu ones. Eleanor Rathbone, the aunt of Cornelia's Elena, who had reviewed *Mother India* favour-ably, complained of the later book that it lost its usefulness because it was too keen to present the evils of child marriage as solely Hindu. The later book used Cornelia's technique of telling stories about women and children. It is even pos-sible that she got the idea from Cornelia. But in Cornelia's stories her love for the women and children shines through, and the stories are told so charmingly that it would indeed take a drain inspector to dredge any anti-Hindu message from them. Cornelia cherished all the religious practices that were not actually handicapping people and wanted her wards to keep them, while they came to see for themselves the value of reforming other practices. Eleanor Rathbone by contrast sided with Mayo against Cornelia on Hinduism, which she described as a dead weight that needed to be thrown off wherever it had social ill effects.[24]

THE BOOK'S EFFECTS

Did *Mother India* achieve the intended effect of bolstering British rule? It may have had some powerful effects in the West, since on one view, it changed Churchill from being a friend to being a foe of India.[25] But in India the effect that Cornelia expected and hoped for was that it would lead to improving the lot of orthodox women. She could not bear to think otherwise. New efforts at alleviation were certainly what the book inspired in Cornelia herself. She began many new lines of social work which will be described in the next chapter, and even gave them priority over her legal practice.[26] It was also true of Eleanor Rathbone. In response to *Mother India*, for the next ten years she worked in England for Indian women,[27] although, like Cornelia, she was handicapped in doing so by her support for Mayo's book. Eventually, Cornelia's sister Alice and her brother Dick were involved, we shall see,[28] in yet other groups planning to help Indian women, and Cornelia became anxious that they would all be in competition for funding. Besides these movements to help at the social level, there was an unexpected movement for *legislative* reform, which Cornelia attributed to Mayo's influence.[29] Cornelia's favourite candidate, the Sarda Bill to raise the age of consent to marriage, was already being debated when Mayo wrote, and some of her juiciest revelations were drawn from the debate. The British certainly thought Mayo relevant to the Sarda Bill, because when the Government put questions to Cornelia with a view to legislation on the age of consent,[30] some of them bore on Mayo's claims.

Reform, however, was not the result that Mayo wanted at all. She wrote a volume II sequel to *Mother India*, which *The Statesman* newspaper regarded as unfair to Hindus, and Cornelia wished that Mayo would instead stay quiet and simply take credit for the passage of the Sarda Act.[31] But Mayo revealed her attitude even more clearly when she offered to raise funds for Cornelia's proposed Bengal League of Social Service, on condition that it stuck to improving health and the things she wrote about, but did nothing to encourage a sense of citizenship, or social service on the part of Indian secluded women, educationally or generally. At least Cornelia recognised this time the incompatibility with her own ideals. She commented, 'Yet unless you give them the civic sense, will they be able to rectify the things that are wrong in any direction?'[32] Mayo wanted them to remain passive recipients of Western aid, but Cornelia's League, we shall see,[33] was to be unique in getting them to perform social service for their poorer sisters, and she did not take up Mayo's offer.

Cornelia's own attitude to the Sarda legislation to raise the age of marriage was entirely unlike Mayo's and was very interesting. It will be further described in Chapter 19. But in brief, she treated it as one of two exceptions, along with the very early British ban on suttee. Sometimes it is good, she thought, to pass legislation in order to establish an ideal, even though it may not be effective for a very long time without education and a change of attitude, which should normally come first. She was sure that age of consent legislation would not be actually effective when there was no registration of births, marital age, or deaths,[34] and an orthodox wife would never betray her husband to a stranger's inquiries. But her insistence that legislation on its own would not put an end to the evil should not be allowed to conceal that her official opinion, which was sought, was in favour of the bill, and of specifying a high age for marriage in order to set a high ideal.

Mrinalini Sinha has thrown the most interesting further light on the fate in India of Mayo's campaign. So far from strengthening British rule, she has argued,[35] Mayo's book led directly to its being weakened. It was an Indian man, Sarda, an Indian woman's movement and an Indianised legislature that passed the marriage age reform, while the British obstructed it. The British were bound by their reaction to the Uprising of 1857, which they called the Indian Mutiny, but in which they recognised their role in inflaming Indian religious feeling. As a result, Queen Victoria had declared that the British would not in future interfere in religious matters, and this gained them the support or acquiescence of the orthodox. To the world it now appeared that Indians and an Indian legislature might be more effective than British rule at getting rid of social evils. In fact, Cornelia was right that the legislation on its own did not get rid of the evil, but the case for Indian self-government had been enhanced, in direct opposition to Mayo's intention. Cornelia regarded the Indian speeches in the Legislative Assembly in favour of social legislation as more courageous than the literary response to Mayo, even though she was worried about the strife it might cause with the orthodox.[36]

DAMAGE TO CORNELIA

The damage to Cornelia from her association with Mayo was enormous. By the beginning of 1928, she knew that there was a boycott against her. It turned out that a young graduate woman who had written against Mayo, Latika Basu, was collecting signatures, going from house to house, to get graduates to boycott any society, committee or work in which Cornelia was involved. According to Cornelia, she was being paid 350 rupees a month for her work for Swaraj, or Home Rule. That was Swaraj work on Gandhi's pattern, which meant not accepting political office proffered by the British, and non-violent breaking of British law. In her house-to-house campaign, Basu used a blank piece of paper so that the indictment was not available to read, but she alleged that Cornelia was 'joint author' with Mayo, and that Cornelia was getting graduates to violate the boycott on talks with the John Simon Commission on India's constitution. That commission was being boycotted for its ill-conceived all-white membership. Cornelia wrote to Elena, 'To what good does one stay on here?' But Mr S. R. Das, the Calcutta judge, currently Law Member on the Viceroy's Council, refused to sign Basu's petition point blank, saying that Cornelia worked for India and the Swarajists did not, and Mrs P. K. Roy withheld the signature which Basu spent three hours trying to get.[37]

The boycott had a powerful effect. Cornelia's main response to Mayo was to set up a League of Social Service for Women with many activities and with support from the wives of the Viceroy and Governor of Bengal, Lady Irwin and Lady Jackson. But, as will be described below,[38] a member of the Governor's staff was told, 'No one will support anything initiated by Miss Sorabji' and he repeated to his superiors that nothing Cornelia did 'lived'. Cornelia had already been worried that the two ladies would not be able to support her, although in fact they did, as did some Indians, Mrs Reddi and Sarojini Naidu's sister.[39] But because of Mayo, she had to struggle against the scaling down of the launch of her League of Social Service.[40] One of the most innovative activities of her league, visits of assistance to villages accompanied by her own purdahnashin supporters, was disrupted on its first attempt, as we shall see,[41] and she was told that this was because of the Mayo connexion.[42] The legal work was also impeded. Her legal clerk who did her so much damage, as described in the last chapter, 'borrowed' her fees for himself, and subjected her to a vexatious prosecution which was financed, she thought, by Swarajist followers of Gandhi, who were enraged by her association with Mayo.[43] The all-white Simon Commission caused so much ill feeling that it would not have helped her reputation to appear before it. But one afternoon she met with Simon, whom she had known at Oxford, and was invited by him to appear before a sub-committee to advise on education.[44] When, to her disappointment, she was not called after all, she learnt that the Swarajists had got her name struck off from a Commission which was by then somewhat on the defensive,[45] although her sister, Lena, had been seen and she described Lena's interviews as 'thrilling'.[46] The boycott also affected Cornelia's work on the Federation of University Women. The original founder of the Federation's Calcutta branch, Mrs P. Chaudhuri, 'spat venom' at Mayo at a Federation meeting and said, and subsequently wrote, that Cornelia was the most unpopular woman in India and no Indians could stand her, because she had supplied Mayo with her vilifications. Cornelia refused to submit Chaudhuri's views on Mayo as a Federation opinion. But she commented that Mayo little knew the bitter depths of feeling in Bengal.[47] The boycott over Mayo affected something even closer to Cornelia's heart, when two women were very rude to her and defected from her Bengal League of Social Service for Women. This was almost the last straw before she gave up her work in India.[48] On a later US lecture tour Cornelia's Indian abusers called her Judas and spoke of her dark, cruel hands around the throat of Mother India.[49]

Mayo continued to identify Cornelia by word of mouth, saying that 'a brilliant Indian woman' had written, 'the measure of resentment will be the measure of truth you have spoken'. It made Cornelia angry that she quoted from a letter that Cornelia had marked 'Confidential' and in the same letter she reported someone else's remark about 'barking dogs', with the result that both quotations were attributed by *Forward,* C.R. Das' paper, to Cornelia. The *Modern Review* put out an article saying that Cornelia was the C. S. who had praised Mayo's book in the *New Statesman*, when in fact that was written by the editor. At the same time, the author of a book against Mayo, *Father India*, dismissed Mayo's quotations from Cornelia's *Between the Twilights*, by saying that Cornelia's book of stories had long been discredited in India as the vapourings of an unbalanced and uninstructed mind.[50] Mayo's belated disclaimer of Cornelia's complicity was published in *The Statesman*[51] two years later in 1929, but the damage was done.

Mayo went on trying to use Cornelia, asking her for more statistics. But in self-defence Cornelia asked Elena to act as intermediary and say that that was impossible. Mayo had said enough and if she mentioned Cornelia's cherished social service scheme, it would die. She wrote to Elena again as intermediary to pass on a request to forgive her silence, but now she was going to return to the social work she had started in 1912, long before *Mother India*, and move to the category of *work*, not argument. Later she plucked up courage to write a letter to Mayo, but sent it indirectly via Elena, in case her mail to Mayo was opened.[52] Her rogue clerk had been copying her letters and forwarding the copies to his political backers.[53]

CORNELIA'S CONTINUING ILLUSIONS

Inspite of all she had suffered, Cornelia saw Mayo on her US lecture tours in 1930 and 1932, while 'keeping it dark', and in 1935 Mayo was back in England, and came again to 'pick the brains' of Cornelia carrying off her information on terrorism.[54] The situation was now a new one. Cornelia was lecturing in America to counteract the influence of Gandhi, whose followers, by the time of her second lecture tour, had destroyed her Bengal League of Social service by intimidating her leading purdahnashin worker and facilitator, Peri Banu. Cornelia no longer believed that Mayo could rally helpers for Indian women. Instead, it was her doomed opposition to Gandhi for which she was desperately seeking an ally in America. She still believed that Mayo's intention had been to help the oppressed, and she credited her book with real achievements in social reform. She said in 1930 that she would act as 'Scarlet Pimpernel' for Mayo's future books against Gandhi's Nationalist Movement,[55] and she had reason to think that Mayo needed such help because she needed to be better informed if she was to have any effect against that movement. Cornelia never lost her love for Mayo, however much it damaged her, as is clear from her comments on hearing a report in 1940 of her death. To understand this, one must remember how perfectly Mayo had expressed Cornelia's hopes and values in the seminar in Cornelia's garden, and the background of loneliness against which Cornelia originally felt that at last she would have a fellow worker who would help her recruit other workers.

The consequences of her attachment were to make Cornelia even more lonely than before. Her entanglement with Mayo wrecked her life at the bar in India, as described in the Chapter 18. Yet without it there would not have been her unique experiment with the Bengal League of Social Service, to be described in the next.

CHAPTER 1 9

SOCIAL SERVICE, 1924–1931:
THE INNOVATION OF
PURDAHNASHINS AS SOCIAL
WORKERS

Cornelia's response to Mayo's book was a series of social service campaigns. For four years from 1927–1931, she tried to make good what she believed to be the book's objective. In November 1929, when she was 63, she could no longer maintain the work load, and on doctor's orders, she gave up the sabotaged legal work and chose the social work alone,[1] although it was not a source of income. The culmination of her work was the enlistment of purdahnashins to undertake social work themselves. But by the time she introduced that, she had had a great deal of experience in social work. At the end of 1927, the year of Mayo's book, she was made Convenor of Boarstal committees[i] for young offenders, and she served on the Boarstal and juvenile jails committee.[2] This involved her with male and female juvenile delinquents, reformatories and beggar boys. More relevant to her later work was her appointment in 1929–1930 to the Bengal Government Labour Commission looking at the working conditions of mill- and dock- workers.[3] Women's working conditions were also studied by the National Council of the Women of India, of which Cornelia was organising Vice-President in 1925.

AGE OF CONSENT FOR PROSTITUTION

Initially, the centrepiece of Cornelia's social work in this period concerned the age of consent in two different contexts – prostitution and marriage. Girls

---

i These came under the title 'Public Services' for the Bengal Presidency Council of Women, a branch of the National Council of Women of India (NCWI).

314

working as prostitutes had often been abducted as a source of income. But the plea of enforced prostitution was allowed only for girls *under* the age of 16. By contrast in disputes about early marriage new legislation had begun to allow marriage only to girls *over* a certain age. Alleged prostitutes were examined by a doctor to estimate their age as well as test virginity. If the doctor declared the girl under 16, ribald lawyers for the other side could make her remove clothes to show her figure in a crowded court, and the doctor himself might be accused. Moreover, the doctors were male, and this alone caused the deepest humiliation to the girl. Cornelia wanted the court to be a family court, without adversarial lawyers, and cleared of the public, and she wanted the doctor to be a woman. But some women opposed the last, on the ground that then the woman doctor would herself be subjected to cross-examination.[4]

As Cornelia had urged, a woman Probation Officer was appointed for the Calcutta area,[5] and in Cornelia's own work for children on probation, the old grandmothers, mothers and aunts were soon holding Cornelia's feet and saying to their girls, 'Tell the mother,' referring to Cornelia, 'She will understand.'[6]

AGE OF CONSENT IN MARRIAGE

The age of consent also concerned child marriage and Cornelia was asked to give an opinion on that more than once. Amongst the official opinions she gave for the bar library, she offered answers to two different inquiries, one for the purpose of reconsidering the Indian penal code on the age of consent,[7] the other in connexion with the protection of children.[8] This second opinion, though commissioned by a sub-committee of the Government of Bengal, was sent on to the Government of India and shown to the Viceroy.[9] A third question was raised by the Government of India, about Sarda's age of consent to marriage bill shortly before the bill's passage: was the legislation enforceable?[10]

Cornelia's official answer, partly explained already,[11] was that raising the age of consent should be treated as an exception, like the ban on suttee, the burning alive of widows. Although she in no way abandoned her life-long view that social legislation would not work without education, she corresponded with her former Oxford teacher, Sir Frederick Pollock, and drew from his writing the idea that sometimes a law can usefully set an ideal.[12] The ban on suttee had set an ideal, even though it took, by her reckoning, 50 years to take effect. Similarly, she recommended that a high age of consent to marriage be set, since she thought that the exact figure would not be the source of difficulty. The task would be the necessary education.[13] Child marriage was not just an 'ingrained habit'. The priests taught that it was required by the gods,[14] and education would have to be brought in Cornelia's manner from house to house.[15] All of this was a long way off.

This was the context in which Cornelia made her discovery that the current law had overlooked the protection of child widows, since it protected only married and never-married children.[16] She also urged that it was no good trying to set an age for intercourse within marriage.[17]

The backing of age of consent legislation as an ideal, with a high age, was, despite appearances, absolutely compatible with her answer that the Sarda Bill would be unenforceable without the required registers and without education. The education would have to start, she thought, through those members of the orthodox community who had become enlightened on the subject.[18]

In no other cases did Cornelia favour social legislation as an ideal, when it affected her purdahnashins. She was against inheritance by a sister's son,[19] against women's suffrage,[20] against temple-entry where it was forbidden to Dalits[21] and against divorce for Hindu women,[22] even though on this last issue she had been moved to suggest divorce for the Eurasian (half-Indian) wife of an English husband. In this horrifying case the husband had refused to pay medical costs for a prolapse of the womb after childbirth, then complained of his wife and took another woman, forcing the wife to sleep in a corridor separated from them only by a curtain.[23]

Cornelia still took the same view much later in 1936. She wrote a letter to *The Times* in reply among others to Eleanor Rathbone, the aunt of her friend Elena. One had to get the priests on one's side, perhaps by getting Scripture reinterpreted. But the Sarda Act of 1929 had merely put on their guard. Dick wrote a letter supporting Cornelia.[24] In 1937–1938, Cornelia recorded protests by thousands of villagers against the Sarda Act and cited the refusal of the Maharaja of Mysore to introduce the Act into his own Princely State, where the law did not apply, a refusal which contrasted with the exceptional tradition of social provision in that State.[25]

BOYS DOWN HOLES IN SEWERS

Through the same organisations, Cornelia also started helping boy sewage workers. Small boys were used, because neither adults nor mechanical dredgers could fit into the holes down into the sewers.[26] This mirrored the nineteenth century practice in England of using small boys to clean out the insides of chimneys. Cornelia's delinquency group agreed to help the boys, and she arranged that the boys should be hosed down and given clean clothes for evenings. She visited their homes, and the parents agreed with her ideas, that night schools should be arranged, and Calcutta Corporation barracks for them to rent.[27] Cornelia's help for sewage workers was something of which Florence Nightingale would have approved.

PURDAH

Cornelia continued to arrange purdah facilities. She got the big stores in Dacca to arrange purdah shopping occasions for the first time. Her wealthy purdahnashin supporter, Peri Banu, spent hundreds of rupees and gave every serving girl a 5 rupee tip[28] After Cornelia saw two Muslim women in purdah stranded without money, when they missed the steamer taking them on pilgrimage abroad, she got the Bengal Presidency Council of Women to form a sub-committee to help, and wrote an article on the protection of Muslim women on pilgrimage.[29] She failed, however, to persuade the banks to open accounts for purdahnashins.[30]

By the late 1920s, changes were being contemplated in the very institution of purdah as practised by Hindus, but this was only a small beginning, and Cornelia thought it often involved more talk than action. It has already been described how advanced was legislation in the Princely State of Baroda in 1894–1906, and how the Princely State of Bharatpur was in 1926 breaking down some of the Hindu purdah customs by its own choice.[31] The Nationalist Movement was also against the practice of purdah by Hindus. In 1928, Cornelia reported a 'purdah must go' movement of some men in Bihar encouraged by Brahmo women and former pupils of Christian Diocesan schools.[32] It was also the view of a Muslim purdahnashin that purdah must go, although Cornelia regarded her as a very lax purdahnashin. She was Mrs P. Chaudhuri, who had accused Cornelia of responsibility for Mayo's calumnies.[33] In 1933, the Congress Party at Lucknow had a meeting at which they claimed 5000 purdahnashins renounced purdah, but Cornelia thought that the few purdahnashins present had been bribed or threatened to come and returned to a purdah even stricter than before, while the votes of entire progressive families were counted. The next month, Cornelia spoke to the Muslim wife of a High Court judge who was just out of purdah, but who explained that the more usual pattern was for mothers to stay in purdah, but let their daughters out, who then despised their mothers. Cornelia also went to the party of a Muslim lady in London for progressive Indian ladies to meet the aristocratic supporters of the English suffragettes. A progressive Indian lady said, 'purdah is dead.' The Vicereine Lady Linlithgow was at the party and said, 'I suppose purdah is quite dead now.' A Bengali replied, 'Look around you. You have proof of it.'[34]

However, this treatment of purdah as something that had been swept away did not correspond to what was happening among Cornelia's clients or in places like Bharatpur. On the contrary, the interest in those circles in reforming purdah was actually incompatible with the Nationalist interest in sweeping it away.

PLANNING THE BENGAL LEAGUE OF SOCIAL SERVICE FOR WOMEN, 1927–1929

Cornelia's friendships with purdahnashins combined with her experience of social work to make possible her final innovation, the creation of the Bengal League of Social Service for Women. Mayo's book reached Cornelia in August 1927 and by October she had told her plans for the new League to the wife of the Governor of Bengal, Lady Jackson, and to the Vicereine, Lady Irwin.[35] She put in a bid for Hastings's House, for which she had competed unsuccessfully since 1912,[36] in order to accommodate her proposed League. Warren Hastings's house had at that time been carved up for use merely as flats for Government of India officers, which spoiled the interior and was not a very inspiring purpose.[37] But she failed again to get the house, in the competition for alternative uses.[38] The history of past competition may have made her over-anxious about competition in general. At any rate, she saw it as competition when her sister Alice and her brother Dick proposed schemes which they saw as complementary to hers.

COMPETITION FOR FUNDS

Cornelia was Honorary National Secretary of the Federation of University Women of India whose central body was due to vote on her League with Lady Irwin's full knowledge. But Alice was secretary to a sub-committee of the Delhi branch and was asking Lady Irwin as Vicereine to get the support of the central body for a different scheme for training primary school teachers. Cornelia saw this as leap-frogging, because all the branches had to be consulted before a proposal could be put to the central body. She reluctantly offered to put Alice's proposal to the branches before putting her own scheme to the vote. But she was upset by what she saw as competition and Alice's irregular procedure, all the more when Alice came and stayed with her in Calcutta and turned out to have been distributing leaflets for her scheme. Things were resolved when Lady Irwin said she was interested in Cornelia's scheme, and would not hear the education proposal, and the Delhi sub-committee agreed to follow the proper procedure. Later, Lady Irwin offered support to Alice's scheme as well,[39] and Alice was to have many other projects funded, including an eye clinic in Lady Irwin College in Delhi.[40] Some of her social work seemed close to Cornelia's,[41] although it did not involve the use of purdahnashins.

There was a second scheme which Cornelia saw as competing for funds with hers, the Indo-British Social Welfare League. It was started in England with Dick as Secretary, who intended it to support Cornelia's project, and who resigned when she objected. The Chair was Lady Lutyens, wife of the architect of New Delhi. Lady Minto, the former Vicereine and Cornelia's great friend, was Patron. It was affiliated with the Saroj Nalini Dutt Women's Institutes in India. Mrs Dutt, a Bengali, was a central figure. Once again Alice helped with the formation of the group. The aim was to train social workers in England who could go out to India for social service in support of schemes like Cornelia's. But Cornelia's new scheme envisaged that learning about customs should be done in India, and she was afraid that a committee in England could not adjudicate which social schemes in India were frauds. Meanwhile the group was raising money from the same clientele as might have supported her.[42]

THE LEAGUE'S NEW SOCIAL OBJECTIVE

The most original part of Cornelia's scheme[43] was the idea of purdahnashins as 'forerunners' speaking the vernacular and going out into villages and mill towns, accompanied by a doctor or baby welfare worker, to persuade women (whether purdahnashin or not) of the value of the knowledge and services being made available, so that they would use them. This new approach was significant in two ways. First, Cornelia was bringing help for the first time not just to women of the land-owning classes, but to women of the poorest classes. But secondly, she was elevating the perspectives of the purdahnashins to new levels. For the purdahnashin workers, having once been recipients of help, were now actively taking responsibility for service to other, poorer women, a commitment which Cornelia had once seen as beyond the reach of the orthodox. She had already innovated by training secluded women to help secluded women, when she started a scheme for training them as nurses.[44] They would now be trained to help others and on a much larger scale. A purdahnashin, Peri Banu, was President of the purdahnashin sub-committee. This sub-committee would also arrange making garments for the poor, and if once welfare workers started coming in from elsewhere, would teach them the customs of the orthodox, although this last stage was not reached. Should it come about, Lady Minto had agreed to be the London chairwoman to arrange a diploma course for training salaried Indian women welfare workers in Bengal, if they had not been trained elsewhere.

AN EARLIER DEBATE ON SOCIAL ATTITUDES IN THE PURDAHED HOUSEHOLD

In November 1925 Cornelia had been asked to open a debate in the so-called 'Calcutta parliament', and move the motion that, 'An orthodox Hindu cannot be a true democrat.' She had already urged the Court of Wards to prepare landowners for home rule, by training them in duties to district and nation.[45] This was what she was trying to do herself on a small scale with her own wards. She had felt for some time that the strictly orthodox household had not readied its members for social roles outside the household, and that democracy required that.[46] She thought the role of women was crucial because they reared the children.[47] She had been trying to change the situation when she arranged for purdahnashins to be trained as nurses and now again when her purdahnashin wards were to go out to help villagers and mill workers. Her idea was that until that happened there would not be a civic sense. Her further rather doubtful idea was that there had been a kind of fatalism in her households about the influence of past incarnations which would militate against civic action. She was apparently not alone, because she won the motion in 1925. But now she felt that a remedy was beginning.

OPPOSITION TO THE LEAGUE OVERCOME, 1929

The first and most original part of the scheme got going successfully, despite opposition. In December 1928, the Vicereine, Lady Irwin, visited Calcutta and Cornelia got her approval as well as that of the Governor's wife Lady Jackson. Lady Irwin had a summary of the scheme printed and a finance committee created.[48] The opposition came from some of Lady Jackson's advisers, especially Major Higston, who had heard of the boycott against Cornelia. He was the one who warned that no one would support what Cornelia did. Similar advice came from two others: one an Englishman who had been persuaded by opponents of British Government education and the other a Swarajist. The opening was on March 11th 1929 in Calcutta, but Higston wrote the speech for Lady Jackson, omitted any outline of the scheme, ruled out any fund-raising initiative by Lady Jackson and forbade reading out the Queen's message of interest. On top of all this he refused to provide physical help, so that Cornelia had to lift all the chairs. But Cornelia had given the outline of the scheme to Reuters. She insisted on reading out a letter offering 400 rupees from Peri Banu, which disclosed that she had already raised 1000 rupees. Moreover, excellent speeches in support were made by the Mayor of Calcutta and by Father Holmes, Cornelia's ally since the time of Nogen's arrest. The lecture room and purdah room were both packed and there were more Indians than English, even though the executive (as opposed to the purdahnashin) committee were all English. Cornelia, who had in January 1927 been made adviser on radio broadcasts to villages, devoted to the League the first of three radio broadcasts she was giving and finished with an appeal for funds, naming *The Statesman* as the body to which subscriptions should be sent.[49] Peri Banu gave a reception on behalf of the purdahnashin committee for Lady Jackson, who had resumed her enthusiasm. At the reception a film was shown of the purdahnashins' first village visit. Lady Jackson said perceptively that the purdahnashin sub-committee on its own made the whole project worthwhile. The Viceroy joined his wife in serving as Patron. Fifty thousand rupees were needed over the first five years. Lady Irwin contributed 1500 from her charitable funds collected from Princes. Cornelia easily exceeded the amount needed for the first year, reaching 17,000 rupees by February 1930.[50]

THE LEAGUE'S SUCCESSFUL FIRST YEAR

Cornelia described five visits in the first 12 months with Peri Banu and her purdahnashins travelling in purdahed cars along with non-purdahed Indian women to villages and mill towns. The villagers were not themselves normally in purdah. The first visit appeared to be a great success. Peri Banu led it with two other purdahnashins, and 140 women and children attended. The head man had given them the women's courtyard in an ancient house with arches of the Moghul type. Peri Banu spoke first and then one of the graduates from the Federation of University Women. The subject was sanitation and they illustrated it with lantern slides. They had a box of garments that they had made for distribution and toys for children and they filmed the visit. They were entreated to come again and planned to provide a baby clinic next time. Peri Banu contributed nearly half the cost so that they could buy their own slide projector for future trips.[51] But then the head man of the village was persuaded to forbid a return. Father Holmes reported that this was due to protests at Cornelia's association with Mayo, and an allegation that male honour had been hurt by a gift of 10 rupees being given to a village widow.[52]

Nonetheless, visits continued elsewhere. The next one, on nutrition, was in a mill area. After a third and a fourth, the fifth had record numbers. Of the 1500 women who wanted to come, only 400 could be admitted. The subject was ante-natal care, and though Peri Banu could not come, a nurse attended, and funds were sought to provide her a wage for the future.[53] The visits went on through the hot weather and the purdahnashins did not take their usual retreat to the hills. Moreover, they arranged a successful purdahed fair.[54]

AN INITIAL SETBACK TO THE LEAGUE

In spite of the initial year of success, things began to go wrong. First, the ill health which had led Cornelia to give up the law required a visit in May 1930 to Vienna and London for treatment.[55] The purdahnashins and Father Holmes begged her to return afterwards,[56] but she was diverted into the first of two lecture tours to the USA from August to December, to promote the lost cause of defending the British against the criticisms of Gandhi's Nationalist Movement. The cause was dear to her heart, but so also was the Bengal League which she was neglecting. She may have been influenced in her choice by the thought of emulating Susie, whose strenuous lecture tours in America had been so successful back in 1902.[57] She also saw Gandhi's movement as a direct threat to her work with purdahnashins. But when she returned to India in January 1931, the boycott against her had resumed and two women in her League were very rude to her and defected to the rival social service scheme, the Saroj Nalini Dutt.

FINAL DEFEAT

Already Cornelia began to wonder if it was time to stop.[58] But something much more serious happened. Peri Banu's life was repeatedly threatened by people whom Cornelia called Bengal Congress workers and followers of

Gandhi, although they were working against his principles. They were trying to get Peri Banu to make financial contributions 'for political purposes to save the country'. If Peri Banu did not comply, she and her children and grandchildren would be 'done in'. They warned her not to tell the police, but she did and the police provided a guard for the Dacca property, but they said they could not offer fortification, because there were rent strikes organised by Gandhi's followers all over East Bengal. When Cornelia had to leave Calcutta for Poona, Peri Banu was deterred by threats from continuing the village work. The next year, she had to leave Calcutta altogether to avoid them.[59] This put an end to Cornelia's social service work, and she herself ascribed the end of her scheme to the threats.[60] She saw the contribution of purdahnashins as unique to her scheme,[61] and it was all the more remarkable that wealthy landowners should have been working for peasants and labourers who were not even their own. Cornelia's work for women had now been obstructed from both sides – first by certain British officers, when she rectified Peri Banu's finances, and now by Congress workers, who torpedoed Peri Banu's facilitation of the Bengal League of Social Service.

There was a final disruption. Cornelia's sister Susie died in Poona on March 15th 1931, and Cornelia had to go to there to act as headmistress until the end of the summer term and wind up Susie's home and affairs. Peri Banu, but for her subjection to intimidation, might have been able to take over the forerunner work in the villages and mill towns. And before Susie's death, Cornelia still looked for still other ways forward. She went to see the Viceroy in Delhi and she hoped they might be able to hire a small house with a warden,[62] because hitherto they had been using Peri Banu's Calcutta house as the base to prepare visits. But with Susie's death, Cornelia had to sell her own car and try to deal with the League by letter, and she was afraid of the League's collapse. She finally decided to give up and buy a one-way ticket to London, where all the family now were except for Alice, who was to follow later. The work of winding up Susie's affairs and ensuring the continuity of her school was hectic, and Cornelia had only five days after that in which to visit Calcutta to deal with her own affairs and the League before sailing on July 29th. She hoped briefly that Tehmina Cama, who had been educated in her mother's schools and was now the only woman factory inspectress, might come in. But the League was handed over to a Mrs Mokherjee as organising Secretary.[63] When Cornelia returned on her tours round India, starting in 1932, there were no orthodox women left in the League, and she feared that Lady Irwin's funds were going principally into Lady Irwin College instead.[64]

The success of Susie's school must have supplied a contrast to Cornelia's own lot. Susie was loved by parents and pupils alike, and, as described in Chapter 3, her closest colleague and teacher showed her devotion by announcing at the burial, at the risk of personal ostracism, that she was converting from Zoroastrianism to Susie's Christian faith. Susie was the one most loyal to their mother, who had re-created her schools in 1906, when the other sisters decided they could not continue. She was to leave a monument more lasting than that of any other sister, since her main school would still be flourishing at its centenary in 2008.[65]

VARIETY AND SCOPE OF CORNELIA'S SOCIAL SERVICE

The variety and scope of Cornelia's social service work had been enormous in her second career up to 1931. By 1929 she had launched the most original of all her schemes, the Bengal League of Social Service. But politics was changing things. Most tragic for Cornelia was its impact on her use of purdahnashins for social service. The political changes stemmed from Gandhi's Independence Movement, which will be the subject of the next two chapters.

CHAPTER 2 0

CORNELIA'S FIRST REACTIONS TO GANDHI AND RELATIONS WITH OTHER NATIONALIST LEADERS

G andhi is such a great figure both in Britain and (with ups and downs) in India that it may be hard in retrospect to imagine how in 1920 any lover of India could have been against him. Cornelia was, and it needs to be asked why. Not only did he become the acknowledged leader of India's successful Independence Movement, but his methods in themselves compel comparison with sages of other times and places. He acquired the indifference to his own death cultivated by ancient Stoic sages. He combined that with an ideal, such as that professed by Christianity, of love, which he showed especially to his opponents, including Cornelia herself. As regards family love, Gandhi's relation to his sons and family members has caused surprise.[i] But a certain detachment in family love, which Gandhi learnt from the *Bhagavadgita*, is also familiar from Stoicism.[ii] The Stoics doubted whether anyone had yet lived up

---

i Gandhi's relation to his sons is discussed by his grandson, Rajmohan Gandhi, in *Mohandas, The True Story of a Man, his People and an Empire*, Penguin Books, Delhi 2006, and is the subject of a 2007 film, *Gandhi My Father*. In 1920 he wrote, 'If my son lives the life of shame..., my love for him requires me to withdraw all support from him, although it may mean even his death', M.K.Gandhi, *Non-violent Resistance (Satyagraha)*, Schocken Books New York 1961, p. 161. Compare Epictetus *Discourses* 2.22.
ii The Stoic Epictetus held that character is the only thing that matters for its own sake and that true family love will focus on character. Gandhi's equally restricted view about what really matters was a source of strength – neither imprisonment, nor death could deter him. But was it not also a source of family tensions? A liberator may need to think that few things matter; a family needs one to think that many things matter. See Richard Sorabji, 'Gandhi and the

325

to their ideals. In some ways Gandhi reveals what Stoic sages would have been like by providing a living example.

Married love was also reinterpreted by Gandhi. Like some of the ancient Christians, Gandhi combined marriage with sexual abstinence after the birth of his children. He treated the control of sexual thoughts as a first step in the necessary process of self-mastery, and, like some ancient Christians again, he had to struggle with 'bad thoughts'.[1]

A further attitude was Gandhi's passionate belief in non-violence, in complete contrast to the methods of terrorism, to which he provided an unimagined alternative of even greater power in that context. From Tolstoy he learnt to think of non-violence in a positive way as love, even if his love may have been a detached one, impartial as between family and foes. Non-violence, he learnt from Tolstoy, also involved willingness to disobey unjust laws if they were imposed by force and to accept the consequences of disobedience. In facing the consequences, emotional detachment became relevant again, bestowing a kind of freedom on Gandhi, since the British were often more anxious about their prisoner's physical welfare than he was himself.

Cornelia was mistaken in complaining to Gandhi that he could not be a Mahatma as well as a practical politician, although the combination was innovative. Gandhi's willingness to experiment by trying his ideals out in practice was one of his unique contributions, and only experiment could reveal the practicality and the limitations of his ideals. But in the interview to be described in the next chapter, Cornelia was to confront him on two issues where there were limitations. One was the issue of violence committed by his followers from which her own work had suffered so much. How many people, she wanted to know, had he persuaded to be non-violent? He had shown a remarkable concern for truth on this subject by starting a debate through the pages of one of his weekly journals about responsibility for harm caused in the fulfilment of non-violent intentions.[2] He did not excuse the violence which Cornelia was to draw to his attention, but he was surprisingly unaware of its existence. Cornelia also found him unrealistic concerning a further issue: the unanimity of Indians about his leadership.

Despite the limitations which Cornelia was to insist on, all of Gandhi's attitudes were remarkable and many admirable, so that it is a matter for regret that

---

Stoics: squaring emotional detachment with universal love and with political activity' published by the Gandhian Studies Centre, Dept. of History, Calcutta Universtiy, and forthcoming in *Philosophy as Samvada and Svaraja*, ed. Shail Mayaram et al. and my tentatively entitled *The Stoics and Gandhi: Modern Experiments on Ancient Values*, in preparation.

Cornelia should have been wholly opposed to him, as she was. The differences between them will be all the more revealingly displayed when we reach Cornelia's interview with Gandhi. But that will be in the next chapter.

EARLIER NATIONALIST LEADERS AND CORNELIA'S ORTHODOX CLIENTS

I come back to the question, why Cornelia should have been opposed to Gandhi, and one factor was that she had been used to a very different type of Nationalist leader and had accommodated herself only to some of these. We must step back a little in time. Gandhi was only coming to the fore in India in the last three years of Cornelia's career as legal adviser in 1919–1922, and these were early days for him. He was experimenting and had his own successes and failures. Like any pioneer, he took time to persuade people and there was no foreseeing his eventual success. Naturally, the leaders that Cornelia took seriously in 1920 belonged to an earlier generation. Among these, I have explained in Chapter 9 how much she admired Gandhi's guru, her friend Gokhale, who encouraged the study of politics, but not the pursuit of revolution.[3]

Another prominent movement at the time was the Home Rule League for India. This had been started by the Englishwoman Annie Besant. Among the members of her League were such major nationalists as Dick's colleague and friend Sapru and Tilak, who had twice been jailed by the British. Another member was Jinnah,[4] who has been described as a nationalist at that time, and far removed from his later insistence on a separate Pakistan.[5] Besant's Home Rule League had an approach extremely different from the one that Gandhi would develop, and although Cornelia disagreed with the League, there was also an area of agreement.

The basis of Cornelia's disagreement with the League was not merely a continuation of her dispute with Dick from student days as to whether Ireland should have Home Rule. It was connected with her gradualism. She believed that cultural and religious orthodoxy was as yet too distant from democracy. Home Rule must come more slowly, to allow time for commending new democratic attitudes to the orthodox. I have mentioned above her belief that her orthodox wards lacked the idea of social duties outside the household, an idea which she believed necessary for a democratic India.[6] She was to express this idea in 1925, when she was asked to speak in Calcutta for the motion that an orthodox Hindu cannot be a true democrat. She argued that the provisions of caste precluded the idea of equality of opportunity.[7] As regards the idea of her women wards voting in a democracy, she thought that one who may not even speak her husband's name was not likely to vote independently of him. The orthodox and purdahed Muslim, the Begum of Bhopal, who was a powerful woman ruler in her own right, agreed. Though a promoter of women's rights, who had presided in 1928 at the annual meeting of the All India Woman's Conference in Delhi, the Begum did not approve of the British suffragettes seeking a democratic vote for women. When she visited London, she approved rather of my mother, newly married to Dick, who, when asked what she was doing, replied, 'learning to be a good wife'. Dick was not even allowed to be at the meeting with the Begum, since it was held in purdah.[8]

Cornelia's aim was to educate her men wards in the direction of democracy. As noted earlier, one such ward built a hospital for women, while another was freeing his peasants from money lenders.[9] Eventually her women wards, we have seen,[10] would join her in bringing help to villagers. It is not surprising that Montagu said of one of Cornelia's suggested methods that it was too slow.[11] But she thought that such a large proportion of India was orthodox that democratic change could not be suddenly imposed.[12] If Mayo's figures were taken from Cornelia, she will have estimated that in 1927 of the 40 million in purdah, between 11 million and 17 million never saw the outside world at all.[13]

What was Cornelia's common ground with the nationalists of the Home Rule League? They were nearly all constitutionalists, who believed in the law and believed that India could and should get independence by negotiation within the law, in which many of them were engaged. Their predecessor Gokhale had admired English law. Tilak, ten years older than Gokhale but like him associated with Poona, had a more robust view which allowed for tax refusal.[14] But Sapru, whom Cornelia suspected of not believing in the law, did in fact believe in it as strongly as she did.

Tagore was another nationalist leader of the earlier generation and Cornelia's three descriptions of him have been quoted above.[15] Immediately following the first description of him appearing in Tussore silk to speak to young nationalists in 1921, Cornelia described her feelings about the kind of leadership available.

'As I looked at that packed Hall of young Bengali boys, I can't tell you how I felt. The pathos of their need held me by the throat and something strained at one's heart. How terribly in need they are of a leader! How eagerly they listen to any voice! How terribly important it is that they should hear the right voice! They pour out adoration, discipleship, even sacrifice – the thing which women,

and not men, are trained to give in India. And whom have they had so far?...
Gandhi...Tagore...neither of them fit to lead. It's a leader that every section
of the country wants just now. What a chance.... And whence will he come?
For come he must'.

Cornelia did not think Tagore was right. He was too critical of the British and
his picture of Bengali women so romantic as to be out of touch with their
needs. But for Cornelia, Gandhi was out of the question.[16]

GANDHI'S INNOVATIONS, 1919–1922

Gandhi changed the old constitutionalist approach in two very clever ways.
While agreeing with the constitutionalists in utterly rejecting terrorism, he
advocated two methods that fell short of constitutionalism. The method he
used first was Non-cooperation, which meant, among other things, rejecting
the political posts which the British like Montagu were beginning to offer to
Indians. The other method was Civil Disobedience, deliberately breaking the
law and taking the consequences. Gandhi introduced Civil Disobedience in
1921, by planning a refusal of tax payments in Bardoli, although he called the
initial campaign off, in order to control unpredicted violence.

   According to the main accounts I have cited, Gandhi prepared the way for
these new policies in 1920, partly by introducing changes into the goals of the
Home Rule League, of which he was President for the year, and of the Congress
Party. For the first he used the term 'Swaraj', in place of Annie Besant's 'Home
Rule'. In both organisations he removed commitment to remaining within the
Empire, and in Congress he gained agreement to Non-cooperation with the
British. But Besant broke with Gandhi over this and 19 people resigned from
the League, Jinnah from both League and Congress. Sapru was against Civil
Disobedience, and it has been said that he was one among a number of prominent politicians driven into political limbo in 1920 when Gandhi's different
policy prevailed, although he returned to work at the bar with a good grace.[17]
Nor was Sapru in agreement with Non-cooperation, since he accepted a three-
year appointment in 1920 to the highest Council of all, the Viceroy's Council,
and he only announced his resignation, to be postponed until the end of his
term of office, when in 1922 Gandhi was arrested.[18]

   Gandhi's new approach was shocking to Cornelia in other ways too. For
one thing, she had been received in England, far more closely than Dick or her
sisters, by leading figures of the Empire and could not bear to think of India,

however independent, being separated from Empire altogether, as Gandhi was willing to contemplate. Gandhi was up to 1929 ready to accept Dominion Status, that is, a high degree of independence within the Empire,[19] and this is what Cornelia's brother Dick hoped for at the time.[20] But later, Gandhi repudiated any such affiliation.

The attitude to Empire was not the only thing that upset Cornelia. The idea of Civil Disobedience went against her constitutionalism, and Non-cooperation shocked her, because it rejected the beginnings of the transfer of power which the Montagu-Chelmsford Reforms had introduced through legislative councils open to Indians. As described in an earlier chapter,[21] Cornelia had been a slow convert to these reforms, writing at length to Montagu in March 1919 to persuade him to incorporate safeguards for the purdahnashin community. But once the reforms were announced, she was in November determined to do everything she could to make them work.[22] Gandhi, by contrast, organised a successful boycott of elections to the new legislative posts in 1920 as part of his Non-cooperation Movement.[23]

Gandhi's innovations can be seen in retrospect to have succeeded. They turned the Independence Movement into a mass movement. But at the time they were startling not only to the British and to Cornelia, but, if the historical accounts I have cited are correct, to many of the most prominent Indian nationalists, who at that point saw themselves as capable of succeeding in negotiation with the British.

There was another reason for Cornelia's attitude to Gandhi. His campaigns directly impeded her work for her purdahnashins. As Gandhi was all too painfully aware,[24] it was extremely difficult, after mobilising people as he did, to make them stick to the non-violence in which he so passionately believed. Gandhi called off his first big Civil Disobedience campaign in Bardoli, against the wishes of his followers, in the hope of correcting the violence that had broken out, and at other times he fasted by way of penance for his followers' violence. His own estimate when Cornelia interviewed him, we shall see,[25] was that he had got only 30,000 out of 365 million people to abide by non-violence. Thirty thousand is a very remarkable figure, but it did not meet Cornelia's concern that the overwhelming majority of his supporters were not committed to non-violence.

Cornelia's first encounters with his Non-cooperation Movement were amusing. Her chauffeur punctured the tubes and a tyre of her car and said that he had vowed not to work for her after May 31st 1921. But could he be re-employed later? In November of that year, her tyres were slashed, her car battery removed and her driver forbidden to drive her again. But she said that she herself would drive and that he was to sit beside her.[26] This was also the year in which supporters of Gandhi, as she identified them, interfered in various ways with the attempt to rescue the Rani of Ramgarh and her two sons, as described earlier. Among other things, they stoned the car carrying Cornelia and the second time hit the driver.[27] The following year, the train carrying Cornelia was stoned and it had to travel slowly because of previous attempts at derailment.[28] One inevitable problem in organising a mass movement is that workers need a livelihood and so money had to be raised. Cornelia tells her own stories of it being raised forcibly from her wards by Gandhi's supporters, but contrary to his principles.[29]

There was a more direct animus against the land-owning class to which Cornelia's wards belonged. Certainly, the wealth of some of them was enormous. Moreover, the landowners were seen, even by some British critics, as having gained enhanced revenues under the Court of Wards' supervision, at the expense of tenant peasants. These British criticisms had been made at a time of famine in 1874 about a wardship of the Hatwa estate in Bihar.[30] But attacks were falling in 1921 on the very land-owners whom Cornelia had educated to do social work for others. There was thus a headlong collision between her vision of what should happen to this class and what Gandhi's policy called for. Her former Churamaon ward, Bhopal, the one who was building a hospital with a woman's wing, had Civil Disobedience workers come to urge his peasants not to pay rent. Another, the Maharaja of Tajhat suggested that the landowners should combine against Gandhi.[31] The Princely States also turned away Gandhi's followers, according to Cornelia. She claimed that this was true of the State of Bharatpur, which was beginning to practise the social reforms which she was advocating.[32]

There were even worse conflicts, we have seen. In the wake of Cornelia's association with Mayo, Cornelia's two most central projects were wrecked. She was subjected to a vexatious prosecution and a boycott in legal work by her dishonest clerk,[33] and to boycott and defection from her Bengal League of Social Work,[34] and in both cases, the damage was brought about, she believed, by Swarajists. Worst of all, in 1931, the purdahnashins' crucial work in Cornelia's Social Service League was stopped, when followers of Gandhi, as Cornelia called them, repeatedly demanded money from Peri Banu on pain of death.[35] In 1938 Cornelia reported that the election promises of the Congress Party included abolishing the land-owning class for whom Cornelia worked.[36]

Thus the nationwide movement created by Gandhi was a far greater threat
to Cornelia's whole life's work than that created by the few thousand Bengali
progressives, whom she had earlier feared on the grounds that they would treat
her purdahnashins as practising anachronistic superstition. This was the background against which Cornelia agreed with the description of Gandhi as an
extremist. But the highest of the British with whom she worked did not necessarily agree. The Viceroy, Lord Reading, told her in 1922 that Gandhi was not
a fanatic. The same month, Lord Montagu resigned when Gandhi was arrested,
and many years later Cornelia was told by a Mr Fieldson something remarkable about Reading's successor as Viceroy, Lord Irwin, later Lord Halifax. Irwin
supposedly said that his greatest regret in his dealings with Gandhi was that he
had not joined him in a fast.[37] Such was the influence of Gandhi over the more
liberal-minded of the British administrators whom he opposed.[iii]

King George V was more inclined to Cornelia's view. We have seen that in
1924 he confided to her that he had refused that year to see Mr C. R. Das, the
recent Law Member of the Viceroy's Council, because he considered him an
extremist.[38] What is better known is that the King tried on the same grounds
of extremism to refuse to include Gandhi in an invitation to tea at the second
Round Table Conference in 1931, but Ramsay Macdonald said that that was
impossible, so the King confronted Gandhi with accusations at the tea party
instead, which Gandhi easily deflected.[39]

Cornelia herself had more in common with Gandhi than she acknowledged
when it came to social reform.[iv] In 1922, Gandhi was arrested and imprisoned
with a six year sentence, and, although he was released in 1924 on grounds of
health, he said that he would not resume his Non-cooperation for the six year
period. During that time, he concentrated on social reform. His 'Curse of child
marriage' was published in 1926.[40] Both Mayo and Cornelia reviewing Mayo
in 1927 acknowledged the value of his opposition to child marriage. Cornelia
thought that Gandhi was a spent force, but she found he was to become as
prominent as ever in 1930–1932, in connexion first with the Salt March to
defy the tax on taking salt and next with the treatment of Dalits, who were
then called 'Untouchables', until Gandhi renamed them 'Harijans' (children
of God). At the second Round Table Conference she interviewed him on that

iii The same liberal-mindedness may not have stood Irwin in good stead, when later, as Lord
Halifax, he lost to Churchill as his rival to become Prime Minister for the war against Hitler.
iv See also on village councils in Chapter 12.

subject in the presence of the Dalits' leader, Ambedkar. But that belongs to the theme of the next chapter.

Despite Cornelia's opposition to Gandhi, she was very curious about him. She knew personally three of his best known women associates, Mirabehn, Sarojini Naidu and Annie Besant, and partly through them she sought further encounters with Gandhi or his institutions.

MIRABEHN: GANDHI'S PRAYER MEETING AND ASHRAM

Madeleine Slade, daughter of a British Admiral, came to India in 1924, and when she joined Gandhi, he renamed her Mirabehn, the spelling she uses in a letter to Cornelia. She had once lived next door to Cornelia in London and wrote to her around New Year 1925–1926.[41] She was Gandhi's close personal attendant and he depended on her. But in December 1926, she had been sent by him to Delhi to learn Hindi away from people of her own kind. Gandhi sent Mirabehn away again in 1936 to live in a village, on the grounds that her dependence on him was interfering with her development.[42]

Mirabehn's letter to Cornelia from Delhi during the first absence is the one fully preserved.[43] Cornelia had been interested in the ascetic life of Gandhi's ashram and had asked about it in her reply. Mirabehn now described life during her year in the ashram and wrote that she did all her own cleaning, cooking and laundering, and studied ginning, carding, spinning and Hindi grammar, wearing a home-spun white or cream Gujarati saree without a border. Her food was very plain Indian food and she had never been so well. She had a room of her own with the bare necessities: no chairs, high tables or carpets. Soon after writing this letter, she was moved on by Gandhi to Hardwar, the sacred town in the North, and Cornelia found that she was at a school of the Arya Samaj Movement, which, whatever its other aims, Cornelia approved as using Hindu scriptures to reinterpret and ameliorate the lot of women. But she was the only woman there and the school was in an area not suitable for a lone English woman, so she wrote to Mirabehn and to Narayani, her Sadhuin friend,[44] to arrange for them to meet. She also learnt at that time from several sources, including Sarojini Naidu, more about Mirabehn's life in the ashram. She had learnt to chant while swaying and to weave an extra cloth every week, and she was set to clean the latrines, which Sarojini said was Gandhi's test for foreign disciples.[45]

The next meeting took place in Delhi at a crucial moment in 1931. Gandhi, newly released at the urging of Sapru from his imprisonment after the Salt March, was engaged in the 16 days of consultation with Viceroy Irwin, which led to the famous Gandhi-Irwin pact and to his agreeing to attend the second of the three Round Table Conferences in London.[46] Cornelia had also gone to Delhi, to see Irwin about her Social Service League and was staying in her sister Alice's pleasant house in Delhi. It was also the month in which Cornelia reported the threats by Gandhi's followers to her wealthy wards in Dacca.[47] The day that Gandhi returned from the second of his meetings with Irwin, Cornelia decided to go to the palatial house of Dr Mukhtar Ahmed Ansari where Gandhi was staying with Mirabehn.

Cornelia saw Mirabehn looking well and was told to come back at 6.30 after Gandhi's afternoon with Irwin.[48] There were by that time about a hundred people outside, mostly women, hoping to catch a glimpse of Gandhi. Cornelia was in Alice's car and sent a message to Mirabehn and they were both invited in and to the evening prayer, which was conducted in the same way as when Gandhi was at his ashram in Ahmedabad. There was a crowd seated in the garden and the electric light had failed. It looked all the more impressive in the semi-darkness, as if they were so many 'silent, waiting bundles.' Gandhi was at the front of the semi-circular concave entrance with his disciples and ashram members, Cornelia among the women visitors to one side, while the crowd squatted in the garden facing him. They started with chanting a series of hymns, mostly in Hindi, sung some by soloists, some by the ashram women, with men visitors occasionally joining in. Then Gandhi stood up and 'the crowd, very orderly, swept forward in a movement of adoration', as Cornelia put it. Mirabehn fell at his feet as the lights came on and that was the end. She picked up his cushions and accompanied him back inside. But she returned to the side verandah to speak to Cornelia.

She talked of their last meeting in London and said how busy she now was. She did all the housekeeping for the feeding of guests and was Gandhi's chosen attendant. He did not stir without her in his domestic activities, and while they were talking, men came to say she was needed because she was to attend him on a drive and a walk. She also walked with him in the mornings. But she had fitted in a discussion of their different attitudes, and started by saying, 'Since we met last, we have gone opposite ways. . . . Knowing what you write and say about Gandhi, all which things are sent me, I wondered when your card was brought in.' Cornelia said what she thought about Gandhi's Non-cooperation and Civil Disobedience Movements and added that as a professional woman lawyer, it seemed to her amazing that he, as a professional lawyer himself, should seek to spoil by non-payment of tax and Civil Disobedience a going concern (India) just at the moment when it was about to go into the hands of his client (the Indians). 'The till will come to you empty', Cornelia said, 'if you continue your tactics'. 'Oh, we will fill it again,' was the reply. 'Taxes there will have to be when Indians rule, but it will not be as now, all the money spent on foreigners and the army. You should see the people in the villages starving not because there is nothing to eat, but because the British Government and officials oppress them and take what they have.' Cornelia reminded her that she knew the villages and had lived and worked and wandered solely among them for over 20 years in a life of which over 35 had been devoted to the service of Indian women. Mirabehn replied yes, but perhaps Cornelia had judged in all that time against India, like Katherine Mayo in her few months. Cornelia replied that her continuing to work in India as an old woman showed what an absurd charge that was and returned to her point that there was no reason to fight for self-government when it was already on offer. Mirabehn said the offer was not meant, and that the first Round Table Conference under Sapru would have elicited nothing without Gandhi's Civil Disobedience Movement, and that she had heard with her own ears the delegates themselves say so. Cornelia concluded not only that Gandhi was, in his current talks with Irwin, using Civil Disobedience as a weapon, but also that Dick's friend Sapru was, though admittedly a moderate, hand in glove with him.[49] Cornelia's opinion of Sapru's politics only really improved in 1940.[50]

Mirabehn said that coming to Gandhi after her upbringing was like coming from darkness into light and she could never go back. Cornelia found even her diction changed, as she spoke like a foreigner, slowly and in a sing-song way and as if she were making a speech. Cornelia planned to visit the ashram in Ahmedabad, which she did the following year. She would also have liked to talk to Gandhi himself, but that was to come later in the year, and would in any case have been difficult while she was staying with her sister, Alice, 'who still takes of me in things political her old view, I fear'. Alice did not agree with Cornelia's politics.

Much had happened, as will be seen in the next chapter, by the time Cornelia visited Gandhi's ashram in Ahmedabad in December of the next year, 1932, with the failure of the second Round Table Conference, Gandhi's resumption of Civil Disobedience, and imprisonment and his fast in prison over the con-stitutional provisions for Dalits.[51] Mirabehn had also been imprisoned in 1932. When Cornelia visited the ashram in Ahmedabad,[52] she was out of jail, but away working on the campaign for Dalits in the South of India. A fourteen year old girl with head bare and hair cut short let Cornelia in and asked if she had come to see the ashram. There were only 100 men and women there instead of the usual 250, because the rest had been jailed, or were picketing, or helping with Gandhi's programme for Dalits. The members wove, spun and learnt to read or write, and the men also did accounts or wrote books, and the atmosphere was pleasantly busy. The girl was kept at sweeper's work and not always allowed to go picketing, which she liked best, but Gandhi (Bapuji) said that sweepers' work was the way to convince the world that they were right. There were gardens with fruit and vegetables for the community. Cornelia was shown where Gandhi lived when at home, 'a really attractive open-doored, wide-verandahed low house on the banks of the river, with a dear little garden in front and to the side, secluded and quiet, away from the noise of the work-sheds'. That was where he gave interviews, slept, sat, wrote and spent his days. 'A suitable retreat', she called it, 'for a holy man'. There were rooms in the house too, but only Mirabehn slept there. Mrs Gandhi lived at the far end of the grounds in her son's house. Cornelia was shown Mirabehn's room, which had no comforts. It had one door leading to the side garden and, so that she could attend to Gandhi closely, was removed from his premises only by the width of his secretary's room. She had a string bed, a cupboard of books, a water vessel and a low Indian writing desk on the floor at which she had to sit cross-legged. She had told Cornelia, when visited in jail, that she could no longer sit on a chair without discomfort. The ashram sold Gandhi's publications, some not obtainable elsewhere, as well as their sewn and woven work and milk. The ashram press had been closed by the Government, but they got everything privately printed. Cornelia remarked that the organisation was wonderful and was spread to other parts of India by Gujarati women sent out to establish similar centres elsewhere. Once again, everyone she met was courteous and friendly, although she did not know if they recognised her.

SAROJINI NAIDU

Cornelia knew much better another close associate of Gandhi, Sarojini Naidu, the poet and central figure in the Independence Movement who was elected President of the Congress Party in 1925 in succession to Gandhi. She was 13 years younger than Cornelia, initially admired her and continued to reach out to her even after the connexion with the Congress Party created a distance between them. In the dark hours of 1940, it will be seen in the final chapter, it was Cornelia who tried to reach out to Sarojini.

Born in 1897, Sarojini got a scholarship to study in England in 1895, just after Cornelia left England, but in 1904 she asked Cornelia to stay in Hyderabad. Cornelia in 1904 was just leaving Sri Lanka to explore the interest among Madrasi lawyers in her case for appointing a woman lawyer. She accepted the invitation to stay and later that year found Sarojini enjoying an excellent 'spurt of song'.[53]

Two years later, Sarojini was recommending a Muslim girl to Cornelia for a Dufferin scholarship, and she saw Cornelia continuously during the December 1907 meeting of Congress in Calcutta and had a number of meals with her. Cornelia drove her to one of the meetings. She was herself disappointed in it, but she found one of the Congress leaders good to talk to, when she gave a final party for people to meet Sarojini. She also heard Sarojini give a very good lecture of her own. She had always thought of her as 'a dear little thing', but in the years after the 1907 Congress she began feeling a political difference which she regretted, and by their next meeting Cornelia was distinctly distant and suspicious.[54]

The next meeting was in 1914 in London, which was when Sarojini first met Gandhi. Cornelia visited Sarojini in a London nursing home and talked to her about her own writing in support of the war effort.[55] She also had Sarojini to tea, but felt she was quizzing her about quotations of what she had said and about her friends, like Una, and trying to get to know them.[56] This cagey attitude to Sarojini was not shared by Cornelia's sister Alice, but Cornelia later believed that Sarojini was funded to stir up student opinion in England in 1912–1914.[57] By 1917, Sarojini was Vice President of Annie Besant's Home Rule League. Though criticising Besant (Cornelia called it abuse), Sarojini also supported her with impassioned eloquence when she visited Cornelia.[58] In 1920, she had moved over to Gandhi's Non-cooperation Movement and reached the pinnacle of the Presidency of Congress in 1925.

After her Presidency of Congress, she was famous, and Cornelia, reading of the speech she made when she was honoured by the City Corporation in Calcutta in 1926, admitted that it must have been brilliant, like a poem, and that she must have improved vastly. Sarojini had been trying to promote peace after Hindu–Muslim riots in Calcutta.[59] Cornelia had her to lunch and Sarojini offered a rather human picture of Gandhi's life, with Mrs Gandhi complaining of the asceticism and the dirty, bad food imposed by an ageing Gandhi on himself and on the young men. Gandhi and his wife referred their differences to Sarojini and she said she would not stay there because he gave the boys in the ashram dog food. But he himself promised to cook her delicacies and he was a superb cook. He also gave her a bed, but she was more comfortable on the floor. Sarojini also tried to commend Gandhi to Cornelia by comparing him with Christ.[60]

In 1928, Cornelia, was on the advisory board of the first Broadcasting Company to be installed in Calcutta in the early days of radio. She got Sarojini to broadcast her poems, which she thought charming and beautifully read.[61] Meanwhile, Sarojini had castigated Katherine Mayo,[62] and was sent to the USA in 1928–1929 to give lectures against Mayo's picture of India, just as Cornelia was to be sent by the British to give lectures against Gandhi's view in 1930–1931 and 1931–1932. Sarojini also came to the second Round Table Conference in this period, after being released from imprisonment for her courageous part in Gandhi's Salt Tax campaign. She crossed swords with Cornelia, when Cornelia interviewed Gandhi in London during the conference.[63] When the conference failed to support Gandhi, and he returned to Civil Disobedience in India, both Gandhi and Sarojini were imprisoned, and Cornelia visited her in prison.[64] Sarojini was also Gandhi's nurse when he fasted in 1933.[65] At that time, Cornelia was asked by the *Evening News* to write Gandhi's obituary,[66] but he survived his fast. Cornelia and Sarojini continued to meet, but I shall come back in the final chapter to Cornelia's last communication.

ANNIE BESANT

Annie Besant (1847–1933) was 19 years older than Cornelia and had already had a remarkable career of free-thinking and social reform in England before she first went to India in 1893, the year Cornelia returned from her studies in England. Cornelia never knew her well, but they first met on the boat to India in 1907, the year Cornelia was returning after Falkner Blair's death and Besant was about to take over as President of the Theosophical Society. That had been the source of Besant's interest in India. Theosophy incorporates much of Hinduism and Besant came to believe that in her last incarnation she had been an Indian. On the boat she discussed this new religion, which she saw as India's gift to the world. Politics was no part of the conversation.[67] Seven years later it was different, and Cornelia received the formal reprimand for engaging in politics partly because she replied in *The Times* of 3 June 1914 to Besant's charges of British injustice.[68]

In 1916 during the First World War, Besant founded the Home Rule League in India and became its President. In that capacity she was interned by the British in June 1917, which drew Jawaharlal's father Motilal Nehru and, for a year, Sapru, into her movement, and led to such pressure that Besant was released in September and promptly elected President of the Congress Party for a year from December. Cornelia found herself in the same railway carriage as her on two long trips in this period. The first was to Bombay soon after her release in 1917, she looking very picturesque in her own version of Indian dress, and the second some of the way to Monghyr in 1918.[69] On that trip, Besant wore a white Madras (Chennai) saree, gold-bordered, a big moonstone brooch and a big jade ring on her forefinger. She read a novel till late, but Cornelia excused herself as she needed to go to sleep.[70]

In March 1919, Cornelia wrote of Besant denouncing Gandhi for having encouraged the riots in the Punjab which were to lead up to the Amritsar Massacre, and upon meeting her at Viceregal Lodge in 1922, she described her as a dear old lady who genuinely opposed Gandhi. She heard her examined there before the Racial Distinctions Committee and called her brave and good.[71]

The approval did not last indefinitely. In 1925, there was an application to let Mrs Besant set up in Madras a unit of the National Council of Women of India, for which Cornelia was the organising Vice-President. The National Council was established for social service, and Mrs Besant would have created a much more political unit, and the resulting alarm caused some units elsewhere in India to be disbanded. The application came from the Secretary of the Bombay unit although the Bombay Chairwoman tried in vain to deny this. Cornelia scotched the application by insisting on the constitutional procedure of submitting it to the Governing Body of all the Indian units.[72]

In 1925, Besant was also drawing up her Commonwealth Bill which Sapru helped her to draft, although Gandhi's followers did not support it. She was seeking for India the comparative independence of Dominion Status enjoyed by certain other countries in the Empire like Canada, where the British Governor General was responsible to a Canadian Parliament. This was something that Sapru was trying to bring about and Dick supported him. Gandhi got the Congress Party to keep the door open for a while, but politicians back in England were not ready to agree to Dominion Status. So Lord Irwin as Viceroy could not promise it and in 1929 the Congress Party rejected it. Cornelia was not in favour of Dominion Status, but what she chiefly objected to in Besant was not that, but Besant's preliminary pamphlet, 'Shall India live or die?', in which she blamed the British for the poverty and other disadvantages that

Indians faced. Cornelia wrote an unpublished 27-page response,[73] arguing that
a proper knowledge of Indian pre-Moghul and Moghul history would show that
the problems went back much further than the British. She posted this to Elena
from aboard ship in July 1925. Cornelia still recognised how magnetic Besant
continued to be, and the last mention is of Besant's manifesto in response to
Mayo's calumnies against India.[74]

Of the three women described, Besant was a leader whom Gandhi pushed
aside; Mirabehn was a personal disciple. Only Sarojini became a national
leader in Gandhi's Independence Movement. She will play a further role in
Chapters 21 and 23, first as trying to terminate the interview in which Cornelia
cross-examined Gandhi. The context of that cross-examination was the second
of the three Round Table Conferences about India's future, held in London in
1930–1932. Cornelia interviewed Gandhi at the second conference. She and
Dick were more closely involved in the third. With Cornelia's initial reactions
to Gandhi explained, the scene is set for turning to the three conferences.

CHAPTER 21

INTEREST GROUPS AT THE ROUND TABLE CONFERENCES: GANDHI INTERVIEWED, AMBEDKAR ENTERTAINED, PRINCES AND THE ORTHODOX REPRESENTED 1930–1932

G andhi was to tell Cornelia in her interview with him that his followers numbered all 350 million Indians. But in a way the achievement of Indians in giving India as much unity as they did was all the greater because the interest groups started off being so diverse. It took Gandhi, but also others besides Gandhi, to achieve this degree of unity. This chapter will consider only the three interest groups with which Cornelia and Dick were concerned: strictly orthodox Hindus, the Princes and the Dalits, who were ranked below any Hindu caste.

A series of three Round Table Conferences with the British Government was brought about in London between 1930 and 1932 at the urging of Sapru and Jayakar.[1] Sapru was interested in the all-important task of bringing disparate groups together with Gandhi and Gandhi's Congress Party in constitutional plans for the future of India. The first conference was held in 1930. Gandhi missed it because he had undertaken one of his most famous campaigns of Civil Disobedience and was in prison.

The Viceroy, Lord Irwin, had declared in 1929 that Dominion Status, the degree of independence from Britain enjoyed, for example, by Canada, was 'the natural issue of India's constitutional progress' and that he would hold the Round Table Conference in London, as desired by Sapru and Jayakar, in order to frame proposals to that end. But at the end of the year Irwin had no undertaking from the Government in London that it would give India Dominion Status. Viceroy and Cabinet did not necessarily agree. Gandhi had pre-arranged with Congress that without such an undertaking, they would seek a still greater degree of independence and for that purpose would resume Civil Disobedience. This took the form of defying the British tax on salt. Gandhi led a long march to the sea, where he picked up a nugget of salt and mud and symbolically boiled it for use, tax free. This was followed by raids on salt depots, and that led to Gandhi's imprisonment. [2]

SAPRU AND THE FIRST ROUND TABLE CONFERENCE, 1930

With Gandhi imprisoned, Sapru and Jayakar had to proceed without him or his Congress Party at the first Round Table Conference. Sapru had secured the participation of Hindus, of Muslims and of rulers of some Princely States. The first conference was held in London in November–December 1930. The inclusion of the Princes, it has been said, mollified sceptical politicians in Britain. [3] The Princes represented a third of India, and their willingness to join a federation with an elected central legislature made the necessary changes of constitution appear to sceptics less impractical.

After the conference, Irwin, at Sapru's urging according to Cornelia, [4] unconditionally released Gandhi and his associates, to facilitate discussion. This was when Gandhi had his 16 days of talks with Irwin in Delhi, [5] finishing with the Gandhi-Irwin pact. The pact provided that Congress would suspend Civil Disobedience and would send its representatives to the second Round Table Conference in London, while the British would release those arrested for the 1930 disobedience and make concessions on the salt tax and other things. [6]

GANDHI AT THE SECOND ROUND TABLE CONFERENCE, 1931

But according to the source already cited on Gandhi, [7] the second Round Table Conference of September–November 1931 resulted in Gandhi's saying that he had never felt more humiliated. Five minority groups among the Indian delegates declared against him that they wanted separate electorates for their minorities in a future constitution. A separate electorate had already been agreed for Muslims by all parties since 1916 and accepted by the British. The plan has been ascribed to the earlier generation of leaders, Tilak, Besant and Jinnah,[8] and according to Cornelia, Gokhale had requested such communal representation from Lord Minto as early as 1907.[9] What was new, however, was that other groups demanded the same, including Ambedkar for the Dalits, and Ambedkar denied Gandhi's right to speak for them. Gandhi thought that separate electorates would prevent the unification of India, which he believed Congress could provide, and that it would keep the Dalits isolated.

CORNELIA'S INTERVIEW WITH GANDHI, 1931

It was during the second Round Table Conference in London that Cornelia had the interview with Gandhi she had wanted. It was at 7 Park Place, St James, a flat she described as charming. Gandhi used it at the conference during the day. He was wearing only his loin cloth and a Kashmir shawl and he was spinning. With a welcoming smile, he kindly stood up to receive Cornelia and her friend Nina Musgrave, remarking that it was not his custom to stand for visitors. Ambedkar was present at the interview, as was Sarojini Naidu and the industrialist Birla,[10] who was said to be a major funder of Gandhi's campaign. The spinning was symbolic of Gandhi's boycott of British, and even Indian, manufactured cloth in favour of homespun. Cornelia had first heard from a friend ten years earlier that the attendants accompanying Gandhi on a train journey were required to use spinning wheels day and night.[11]

We have only Cornelia's account of the interview, but according to her, she started by saying that they were both barristers and suggested that during the interview they should treat each other as fellow professionals, speaking their minds without fear of offence given or taken. He consented, but reminded her that he had been disbarred from the law courts. Cornelia also objected to the title 'Mahatma' being used for a politician. But Gandhi himself deprecated that title. Cornelia was no doubt influenced by admiration for her Sadhu and Sadhuin friends whose holy way of life was socially engaged, but non-political.

The two most burning questions in the interview were about things that had affected the work Cornelia had just abandoned. The first concerned violence on the part of Gandhi's followers. According to Cornelia, his homespun campaign had boycotted even Indian manufactured cloth and

this had led to such cloth being burnt by his followers, which ruined the sell-
ers. Besides, homespun cloth cost much more to produce, and many poor
Indians were unable to afford it. Cornelia tells of death threats against those
who could not afford to wear it. Remarkably, the Bengal Home Industries
Committee, on which Cornelia served, tried to solve the problem of cost
by giving looms and materials and a standard pattern free to the workers,
but even then, the homespun cost twice as much to produce.[12] In the interview, Cornelia raised only the question of burning. She deliberately chose
an example of something that harmed Indians. Gandhi had in his newspaper
openly reflected on harm caused by non-violence and invited discussion. But
Cornelia was taking the hardest case, not harm to British textile workers,
but to Indians.[i] Gandhi seemed genuinely not to believe that cloth had been
burnt. Violence was a sore point with Cornelia, because that was the year she
had lost through intimidation Peri Banu, the key worker in her social experiment of having purdahnashins go out and help villagers and mill workers.[13]
Gandhi insisted to Cornelia that his following was all 350 million of India's
inhabitants, but pressed to say how many would abide by his non-violent
principles, he estimated 30,000.

Towards the end of the interview, Cornelia took the side of Ambedkar,
leader of the Dalits. Their common ground was the belief that no one could
preserve the caste system while abolishing Untouchability. The privileges of
caste depended, they agreed, on denial of rights to the casteless. Cornelia's
secluded families wanted caste preserved; Ambedkar wanted it abolished. They
both rejected Gandhi's attempt to have things both ways and Cornelia tack-
led Gandhi on the question. She asked if Gandhi believed (like her wards) in
caste or in abolishing 'Untouchability', since one could not have both. Gandhi
said one could have both, since what he believed in was the original conception of caste as (four) main occupational divisions. Cornelia said that everybody believed in trade guilds, but that was not what caste had meant since the
second century and her orthodox clients took him to mean that he believed
in caste as it now was, while the 'Untouchables' believed that he meant the
opposite. In the longer run, but very much later, Ambedkar got Gandhi to
switch to his own view and in the *Harijan* for November 16th 1935 Gandhi
eventually wrote an article entitled, 'Caste has to go'.[14] Here is an extract from

---

i One of the arguments he developed elsewhere could have applied to harm done to Indians,
that the harm was an unintended consequence of a legitimate activity, which he would rectify if
he could. See Bhikhu Parekh, *Colonialism, Tradition and Reform*, Ch. 4.

Cornelia's discussion, as presented by Cornelia in her uncorroborated account to an American readership.[15]

'I went on to inquire how many disciples he had. "You are always saying that you speak for 'the dumb millions of India'. Of course you and I know that this cannot be so. You speak for a certain number of English-educated Indians who are most extraordinarily vocal themselves. What is your real following, Mr Gandhi?"

"Three hundred and fifty millions."

"Ah, do be serious. I want to know the number of your disciples, not the population of India."

'He repeated, "Three hundred and fifty millions."

"Deduct at least one individual from that total," I said, indicating myself. "Come now, what is your following?"

"Three hundred and fifty millions, whether you like it or not."

'It seemed hopeless to pin him down, so I tried another tack. "What is the membership of the Congress of which you are the accepted leader?"

"We have no list of members – all India."

'I tried again. "How many people were imprisoned when you came to Delhi last year to negotiate with Lord Irwin?"

"The entire Congress."

"Yes; I remember you said so at the time. How many people would you say were then in prison?"

"Lakhs and lakhs." [ii]

"And why were they in prison? Didn't you invite them to qualify for prison by breaking the law? Yes, I heard you myself. They obeyed you, and committed acts of violence punishable under the Indian Penal Code – murder, assault, the wrecking of trains, arson, the burning of imported or mill-made cloth, which ruined the poor, smaller Indian merchants. How was it that the apostle of passive resistance had disciples who committed violence?"

"I deny that cloth was burned."

---

ii Hundreds of thousands.

"But it *was*, Mr Gandhi. Your disciple here," said I, indicating a wealthy cotton merchant and mill owner who sat beside me, a mill owner who is commonly believed to have been excused from Gandhi's ban because, like the mill owners of Ahmedabad, near Gandhi's home, he is said to subsidize the Congress, – "your disciple here knows that this is true."

"Yes, Mahatmaji", he said, "cloth was burned in Bombay."

"Well, I never commanded violence. I repudiate all who committed violence."

"You can't repudiate your followers and agents. 'What you do through another you do yourself'. You and I are familiar with that principle. You certainly commanded picketing. What did you mean by picketing?"

"I meant for them to fall at the feet of persons using or selling foreign cloth or mill-made cloth, and say, 'please do not do this.' That is not countenancing violence."

"But surely you knew that that was not the way they would do it. And those who committed violence said that you paid them to do it. That was revealed when they were let out of prison in 1931 after the Irwin-Gandhi pact. They complained that if the boycott could not be renewed they would starve, since they would lose both their wages from you and their gains from looting. You held a meeting to decide how many of these people you could continue to pay."

"Yes, I paid them. But I repudiate those who committed acts of violence. They were hooligans."

"Exactly. Many people have thought all along that your following was swelled by the hooligans who live on the edge of social unrest in all countries, but I didn't expect you to say the same thing. However, deduct the hooligans from the 'lakhs and lakhs' – how many are left whom you would regard as your followers?"

"Thirty thousand."

"Thank you, Mr Gandhi. When I am asked in America, 'what is the number of Mr Gandhi's real discipleship?' I shall say, "thirty thousand; he told me so himself".'

Cornelia felt throughout that Gandhi wanted to be friendly and that there was an attractiveness about him. It was only Sarojini Naidu who expressed horror at Cornelia's line of questioning, especially when Cornelia rejected the title of 'Mahatma', which Gandhi himself deprecated, and insisted that he had made himself outcaste – no longer a Hindu caste member – by associating with an

'Untouchable'. This was a serious part of her argument, intended to convey that Gandhi could not represent strictly orthodox Hindus, if he represented 'Untouchables'.

> '"What have you done for Dr Ambedkar's community?" I asked. " I have an outcaste girl at my *Ashram*. You will see her when you come to Allahabad". "What is that? The missionaries take hundreds of thousands of outcastes under their protection, clothe and educate them, and fit them to stand on their feet. Besides, you are an outcaste yourself now. What credit can be claimed by an outcaste for adopting an outcaste child?" Horrified disciple: "She calls you an outcaste!" "Are you not one, Mr Gandhi? You boast of eating with them. Any Orthodox Hindu will tell you that by that act alone you have lost whatever caste you once possessed". "Yes, I have eaten with them. They are my people."'

Cornelia felt that Sarojini interrupted her just when Gandhi was about to make an admission useful to her (she really did see it as a confrontation between lawyers). She even thought Sarojini malicious and acknowledged that her vitality was overpowering.[16] But Gandhi's approach was different. He made use of something more powerful than Sarojini's vitality, or Cornelia's skill at cross-examination: what she experienced directly was the force of *love* towards his opponents. Cornelia may have won intellectually, but who had won overall when at the end Gandhi practised on the unsuspecting Cornelia his belief in love for all mankind, especially for your enemies? According to her description in the *Atlantic Monthly*,

> 'We rose to leave, and I was saluting him Indian fashion, when he seized my hand and took it in his own. "No, I will have your hand", he said, and invited me to become his disciple. We parted laughingly, he threatening that he would yet convert me. He indicated clearly by his manner that he held no grudges in his heart for the candour which I had felt bound to use in questioning him'.

GANDHI, AMBEDKAR AND THE DALITS

To follow a well received account, when negotiations broke down at the second Round Table Conference in 1931, Gandhi warned the British that he would return to Civil Disobedience as the only alternative. A new Viceroy, Lord Willingdon, had him arrested and imprisoned on return to India.[17]

In August 1932, the Prime Minister, Ramsay Macdonald, offered the Dalits the separate electorates for which they had asked, and Gandhi, imprisoned in

Poona, warned him that he would fast unto death unless this was changed.[18] The fast began in September and put tremendous pressure on Ambedkar, as the Dalits' leader, especially as Gandhi entered the danger period. But Gandhi offered a compromise, which Ambedkar accepted. There would be reserved seats for Dalits in a future legislature, and nearly twice as many as the Round Table Conference had envisaged, but candidates would have to win the votes of a joint electorate, not just those of Dalits. This so-called Poona Pact was signed by Ambedkar and also by Malaviya, a member of the Congress Party who represented strictly orthodox caste Hindus. Malaviya's constituents later pressed him, according to Cornelia, to tell Gandhi that his campaign for Dalits to be admitted to all temples was not part of the Poona Pact, although Gandhi did not agree.[19] The signed compromise was accepted by Ramsay Macdonald. Gandhi now called Untouchables 'Harijans' or 'children of God'.[20] The name 'Untouchable' has long since disappeared. In so far as it is used here, this is only because it was the name at the time and was an unconscious indicator of the depth of their social disadvantage. The modern name, 'Dalit', is Ambedkar's designation, meaning *oppressed*.

Cornelia had already met Ambedkar the preceding Christmas of 1931, when they were both lecturing in America. She had then had him to tea, smartly dressed, genial and self-assertive. She disliked his criticisms of the British, but when she gave him Christmas cake, he enjoyed it without scruple. According to Cornelia, he was raising funds for his Dalits programme, and he said that Gandhi would fail in his efforts to detach the Dalits from him. But he was also against the British. Cornelia argued that the British had given Dalits equal opportunities, he himself being one example among others. But he attributed these advances to Indian members of the legislatures or to his personal intervention. The spirit was one of banter.[21]

GANDHI'S VILLAGE FOR HARIJANS (PREVIOUSLY 'UNTOUCHABLES')

The question of 'Untouchables' continued well beyond 1930–1932. Cornelia recorded with interest Ambedkar's later plans to convert them away from Hinduism. In 1935, Cornelia commented, his proposal attracted overtures from Christians among others.[22] She had mentioned in her interview what Christians were doing for 'Untouchables'. But Ambedkar had long had a serious interest in Buddhism and that is where in the end he led many Dalits.

Cornelia's curiosity took her in 1936 to see one of Gandhi's attempts to provide for Dalits— his village for 'Harijans'. She was very impressed.[23] She visited his village while she was once again staying at Alice's house in Delhi. She was struck at the genuine experiment in teaching industry to them. There were 35 boys aged from 14 to 18, chosen from all over India by local Congress committees. The boys were taught tailoring, carpentry, or shoemaking for two years and then sent back to village or town. Gandhi had raised 800,000 rupees for Harijans, part for the village, and Birla had put up the workshops, dining and hostel block and dormitory. There were five and a half hours of instruction in the workshops and two and a half devoted to Hindi, arithmetic, history and general studies, including politics. She called it 'an A1 arrangement'. The food was good, though simple, and the boys helped the cook. There were prayers and readings in Gandhi's style held round the Independence flag he had designed.

The superintendent, Mr Salkani, also impressed her and surprised her by his attitude to violent self-sacrifice. He was an ex-professor of Economics from Muzzafarpur University in Bihar and now worked for the village for bare maintenance. He had a little house with a study on the roof and lovely, wide views. He was a cultured and charming man, thoughtful and full of humour. He had been twice in prison and was serving Gandhi faithfully, but talked about him frankly. He thought that Gandhi's fads would some day kill him. He was torn between Gandhi and Jawaharlal Nehru – Nehru 'a perfect gentleman', he would not hit below the belt', but Nehru believed in Communism, when so many Communists, unlike Nehru, believed in terrorism. As for Salkani himself, though mild and pacific, he said that in his youth he had believed in terrorism, and what was left now was that he might at any moment feel he must rush out and seek a bullet or imprisonment to prove that he really cared for his cause. Although, he agreed, he was serving the cause in the Harijan village, he might feel urged to prove that he could do without ease and comforts and could court death.

CORNELIA, DICK AND THEIR DIFFERENT CONSTITUENCIES AT THE THIRD ROUND TABLE CONFERENCE, 1932

The Dalits were one constituency, but there were others. Back in 1932, Sapru's third and last Round Table Conference and its aftermath saw Dick and Cornelia working for different constituencies from each other: strictly orthodox caste Hindus and the Princes. The strictly orthodox had not been separately

represented at any of the Round Table Conferences. The recommendations of
the third conference were to be debated in Parliament and put on the statute
book by the summer. Cornelia learnt in February 1933, after the conference,
that if the strictly orthodox were to be heard before the Parliamentary debate,
they must get their views to England by May. But their official leaders were
not effective, although she set about meeting them and looking for other possible leaders to alert.[24] M. K. Acharya, a very orthodox former member of the
Madras Legislative Assembly, came to see her. He had once worked with Tilak
and been in the Congress Party, but left it, and he had opposed raising the age
of marriage. He was old, grey-bearded, but strict in law, with perfect English
and, according to Cornelia, had successfully resisted the attempt to bring about
temple entry for Dalits at Gandhi's chosen temple. He had written an open letter to Gandhi in the *Madras Mail*,[25] in which he denied that Gandhi's movement
had succeeded in entering any of the more sacred temples and complained that
the orthodox had not been consulted when Gandhi and Ambedkar signed the
Poona Pact about the future of Dalits. He did not accept Malaviya as a leader of
orthodox caste Hindus, but his letter of protest about Malaviya had not been
accepted by any of the Nationalist newspapers. He had himself offered to purify
Dalits into the path of the love of God, so that they could enter, but Gandhi had
replied that they were already pure.

Acharya said he would have the courage to go to England if Cornelia chaperoned him. The orthodox went on to set up headquarters for propaganda especially in holy towns in India. The Secretary of State for India, Sir Samuel Hoare,
told Cornelia that, although he could not co-opt orthodox representatives,
because others would be disappointed, they should come and give evidence
and he asked Cornelia to influence them to do so. Acharya was put off, but the
Joint Select Committee cabled him to come and give evidence with others and
he agreed. As a strictly orthodox Hindu, he would bring his own cook and he
asked Cornelia to find him a kitchen that would be purified and to meet his
train. Cornelia meanwhile wrote an article on these developments in the *Indian
Mirror*, and was asked to be their correspondent.

Acharya settled in a flat at 4 Park Lane, 'a picturesque figure, bearded, with
the marks of his "puja"[iii] on his forehead'. He wore a turban and regretted that
the climate would make him add an overcoat. He came with the Bombay orthodox representative and there was a third expected to follow. Sapru was against

---

iii Prayer marks.

him, saying that his group were politicians hiding behind religion. Cornelia coached him and helped him write up his evidence. She reported how he faced fierce questioning in meetings with members of the recent Round Table Conference, including Jayakar and the young British Under Secretary for India, R. A. Butler.[iv] Did Acharya approve suttee (the burning of widows alive)? Had he not been a member of Congress? How could he now claim to represent the Hindu majority? Why was there no protest about Gandhi's Poona Pact with Ambedkar? In fact, he was himself one of the protesters in his *Madras Mail* open letter. Two students called on him and said, 'Get out, you old man, you and those with you. Your day is over.'[v]

Dick, unlike Cornelia, had attended the Round Table Conference in November–December 1932, working with a completely different group in close collaboration with Sapru. It was still part of Sapru's aim to draw in the Princely part of India, and Dick was there as unofficial adviser to the Princely State of Datia, which was represented at the conference as part of the Princely State delegation. Datia was near Bharatpur, and Dick had been working for them back in 1921, when he left the Bharatpur festivities early, to go and see them.[26] They, like Bharatpur, still preserved picturesque traditions, such as having their gates guarded by live panthers. But here they were in discussions on a modern constitution. Dick wrote a glowing newspaper article on the Round Table Conference.[27] He described it as a working conference in which speeches were not reported, but, for example, a committee of Indians had meetings with the Bank of England on the future of India's finances, bringing the possibility of a final settlement closer. Congress was not represented. The Princes, who were represented in many cases by their Chief Ministers, were still considering federation to a central legislature, but like Sapru himself, they wanted Home Rule to be within the Empire. All delegates, including Sapru and Jayakar, were determined to go back and persuade the absent Congress leaders, whom Dick also described as extremists, of what had been agreed. The future, of course, was to take a very different direction, and not everyone thought the conference important. But the enormous task of bringing together such disparate parties as the Princely delegation for detailed discussion of practicalities has been seen by some as a step towards the distant final settlement.

The conference was held in the King's panelled Robing Room beside the House of Lords, with the delegates, according to Dick, not sitting in a circle,

iv Later to be a candidate for Prime Minister.
v For Acharya's conclusions from his visit, see reprint from *Madras mail* of 1933, in 165/233.

but in a square. Sir Samuel Hoare as Secretary of State for India had chaired and Lord Sankey as Lord Chancellor read the King's farewell message on Christmas Eve. Included on one adjacent side of the square were Sapru and Jayakar, on another Lord Irwin, whom Dick described as almost worshipped by the Indian delegates, and on the side facing the chair was Lord Reading, now representing the Liberal Party, who received applause little short of that given to Irwin.

Dick's friendship with Sapru had been further cemented since 1925, when Sapru asked Dick and his new wife to take in his 16-year-old grandson and act *in loco parentis*, while he went to school in England and on to Balliol College, Oxford. Dick forbade Sapru to send young Jai Atal excessive pocket money, saying he was ruining the boy, and he made the boy overcome his fears by training him to welcome unknown guests at the railway station, when they lived at Mill Hill, and later to run every night round a dark wood, when they lived in Woodstock.[vi]

THE AMERICAN ARENA: LECTURE TOURS FOR AND AGAINST GANDHI

The time of the Round Table Conferences was also when Cornelia made her two lecture tours to America. America was the arena for lecture tours for and against Gandhi. As already mentioned, Sarojini Naidu had been on a tour at Gandhi's suggestion and during Cornelia's tours, Ambedkar and Tagore went too.[28] Each of them agreed with Gandhi on the need for independence from Britain, but while Ambedkar disagreed with Gandhi on the future of the Dalits, Tagore differed on the burning of cloth, Non-cooperation and Civil Disobedience. Cornelia was not paid for her tour, since the British Government was more cautious in every way after Mayo revealed its involvement with her book. But she discussed the tour with a Member of Parliament, Mr Eustace Percy, who tried to arrange a meeting with Prime Minister, Ramsay Macdonald. Lord Peel, Secretary of State for India, expressed interest in her second tour.[29] The tours were as strenuous as her sister Susie's American tours had been many years before, and early in the first one, she commented that she had given 25 talks, all different, in 22 days in different parts of America.[30] But much of

---

vi It was this grandson, later Nehru's ambassador to Pakistan, who was eventually to give Cornelia's nephew – the author of this work – his first introduction to India.

the entertainment was lavish, not least when she stayed with the Henry Fords of the Ford Motor Company, who had lifted a house bodily from the Cotswolds in England, furnished to the last item and supplied with sheep, sheepdog and kittens.[31] There were also many expatriate Indians at her talks, who were very hostile to the British. At one meeting, as she tells it,

'They wanted to attack me in the hall after the meeting. One man wrenched open the taxi door and said, "You are doing great harm to India. You ought to be killed". He is a Guzerathi. (I had two women friends with me who exclaimed in horror and tried to make him go away, but) he had hold of my hand. I spoke to him quietly, greatly interested in meeting one of these youths at close quarters for the first time. He has done nothing, you see, so far! . . . England is great. I felt so proud to be abused as her friend'.[32]

On return from her second lecture tour in America, Cornelia devised a new series of tours in India, to inform herself of the situation there.

CHAPTER 2 2

CORNELIA'S CRITICISM OF BRITISH PROTECTION OF WOMEN IN THE PRINCELY STATES, 1925–1938

FACT-FINDING TOURS IN INDIA, 1932–1938

With her fact-finding tours in India of 1932–1938 Cornelia hoped to influence English opinion. But she also found herself learning about parts and aspects of India she had not known before. And no longer having employment in British-ruled India, she finished as she had begun in the 1890s working on British legal supervision in the Princely States, where Indian Princes ruled.

She found her tours surprisingly rewarding. One was to check on the Bihar earthquake which had flattened the homes of some of her former wards. Other tours were political. It was at this time that she made her visits to Gandhi's institutions, his ashram and his Harijan village.[1] On several other tours she visited jails with political prisoners. I have already described[2] how well the prisoners received her after initial hostility, one even saving her from a confrontation when he recognised her as the saviour of the self-proclaimed bomb-thrower, Nogen.

On her tours Cornelia stayed for part of each visit with the cheerful and attentive Alice, who had landed again on her feet in a spacious, comfortable and inviting house in Delhi. It had a charming drawing room with many books, Persian rugs, cosy sofas and chairs, her piano and big glass doors to a lovely park-like garden with trees and shadows on the lawn. One half of the house was occupied by a Maharani who was comforted by Alice who had cured her health. Apart from initial friction over the arrangements after Susie's death, Cornelia and Alice had now learnt how to live together by not discussing politics or what exactly their projects were.[3]

One major activity on these tours was investigating social welfare provisions made by the rulers of certain Princely States.[4] Cornelia found these better in some Princely States than in British-ruled India. Particularly impressive were the facilities going back to the nineteenth century in the Princely State of Mysore.[5] She had not known very much about Princely social provisions, since the Princely States in Kathiawar and at Tihur where she did some of her earliest work had not seemed to be very well provided, although she had known as a student that the Nizam of Hyderabad appointed a woman interpreter for purdahnashins, and she had worked briefly for the educational schemes of the Gaekwar of Baroda, a major reformer.[6] Her hopes had also more recently been raised by the Maharani of Bharatpur.[7]

BRITISH PROTECTION OF WOMEN IN THE PRINCELY STATES

Newly impressed by some of the Princely rulers, Cornelia was less satisfied with the arrangements for British supervision in other Princely States. The British had left themselves only limited control over the administration of justice in these Princely States. The theory was[8] that Princely courts were subject to the veto of a British Political Agent. There were Agency courts to which Indians could appeal, if the Princely courts did not give satisfaction. The Political Agent himself fell under a British Political Department and his decisions could in turn be appealed up to the Viceroy and eventually to the Privy Council in London.

Cornelia's question was how well the system of appeal to the British worked in cases where women had legal grievances. She had had a good impression of the system back in the 1890s , because she had been successful in appealing to the Viceroy to get a maintenance allowance restored, when it had been wrongly withheld from her Kathiawar Rani (the one who said 'God will resent it for me').[9] But even in that successful case, the allowance had been withheld for 30 years, and Cornelia got it back only in 1906. Moreover, W. R. Gourlay had warned her, soon after they met, that lists were kept by the British of disputes marked 'not to be resolved'. Nonetheless, Cornelia thought that, by the mid 1920s, the Political Department had changed, under the pressure of the Independence Movement in British India, to a political agenda of trying to keep the Princely States loyal. For that reason, it was not exercising effective supervision in cases where women appealed from the Princely courts to the British. The relations of the British with the Princes were too cordial. The Political

Department was also making decisions on legal matters without having been legally trained, and unlike judges, they did not have to give reasons.[10] Cornelia had started her career in Princely States in 1894, although her later post in the Court of Wards had operated in British India. Once she returned to India after retirement, she began two cases almost at once in 1925 for women in the Princely States of Bastar and Janjira. She continued work for women in the Princely States right up to 1939, when she was 72, on behalf of the Maharani of Dholpur. If we hear only Cornelia's interpretation of the cases, that is sometimes because the British responses to her questions were evasive rather than informative.

DHOLPUR: A MAHARANI'S ALLOWANCE WITHHELD

According to Cornelia, when the popular Maharaja of Dholpur came of age and took the throne, he was induced by imperfect British record-keeping to believe that the widow of the former Maharaja, his brother, had taken a piece of State jewellery. He consequently refused her the maintenance due under Hindu law over a period of 23 years, in order to make her return it, and the British allowed him to raid her property. Nobody could describe the piece of jewellery, and the Maharani was never shown to have possessed it. The British had lost the records of a sale they had made themselves through the dealer Hamilton's, and Cornelia complained that they might have disposed of the jewellery themselves in that sale. Cornelia held that responsibility for redress lay entirely with the British, because while the heir who now held the throne was a minor, the British Political Agent was fully in charge. During this period the widowed Maharani had complied at every point with British attempts to make an inventory of valuables and had supplied an inventory which the British had lost. It was this inventory of hers, voluntarily supplied, that became the source of the idea that there was a piece missing. The widowed Maharani did not know of any piece missing, and she submitted a memorial to the British first in 1914 and then another written by Cornelia in 1934. In this memorial Cornelia asked that, whatever the piece might be, its value should be deducted and the residue paid as maintenance under Hindu law. This was refused by the British without reason after two years.

In 1936, Cornelia went to see the new Viceroy, Lord Linlithgow, and the Head of the Political Department about this.[11] The Head at first refused to discuss the case. He turned out to have no idea what legal channels of redress might be open to women in Princely States and had no knowledge of the widowed Maharani's compliance. When Cornelia referred him to her memorial, he said it was a long time since he had read the case, but he was not a fool, and he offered crossly to send for the file and show her what he meant, if she would wait next door. He then called her in and read out an irrelevant letter from before the date of any quarrel, a letter she knew because she had filed it herself when preparing the memorial. Left no further chance to speak, she wrote to tell him that the letter he read her was of the wrong date to be relevant.

Cornelia was staying with Alice in Delhi, when the Dholpur widow finally died there in 1938 without enough money for more than a night nurse.[12] Alice managed to supply her two nurses. When she died, according to Cornelia, the Maharaja took over the widow's house, her cremation and the disposal of her ashes against her wishes and without paying the costs. Cornelia got from the British Resident in Lahore enough to cover medical expenses, death rites and other outstanding costs and tried to reassure members of the widow's household.

Cornelia sent to the Viceroy's Private Secretary a scheme, which is preserved,[13] for the future protection of women in Princely States. Correspondence with the Viceroy followed in which Cornelia repeatedly protested into 1939, but at that stage, with the Second World War under way, there was no further answer.[14]

BASTAR: A BRITISH OFFICER CHOOSES THE BRIDEGROOM

Cornelia's earlier cases in 1925 were much more colourful. In the Princely State of Bastar,[15] the case was unlike the other two, in that the Political Agent was interfering too much, not too little. He overrode the wishes of the local Rani in favour of a social experiment. The case surprised Cornelia, because she thought it involved ill-informed interference by a British official in what she saw as a religious matter. The British had been very cautious about such interference since the Uprising of 1857, which they recognised they had provoked partly by violating religious sentiment.

Cornelia complained that the Political Agent, Mr Ley, was insisting on marrying an orthodox girl in purdah, Praful, heir to a throne, to an unorthodox man, not a land-owner, but, according to Cornelia, a Brahmo. The prospective bridegroom had been chosen by the British administration, against the wishes of the blind Rani step-mother who had brought the heiress up from infancy when her natural mother died, and who was regarded as her mother. The step-mother had offers for the girl's hand from land-owners and Rajas. Since the Rani step-mother objected to the Political Agent's choice, Mr Ley had banished her from her own State, had docked her allowance and forbidden her to return until after the marriage or to correspond with her step-daughter. According to Cornelia, he laughed at her blindness. He had hurried through the betrothal ceremony, although Cornelia had the written opinion of 20 Benares (Varanasi) Pundits and many precedents to show that the betrothal could be set at naught. Contrary to custom, he had replaced the maidservants left by the step-mother with maidservants from the prospective bridegroom, had allowed pictures of the bridegroom in the house and had encouraged correspondence with the bridegroom. His behaviour had already caused anti-British propaganda in the press, although Cornelia had stopped it. And she had persuaded the step-mother to abide by the banishment, although she did not consider such an order valid. But she insisted on seeing the girl alone, and not in the presence of a male British administrator, as the Political Agent tried to prescribe.

The Political Agent had sat while Cornelia stood and been rude in other ways, but Cornelia evidently began to make him feel nervous. He wrote afterwards to say there might be concessions if she did not publish her interview with the girl, and then in a second letter that he would be retiring shortly and did not want to leave bitterness behind. Cornelia spoke to the Governor and to the Viceroy, although she was rebuked for the latter, and she wrote a memorial about the case to the Secretary of State for India, which she explained to the blind step-mother, and had signed by her and blessed by the devout courier.

The solo interview at Bastar was granted and she was met on her journey there at Raipur by the very nice new Political Agent, Mr Hamilton, and driven 88 miles in state cars through hot black bouldery country to the first night's stop in Kanker. There they were escorted to the palace by outriders to meet the new three year old Raja, 'a dear little boy', and his family, and were given a gun salute. But they stayed in the British Guest House, which was

'all beflagged and adorned as if for royalty. "God Save". "God Save" shouted the flags. And it was only in the cool of the evening that I discovered that below the gay red and blue lettering was to be found in white letters on a white ground the words "The King"! I expect this arrangement was designed to suit all comers. The Rajah, or we, or anyone might imagine the flags were saving them!'

Cornelia would have been pleased to know what happened to the British Guest House at Kanker later. It was first refurbished in 1937. Subsequently, the Royal family of Kanker took part of the Guest House as their own palace and entertained paying guests in the other part, so that Cornelia's nephew was himself to stay there, eating in the same dining room with a large punkah fan. Moreover, the Royal family's own coat of arms preserved the British lion and unicorn, while adding the god Hanuman, and used the family motto not so different from the British one: 'Loyalty to the Kingdom and Stable Government'.

It was a further 99 miles the next day through beautiful jungle to Bastar. At Bastar there was as yet no bridge across the Indravati River.

> 'Our car was put on a raft and punted across, while the Police Band played to us. Bastar is lovely. Everything grows there, even in the heat: flowery shrubs and trees, frangipani, chumpa – white and pink, poinsettia, (luxuria?) were all still a-bloom, and the Guest House verandah was a mass of Easter Lillies.'

Cornelia interviewed the Bastar girl alone. But the damage had been done. She had pictures of the intended bridegroom all over the house and on her dressing table and wore his miniature displayed in a brooch, contrary to the orthodox custom she had followed eight months earlier. Cornelia believed the priests had been bribed to agree. Another marriage had already been arranged of an orthodox boy into the bridegroom's Brahmo family, but it was more disturbing to custom to bring an unorthodox boy in to join the family of an orthodox girl heir, and Cornelia feared the worst.

The Secretary of State's decision was sent in November to the blind Rani who could not read it, but it turned out to reject her memorial. The stepmother now became seriously ill and Cornelia was refused permission for her to be allowed to return. She died before the wedding, without seeing her daughter again. Cornelia thought that Political Agents could do worse things than anything done by the Court of Wards in British India.

At first, the marriage seemed a success. The girl saw Cornelia and declared she was pleased to be out of purdah.[16] She built a new palace adjacent to the 300-year old one, and its drawing room still contains a photograph of the younger Rani, a tiny, very young-looking figure sitting in the same chair as her large husband, who towers over her. But 11 years later, Cornelia heard the sequel from a British officer who had served as Chief Secretary to the Central Provinces.[17] 'Don't say you don't know me,' he said. 'You championed the Bastar Rani and fought us over the marriage planned for her daughter.' He added, 'and

Government acknowledges you were right'. What had happened, he said, was that the priests tried to impose orthodox Hinduism on the incoming bride-groom. But the husband carried the girl away from Bastar and introduced her to the unsecluded world outside. He also campaigned to be recognised as co-ruler in Bastar with his wife. The liberated Rani lived part of each year in London, while her husband spent time in Cambridge. The husband, who was penniless, had been exiled from the Central Provinces by the British adminis-tration, which also took the children in care. So in the part of the year that the Rani spent in Bastar, her husband was not with her. She died in London in 1936 from infection after the removal of her appendix, but controversy over her husband still continues.[18]

The official reason given for the suitability of the marriage had been that the bridegroom had come first in his college diploma exam. But Cornelia believed that the reason for favouring him was that his cousin had offered a donation to the Chief Secretary's college at Raipur.[19] Cornelia used the example of Bastar, and of the next case (Janjira), when giving an opinion for the bar library to the Government on British oversight in the Princely States.[20] She said that it showed the need for having a legal adviser in the Princely States as well as a Political Agent.

JANJIRA: AN UNAUTHENTICATED DIVORCE ALLEGED

Another case of trying to rectify a British decision concerning a woman in a Princely State began to occupy Cornelia in the same year, 1925. The Begum of Janjira[21] had contributed funds back in 1905 to the project of Cornelia's sister Susie of re-establishing one of her mother's schools.[22] To the Begum, as to the other women, Cornelia offered her services free.[23] She investigated the diversity of Muslim divorce customs and showed her findings among others to Gertrude Bell, who re-drew for Britain the map of Muslim Mesopotamia. Cornelia had found that under Shia law, a husband cannot divorce his wife by pronouncing to others his intention three times. He must deliver the pro-nouncement to his wife and there must be witnesses.[24]

In Janjira, the Nawab, having no child by his first wife, had eventually, not long before he died, taken a second wife. Cornelia unwisely described her as having been enslaved to a dried-fish-selling family when she was rescued and taken on as lady-in-waiting by the first wife. But the British refused to discuss Cornelia's memorial petition unless she withdrew that description.[25] Cornelia also said that the Nawab was an opium addict and that his first wife as Begum had in effect ruled most of the 28 years since she married him. With this the Commissioner of Janjira agreed.[26] Cornelia continued to call the first wife 'the Begum', having known her by that title at least since 1905.

Two years after the Nawab died, the Begum gathered that the Government believed she had been divorced. The Chief Political Secretary in Bombay alleged to Cornelia that the Begum was divorced, but refused to reveal his grounds. He later said the rumour was very strong. His Political Department said that the matter was confidential, but then claimed that the Maharaja had announced the divorce to them. The second wife also claimed there was a divorce, but Cornelia asked for the evidence. Later the Political Secretary tried to bully the Begum into saying that she herself had signed a receipt for delivery of the divorce papers, a claim never made before, but he would not show her the alleged letter or signature. As for the Prime Minister of Janjira, he claimed to Cornelia that the letter was in the Janjira records. Cornelia found evidence against the divorce in that the Begum's grants were still entered on the State budget, although someone else drew them.[27]

There was chaos as to whether redress should be sought from the British, and if so, from whom, or from the Princely Durbar court. So long as Cornelia received from the British a claim of divorce only in informal letters, she was not allowed to challenge the claim in a court of law.[28] Cornelia thought she might be able to prove the Begum's status by going to court with a different case, to claim the Begum's village for her from the State of Janjira, although even for that permission would be needed from the British Political Department.[29] In 1928, she was told that the Viceroy could not intervene in response to her memorial, but she could try the Princely Durbar Court. But she already had,[30] and a further hazard of going beyond their lower court was that in the High Court of the Princely State the second wife sat in judgement, wearing a burqa, although Cornelia got a letter saying that if both those courts left a grievance, she could then appeal to the British.[31]

The Begum did not want money, and she was content for the second wife to be regent for the son and heir she had produced, although in her disappointment at the British decision, and perhaps mis-advised by her younger sister Atiya, she was now inclined to deny Cornelia even expenses. She had a house on Malabar Hill in Bombay, a deluxe car and a new Chevrolet, and had paid for a trip by her sister to England. All she wanted was the promised State Guard and two months arrears of allowance.[32]

Cornelia had two exotic visits to the Begum's properties, one to her elegant house in Bombay, and one hair-raising expedition to plead at the lower court in the remote fastness of Janjira, which rises out of the waters of the Arabian sea. Of the Bombay visit, Cornelia wrote:[33]

> 'I am staying with my client, the Begum Sahiba of Janjira in a house which I must have described when I last wrote from Bombay. It is built of red Delhi sandstone in the old Muslim style – arches and pierced openings in place of windows, and cool marble halls, with fountains playing and runlets for water. The pillars are all beautifully carved as in old Delhi work; so are the doors and the arches are all crimped – you know the way. The lighting pleases me – white marble lotus flowers on ball pedestals holding the electric bulbs, which give you that nice overhead lighting. Happily, the furnishing is English, so one has beauty and comfort combined. The Begum's garden is at its best, roses everywhere and little trees of orange blossom and small oranges – most decorative – and pansies and carnations and antoninum in lovely colourings. So England and India meet in the formal 'Delhi' garden also.

> 'It has been lovely on the terrace just about sunset times. Bombay lies in a semi-circle at our feet, all grey and misty. The tide at this hour has receded, and the grey, crumpled mud is all wet and shiny, and the boats are at rest, grey and trans-formed in the silvery light, and the mists are light enough to show you the wavy lines of the hills round Bombay and dense enough to hide all the ugliness of the crowded city. And Atiya Begum, a study in grey and silver, sits against the back-ground, still perhaps for the only moment in the day. And one feels the utter peace of the hour. Then 6 o'clock, or whatever is the hour of the sun's setting, calls to prayer and Atiya runs to her room for a soft white shawl and her prayer rug, and the kind Begum lets me mount to the roof with them and I sit apart on a parapet whence I can see both the flaming glory in the West and the quiet greyness of the world which has lost its sunshine – and I think many thoughts thridded with the names of those I love, as you will guess.

> 'Prayers over and the little ladies kneel and huddle and stand, just like the men one sees praying at mosques all over India. We sit on awhile on the roof and big Begum tells me scraps of ancient Persian or Arabic verse which she translates, or Atiya explains the mysticism of Sufi, or her theories about Indian music (her great subject), until it's time to dress for dinner'.

The journey to Janjira seven hours South down the coast, accompanied by Sabrus, a vakil, could hardly have been a greater contrast. In Cornelia's description:[34]

> 'We had to be up before four o'clock on Monday to take the boat and were up and away, to find that the boat just that day had changed the hour of departure to

9 a.m. (It proved to be nearer 10). They are so casual. I sped back to the Begum's and wired to the Judge, telling him what had happened, because I feared he might deal with the case *ex parte* in the absence of a message.

'It was a weary journey when we did start – 7 hours on a miserable steamer, not like our nice Bengal river and coasting boats. No accommodation except hard benches and no retiring rooms and no food. The last did not matter, as I had fruit and biscuits and dates and little meat patties made by the Begum and could supply Sabrus,[i] his clerk and my chuprassi.[ii] But it was a very tiring journey and I had need to be thankful that I am a good sailor. The route is rather lovely. Palm trees abound and the little low-lying beaches at the stopping places seemed to lead to the isles of peace.

'Janjira itself from the sea looks like a pirate's fortress, which I believe it was, set on an inaccessible rock. Our Begum built a lovely new palace on the mainland, separated by a creek from the rock fortress, in the quieter palm-covered slopes between mountain and sea. There is no harbour, so the boat cast us off (literally) onto a sailing boat, and this again threw us onto a rowing boat. We found a narrow road on landing, which ran for 2 miles to the creek which had to be crossed before we got to Janjira. Miserably springless *ekkas* awaited us and we waded up and went as fast as we could to the creek, to be ferried across. But the tide was low and we could not land. So some greasy men made chairs of their arms and carried us through the *wash* of the waves onto Janjira soil.

'It was now 5 p.m., the hour when the Court *rises*. But we gat us again into ekkas and travelled with Hope to the Court. The Judge was very kind. He had left Court, but returned to sit, so as to release us for our return journey next morning. Sabrus made me wear my wig and I robed hastily and went in. The Judge said the High Court must really allow me to plead, that is, give me a sanad,[iii] before he could hear me, and that the High Court (the Begum number 2 and her Prime Minister) had left for Bombay the day before. I felt I must take this smiling, which I did, asking only that Sabrus, as being a Bombay vakil, who I said from Janjira rules had a right to appear in Janjira courts, might address the Court. I had arranged with Sabrus to tell him what to say. This was allowed, and after all there was little to be said. For, the other side not being ready with evidence, or documents, or lists of witnesses and of admissions, etc., was making objections to our plaint in order to gain time. I said (the judge allowing me

---

i The accompanying vakil.

ii Attendant, henchman.

iii Permission.

to speak) the objections must be put down in writing and we must have time to consult our client, which was allowed.

'I must say the Judge was very courteous to me, though he snapped at Sabrus. Sabrus himself was in a very bad temper, saying, "damn-fool-judge", "damn-fool-place" all the time under his breath. The language of the Court is Marathi, which, thank God, my mother made us learn as children. But the Counsel is allowed to plead in English, though all papers are in Marathi, or Mori (written Marathi).

'It was 7.45 p.m. when the judge rose. . . . We set out for the Dak bungalow [iv] after Court. I'd wired to the Dewan [v] and before he left Janjira, he had written me a letter which awaited me, saying that I should go up to the Dak bungalow. This is in a remote spot on a hill – jungle all round. We got there in darkness, but found a very nice bungalow built by our Begum, nicely furnished, and with two sides to it. So Sabrus took one and I the other. I had my chuprassi and Begum had sent a man ahead to fill water, etc. So we got some tea and some dinner (of a sort) and my bedding and mosquito net made a good prospect for whatever sort of night lay ahead. The bedsteads were quite decent iron ones. But the loneliness of the place was rather alarming. Sabrus was quite nervous.

'"They will send men to loot and injure us, pretending they are thieves. The Begum number 2 and the Dewan are away and went away on purpose, so as to plead ignorance. I wish I had brought my rifle".
Cornelia. "Never mind, you have your stick. We'll put up a fight".
He. "My stick is left in Court".
Cornelia. "No matter, I have an umbrella"'.

'But it really was rather alarming. They might have done something just to discourage Counsel and Attorney from Bombay and Calcutta coming to that God-forsaken place. The case would then have to be left to local pleaders, with a certain result.

'However, as I watched the hillside, I saw an old man like Aaron in picture Bibles walking onto our plateau and towards the house in the wake of a lanthorn and a man or two (or rather, leading these). "Good evening, Aaron", I said. "My name is Reuben", was his answer. It was really very funny, for there really was nothing save his likeness to Aaron to mark him a Jew. He was Superintendent, he said, of the Dak bungalow. So I told him he must send up men to guard us and that the British Government would ask for an explanation if anything happened to us.

---

iv Rest house.
v Chief Minister.

'He sent up the men and I, for one, slept peacefully, being dead beat. He forgot, however, to call us at 2.30 a.m. as promised. But I managed to wake myself at the hour and to get all ready for the road by 3.15, so that it was all the greater chance, as I've told you, that all means of transport failed us and that we therefore missed the boat. Did I tell you that close on 4 a.m. one ekka appeared? Into this I piled all the luggage and servants and set out walking downhill. Sabrus too, but he got lost. He had a lantern and guide to himself. I went with Reuben, another lantern and another guide. It was pitch dark and the lantern blinded me. It would go ahead, instead of keeping behind and I went stumbling among the rocks on the hillside. It was three miles to the creek. I got there and crossed it and was on the road to the Bund,^{vi} feeling I could hold the boat for Sabrus, when the whistle sounded departure! There was nothing for it but to post back. I'd heard that a postal car left at 6 a.m. and I hoped we might get seats in this to some other port along the shore.

'We found Sabrus at a motor garage – there is one – bargaining for a special car to take us along the coast. We got one for eight rupees (!) and sped like the wind. It was bitterly cold, but I loved the adventure of it. At a really lovely spot we "de-trained" and found a little paddle boat and sat in the bottom of it with the villagers and their baskets of vegetables crossing to the other side. There we got a sailing boat and now our steamer was in sight and we met it in mid-stream and got taken on board! So our troubles were over and we got to Bombay by midday. I must say I was glad of the Begum's house, of a hot bath and some food – we'd had none and I'd been up since 2 o'clock.'

Cornelia had to leave the vakil to plead the next stage, and the case was pleaded and lost in her absence in January 1931.[35] An appeal was also lost.[36] The case gave her more colourful experiences than the other two cases, but it too had to be added to those in which there was no redress for women against British decisions in the Princely States.

Cornelia finished her tours of 1932–1938 with a wider knowledge of the variety of India. But her interventions on behalf of women in the Princely States, both before and during the tours, left her with a sense that Britain's anxiety about losing India was making it less attentive to the supervision of justice in the provinces it considered loyal.

---

vi Wall.

PART VI

FINALE

CHAPTER 23

SECOND WORLD WAR, 1939–1946: ABLAZE IN LONDON'S INNS OF COURT

A fter the 1938 tour, there could be no more travel to India. Cornelia was 70. The war with Hitler was imminent. In 1934, Dick and his wife were expecting a second child. The first having been a daughter (Francina), the great feminist Cornelia devoutly hoped for a son and was not disappointed when on November 8th 1934, her nephew was born.[1] She started planning for his long-term educational future, to give him the best chance in life.[2]

THE FAMILY

Dick was not very well. I first realised this, when a student of mine got me a copy, second hand, of Cornelia's *India Calling*, with press cuttings stuffed inside concerning Dick's controversy of 1936 with Lord Irwin, now elevated to be Lord Halifax and from 1938 the Foreign Secretary, and related letters from Dick to the Prime Minister Stanley Baldwin. Dick was objecting that Indian students arriving in Oxford were not being looked after by anyone but the Communist Party, who turned them against British policy to India.[3] But the letters showed a certain excessive excitement and were dated just before Dick's depressive breakdown of 1937. It was Lena who first alerted Cornelia to the fact that he was having mood swings as if he had two personalities,[4] and Cornelia thereafter recorded them along with his diabetes, which, being untreated since he ate sugar as gaily as before, could have added to unstable moods. Most of the time, he was as ebullient as he had been described when head of the Law College in 1909,[5] and as hospitable. His wife laid extra places each night for strangers whom he had invited home from the train.

369

His family moved to Oxford in 1938, and Cornelia visited them all there, as well as her old Chief, Mr Lyon, and her Somerville friend in the next road, Alice Bruce. Dick's straight-speaking mother-in-law, May Monkhouse, lived with Dick's family in Oxford and Cornelia had crossed swords with her, because Cornelia's descents on the family had been rather in the style of her descents on her clients' palaces, timed for her own tight programme and sometimes designed to create surprise.[6] But Alice poured oil on troubled waters, saying what a good effect Dick's mother-in-law had on the children.[7]

I remember the four surviving aunts as the brightest thing in London during the war, apart from the red double-decker buses. All windows in England were blacked out against German bombers, and the lights of the very few permitted cars (mostly taxis) were hooded to conceal inhabited areas. Zuleika and Lena had died since Susie, but the four surviving aunts, Pheroze, Mary, Cornelia and Alice, wore, as they always had, brilliant coloured sarees.

Cornelia had been staying in her sister Mary's flat. Mary was rather particular and only tolerated sharing because she was often away on speaking tours.[8] But it helped that Alice now joined the flat, and she also read the newspapers to Cornelia, whose sight was getting very poor.[9] By August 1940, few people wanted to live with the bombs in the middle of London, and Cornelia was able to move to where I remember her, within the medieval law college at 22 Old Buildings Lincoln's Inn.[10] Her letter to Sarojini quoted below reveals what was obvious to all at the time, that it was a source of pride to her to be living within the Inn, where it had taken her so many decades to get called to the bar.

PREPARATIONS FOR WAR

Britain finally declared war on Hitler on September 3rd 1939, after his annexation of Austria and Czechoslovakia and his invasion of Poland. But there had been and would still be a long period of preparation for war, because British armaments were not ready. On September 28th 1938, Cornelia felt two hours away from war, but Hitler's fraudulent agreement at Munich postponed it. Nonetheless, she volunteered the same day for work on Air Raid Precautions. Gas masks were distributed and there was drill against gas attacks the next month.[11] When war came, she took a job in the citizen's advice bureau in Battersea. But she was soon transferred to legal work, concerned with the Unemployment Act, and she obtained hearings for distress caused by war. It made a big difference to the poor when the family earner had been called up for war and the price of fish had risen.[12] Besides giving talks for the Ministry of Information, she led a series of discussions and debates on the future of India at Chatham House.[13]

WAR STARTS

In September 1940 the bombs started falling and Lincoln's Inn was hit on the 11th. Cornelia's bedroom and bathroom windows were smashed to smithereens, but she was saved 'as by a miracle', since she was sitting up late writing. She later showed me where the glass fell. She postponed a visit to see Dick's family at Oxford, because the Prime Minister asked people not to travel then.[14] But she arranged a visit a few days later, thinking it might be the last visit before Hitler's invasion. The railway line had already been bombed.[15] She expected the invasion again in a letter of December 9th. After one of the invasion warnings, Dick's family house was the only one covered by a smoke screen, since the family burnt its smoke bricks, not having heard that the invasion warning was cancelled.[16] Four days later in December, her friend Elena lost her nephew in air action.[17] On the 15th Cornelia got to Oxford again, after queueing for 45 minutes for a ticket and waiting an hour on return for ammunition trains to go first. The danger siren was sounding on arrival back in London and there were no lights, but a porter found her a taxi at a distance.[18] The Government again asked people not to travel at Christmas for fear of invasion.[19] One of the memorable war time posters read, 'Is your journey really necessary?'

APPEAL TO SAROJINI NAIDU

Cornelia saw a lot of the Secretary of State for India, Leopold Amery,[20] who had been a fellow student with Dick at Balliol. His wife was housing her own sister and eight others who had been bombed out of their own house.[21] He helped Cornelia with two contributions to the war effort. The first was an appeal to Sarojini Naidu to get the women of India to persuade the men to join the war effort. Gandhi had refused support and Sarojini was the leading woman symbol of his Independence Movement. Amery had the letter sent to India in the Viceroy's diplomatic bag. Sarojini had first been an admirer of Cornelia, who was older, and had then wanted to win her to Gandhi's cause.[22] But now Cornelia needed her. The letter shows, that, for all Cornelia's political reservations, Sarojini knew the whole family and especially admired Susie, so that family details could be mixed with exhortation. Cornelia wrote carefully, while not telling Alice who might have disagreed, and casting herself as Indian, as she did another time to Mirabehn.[23] A draft survives.[24]

'Oh Sarojini dear, my "Singing Bird",

How are you? Nor public nor private news have we had of you since 1939, and as in the last war, one particularly wants news of friends. When enemies are ramping around and breathing hate and bitterness, one wants to reach out a hand and feel that friendliness and kindness are still in the world, especially among those one has known longest. So I write. Do you remember how in 1914 I sought you out in Park Lane with the very same intent and found you in a "swell" nursing home surrounded by flowers brought by your admirers?

'The admirers still throng, I am sure, but I trust you need not receive them now in a sick room! How is the nice little daughter whose chest was bad and who stayed at the Poona Hotel when I was there? And the one very clever whom I met in Lucknow? And is your husband still troubled with his eyes? I hope not, or at any rate if trouble there must be, that he has you or one of the girls to read to him. Mine eyes grow dimmer, alas! But they have served for my work so far and I can trust God to let them carry me through to Journey's End, which cannot now be far off.

'The second reason why I write is because, recalling the wonderful poem you wrote in 1914, I felt, "We must have some authoritative statement from Sarojini in prose or verse this time also – or, maybe, for that is most needed, some *act of leadership* of Indian women, which will be more lasting and remarkable still". And as if I'd heard it in Susie's voice – you know how truly she loved you, and I think you loved her too and valued her – I knew what message I was to send you. "Let Sarojini rally all Indian women now, at once, to say to their men of the Congress and of all political parties – 'Lay aside friction for now, and because we, your women, the women of India, ask it – co-operate whole-heartedly in the war which you believe to be a righteous war for Justice and Freedom against Force and Oppression, our war equally with England's, since Mahatma Gandhi and Pandit J. Nehru have declared this to be their conviction in rejecting the bribes of the Naziists and Fascists. We've declared our demand – Independence, and we stick to that, but "without prejudice" to renewal of discussion on the issue when the war is over, we come in now with our might, retaking the Government if the Congress (allows?), and proving our ability to rule in a crisis, accepting at the same time the Viceroy's invitation to representation on the Central Executive'".

'It would be great – if they consented. Political men in India have always been nice to their womenkind. – "Indian women to the rescue under Sarojini Naidu's leadership" – I'd love to see that – such a grand tribute to the place you've taken already in the more active years of your life.

'English women in the last war did the putting aside of the moment's disagreements and by proving their ability to work – got their demands without further strife when the war was over.

'All political parties in England and throughout the Commonwealth have done the same. Think how the world would acclaim such a gesture! It would be treated as evidence of the spiritual self-abnegation which Gandhi preaches. When the war is won and over, we'd hate not to have had our share in buying freedom for the world. To have sat outside making terms which could not be thrashed out because the enemy was at the Gates of our Joint Family House at the moment – would in the light of retrospect and history fill us with shame.

'You can save us from that shame now before it is too late. And you will do it.

'I'm not telling even Alice that I'm asking you to do this. – I want it to be your surprise and gift to the troubled world.

'You will know best how it should be done. – A broadcast? Addressed to the menkind? A resolution passed at a big meeting of women? I hope for the former, because then we could all hear your voice here – but at any rate it would be Sarojini to the rescue.

'That I am genuine in believing it's *your* job, that you alone could do it successfully, you will realise when you reflect how *gladly* I would have such an act to my credit in my overdrawn account with life. But it's you we want – and we'll all be so proud of you and the success of your appeal.

'I wish letters did not take so long to get to India now. I want to hear your voice directly (this) minute.

'Alice is much better than when in Delhi and is hard at work – First Aid lectures, and doctoring refugees. Mary continues her Mission talks. I am "poor man's lawyer" for those hit by the war, and also have work connected with the Ministry of Information. We are of course Honorary workers.

'…Dick is not quite well yet.' (News is added of his two children). '…I am settled in Chambers in my Inn. I long for you to come and see me here. All my life I've wanted this last "setting" before I am carried to Golders Green' (the crematorium).

'With my love – and Go to it! I beg. Think how happy you would make your old friend SS' (Susie Sorabji) 'as well as all of us

'Yours CS'.

Sarojini did not answer the plea, but mails were unreliable in the war, and
Cornelia also heard that Congress women had sworn to follow Gandhi.[25]

QUEEN MARY'S BOOK FOR INDIA

Cornelia's other contribution to the war effort through Amery was the creation
of *Queen Mary's Book for India*, London 1943, designed to thank the one and a half
million Indians who had fought in the war. Queen Mary, now the Queen Mother,
and Amery wrote introductory pieces and there were contributions from leading British politicians, Churchill and Bevin, leading poets, Eliot and de la Mare,
leading writers, Dorothy Sayers and Helen Waddell, both Somervillians, and
the archaeologist Leonard Woolley. The most discussed contribution was that
of T. S. Eliot, whose poem, 'To the Indians who died in Africa', finished with
a phrase from the *Bhagvadgita*, 'the fruit of action'. The Gita repeatedly tells us
not to be attached to the fruit of action.[26] What were Indians doing dying, like
Englishmen, in Africa, a land that belonged to neither of them? The point was that
by dying bravely the Indian soldier was following his destiny (*dharma*). Whether
or not it would bear *fruit* for the Indian, the Gita tells us not to be worried about
such consequences, and Eliot adds that until after death we cannot know.

THE SEE-SAW TILTS BACK UP

Despite the obstruction to Cornelia's work in India in the wake of Mayo in 1927
to 1931 and her eclipse in India's drama for the rest of the century, the see-
saw of her life had now in England swung upwards again, although there was
to be a final tilt down. Hesitation in England about her utility after the Mayo
episode had already been somewhat assuaged by her lecture tours in America
of 1930–1932, on which the then Secretary of State for India, Hoare, congratulated her,[27] and she herself commented that she was being better treated.
British officials were happy after that to facilitate her fact-finding tours in India
up to 1938. But now her consultations with Amery as Secretary of State and
with the Queen Mother were both on the life or death question of the war
effort and gave her a new status again. The aura of success was noticeable to her
nephew and to her niece, Francina. Her location in the Inns of Court fascinated
one, her occasional teas with the Queen Mother the other, and her wonderful
sarees and ornaments led Francina to call her a golden cloud.

THE BOMBING OF LONDON CONTINUES

The blitz bombing of London continued for nearly a year after Cornelia escaped with her life from her windows being shattered in September 1940. The same month, the white-headed ex-soldier who sold fruit and matches at the gate of the Inn, and was the fourth generation of his family over a period of 150 years to do so, was buried in the rubble of his house, but Cornelia found him back at work as usual in the morning.[28] One night at 2 a.m. a bomb fell in Lincoln's Inn with a terrific noise. Cornelia dressed and opened her outer door to see raging fire and burning sparks and splinters falling like rain. She got to the Inn's air raid shelter unaided through the rain of fire, as it was brighter than day, and rested in a deck chair until 6.15, when the fires were out. Then she was helped back through the hoses, fire engines and drenched grounds. Two further incendiaries had fallen on the Inn meanwhile, one on her roof, along with a land mine and a time bomb not yet defused.[29] She wrote later, to the sound of screaming bombs, about the effect of that night on her friends, the Broadribbs.[30] The offices of *The Times* newspaper where Mr Broadribb slept close by were hit and he left to go to his flat in Lincoln's Inn instead, only to find that that too was ablaze. He was discovered in the garden an hour later in a state of shock, saying only, 'How shall I tell Sylvia?' (his wife, whom he had sent away to the comparative safety of the country). When the demolition workers found a silver tray still intact, he gave it to them. They asked his wife if it was alright to take it, but he said, yes, he had given it. What use was silver when they had no home? He remained in a state of shock, but Mrs Broadribb coped with everything.

The next month, October, Cornelia's laundress disappeared, it was feared from a land mine, and although a laundress was in evidence again next year, a maid was then missing. The nights were often filled with the scream of bombs and the thunder of gunfire. All the passengers on the top deck of a bus in Chancery Lane, which ran past the Inn, were killed instantly by a bomb.[31] The month after that, November, while returning from speaking to women soldiers at Greenwich, where the Naval College was devastated, Cornelia passed through a raid on a poor quarter and saw the cheap furniture, stray garments and children's toys lying in the road.[32] On her birthday, during an all-night bombardment, incendiary bombs were dropped in Chancery Lane outside, the opposite side was on fire and her windows were hit by shrapnel. But the shutters over one window held and the other window was hit only where the glass had already been replaced with a patch, although the floor heaved and in the morning was sloping.[33] People talked very freely in the streets and a foreigner came up to Cornelia to tell her of the loss of his beloved wife in a raid.[34] At the end of the year, with a bomb practically throwing her out of her chair, everything round about was hit. St Brides's Church was gutted, and much was damaged beyond repair: many old churches, the municipal Guildhall, the Syon College theological library. But St Paul's Cathedral was saved by firemen.[35]

In the new year, she had her worst personal experience. Landmines on the neighbouring Inns of Court to North and South shook the earth and made her feel 'wrenched apart'.[36] In April, a neighbour reported that Cornelia tended not to go to the air raid shelter because of her failing sight, but chanced things in her bedroom.[37] In the raids of May, Cornelia's building shook and she thought a wall was going to fall, but it righted itself after quivering. The ancient Temple Church was destroyed that night in a neighbouring Inn. St Clement Danes Church was hit, and two of the Inns of Court, one of them being nearly demolished by this and previous hits. But she read the prayer book during the raid and went to St Dunstan's Church as usual for early morning service. The old padré had been up all night helping to put out fires, when the fire engines failed through lack of water. But she had him conduct a service for her amongst the ruins to his great surprise.[38] St Dunstan's had recently had a time bomb on a night when many shops and trams were set on fire and left burning in the morning.[39] The next week she went on after early service to Westminster Abbey, to give thanks that it was still standing. Light came into the chancel and choir through the open roof. The cloisters, deanery, the school and its houses were in ruins and the Archdeacon's family, who showed her round, had lost almost everything. The House of Commons had also been hit and was closed.[40]

Water, gas, heat and light often remained off after a raid. And bomb craters might mean there were no taxis and one had to walk long distances by side roads.

Two of Cornelia's sisters were affected by the raids. Alice was running a refugee hospital which got bombed out.[41] Mary had been evacuated in November 1939 to Hindhead in the country, where Cornelia's beloved Falkner Blair had finished his days. The intense fire bombing of May 1941 cut the telephone wires, and made it impossible to warn Mary not to try to return to her London flat on May 12th. But Cornelia got through to Hindhead by coach and found her quite ill. Cornelia returned to get Mary's flat ready and enlist her own helper, Alpy, and Alice brought Mary there, until they could find her a nursing home away from the bombing. On June 4th, Mary was critically ill, but the previous night's bomb damage meant that it took three to four hours for Cornelia to get from Lincoln's Inn to see her in Chelsea, a journey which in those days should have taken only a few minutes by taxi.[42]

The news of the bombing had an effect on her self-declared terrorist pro-tégé Nogen in India, who now sent her a message received on Christmas day 1940, acknowledging how much he owed her, more than to anyone else, in her directing his work and preparing him for his period of study in England.[43]

PERSUASION TO FOLLOW THE LEGAL PROFESSION

Cornelia did for me, her nephew, what Lord Hobhouse had done for her back in 1893, fifty years earlier. In 1943, she had me, aged 9, to lunch in Lincoln's Inn at Barristers' mess and asked in front of the judges and barristers what I would be when I grew up. Unfortunately, I gave the wrong answer, because I had already decided to be a teacher. Undaunted, she then had me attend a trial. When it was over, the judge came up and asked me if I had believed the man. 'No', I said. 'What a relief', he replied, 'neither did I'. This was Judge Cyril Atkinson, who in 1940 tried the assassin who had killed O'Dwyer, Lieutenant Governor of the Punjab, at the time of the Amritsar massacre.[44] He gave Cornelia a contribution to *Queen Mary's Book for India*. Later, she had him invite my sister Francina and me to tea in the grand judge's lodgings in St Giles in Oxford where he used to come on circuit, and there he told us the most wonderful murder stories. If anything could have persuaded a boy to become a lawyer, those stories would have done. But although I saw the attraction, I stuck to my plan, so in this respect must have disappointed her.

HEALTH AND THE FINAL TILT DOWN

Cornelia bravely underwent two eye operations in these years, by which Sir Richard Cruise, who had earlier examined Susie, partially restored her sight.[45] She also had her leg repaired with what was called a 'silver pin' after being run over in the street. In both cases, Queen Mary asked after her.[46] She was fit enough apart from the operations, and late in 1944 was corresponding with the current Vicereine, Lady Wavell, about her ideas on agricultural training in India and women inspectors of health for the Court of Wards.[47] But there was to be a final tilt down. Her leg operation was done at the time of her correspondence with Lady Wavell. Whether or not the anaesthetic had affected her, it became apparent very soon afterwards in 1945 that her mind was rambling.[48] She had twice written in 1933 and 1934, that the one thing she prayed to avoid was outlasting her powers.[49] But many years later, this was one last misfortune that caught up with her and she was in nursing homes for nine years. I visited her there and introduced myself by the name she used for me, 'Rustom'. But she did not recognise the 16-year-old schoolboy as the Rustom on whom she had pinned her hopes and imaginings. Ignoring the schoolboy's self-introduction, she told me that Rustom was leader of the House of Lords and had made a wonderful speech that day in the House.

She died in 1954 at the age of 87, the last in the family of seven sisters and one brother. Many of her papers passed through our house on their way to what is now the British Library collection and some of them stayed in the house. It was then that I first read how beastly the external examiner had been to her in the interview for the Oxford Bachelor of Civil Law sixty two years earlier. By the time I read that in 1954, she had opened every door she could in the context of the Raj. New doors were being opened by the new India.

RETROSPECT

Was Cornelia's work a success or a failure? One has to see it as a whole with its giddy lurches up and down, and one has to decide what was its central enterprise. I see the central task as her work for the purdahnashins and this gives her life a unity. There was a ten year campaign to get the British to give her the job in 1904. Then there were 18 years in which she carried it out with a huge number of successes until 1922. It was only the acknowledgement of success that was denied from 1913 onwards by opponents whom she had crossed, and who had reached top positions where they could to some extent withhold recognition. But the truth broke through in the 1918 report and the second award of the Kaiser-i-Hind medal in 1922, which was due to the Secretary of State for India, Lord Montagu. The annual reports from 1904–1913 and the accidental revelations of 1918 display a level of achievement beyond the wildest dreams of the ordinary person, lasting the length of a whole career from 1904–1922. Of the purdahnashins she had a unique understanding and she did them unique good.

With her social service work,[1] there is a temptation to dwell on her frustrations, because they were such a harrowing part of her personal story. But in fact from the beginning the British appointed her to social service organisations and she created others of her own. Her social service from 1905 until her retirement in 1922, especially under the Vicereines Lady Minto and Lady Chelmsford, had a tremendous impact and the recommendations of her booklet, *The Purdahnashin*, became for a while official policy.

Her return to India after retirement to practice law met with far higher opposition to a woman than she had encountered before. There were two major political reverses: the entanglement with Mayo and the intimidation of Peri Banu, the purdahnashin who spear-headed her new social service experiment. In this period of seven years from 1924–1931, the successes that Cornelia did gain chiefly involved her purdahnashins and other women: the protection of the Narhan estate against Sapru, the legal opinions on women's welfare, the unparalleled experiment of wealthy purdahnashins helping poor villagers and mill workers, which also began to transform the social sense of purdahnashins themselves. The Mayo debacle turned out not to be unrelievedly bad, because it inspired Cornelia to this final experiment in social progress, which was the very last thing Mayo wanted to see. After the confrontation with Sapru, she might also have fulfilled her early wish of a successful practice as a woman barrister, if she had gone back to Allahabad, but by that time she was too committed to social welfare in Calcutta.

Cornelia also gained in this period a rare insight into the imperfection of British supervision in the Princely States of India. She found British relations with the Princes sometimes a little too cosy.

As regards her failures, her biggest disappointment was that she was finally denied the successor that had originally been envisaged, so she left no institution behind her. But by that time, the political scene had changed so much that it is unclear whether a successor could have operated successfully. Her work for women was conducted against the unusual difficulty of obstruction from two opposite sides. First there was opposition from certain British officials and then opposition from the Indian Nationalist Movement, partly because of her connexion with Mayo, and finally and decisively because of political intimidation directed not at her, but at her chief collaborator, Peri Banu.

If instead one were to see as the centrepieces of her career the opposition of some British officials from 1913, when she was 47, her struggles for the lost cause of opposing Gandhi from 1919, the frustration of her work as a barrister from 1924, her entanglement with Mayo from 1927 and the huge injustices she suffered as a result, then her career could look like a failure. And it is true that the political changes in India did eclipse her name there for nearly 60 years after Independence. But in Britain the situation was more nuanced. There was some embarrassment about using her services, certainly in any open way, in the 1920s. But her lecture tours in America in 1930 and 1932 were much appreciated, and her fact-finding tours in India from 1932–1938 were facilitated by the British. Her enormous knowledge of India was valued in the desperate war years of 1939–1945, when she was in consultation on Indian matters with the Secretary of State for India, Lord Amery. As late as September 1944, she was corresponding through him with the Viceroy's wife in India, Lady Wavell, about an agricultural training proposal.

Certainly, Cornelia's love of the British Empire was a lost cause, but it was at most indirectly the source of her failures. In understanding it, one must remember that Dick and Alice held a different view from hers, Dick supporting Sapru, who wanted a constitutionally negotiated independence. Why was Cornelia so much more supportive of British rule as it was? I think that it was her exceptional treatment as a student and then adult in England, which is why I dwell on that at the opening.[2] All three siblings, indeed the whole family, were very well treated. But only Cornelia was treated as the darling of the late Victorians who had been leaders of Empire. She could not bear to think that their whole enterprise must go. She switched within a few months in her student days from disliking the future Conservative Prime Minister, A. J. Balfour, to admiring him and calling herself a Conservative. This departure from the position of most of her English friends was perhaps chiefly because of Balfour's rejection of Gladstone's Home Rule policy for Ireland, which she too rejected.[3]

One thing already noticed above,[4] but comparatively unfamiliar nowadays, was her association so much of the time in England with the aristocracy, in contrast to Dick's custom of inviting anybody and everybody, whatever their rank, to his table. But it was the aristocracy who welcomed her in England and it was in those days the aristocracy who held the power, as illustrated by the ten year campaign to get her job. Without the aristocracy, the ten year campaign would not have had the slightest chance.

Cornelia's uncompromising personality played a role in her successes and her failures. She immediately saw ways around the quarrels of her purdahnashins, but not so easily around her own quarrels, and compromise might have occasionally gained more, not in all cases, but in the case of the quarrel with her old friend Barbara Stephen and the wives of other officials.[5] Compromise might also have secured more in the competition with Alice and Dick over funds for social service.[6] There the originality of her new social experiment and her wish to be the pioneer got in the way. What she did not have was her sister Alice's easy charm, which won so much so easily. It was, however, the same uncompromising personality that got her the job as legal adviser against such odds and enabled her to continue. Whatever the opposition, she never gave up. She was helped in standing up to British opponents by her belief that those opponents were themselves falling short of the standards she attributed to the Britons she admired from her early days.

Her ability to endure also depended on her religious belief and she repeatedly tried to imagine how God would view her conduct or her tribulations and whether she had distanced herself from God, or was close. Her spirits could be restored by attending services in the cathedral in Allahabad or Calcutta. She would also not have survived without the support of her confidants, and she gained relief just from their listening by letter to her troubles. She had a capacity for very intense friendships. In her letters, she is able to express to her friends her feelings about those friendships. I am struck also by the honesty with which she acknowledged her own feelings to her diary, even when she thought them discreditable. In both ways she showed herself a highly emotional person. Sometimes her emotions could mislead her, as they did with Mayo and perhaps in her hopes about Gourlay.

The letters to family or confidants, which she wrote day by day, and of which an almost continuous succession survives, formed only a small part of her voluminous writing. For 44 years, she wrote a daily personal diary, adding a work diary for 14 of those years. When one adds the colossal volume of her articles and books, and her official Civil Service and legal reports, it is hard to imagine how this amount of writing was fitted in to her already crowded life.

Another salient feature of Cornelia's personality was her quickness of wit, which was put to use a thousand times over. It first fascinated the salons of Oxford and London. It was then used, for example, in her rescues of women from Tihur fort and from Ramgarh, or again, in her confrontation with Sapru, and, if she has faithfully recorded it, in her interview with Gandhi.

I have centred Cornelia's life on the work she did for purdahnashins. That was where she made good, but what did the good consist in? In Chapter 10, we found the son of one of Cornelia's wards saying that the Court of Wards had saved his family, when his defenceless grandmother was widowed at the age of 13, by securing the succession of the rightful proprietors against rival claims. What I added was that it took Cornelia's expertise in many cases to get to the bottom of the question of who was the rightful proprietor.

What were the numbers involved? Cornelia had 600 women and children at any time among her wards. Of course, new generations were being born all the time, so the number was much larger, but limited even so. Is 600 a large or a small number? I was impressed early in my own career by a student who brought to an end a discussion on improving the world, by saying that he found it hard enough to help six people. Anyone who has really helped 600 women and children per year has done something very important, as I now think. To those generations of purdahnashins that she helped we must add the huge range of non-purdahed poor that she supported in her social work.

Some things, I believe, were more lasting than that and continue to be relevant to multi-cultural societies. One was Cornelia's method of changing custom through custom. There are always cases in which harmful customs cannot be changed by simply trying to impose change, and I have noticed cases in which Cornelia's method of changing custom through custom would have been far more effective. When a brief imposition of compulsory sterilisation set back the cause of voluntary contraception in India, what was needed to regain people's confidence in contraception was Cornelia's kind of understanding of, and sympathy for, religious belief and her ability to spot how to change custom through custom. Another part of her method was the approach of love for other cultures, which is something she learnt from her mother, and applied to the restricted case of her purdahnashins. Cultural change is not likely to be produced by criticism from the outside.

There is a lesson here for the attempts of thinkers to find social norms that everyone in the world ought to be able to agree to.[i] Cornelia's child brides might regard it as sinful for women to be educated, and right and proper that they should practise austerities for the rest of their lives if their husbands died. They would not agree to different norms, however much they were accepted by others. Different norms cannot be imposed by force or by legislation. Cornelia's method of changing custom through custom has the merit of circumventing such problems.

A further good was displayed by Cornelia's ten year campaign to get her job, a model of planning, but also of patience and determination. The same determination was shown in her standing up, whether rightly or wrongly, to those who opposed her or seemed to be harming her wards, equally to British and to Indians, since she had to fight unendingly on every front.

From the beginning and throughout all her struggles, Cornelia took enormous care over her appearance. In some of the youthful photographs taken with Alice, Cornelia is impeccably dressed, while Alice's saree looks thrown together. Cornelia cared what her family wore. She was concerned not only that her sisters wear sarees, but what colours, materials and borders they chose, and she wanted her brother to appear to best advantage by wearing Persian costume.[7] Dick wore a flower in his buttonhole, Cornelia, for occasions, flowers to her throat. When young she was beautiful, when older formidable, as the photograph of her in legal wig shows,[8] but still elegant. In the bewigged photograph, she is at least 55, but the face is still handsome. Even into the 1940s, when she was well into her seventies, she continued to wear her dazzling draperies and ornaments. That and her celebrity status in England caused her niece, Francina Sorabji (Dick's daughter), to call her 'my golden cloud'.

---

i The author of the most influential Western approach of recent times, John Rawls, increasingly accepted that his method for finding such norms could not appeal beyond the circle of those who started with enough values in common already.

William Dalrymple has written a number of books showing the change in British–Indian relations from British admiration and intermarriage in the eighteenth century to almost total separateness in the nineteenth to twentieth.[9] Cornelia partly broke through this separateness, as the only Indian woman invited to English dinner parties in her early years in Calcutta. But when it came to marriage, the barriers were as strong as ever. She naively thought that she could attract older men with no sexual danger. When that proved an excruciating mistake in Allahabad, at least she experienced with Falkner Blair fully reciprocated love once in her life, and in a way that may have seemed to her the nobler for not being fully consummated. Marriage with Falkner Blair was never even considered a possibility. Cornelia allowed herself thought of marriage with someone nearer her own age, Gourlay. But it is hard to imagine what the outcome of marriage would have been. It could very well have ruined Gourlay's career. When Dick married an English woman back in England a quarter of a century later, attitudes had changed in a way that could not have been predicted. The anxiety of Lady Reading about what would happen to the children of the marriage[10] was very reasonable for the periods which Dalrymple has described and for Cornelia's own period. Fortunately, however, the period and place in which Dick's children grew up were different. It was then easy for a child brought up in England on the romance of Indian stories to rejoice in both affiliations instead of being battered, like Cornelia, between the two.

As things turned out, Cornelia's unmarried and solitary life enabled her to do incalculably more for her purdahnashins. But the loneliness of her life and work took a heavy toll. It caused her sadness, and sometimes a sense of worthlessness in comparison with Alice, and anxiety when she saw Alice as competing for funding. The loneliness may have given her attention to work plans an obsessive quality and led her to neglect not only Barbara Stephen, but also sometimes, when in London, her family, their schedules and their celebrations.[11] She felt guilty about this, although on the whole the family did no more than make private jokes about Cornelia's grandeur.[12] Loneliness, I have already suggested,[13] may have made her over-attached to Katherine Mayo, when she imagined that at last she would have a supporter who shared her ideals of service to women.

Cornelia made different statements to different people under different pressures as to whether she felt English or Indian, both, or neither.[14] Even her clothes, we saw, often combined Indian saree with stylish English blouse. To Mrs Darling she wrote in 1897, 'Jowett said my duty in life was, as far as possible, to interpret the East to the West. But 'tis an almost impossible task. The

East is so conglomerate and the west as a nation so insular, and I seem to stand midway between the two, my birth allotting me to one hemisphere, my education, instincts and friendships allotting me to the other.'[15] She liked the company of the British at a time when there was little mixing. But she was proud of being Indian[16] and she deliberately entitled her second book in 1908, *Between the Twilights: Being Studies of Indian Women by One of Themselves.* She was also intent on serving Indians[17] at a time when the British could provide the facilities for such service and could benefit from it. She did serve Indians, but sometimes she was excluded from both sides.

Whatever her sorrows and shortcomings, there is something inspiring about Cornelia's life. It shows what can be done by a woman not born into the dominant group in society. If she had no fixed feeling about whether she was English or Indian, this was partly because, while inspired by both affiliations, she also transcended them. She was motivated not simply by being British or Indian, or of one religion rather than another, but by a moral ideal of social service, gained from Christianity, in a multi-cultural society, from parents who themselves came from different cultures. She had to negotiate her way among many different groups, the British aristocracy, purdahnashins, the world of lawyers, Gandhi's Independence Movement and her family. The negotiations called for many different qualities. If she had not been clever and fascinating, she would not have gained her initial support, but she had to go far beyond that. All her life, she had to exercise exceptional determination. Her work with purdahnashins required the right mixture of tact and firmness. She stood up fearlessly to enemies, both among British officers and in the Gandhian phase of the Independence Movement. The larger drama of that movement may have submerged her recognition in India for a time. But in England she received recognition, apart from some temporary setbacks during the 1920s. Most important of all was the main task she set herself, her astonishing legal and social work with and for purdahnashins. This was recognised by the purdahnashins themselves, by most British administrators, and at the highest levels in England and she remained the biggest single contributor to the purdahnashins' legal and social well-being.

APPENDIX 1

ALICE AND CORNELIA'S OTHER SISTERS

I did not know my Indian grandparents but, of the seven sisters from that marriage, I remember from the time of the Second World War Pheroze, Mary, Cornelia and Alice. Although Alice was the youngest sister, she had the most impact on Cornelia and I shall tell her story more fully.

Back in their time, the invisible circle of being Indians, yet English-educated Christians, made it very difficult for the sisters, and for their brother Dick to find spouses, and this was even more difficult for women who wanted careers. Yet they were naturally as susceptible as anyone else, and the first two daughters, Zuleika (or Jane, Janie) and Pheroze (or Phiz), the two denied university admission, may not have been prepared for this problem. Some of Cornelia's later experiences were due to her plan for avoiding the pitfalls of Zuleika and Pheroze by befriending only older men.[1]

ZULEIKA SORABJI: TWO 'SCANDALS'

Zuleika was the first child after the marriage of 1853. Cornelia describes her as having big eyes, thick black eyebrows, a kindly face, a gentle nature, as spoiling the younger children and being good at pacifying their parents.[2] Zuleika came to England in 1885, a year before Dick, and went to Tunbridge Wells where her adoptive grandmother, Lady Ford, was living and stayed at 1 St James Villas, Stone Street.[3] Pheroze and Mary were to follow later in the 1880s.[4]

In 1889, Zuleika was back teaching in her mother's school and in 1890 she had a close relationship with a man of whom the family did not approve. Zuleika was also called Jane, and she wrote a heart-rending letter under that name from the Poona home on January 27th 1891.[5] It tells us much about Cornelia's subsequent attitudes to men and to some of her sisters.

'My Dear Mrs Barrett,

...I will send for the book you kindly suggest and will read it word for word and think and pray (if I *can* pray). The step, if taken at all, shall not be done hastily, but I *will not* be a hypocrite. Perhaps I ought to tell you that circumstances around me, and my own embittered life, have helped in a great measure to bring me to this sad crisis and perhaps I *ought* to rise above it all and say, "It is the Lord. Let Him do what seemeth to him best", but I *cannot*. Energy, strength, all, all is gone and only bitterness remains, the bitterness of death. One cannot explain in writing for it would all look so uncharitable to tell you facts which exist and yet out of filial affection and duty must needs be as if they were not. I tell you because I was drawn *to* you, inasmuch as *you* did not preach to me, and you were not a canting Christian. Oh, if people *only* knew the harm they do by quoting righteous phrases and saying off Psalms and hymns ad lib, they would ever after hold their peace, but the world must go on and *such* people must exist ... What is the end of it all! Am I creating a hard deathbed for myself, I wonder? I would that I could see into the future for a brief moment.... Mary prays as usual for 6 hours a day, and sighs and groans over *my* sins – !!

With love,

Ever yours gratefully and affectionately,

Jane Sorabji'

This agonised letter will give some idea of the criticisms that Cornelia hoped she herself would never face and what she might anticipate from some of her family such as her sister Mary, when she in fact incurred such criticisms later. The 'step' Zuleika contemplates is not explained, but she took an early opportunity of leaving the family home and school. Although she wrote from the Poona home in January 1891, she had already in 1890 secured a teaching job away from home,[6] and in 1892 took a job in a Bombay hospital.[7] The family could still easily visit her there, but the big change came in 1893, when she was chosen to go to Chicago for the first of the continuing meetings of the World Parliament of Religions, which set out to explore 'wells of truth' outside Christianity. It was at that meeting that Swami Vivekananda's account of *Vedanta* impressed so many Christians. Zuleika seems never to have returned to India after that. It may have been in Chicago that she met the American Herbert (or H C), whose unrecorded second name was French. In 1895, Herbert and she were together back in England and Zuleika was speaking for Dadabhai Naoroji, the Parsee who had become the first Indian Member of Parliament in England as a Liberal in 1892.[8] But on August 6th 1895 another blow fell.[9]

Ramabai called and told Cornelia's mother a story about Zuleika which had come from a Mrs Andrewes. The family was very unhappy and wrote to 'C J C' in Bombay, only to hear back on August 19th that the story was indeed true. Cornelia in Poona writes on August 22nd, 'Tis hopeless. Nothing but death can undo it.' What can it have been? By September 22nd, Dick and Pheroze, who were in England and meeting Zuleika and Herbert, knew the news, but Zuleika denied it. On December 2nd, Herbert wrote to the Poona family 'rather extraordinarily'. Dick had liked Herbert on meeting the two of them earlier in 1895 and had written kindly about them. Pheroze commented that Zuleika had become stout and unwieldy. On March 2nd 1896, Cornelia commented that Zuleika was very happy about 'things coming right', and she prayed, 'God keep her straight now.' But on September 24th 1896 she wrote, 'the whole story is out' and the family was very troubled about the effect of the story on the orphan boys whom they were educating at home. What was happening?

No further clue emerges until 1900, when on April 21st there was 'news by wire of something wrong about Zuleika'. By May 3rd, Lord Hobhouse had heard about it in England, and on September 9th, Cornelia found 'a horrid article about Zuleika in *The Queen*'. The only thing I find in *The Queen* for this period is a leader of July 21st 1900, which purports to be giving the case of an English widow, but cites it as typical of cases which have occurred in recent years, and may be concealing identities. The story had to do with legally invalid marriages. The woman was described as living in Paris and being offered marriage in that very year, 1900, with the proviso that the wedding should be held in England. Dick had earlier reported that Herbert and Zuleika were thinking of going to France and that Herbert hoped she would learn French.[10] On return to France, the report continued, after the English wedding, it turned out that the man had known all along that the marriage would not be recognised in France, because French law required the consent of parents or grandparents. He said he had thought the lady knew this herself. The man declared himself an American citizen, and the question now to be determined was whether the French courts would recognise the marriage as valid in the case of an American citizen.

The most likely explanation is that in 1895 Zuleika had by Herbert a baby who died (is this the death that could undo it?). Whether she then believed herself validly married or not, she must have believed herself to be validly married by 1896 when things seemed to have come right. The discovery that her wedding was not recognised in France may have occurred in 1895, or, as envisaged in *The Queen*'s story, in 1900.

Zuleika continued to adore Herbert,[11] and they lived together for a considerable time. She loved music and put on concerts.[12] But in 1918 he seems to have left her, sending letters of complaint all the way to 1922. Cornelia was convinced that the complaint, whatever it was, was not the fault of poor Zuleika.[13]

In 1913, Zuleika performed the kindness described in Chapter 16 of persuading the young lady in England, Joan Butler, to consider seriously marriage with Dick, and she put Dick up during his visit to England.

Zuleika nearly died later in 1913 from a lung haemorrhage and was never well again. She lived in Sevenoaks, needed an attendant and was slightly odd. When Dick finally did marry at the age of 52 in 1924, his bride, my mother, went to see Zuleika at a home in Crystal Palace and all she said was, 'Will she stick to you?'. My mother knew there had been an earlier proposal, but was somewhat mystified. It could have been a reference to Joan Butler's change of mind, even though that came as a relief to Dick.

Zuleika died in January 1938 at a time when, by an irony, the only family member available at the deathbed she had feared was her sister Mary, who had prayed 47 years earlier for her sins.

PHEROZE: WIDOWED, SINGING CAREER
IN ENGLAND, 'SCANDAL' AVERTED, REMARRIES

Pheroze, the other sister whom Cornelia saw as running into difficulties with men, was born in 1858. Like Zuleika, she had a kindly face.[14] In 1882, at the time of Sir William Hunter's commission on Indian Education, she was head of a college in Ahmedabad, and her sister, Mary, had taught there with her.[15] On January 8th 1884, she married in Poona Morgan Thomas, who was 36.[16] Cornelia was annoyed at *The Queen* calling him a Eurasian (half-breed) and says he was related to the Tredegars of Wales.[17] He was born in Wales at Builth Wells.[18] Pheroze and Morgan were in India when their daughter Elsie was born on the October 3rd 1884. A birth less than 9 months after the wedding could suggest something that the family would have considered shocking, conception before marriage, and if so, this will have contributed to Cornelia's determination not to follow her two oldest sisters. Later Pheroze and Morgan stayed in England at Rossie Priory, the Scottish home of the missionary family Kinnaird, overlooking the River Tay, and Pheroze knew the Christian Mothers of Dundee.[19] During this period, she and her sister Mary also stayed with their adoptive grandmother, Lady Ford, near Tunbridge Wells where their music-making was remembered, and at the convent in Wantage where Pandita Ramabai stayed at about the same time. Their mother came over in 1886 and they would all have been together.

In 1889 back in Poona, Morgan was ill, and, leaving Elsie in the Poona family home, they sailed for England in the ship behind Cornelia's. But Morgan died on the way and was buried at sea, leaving Pheroze a widow.[20]

Pheroze returned to Poona and in 1890 accepted a post providing education for the palace ladies of the Gaekwar of Baroda, where Cornelia was later to serve briefly.[21] But by mid-November 1890, Pheroze had returned to London, aged 32, with Elsie, aged 6, in the hope of making her living by singing, and had called on Dick and Cornelia in Oxford. Much of this period has been described as part of Cornelia's life in Oxford and London.[22]

Elsie was very charming, but naturally also very clinging with Pheroze. There is a photograph of the musical Elsie from about this time with her violin. Pheroze's singing lessons were to take longer than expected, over two years, but eventually successful concerts were held, and she learnt from Cornelia how to wear beautiful sarees to effect. Cornelia regretted the choice of profession and wished she would teach singing instead, which naturally annoyed Pheroze. But one concert was in the Albert Hall and another was much appreciated by the Duchess of Teck and her daughter, the future Queen Mary. Even so, Pheroze had also to take up embroidery to make ends meet.[23] And later on she practised massage, which the family continued to recall with distaste.

In 1893, Pheroze assumed that a handsome and prosperous medical doctor, Dr Bowie, intended to marry her. He visited her room in the evenings, seen by the other members of the household, both when he passed through their rooms and when they knocked on Pheroze's door. Cornelia was afraid that the same would happen as with Zuleika in 1890, and got Pheroze to ask him point blank whether he intended to marry her, which he did not. After that Pheroze dropped him and accepted the company of admirers of greater propriety.[24]

On February 4th 1902, Pheroze married Beckham Arthur, a New Zealander and soldier.[25] He was then, however, working for the Windsor Goldmining Company in Krugersdorp, Transvaal. She went to join him in South Africa on June 7th 1902.[26] She left Elsie to stay in London with Cornelia, who found Elsie's moral welfare almost as much of a problem as her mother's. First, Cornelia wrestled with Elsie's being stage-struck. Cornelia persuaded her to cry off a theatre engagement, in return for introductions to Alexander, the actor and theatre manager, and to the Lyceum. On January 2nd 1903, Cornelia persuaded Elsie to do as her mother wished and sail to South Africa to join her, and by the end of the year Elsie had got married there. But this was not the last time that Elsie caused the family anxiety. At some later date, she went to Paris as a Bluebell girl. The Bluebell girls kicked up their legs on stage just as much as those at the Folies Bergères, but the difference was that they were chaperoned by a padré of the Church of England. The family were not persuaded that this made a sufficient difference.[27] Cornelia does not mention the episode explicitly, although there is a much later reference to Elsie 'going off with Mr S' in 1912, when she was 28.[28]

Pheroze and her husband did not stay permanently in South Africa.[29] In England in the First World War in 1914, she became a nurse, while her husband served in the forces and won the D. S. O.[30] In 1922, Cornelia admired Pheroze for the way she had withstood the loss of her husband, Arthur, who survived the First World War,[31] but died a little after of wounds received.[32]

In the 1930s, Pheroze was in a house called 'Why Worry?' at Storrington on the Sussex Downs,[33] where Lena was to be buried in 1935. She used to visit Dick's family in Oxford in the 1940s[34] and was then living with her daughter in Brighton. Her saree caught fire and I remember the final telegram coming in February 1941, since it had to be explained to me, 'Dearest Pheroze at rest'.

LENA SORABJI: THE SUPPORTIVE FUTURE HEADMISTRESS

If Cornelia was accurate in saying that her mother thought there was a particular thing that each of the girls could do for India,[35] then by that standard the first two girls were not successful, because they were overtaken by love and marriage. But the subsequent six children became professionals, with varying consequences for love and marriage, Dick and Alice being the only two remaining ones who married, while Dick and Pheroze were the only ones to have children.

Lena was the third daughter, born in 1863. Because she was thin, she was known as Caves, Robin Starveling or Thinnie. She was very attached to her father, keeping all his letters and some of his clothes after his death in 1894. By 1896, she was in charge of the vernacular teaching in her mother's school, apart from a brief trip she made that year to England, and she paid for a Muslim woman to bring the Muslim girls to school. Later, she played a bigger role, as her mother did less, and took charge of the main English language school from 1902 or earlier, until she retired to England to recuperate in 1904–1905. After a brief return to India, she decided in 1906 that she could not continue after her mother's retirement and she left again for England.[36]

Then a new opportunity arose. Cornelia's friend and mentor Mr LeMesurier, then officiating Secretary and Secretary to the Government of East Bengal, asked Cornelia to interest Lena in being Principal of Eden College in Dacca, East Bengal, now in Bangladesh. The appointment was confirmed in 1909, and Lena arrived in January 1910.[37] This was the start of a co-operation between Cornelia and Lena, in which Lena accepted as girl boarders some of Cornelia's Muslim wards along with non-purdahed Hindus, and tried to prolong their education and postpone marriage. In one case the girl's betrothal was celebrated there on the understanding that the wedding would be postponed. In another case they lost, because a local Nawab removed a Muslim girl when he found his control over her was diminished.[38]

Lena's presence in her region was also very cheering for Cornelia. Dick and Lena lived close enough to come and stay with Cornelia each year after Christmas. Cornelia was always enthusiastic about her own visits to Lena. In Dacca, Lena was always 'kind' and a 'wonderful hostess'. Her house and garden were 'lovely'; she had made the school 'a model' and was 'admired' and 'popular'. Eight of the teachers had eventually been appointed by Lena, and they included resident orthodox Hindus, progressive Brahmos and English teachers. She organised teacher training, she ensured the pupils had very good English, and she taught them to sight read music. She was also good with her hands and taught local industries, and lace-making.[39]

In 1917, she went shortly before Cornelia to visit Alice in Bannu on the Afghan frontier, and her very full report to Mary, reflected in one of Mary's letters, provides some of the information below about Alice's work.[40]

On July 1st 1919, she retired from the Eden High School, although the Government had earlier asked her to stay on, and the selection committee would have liked her to do so. She reached England on August 26th 1919.[41]

Lena was a very supportive person. She was particularly helpful in 1908 with Mary, and later in 1916 with Dick, when they suffered depressions, and she came back from retirement in England in 1923–1924, to take over Susie's school in Poona, so that Susie could make a fund-raising trip to America.[42]

Although I do not remember her, her last act before her fatal stroke was to tuck Cornelia's one-year nephew into bed in the family's Sussex home. She was by chance taken to the place where she had said she wanted to die, the Convent of the Holy Rood at Findon in Sussex. She had been at its opening ceremony. The Reverend Mother was a cousin of Theodore Pennell and knew Pheroze and Mary. Dick visited her every day, until she died in January 1936 at the age of 73, and was buried where Pheroze lived in Storrington.[43]

MARY SORABJI: THE ANXIOUS SISTER

Mary, the fourth daughter, was a teacher. She had been Cornelia's official mentor as a child, which did not always make for good relations. But she taught Cornelia for matriculation and supported her in print when Cornelia provoked controversy by claiming that social legislation was useless in India without education.[44] She was also known as Misery, and she was the quiet one, who worried whether the prize giving would go all right, and who later suffered for a while from depression. She was teaching in Ahmedabad, first under the headship of Pheroze in 1882,[45] and then when Pheroze had left in 1884, as First Assistant to the Head of what may have been the same institution, a teacher training college for women. But her services were loaned that year to the newly opening High School for Indian Girls in Poona and she was summoned to the opening.[46] We have seen her in England with Pheroze in 1886 at her adoptive grandmother's and at the Wantage convent.

On returning to India, Mary helped with her mother's school for a long time. But she repeatedly looked for a more senior teaching post and eventually returned to Poona's High School for Indian Girls. When she first taught there in 1884, the school had been surrounded by controversy for venturing to educate women, though it had had the support of the reformer Ranade and his wife. Miss Anne Hurford had been head, but when there appeared to be a vacancy in 1890, Mary applied for the headship. In fact Miss Hurford went away only temporarily, but in 1891 Mary got a post at the school and was acting head in Miss Hurford's absence.[47] Mary lived near her school, but within reach of the family home. She was absent teaching in Baroda in 1897–8, and in 1898 had her dire experience of plague with the child of her butler,[48] as described in Chapter 1. But she was back before long at her Poona school. In 1904 she is described as coming across town for dinner at her mother's home every evening.[49] Her years at the Poona High School were perhaps her most successful, and in 1932, she was still being referred to there as 'mother' and her pupils had become Principal and teachers there.[50] She describes how at first only twelve female pupils could be found whose relatives would let them attend, but in the end the school had grown to 1500 pupils, and the first girl they sent up for university matriculation came top of all 400 candidates in the Bombay Presidency.[51]

The year 1906 was a turning point in the family. Some decided to retire from their current work, just as 1922 would later mark such a retirement for Cornelia, Dick and Alice. By 1906, their mother was no longer running her schools. Mary, like Lena, decided to stop and go to England after 15 years mostly at the Poona High School and a teaching career of at least 24 years. She finally sailed from India on December 4th 1906, leaving only Susie in Poona. But whereas Lena would return to India to a new teaching career, Mary, always seen as a little forlorn, collapsed in the new situation, and by August 1907 was in an English nursing home with depression. Apart from a visit to Poona and to see her mother in her last two years in Nasik from November 1908 to May 1910,[52] she remained in England, and from 1911 to at least 1914, when she was nearing 50, needed a personal attendant.[53]

In time, however, she converted her teaching skills and became a sought-after
public speaker. After hearing Mary in England a few years later in 1918, Cornelia
declared, 'Mary is *wonderful*'[54] and she recommended her the next year to her friend
Elena to speak about India to Elena's India study group.[55] Much later, when Cornelia
shared Mary's London flat at 1 Ashburnham Mansions from 1936–1939, Mary, who
was neat and particular, found Cornelia got on her nerves, while Cornelia was painfully reminded of Mary's childhood tutelage. But Mary dealt with the friction by going
off on her lecture tours,[56] some of them for the Conservative Party.[57]

Her evacuation to Hindhead in the war from 1939–1941, and her rescue by Cornelia and Alice during the bombing of London in 1941, was described in Chapter 23.
By August 1941, Cornelia and Alice got her a place at a nursing home at Pitchcombe
in the Cotswolds.[58] But she did not last much longer than Pheroze, who had died in
February that year.

SUSIE SORABJI, THE FUND-RAISER WHO RE-ESTABLISHED HER MOTHER'S SCHOOLS FOR A CENTURY

The youngest three daughters were the most successful and Susie's success in
re-founding her mother's schools had the most lasting consequences of all. She was
the sixth daughter, born on May 15th 1868, but in the interim Cornelia had been
born, the fifth daughter, on November 15th 1866. Susie was a teacher and the one
who ensured that her mother's school projects were re-started on new sites, when
they would otherwise have been discontinued. It was when Cornelia had to ensure
the continuation of Susie's projects, many years later in 1931, that she finally discontinued her own second career.[59] It was also about this time that Cornelia emulated
Susie in her strenuous lecture tours round the USA and Canada.[60] Surprisingly, in the
memoir that Cornelia wrote about her,[61] she said little about Susie's most stupendous
feat, the fund-raising in America that re-established the main school for a century
and more.

The story has already been told of the seven year old Susie and two other little girls
out-staring the tigress in the Mahableshwar woods.[62] It can be taken as a foretaste of the
triumph against odds in the rest of her life.

At the age of 17 in 1886, Susie was struck by a painful illness which nearly removed
her sight, and she suffered from this for the rest of her life. But she worked in her
mother's schools. She, like her older sisters, was not immune to masculine attention, and in 1897, according to Cornelia, 'Susie wrote about E. W. P. I fear she is a bit
touched about him. Men should not be such *very* great friends with women, unless they
mean developments of sorts'.[63] But Susie was soon concentrating again on her teaching
and beginning to take over from her mother the vernacular teaching in the Hindu and
Muslim schools.

American trip for the vernacular schools, Rockefeller mansion and the White House, 1902

As early as 1902, Susie had foreseen the danger to the Poona schools that would arise from her mother's eventual retirement, and she set out on her astonishing venture. Despite her bad health, a Reverend Mr Yatman had encouraged her in 1899 to visit America and had offered to arrange pulpits for her to talk from. Her mother insisted that she was too ill, but she set out in 1902, hoping to raise funds to revive her mother's vernacular schools which used Marathi and Urdu language, catering for poor Hindu and Muslim children. She stopped off in London where Alice was studying medicine and Cornelia was campaigning for the creation of her own post. She had never seen such crowds before, but her sisters warned her that New York would be worse and that she was too ill, as her mother had said. She was indeed ill all the way on the boat from London to New York, and when she got there, there was no sign of Mr Yatman and no one to meet her. He had not even alerted Dr Louis Klotch, editor of the *Christian Herald*, whom he had described as the man to finance and organise her tour.

She found on deck the brother of a Poona friend, who was able to give her the address of a lodging house and put her in a taxi. She was startled when the door was opened by a black servant, and she was given the worst room, too dark for her to write, except in a passage outside.

The next day she made her way to a Wall Street bank to which she had advanced money. They were surprised to see a woman there, and she turned out to have no letter of credit to identify herself, but they took pity on her and advanced her some of her money. Mr Yatman had still not sent a letter of introduction to Klotch. When at last she got it, she went round to the offices of the *Christian Herald*, only to be told by the clerk that Mr Klotch had gone to England. She sat down and wept, but the clerk fetched an editor and soon she was with the woman's editor, Miss Freer, who took charge, first driving with her to her landlady's to insist on a better room, as she was paying the full price charged to others.

Through Miss Freer, the *Christian Herald* offered to pay her speaking expenses, if she agreed to speak not only for her vernacular schools, but also for their own project for 25,000 orphans, which included the orphanage run in Poona by the family friend, Pandita Ramabai. At the very first talk arranged, however, the audience wanted to give all the money to her own vernacular school project, and she felt obliged to decline expenses from the *Christian Herald*.

At her first conference she spoke seven times, and she noticed a man in the audience every time, who turned out to be a Mr Hatton from a group called 'New York 400'. He formed a committee with a woman Susie called her guardian angel, Miss Marsh, to handle the invitations that flowed from her first engagements and to collect funds. She was invited by over 100 churches, by 500 smartly dressed ladies for lunch at the Waldorf Astoria Hotel and by the colleges or universities of Bryn Mawr, Columbia, Radcliffe and Cornell. Miss Marsh had a letter waiting for her at every stop, and heard her report after every journey.

She found misconceptions about India. One Swami had persuaded a Bishop that there were no child widows in India. One Vicar had allowed a lecture in favour of Shiva worship, which secured a following.

Astonishingly, Susie found herself talking to the Rockefellers and to the President of the United States. She was invited by the Rockefellers to a gorgeous assembly in the beautiful rooms of their New York house. Mr Rockefeller himself came up and modestly asked to be introduced to her. Next, she was invited to the White House by Mrs Roosevelt. Ethel Roosevelt, daughter of the American President Teddy, had given up candy for a month at her school in order to make her gift to Susie's schools and that is why Susie was invited. The President himself came out to meet the Indian of whom their daughter had talked.

As the cold weather approached in America, Susie had a very bad cough, and her committee insisted that she must return to India. But she was still $3000 short of the $21,000 she was seeking. From a group that was praying for her return to India she received cheques of $1000 each from two ladies and after that a further invitation to speak, despite her being very weak, made up the full amount. Then, as there was still time to go before her boat sailed, she agreed to give talks in Canada and exceeded her total by $2000.

Throughout the very strenuous programme with ill health in unfamiliar surroundings, she kept going by reading passages of the Bible at random and taking them as her guide and reassurance.

Her tour paid for building the two schools in Poona for poor Hindus and Muslims in Covent Street and for the furniture of her mother's Victoria High School. Some missionaries described the schools for Hindu and Muslim children as 'vernacular', as if that were a term of abuse. But the Marathi language school for Hindus has been described as having given the highest standard of education available in the language, since Government and Mission schools were all English language schools.[64] The vernacular schools came to be called the St John's School. Susie herself supervised the vernacular teaching there, and St John's School is still standing and in use, though now independent of the English-language school that Susie went on to found.

Susie had now secured the future of her mother's two vernacular schools and Lena was running her English-language Victoria High School. So Susie next turned her attention to her mother's fourth school, the Gujarati-speaking preparatory school for Parsees, chiefly for infants who were waiting to move on to the English-language school. It was in the grounds of 80 Civil Lines, which also contained the English-language Victoria High School and the family home. It had had only 30 pupils, but when Susie started teaching there as well, the numbers doubled. Susie got her former pupil, Naja Kabraji, to join her in the teaching. Naja, a Zoroastrian, had become her pupil along with two sisters only after a long hesitation on her father's part about sending his Zoroastrian daughters to a Christian school. For Susie and Naja it was a problem how to accommodate all the children of the preparatory school. For a while, Pandita Ramabai lent part of her building, when she moved her school, but when she needed it back, a different solution was required.

30. Susie Sorabji (right) with Naja Kabraji, her lieutenant.

Susie had only 5000 rupees left when a bungalow with large grounds came on the market for 36,500 rupees. She was determined to borrow and raise the funds to pay back. Not being experienced, she was tricked into accepting a loan at 9 per cent interest, after rejecting one at 7 per cent. She raised separately a further 450 rupees to repair the floors and provide matting. But to pay back the loan, she needed to make a fresh trip in 1905 to America and she sailed on February 23rd 1905.

Second American trip: Helen Gould's blank cheque, the Parsee school 1905, St Helena's 1908

Stopping off in London from May 5th to 12th, where Alice was taking exams,[65] she learnt that her guardian angel, Miss Marsh, had died. But Miss Freer took over the role, met Susie in New York and took her to the Martha Washington Hotel. A Miss Helen Gould (later Mrs Finlay Sheppard) asked her to speak to various Christian missions and Young Men's Christian Associations for sailors and then Susie moved to Canada, speaking sometimes three times a day. She was terribly cold, her health broke down and her doctor said she must go home. But she refused so long as the huge sum of money was not raised. A friend of Helen Gould arranged for Helen to be approached. She said she had not realised that the money was needed and sent a blank cheque.

Susie was able to buy the new premises for the preparatory school, and she held classes in the drawing room and dining room of the bungalow, where she lived with Naja Kabraji. There were now 100 children and they included boarders from all parts of the Deccan. She gave a party under a coloured canvas with the Bishop of Poona to advertise the school, and she wrote in the *Church Missionary Society Journal*, stating her wish to convert Parsees (she was not speaking of Hindus or Muslims) from Zoroastrianism to Christianity. She was to supply every child with a Bible. Lena gave up the main Victoria High School in 1906, and the boys from that school were sent over and swelled Susie's numbers.

The final school, St Helena's, was established, when Miss Helen Gould asked to be sent a photograph of the existing school, and was astonished to find that it was only a bungalow. She immediately sent more money in 1906 and this provided the library, the tower, which had a guest room with views towards the hills and the building which was to form the centre of the new English-language school. Susie supervised the building work. She found that in two hours in Bombay she could memorise all the contractor's specifications for quantities of materials. The main door was inducted with Hindu as well as Christian rites. A coconut and egg were broken and mixed with red pigment and money was buried. Susie's home remained in the bungalow, although that is no longer standing. She now taught in the main school, but she would leave every day at 3.30 to teach in the schools for the poor. The substantial Helen Gould building, which still stands, was opened on October 3rd 1908 by Lord Sydenham, the Governor of Bombay, and the school was called St Helena's after Helen Gould.

Susie's loss of sight, 1908

Five days later, Susie went down with fever, which lasted for eight months and was followed by pain and blindness for over a year more, while Naja ran the school. After an emergency operation, Susie waited for six weeks in bandages to see if the operation had restored her sight, which it had not, and a course of 11 injections was equally unsuccessful. For a year she had to wear a shade against glare and change her bandages every ten minutes. More than once she tried to read, but her sisters, asked to check her attempts, had to disappoint her. Meeting with no success, she took comfort from a hymn written by the blind George Matheson, 'O love that will not let me go', and she tried a service of faith healing. On her return from that, she asked Naja if there was light blue above the dark blue on the house opposite. Naja confirmed that there was, but wanted more proof that Susie could see. Soon Susie found that she could once again find her place in the hymn book. Moreover, in response to Naja's challenge, on April 13th 1913, she went to Sunday School at midday without her eye shade. From that point, she found she could write again, using a magnifying glass. Cornelia, impressed by Susie's faith, stresses her confidence during sickness rather than her despair, but the alternating despair would have given them something in common.

Angela Grote's legacy, 1923–9

In 1923, Susie made her third and last tour abroad, first to see Sir Richard Cruise in London, who would later treat Cornelia's eyes. Cruise said he could not help, and Susie went again to be anointed by a faith healer, which was followed by an improvement. Cruise, had no explanation, but agreed to write a letter to Cornelia saying that the improvement in Susie's eyes was 'marvellous'. Susie's wish to convince Cornelia should be seen against the background of Cornelia's earlier remark[66] that she herself was not 'saved', but her sister Susie was. Lena moved from retirement in England to take Susie's place at the Poona school, so that Susie could go on to America. At the border, the immigration authorities gave her a health check and questioned her eyesight, but a letter sent by Helen Gould immediately cleared the way for entry. On this trip, she failed to raise any more money, and on return to Poona she needed another major operation, but when she got back home from that there was a legacy waiting for her from Miss Angela Grote, and with that she built a new science block, matching and facing the Grote building. The foundation stone was laid on July 26th 1929 by Lady Sykes, wife of the Governor, and at the ceremony three white pigeons were released.

Recollections of pupils and others

Susie's life was enacted in 2007 by the teachers at St Helena's, the English-language school she founded, now confined to girls and grown from the 250 in Susie's time (plus 300 in the poor schools) to 3000 pupils, and celebrating its centenary in 2008. Even though very few of the girls are now Christian, the school maintains Susie's tradition of singing Christian hymns. This tradition of hymns, as well as Susie's telling of Bible stories, remained in 2007 the delight of two non-Christian Parsee ladies who had been Susie's pupils, Tehmi and Franie Darukhanavala. The Parsee pupils I met in 1988, Rustom Kabraji and others,[67] who were all non-Christian, spoke of her influence in the same way. Rustom Kabraji visited Susie on her death bed and asked, 'How are you, Miss Susie?' '*Sing a hymn,*' she said. To him she conveyed a love not only of hymns, but of music in general. He remembered her in pink as her favourite colour, and wearing sarees that flowed like a bride's train, accompanied by much jewellery round her neck. She rode in her Victoria carriage drawn by a white horse, stopping to speak to anyone who greeted her. Her two dogs would herald her arrival in the classrooms. The portraits one in oils by Pimputkhave, who was appointed to Queen Victoria, one in pastels, and the photographs[68], show rounded features suggesting kindliness, along with total conviction.

Dick used to visit Susie's school and speak once a year and the pupils all looked forward to his visits because after that a holiday was declared. Susie continued the family practice of holding purdah parties for secluded women, and she had the same sympathy as Cornelia about the hardships of secluded orthodox life. Among the episodes re-enacted by St Helena's teachers, in this case by a Muslim teacher, was that of a Muslim whom Susie had called beautiful. 'Do you think so?', she said. 'My husband does not think so because I have not given him a child.'

Susie's death and Cornelia's difficulties with her pupils, 1931

Susie's health never came right, and Alice, the ever useful doctor, was with her in the three days before she died in her original bungalow at the age of 62, on March 15th, 1931, which became St Helena's Founder's day. There was an 'immense' crowd for the funeral at St Paul's church, as Alice tells the story:[69] 'Just then Naja gripped me and said,

"Miss Alice (as she still calls me often!), I have decided to become a Christian and I want to have it announced now or at the cemetery, but in her presence" (or words like that)'. Alice tried to persuade her not to decide under stress of emotion, but to wait. But Naja insisted when they moved on to the burial at the cemetery that Canon Butcher should make the announcement in front of Susie's coffin. All but one of Naja's cousins sobbed and told her she had broken their hearts. But one of them embraced her, according to Alice, and said what a glorious thing she had done. Franie Darukhanavala was at the burial. As she described it in 2007, she had never seen or heard of a burial, since the Zoroastrian custom is consumption by vultures in the towers of silence. Her parents told her that Naja's conversion was not something that concerned her. But some of the stricter Zoroastrian parents were put off by the conversion, and Naja was right that an earlier announcement could have disrupted Susie's work.

Cornelia missed the death and burial. She was brought in to take over the school from March until July, but the conqueror of Sapru could not keep order with the children like the kindly Susie, according to Rustom Kabraji, and this is borne out by her own comments on the children's behaviour.[70] Cornelia describes the unwillingness of either pupils or teachers to leave at the end of term on April 20th, because they wanted to go on talking about Susie. Cornelia's final task on June 16th was to introduce the new headmistress for the next term. By that time Cornelia had decided to end her own second career in India.

Naming of Susie Sorabji Road, 1932

On October 26th 1932, Lord Willingdon with Lady Willingdon, as almost his last act as Governor before becoming Viceroy, opened the road outside the school, renamed Susie Sorabji road, as it is to this day, and this opening too was re enacted by the teachers of the school. Susie was given a common tomb stone in St Sepulchre's Cemetery, Poona, with her mother, whose body was moved from Nasik,[71] while a plaque to Susie was added in St Matthews Church to the plaque to her father.

Susie's achievement was getting all the Poona schools funded and re-established on a lasting basis in seemingly hopeless circumstances. Cornelia's memoir emphasises instead her faith throughout adversity. That was an important factor, but one that can be seen a necessary prerequisite for her achievement.

The next surviving child, after the loss of another boy baby – one had died before the birth of Zuleika – was Dick, whose life with Cornelia in Oxford and Allahabad and simultaneous return to England has been separately described, and the eighth and last child was Alice.

ALICE, FUTURE HEROINE OF THE FRONTIER

Alice, also known as Ailsa, was born in 1873. She was Cornelia's youngest sister and probably the most significant sister for her. Her success in many of the same spheres as Cornelia was partly unexpected and personal success was not something that interested her. It is not surprising that she was the one before whom Cornelia came to feel pangs of jealousy and even a sense of failure, so that the very different sense in which Alice's life was successful throws light on Cornelia's own feelings. Alice differed from Cornelia not only in her interest in Christian conversion,[72] but also in her experience of the warrior tribes of the Afghan frontier, which acquainted her with a very different India from that of Cornelia's career. The story of Alice's success needs telling because Cornelia's life was at intervals conducted in reaction to it.

Alice's medical training and overlap with Cornelia in London, 1897–1905

Things started well, with Cornelia writing from England that Alice must work hard, and at the same time defending her from being drawn away from study to helping in the family school. She was to be the doctor that their mother wanted.[73] This may suggest that Cornelia had been appointed as the one to mind the young Alice. Alice, like Dick, teased Cornelia affectionately in return. She gained university admission at age 14, the 19th out of 3000 candidates, and in 1896 became the first woman Bachelor of Science (B.Sc.) in India with 16 and a half marks more on her exam than any male candidate.[74] Alice, like Cornelia before her, had her picture in *The Queen*.[75] On January 9th 1897, Cornelia and Dick saw her off in her pink saree from Bombay to study in London.[76]

Their father being dead, money was short, and Cornelia and Mary both subsidised her. Cornelia was indignant when, instead of going straight to medicine, Alice took a preliminary course in Bedford College, London, which included general science. But Dick defended her and she replied uncompromisingly, going on to collect her own scholarships from Bedford College, from the Society for Promoting Christian Knowledge (SPCK) and from Dufferin medical funds.[77] She was very happy in College Hall, Byng Place,[78] which was next to University College where, unknown to her, her future husband had completed his medical studies five years earlier. She herself finished at Bedford with a first class matriculation in January 1898 and a second class in preliminary science in July, and moved to the London School of Medicine for Women.[79]

In 1901 she had her first failure in a medical exam,[80] but medical exams can be taken again. Cornelia sailed to London in May and was soon to see Alice cutting up a frog.[81] For several months, they were allowed to share together the flat of the Hobhouse's daughter, Emily, who had gone out to South Africa, with her family's approval, to protest about British treatment of the Boers in the Boer War, and on being turned back – which shortened the vacancy of the flat – sued Lord Kitchener.[82]

In 1902, Alice was hospitalised from February to August with rheumatism, and was told, as Cornelia had been told of women in general, that she was not strong enough to do medicine.[83] But in January 1904, she wrote home about having taken her next set of exams, although she was so nervous that she had to ask others to verify that her name really was displayed on the list of those who had passed. She remained nervous about the next exams, reminding home that there had been recriminations about earlier failure.[84] She did indeed fail a second time in summer 1904, and this provoked a quarrel with Cornelia in which Alice replied accusingly.[85] In letters home, Alice defended having taken out a loan in order to continue, as if she had been told to give up, and protested that the loan was not from a man.[86] In May 1905 she was worried that the need to welcome Susie on her way to raise funds in America fell just before the final exams that month and again she got others to look at the list of successful candidates in June, but she had passed. She started writing for jobs and contested Cornelia's view that she would only be able to work under supervision.[87]

Alice head of a Delhi hospital, 1906

Alice got back to India on August 2nd and joined the Poona family, but relations with Cornelia were strained and by November 23rd she had left for a very satisfactory job in Bahawalpur in what is now Pakistan. Like Cornelia, she was warmly greeted by Princess Mary, when the future Queen, visited India in 1905, and by Lady Minto, the Vicereine.[88] By mid-1906 she had got an even better job as head of the Victoria Memorial Hospital in Delhi, and Cornelia on one of her journeys through Delhi stopped off at Alice's house, calling it a dear little place with her room looking even nicer with the piano in it. Stopping again on her return journey, she found Alice looking charming, dressed for a dance at her club.[89]

August 1907 was when Alice applied, to Cornelia's consternation, to the Dufferin Hospital in Calcutta. As a member of the hospital committee, Cornelia warned Alice that the application would cause 'awkwardnesses'. Alice still applied, but nothing came of it.

Marriage to Theodore Pennell, 1908

Next arrived the really transforming news. Alice cabled Cornelia on July 7th 1908 that she was engaged to be married to Theodore Pennell, an English missionary doctor on the Afghan frontier. Theodore, well over six foot tall, wore Pathan clothing and head dress and was the only unarmed man to travel in Afghan territory. His achievements explain Alice's calm ability, unlike Cornelia, to treat her own exploits as unimportant.

Theodore knew the ways of all the tribes, and even conducted debates with them about their respective world views. They found his scientific explanation of why the sun is colder in winter absolutely ludicrous, and preferred their own explanation, that the devil is short of firewood in the winter to stoke it up. He cured them in thousands in the villages and when they crowded around him on the roadside. But the more serious cases, often gunshot wounds from continuous feuding, made gangrenous by flayed sheepskin dressings, needed to come to his hospital for surgery. Another hazard was the slicing off of a nose, a standard response for a wife's suspected infidelity, which required plastic surgery. The complication for nomadic patients who went off for months at a time was that the nose grew back too big while they were away, and the surgery often had to be repeated. There were then, and are today, military operations in the frontier area of Bannu. The British of the time considered him worth two battalions, and, as history repeats itself, their successors would be well advised to read his book, *Among the Wild Tribes of the Afghan Frontier.*[i]

Mrs Croker Pennell, Theodore's mother, had called on Alice in London in 1902,[90] possibly to look her over, but he himself says in his letter to Alice's and Cornelia's mother[91] that he met her first much later at Bahawalpur. Theodore's companion on the frontier was his mother while she lived. He needed a woman helper for his women patients, but she had opposed his marrying an Indian. As soon as she died, however, he wrote his proposal from sick leave in England, and Alice cabled acceptance.

They were married three months later in Dick's city, in the cathedral at Allahabad, on October 17th 1908, and were to visit Cornelia in Calcutta for a week the following year.[92] Alice was then very slim. Cornelia found Theodore shy at first, which is borne out by Alice's descriptions.

The Afghan frontier: adventurous tours as doctor for women

Bannu was an emerald oasis beneath the Afghan mountains.[93] They were back there 12 days after their marriage and from then on did all the work together.[94] In Bannu, Alice was consultant for the women and operated on them with Theodore as assistant. In Bannu itself, women were veiled from head to toe. When Alice and Theodore went out from Bannu, and were stopped on the roads or reached the villages, they took turns at examining and writing prescriptions. Soon after their marriage, she describes one remote village where their hosts gave them for night time privacy only some turbans, sheets, rugs and a coat at intervals on a clothes line, with curious inquirers peering through the gaps.[95] The only room was 30 foot long, with the horses occupying 12 feet. They had a rope tied across to create the screen in part of the room, with their police escort just outside the curtain, and beyond cows, sheep and the family.

At this time Theodore was choosing a site for a small outpost hospital at a much more remote and dangerous place to the North, Thal. Patients would surround them at every stop on the way and would lie in wait for them in every street in Thal. Once the hospital was built, they were able to do operations on their visits there. They both went together many times, but only the first time were they allowed to take the direct 34 mile route through Waziristan. After that, the direct route was declared too dangerous, and they were not able to circumvent that as they sometimes circumvented the night curfews on the roads. The other remote settlement was to the North East at Karak, where Theodore had established a dispensary, later to become a hospital, but where his chief aim was to house converts and provide teaching for them. It was at Karak that a mullah had converted, and, after he offered Theodore land for a church

---

i His further book, *Things Seen in Northern India*, London 1912, describes his travels in 1904–5 with a Muslim, both disguised as Hindu sadhus, and carrying no money, in order to learn the ways of Hindu asceticism.

to be built there, suffered an axe attack. When the foundation of the church was laid, there were 40 Christians in the settlement, and there were by 1910 a hundred in the Bannu Mission complex with its school and hospital.

In the hospital, a patient involved in feuds would sometimes be surrounded by men with loaded rifles. On one occasion the wounded from opposite factions reached Bannu with their armed guards at roughly the same time and had to be kept at opposite ends of the hospital to reduce their anxiety.

Theodore not only ran the hospital, but he and his mother had substantially contributed to the cost of the buildings. Moreover, he was equally devoted to his work as Principal of the Mission school for 650 boys, and though there was a headmaster under him, he attended to the school every day.

Widowed, 1912, but returns to the frontier, 1913–22

Theodore was seriously ill more than once, and when his life was in danger in 1909, work in the city of Bannu came to a stop with crowds around the hospital awaiting every report. This illness resulted in 1910 in a leave in England, where Alice in turn became seriously ill. But Theodore's final illness in 1912 was very sudden. He had just had time to have the foundation laid for the new woman's hospital which Alice was to run, when he caught a colleague's infection by cutting himself when operating on him. Alice was only just up from surgery on herself, and Theodore died in three days on March 21st 1912.

It was Dick who came at once from Allahabad to comfort Alice. Cornelia wanted to go, but was advised by a friend not to. She saw Alice instead the next month wearing black in Allahabad, cheered only by talking of Theodore.[96] Alice's first task was to write about him *Pennell of the Frontier*, which was published in 1913. One remarkable feature of the book is that she was too self-effacing to mention that she was the wife who shared Theodore's last three and a half years. But others recognised her and in the New Year's honours for 1913 she was awarded the silver medal of the Kaiser-i-Hind, an honour which Queen Victoria had established to reward civilian service in India.

The book was written by Alice during health leave. With a suspected patch on the lung,[97] she planned to winter in Egypt, leaving Bannu on October 25th 1912.[98] But a year later in November 1913, she was ready to return and she offered to work as honorary surgeon for women and to pay two thirds of the cost of completing the women's block.[99] For the next ten years after Theodore's death until 1922, her main work was for the hospital, with some inevitable absences. She returned to Bannu on February 7th 1914, built herself a new house behind the cemetery and took part in the opening of the outpatient's block in the new Pennell Memorial Hospital later that year.[100]

First World War, killings and kidnappings. Alice escapes kidnap and takes over male surgery

The year 1914 was not a safe time to return. The First World War of 1914–18 greatly increased the dangers on the frontier. The Germans were trying to persuade first their allies the Turks and then the Amir of Afghanistan to join Indian Muslims in a Holy War

Invoice for Dd4YWrJqR 18.06.2010

amazon.co.uk

www.amazon.co.uk

Invoice/Receipt for:	Paid by:	Delivered to:
[illegible]	[illegible]	Jack Wigglesworth 3 Deacons Heights Barnet Lane Elstree BOREHAMWOOD, Herts WD6 3QY United Kingdom, GB

Qty.	Item	Our Price (excl. VAT)	VAT Rate	Total Price (excl. VAT)
[illegible]	[illegible]	£15.75		£15.75

Shipping Subtotal (excl. VAT)	£0.00
Subtotal (excl. VAT)	£15.75
Order Total	£15.75
[illegible]	£15.75
Balance Due	£0.00

[illegible]

[illegible] at the top of each page of our site.

Thinking of Returning an Item?

PLEASE USE OUR ON-LINE RETURNS SUPPORT CENTRE

[illegible] Returns Policy and provide you with a [illegible] order summary, above). Our Returns [illegible]

[illegible]

[illegible] Luxembourg
VAT number [illegible]

[illegible] returns centre

2010060973750l_66700_2

against the British in India, and many Afghans liked the idea.[ii] One of Alice's novels describes the replica gun factories in Afghanistan that were preparing for the war.[iii] Cornelia told Elena on May 13 1915 that when Alice first returned to visit the outlying hospital at Thal, martial law required her to reside for her protection in the fort. On September 23 Cornelia reported the murder of the doctor, Mehr Khan, at Thal, a Pathan convert, and of the kidnapping of his five and a half year old boy, Joel, who was carried off to the mountains for a ransom of up to £1000. It was said that, required to join in the Afghans' prayers, the boy only knew how to say the Lord's Prayer. He was eventually recovered when one of the brigands was captured and released on security of almost £1800 in order to recover Joel. Even then, the brigand had to shoot dead another of the brigands who resisted.[101]

In 1916, there was an attempt by Mahsud tribesmen to kidnap Alice herself for ransom, with a view to forcing the government to drop various murder charges against them. Fortunately, Alice was away doctoring at an eye hospital camp in Shikapur and merely lost many of her most valued possessions. She was asked then by the British to abandon her visits to the outlying hospitals at Thal and Karak and to entrust visiting to Dr Vosper, which meant that she had to take over from him the male surgery in Bannu. She wrote,

> 'A Pathan is always a gentleman, and I have enjoyed having the care of the men as much as any of my work, especially as most of them remember my husband and love his memory, so find my ministrations welcome. Their courage and cheerfulness in pain are always inspiring, and though they may not agree with us in their ideas of right and wrong, their manliness and hearty good fellowship are very attractive'.[102]

War hospital work, Bombay 1917–18, sole charge on frontier 1919

As described in Chapter 16, Alice was moved by the Government on November 17th 1917 for some months to a war hospital for the wounded in Bombay, and Cornelia visited her there and saw where the wounded were taught trades. After that duty in 1918 Alice was awarded the gold medal of the Kaiser-i-Hind, which was awarded to Cornelia in 1909 and 1922,[103] and which Theodore had received in 1910, having, like Alice, received the silver medal earlier.[104]

Alice returned from Bombay on September 17th 1918 to the Bannu hospital, but the military situation was getting worse. In 1919, she was for some time in sole charge in the absence of Drs Cox and Wigram.[105] Her friend, the commanding officer, General Bruce, was invalided out of Bannu, and Alice's hospital was the Brigade General Hospital,[106] so that Mahsud and Waziri women could not be treated, though they begged to be admitted.

---

ii Peter Hopkirk, *On Secret Service East of Constantinople*, London 1994.
iii *Children of the Border*.

Outlying hospitals destroyed, 1919–20

Things were to get worse after the war. Both Alice's outposts at Thal and at Karak were attacked and Thal burnt down, as she describes in a letter and in one of her novels.[107] At Thal on May 28th 1919, hundreds of Afghans under Nadir Khan poured over the hilltop with elephants drawing their guns. They fired on the hospital and set it alight, and the villagers, seeing the flames, looted it, removing even windows and doors. The Afghans occupied the hospital, drawing the defenders' fire in return down from the British fort, which caused further damage. Telegraph wires were cut and the little railway to the village destroyed. One woman with her baby escaped from the hospital to the village disguised as a Pathan. The Indian commander of an outnumbered constabulary post negotiated safe conduct to the village for other hospital workers. The attack ended suddenly, when relief aeroplanes were heard overhead. The elephants stampeded, and the astonished Afghans who had never heard such a thing, fled with them, leaving guns and ammunition behind. When the relieving force arrived on foot, the villagers all proclaimed their restored loyalty. But the hospital had been burnt to the ground. The relieving officer was General Dyer, who was to become notorious later that year for his massacre of unarmed civilians in Amritsar.

At the remaining outpost in Karak on January 3rd 1920, 700 Wazirs and Mahsuds with a few Khattak outlaws, attacked. Two hundred of them entered the village. They climbed to the top story of the hospital calling for Jahan Khan, Theodore's dependable convert, who ran the establishment. He and his family were next door, and, as Alice records, when he said to them, 'we'll test our faith by praying', one of his children replied, 'I have been praying a long time, Father'. A diversion was created when Indian soldiers in the police post next to the hospital fired, and in the end one wazir convert was stabbed to death in the church, but it was the wealthier Hindus who suffered the main losses. After these excitements, Alice took leave, and left Bannu on February 18th 1920 and sailed for England in March, returning to Bannu only in 1922.[108]

Cornelia's visits to Alice, 1917 and 1922

Cornelia made two visits to see Alice on the Afghan frontier during the war. In 1917, she and Lena both made trips to see Alice there, and both went on over the mountains to experience the incomparable beauty of Kashmir.[109] Cornelia arrived on May 22nd 1917 and found Alice on the verandah to meet her, 'looking, as usual, very young and bright'. This was the time when the hospital, normally open for the whole neighbourhood, was to become a war hospital for British troops on the frontier. General Bruce, brother of Cornelia's college friend, dined the first two nights, and they were told of a fort 50 miles off that was to be attacked that night. But another fort had been captured by Afghans disguised as women and Cornelia did not hear of its recapture until June 11th. Hostilities were continuing even though the Amir's Afghan government had supposedly decided to remain neutral in the war.

One day Cornelia and Alice had an accident in Alice's car on the road to Kohat and were stranded overnight, but Alice's fluent Pushtu saved the situation and the car was retrieved another day. Cornelia stayed in Alice's house and was shown everything: the hospital, the buildings erected in memory of Alice's and Theodore's parents, water sports at the nursery school, the main schools, the original house built by Theodore, the room where Theodore died and the cemetery where he was buried. They visited a girls' school in the city, and met the other two doctors, Wigram and Cox, as well as nursing sister, Hillman, who was to remain Alice's friend in her retirement in London after 1938. Cornelia thought it 'lovely' to see Alice 'so loved and so efficient',[110] and yet at a time when she herself was suffering enormous opposition from officials to her work, she confided to her diary, 'it's dreadful feeling a failure and *despicable*, as Alice somehow makes one feel'.[111]

Cornelia's second visit was in 1922, the year that Cornelia and Dick were to leave India. Alice had returned to Bannu from her leave and Cornelia made her second and last visit to see her on the frontier, as described in Chapter 16.[112] The other doctor, Wigram, and sister Hillman were there, but the new meeting was with the Bahadur Khan, a convert and friend of Theodore and Alice.

The Bahadur Khan's claim on the property

In 1922, the Bahadur Khan took Cornelia out driving in his *Overland 4* two days running. Many years later, when Alice left her house and 200 acres to her schoolboy nephew (myself), the Bahadur Khan used a forged letter in pidgin English assigning to himself the property and adding in a Rolls Royce, which, he complained, had not yet come. The Rolls Royce may have been suggested by Lord Montagu's arriving with Cornelia in a Rolls Royce on her 1922 visit.[113] The trustees of Alice's estate, acting for her nephew, did not understand why the lawyers whom they employed always died when the case reached the High Court, but when I had read the first page of Theodore's book, the explanation seemed obvious and I stopped the litigation. The Bahadur's descendants rented the land to the Pakistani government, and it became valuable building land for the cantonment area. The name 'Bahadur Khan' was used in Alice's first novel for an Afghan hero, who, however, had not entirely abandoned the feuding beliefs of his people, and indeed I have read a letter to Alice asking her to replace the chaukidar or guard on the property, who had been shot in her absence. I received a loyal warning from a brave and faithful gardener about the property being looted 'even up to bricks'.

New work for refugees in Greece, 1923–1925

That year, 1922, with both Dick and Cornelia retiring, Alice too offered her resignation, so that all three prepared to leave India and, like 1906, the year was a turning point in the family's history.[114] Cornelia could not help noticing competitively the fond farewells that Alice received from the Viceroy and Vicereine, Lord and Lady Reading.[115] Alice never lost her commitment to the Bannu hospital and school and there were to be many visits back to Bannu every year from 1926–1928 and again in 1936, while in 1939 she gave a generous gift to save the Bannu high school from closure.[116] Dr Effie Bolton describes the 1927 visit as follows:[117]

> 'Imperious Mrs Pennell came to pay us a visit. It is 4 years since she left Bannu having worked as a doctor here after her husband's death in 1912.... When the news of

Mrs Pennell's visit was noised abroad, crowds came to pay her their respects in true Oriental fashion. I turned out to let her have my little suite of rooms, as most convenient,
and all day long, on her verandah, queues of people came to call on her. How she kept
up her spirits and vitality I don't know. She is a charming Parsee lady, very stout and
very lively with an endless store of repartee! She always wears a silk saree, which is most
becoming.... On Thursday Mrs Pennell drove away in great style'.

In the meantime, a new opportunity had opened up for Alice. It is first mentioned on
October 7th 1922.[118] On September 9th 1922 there had been a massacre of Greeks in
Smyrna, now Izmir on the modern Turkish mainland, and there were huge movements
of refugees and population exchanges over the whole region. The facts of the massacre
are still disputed, but the Church Missionary Society asked Alice to go to Smyrna. After
a brief stay at Dublin University's institution in Hazaribagh, Bihar, into early 1923,[119]
Alice reached Greece and met the new King and Queen of Greece in Athens.[120]
Alice returned to Greece in 1924–5 after a four-month stay in England.[121]

Queen Elisabeth of Greece was daughter of the Romanian Queen, and their friendship led Alice to visit Romania, in 1931 and 1936, to stay at least on the first occasion
with Queen Elisabeth.[122] She was the source of Alice's presents to the family which
Dick had started by that time. Alice's niece Francina (my sister) got a pretty Romanian
dress, and Dick's wife Mary (my mother) received a Greek-style bangle of green and
white enamel, with two gold-coloured rams' heads with ruby eyes. It disappeared in
Mary's old age after one of the cups of tea she gave to visiting burglars.

Overland through Persia

A pleasure that arose from the new location was trips between India and England that
passed through Europe and Persia. There were overland trips passing through Persia in
1926, 1928, 1929 and 1931.[123] The last trip of 1931 is recorded in a 21 page memorandum, 'Memories of Persia' dated September 20th 1941.[124] Alice stayed in old cara-
vanserais with parking below, rooms above and delicious cook shops just inside. A few
days before her arrival, two women members of the Reza Shah's household had visited
the shrine of Fatima at Qum for the New Year festival, Navroz. They wore not black,
but bright colours and exposed their faces, which drew a public rebuke from one of
the priests. They went out and used the telephone, a new instrument then, to the Shah,
who appeared in no time, booted and spurred, with his men at arms, entered the
mosque in his boots, and personally whipped the mullahs who were still there, even
though they were clinging to sanctuary rails. Alice reports that as she travelled, inn
keepers, shopkeepers, petrol station attendants, bakers and greengrocers all rejoiced
as if at a release from oppression. By 1979 the Shah's son was no longer welcome, and
the mullahs regained their place.

Alice's novels from 1926

Alice also wrote her three novels during this period published by John Murray. *Children
of the Border* in 1926 celebrated the heroism and endurance of the Afghan tribesman's

life of blood feud and showed an intimate knowledge of domestic custom as well as of their methods of crime. Her admiration for these austere and hardy people contrasts with Cornelia's love of the pageantry in her palaces. Alice drew in her novels on real life stories and names from frontier life and made no attempt to draw Christian conclusions about the way of life. The contact with England through service in the First World War is presented not as redeeming, but as disorienting. Her novel shows what huge social differences India contains, when one compares the lives described in Cornelia's books.[125] In *The Begum's Son*, which followed in 1928, Alice described a Muslim family and disagreed with Cornelia's attitude that the veiled seclusion of women was acceptable, if suitably reformed. She thought on the contrary that it needed to be swept away. Freedom from Britain would come to India, she thought, when it followed the unsecluded practices and the grasp of administration that she described in more enlightened Muslim families further South in India. In 1931, *Doorways of the East* again used the name of one of Theodore's converts, Ram Ditta, who in real life made a pilgrimage to Theodore's old school, Eastbourne College, in 1965.[126] It was about Hindu families and the tensions created by the juxtaposition of traditional family values with Westernisation in its very varied forms, only some of them desirable, according to Alice. The seductive dancer could reflect earlier family anxieties about Pheroze's daughter, Elsie, as a Bluebell Girl. In the novel Alice defended the explicit teaching of Christianity, which only the missionary schools practised, and opposed non-interference in religion, at least for those Hindus and Parsees who had already abandoned orthodoxy, and whom she saw as lacking clear guidance. She agreed with Cornelia in not approving the guidance offered by Gandhi, although she saw him as incorporating some of the better ideals of the West.

Social and medical work in Delhi under Lady Irwin, 1927–1938

By 1927, Alice had started a new phase. She was then living in Delhi and persuading the Vicereine, Lady Irwin, to fund projects in education. The competition this caused with Cornelia has already been described.[127] Later, the Lady Irwin College grew out of Lady Irwin's consultations and Alice was able to open an eye clinic there by 1933.[128] She had, perhaps by way of preparation for the eye clinic, made a visit to a Baltimore hospital some time before she started it and made a great impression there, as a queenly figure in glorious clothes.[129]

In 1938, she accompanied the Vicereine to open the children's home which she had got established. Cornelia, as guest, remarked, not for the first time, how self-effacing she was.[130]

It was at this time that Alice had the spacious and comfortable house, Racquet Court House, in Delhi with shady lawns where Cornelia stayed so often in 1931–1938, after giving up her own main work. Cornelia very much liked staying in Alice's house in Delhi. Alice would arrange the comforts of tea and massages and make delicious pakora pastries for Cornelia in between her committee meetings.[131]

Second World War in London, 1939–1945

The end of 1938 saw all four surviving sisters in London on the eve of the Second World War.[132] Cornelia offered to share her flat with Alice, and for a while they were both in Mary's flat. They both prepared for Air Raid Precaution work and both met Indian troops, on one occasion joining forces to get Punjabi troops to sing. The refugee hostel in Cheyne Walk in Chelsea, where Alice did her main war work, was bombed out, and the window by the bed in her flat in Chelsea was also cracked by bombing.

Though Alice had no children of her own, she was a family person by temperament, good at seeing what was needed by Dick's family. She was the most comfortable one of the four, being plump, whereas the others were lean and wiry. She became a provider to Dick's family in Oxford, coming down with delicious lentil pakoras and being consulted on health matters, Dick's depression, her niece Francina's meningitis and her nephew's illness after eating mushrooms. She kept her nephew informed on the war by sending him the magazine *Everybody*, and on the most colourful side of India by giving him *Indian India*, a magazine about the Princely States after Indian Independence. She supplied when he was eight *The Pilgrim's Progress* and when he was nine his first bicycle. Alice's lectures as late as 1947 at Theodore's school, Eastbourne College, were on the future of the new India and on Theodore, and she is remembered there as stately with silky grey hair.[133] I stayed with her for three days in a holiday home called Malabar in Ashtead, Surrey, in May 1948, and talked cricket with nursing sister Hillman from Bannu. She died on 7th March 1951 in the same convent of the Holy Rood at Findon in Sussex where her sister Lena had died in 1936, and whose Reverend Mother was a cousin of Theodore Pennell.

Throughout Alice was a counterpoise to Cornelia, obtaining by charm, confidence, modesty and ability some of the same things that Cornelia secured by continuous battle with opposing forces.

OFFICIAL REPORTS BY THE COURT OF WARDS ON CORNELIA'S WORK, 1904–1909

Extracts relating to Cornelia from annual reports on the Court of Wards (all italics added), India Office Records/V/24/2532-3 and V/24/2602.

Bengal 1905–1906. 'She was *able to prevent litigation* between the proprietrix of the Narhan estate and her son-in-law and has devoted much attention to the health and education of the daughter of the proprietrix . . . It is proposed that *she should periodically visit all the estates* in the Province which are the property of purdahnashin ladies, or of which the proprietors are under the guardianship of purdahnashin ladies. Arrangements are now being made to give effect to these proposals. The Board consider it desirable that Miss Sorabji should *not merely be employed to settle difficulties after they have arisen, but that she should gain confidence beforehand*, so as to be able to prevent troubles from occurring or from assuming serious proportions'.

Bengal 1906–1907. 'Miss Sorabji has been instrumental in *preventing the litigation* which, but for her, would certainly have taken place in some of the estates visited by her. She has, by the exercise of great tact, been able to prevent family quarrels and to reconcile relatives who had become estranged. Her continued efforts for the improvement of the health and education of the ladies and minor wards of the families visited by her have been signally successful'.

Bengal 1907–1908. 'Her services have been successful in many cases in *obviating or healing family quarrels*. She has devoted much attention to the health and education of the ladies and minor wards of the estates visited by her and her visits and companionship have in all cases promoted the welfare of the ladies with whom she has come in contact. She has also done a considerable amount of *legal business* in connexion with some of the ladies.'

East Bengal 1908–1909. ' . . . She has been invaluable to the Court in the administration of these ladies' affairs. A set of provisional rules has recently been issued with the concurrence of the Board of Revenue, Lower Provinces,[i] defining more precisely the duties and position of the lady assistant. It is hoped that the effect of these rules will be not only to *give her a definite place in the chain of officers* engaged in the administration of the Wards' Department, but to *secure for her the co-operation of Managers and Collectors* which is necessary to enable the Court to obtain full value from her visits to the zenanas in the mofussil.[ii] Proposals are under consideration which will *secure the whole-time services* of Miss Sorabji, and will provide her with *an assistant to be trained by her and eventually to carry on the work which she has so ably begun'*.

Citation from first award of gold first class medal of the Kaiser-i-Hind, 1909, India Office Records/L/PS/15/32 and 55.

'Miss Sorabji has done most exceptional valuable work in the zenanas as Assistant to the Court of Wards in Bengal and Eastern Bengal and as a Legal Adviser to Ladies who come under the Court of Wards. This is a new line of work of very great merit which she has struck out for herself under the aegis of Government, and her sympathetic and untiring work has been most beneficial in furthering the interests of these ladies, explaining to them the object and intentions of the Court of Wards and protecting their interests'.

---

i i.e., the Greater Bengal area.

ii Rural areas.

APPENDIX 3

STRUCTURE OF ADMINISTRATION IN BRITISH INDIA AND PRINCELY STATES

APPOINTED FROM OUTSIDE THE INDIAN CIVIL SERVICE:

All of India

1. Secretary of State for India in London, a member of the cabinet.
2. Viceroy of India, with his Council, reporting to the Secretary of State for India in London.

British India

3. Governor of Bengal when enlarged after its reunification in 1912, or of another major Province in British India, with his own personal secretary, reporting in concert with his Council to the Viceroy of India.

BRITISH INDIA

Three tiers of Civil Service in British India

First tier

1. Indian Civil Service officers

From 1892 very slow entry for Indians from the lower Provincial Service
Entry by prestigious examination in England normally for English and assignment to one of the British-ruled provinces.

Five major grades

    i.   Sub-divisional officer (lowest)
    ii. Collector in charge of a whole district with big responsibilities
    iii. Commissioner in charge of the larger division
    iv. Senior roles at Provincial Headquarters, including the secretary of the Board of Revenue, which was in charge of the Court of Wards.
    v. Provincial Governor's Council, which included the honorary 'Member' of the Board of Revenue and the Secretary to the Government of the Province.

Second tier

Provincial Service open to Indians, but highest grade Deputy Collector, below Collector, the latter being the most coveted post for junior Indian Civil Service officers.

Third tier

Subordinate Service, open to Indians, but highest grade Munsiff, or local judge for legal cases involving small sums of money, or Tehsildar, a sub-collector for a sub-district.

PRINCELY STATES

A third of India was governed by Indian Maharajahs, or, below that, by Rajas and their near-equivalents, e.g., Thakurs, or by their Muslim counterparts, e.g., Nawabs, or (female) a Begum in the case of Bhopal. They were merely subject to the veto of a British Political Agent (also called a Resident)[i] and to British Agency courts which heard appeals from their jurisdiction. Appeals could go beyond the Agent to the Viceroy, or to the Privy Council in Britain.

---

i Michael Fisher, *Indirect Rule in India*, Oxford University Press, Delhi 1991.

CHRONOLOGY OF
CORNELIA'S LIFE

November 15th 1866   Born in Nasik

1867   Moves to Sholapur

1868   Moves to Belgaum

1876   Mother starts schools in Poona

1883–7   Cornelia at Deccan College, Poona, finishes top student with B.A. first class, but scholarship denied to woman

1886   Mother raises funds for her schools by speaking in England and Cornelia's only brother Dick starts schooling in England

1888   Question in Parliament on denial of scholarship to Cornelia, funds raised privately by English ladies

1889–92   Somerville Hall, Oxford. Under Benjamin Jowett's patronage, meets leading Victorians and becomes first woman to sit Oxford's Bachelor of Civil Law exam – passes, but degree not awarded to women

1890   Dick joins Cornelia as student at Balliol College, Oxford. Family in Poona 'scandalised' by a relationship of oldest sister, Zuleika. Zuleika leaves India 1893, visits America and France, settles in England. 1900 second 'scandal'. Second oldest sister, widowed Pheroze with daughter, joins Dick and Cornelia in England. Cornelia's fears of new scandals, 1893. Pheroze remarries, 1902

1891   Cornelia publishes in *The Nineteenth Century* on the need for women's education, the first article in a life of writing

1892–3   Trains at Lee and Pemberton, solicitors, London. Meets Tennyson, Florence Nightingale

1893   Returns to Poona. Chief Justice, Bombay, opposes woman working as solicitor

1894   Starts ten year search for legal post in India

1894–7   Cornelia prepares cases for women especially in Princely State of Kathiawar

1895	Father dies
1895–6	Passes Bachelor of Laws, Bombay, only at second attempt. Refused permission to plead in British courts
1896	Youngest sister Alice becomes first woman Bachelor of Science in India, beating all male candidates
1896	First appearance of a woman to plead in British court in British India – Poona. Dick called to the bar at Lincoln's Inn in London in the same batch as Jinnah
1897	Moves with her brother Dick to Allahabad to set up law practice
1898	In love with older High Court judge, Harrison Falkner Blair
1899	Allahabad High Court reneges on promise to enrol her as barrister, starts five year campaign for post as woman legal adviser
1901–4	Exiled to England. Interacts with G. F. Watts, Mrs Patrick Campbell, Bernard Shaw and other artists and writers
1901	Success of her first book on purdahnashins, *Love and Life Behind the Purdah*
1902	Orchestrated case in *The Times* and question in Parliament on need for post of woman legal adviser. Cornelia's sister Susie raises funds in Rockefeller mansion and White House for her mother's vernacular schools
1903	Brodrick becomes Secretary of State for India and supports campaign for advisory legal post. Dick becomes law lecturer at Muir College as well as barrister in Allahabad
1904	Cornelia's probationary appointment as legal adviser for purdahnashins under Indian Civil Service Court of Wards in Bengal, Bihar, Orissa and later Assam. Assigned hardest cases. Immediate success. Falkner Blair retires to England. Monthly visits to Dick in Allahabad until retirement
1905–13	Glowing annual reports on Cornelia, Kaiser-i-Hind gold medal awarded 1909
1906	Appointment confirmed, office in Writers' Buildings, Calcutta. Mother retires from Poona schools. Sisters Mary and Lena stop teaching and leave for England. Susie begins to re-establish all her mother's schools in Poona. Alice qualifies as doctor in London and becomes head of a hospital in Delhi
1907	Falkner Blair dies in Cornelia's arms on visit to Oxford
1908	Alice marries distinguished English missionary doctor on Afghan frontier, Theodore Pennell. Adventurous medical

	tours among the Afghans. Cornelia feels her own solitude. Susie founds St Helena's school in Poona
1909	Dick by now also Principal of Law College, Allahabad
1910	Mother dies. Cornelia's sister Lena becomes headmistress of school in Dacca for non-purdahed Hindu girls, Muslims and Christians, with Hindus predominating. Regular visits
1912	Alice widowed
1913–22	Cornelia's quarrels with some British officers, annual reports change, but work for purdahnashins just as effective
1914–18	First World War. Cornelia sees first and last day on short visits to London
1916	Alice escapes kidnap
1917	Cornelia's booklet, *The Purdahnashin*, gives definitive account of purdahnashins' needs. First of two visits to Alice on the Afghan frontier
1917–18	Visits Alice who is temporarily seconded to help war-wounded in Bombay. Alice awarded gold medal of Kaiser-i-Hind 1918
1919	Cornelia starts scheme for secluded training of purdahnashins as nurses in Calcutta. Plea for training in vernacular language eventually becomes Government policy. Lena retires and returns to London. 1919 Alice's main frontier hospital becomes brigade headquarters. Alice in sole charge for a year
1919–20	Alice's hospital outposts at Thal and Karak destroyed
1921–3	Dick discusses future Indian constitution with Sapru, currently on the Viceroy's Council
1922	Farewell visit, the second, to her sister Alice on the Afghan frontier. Dick and Cornelia retire to London, Cornelia receiving bar to Kaiser-i-Hind gold medal. Alice also resigns. In Oxford Cornelia receives BCL degree withheld from women until 1920
1923–5	Alice works for refugees in Greece
1923	Cornelia called to the bar at Lincoln's Inn, opened to women the previous year and collects through Somerville her BCL degree from Oxford
1924	Returns to Calcutta, enrolled as barrister in Calcutta High Court. Dick marries and stays in England
1924–9	Cornelia meets opposition to a woman pleading in Court
1925–38	Criticises British supervision of women's grievances in Princely States

1926	Cornelia on infanticide, first of a series of acclaimed legal opinions. Alice's first novel of three published
1927–38	Alice in Delhi, 1933 opens eye clinic, 1938 helps open children's home
1927	Katherine Mayo controversy damages Cornelia's work
1928	Cornelia defends the estate to which she was first assigned in 1904 from takeover. Sapru opposes her. 1933 case won on appeal
1929	Gives up legal practice, to concentrate on social work. Founds Bengal League of Social Service for Women with innovation of a purdahnashin secretary spear-heading work for villagers and mill workers
1930, 1932	Cornelia's lecture tours in USA, opposing Gandhi's programme
1931	Interview with Gandhi in London. Purdahnashin secretary subjected to political intimidation and gives up work for League. Cornelia's sister Susie dies and Cornelia called to wind up her affairs at Poona school. Abandons Bengal League and returns to England
1932	Dick and Cornelia support different delegations at and after Third Round Table Conference in London
1932–8	Cornelia makes fact-finding tours in India
1934	*India Calling*, her life recollected in tranquillity
1938	Cornelia and Alice join Dick, Mary and Pheroze in England. War brewing
1939–46	Second World War at Lincoln's Inn in London. War work amidst the bombs. Seeks to persuade nephew to take up law
1945	Hospitalised
July 6th 1954	Dies

CORNELIA'S PRINCIPAL BOOKS AND ABBREVIATIONS

1901   *Love and Life Behind the Purdah*, Oxford University Press, Delhi, 2003, stories about orthodox women, acclaimed in England on publication, new edition by Chandani Lokugé.

1904   *Sun-Babies* (First series): *Studies in the Child Life of India*, John Murray, London, the first three studies being drawn from the domestic servants of the joint household with Dick in Allahabad.

1908   *Between the Twilights*: *Being Studies of Indian Women by One of Themselves*, Harper, London, stories illustrating the position of women.

1916   *Indian Tales of the Great Ones*, Blackie, London, told to children of other countries.

1917   *The Purdahnashin*, Thacker, Spink, Calcutta, Cornelia's definitive account of the needs of the purdahnashin, written for Lady Chelmsford.

1918/1919   *Sun Babies* (Second series), Blackie, London, drawing on work with Cornelia's child wards since 1905.

1920   *Shubala – A Child-mother*, Baptist Mission Press, Calcutta, on child health, written for Lady Chelmsford.

1924   *Therefore*, Oxford University Press, London, an account of Cornelia's parents.

1932   *Susie Sorabji*, Oxford University Press, London, the life of Cornelia's sister Susie.

1934   *India Calling*, Nisbet, London, an autobiography, new editions by Chandani Lokugé, Oxford University Press, Delhi 2001, and by Elleke Boehmer, Nottingham 2004.

1936   *India Recalled*, on ceremonies in purdahnashin families, Hindu and (Ch 5) Muslim, reprinted as *India: Ancient Heritage* by SWP publishers, Delhi 1992, new edition in preparation by Sonita Sarkar.

1943   *Queen Mary's Book for India*, Harrap, London, to celebrate the Indian war effort in the Second World War.

F165/ followed by a number, here shortened to 165, refers to the main collection of Cornelia's papers in the British Library, Asia, Pacific and Africa Collections, European Manuscripts. I intend, as requested, to add the Richard Sorabji Collection to that collection, when I have finished with it.

419

GLOSSARY

A

Amir, Emir. Title of former rulers of Afghanistan

Ayah. Nursemaid, nanny, here 'nurse'

B

Basti. Village or hut

Begum. Muslim title for wife of Muslim ruler, occasionally ruler in her own right

Brahmin. Highest caste of Hindu

Brahmoism. A socially progressive revision of Hinduism, founded in Bengal in 1828 by Ram Mohun Roy, monotheistic and influenced by Christian Puritanism

C

Chaprassi, Chuprassi. Carrier of messages, wearer of badge, attendant, 'henchman'

Chattri. Domed turret

Chudder. Head to foot veil

Collector. Officer of the Indian Civil Service in charge of a district in his first major appointment

D

Dacoits. Assassin-robbers, here 'assassins'

Dak bungalow. Rest house for travellers

Dalits. Hindus below any of the castes ('the oppressed'), modern designation replacing 'Untouchables'

Dewan. Chief minister of ruler

Dharna. To sit dharna is to sit fasting unto death near the person you intend to blackmail

Dhoti. Male drapery over the legs and shoulders

Divisional Commissioner. Officer of the Indian Civil Service, above rank of Collector, in charge of a division or sub-province

Durbar. Assembly

E

Ekka. Ox cart without springs

G

Gaekwar. Title of the ruler of Baroda

H

Harijans. Gandhi's designation ('children of God') replacing 'Untouchables'

Howdah. Box with awning for carrying passengers on an elephant's back

K

Karma. The Hindu system of good and bad consequences incurred by conduct in an earlier incarnation

Khansama. Head of household management, here 'head servant'

Kharghosh. Rabbit

Khitmagar. Waiter, server at table, here 'table servant'

Kothi. Audience chamber or other premises

L

Legal Remembrancer. A legal official who supplied legal briefs on Government business

M

Maharaja. Ruling prince
Maharani. Wife or widow of Maharaja, occasionally may rule in own right
Mahout. Elephant driver
Mali. Gardener
Memsahibs. Wives of British in India
Mullah. Muslim priest
Munsiff. Local Indian magistrate for cases involving small sums of money

N

Naubat Khana. House of music
Nawab. Muslim ruler (male)

P

Pakora. Small pastry filled with meat or vegetable
Palanquin. A litter for carrying people over long distances
Palki. Palanquin
Puja, Pooja. Prayer
Punkah. A fan consisting of a curtain pulled by a string
Purdah, Purdahnashin. Literally, curtain, and one who sits behind the curtain – secluded woman

R

Raj. Royalty, rule
Rajbari. Palace, sometimes shortened to 'bari'
Reversioner. Person to whom an estate will revert, if anything befalls the heir.

S

Sadhu, Sadhuin. A type of holy man or woman

Sal tree. Tall and straight with sparse foliage like a birch, but with orange-brown trunk
Sanad. Legal permission
Sannyasi. Hindu ascetic
Shampini. Sprung bullock cart
Shias and Sunnis. The two main sects of Islam
Sub-Divisional Officer. Starting rank for members of the Indian Civil Service
Suttee, Sati. The burning alive of Hindu widows on their husband's funeral pyre

T

Tehsildar. Indian sub-collector for a sub-district. See Collector.
Thakur, Thakurani. Ruler of certain dependent States, and wife or widow
Thanedar. Indian officer in charge of local police station
Tonga. A low trap drawn by ponies
Tulsi. Sacred basil plant

U

Untouchables. Hindus below any of the castes, renamed by Gandhi as 'Harijans', children of God, by Ambedkar, 'Dalits' (the oppressed)

V

Vakil. Indian pleader trained in India, below the rank of barrister

Z

Zenana. Women's quarters in a household

NOTES

INTRODUCTION

1 When the papers come from my own collection of Cornelia's work, I shall say so, but I plan to convey virtually all those papers, as has been requested, to join the main collection in the British Library, when I have finished with them. The British Library collection of Cornelia's papers is in British Library, Asia, Pacific and Africa Collections (formerly Oriental and India Office Collections), European manuscripts F165/. I shall normally shorten F165 to 165.

2 Cornelia Sorabji, *India Calling*, Nisbet, London 1934, repr. Oxford University Press, Delhi, 2001, Trent editions, Nottingham 2004.

3 Suparna Gooptu, *Cornelia Sorabji, India's Pioneer Woman Lawyer*, Oxford University Press, New Delhi, 2006.

4 Chiefly the happy student letters home corresponding to Chapters 2 and 3 and the more agonised ones after the happiest years of her career were over corresponding to Chapters 15 and 17–21.

5 Gooptu, pp. 2, 6, 196, 205–207.

6 Sukanya Banerjee is one in 'Empire, nation and the professional citizen: reading Cornelia Sorabji's *India Calling*', *Prose Studies* 28, 2006, 291–317.

7 Chapters 1–3.

8 Chapters 4–16.

9 Chapters 17–20.

10 Chapters 4, 8 and 10.

11 Chapters 8 and 12.

12 Chapters 4, 8, 10 and 11.

13 Chapter 1.

14 Chapter 4.

15 Chapter 9.

16 Chapters 7, 8 and 10.

17 Chapters 14 and 15.

18 Chapter 13.

19 Chapter 9.

20 Chapters 21 and 22.

21 Chapter 21.

22 Chapters 4, 20 and 22.

23 This isolation is well brought out by Gooptu.

24 Letters home, 165/7, Nov 8, 1892, cf. 165/3, Aug 10, 1890; Letters to Blair, 165/24, Feb 10, 1904, cf. 165/21, Jun 27, 1901, where she wants him to keep her letters to serve as a diary in her old age.

CHAPTER 1

1 Letters home, British Library, Asia, Pacific and Africa (formerly Oriental and India Office Collections), European manuscripts F165/1, Sep 19, 1889. I shall normally shorten F165 to 165.

2 Personal diary, 165/98, Feb 9, 1936.

3 I shall be using three sources for Sorabji Kharsedji, except where otherwise indicated: Cornelia Sorabji, *Therefore*, Oxford University Press 1924, is an account of her parents. 165/205 contains Sorabji Kharsedji's 35-page account of his life. Farshid Namdaran kindly sent me a draft of part of his M.Th. dissertation, University of Edinburgh, on the Christian Mission to Zoroastrians. A fourth source that I shall use throughout Chapter 1 is Mrs E.F. Chapman, *Sketches of Some Distinguished Indian Women*, W.H. Allen, London and Calcutta 1891, Ch. 6, pp. 113–39, of which Dr Aroon Tikekar showed me his own copy, now in the library of the University of Mumbai. He draws on it himself in his 'Cornelia Sorabji (b. 1866-d. 1954): the emergence of a "new woman", in Mariam Dossai, Ruby Maloni, eds, *State Intervention and Popular Response, Western India in the Nineteenth Century*, Mumbai, 1999, Ch. 11, pp. 205–16.

4 John R. Hinnells, 'Social change and religious transformation among Bombay Parsis in the early twentieth century', in P. Slater, D. Wiebe, eds, *Traditions in Contact and Change*, Winnipeg 1983, pp. 105–125; cf. his 'Parsi attitudes to religious pluralism', in H. Coward, ed., *Modern Indian Responses to Religious Pluralism*, Albany NY 1987, Ch. 10, pp. 195–233.

5 F. Namdaran, Draft.

6 Namdaran has consulted five reports by Sorabji of his missionary work round Nasik from 1850 to 1861, held in Church Missionary Society records at Birmingham University Library, category no. C13/o46/1–5.

7 Namdaran, Draft and Cornelia, Letters home, 165/8, Jan 1893.

8 Letters to Lady Hobhouse, 165/16, Sep 19, 1894.

9 Richard Sorabji collection.

10 Letters to Elena, 165/31, Apr 10, 1919.

11 I take the evidence on Cornelia's mother, except where otherwise indicated, from Cornelia Sorabji, *Therefore*, *Susie Sorabji* and *India Calling* and Chapman, *Sketches, 1891*.

12 Chapman, *Sketches*, 1891 and Hobhouse appeal, reprinted by Suparna Gooptu, *Cornelia Sorabji, India's Pioneer Woman Lawyer*, Oxford University Press, Delhi, 2006, p. 224.

13 See Illustration, p. 9.

14 Manoranjan Jha, *Katherine Mayo and India*, New Delhi 1971, p. 92 makes sense only if it is talking about Franscina's mother, not Cornelia's mother, as dying early and being a Chamar. The claim is said to have been made in 1926 by Basil Blackett, finance member in the Government of India, talking to Katherine Mayo's associate, H. H. Field, as recorded in Field's diary. It is said to have been confirmed by the Maharaja of Datia, who was a friend of Cornelia's brother, Dick. Blackett's other claims are clearly mistaken,

however, so this one remains only a possibility. Cornelia herself ascribed Rajput blood to her mother's mother after discovering that the family name on her mother's side was to be found among the oldest Rajput feudal lords and was mentioned in Tod's classic *Annals and Antiquities of Rajasthan* of 1832 (Letter to Blair 165/25, Dec 12, 1906). But this is inconclusive given the character of the Rajput records.

15 Personal diary, 165/100, Dec 26, 1938; Records of Franscina's death, 165/204, including photographs of the inside of the cottage.
16 Letters home, 165/5, Dec 28, 1891.
17 Letters to Blair, 165/24, Feb 28, 1904.
18 *Susie Sorabji*, pp. 7–8.
19 *India Calling*, London pp. 8–9, Nottingham p.14, New Delhi p.16.
20 Letter to Jowett, Jun 24, 1893, original in the Balliol College, Oxford, collection, II C 1/155.
21 Letters home, 165/1, Dec 31, 1889; 165/2 May undated 1890.
22 Letters to Elena, 165/50, Jun 10, 1938.
23 *Susie Sorabji*, p. 5 and Chapman *Sketches* 1891.
24 Letters home 165/1, 1889.
25 Letters home 165/5, Sep 23, 1891.
26 Personal diary, 165/58, Nov 4, 1897.
27 Personal diary, 165/57, 58, 60, May 2, 1896; Jan and Feb 9, 1897. Feb 1, Mar 14, 1899.
28 Mary Sorabji, Opening of Victoria High School, Richard Sorabji collection.
29 Letters home, 165/4, Jan 6, 1891, said by the Kennaways of Escot House; cf. 165/1, Nov 24, 1889.
30 Letters home 165/1 from Sep 1889.
31 *Therefore*, pp. 68–70. On the plague in Poona, see also Letters to Lady Hobhouse, 165/16, 17, Mar 5, 1897, Aug 10, 1899.
32 Personal diary 165/58, Jul 9, 1897 and ff.
33 Letter to Mrs Darling 165/20, Oct 17, 1897.
34 Letter to Mrs Darling, 165/20, Oct 20, 1898.
35 Personal diary, 165/58, Feb 11, Mar 22, 1898; Letters to Mrs Darling, 165/20, Feb 17, 1898, from Dick; Mrs Darling to Dick, Jun 4, 1898, Richard Sorabji collection.
36 Cornelia Sorabji, 'An Indian Plague Story', *The Nineteenth Century*, Sep 1899, pp. 410–421, reprinted in her *Between the Twilights*, Harper, London, 1908.
37 Letter to Mrs Darling, 165/20, Nov 30, 1898.
38 Letters home, 165/1, 2 and 3, Sep 21, 1889, Feb 9 and Sep 24, 1890.
39 *India Calling*, London pp. 6–7, Nottingham p.12, New Delhi pp. 14–15.
40 Personal diary, 165/67, Oct 16 and 27, 1906.
41 See Appendix 1.
42 Chapter 5.
43 Chapter 9.
44 Chapter 16 and Appendix 1.
45 This chapter and Appendix 1.
46 Included, along with the prospectus of payments, in Letters to Lady Hobhouse, 165/17, pp. 245–255.

47 Jhama Gourlay, Florence Nightingale and the Health of the Raj, Ashgate, Aldershot 2003, esp. Chapters 9 and 10.

48 Except where otherwise indicated, the following material and that in Chapters 2 and 3 is taken from Cornelia's letters home to her Poona family, British Library 165/1–8.

49 Letters home, British Library, Asia, Pacific and Africa (formerly Oriental and India Office Collections), European manuscripts 165/1, Sep 19, 1889.

50 This photograph is reproduced in Antoinette Burton, At the Heart of Empire, University of California, Berkeley and Los Angeles 1998.

51 Letter from Lady Ford, 165/203, Dec 4, 1886.

CHAPTER 2

1 Cornelia Sorabji, India Calling, Ch. 1, Nisbet, London 1934, and Trent editions, Nottingham, p. 16, Oxford University Press, Delhi, 2001, p. 21.

2 India Calling, London, p. 14, Nottingham p. 16, Delhi p. 19.

3 Letter to Lady Hobhouse, 165/16, Jun 16, 1889.

4 India Calling, Oxford p. 33, Nottingham p. 26, Delhi p. 32.

5 India Calling, London p. 22, Nottingham p. 20, Delhi p. 25.

6 Antoinette Burton, At the Heart of Empire, University of California, Berkeley and Los Angeles 1998, p. 120.

7 165/2 begins here.

8 Nettleship's portrait is in the Corpus Christi Senior Common Room; Hunter's bust in the Indian Institute Library in Oxford.

9 By Mrs Hoare, wife of the MP for Norfolk, whose son was to play a role as Secretary of State for India in Cornelia's life later, Chapters 18 and 21.

10 Therefore, Oxford 1924, p. 61; India Recalled Ch. 18, pp. 269–270.

11 Letters to Lady Hobhouse, 165/16, Mar 5, 1897; Personal diary, 165/61, Sep 23, 1900.

12 Appendix 1.

13 See Chapter 12.

14 Personal diary, 165/84, Mar 28, 1922.

15 Cornelia Sorabji, India Recalled, pp. 268–271.

16 Letters home, 165/1, Sep 1, Oct 8, Dec 11, 1889; 165/2, Jan 26, Feb 2, 1890; 165/4, Jun 2, 1891; 165/6, Jul 15, 1892; Personal diary, 165/56, Jan 16, 1895.

17 Daniel Sanjiv Roberts, ' "Merely birds of passage": Lady Hariot Dufferin's travel writings and medical work in India, 1884–1888', Women's History Review 15, 2006, pp. 443–457, at 453.

18 Antoinette Burton, At the Heart of Empire, University of California, Berkeley and Los Angeles 1998, n. 52, p. 124.

19 Jhama Gourlay, Florence Nightingale and the Health of the Raj, Ashgate, Aldershot 2003, pp. 226–227.

20 India Calling, London pp. 78–80, Delhi pp. 62–63, Nottingham pp. 53–54.

21 Letters home 165/2, Jun 1, 1890.

22 Nov 19, 1890 is misplaced in 165/3, p. 277.

23 Letter home from Dick, November 16, 1890, included with Cornelia's letters in 165/3.

24 165/3 begins here.

25 Cornelia Sorabji, Letters to Falkner Blair, June 19, 1901, British Library 165/21.

26 Chapter 7.

27 Jane Abdy, Charlotte Gere, *The Souls*, London 1984, p. 10. See also Angela Lambert, *Unquiet Souls*, London 1984.

28 See Richard Symonds, *Oxford and Empire*, Macmillan 1986, Oxford 1991.

29 Letters to Blair, 165/22, Jun 19, 1902.

30 Letters to family, 165/11, Mar 13, 1918.

31 165/5, Nov 28, 1891; 165/6, Feb 14, Mar 6, 1892.

32 Personal diary, 165/59, Mar 24, 1898.

33 165/1, Nov 3, 1889; 165/7, Dec 13, 1892.

34 165/4 begins here.

35 165/4, Jan 18, 1891; 165/5, Nov 28, 1891; 165/6, Jan 21, 1892.

36 Letter to Mrs Darling, 165/20, Feb 17, 1898.

37 Letter home, 165/6, Jan 21, 1892; 165/7, Dec 25, 1892.

38 Cornelia Sorabji, *India Calling*, London 1934, pp. 50–51; Delhi 2001, pp. 43–44; Nottingham 2004, p. 36.

39 Chapter 12.

40 Jhama Gourlay, *Florence Nightingale and the Health of the Raj*, Ashgate, Aldershot 2003, esp. pp. 237–238.

41 See Chapter 6.

42 Letters to Elena 165/41, Oct 6, 1926.

43 165/6, Jan 21, 1892.

44 Chapter 22.

45 165/5 begins here.

46 *India Calling*, London p. 33, Nottingham p. 26, Delhi p. 32.

47 165/6, Jul 15, 1892.

48 See e.g. M. Richter, *The Politics of Concience:T.H.Green and his Age*, London 1964, Ch. 3.

49 Richard Symonds, *Oxford and Empire*, London 1986, p. 24, and Oxford 1991.

50 Antoinette Burton, *At the Heart of Empire*, University of California Press, Berkeley, Los Angeles 1998, Chapter 3, 'Cornelia Sorabji in Victorian Oxford' pp. 110–151, referring to Rukhmabai, 'Indian child marriages: an appeal to the British Government', *The New Review* 16, 1890, pp. 263–269.

51 Jhama Gourlay, *Florence Nightingale and the Health of the Raj*, Ashgate, Aldershot 2003, pp. 226; 232.

52 165/7, Sep 20, 1892.

53 Appendix 1.

54 165/7, Oct 27, 1892.

55 165/8, Mar 1, 1893.

56 Chapter 4.

57 165/6 begins here.

58 165/7, Sep 20, 1892.

59   Family information.

60   She gives accounts in her letters home of June 16 and 23, 1892 (165/6, pp. 80–85), and much later in *India Calling*, London pp. 27–29, Nottingham p. 24, Delhi pp. 29–30.

61   *India Calling*, London pp. 28–29, Delhi, p. 29, Nottingham p. 24.

62   Letters home, 165/6, Jun 16, 1892.

63   Letters home, 165/6, Jun 23, 1892.

64   E.g. *India Calling*, London pp. 22–28, Delhi pp. 26–29, Nottinham pp. 20–24.

65   Letters to Blair, 165/23, Jun 12, 1903.

66   Letters from Jowett, 165/18, May 21, 1892 and May 6, 1893, as well as two letters in the Balliol College collection, although most of the letters he received were destroyed as he wished.

67   Cornelia, 'Benjamin Jowett – Master of Balliol College, some recollections', *The Nineteenth Century* 1903, proof pages 1–9, quoting his letter of 21 September 1892, of which the original is in Balliol College library, Oxford.

CHAPTER 3

1   Except where otherwise indicated, material in Chapters 2 and 3 is taken from Cornelia's letters home to her Poona family, British Library 165/1–8.

2   Chapter 2.

3   Letters home, 165/5, Sep 9 and 23, 1891. The letter was borrowed from Cornelia's mother by a Mr Kirkham, who may have gained leverage after favourably assessing her Poona school for a grant from the Church Missionary Society.

4   Letters home, 165/7, Nov 8, 1892, cf. 165/3, Aug 10, 1890; Letters to Blair, 165/24, Feb 10, 1904, cf. 165/21, Jun 27, 1901, where she wants him to keep her letters to serve as a diary in her old age.

5   Dick Sorabji, Allahabad Dec 31, 1918, Bluebird series of letters to children, privately printed, Richard Sorabji collection; visit announced, Kirkham's appropriation, 165/6, Jul 15, 1892, Nov 8, 1892 *India Calling*, London pp. 48–49, Nottingham p. 35, Delhi p. 42. Funeral 165/7, Oct 18, 1892.

6   Letters home, 165/5, Oct 18, 1892.

7   165/8, Feb 16, 1893; 'A new story about Florence Nightingale' typewritten account in Richard Sorabji collection of the story as told by Cornelia to a group of American friends. See also *India Calling*, London, Delhi, pp. 31–32, Nottingham pp. 25–26.

8   Chapter 1.

9   165/7, Aug 4, 1892.

10   Therefore, Oxford 1924, p. 58.

11   *India Calling*, London p. 38, Nottingham p. 29, Delhi p. 35.

12   165/8, Mar 1 and 10, 1893; Letters to Elena 165/35, Feb 3, 1921.

13   165/7.

14   Family information.

15   Chapter 1.

16 *Therefore*, Oxford University Press 1924, p. 61 and *passim*, F. Namdaran, M.Th. dissertation, Edinburgh University, on the Christian Mission to Zoroastrians. See also Chapter 1.

17 *India Calling*, London p. 52, Delhi p. 44, Nottingham p. 37.

18 *Susie Sorabji*, p. 7.

19 *Therefore*, Oxford University Press 1924, e.g. pp. 17, 61, 77.

20 *India Calling*, London p. 14, Nottingham p. 16, Delhi p. 19.

21 In the 1890s, there were 12 rupees to the pound.

22 Chapter 16.

23 The Indian Female Normal School Society.

24 For the preceding see 165/1, Oct 8, 1889; 165/3, Aug 4, 1890; 165/4, Mar 10, Apr 12, 1891; 165/7, Sep 29, 1892; 165/8, Mar 10, 1893; Personal diary, 165/57, Oct 24, 1896; *Therefore*, Oxford 1924, pp. 59 and 61.

25 Letters to Elena 165/46, Apr 2, 1931.

26 See Appendix 1.

27 Appendix 1.

28 All this is in Alice's book, A. M. Pennell, *Pennell of the Afghan Frontier*, London 1914, pp. 345–453. There is more in his own, *Among the Wild Tribes of the Afghan Frontier*, London 1909.

29 Alice in *Mercy and Truth* 1916, p. 282.

30 Appendix 1.

31 *India Calling*, London pp. 174–175, Delhi pp. 128–129, Nottingham pp. 110–111.

32 That was before he had created his own village for Dalits ('Harijans', as he called them), which impressed her in 1936, Chapter 21.

33 For these two incidents, Personal diary, 165/70, Jun 14, 1909; Letters to Elena 165/41, Dec 31, 1926; 165/51, Oct 2 and Nov 26, 1939.

CHAPTER 4

1 Personal diary, 165/84, Aug 27, 1922.

2 Letters home, 165/7, Dec 13, 1892; Personal diary, 165/56, Oct 12 and 21, 1895; 165/57 May 3, 1896.

3 Letters home, 165/4, Mar 10, 1891.

4 On the rank of Collector, see Chapter 10.

5 Edward Blunt, *The Indian Civil Service*, I. C. S., London 1937, pp. 48–53; L.S.S.O' Malley, *The Indian Civil Service, 1601–1930*, London 1931, pp. 83–84, 218–219.

6 Letters to Lady Hobhouse, 165/16, Oct 13, 1895, printed in Klaus Stierstorfer, *Women Writing Home, 1700–1920*, London 2006.

7 Chapters 7 and 10.

8 Personal diary, 165/57, May 3, Nov 15–17, 24, Dec 16, 19–20, 30, 1896.

9 Letters home, 165/7, Nov 11, 1892. Lord Reay had been Chancellor of Bombay University.

10 Letters to Lady Hobhouse, 165/16, Nov 16, 1893, in *Women Writing Home*.

11 Letter to Jowett, June 24, 1893, original in the Balliol College, Oxford, collection, II C 1/155. See also Letters to Lady Hobhouse, 165/16, Aug 9, 1893–Feb 16, 1894, in *Women Writing Home*, for thieves and revolvers Aug 9, Nov 16, Dec 6, 1893.

12 Letters to Lady Hobhouse, 165/16, Jan 18, 1894 in *Women Writing Home*.

13 Letters to Lady Hobhouse, 165/16, Apr 18, 1894 in *Women Writing Home*.

14 Personal diary, 165/56, 57, for these dates.

15 *India Calling*, London p. 64, Delhi p. 52, Nottingham p. 46.

16 Letters to Lady Hobhouse, 165/16, May 7, 1896; and with variations in *India Calling*, London 1934, pp. 94–99, Delhi pp. 75–77, Nottingham pp. 63–66; Cornelia, 'The elephant named "Folded Rosebud"', *St Nicholas*, February 1924, pp. 399–404, in Richard Sorabji collection. What Cornelia first understood was that it was not the Raja who was at fault, but the elephant's custodian, who wanted to sell off the elephant's land, and who was claiming that the original elephant was dead. There are also discrepancies in Cornelia's accounts about the number of generations back that the grant was made. The discrepancies in this case may have been due to the original letter having been written before it was clear who was telling the truth, and before deeds and the identity of a long-lived elephant could be checked. Other changes are merely literary: the patting of the bulldog got moved from the preliminary meeting with the Raja to the official hearing, and the musical box changed location.

17 Personal diary, 165/57, Jul 1–3, 1896; Letters to Lady Hobhouse, 165/16, Jul 16, 1896; and with variations in *India Calling*, London, 59–63, Delhi pp. 49–52, Nottingham pp. 43–45. The variations in Cornelia's descriptions of this case have been ably noted and discussed by Mary Jane Mossman, 'Cornelia Sorabji: a "Woman in Law" in India in the 1890s', *Canadian Journal of Women and the Law*, 16, 2004, pp. 54–85, at 80–82. The unparalleled suspense of waiting for the jury is similarly described both early and late. But was the accused the victim's wife, or friends and relatives of the *criminal*? Again, was the victim beaten to death, or killed with a cutting instrument for vegetables? Mossman concludes that *India Calling* may have amalgamated several cases, either to protect privacy or for literary reasons and in a way that would imply the justice of British India. Nonetheless, she points out, the truth remains that Cornelia was the first.

18 *India Calling*, London pp. 86–93, Delhi pp. 68–73, Nottingham pp. 59–63; Personal diary, 165/68, Apr 29, 1907; and (with a rather different-sounding account of early stages) Letters to Lady Hobhouse, 165/16, Nov 2, 1894, May 7, Jun 18, 1896, 165/17, Apr 12, 1900, Jan 12, 1905, the first three printed in Klaus Stierstorfer, ed., *Women Writing Home, 1700–1920*, London 2006; recalled much later in papers on Dholpur case 1935–1944, 165/138.

19 *India Calling*, London pp. 229–230, Delhi p. 165, Nottingham p. 148.

20 *India Calling*, London p. 84, Delhi p. 66, Nottingham pp. 56–57.

21 Personal diary, 165/58, Jun 15, Sep 9, 1897.

22 Cornelia, 'The legal status of women in India', *The Nineteenth Century*, Nov 1898, 854–866.

23 Personal diary, 165/58, Mar 4, 9, 11, 1897.

24 Letters to Dick and Family, Jan 4, 1933, Richard Sorabji collection.

25 Letters to Elena, 165/50, Jan 13, Feb 23, Mar 12, 1938.

26 Personal diary, 165/58, Mar 18–19, Apr 23, 1897.

27 Cornelia, 'Fleetfoot', in *Sun-Babies*, First series, John Murray, London 1904, pp. 47–73.

28 Personal diary, 165/58, 59 and 60, Apr 4–5, 17, 1897; May 19, 1898; Jan 23, 1899; Letters to Blair, 165/21, Dec 12, 1901; *India Calling*, London p. 105, Delhi p. 81, Nottingham p. 69; *Sun-Babies*, First series, John Murray, London 1904, Chapters 1 and 2.

29 Chapter 5.

30 Dick, Bluebird series of letters to children, Allahabad, series 1, Jun 10, 1918; series 2, Apr 19, 1920, privately printed, Richard Sorabji collection.

31 Personal diary, 165/58 and 60, Mar 18–19, Apr 5, 7, 8, 10,12, 14–17, 27, May 10, Oct 30, Nov 2, 30, 1897, Jan 23, 1899; Letters to Mrs Darling, 165/20, Oct 20, 1898; Other correspondence of Cornelia 1890–1944, 165/54, p. 9.

32 Letters to Dick and family, Jan 4, 1933, Richard Sorabji collection.

33 Personal diary 165/58, Mar 19, 25, 27, Apr 6, 13, 18, 1897.

34 Personal diary 165/58 and 59, Mar 26, 1897; Feb 15 and 25, 1898; Letters to Mrs Darling, 165/20, Mar 9, Nov 2, 1899.

35 Personal diary 165/58–60, Apr 17 and 27, May 1 and 13, Jun 2, 11 and 22, Jul 15, Nov 4, 16 and 27, Dec 1, 3 and 6–7, 1897, Jan 1, 10 and 26–27, Feb 21, Mar 9, 15, 27 and 29, Apr 12, 14, 16, 18, 20–21, 23 and 26, May 5–7, 9, 27, 30, Jun 11–12, Nov 10, 28, Dec 4, 6, 7, 14, 1898, Jan 12, 18–20, Feb 1, Feb 14, Mar 10, 1899; Letters to Mrs Darling, 165/20, Feb 24, Dec 6, 1898.

36 Personal diary, Jul 1–2, 1911; Letters to Elena Dec 3, 1919, Jul 25, 1928. Wallach stands behind Dick in the photograph of Dick's wedding, p. 283.

37 Chapter 7.

38 Letters to Mrs Darling, 165/20, Feb 17, Mar 24, Dick's letter to Mrs Darling Feb 17; Letters to Lady Hobhouse 165/16, Mar 30, 1898; *Sun-Babies*, First series, John Murray, London 1904, pp. 22–49.

39 Chapter 7.

40 Chapter 5.

41 Personal diary, 165/60, Feb 10, 1899, Letters to Mrs Darling 165/20, Feb 15, 1899.

42 Cornelia *India Recalled*, London 1936, 193–197.

43 Personal diary, 165/58, Apr 26, 28, 30, May 8, 12, 1897.

44 Personal diary, 165/ 59, Feb 11, Mar 22, 1898; Letters to Mrs Darling, 165/20, Feb 17, 1898, from Dick; Mrs Darling to Dick, Jun 4, 1898, Richard Sorabji collection. Dick got a further Cawnpore case in 1900, Personal diary, 165/61, Aug 22, 1900.

45 Personal diary, 165/60, Mar 7, 1899; Letters to Mrs Darling, 165/20, Mar 9, 1899.

46 Letters to Lady Hobhouse, 165/16, Jul 6, 1899.

47 For the above, see Personal diary 165/57 and 58, Apr 14, and 27, May 10 and 15, Jun 1, Jul 16–19, 1897, Jan 19, 1898, Apr 4–10, May 1, 1899, Letters to Mrs Darling, 165/20, May 26, 1898, Jan 11, Feb 3 and 9, Mar 9 and 23, Apr 6 and 27, Jul 6, 1899; Letters to Lady Hobhouse, 165/16, May or Jun 13, Jul 6, 20, Aug 10, 15, 1899; Letters to Blair, Jun 27, 1901; *India Calling*, London 100–101, Delhi 79, Nottingham 67.

48 Letters to Blair, 165/21, Jun 27, 1901.

49 Chapter 5.

50 Letters to Mrs Darling, 165/20, Feb 9, Apr 27, May 4 and 25, Jun 1, Jul 6, Aug 3, 1899; Letters to Blair, 165/22, May 11, Jun 19, 1902.

51 Letters to Blair, 165/22, May 11, Jun 19, 1902.

52 Letters to Mrs Darling, 165/20, Aug 7, 15, Oct 24, 1918, and a missing one lost in the post; Letters to Lady Hobhouse, 165/16, original of Oct 5, 1899, pp. 355–356, 358, last page of 165/16, original of Nov 21, 1899, pp. 366–374 and 381 to end (out of order); Letters to Lady Hobhouse, 165/17, fair copy of Aug 15, 19, Oct 5, 1899, typed up in a later year, pp. 206–226; Hobhouse letters edited with reference to Darling letters in, 'Concerning an imprisoned Rani', *The Nineteenth Century*, 1901, pp. 623–638, which corresponds roughly to letters of Aug 15, 19 and Nov 21, 1899; Personal diary 165/60, Aug 17–20, Oct 16–19; reminiscence in *India Calling*, London pp. 104–115, Delhi pp. 82–89, Nottingham 69–75, omits some details of the journeys and gives a different account of switching the palanquins. A shorter version is included in 'Portraits of some Indian women', *The Nineteenth Century*, 1905, repr. in *Between the Twilights*, Harper, London, 1908, pp. 128–149, and an extra detail in *Shubala – A Child Mother*, Baptist Mission Press, Calcutta, 1920, p. 18.

53 See Chapter 10, p. 1 for further details.

54 For another description of the palanquin, see Work diary, Jan 29, 1917, Richard Sorabji collection.

55 Letters to Lady Hobhouse, 165/16, Aug 19, 1899. The thirst is not mentioned in the edited version in *The Nineteenth Century*.

56 Letters to Lady Hobhouse, 165/16, Aug 19, 1899.

57 Letters to Lady Hobhouse, 165/16, Aug 19, 1899.

58 Letter to Lady Hobhouse, but to Mrs Darling she wrote by mistake 'Khitmagar' (table servant).

59 Letters to Mrs Darling, 165/20, Oct 24, 1899.

60 Letter to Mrs Darling, 165/20, Oct 24, 1899.

61 Letters to Lady Hobhouse, 165/16, Nov 21, 1899.

62 Letters to Lady Hobhouse, 165/17, Mar 10, 21, Jul 17, Oct 5, Nov 21, 1900.

CHAPTER 5

1 Personal diary, 165/58, Mar 27, 1897; Letters to Mrs Darling, 165/20, Feb 15, 1899; Letters to Blair, Nov 28, 1901.

2 Personal diary, 165/58 and 59, Dec 27 and 30, 1897; Jan 2, 1898.

3 Personal diary, 165/59, Jan 22, 1898; Letters to Mrs Darling, 165/20, Jan 25, 1898; Letters to Lady Hobhouse, 165/20, Jan 20, Feb 10, 1898.

4 The agonies are recorded in her personal diary from Jan 11, 1898 until her exile, but the attractive side of the relationship is explained in the letters to Mrs Darling.

5 Personal diary, 165/59, May 15, 1898; Letters to Mrs Darling, 165/20, May 15, 1898.

6 *India Calling*, London pp. 42–49 and 117, Delhi pp. 38–42 and 90, Nottingham pp. 31–35 and 79.

7 Letters to Blair, 165/22 and 23, Jun 4, Jul 10, Aug 28, 1902, Dec 26, 1903.

8 Letters to Blair, 165/21 and 24, Dec 12, 1901; Feb 27, 1904.

9 Letters to Blair, 165/23, Jan 15, 1903; Personal diary, 165/64, Jan 10, 1903.

10 Letters to Blair, 165/21, Dec 12, 1901.

11 Letters to Blair, 165/22 and 23, May 18, 1902, May 14, 1903.

12 Letters to Blair, 165/23, Jul 23, 1903.

13 Letters to Blair, 165/21, May 13, 1901; cf. 165/22, May 18, 1902.

14 Letters to Blair, 165/24, Mar 4, 1904.

15 Letters to Blair, 165/22 and 24, Dec 3, 1902, Jan 7, 1904.

16 Personal diary, 165/63, Feb 1–2, 1902.

17 Letters to Blair, 165/21, Dec 25, 1901.

18 Letters to Blair, 165/21 and 22, 1901 and Jul 3, 1902.

19 Personal diary and Letters to Blair for this period.

20 Letters to Blair, 165/22, May 8, 1902.

21 Letters to Blair, 165/22 and 23, May 11, Aug 14 and 20, 1902, Jul 24, 1903; Personal diary, 165/63 and 64, Aug 16–22, 1902, Jul 17–23, 1903.

22 Letters to Blair, 165/23, Aug 17–Oct 3, 1903; *India Calling*, London p. 41, Delhi p. 37, Nottingham pp. 30–31.

23 Letters to Blair, 165/23, Oct 3, 1903.

24 Letters to Blair, 165/24 and 25, Aug 26 and 30, 1904, Oct 12, 1905; Personal diary, 165/65 and 66, Dec 27 and 30, 1904, Mar 25, 1905.

25 Letters to Blair, 165/25, Mar 23, Apr 4, 19, Jun 26, 1905, Aug 8, 1906; Personal diary, 165/66, Apr 7, 1905. The photograph of Cornelia with horse and buggy in the foreground is in 165/212.

26 Personal diary, 165/68, Feb 13, 1907.

27 Work diary, 165/101, May 25, 1907, p. 76ff.

28 Personal diary, 165/68, Jun 4 and 26, Aug 12, 1907.

29 Letters to Blair, 165/25, Jul 6 and 12, 1905.

30 The letters are in: Other correspondence of Cornelia Sorabji 1880s–1944, 165/54, nine letters from 1908 to March 1909, and four from 1911, pp. 22–43. All other information is from the Personal diary for the periods and dates indicated, 165/69–72.

31 Personal diary, 165/72, Jun 18, 1911.

32 Other correspondence of Cornelia Sorabji 1880–1944, 165/54, p. 41. The following information for 1912 is taken from the Personal diary for that year, 165/73.

33 Booklet of Cornelia's poems, Richard Sorabji collection.

34 Chapter 15.

35 Chapter 15.

36 Personal diary 165/74, 1913.

37 Personal diary, 165/77, Jan 8–16, 1916. Chapter 14.

38 Work diary, 165/108, Oct 12, 1914. Chapter 14.

39 Letters to Elena in Richard Sorabji collection, Apr 27, Jun 17, Aug 6, 1915. Chapter 13.

40 Personal diary, 165/77, Aug 19, Nov 28, Dec 4, 22, 26, 1916. Chapter 14.

41 Personal diary, 165/78, Apr 9–10 1917.

42 Other correspondence of Cornelia Sorabji 1880–1944, 165/54, Sep 18, 1911, p.45.

43 Personal diary, 165/80, Jan 7, 11, 13, Mar 4, 1919.

44 Letters to Lady Hobhouse, 165/16, Mar 30, 1898.

CHAPTER 6

1 Letters to Blair, 165/23, Feb 4, May 14, 1903.

2 Chapter 2.

3 Una Taylor is described in Letters to Falkner Blair, starting in 165/21, Nov 28, 1901, and in her Personal diary, starting in 165/62, Dec 5, 1901.

4 Personal diary, 165/63, Apr 30, 1902; Letters to Falkner Blair, 165/22, May 2, 1902.

5 Chapter 5.

6 Letters to Blair, 165/22, Apr 17, 1902.

7 Letters to Blair, 165/22, May 11, 1902.

8 But spreading – she also heard one the next year, Letters to Blair, 165/23, Feb 12, 1903.

9 Letters to Blair, 165/22, Apr 17, 1902.

10 Letters to Blair, 165/22, Jun 12, 1902.

11 Letters to Blair, 165/22, Jun 12, 1902.

12 Letters to Blair, 165/22, 165/25, Jun 4, 12, 1902, Apr 4, 1905; Personal diary, 165/66, Apr 2, 1905.

13 Letters to Blair, 165/22, Jun 19, 1902.

14 Letters to Blair, 165/22, Jun 27, 1902.

15 Richard Sorabji collection.

16 Letters to Blair, 165/22, Jun 19, 1902.

17 *India Calling*, London p. 47; Delhi pp. 40–41; Nottingham pp. 33–34.

18 Letters to Blair, 165/24, Apr 20, 1904.

19 I thank Isabelle Onians for the information.

20 Letters to Blair, 165/22 and 24, Apr 17, 25, May 2, 11, 18, Jun 4, 12, 19, 1902, Apr 20, 1904; *India Calling*, London pp. 46–48, Delhi pp. 40–42, Nottingham pp. 33–35.

21 Richard Sorabji collection.

22 See photograph, p. 108.

23 Letters to Elena, 165/47, Jul 8, 1933.

24 Letters to Blair, 165/22, Mar 27, 1902.

25 Letters to Blair, 165/22, 23, Aug 14, 28, 1902; Nov 26, 1903.

26 Visiting book, somewhat despoiled, Richard Sorabji collection.

27 Letters to Blair, 165/23, Nov 26, 1903.

28 Letters to Blair, 165/22 and 23, Mar 27, Jun 12, Jul 3, 17, Aug 14, 28, 1902, Jan 15, Nov 26, 1903.

29 Letters to Blair, 165/22, Jun 27, 1902.

30 Letters to Blair, 165/21 and 23, Jun 19, 1901, Jan 30, Feb 4, Apr 3, 1903; Personal diary, 165/64, May 20, 1903.

31 Letters to Blair, 165/22, Oct 3, 11, Nov 15, 1902.

32 Personal diary, 165/63 and 64, Nov 28, Dec 6, 1902, Oct 17, 24, Nov 8, 1903.

33 Cornelia Sorabji, *Love and Life Behind the Purdah, Freemantle*, London 1901, reprinted C. Lokugé, ed., Oxford University Press, New Delhi 2003.

34 Letter to Blair, 165/22, May 30, 1902.

35 Personal diary, 165/64, Jan 23, 1903.

36 Letter to Blair, 165/22, Jan 16, 1902.

37 Letter to Blair, 165/22, Jan 23, 1902.

38 Letter to Blair, 165/22, May 30, Jun 12, 1902.

39 Letter to Blair, 165/22, Jul 17, Dec 18, 1902.

40 Chapter 10.

41 Letters to Blair, 165/21 and 22, Dec 25, 1901, Jan 9, 1902.

42 Chapter 1.

43 The Kennaway papers are now in the Devon record office at Exeter and Adam Matthew publications has a microfilm for sale.

44 Personal diary, 165/80, Mar 18, 1919.

45 Letters to Blair, 165/22, Sep 30, 1902; Letters to Lady Hobhouse, 165/17, May 1, 1905.

46 Letters to Blair, 165/22, Aug 14, 1902.

47 Letters to Blair, 165/23, May 14, 1903; Personal diary, 165/64, May 8, 1903.

48 Letters to Blair, 165/22, Aug 7, Dec 18, 1902, Personal diary, 165/67, Jan 30, 1906. Her letters to Cornelia from 1902–30 are preserved in 165/26.

49 Personal diary, 165/64, May 5, Jul 16, Oct 10, 1903; Letters to Blair, 165/23, Feb 4, Apr 23, 1903.

50 Chapter 7.

CHAPTER 7

1 Chapter 4.

2 Report by Cornelia to Court of Wards 1915–16, 165/132, Presidency division, p. 8.

3 Anand A. Yang, 'An institutional shelter: the Court of Wards in late Nineteenth Century Bihar', *Modern Asian Studies* 13, 1979, 247–264.

4 Report by Cornelia to Court of Wards 1915–16, 165/132, Chota Nagpur division, p. 20.

5 Letters on the Purdahnashin question, 165/119, 1902–3.

6 Letters on the Purdahnashin question, 165/119, pp. 17–19, 21–22, 26, 44–53, 56–61a, 61b, 65, 69–71, 73–74, 87ff., 92 and 92a–94; Letters to Blair, 165/22, Apr 17, Jun 4, Aug 7, 1902.

7 Letters on the Purdahnashin question, 165/119, pp. 3, 11–12, 32–35, 38, 92a–94; Letters to Blair, 165/22 and 24, Nov 13, 1902, Feb 20 and 21, 1904.

8 Letters to Blair, 165/23, Feb 20, Jun 19, 1903.

9 Letters to Blair, 165/22, Apr 17 and 25, 1902.

10 Letters to Blair, 165/22, Jun 19, Jul 17, 1902, Letters on the Purdahnashin question, 165/119, p. 30.

11 Chapter 4.

12 Letters to Blair, 165/22, 23 and 24, Feb 13, 20, Mar 7, Apr 17, Jun 19, Jul 10 and 17, Aug 7, Oct 23 and 30, Nov 28, 1902, Jan 23, Jan 30, Feb 4, 1903, Jan 12, 1904; Letters on the Purdahnashin question, 165/119, p. 87ff.; Personal diary, 165/66, Jan 4, 1905.

13 Chapter 2.

14 Letters to Blair, 165/22, Aug 7 and 14, Sep 4, Nov 28, 1902.

15 Chapter 4.

16 Letters to Blair, 165/22, Jan 23, Feb 6, 28, Apr 17 and 25, May 2, 1902; Letters on the Purdahnashin question, 165/119, p. 25 (Nov 20, 1902).

17 Chapter 4.

18 Chapters 4 and 6.

19 Several drafts of it exist, Letters on the Purdahnashin question, 165/119, pp. 73–84, 120–127, 136–152; Official correspondence on conditions of employment, 165/124, pp. 14–15.

20 All *The Times* entries for the day are reprinted in 165/124, Official correspondence on conditions of employment, pp. 16–18.

21 Letters to Blair, 165/22, May 8 and 30, Oct 12, 16 and 30, 1902.

22 Reprinted in 165/124, Official correspondence on conditions of employment, pp. 15–16.

23 'Women and the law in India', *Juridical Review*, 1903, with review by John P. Coldstream; 'The Purdahnashin question', *India Review*, 1903, Madras, which gave rise to a very supportive response from a Parsee lady, Khurshedree Shavaksha, who had taken evidence from two secluded widows of a Nawab; Letter in *The Times of India*, 'Purdahnashins. The proposed legal safeguards', which attracted the editor's opposition, but support from one lady. See Letters on the Purdahnashin question, 165/119, pp. 17–19, 21–22, 36, 87ff., 92–94, 96 (December 1902, January, February, July 1903); Letters to Blair, 165/22 and 23, Nov 28, Dec 25, 1902, Jan 15, Feb 4, 1903.

24 *The Queen* had a favourable editorial on October 11 1903, and a lawyer wrote a supportive article in the *Indian Ladies' Magazine* for 1903. Letters on the Purdahnashin question, 165/119, pp. 99 (Oct 11, 1902), 92a (1903); Letters to Blair, 165/22, Oct 16, Nov 6, 1902.

25 Letters on the Purdahnashin question, 165/119, pp. 92–94; Letters to Blair, 165/22, Oct 23 and 30, Nov 13, 1902.

26 Letters to Blair, 165/22, Nov 20 and 28, 1902, Jan 9 and 15, 1903.

27 Chapter 2.

28 Letters to Blair, 165/23, Oct 12, 23, and 29, Nov 19, Dec 9, 1902; Letters on the Purdahnashin question, 165/119, p. 7.

29 Letters to Blair, 165/24, Jan 12, 13, 1904; Letters to Lady Hobhouse, 165/17, Dec 29, 1903, Feb 1, 1904.

30 *India Calling*, London p. 122, Delhi p. 93, Nottingham p. 81.

31 The Ceylon trip is described in Letters to Blair, 165/24, Jan 7, 12, 17, 21, 23, 25, 29, Feb 1, 4, 10, and 12, 1904, Personal diary, 165/64–65, Dec 4, 1903 to Feb 17, 1904, with further comment on the Watson's bank crash, Feb 28, Mar 3 and 14, 1904 and the chamois leather sheets, Letters to Lady Hobhouse, 165/17, Dec 11, 1903.

32 Chapter 2.

33 Letters to Blair, 165/24, Feb 18, 20, 21, 24, 28, Mar 9; Letters to Lady Hobhouse, 165/17, Feb 23, 1904.

34 Personal diary, 165/65, Jan 15, Jul 2, 1904. See Chapters 20 and 23.

35 The opinion-seeking in the South is described in Letters to Blair, 165/24, Feb 18, 20, 21, 24, and 28, Mar 9, 1904.

36 Personal diary, 165/65, Feb 27–30, 1904; Letters to Blair, 165/24, Feb 21, 1904.

37 Letters to Blair, 165/24, Mar 9, 1904.

38 Personal diary, 165/65, Apr 12, 15–17, Aug 17, 18, and 31, 1904.

39 Chapter 17.

40 *India Calling*, London p. 177, Delhi p. 130, Nottingham p. 115; 165/124, Official correspondence on terms of employment, p. 14.

41 The interviews are described, Personal diary, 165/65, Mar 25–29, 1904; Letters to Blair, 165/24, Mar 28–30, 1904.

42 See Personal diary for April and start of May 1904.

43 Letters to Blair, 165/25, Nov 25, 1905. After 1905, with Curzon's experimental division of Bengal, the area would be even larger. See Chapter 10.

44 Personal diary, 165/65, Mar 29, 1904.

45 Photograph in Richard Sorabji collection.

46 Personal diary, 165/65, May 6–18, 1904; Letters to Elena, 165/30, Aug 8, 1917; *India Calling*, London pp. 124, 180–182, Delhi pp. 94, 132–133, Nottingham pp. 82–83, 117.

47 Two political representatives of the orthodox, Malaviya and M. K. Acharya, are discussed in Chapter 21. For use of the term 'orthodox', see e.g. Rajmohan Gandhi, Mohandas, New Delhi 2006, pp. 377; 379.

48 Letter to *The Times*, 'Purdahnashins in India', Sep 20, 1902.

49 Chapter 2.

50 Letters to Elena, 165/50, Jan 6, 1937.

51 Chapter 19. For Cornelia's earlier social work for the poor, see Chapter 12. She also defended a peasant against encroachment by a British mill owner in Kasimbazar.

52 Tajhat in Chapter 8.

53 Work diary, 165/109–110, Nov 11, 1918; Letters to Elena, 165/33, 34, Oct 30, early November (undated), Nov 13, Dec 10, 1919, Jan 14, Mar 11, Apr 20, Aug 19, 1920.

54 'Effects of ignoring Cornelia's expertise'. Chapter 15.

55 Churamaon in contrast with Narhan, Chapter 8.

56 Peri Banu was the ward, Chapter 14.

57 At Kasimbazar, Chapter 8. See also under 'Hardships of secluded women', in Chapter 12.

58 At Ramgarh, Chapter 10.

59 The Kasimbazar cases are supplemented in 'Education through custom against custom', in Chapter 12.

60 'Once a corpse, always a corpse' in Chapter 12.

61 'Success with Court of Wards estates' in Chapter 17.

62 'Adoption and peacocks', Chapter 10.

63 'Wills inside caskets' in Chapter 10.

64 'Janjira' in Chapter 23.

65 Narhan and Churamaon in Chapter 8.

66 Tajhat, Chapter 8.

67 'Ideas about reincarnation', Chapter 12.

68 Churamaon, Chapter 8.

69 'A case of succession: bones, mines and parrots', Chapter 10.

CHAPTER 8

1 Letters to Elena, 165/34, Oct 13, 1920, quoted by Suparna Gooptu, *Cornelia Sorabji*, pp. 104–105.

2 Chapter 19.

3 *India Recalled*, pp. 33–34.

4 This knowledge of variant laws is particularly apparent in Cornelia's annual reports to the Court of Wards, 165/131–134.

5 Especially Chapters 13–15.

6 As in this chapter.

7 See Chapters 13–15, and after her service with the Court of Wards see on the Rani of Bastar, a Princely state, Chapter 22.

8 See on Narhan and Tajhat in this chapter, and on Ramgarh, Chapter 10.

9 *India Recalled*.

10 Richard Sorabji collection, now published by Suparna Gooptu, 'Women's world in folk narratives of Bengali: view from an early twentieth century private collection', *The Calcutta Historical Journal*, 26, 2006, 19–62.

11 See Chapter 3 on the pageantry of Tennyson's funeral and Chapter 9 on the pageantry of the 1905 visit to Calcutta of the future British King and Queen.

12 Annual reports by Cornelia to the Court of Wards, 165/131–134.

13 Suparna Gooptu, *Cornelia Sorabji*.

14 Sukanya Banerjee, 'Empire, nation and the professional citizen: reading Cornelia Sorabji's India Calling', *Prose Studies*, 28, 2006, 291–317.

15 See this chapter and 'A case of succession: bones, mines and parrots' in Chapter 10.

16 *India Recalled*, pp. 112–119, 140–161, 263. For Bawaji, see Chapter 14 and *Between the Twilights*, pp. 74–81, for Mathaji Chapters 12 and 18 and *Between the Twilights*, pp. 61–73, for Narayani Letters to Elena 165/29, Aug 5, 1915, pp. 27 and (out of order) 23; also Chapter 12. In an unpublished story not told in *India Recalled*, Narayani renounced her lifelong guru in Cornelia's presence, after Cornelia's interrogation convinced her that the guru was shielding the perpetrators of a religious riot, while innocent bystanders went to jail in their place, Letters to Elena, 165/32, 33, esp. Nov 13, also Sep 19 and 24, Oct 1, Nov 20, Dec 3 and 18, 1919, Jan 8, Feb 12, May 20, 1920.

17 Notebook 1903–5, Richard Sorabji collection; Personal diary, 165/65, May 24–Aug 18, 1904; Letters to Lady Hobhouse, 165/17, May 31, Jul 4, Aug 4, 10, 17, 1904, fair copy: pp. 227–239; Letters to Blair, 165/24, May pp. 139–140 misplaced, May 27, 28, 30, 31, Jun 2–4, 1904: 'A child or two', in *Between the Twilights*, Harper, London 1908, pp. 164–174, *India Calling*, London pp. 142–152, Delhi pp. 108–114, Nottingham pp. 93–99.

18 Bisheswari Koer, Annual reports by Cornelia to the Court of Wards, 1914–15, 165/131, Bihar estates, p. 11. The 14-year-old daughter was Chandrabati Koer.

19 The division was larger than the district. See Appendix on structure of administration.

20 The explanation comes from a later case described in Cornelia's *Between the Twilights*, p. 59.

21 Chapter 17.

22 Personal diary, 165/66, Aug 2, 1905.

23 Chapter 17.

24 Letters to Lady Hobhouse, 165/17, Aug 4, 10, 17; more briefly, *Between the Twilights*, pp. 57–8.

25 *Between the Twilights*, p. 59.

26 Notebook 1903–5, Richard Sorabji collection; *India Calling*, London pp. 148–151, Delhi pp. 111–113, Nottingham pp. 96–98; *Between the Twilights*, pp. 58–59.

27 For what follows, see Personal diary, 165/65–68, Jul 20–Aug 13, 1904, May 30, Jul 1, 3 and 15, Aug 2, 9 and 13, Sep 25, Oct 11, 1905, Jan 17, May 16, 1906, Jan 27, Nov 27, 1907; Work diary, 165/102, Jan 5, 17, 22–23, 25–27, 30, 1907; Letters to Blair, 165/25, May 10, Jul 6, Aug 2, Nov 9, 1905; Letters to Elena, 165/33, Jan 21, 1920; 'A child or two' in *Between the Twilights* 1908, pp. 173–174; *India Calling*, London pp. 143, 148–152, Delhi pp. 108, 111–114, Nottingham pp. 93, 96–99; *The Purdahnashin*, Thacker, Spink, Calcutta 1917, in Richard Sorabji collection, p. 15.

28 *India Calling*, London p. 206, Delhi p. 149, Nottingham p. 131; 'The slave of Kali', in *Sun Babies*, Second series, Blackie, London approx. 1919, p. 24. See 'A case of succession: bones, mines and parrots' Chapter 10 for a repeat of the strategy.

29 There is a sketch of Wanglo in *Sun Babies*, Second series, Blackie, London approx. 1919, pp. 45–47, cf. Letters to Blair, 165/25, Apr 19, 1905.

30 *India Calling*, London p. 151, Delhi p. 113, Nottingham p. 98.

31 Annual reports by Cornelia to the Court of Wards, 1914–15, 165/131, Bihar estates, p. 11.

32 *India Calling*, London p. 152, Delhi pp. 113–114, Nottingham p. 98.

33 Work diary, 165/107, Oct 29–30, Nov 9–13, 1913.

34 Work diary, 165/107, Nov 11–12, 1913.

35 Annual reports by Cornelia to the Court of Wards, 1914–15, 165/131, Bihar estates, p. 11.

36 Annual reports by Cornelia to the Court of Wards, 1915–16, 165/132, Bihar, Tirhut division, p. 7.

37 Work diary, Feb 16, 1916, Richard Sorabji collection; Letters to Elena May 13, 1920, transferred to file on Nogen, 165/140; *India Calling*, London p. 152, Delhi p. 114, Nottingham p. 99. For the history of the Rani title, Notebook 1903–5, Richard Sorabji collection; Letters to Elena, 165/33, Jan 21, 1920; 'The mothers of fighters' in *Between the Twilights*, Harper, London and New York 1908, Ch. 9, 106–114; *India Calling*, London p. 142, Delhi p. 107–108, Nottingham p. 93.

38 Chapter 17.

39 Notebook 1903–5, Richard Sorabji collection; Personal diary, 165/65, Aug 12, Sep 16–24, 1904; Letters to Lady Hobhouse 165/17, Oct (undated) 1904.

40 Photo p. 142.

41 Notebook 1903–5, Richard Sorabji collection; Letters to Lady Hobhouse 165/17, Oct (undated) 1904; *India Calling*, London p. 128, Delhi p. 97, Nottingham p. 84.

42 Personal diary, 165/66, Jan 4, Dec 18, 20, 1905.

43 *India Calling*, London p. 129, Delhi p. 97, Nottingham p. 85; *India Recalled*, pp. 104–107, 84–85.

44 Personal diary, 165/66, Jan 7, 9, 20, Aug 15 and 17, 1905.

45 Letters to Blair, 165/25, Aug 16, 1905; Personal diary, 165/66, Aug 10 and 11, 1905; Letters to Elena, 165/50, Oct 2, 1938; *India Calling*, London 127–141, Delhi pp. 97–102, Nottingham pp. 84–89; *India Recalled*, p. 37.

46 *Mashima*. 'Aunt-mother' is the translation intended also by Amitav Ghosh for *mashima*, *Sea of Poppies*, John Murray London 2008, p. 61. I thank Niharika and Narayani Gupta for checking this with him.

47 *India Recalled*, p. 37.

48 Letters to Blair, Aug 24, 1905; *India Calling*, London pp. 132–133, Delhi pp. 99–100, Nottingham pp. 87–88; *Between the Twilights*, pp. 33–35.

49 Work diary, 165/101, Jan 15, 1907; Personal diary, 165/66, Aug 31, 1905; *India Calling*, London pp. 133–136, Delhi pp. 100–102, Nottingham pp. 88–89.

50 Personal diary, 165/67–68, Dec 19 and 21, 1906, Apr 7, 1907; Work diary, 165/101, Jan 8 and 10, Feb 7, Mar 31, Apr 2 and 7, 1907; *India Calling*, London pp. 136–140, Delhi pp. 102–105, Nottingham pp. 89–91.

51 The first description here is based on Cornelia, *Sun Babies*, Second series, Blackie approx. 1919, pp. 41–44, 'Shubala'; an extract describing the bullock cart journey is quoted here from Letters to Lady Hobhouse, 165/17, Feb 2, 1905. A third description is quoted in full in Chapter 11.

52 Work diary, 165/107, Feb 7, 1913.

53 Personal diary, 165/68, Feb 10–11, 1907.

54 Letters to Lady Hobhouse, 165/17, Feb 2, 1905.

55 Work diary, 165/101, Jan 7, 1907.

56 For what follows, see Personal diary, 165/67, Apr 4, 1906; Work diary, 165/101–103, 104–105, 107, Jan 16 and 19, Feb 2, 3, 9–11, Jul 27, 1907. May 1–3 and 11, Sep 19 and 22, 1908, May 21–22, Jul 30, 1910, Feb 28, Nov 24, 1911, Feb 7 and 13, 1913; Letters to Blair, 165/25, Aug 19, Nov 7, 1906; Letters to Elena, 165/33, Apr 28, 1920; 'Shubala' in *Sun Babies*, Second series, Blackie, London approx. 1919, pp. 41–44; *Shubala – A Child Mother*, Baptist Mission Press, Calcutta 1920; *India Calling*, London p. 234.

57 Work diary, 165/101, Feb 9–11, Sep 30, 1907; Letters to Blair, 165/25, Apr 10, 1906.

58 'Shubala' in *Sun Babies*, Second series, Blackie, London approx. 1919, pp. 41–44.

59 For Barisal, see Chapter 11.

60 Bhopal Chandra Roy Chaudhuri, Cornelia's reports to the Court of Wards, 1915–16, 165/132, Churamaon, p. 23.

61 Work diary, 165/101, Feb 9–11, Aug 27, Sep 30, 1907; Letters to Blair, 165/25, Apr 10, 1906.

62 Cornelia's reports to the Court of Wards, 1915–16, 165/132, Churamaon, p. 23.

63 Letters to Elena, 165/33, Apr 28, 1920.

64 Letters to Elena, 165/35, Feb 17, 1921.

65 Letters to Elena, 165/33, Apr 28, 1920; 'Shubala' in *Sun Babies*, Second series, Blackie, London approx. 1919, pp. 41–44; *Shubala – A Child Mother*, Baptist Mission Press, Calcutta 1920.

66 *Shubala – A Child Mother*, Baptist Mission Press, Calcutta 1920; Work diary, 165/101, 104, 105, May 1–2, 1908, Jul 30, 1910, Feb 3, 1911; Personal diary, 165/69, May 2–3, 1908.

67 Personal diary, 165/71, Jul 30, 1910; Work diary, 165/105, Feb 3, 1911; *Shubala – A Child Mother*, Baptist Mission Press, Calcutta 1920, pp. 6–8; *India Calling*, London p. 234–6, Delhi pp. 167–169, Nottingham pp. 151–152; *The Purdahnashin*, Thacker, Spink, Calcutta 1917, in Richard Sorabji collection, p. 15–16.

68 See Chapter 12.

69 Cornelia's reports to the Court of Wards, 1914–15, 165/131, Churamaon, p. 30.

70 *Shubala – A Child Mother*, Baptist Mission Press, Calcutta 1920, p. 10; Work diary, 165/106–107, Jul 19, 1912, Feb 13, 1913; Letters to Elena, 165/45, Feb 12, 1930.

71 Rani Sarojini.

72 *India Calling*, London pp. 185–188, Delhi pp. 135–138, Nottingham pp. 119–121; *India Recalled*, pp. 11–14. For her position in the Kasimbazar family, see Annual reports by Cornelia to the Court of Wards, 1914–15, Bengal estates, p. 11.

73 She is called Prithivi Maharani, while the name Chundi is used only on p. 93 and otherwise is kept for a Muslim and a strictly orthodox Hindu lady, pp. 75 and 92. For the references in *India Recalled*, see pp. xi–xiii, 55, 58, 62–67, 71–72, 93, 98, 119–130, 218–223.

74 *India Recalled*, p. 55.

75 Annual reports by Cornelia to the Court of Wards, Bengal 1919–20, 165/133, p. 110.

76 *India Calling*, London, p. 231–234, Delhi pp. 166–167, Nottingham pp. 149–150; *The Purdahnashin*, Thacker, Spink, Calcutta 1917, in Richard Sorabji collection, p. 8–9.

77 See Chapter 19 for the more extensive example of Peri Banu.

78 Letters to Elena in Richard Sorabji collection, Feb 9, Aug 27, Sep 23, Nov 12, 1915; Letters to Elena, 165/29, Jun 11–13, 1914.

79 Letters to Elena, 165/33, Jun 24, 1920.

80 Letters to Elena, 165/33, Sep 1, Oct 28, 1920.

81 Letters to Elena, Jul 17, 1919, Mar 11, Apr 28, 1920.

82 Letters to Blair, 165/25, Apr 4, 1905.

83 Letters to Blair, Apr 19, 1905, Jan undated 1906; *India Calling*, London pp. 128–130, Delhi pp. 97–98, Nottingham pp. 85–86; 'Kamala Ranjan', in *Sun Babies*, Second series, Blackie, London approx. 1919, pp. 19–21.

84 Annual reports by Cornelia to Court of Wards, 1915–16, 165/132, Presidency division, p. 10.

85 Work diary, Dec 16, 1917; Letters to Elena, 165/31, Aug 5, 1919.

86 Letters to Elena, 165/44, Sep 19, 1929.

87 Letters to Elena, 165/47, Jan 18, 1933; Letters to Dick and family, Jan 17, Feb 2, 1933, Richard Sorabji collection.

88 Chapter 10.

89 Chapter 12.

CHAPTER 9

1   See Peter Hopkirk, *The Great Game*, London 1990; Charles Allen, *Duel in the Snows*, London 2004.

2   Personal diary, 165/65, Jun 17, 21, 1904; Letters to Blair, 165/24, approx. May 23, p. 178, and approx. 25, misplaced at p. 139, 1904; Letters to Lady Hobhouse, 165/17, Jun 8, 1904. The Daily Mail correspondent's account of the massacre is quoted e.g. in Charles Allen, *Duel in the Snows*, London 2004, p. 119.

3   *India Calling*, London p. 173, Delhi p. 127, Nottingham p. 110.

4   Letters to Blair, 165/25, Mar 7, 1907.

5   Annual reports by Cornelia to the Court of Wards, 1915–16, 165/132, Part A, p. 2.

6   Official correspondence, 165/126. See photograph, p. 170.

7   Letters to Elena, 165/29, 36, Nov 14, 1914, Dec 29, 1921; *India Calling*, London p. 244, Delhi p. 174, Nottingham p. 156.

8   'Pundit-je', in her *Love and Life Behind the Purdah*, Freemantle, London 1901, pp. 231–239, repr. Oxford University Press Delhi 2003, pp. 106–110.

9   Letters to Blair, 165/25, Nov 1, 1905; Personal diary, 165/66, Oct 27, 1905; 'Garden fancies', in *Between the Twilights*, Harper, London and New York 1908, pp. 150–155.

10 Letters to Elena, 165/39, Oct 20, 1925; subsequently turned into an article in *Country Life*, April 1926.

11 Personal diary, 165/66, Feb 18, 1905.

12 Letters to Blair, 165/25, Aug 25, 1905.

13 Letters to Blair, 165/25, Jul 25, 1905.

14 Personal diary, 165/66–67, Dec 29, 1905–Jan 5, 1906 (some misplaced).

15 Letters to Blair, 165/25, approx. Jan 9 (undated) 1906.

16 Letters to Blair, 165/25, Mar 28, 1906.

17 India Office Records/ V/ 24/2602, annual report by Board of Revenue, Eastern Bengal and Assam, 1905–6.

18 Letters home, 165/9, Jan 8, 1906, to Mary.

19 Chapter 12.

20 Personal diary, 165/70, Jan 5, 1909.

21 Personal diary, 165/71, Mar 9, 1910.

22 Personal diary, 165/25, Nov 22, 1905.

23 Chapter 22.

24 See Chapter 8.

25 Letters to Blair, 165/25, approx. Jan 9 (undated) 1906, Letters home, 165/9, Jan 8, 1906, to Mary; Personal diary, 165/66–67, Dec 29, 1905–Dec 5, 1906.

26 Chapter 15.

27 Letters to Blair, 165/25, Jan 24, Feb 8, 1906; Letters home, 165/8, May 6, 1906, to Mary; Personal diary, 165/67, Jan 21–Feb 6, 1906; Letters to Family, 165/10, Jan 8, Feb 2, 5, 1906.

28 Newspaper cuttings, 165/233, *The Statesman*, May 21, 1906.

29 Letters to Blair, 165/25, Oct 12, 1905.

30 Personal diary 165/25, Letters to Blair, Apr 16, 1905.

31 Letters to Blair, 165/25, May 16, 1905; Letters to Lady Hobhouse, 165/17, Dec 8, 1904.

32 Chapter 14.

33 Jhama Gourlay, *Florence Nightingale and the Health of the Raj*, pp. 245–249.

34 Letters to Blair, 165/25, Mar 30–Apr 1, 1904.

35 Letters to Blair, 165/25, Jan 24, 1906.

36 Letters to Blair, 165/25, Apr 1, 1904.

37 Letters to Blair, 165/25, Nov 15, 1905, Feb 21, 1906; Personal diary, 165/69, 70, 71, 73, Mar 27, 1908, Jan 8, 1909, Oct 13, 1909, Mar 24, 1910, Feb 27, 1912.

38 Personal diary, 165/69, Jan 8, 1909.

39 Personal diary, 165/70, Oct 13, 1909, 165/73, Feb 27, 1912.

40 *India Calling*, London p. 271, Delhi p. 192, Nottingham p. 172.

41 *The Statesman*, Mar 16, 1929, clipping in Richard Sorabji collection.

42 Letters to Dick's family, Feb 21, 1933, Richard Sorabji collection.

43 Letter to Elena, 165/41, Aug 19, 1926.

44 Personal diary, 165/75, Jan 29, 1914.

45 Letters to Elena, 165/36, 39, 43, Aug 18, 1921, Dec 16, 23, 1925, Jan 5, 1928, misplaced at pp. 43–48.

46 Discussion of the first in Letters to Elena, 165/31, approx. Sep 1 (undated) 1919; draft review enclosed in Letters to Elena, 165/32, 1919; wanted by *The Pioneer*, according to Personal diary, 165/32, Nov 20, 1919. 'Rabindranath Tagore's *Gora* the revolutionary', also in Richard Sorabji collection, written in 28 Chowringee, i.e., 1924–6, unpublished.

47 Letters to Elena, 165/36, Aug 18, 1921.

48 Letters to Elena, 165/39, Dec 25, 1925.

49 Letters to Elena, 165/43, Jan 5, 1928, misplaced at pp. 43–48.

50 Letters to Blair, 165/25, May 23, 1905.

51 Personal diary, 165/68, 70, Aug 7, Sep 3, 1907, Aug 30, 1909.

52 Cornelia, 'Zenana education and the Report of the Calcutta University Commission', *Statesman*, Oct 9, 10, 1919, typescript in Richard Sorabji collection.

53 Annual reports by Cornelia to the Court of Wards, 1914–15, 165/131, Bengal estates p. 22, further discussed in Chapter 15.

54 See Appendix 1 for further details.

55 See photograph, p. 180.

56 Personal diary, 165/64, Jan 10, 1903; Letters to Blair, 165/24, late January 1904 undated, p. 31.

57 I am grateful to Professor Pandey, head of the Philosophy Department, University of Allahabad, in 1989, for helping me to reconstruct his movements.

58 Chapter 4.

59 Personal diary, 165/65, 66, Sep 3, 1904, Jun 4, 1905.

60 *The Leader*, Saturday Dec 25, 1909.

61 Richard Kaikushru Sorabji, 165/206.

62 Molly Whittington-Egan, *Khaki Mischief*, London 1990, pp. 209, 213, 221–223.

CHAPTER 10

1   Letters to Elena, 165/30, Aug 29, 1917.

2   *India Calling*, London pp. 177, 181, Delhi pp. 130, 133, Nottingham pp. 115, 117.

3   Annual reports by Cornelia to the Court of Wards, 1915–16, 165/132, Part A, p. 2; 1919–20, 165/133, Part A, p. 2.

4   Annual reports by Cornelia to the Court of Wards, 1915–16, 1919–20,165/133, Part B, p. 29.

5   Letters to Lady Hobhouse, 165/17, May 1, 1905.

6   Letters to Blair, 165/25, Oct 12, 1905, Nov 15, Dec 20, 1906; Personal diary, 165/66, Apr 20, Jun 4, 1906; *India Calling*, London p. 177, Delhi p. 132, Nottingham p. 115.

7   Correspondence 1890s to 1944, 165/54, Jan 11, 1906.

8   Philip Mason, *The Men who Ruled India*, London 1971, vol. 2, Ch. 4; Edward Blunt, *The ICS, The Indian Civil Service*, London 1937; *India Office List* (annual gazetteer with annually revised article on India); Cornelia, *India Calling*, London pp. 178–180, Delhi pp. 130–132, Nottingham pp. 115–116.

9   *India Calling*, London pp. 178–179, Delhi pp. 131–132, Nottingham pp. 115–116.

10   Letters to Blair, 165/25, Nov 25, 1905.

11   Personal diary, 165/70, Jun 25, 1909.

12   Personal diary, 165/76, May 18, 1915; Letters to Elena, 165/32, 33, Oct 30, 1919, Jun 24, 1920.

13   Letters to Elena, 165/35, Apr 27, 1921.

14   Letters to Elena, 165/32, 33, 35, 36, 49, 51, Oct 30, 1919, Feb 5, Jun 13, 20, 24, 1920, Apr 27, May 23, Jun 1, Jun approx. 8, Jun 15, 22, 29, 1921, Aug 11, 18, Sep 29, Nov 2, 1921, Jan approx. 8, 1936, Apr 17, 1941; Annual reports by Cornelia to the Court of Wards, 1919–20, 165/134, p. 61.

15   Letters to Elena, 165/36, Oct 10, 1921.

16   Work diary, 165/101, 102, 108, Mar 26, 1907, Apr 28, 1908, Jan 16, 1914; Personal diary, 165/68, Mar 25–26, 1907; 'The slave of Kali', in *Sun Babies*, Second series, Blackie, London approx. 1919, p. 23–26; *India Calling*, London pp.202–209, Delhi pp. 146–152, Nottingham pp. 128–134.

17   Chapter 14.

18   *India Calling*, London pp. 157–161, Delhi pp. 117–119; Nottingham pp. 102–103. The visit seems to be described in Personal diary, 165/68, Oct 24–25, 1907.

19   Letters to Elena, 165/35, Mar 17, 1921.

20   Rajendra Nath Rana, Annual reports by Cornelia to the Court of Wards, 1914–15, 165/131, Bihar estates, p. 24.

21   Quoted from 'The adoption' in *Sun Babies*, Second series, Blackie approx. 1919. See also Work diary, 165/107, Jun/Jul(?) 10, 1913; Personal diary, 165/74, Jul 10, 1913; Letters to Elena, 165/33, Jun 10, 1920; *India Calling*, London p. 194, Delhi p. 142, Nottingham p. 124; *India Recalled*, pp. 206–213.

22   Work diary, 165/107, Jul 10, 1913.

23   Letters to Elena, 165/31, Jul 17, Aug 28, and (undated) approx. Sep 1, 1919.

24   Work diary, Aug 9, Sep 5, 1918; Letters to Elena, Aug 5, Sep 8, 1919; Personal diary, 165/80, Sep 5, 1919.

25 Cornelia, 'A Prince of Oudh', *The Times*, Aug 3, at the time of his death, year not supplied, Richard Sorabji collection.

26 Work diary, Aug 9, Sep 5, 1918; Letters to Elena, Aug 5, Sep 8, 1919; Personal diary, 165/80, Sep 5, 1919.

27 Chapter 6.

28 Letters to Elena, 165/34, 45, Oct 28, 1920; Mar 6, 1930.

29 Letters to Elena, 165/29, Jun 11–13, 1914, Undated 1915 after Aug 6, 165/33 and 34, Apr 20, Sep 9, 1920; Work diary, 165/104, Oct 30, 1910. Only the early part if the story is told in Letters to Blair, 165/25, Jun 26, 1906 and 'Tum-ta', *The Nineteenth Century* Aug 1913, pp. 413–418.

30 Tihur, see Chapter 4; Bettiah, see Chapter 14. See also 'Selflessness and forgiveness admired' in Chapter 12, and Work diary, 165/104, Jan 27, Apr 2, 1910.

31 At Canipore in 1908, the insanity of a millionaire widow, attested by three doctors out of six, was also accepted by the claimants to her estate, see Work diary, 165/102, Jun 8, 1908.

32 Letters to Elena, 165/36, Jul 9 and 27, Aug 4, 1921.

33 Letters to Blair, 165/25, Mar 19, 1907; Work diary, 165/101, Mar 16, 1907.

34 Chapter 7.

35 I thank him for permission to quote.

36 Annual reports by Cornelia to the Court of Wards, 1914–15, Part A, p. 4; Part B, p. 9; 1915–16, 165/132, Part A, p. 4; Chota Nagpur division, p. 20; 1919–20, 165/133, Part A, p. 2; Part B, p. 29.

37 Annual reports by Cornelia to the Court of Wards, 1915–16, 165/132, Patna division, p. 14.

38 Annual reports by Cornelia to the Court of Wards, 1914–15, Part A, p. 3.

39 Annual reports by Cornelia to the Court of Wards, 1919–20, 165/133, Part A, p. 20, Part B, p.22.

CHAPTER 11

1 Annual reports by Cornelia to the Court of Wards 1915–16, 165/132, Part A, p. 2.

2 See for the list of seven qualifications Chapter 15.

3 Letters to Elena, 165/32 and 33, Oct 23, 1919, Apr 28, 1920, Personal diary, 165/68, 70, 73, Feb 9–11, Oct 21, 1907; Feb 21, Aug 21, 1909, Feb 4, 1912; Work diary, 165/101, 102, 104, Feb 9, Sep 11, 1907, Apr 11, 1908, Apr 20, 1910.

4 Letters to Elena, 165/30, Sep 25, 1917.

5 Chapter 10.

6 See further Work diary, May 16–17, 1916, Richard Sorabji collection; Personal diary, 165/73 and 77, Jan 16, 1912, May 16–17, 1916; Letters to Elena, 165/32, Oct 30, 1919.

7 Work diary, 165/104, Apr 1910.

8 Letters to Elena, 165/35, Mar 17, 1921.

9 Letters to Elena, 165/33 and 34, Feb 12, Sep 16, 1920, *India Calling*, London pp. 228–229, Delhi p. 164, Nottingham pp. 147–148.

10 Letters to Blair, 165/25, Feb 14, 1907.

11 Letters to Blair, 165/25, Jun 6, 1906; the journey is retold in *Between the Twilights*, pp. 53–54.

12 Letters to Blair, 165/25, Jun 20, 1906, out of order at p. 358.

13 Letters to Blair, 165/25, Jun 20, 1906, out of order at p. 358; Letters to Elena, 165/32, 34, 36, Dec 3, 1919, Oct 7, 1920, Dec 19, 1921.

14 Letters to Elena, 165/32, Dec 3, 1919.

15 Letters to Elena, 165/32, Dec 3, 1919.

16 Personal diary, 165/67, Aug 22, 1906.

17 Personal diary, 165/68, Aug 30, 1907.

18 From *India Recalled*, pp. 171–173.

19 Letters to Elena, 165/32, Oct 23, 1919.

20 Letters to Elena, Apr 14–15, 1915, Richard Sorabji collection; Work diary, Apr 12, 1915, Apr 25, 1917, both in Richard Sorabji collection; Personal diary, 165/73, 77, Feb 18–19, 1912, Mar 10, 1916, Apr 25, 1917.

21 Personal diary, 165/73, Feb 18, 1912.

22 Letters to Elena, Apr 14–15, 1915, Richard Sorabji collection.

23 Chapter 8.

24 Letters to Elena, Apr 14, 1915, Work diary, Mar 11, 1916, both in Richard Sorabji collection.

25 Personal diary 165/67, Nov 13–18, 1906, Letters to Blair, 165/25, Nov 21, 1906.

CHAPTER 12

1 For Narhan and Tajhat, see Chapter 8.

2 For the Maharani of Tajhat see Chapter 8.

3 Chapter 8.

4 *India Recalled*, London p. 13.

5 See Chapter 8.

6 Letters to Elena, Oct 22, 1915, Richard Sorabji collection.

7 See Chapter 4.

8 *India Calling*, London p. 88, Delhi p. 69, Nottingham p. 60.

9 The Maharani of Tajhat, Chapter 8.

10 Work diary, 165/105, Apr 19, 1911.

11 Letters to Elena 165/29 and 32, Oct 13, 1914, Aug 28, 1919.

12 *India Recalled*, pp. 30–31.

13 Chapter 11.

14 *India Recalled*, Chapter 3, pp. 41–51, reproduced from 'Making a will in India', *The Nineteenth Century and After*, Vol. 120, 1936, pp. 80–86.

15 Letters to Elena, 165/36, Dec 19, 1921.

16 *India Calling*, London pp. 287–289, Delhi p. 203, Nottingham p. 182.

17 Letters to Elena, 165/31, Jul 30, 1919.

18 Letters to Elena, 165/43, Jun 20, 1928.

19 *India Calling*, London pp. 287–289, Delhi p. 203, Nottingham p. 182.

20 Letters to Lady Hobhouse, 165/17, Mar 30, 1905; *India Recalled*, p. 21; *Shubala – A Child Mother*, pp. 2–3; 'Zenana dwellers: the selfless women of Hinduism, Keepers of the God rules', *Asia* 1924, pp. 171–176 and 238, at 172.

21 Letters to Elena, 165/35, 48, May 19, Sep 21, 1921, Feb 1, 1934; Work diary Jan 31, Feb 4, 1917, Richard Sorabji collection; Personal diary, 165/85, Mar 31, 1923; Partha Chatterjee, *A Princely Impostor?* Columbia University Press, NY, 2002.

22 *India Calling*, London pp. 187–188; Delhi pp. 137–138; Nottingham pp. 120–121.

23 Chapter 8.

24 Letters to Elena, 165/35, Mar 17, 1921; *India Calling*, without giving a name, runs together the stories of Arnakali Devi's shrivelled finger and Lakshmi Devi's subsequent suttee, London pp. 185–188, Delhi pp. 135–138, Nottingham pp. 119–121.

25 Chapter 4.

26 Chapter 10.

27 Letters to Elena, 165/33, Aug 19, 1920; *India Calling*, London p. 184–185, Delhi p. 135, Nottingham p. 119.

28 Nirad Chaudhuri, *The Autobiography of an Unknown Indian*, London 1951, Chapter 2.

29 Balliol College Library, Letters from Jowett to Cornelia.

30 165/177, 'Necessity for safeguards', typescript, Mar 6, 1919, with covering letter Jun 3, 1919.

31 Chapter 17.

32 For this and other aspects of widowhood, see *India Recalled*, Chapter 1; 'Portraits of some Indian women', reprinted from *The Nineteenth Century*, in *Between the Twilights*, Harper, London and New York 1908, Chapter 11, pp. 128–149.

33 Cornelia was able to use the belief that the wife's past incarnation was to blame in order to calm wives whose husbands had been wrongly arrested after riots in Katarpur on which she was consulted: Letters to Elena, 165/32, Nov 13, 1919, with other references cited in Chapter 8, note xvi.

34 Chapter 17.

35 See on the Narhan mother-in-law in Chapter 8, and Letters to Elena, 165/44, Apr 17, 1929.

36 Chapter 16.

37 'A happy ending', Chapter 10.

38 A. M. Pennell, *The Begum's Son*, John Murray, London 1928. On Alice's novels see Appendix 1.

39 Jhama Gourlay, *Florence Nightingale and the Health of the Raj*, Ashgate, Aldershot 2003, p. 226.

40 Letters to Lady Hobhouse, 165/16, Apr 18, Jul 11, 1894, Apr 19, 1895, Aug 23, 1896.

41 Personal diary, 165/66, Sep 12, 1905.

42 *India Recalled*, Chapter 18.

43 *India Recalled*, pp. 147–158, and Chapters 8 and 18. Cornelia believed Mathaji to be 103 in 1910.

44 See Chapter 8 and *India Recalled*, pp. 140–161.

45 Also used in *Shubala – A Child Mother*, 1920.

46 *The Purdahnashin*, Thacker, Spink, Calcutta 1917; Letters to Elena, 165/30, Nov 16, Dec 12, 1917, published copy and original typescript in Richard Sorabji collection; Letters to Elena, 165/30, Dec 12, 1917.

47 *India Calling*, London p. 68, Delhi pp. 54–55, Nottingham p. 48.

48 Letters to Elena, 165/30, Nov 16, Dec 12, 1917.

49 Chapter 8.

50 *India Recalled*, pp. 170–171.

51 *India Calling*, London 236, Delhi p. 169, Nottingham p.152; *Shubala – A Child Mother*, Baptist Mission Press, Calcutta, 1920, pp. 15–16, *The Purdahnashin*, pp. 16–18, both the last in the Richard Sorabji collection.

52 Letters to Elena, 165/34, Jul 29, 1920; *India Calling*, London p. 221, Delhi p. 159, Nottingham p. 140.

53 *India Calling*, London pp. 199–201, Delhi pp. 145–146, Nottingham pp. 127–128.

54 See Retrospect below.

55 India Office Records, British Library, V/24/2602 for 1906–7.

56 Letters home, 165/8, Jan 8, 1906, to Mary.

57 Personal diary, e.g. 165/68, 69, 70 and 72, Mar 14, 1907, Jan 25, 1909, May 19, 1910, Mar 3 and 14, 1911.

58 Personal diary, 165/68, Jan 2 and 31, 1907, Letters to Elena, 165/32, Oct 30, 1919.

59 She had been on a committee of the Dufferin Hospital in Allahabad in 1897, had become legal adviser to the Society for the Prevention of Cruelty to Children there in 1898 and in Calcutta in 1907, she was getting up a branch of the National India Association, with a view to social work: Letters to Lady Hobhouse, 165/16, Oct 25, 1897; Personal diary, 165/68 and 70, Feb/Mar, 1907, Aug 30, 1909. She had already in her student days in London in 1892–3 represented the Federation of University Women, and in 1915, she was elected President of the University Association of Women in Calcutta and in 1919 the General Secretary of the Federation of University Women for India as a whole: Letters to Elena, 165/29 and 32, Jun 2, 1916, Dec 3, 1919. In 1925 she was the organising Vice-President of the National Council of the Women of India, as well as working on its local unit, the Bengal Presidency Council of Women: Letters to Elena, 165/39, Oct 9, 1925 (out of order).

60 Personal diary, 165/67, Feb 19, 1906.

61 Personal diary, 165/71, May 19, Aug 21, 1910.

62 *Shubala – A Child Mother.*

63 See Chapter 19.

64 Letters to Elena, 165/33, 34, 36, Jan 8, Apr 15, 20 and 28, Jun 3, Sep 9, Oct 28, Nov 18, 1920, Jul 7, 1921.

65 See photograph, p. 224.

66 Personal diary, 165/73, Apr 3 and 21, May 13, Aug 19, Sep 29, Oct 20, 1912; Work diary, 165/106, Jun 30, Jul 1–2 and 4–5, Aug 18, Oct 3, 24, 1912.

67 Personal diary, 165/73, Nov 22, 1912.

68 Letters to Elena, 165/31, 34, 35, Aug 12, 14, 1919, Jul 8, 1920, Mar 3, 1921.

69 Chapter 19.

70 Letters to Elena, 165/44, Feb 27, 1929, Handbook of the Bengal League of Social Service for Women, 1929, Richard Sorabji collection.

71 Letters to Elena, 165/42, 43, 44, 45, Nov 9, 1927, May 24, 1928, Feb 19, Aug 29, Nov 28, 1929, Mar 20, 1930.

72 Letters to Elena, 165/50, Feb 3, 1937.

73 Chapters 16 and 19.
74 Chapter 19.

CHAPTER 13

1 'A Bengali woman revolutionary', *The Nineteenth Century* 1933, pp. 604–611.
2 Work diary 1914, 165/108, 109, Nov 26–Dec 2, 5, 1914; Work diary, Jan 1, 5, 8, 9, 1915, Richard Sorabji collection; Letters to Elena Apr 8, 1915, Richard Sorabji collection; Nogen file, 165/140, Letter to Elena Nov 30, 1914; Personal diary, 165/75, 76, Nov 27, 29, Dec 4, 23, 1914, Jan 5, 1915.
3 Work diary, Jan 28–30, 1915, Richard Sorabji collection, Personal diary, 165/76, Jan 28–29, Feb 1, 1915.
4 Work diary, Jan 8, Feb 2, 4, 6, 8, 19–20, Richard Sorabji collection; Personal diary, 165/76, Feb 1, 6, 1915.
5 Letters from Elena, Apr 8, 1915, Richard Sorabji collection, Work diary, Mar 8–19, 22, 1915, Richard Sorabji collection; Personal diary, 165/76, Mar 8–9, 15, 18, 22, 1915.
6 Letters to Elena, 165/31, Jul 23, 30, 1919.
7 Work diary, Mar 24, 29–30, Apr 2, 4, 6–9, 1915, Richard Sorabji collection; Personal diary, 165/76, Apr 2, 7–9, 1915.
8 Work diary, Apr 8–9, 1915, Richard Sorabji collection, Personal diary, 165/76, Apr 9, 1915.
9 Chapter 14.
10 Letters to Elena, 165/29, Jan 16, 1916.
11 Work diary Apr 1, 21–24, 27, May 4–5, 7, 1915, Richard Sorabji collection; Letters to Elena, Apr 20, 27, May 5, 13, Jun 17, 22, Oct 22, 1915, Richard Sorabji collection; Letters to Elena, 165/29, Jan 19, 1916; Personal diary, 165/76,77, Apr 21, 23, May 5, 1915, Aug 19, 1916.
12 Work diary, May 5, 7, 10, 19, 1915, Richard Sorabji collection; Letters to Elena, May 5, 13, 1915, Richard Sorabji collection; Personal diary, 165/76, May 7, 10, 19, 1915.
13 Work diary, Jul 21, 1916, Richard Sorabji collection.
14 Work diary (supplementary, written up to show trainees), 165/109–110, Aug 2, 1918.
15 Letters to Elena, 165/31, Jul 30, Aug 5, 1919.
16 Work diary, 165/109-110, Jul 14, 1918.
17 Letters to Elena, Dec 31, 1918, Richard Sorabji collection; Personal diary, 165/79, Dec 24, 1918.
18 Letters to Elena, 165/31, 34, 35, Aug 19, 1919, Nov 2, 18, Dec 2, 1920, Jan 4, 5, 27, Mar 31, Jun 22, Oct 26, 1921; Personal diary, 165/80, Nov 7, 1919.
19 Personal diary, 165/84, 85, 86, Jul 25, 1922, Sep 7, 15, 1923, Jan 21, Mar 3, Jun 16, 1924.
20 Letters to Elena, 165/38, 39, Dec 27, 1924, Jan 20, Feb 3, 4, 1925.
21 Letters to Elena, 165/41, Jul 14, 1926.

22 Letters to Elena, 165/46, Jan 29, 1931.

23 Letters to Dick's family, Feb 2, 1933, Richard Sorabji collection, Letters to Elena, 165/47, 51, Feb 1, 1933, Dec 25, 1940.

CHAPTER 14

1 India Office Records/V/24/2532-3.

2 India Office Records/V/24/2602.

3 See Chapter 5.

4 India Office Records/L/PS/15/32 and 55.

5 Chapter 13.

6 Letters to Elena, 165/40, Feb 11, 1926.

7 Some of these are published in Klaus Stierstorfer, ed., *Women Writing Home, 1700–1920*, Vol. 4, Pickering and Chatto, London 2006.

8 Richard Symonds picks out Beatson-Bell as having got what was considered a notable first-class degree in Indian Studies at Oxford, *Oxford and Empire*, London 1986, p. 189.

9 Annual reports by Cornelia to Court of Wards, 1919–20, 165/134, p. 78.

10 Letters to Valentine Chirol, 165/28, Oct 13, 1914, repr. in Klaus Stierstorfer, ed., *Women Writing Home*, *1700–1920*, Vol. 4, p. 209.

11 Letters to Elena, 165/29, 34, Oct 13, 1914, Jul 21, 1920.

12 Letters to Elena, 165/3, Jul 21, 1920.

13 Chapter 19.

14 India Office List.

15 *India Calling*, London pp. 152–169, Delhi pp. 114–125, Nottingham pp. 99–108.

16 Letters to Elena, 165/32, Oct 15, 1919.

17 Chapter 10.

18 Latters to Blair, 165/25, Aug 2, 1905.

19 Work diary, 165/101, Jan 11–12, 1907.

20 Annual reports by Cornelia to the Court of Wards, 1914–15, 165/131, Bihar p. 13.

21 For what follows see Work diary, 165/105, Jan 12–Feb 7, Mar 6, Oct 27, 1911.

22 For what follows see Work diary, 165/105, Oct 27, 1911; Work diary 1917, Jan 7, 17–18, Mar 15, 1917, Apr 5, Richard Sorabji collection; Letters to Elena, 165/30, 32, 33, 36, Jan 25, Mar 23, Apr 7, May 15, 1917, Oct 15, Nov 13, 20, 1919, May 6, Jun 13, 20, 24, 1920, Aug 4, 1921; Personal diary Jan 3, Mar 15, May 14, 1917.

23 Annual reports by Cornelia to the Court of Wards, 1919–20, 165/134, p. 92.

24 Annual reports by Cornelia to the Court of Wards, 1915–16, 165/132, Patna division, pp. 7–8; 1919–20, 165/134, p. 92.

25 Other correspondence, 165/54, Sep 7, 1944 (to Elena).

26 For what follows see Letters to Elena, 165/29, Oct 13, 1914; Work diary, 165/108, Oct 9, 1914; Personal diary, 165/75, Sep 15, Oct 7–8, 12, 20–23, Nov 7–8, 1914; Letters to Valentine Chirol, 165/28, Oct 6, 13, Nov 5, 13, 1914, repr. in Klaus Stierstorfer, ed., *Women Writing Home*, *1700–1920*, Vol. 4, pp. 206–216.

27 Letters to Valentine Chirol, 165/28, Oct 13, Nov 5, 15, 1914, repr. in Klaus Stierstorfer, ed., *Women Writing Home*, *1700–1920*, Vol. 4, pp. 209–216.

28 'A Hindu guru's views of the political situation in India', *The Nineteenth Century* Jul 1914, pp. 76–79, included in Official correspondence on terms of employment, 165/124, pp. 141–146.

29 *India Calling*, London p. 201, Delhi p. 146, Nottingham, p. 128.

30 Letter to Valentine Chirol, 165/28, Nov 5, 1914, repr. in Klaus Stierstorfer, ed., *Women Writing Home, 1700–1920*, Vol. 4, p. 213. Bawaji is described in *India Recalled*, pp. 140–146, 154.

31 See Chapter 12 on the Brahmos.

32 Personal diary, 165/75, Jun 1, 1914; *The Times*, Jun 3, 1914.

33 Chapter 16, and on Mrs Besant's call for allowing Indian immigration in other countries of the Empire, see Chapter 18.

34 Personal diary, 165/75, Oct 22, 1914.

35 Personal diary, 165/29, Nov 8, 1914.

36 Official correspondence on terms of employment, 165/124, pp. 141–146, letter from F. H. Kerr, Oct 22, 1914.

37 Official correspondence on terms of employment, 165/124, pp. 141–146, letter from Marr, Oct 29, 1914.

38 Personal diary, 165/84, 100, May 2, 27–28, 1922, Oct 31, 1938; See also Chapter 16.

39 Chapter 12.

40 For what follows see Personal diary, 165/73, 74, Nov 22, 30, Dec 2, 6, 16–17, 1912, Mar 24, 27–8, 30, Apr 7–9, 14–15, 22, May 12, Jun 24, 26, Jul 26, Aug 2–6, Aug 14, 21, 28, 1913.

41 Chapter 8. For what follows see Personal diary, 165/75, Jan 3, 7, 8, Feb 2, 6, 1914.

42 Personal diary, 165/75–78, Oct 26, Dec 17, 1914, Jan 5, Jul, 5, 1915, Mar 17, 1916, Apr 3, 1917.

43 Personal diary, 165/76–78, Jan 16, 1915, Dec 4, 1916, Jul 4, 1917.

44 Personal diary, 165/77, Feb 13, May 1, 11, 1916.

45 Personal diary 165/76, Jul 16, 1915; Work diary, Jul 16, 1915, Richard Sorabji collection.

46 Letters to Elena, 165/31, Jul 17, 1919.

47 Personal diary, 165/75, Oct 26, 1914.

48 Personal diary, 165/76, Aug 3, 1915.

49 Personal diary, 165/75, Oct 25, 28, Nov 4, 1914, Feb 22, 1915; Work diary, 165/108, Oct 26, 28, Nov 2, 17, 1914.

50 Personal diary, 165/78, Jul 5, 1917.

51 Personal diary, 165/77, Nov 28, 1916.

52 Personal diary, 165/77, Dec 22, 26, 28, 1916; Letters to Elena, 165/29, Dec 28, 1916.

53 Personal diary, 165/78, Apr 9–10, 1917; compare Mar 25, 1917.

54 Letters to family, 165/11, Apr 24–30, 1918.

55 Work diary, May 31, 1916, Richard Sorabji collection; Letters to Elena, 165/29, Jun 2, 1916.

56 Letters to Elena, 165/29, Jan 19, 1916.

57 Letters to Elena, 165/29, Jun 2, 1916.

58 Letters to Elena, 165/29, Nov 23, 1916; Personal diary, 165/77, Oct 23, 1916; Work diary, Jul 13, 1917, Richard Sorabji collection.

59 Letters to Elena, 165/29, Jun 2, 1916.

60 Letters to Elena, 165/29, 30, 31, 34, Nov 23, 1916, Jan 11, Mar 23, Dec 12, 1917, Jun 24–25, 1919. The surviving typescript, after one copy was lost by her clerks, is in the Richard Sorabji collection. Both booklets are there in the Bodleian Library, Oxford.

61 Letters to Elena, 165/33, Jan 8, 21, Feb 5, 1920.

62 Personal diary, 165/78, Jul 10, Sep 3, 1917.

63 Letters to Elena, 165/30, Jan 11, 1917.

64 Letters to Elena, 165/30, Mar 23, May 18, 1917.

65 Letters to Elena, 165/34, Jun 24–25, 1919.

66 'What English women have done in India', *The Queen* Nov 18, 1924, in Richard Sorabji collection.

67 Letters to Elena, 165/33, Feb 26, 1920.

68 See Chapter 12.

69 Letters to Elena, 165/36, Jul 7, 1921.

70 Annual reports by Cornelia to the Court of Wards, 1919–20, 165/133, Part A, p. 20, Part B, p. 22.

71 Letters to Elena, 165/35, Jan 27, Mar 31, 1921.

72 See Chapter 10.

73 Letters to Elena, 165/31, Jun 11, 1919.

CHAPTER 15

1 Official correspondence on terms of employment, 165/124, pp. 41a–41b, Letter from J. H. Kerr, Secretary to Government of Bengal.

2 Official correspondence on terms of employment, 165/124, pp. 2–3 of a letter of 1909.

3 Official correspondence on terms of employment, 165/124, Huda, Oct 12, 1912, F. W. Duke, Sep 12, 1912.

4 Annual reports by Cornelia to the Court of Wards, 1914–15, 165/131, Bengal estates, p.22.

5 Unfortunately Khatun eventually fell victim to multiple intrigue to grab her estate, both from her husband's Muslim family and from her mother's Jewish associates, and after a poisoning, an enforced divorce and remarriage, and a disappearance, Cornelia finally located her in what she called one of the filthiest quarters of Calcutta, Letters to Elena, 165/34–36, Dec 2, 1920, Jan 27, Mar 17, 31, Sep 21, 29, 1921.

6 Letters to Elena, 165/29, Apr 1, 1916, *India Calling*, London pp. 177–180, Delhi pp. 130–132, Nottingham pp. 115–117; Official correspondence on terms of employment, 1909–18, 165/124.

7 Work diary, 165/102, Jan 25, 1908; Personal diary, 165/70, Mar 21, Apr 3, 1909.

8 Official correspondence on terms of employment, 165/124. Much of the correspondence was carried on through the secretaries to the governments under the two Lieutenant Governors: in Assam by P. C. Lyon, and in Bengal by Sir Charles Allen and later J. H. Kerr, e.g. pp. 2, 5–6, 10.

9 Official correspondence on terms of employment, 165/124, Letters of Lyon, May 29, 1909, of Allen, Aug 11, 1909; *cf.* Personal diary, 165/70, 75, Jul 28, 1909; Jul 28, 1914.

10 Official correspondence on terms of employment, 165/124, pp. 2, 10.

11 Work diary, 165/105, May 6, 1911; Personal diary, 165/72, May 6, 1911; Official correspondence on terms of employment, 165/124, pp. 21–23, Viceroy's Council reporting Lord Crewe's decision of Mar 24, 1911, response by Cornelia of Jun 21, 1911 enclosed.

12 Correspondence on employment sent for opinion of Counsel, 165, 126, Letter by Kerr on behalf of Carmichael, Nov 27, 1912; Official correspondence on terms of employment, 165/124, pp. 24–25, letter from Kerr on behalf of Carmichael to Government of India, p. 43, letter stating Carmichael's proposals, Oct 22, 1912, pp. 118–137, Letter of Cornelia of Oct 14, 1914.

13 Work diary, 165/106, 107, Jul 27, 1912, May 9, 1913; Personal diary, 165/73, Jul 29, 1912.

14 Personal diary, 165/73, Dec 26, 1912.

15 Work diary, 165/107, 108, Mar 5, 1913, Mar 22, 1914, Work diary, May 31, 1916, Richard Sorabji collection; Letters to Elena, 165/29, May, 25, Jun 2, 1916.

16 Personal diary, 165/75, Jun 8, 1914.

17 Personal diary, 165/75, Jul 29, 1914; Letters to Elena, 165/29, Jun 7, 1916.

18 Personal diary, 165/76, Nov 11, 1915; Letters to Elena, Nov 12, 1915, Richard Sorabji collection.

19 Work diary, Feb 23, 1916, Richard Sorabji collection; Letters to Elena, 165/29, Jan 7, Mar 8, 1916; Personal diary, 165/77, Feb 22, 1916.

20 Letters to Elena, 165/29, Mar 8, Apr 1, 1916; Personal diary, 165/77, Mar 24, Oct 17, 1916.

21 Letters to Elena, 165/29, Mar 8, Apr 7, Jun 7, 1916.

22 Work diary, 165/107, Mar 5–10, 1913.

23 Letters to Elena, 165/35, Apr 20, 1921.

24 Letters to Elena, 165/29, Apr 1, 1916.

25 Chapters 8, 10, 12 and 14.

26 Chapter 14 and Appendix 2.

27 Letters to Elena, Feb 9, 1918, Richard Sorabji collection.

28 Work diary, Jan 24–25, Apr 19, 1917, Richard Sorabji collection; Letters to Elena, 165/29, 30, May 25, 1916, Jan 25, Mar 23, Aug 8, 1917; Personal diary, 165/78, Apr 19, 1917.

29 Letters to Elena, 165/29, Jun 2, 1916.

30 Letters to Elena, 165/30, Jan 25, 1917.

31 Work diary, Apr 19, 1917, Richard Sorabji collection; Personal diary, 165/78, Apr 17, 1917, Letters to Elena, 165/30, Mar 23, 1917.

32 *India Calling*, London p. 180, Delhi p. 132, Nottingham pp. 116–117.

33 India Office Records V/24/2602 quoted in Appendix 2.

34 Personal diary, 165/79, Jun 19, 1918.

35 Work diary, 165/105, Apr 8, 1911.

36 Personal diary, 165/71, Feb 3, Mar 9, 1910; Work diary, 165/105, Apr 8, 1911; Official correspondence on terms of employment, 165/124, pp. 47–62, letter of Cornelia, Oct 17, 1917; Letters to Elena, 165/29, 30, Mar 8, 1916, Jan 25, 1917.

37 Work diary, 165/107, Dec 8, 1913.

38 Letters to Elena, 165/30, Sep 25, 1917.

39 Work diary, Jan 24, 1917, Richard Sorabji collection; Letters to Elena, 165/30, Jan 25, 1917.

40 Personal diary, 165/78, 79, Apr 4, 1917, Sep 28, Dec 1, 1918; Work diary, 165/109–110, Feb 18, May 28, 1918; Letters to Elena, Jan 24, Jul 18, 1918, Richard Sorabji collection.

41 Letters to Elena, 165/30, Aug 5, 8, Sep 25, 1917.

42 Personal diary, 165/79, Mar 18, 29, 30, Apr 30, Nov 28, Dec 2, 1918; Letters to Elena, 165/32, Oct 30, 1919.

43 See photograph, Chapter 9, p. 170.

44 As more fully described by Dick Sorabji, *Bluebell Letters for Children*, privately printed Allahabad, Aug 12, 1918, Richard Sorabji collection.

45 Letters to Elena, Jan 24, 1918, Richard Sorabji collection.

46 Work diary, 165/109–110, Sep 12, Oct 18, 1918; Personal diary, 165/79, May 25, 1918; Letters to Elena, 165/31, Jul 10, Sep 8, 1919.

47 Letters to Elena, 165/31, 32, Sep 8, Oct 15, 1919.

48 Letters to Elena, 165/34, 35, Dec 9, 28, 1920, Jan 5, 27, 1921.

49 Personal diary, 165/65, Aug 15, 1904

50 Personal diary, 165/71, Apr 6, Aug 31, 1910; Work diary, 165/104, 105, 106, 107, Aug 17, 1910, Apr 8, 1911, May 23, 1912, May 23, 1913.

51 Annual reports by Cornelia to the Court of Wards, 1915–16, 165/132, Part B.

52 Letters to Elena, 165/30, 31, Jan 25, Aug 28, 1917, Jul 17, 1919; Personal diary, 165/78, Jan 24, 1917; Work diary, Jan 24, Feb 16, 1917, Richard Sorabji collection; Work diary, 165/109–110, Jul 31, 1918.

53 Work diary, Aug 31, 1917, Richard Sorabji collection; Letters to Elena, 165/31–34, Jul 30, Dec 3, 1919, Jul, 29, Dec 19, 1920.

54 Letters to Elena, 165/31, 33, Jul 10, 1919, Mar 11, 1920; Personal diary, 165/80, Jul 10, 1919.

55 Letters to Elena, 165/32–33, Dec 10, 1919.

56 Letters to Elena, 165/33, 34, Apr 28, Dec 19, 1920.

57 Letters to Elena, 165/33, 35, Jun 30, 1920, Jan 27, 1921; Personal diary, 165/82, Jul 2, 9, Aug 8, 12, Sep 4, Oct 24, 1920.

58 Work diary, Jan 13, 1916, Richard Sorabji collection; Letters to Elena, 165/29, Jan 19, 1916.

59 *India Calling*, London pp. 178–180, Delhi pp. 131–132, Nottingham pp. 115–117.

60 Work diary, 165/106, Oct 19, 1912; Annual reports by Cornelia on Court of Wards, 1915–16, Chittagong division, p. 17.

61 Work diary, Jun 1–2, 10, 14–17, Jul 9–11, Aug 26–27, 1916, Richard Sorabji collection.

62 Compare personal diary, 165/77, Oct 18, 1916.

63 Letters to Elena, 165/31, Jul 10, 1919.

64 Personal diary, 165/84, 85, Nov 21, 1922, Oct 1, Nov 17, Dec 14, 1923; Letters to Elena, 165/36, Dec 15, 1921.

65 India Office List (annual).

66 Personal diary, 165/76, Nov 22, 1915; Letters to Elena, 165/30, 31, Jan 25, 1917, Jun 11 and 12, 1919.

67 Beatson-Bell, she claimed, not only presided over the wastage of 400,000 Rupees (Chapter 14), but also accepted a father's choice of theatre boy as son-in-law, despite the father being suspected of murdering the mother and taking the children's money, and despite contrary promises to the family (Chapters 10 and 14). Monahan's ruling on Cornelia's needing permission apparently delayed a ward's emergency medical treatment (given in this chapter). Morshead, who refused representations about the Maharani of Bettiah (Chapter 14) was also criticised for jeopardising safeguards being imposed upon a potentially murderous grandmother, by renewing her fears about Western medicine (Chapter 10).

68 Chapter 12.

69 Letters to Elena, 165/33, Feb 12, 1920. Compare Letters to Elena, 165/29, 33, undated 1915, pp. 28–30, Mar 17, 1920; Letters to Valentine Chirol, 165/28, Aug 20, 28, 1913, printed in Klaus Stierstorfer, ed., *Women Writing Home, 1700–1920*, Vol. 4, London 2006.

70 Chapter 10.

71 Chapter 2.

72 Personal diary, 165/78, May 26 and 31, 1917.

73 Letters to Elena, 165/29, Dec 28, 1916.

74 Chapter 17.

CHAPTER 16

1 Personal diary, 165/74, Apr 19, Jun 26, 28, Aug 24, 29, 31, Sep 7, 9, 14, Oct 22, Nov 12, 15, 1913

2 See Chapter 9.

3 For what follows see Personal diary, 165/76-80, May 27, Jun 3, Aug 1, 2, 5, 12, 14, Oct 17–19, 22–Nov 2, 7, 14–19, 22–26, Dec 2, 18–20, 31, 1915, Feb 17–18, Apr 4–5, 22, 26, May 27, 30, Jun 1–2, 7, 10, Jul 1–2, Jul 22, 31, 25, Aug 17, 22–25, 28–19, 31, Sep 22, Nov 18, 1916, Jan 14, 28, Feb 11, 17, 21, Mar 1–2, 4, 6, May 19, Jun 22, 24, Jul 29, Nov 10, 24, 29, 1917, Apr 29, May 1, 6–7, 11, 23, 30, Jun 3, 19, Jul 5–6, Aug 17–18, 1918, Jul 5, 1919. Cornelia, Letter to Richard Burn, Aug 13, 1916, Richard Sorabji collection.

4 Letter to Richard Burn, Aug 13, 1916, Richard Sorabji collection.

5 Personal diary, 165/77, 78, Oct 13, 1916, Feb 11, Mar 4, 1917.

6 Work diary, 165/108, Mar 21–22, 1914.

7 Chapter 15.

8 Personal diary, 165/75, Jul 9–10, 1914.

9 Personal diary, 165/75, Apr 8, 1914.

10 *The Times*, May 29, Jun 3, 1914.

11 Chapter 14.

12 Personal diary, 165/75, Jun 30, Jul 5–7, 25–27, Aug 29, Oct 16, 1914; Letters to family, 165/12, Dec 17, 1922.

13 Personal diary, 165/75, Jun 17, Aug 3–4, 7–9, 1914.

14 Chapter 9.

15 Personal diary, 165/75, Jun 25, 1914.

16 Personal diary, 165/75, Jun 29, Jul 16, 1914.

17 *The Times*, Aug 20, 1914; Personal diary, 165/75, Aug 21, 1914.

18 Personal diary, 165/75, Aug 4, 8–13, 28–30, Sep 1–3, 7, 9–10, 1914.

19 Chapter 14.

20 Personal diary, 165/75, Oct 18, 25, 1914; Letters to Elena, 165/29 Nov 17, 1914.

21 Work diary, 165/108, Oct 7–8, 1914.

22 Letters to Elena, 165/29, Oct 13, Nov 17, 1914, Jun 2, 1916.

23 Work diary, 165/108, Oct 26, 28, Nov 2, 1914; Personal diary, 165/75, 76, Oct 25, 28, Nov 4, 1914, Feb 22, 1915; Letters to Elena, 165/29, Nov 17, 1914.

24 Work diary, May 16, 1917, Richard Sorabji collection.

25 Letters to Elena, Feb 9, 1915, Richard Sorabji collection; Work diary, 165/108, Oct 7, 1914.

26 Personal diary, 165/78, Feb 2, 1917; Work diary, Feb 2, 1917, Richard Sorabji collection; Letters to Elena, 165/29, Jul 12, 1915 (pp. 23 and 27 out of order).

27 Personal diary, 165/77, Feb 4, 1916.

28 Letters to Elena, 1915, Richard Sorabji collection; Personal diary, 165/76, May 9, 1915.

29 Peronal diary, 165/76, Nov 16, 1915.

30 Personal diary, 165/76, 77, Jul 2, 1915, May 12, Jun 26, 29, 1917, Aug 29, 1918; Letters to Elena, 165/29, Nov 3, 1916.

31 Personal diary, 165/78, Mar 27, 1917.

32 Personal diary, 165/78, 79, Apr 11, Sep 10, 1917, Jul 31, 1918; Letters to Elena, Jun 13, 1918, Richard Sorabji collection; Letters to Elena, 165/30, Nov 16, 1917. Information on Pheroze from her great granddaughter, Joan King. Nell's son, Geoffrey, is the dedicatee of Cornelia's *Sun Babies*, Second series.

33 Letters to Elena, 165/30, Dec 12, 1917; Personal diary, 165/78, Nov 26, 1917.

34 Personal diary, 165/79, Jun 4, 1918.

35 Chapter 15.

36 Personal diary, 165/79, Aug 25, 29, Sep 4, Oct 5, 1918; Letters to Elena, Jun 13, Jul 18, 1918, Richard Sorabji collection; Work diary, 165/79, Aug 26, 1918.

37 Personal diary, 165/79, Jul 29, Sep 4, Oct 5–Nov 12, Dec 27, 30, 1918; Letters to family, 165/11, Oct 7, 10, 15, Nov 10, 16, 20, 1918; *India Calling*, London pp. 282–284, Delhi pp. 199–201, Nottingham pp. 179–180.

38 Personal diary, 165/79, 84, 85, Nov 28, Dec 2, 1918, Jun 14, 1922, Jul 30, 1923.

39 Chapter 13.

40 Personal diary, 165/80, Jun 6, Jul 2, 1919; Letters to Elena, 165/31, Jun 20, 1919.

41 Personal diary, 165/82, Jul 29, 1920.

42 Dick was appointed legal adviser when there were railway strikes in 1919, and got the men to go back to work, while also securing them all their lawful demands. European, Indian and mixed race employees alike came to him to act as arbitrator. Two years later, he arbitrated again in a railway dispute. He said the men were not wholly in the wrong, and the company had ignored valid requests and grievances. The railway Union Executive decided to postpone their strike, although the goods sheds and smaller hands at

Howrah in Calcutta disobeyed and there were riots. Personal diary, 165/80, Jun 20, 1919; Letters to Elena, 165/31, 35, Jun 24, 1919, Mar 3, 1921.

43 Chapter 9.

44 I have taken information on Sapru from Martin Gilbert, Lecture, 'Churchill: friend or foe of India?', India International Centre, Jan 27, 1905; Rima Hooja, *Crusader for Self-Rule, Tej Bahadur Sapru and the Indian National Movement*, with the Foreword of B. R. Nanda, Jaipur 1999; D. A. Low, *Britain and Indian Nationalism*, Cambridge 1997, Chapter. 8, 'Working with the grain: Sir Tej Bahadur Sapru and the antecedents to the Cripps declaration 1942'; D. A. Low, 'The mediator's moment: Sir Tej Bahadur Sapru and the antecedents to the Cripps Mission to India', in his *Rearguard Action*, Sterling Publishers, Delhi 1996, Chapter. 7, repr. from *Journal of Imperial and Commonwealth History*; Cornelia Sorabji, 'Prospice: the new India', *The Nineteenth Century*, 1931, pp. 176–183, at 178; Rajmohan Gandhi, *Mohandas, The True Story of a Man, his People and an Empire*, Penguin Books, Delhi 2006, p. 319.

45 B. R. Nanda, as above.

46 D. A. Low 1996, 1997, and Martin Gilbert, as above, have described Sapru as gaining support for Indian Independence, against Churchill's wishes, with the American President, Roosevelt, and with the British coalition Government.

47 Chapter 21.

48 Letters to Elena, 165/35, 36, Apr 13, Sep 15, 1921; Personal diary, 165/83, 84, Sep 7, 12, 18, 1921, Jan 25, 1922.

49 Personal diary, 165/82, 83, Dec 24–31, 1920, Oct 13–14, 1921; Letters to Elena, 165/34, 35, 36, Dec 28, 1920, Jan 5, Oct 10, 26, 1921; Cornelia, unpublished manuscript, 'Dashera week, Bharatpur, Rajputana', Nov 17, 1921, Richard Sorabji collection; *India Recalled*, Chapter 17; Dick Sorabji, *The Bluebird Series of Letters for Children*, privately printed, Allahabad, Letter of Jan 19, 1920.

50 Letters to Elena, 165/36, Oct 10, 1921; Dashera Week, Unpublished manuscript, Nov 17, 1921, Richard Sorabji collection.

51 *India Recalled*, pp. 249–254.

52 Letters to Elena, 165/36, 41, 44, Oct 26, 1921, Oct 6, 21, 26, Dec 23, 1926, Nov 6, 28, 1929.

53 Personal diary, 165/84, Sep 20, 1922.

54 Letters to Elena, 165/41, Oct 26, 1921; retold in *India Recalled,* pp. 102–103.

55 Chapter 17. Papers on Bharatpur jewel robbery, 165/146.

56 Letters to Elena, 165/36, Dec 19, 1921; Personal diary, 165/84, Jan 14, 17, 20–24, Mar 2, 1922.

57 Letters to Elena, 165/37, Jan 4, 1922; Personal diary, 165/84, Mar 21, 23, 1922.

58 Personal diary, 165/84, Feb 5–16; Letters to Elena, 165/37, Feb 13, 1922.

59 Letters to Elena, 165/37, Feb 13, 1922.

60 For these reforms, intended to give more political power to Indians, see Chapters 12 and 20.

61 Appendix 1.

62 Personal diary, 165/84, Feb 11, 1922.

63 Personal diary, 165/84, Jul 3, 1922.

64 Personal diary, 165/84, Sep 27, 1922.

65 This continuing theme is found already in Letters to Lady Hobhouse, 165/16, Jul 4, Oct 25, 1897.

66 Letters to family 165/11, 1918–19.

67 Personal diary, 165/84, 85, Oct 20, 1922, Jan 2, 21, May 24, Nov 8, 10, 12, Dec 21, 1923.

68 Letters to Elena, 165/38, Apr 29, 1924.

69 Letters to Elena, 165/38, Sep 18, 1924; Personal diary, 165/86, Sep 4, 1924.

70 Personal diary, 165/84, 85, Apr 5, May 29, Jun 16, Oct 2, 29, Dec 18, 1922, Feb 1, 24, 1923.

71 For her examinations and call to the bar, see Personal diary, 165/84, 85, 86, Apr 26–27, May 1, 10, 11, 17, 26, Jun 15, Oct 17, Nov 3, 7, 24, 28, 1922, Mar 26, Apr 24, May 12, 14, 15, Jun 2, 13–14, Oct 12, 25, 30, Nov 12, 13, 1923, Mar 25, 1924.

72 Letters to family, 165/12, Dec 10, 1922.

73 Personal diary, 165/86, Mar 25, 1924.

74 Personal diary, 165/84, May 2, 27–28, 1922.

75 Personal diary, 165/86, Jan 11, 27, Feb 2, 3, 27, Mar 22, May 29, Jun 1, Jul 11, 12, 26–30, Aug 19, 26–28, Sep 11, 1924. See photo, p. 283, with bride's brother, Allan Monkhouse, left, lawyer colleague Wallach, right rear.

76 Iris Butler, *The Viceroy's Wife: Letters of Alice, Countess of Reading, from India*, 1921–25, London 1969, at p. 142. See Retrospect for further comment.

77 Personal diary, 165/86, Sep 9, 1924.

78 Chapter 12. *India Calling*, London pp. 287–289, Delhi p. 203, Nottingham p. 182.

CHAPTER 17

1 Letters to Elena, 165/38, Oct 6, 10, 1924.

2 Letters to Elena, 165/38, Nov 13, 20, 26, 1924.

3 The guinea was 1/20th more than £1 sterling.

4 Letters to Elena, 165/38, Dec 2, 10, 17, 1924.

5 Letters to Elena, Jul 12, 1925, Richard Sorabji collection; Letters to Elena, 165/38, 39, Nov 13, Dec 5, 10, 1924, Jan 28, Feb 18, Mar 19, Jun 18, Aug 26, Sep 2, 9, 1925.

6 Letters to Elena, 165/39, Aug 26, 1925.

7 Letters to Elena, 165/39, Aug 18, Oct 28, 1925.

8 Letters to Elena, 165/39, Sep 16, 29, 1925.

9 Letters to Elena, 165/39, Nov approx. 25, Dec 2, 9, 1925.

10 Letters to Elena, 165/42, Jan 9, 1927.

11 Letters to Elena, 165/44, Feb 6, 1929.

12 Letters to Elena, 165/40, Jan 13, 1926.

13 Letters to Elena, 165/40, Jan 26, 1925.

14 Letters to Elena, 165/42, Aug 10, 1927.

15 Letters to Elena, 165/42, Jul 19, 27, 1927.

16 Letters to Elena, 165/42, 44, May 10, 1927, Dec 19, 1929.

17 Letters to Elena, 165/40, Feb 11, 1925.

18 Letters to Elena, 165/41, 42, Sep 7, 1926, Nov 9, 1927.

19 Letters to Elena, 165/42, Dec 22, 1927.

20 Letters to Elena, 165/39, Nov 25, Dec 2, 1925.

21 Letters to Elena, 165/41, 42, Sep 22, 1926, Sep 7, 1927.

22 Letters to Elena, 165/42, Feb 22, Apr 27, May 3, 10, Dec 22, 1927.

23 Letters to Elena, 165/44, 45, Nov 6, 1929, Apr 10, 1930.

24 Letters to Elena, 165/41, Jan 4, 1926.

25 Letters to Elena, 165/41, Aug 25, 1926.

26 Letters to Elena, 165/42, Aug 10, 1927.

27 Letters to Elena, 165/42, Feb 2, Mar 10, 1927.

28 Letters to Elena, 165/41, Dec 7, 1926.

29 Letters to Elena, 165/41, Sep 22, 1926.

30 Letters to Elena, 165/41, Sep 22, 1926.

31 Letters to Elena, 165/44, Nov 28, 1929.

32 Letters to Elena, 165/39, 43, 44, Dec 23, 1925, Jan 18, 25, 31, Dec 20, 1928, Jan 30, Feb 6, Mar 27, 1929.

33 Letters to Elena 165/43, early Jan undated, Jan 31, May 17, 1928.

34 Letters to Elena, 165/43, Feb 26, 1928.

35 Letters to Elena, 165/41, Jun 16, 1926.

36 Letters to Elena, 165/41, Sep 22, 1926.

37 Letters to Elena, 165/41, 42, May 26, 1926, Jun 30, 1927.

38 Letters to Elena, 165/39, 41, 42, Nov 10, 1925, Nov 9, 1926, Nov 9, 1927.

39 Letters to Elena, 165/44, Apr 22, 1929.

40 Letters to Elena, 165/41, 42, 43, Sep 22, 1926, Dec 31, 1926, Mar 2, Apr 3, 1927, Feb 29, Apr 12, 18, 26, 29, May 31, Jun 5, 1928

41 Letters to Elena, 165/44, Jan 23, Mar 14, 20, May 8, Jun 26, 1929.

42 E.g. Letters to Elena, 165/43, Apr 18, May 31, Jun 5, 1928.

43 Letters to Elena, 165/42, May 10, 1927.

44 Letters to Elena, 165/41, Feb 11, 1926; Cornelia's opinions on infanticide (etc), 165/143.

45 Letters to Elena, 165/41, Feb 11, Mar 15, 1926.

46 Letters to Elena, 165/41, 42, Jun 23, 1926, Aug 31, 1927.

47 165/164, pp. 1–8, Apr 10, 1928, on Protection of children, as above; 165/143, pp. 55f, 56 draft reply on Protection of children, Apr 10, 1928; Letters to Elena, 165/43, Mar 22, Apr 4, Aug 6, 1928. See Chapter 19.

48 Letters to Elena, 165/42, 44, Apr 27, 1927, Apr 17, Nov 28, 1929; 165/143.

49 165/143, Infanticide pp. 2–10, Slander of women, pp. 11–24, Children's protection, including age of consent, pp. 40–45, 51, 55e, 55f, 56 (and 165/164, pp. 1–8), Civil Service entry for Indians, pp. 25–39, Age of consent, pp. 78–88 (= 165/164, pp. 19–29), Protection of women in Princely States, pp. 101–116.

50 Letters to Elena, 165/41, Jun 26, Sep 22, 1926.

51 Letters to Elena, 165/40, Jan 20, 1926.

52 Letters to Elena, 165/44, 45, Mar 6, Dec 31, 1929, Jan 29, 1930.

53 Letters to Elena, 165/39–43, Jan 25, Feb 11, 18, 1925, Mar 23, 1926, Jul 6, Aug 17, Dec 13, 1927, Jan 11, 25, Feb 21, Mar 8, 1928.

54 See Chapters 14 and 19.

55 Letters to Elena, 165/40 and 41, Feb 3, Mar 10, 23, 24, Apr 28, Jun 16, Aug 19, Nov 4, 1926.

56 Chapter 19.

57 Letters to Elena, 165/43, May 31, Jun 5, 12, 20, Jul 2, 19 (out of order at p. 28), Aug 6, Dec 1, 4, 1928.

58 Chapter 21.

59 Letters to Elena, 165/43, Jul 19, 1928, misplaced at p. 28, emphasis in original.

60 Chapter 14.

61 Letters to Elena, 165/43, Dec 4, 1928; Letters to Dick's family, Jan 4, 1933, Richard Sorabji collection.

62 Letters to Elena, 165/47, Jan 5, 1933.

63 Letters to Elena, 165/43, Jul 19, 1928, misplaced at p. 28.

CHAPTER 18

1   Letters to Elena, 165/40, Feb 24, 1926.

2   Letters to Elena, 165/40, 42, Mar 3, 28, Apr 14, 1926, Oct 6, 1927.

3   Letters to Elena, 165/42, Sep 7, Oct 6, 1927.

4   *Mother India*, Harcourt, Brace, New York, and Jonathan Cape, London 1927, pp. 99–101; cf. 77, 81, 134.

5   Letters to Elena, 165/42, 43, Aug 10, Nov 16, 1927, May 24, 1928.

6   Mrinalini Sinha, *Specters of Mother India*, Durham NC and London 2006, p. 96.

7   *Mother India* 1927, p. 32.

8   Letters to Elena, 165/42, Sep 14, 1927.

9   Mrinalini Sinha has amply confirmed the allegation and uncovered much of the background to Cornelia's entanglement with Mayo in *Selections from Mother India*, Delhi 1998, p. 24; and extensively in *Specters of Mother India*. Much of this background was not clear to Cornelia herself. I shall be drawing on Sinha's two books here and in Chapter 19.

10 Lord Salisbury was very keen to know, but warned her not to tell the over-flamboyant Churchill, while Hoare, Secretary of State, rebuked her for confusing terrorist aspirations with practical realities: Letter to Elena, 165/47, 48, Feb 22, 28, Mar 17, 1933, Feb 7, 13, 1934; Personal diary, 165/97, Jan 7, 1935; Correspondence with Salisbury and Hoare 165/187, Jul 11, 1932, May 27, Jul 13, 28, Aug 12, Sep 16, 1933.

11 More fully described in *India Recalled*, Chapter 11, pp. 147–158.

12 ' "Mother India", The incense of service: what sacrifice can we make?', *The Englishman*, Aug 31 and Sep 1, 1937.

13 Letters to Elena, 165/42, Aug 17, Nov 27, 1927.

14 Letters to Elena, 165/42, Aug 17, Sep 14, 1927.

15 Letters to Elena, 165/42, 43, 46, Aug 10, Sep 21, Oct 6, 1927, Jun 5, 1928, Jun 19, 1931.

16 *The Statesman*, Thursday 18th (month missing) 1927, in Newspaper cuttings, 165/233.

17 Letters to Elena, 165/42, 43, Sep 7, 1927, Apr 26, May 24, 1928.

18 Letters to Elena, 165/42, Oct 6, 1927; Personal diary, 165/90, Oct 21, 1928.

19 Letters to Elena, 165/42, Oct 20, 1927. cf. Margaret I. Balfour, Ruth Young, *The Work of Medical Women in India*, Oxford 1929.

20 Chapter 14; *The Times*, Jun 3, 1914.

21 Mrinalini Sinha, *Selections from Mother India*, p. 16.

22 This was in one of two letters to Eleanor Rathbone, the Member of Parliament whose name was almost identical with the maiden name of her niece, Cornelia's confidant, *Elena* Rathbone, Papers on Katherine Mayo, 165/161.

23 Mrinalini Sinha, *Selections from Mother India*, pp. 26–27; *Specters of Mother India*, pp. 98, 145.

24 Letters to Elena, 165/47, Jun 11, 14, 1933.

25 Martin Gilbert, Lecture, 'Churchill: friend or foe of India?', India International Centre, Delhi, Jan 27, 1905.

26 Letters to Elena, 165/44, Nov 28, 1929.

27 Letters to Elena, 165/42, Dec 22, 1927; Eleanor Rathbone, 'Has Katherine Mayo slandered Mother India?', *The Hibbert Journal*, Jan, 1929.

28 Chapter 19.

29 Letters to Elena, 165/43, 44, Feb 29, May 24, 1928, Oct 31, 1929.

30 Chapter 19, 165/164 and 143.

31 Letters to Elena, 165/46, Jun 25, 1931.

32 Letters to Elena, 165/43, Feb 21, 1928.

33 Chapter 19.

34 165/164, pp. 19–29 = 165/143, pp. 78–88, Aug 13, 1928, Bar library reply to age of consent questionnaire, as above; 165/164, pp. 44–55 re Sarda bill, as above.

35 Mrinalini Sinha, *Specters of Mother India*.

36 Letters to Elena, 165/42, Sep 21, 1927.

37 Letters to Elena, 165/43, Jan 5, Apr 4, 26, 1928.

38 Chapter 19.

39 Letters to Elena, 165/43, 44, Dec 20, 1928, Mar 14, 1929.

40 Letters to Elena, 165/42, 43, Apr 6, 1928, Mar 6, May 16, 1929.

41 Chapter 19.

42 Letters to Elena, 165/43, Jul 7, 1929.

43 Letters to Elena, references in Chapter 17.

44 Letters to Elena, 165/43, Feb 21, 1928.

45 Letters to Elena, 165/43, Feb 21 (p. 67), May 10, 24, 1928.

46 Letters to Elena, 165/43, Jan 5, Feb 21, 1928 (out of order at pp. 43, 67).

47 Letters to Elena, 165/43, Apr 18, Jul 19, 1928.

48 Letter to Elena, 165/46, Jan 29, Feb 5, 1931, Chapter 19.

49 Letters to Dick's family, Feb 27, 1932, Richard Sorabji collection.

50 Letters to Elena, 165/42, 43, Sep 14, 1927, Feb 29, May 24, 1928.

51 *The Statesman*, Mar 5, 1929, in Newspaper cuttings 165/233.

52 Letters to Elena, 165/43, Apr 18, May 24, Jun 12, 1928.

53 Chapter 17.

54 Letters to Elena, 165/45, 51, Sep 8, 1930, Oct 15, 1940; Personal diary 165/47, 48, Oct 12, 1932, Jan 18, Feb 8, Mar 5, May 13, 1935.

55 Mrinalini Sinha, *Specters of Mother India*, p. 144, citing Cornelia's letter in Katherine Mayo's papers at Yale of Sep 1, 1930, folder 55, series 1, box 6.

CHAPTER 19

1 Letters to Elena, 165/44, Oct 17, Nov 13, 28, 1929.

2 Letters to Elena, 165/43, Jan approx. 18, 1928. She was also made Honorary Counsel to the Children's Protection Society, Letters to Elena, 165/43, Jan 31, Feb 8, Jun 12, 1928.

3 Letters to Elena, 165/44, 45, Oct 23–24, 1929, Feb 5, 12, 20, 1930.

4 Letters to Elena, 165/43, May 10, Jun 12, 1928; 165/164, pp. 19–29 = 165/143, pp. 78–88 (Bar library reply of Aug 13, 1928 to Age of Consent Committee questionnaire of July), pp. 9–15 (Letter as Convenor of Public Services Group, Bengal Presidency Council of Women to Judicial Department, Government of Bengal, Jun 26, 1928), pp. 30–32 (Re Bengal's Children's Act, with reference to actions of Bengal Presidency Council of Women, Mar 21, 1929), p. 67 (*The Statesman*'s report, Apr 21, 1929, of Cornelia's speech the day before, 'A child in court'), pp. 68–69 (*The Statesman's* report, Mar 16, 1929, of Cornelia at the first meeting of the Bengal After-Care Association); 165/143, pp. 89–100 (Opinion on Criminal Procedure, Indian Penal Code 552); Cornelia, typescript, 'The traffic in women and children', written as Convenor Public Services Group, Jan 4, 1929, for the magazine of the National Council of Women of India, in Newspaper cuttings, 165/233.

5 Letters to Elena, 165/42, Dec 13, 1927.

6 Letters to Elena, 165/44, Aug approx. 22, 1929.

7 165/164, pp. 19–29 = 165/143 pp. 78–88 (Bar library reply of Aug 13, 1928 to Age of Consent Committee questionnaire question of July).

8 Letters to Elena, 165/43, Apr 4, May 17, 1928; 165/143, pp. 40–56; 165/164, pp. 1–8 (Apr 9, 1928, opinion sent to Judicial Department, Government of Bengal, Apr 10, 1928, re Children's Protection Bill and Amendment of Indian Penal Code sections 375, 376).

9 165/143, May 1, 1928; Letters to Elena, 165/43, May 17, 1928.

10 Letters to Elena, 165/44, Dec 31, 1929; 165/164, pp. 44–55 (reply to question of Sep 7, 1929).

11 Chapter 18.

12 165/143, pp. 55a,b (letter from Pollock).

13 Letters to Elena, 165/43, Apr 4, May 17, 1928; 165/143, May 1, 1928.

14 165/143, pp. 46–49, 55c,d (Correspondence with George Cunningham, May 1, 9, 16, 1928).

15 Letters to Elena, 165/43, Apr 4, May 17, 1928; 165/164, pp. 19–29 = 165/143, pp. 78–88, as above.

16 165/164, pp. 1–8, Apr 10, 1928, on Protection of children, as above; 165/143, pp. 55f, 56 draft reply on Protection of children, Apr 10, 1928; Letters to Elena, 165/43, Mar 22, Apr 4, Aug 6, 1928.

17 165/164, pp. 1–8, Bar library reply, Apr 10, 1928, as above, pp. 44–55 reply to question of Sep 7, 1929 reply to Sarda bill, as above, pp. 19–29 (= 165/143, pp. 78–88), Aug 13, 1928, Bar library reply, as above.

18 165/164, pp. 44–55 reply to question of Sep 7, 1929 reply to Sarda bill, as above.

19 Chapters 12, 16, 17.

20 Chapter 20.

21 Chapter 21.

22 Letters to Elena, 165/47, Jun 11, 1933.

23 Letters to Elena, 165/39, Oct 13, 28, Nov 4, 1925.

24 Letter to *The Times*, Aug 6, 1936 and Dick's letter, 165/171.

25 Letters to Elena, 165/50, Dec 13, 1937, Feb 23, 1938.

26 Letters to Elena, 165/43, Apr 29, 1928.

27 Letters to Elena, 165/43, Jan 31, Apr 26, Jun 5, 1928.

28 Letters to Elena, 165/44, Feb 6, 1929.

29 Letters to Elena, 165/44, Jul 24, 1929, printed in *The Statesman* Jul 31, 1929, cutting enclosed with Letters to Elena of July 1929.

30 Letters to Elena, 165/44, Apr 17, 1929.

31 Chapters 4 and 16.

32 Letters to Elena, 165/43, Jul 2, 1928.

33 Chapter 18.

34 Letters to Dick's family, Jan 4, 1933, Richard Sorabji collection; Letters to Elena, 165/47, Jan 5, Feb 28, Jun 10 (out of order, p. 174), 1933.

35 Letters to Elena, 165/42, Oct 6, Nov 9, 23, 1927.

36 Chapter 12.

37 Letters to Elena, 165/44, Feb 27, 1929.

38 Letters to Elena, 165/42, 43, 44, 45, Nov 9, 1927, May 24, 1928, Feb 19, Aug 29, Nov 28, 1929, Mar 20, 1930.

39 Letters to Elena, 165/42, 43, Oct 6, Nov 16, Dec 13, 22, 1927, Dec 20, 1928.

40 Letters to Dick's family, Feb 1, 1932, Jan 4, 1933, Richard Sorabji collection; Letters to Elena, 165/47, Jan 5, 17, 1933.

41 Letters to Elena, 165/47, Feb 8, 14, 21, 1932.

42 Letters to Elena, 165/43, 44, Dec 20, 1928, May 8, Jun 6, 13 (encloses brochure), Nov 21, 1929.

43 Handbook of the Bengal League of Social Service for Women, Calcutta August 1929, Richard Sorabji collection; Letter to *The Times*, 'Social service in India', Apr 3, 1929.

44 Chapter 12.

45 See Chapter 10.

46 Letters to Elena, 165/30, 31 and 39, Nov 16, 1917, Aug 9, 1919, Nov 4 and 10, 1925; 165/178, Cornelia, 'An orthodox Hindu cannot be a true democrat', Oct 31, 1925, typescript for speech delivered Nov 5, 1925.

47 As she argued in 'Back to the woman', see Chapter 12.

48 Letters to Elena, 165/43, Dec 20, 1928; Letter to *The Times* Apr 23, 1929, Richard Sorabji collection; Chapter 18.

49 Letters to Elena, 165/42, 44, Jan 27, 1927, Mar 6, 14, Apr 11, 1929; Broadcast type-script, 'We take the golden road to Samarkand', Richard Sorabji collection.

50 Letters to Elena, 165/44, 45, Apr 17, Nov 13, 21, 1929, Jan 15, Feb 20, 27, Apr 22, 1930.

51 Letters to Elena, 165/44, Jun 6, 21, Aug approx. 22, 1929.

52 Letters to Elena, 165/44, Jun 26, Jul 7, 1929.

53 Letters to Elena, 165/44, 45, Aug approx. 22, Sep 26, Nov 13, 1929, Feb 27, 1930; *India Calling*, London pp. 238–243, Delhi pp. 170–173, Nottingham pp. 153–155.

54 *India Calling*, London pp. 238–243, Delhi pp. 170–173, Nottingham pp. 153–155; Handbook of the Bengal League of Social Service for Women, Calcutta August 1929, Richard Sorabji collection.

55 Letters to Elena, 165/45, May 12, 17, 1930.

56 Letters to Elena, 165/45, Jul 14, 1930.

57 Appendix 1.

58 Letters to Elena, 165/46, Jan 29, 1931.

59 Letters to Elena, 165/46, 47, Jan 29, Feb 26, Mar 21, 1931, Mar 13, 1932.

60 *India Calling*, London p. 242, Delhi pp. 172–173, Nottingham p. 155. For another example of violent extortion from purdahnashins for the Swarajist cause, see *India Calling*, London p. 268, Delhi pp. 189–191, Nottingham pp. 170–171.

61 Letters to Elena, 165/44, Jul 7, 1929.

62 Letters to Elena, 165/46, Feb 5, 12, Mar 12, 1931.

63 Letters to Elena, 165/46, Mar 21, Jul 3, 23, 1931.

64 Letters to Elena, 165/47, Mar 13, 1932, Jan 17, 1933.

65 Appendix 1.

CHAPTER 20

1 M. K. Gandhi, *The Story of my Experiments with Truth* (an autobiography), translated from Gujarati by Mahadev Desai, 1927–29, Penguin Books, Harmondsworth, 1982.

2 Bhikhu Parekh, *Colonialism, Tradition and Reform*, 2nd edition Delhi 1999, Chapter 4, 'Theory of Non-violence'.

3 Chapter 9.

4 Rajmohan Gandhi, *Mohandas, The True Story of a Man, his People and an Empire*, Penguin Books, Delhi 2006, p. 242.

5 Stanley Wolpert, *Jinnah of Pakistan*, Oxford 1984.

6 Chapter 18.

7 Chapter 17. Draft of speech, 165/178, Oct 1925; Letters to Elena 165/39, Oct 13, Nov 10, 1925.

8 Letters to Elena, 165/32, 39, 41, Sep 20, 1919, Nov 18, 1925, Dec 23, 1926; Cornelia had visited also the court of her less-distinguished mother: Letters to Lady Hobhouse, 165/16, Jan 18, 1896.

9 Chapter 8.

10 Chapter 19.

11 Chapter 12 n. 8: Letters to Elena, 165/30, Nov 16, Dec 12, 1917.

12 Chapter 12, n. 33: Letters to Elena, 165/31, Sep 12, 1911; *India Recalled*, Chapter 18.

13 Katherine Mayo, *Mother India*, Harcourt, Brace and co., New York, Jonathan Cape, London, 1927, pp. 118–119.

14 I am indebted to conversation with his great grandson, Dr Deepak Tilak, Vice Chancellor of Tilak Maharashtra Vidyapeeth. For Cornelia on Tilak, see Letters to Lady Hobhouse, 165/16, Jul 4, Oct 25, 1897; Cutting from *The Times* in Letters to Blair, 165/23, Oct 12, 1903; Letters to Mrs Darling, 165/20, Oct 20, 1897; Letters to Elena, 165/29, Jan 19, 1916.

15 Chapter 9.

16 Letters to Elena, 165/36, Aug 18, 1921.

17 B. R. Nanda, Foreword to Rima Hooja, *Crusader for Self-Rule, Tej Bahadur Sapru and the Indian National Movement,* p. 14.

18 B.R.Nanda, Foreword to Rima Hooja, *Crusader for Self-Rule, Tej Bahadur Sapru and the Indian National Movement,* p. 13.

19 *Mohandas, The True Story of a Man, his People and an Empire*, pp. 315, 318, 323.

20 Family information.

21 Chapter 12.

22 Chapter 12, n. 34: 165/177, 'Necessity for safeguards', typescript, Mar 6, 1919, with covering letter Jun 3, 1919; Personal diary, 165/80, Mar 23, 1919; Letters to Elena, 165/32, Nov 23, 1919.

23 *Mohandas, The True Story of a Man, his People and an Empire*, pp. 248–249.

24 *Mohandas, The True Story of a Man, his People and an Empire*, pp. 225, 262–263, 265–267.

25 Cornelia's interview with Gandhi, excerpt quoted in Chapter 21.

26 Letters to Elena, 165/35, 36, Jun (undated, approx 8th), Nov 23, 1921.

27 Chapter 10.

28 Letters to Elena, 165/37, Mar 2, 1922; Personal diary, 165/84, Feb 28, 1922.

29 *India Calling*, London pp. 267–270, Delhi pp. 188–191, Nottingham pp. 170–173.

30 Anand A. Yang, 'An institutional shelter: the Court of Wards in later Nineteenth Century Bihar', *Modern Asian Studies* 13, 1979, 247–264, at 257–259.

31 Letters to Elena, 165/35, Feb 17, 1921.

32 Letters to Elena, 165/36, Sep 21, Oct 10, 1921.

33 Chapter 17.

34 Chapter 19.

35 Chapter 19.

36 Letters to Elena, 165/50, Feb 23, 1938.

37 Personal diary, 165/84, Mar 12 and 23, 1922; Letters to Elena, 165/48, Aug 28, 1935.

38 Chapter 16. Personal diary, 165/86, Sep 4, 1924; Letters to Elena, 165/38, Sep 18, 1924.

39 Rajmohan Gandhi, *Mohandas*, p. 358.

40 Katherine Mayo, *Mother India*, Chapter 5; Cornelia, Review of Mayo, *The Englishman* Aug 31, Sep 1, 1927, in 165/161; Gandhi, 'Curse of child marriage', *Young India*, Aug 26, 1926.

41 Letters to Elena, 165/40, Jan 4, 1926, one page preserved.

42 Letters to Elena, 165/49, Nov 26, 1936.

43 Letter from Mirabehn, Jan 4, 1926, Dec 26, 1926, enclosed in Letters to Elena, 165/40, 41.

44 Chapter 8.

45 Letters to Elena, 165/41, 42, Jul 29, 1926, Mar 16, Apr 6, 1927.

46 Chapter 22.

47 Letters to Elena, 165/46, Jan 29, Feb 5 and 12, 1931.

48 Letters to Elena, 165/46, Feb 18, 1931, see also Apr 2, 1931, 165/48, Sep 26, 1935. A shorter account of the prayer meeting, ' "The Showing", a silhouette', dated Mar 10, 1931 is in 165/181, perhaps intended for submission to *The Times*.

49 Letters to Elena, 165/45, Jan 15, 1930.

50 Letters to Elena, 165/51, Dec 15, 1940, Jan 8, May 11, 1941.

51 *Mohandas, The True Story of a Man, his People and an Empire*, pp. 360–363, 370–374.

52 Letters to Elena, 165/47, Dec 29, 1932.

53 Personal diary, 165/65, Jan 15, Feb 24–28, Jul 2, 1904.

54 Personal diary, 165/67, 68, Jun 5, 26, 1906, Dec 24, 1906–Jan 4, 1907; Letter to Elena, May 28, 1918, Richard Sorabji collection.

55 Letter to Sarojini Naidu of 1940, quoted in Chapter 23.

56 Work diary, 165/108, Apr 12, 15, 1914.

57 Letter to Elena, May 28, 1918, Richard Sorabji collection.

58 Letters to Elena, 165/30, Nov 16, 1917; Personal diary, 165/78, Oct 19, 1917.

59 Letters to Elena, 165/40, 41, Apr 8, Jul 7, 1926.

60 Letters to Elena, 165/41, Jul 29, 1926.

61 Letters to Elena, 165/42, 43, Aug 31, 1927, Jan 25, 1928.

62 Letters to Elena, 165/42, Sep 7, 1927.

63 Chapter 22.

64 Letters to Elena, 165/47, Dec 9, 1932.

65 Letters to Elena, 165/48, May 7, 11, 1933.

66 Personal diary, 165/95, May 11, 1933.

67 Personal diary, 165/68, May 4, 1907.

68 Chapter 14.

69 Personal diary, 165/78, Nov 23, 1917.

70 Letter to Elena, Jul 31, 1918, Richard Sorabji collection; Personal diary, 165/79, Jul 24–25, 1918.

71 Personal diary 165/80, Apr 21, 1919; Letters to Elena, 165/84, Jan 25, 1922.

72 Letters to Elena, 165/39, Oct 9, 1925 (out of order at pp. 94–100).

73 Letters to Elena Jul 23, 31, 1925, Reply to Besant, Jul 20, 1925, all in Richard Sorabji collection.

74 Letters to Elena, 165/41, 42, Oct 6, 1926, Sep 14, 1927.

CHAPTER 21

1 D. A. Low, 'Sir Tej Bahadur Sapru and the First Round Table Conference', in his *Rearguard Action*, Sterling Publishers, Delhi 1996, Ch. 3, pp. 54–95. Low sees Sapru as the dominant figure.

2 Rajmohan Gandhi, *Mohandas, The True Story of a Man, his People and an Empire*, Penguin Books, Delhi 2006, pp. 323, 325.

3 D.A. Low, 'Sir Tej Bahadur Sapru and the First Round Table Conference', in his *Rearguard Action*, Ch. 3, pp. 54–95.

4 Letters to Elena, 165/46, Feb 12, 1931, cf. 165/45, Jan 15, 1930; Personal diary, 165/93, Jan 26, 1931.

5 Chapter 20.

6 Rajmohan Gandhi, *Mohandas, The True Story of a Man, his People and an Empire*, p. 346.

7 Rajmohan Gandhi, *Mohandas, The True Story of a Man, his People and an Empire*, pp. 360–364.

8 Rajmohan Gandhi, *Mohandas, The True Story of a Man, his People and an Empire*, pp. 201–202.

9 Letters to Dick's family, Feb 21, 1933, Richard Sorabji collection.

10 Letter to Elena, 165/46, Sep 27, 1931; Personal diary, 165/93, Sep 24, 1931; Interview reproduced in *Atlantic Monthly* April 1932, pp. 453–458, copy in 165/181.

11 Letters to Elena, 165/35, May 5, 1921.

12 *India Calling*, London pp. 262–265, Delhi pp. 185–187, Nottingham pp. 167–169.

13 Chapter 19.

14 Rajmohan Gandhi, *Mohandas, The True Story of a Man, his People and an Empire*, p. 401.

15 'Gandhi interrogated, an interview', *The Atlantic Monthly*, April 1932.

16 Personal diary, 165/93, Sep 24, 1931; Letters to Elena, 165/46, Sep 27, 1931.

17 Rajmohan Gandhi, *Mohandas, The True Story of a Man, his People and an Empire*, pp. 360–365.

18 For what follows, see Rajmohan Gandhi, *Mohandas, The True Story of a Man, his People and an Empire*, 370–374.

19 Letters to Elena, 165/47, Feb 22, 1933.

20 Rajmohan Gandhi, *Mohandas, The True Story of a Man, his People and an Empire*, p. 376.

21 Letters to Dick's family, Dec 28, 1931, Richard Sorabji collection; Personal diary, 165/93, Dec 26, 1931.

22 Letters to Elena, 165/48, Oct 28, 1935.

23 Letters to Elena, 165/49, Nov 26, 1936.

24 For what follows see Letters to Elena, 165/47, Feb, 9, 16, 22, 28, May 3, 10, 22, 23, 30, Jun 7, 10, 11, 27, Jul 1, 8, 16, Aug 1, 1933; Personal diary 165/95, May 3, 6, 7, 23, Jun 26, 30, Jul 7, 11, 13, 20, Aug 2, 1933.

25 *Madras Mail*, Oct 5, 1932 in Articles on Gandhi, 165/181.

26 Personal diary, 165/83, Oct 13, 1921.

27 Prof. R. K. Sorabji (=Dick), 'The third Round Table Conference, a priceless experience', The Church of England Newspaper, Jan 6, 1933, cutting in Richard Sorabji

collection; Letters to Dick's family, Feb 14, 1933, both in Richard Sorabji collection; Letters to Elena, 165/47, Jan 4, 1933.

28 For Tagore, Letters to Elena, 165/45, Sep 28, 1930.

29 Letters to Elena, 165/45, 46, Jul 8, 10, 1930, Sep 27, 1931; Personal diary, 165/92, Jul 9, 10, 1930.

30 Letters to Elena, 165/45, Oct 22, 1930.

31 Personal diary, 165/93, Nov 7, 1931.

32 Letters to Elena, 165/46, Oct or Nov? 3, 1931.

CHAPTER 22

1 Chapter 20.

2 Chapter 13.

3 Letters to Dick's family, Feb 8, 1933, undated pp. 5–7 of approx. Dec 29, 1932, Richard Sorabji collection; Personal diary Jan 18, 1938.

4 Letters to Elena, 165/48, 49, 50, Sep 11, 1934, Nov 16, 26, Dec 1, 1936, Jan 6, 19, Dec 20–22, 1937.

5 Letters to Elena, 165/48, 50, Sep 11, 1934, Dec 20–22, 1937.

6 *India Calling*, London pp. 56–57, Delhi pp. 47–48, Nottingham pp. 41–42. Chapter 4.

7 Chapter 16.

8 See Chapter 4.

9 Chapter 4.

10 Personal diary, 165/96, Feb 10, 1934; Letters to Elena, 165/49, Dec 1, 1936 and 165/150.

11 Letters to Elena, 165/49, Dec 1, 1936.

12 Personal diary, 165/100, Jan 25, 1938; Letters to Elena, 165/50, Jan 13, 25, Feb 2, 7, 15, 23, Mar 2, 23, 1938.

13 165/150.

14 165/150.

15 Letters to Elena, 165/39, 41, 42, Feb 11, 18, Mar 10, 19, 25, Apr 2, 15, 22 (p. 55), undated (p. 61), Jun 5, Aug 18, Nov 18, Dec 2, 23, 1925, May 12, 1926, May 18, 1927. Bastar palace was 187 miles South of Raipur in Jagdalpur in the Central Provinces (now Chhattisgarh).

16 Letters to Elena, 165/42, May 18, 1927.

17 Letters to Elena, 165/50, Feb 7, 1938.

18 For opposite views see Nandini Sundar, *Subalterns and Savages*, Oxford University Press 1997, p. 192, and a work of defence by Juga Bhanu Singh Deo, *A man called Prafulla Chandra Banj Deo*, Bhubaneshwar 2005.

19 Letters to Elena, 165/39, 41, 42, Feb 11, 18, Mar 10, 19, 25, Apr 2, 15 (out of order p. 26), Apr 22 (p. 55), Apr undated (p. 61), Jun 5, Aug 18, Nov 18, Dec 2, 23, 1925, May 12, 1926, May 18, 1927, Feb 7, 1938.

20 165/143.

21 The case is summarised in Legal opinions, 165/143, opinions on Princely States, pp. 101–116.

22 Susie, autobiography, 165/209, pp. 33–48, at p. 40, her Ch. 2, see also Letter to Lady Hobhouse, 165/16, Jun 27, 1895.

23 Letters to Elena, 165/39, Oct 9, 1925.

24 Letters to Elena, 165/39, Sep 2, Oct 13, 1925.

25 Letters to Elena, 165/42, 43, Jan 5, 1927, Feb 26, 1928.

26 Letters to Elena, 165/43, Feb 26, Mar 4, 1928.

27 Letters to Elena, 165/39, 40, 43, 45, Mar 19, Oct 13, Nov 10, 1925, Mar 3, 10, 1926, Feb 16, 26, Mar 4, 1928, Jan 15, 1930.

28 Letters to Elena, 165/39, Oct 28, Nov 10, 1925.

29 Letters to Elena, 165/39, 41, Nov 18, 1925, Jun 16, 1926.

30 Letters to Elena, 165/43, Jul 2, 1928.

31 Letters to Elena, 165/45, Jan 15, 1930.

32 Etters to Elena, 165/43, 44, Feb 26, 1928, Sep 19, 1929.

33 Letters to Elena, 165/43, Feb 26, 1928.

34 Letters to Elena, 165/45, Jan 15, 1930.

35 Letters to Elena, 165/46, Jan 29, 1931; Personal diary, 165/91, Jan 27, 1931.

36 Letters to Elena, 165/46, Feb 26, Jul 10, 1931.

CHAPTER 23

1 Personal diary, 165/96, Mar 24, Nov 8, 1934.

2 Letters to Elena, 165/51, Sep 28, 1940.

3 *Yorkshire Herald*, Jun 27, 1936, Richard Sorabji collection.

4 Personal diary, 165/95, Apr 24, 1933.

5 Chapter 9.

6 Personal diary, 165/100, Jul 30, Aug 6–8, 1938.

7 Personal diary, 165/100, Oct 24, 1938.

8 Personal diary, 165/100, Sep 22, Oct 16, 1938.

9 Letters to Elena, 165/51, Oct 2, 22, 1939.

10 Letters to Elena, 165/51, Aug 4, 1940.

11 Letters to Elena, 165/50, Sep 29, 1938; Personal diary, 165/100, Oct 21, 1938.

12 Letters to Elena, 165/51, Oct 2, 22, Nov 26, 1939.

13 Letters to Elena, 165/51, Nov 26, Dec 4, 1940, Jan 8, Feb 1, 1941.

14 Letters to Elena, 165/51, Sep 11, 1940.

15 Letters to Elena, 165/51, Sep 19, 1940.

16 Personal memory here and elsewhere.

17 Letters to Elena, 165/51, Dec 13, 30, 1940.

18 Letters to Elena, 165/51, Dec 9, 1940.

19 Letters to Elena, 165/51, Dec 9, 1940.

20 Letters to Elena, 165/51, Aug 4, Oct 9, Nov 11, 26, 1940, Feb 24, Aug 4, 1941.

21 Letters to Elena, 165/51, Sep 19, 1940.

22 Chapter 20.

23 See Retrospect.

24 Other correspondence 1890s–1944, 165/54, pp. 160–164, draft dated Aug 4, 1940.

25 Letters to Elena, 165/54, Nov 26, 1940, Feb 1, 1941.

26 *Bhagavadgita* 2.47, 4.20, 18.26.

27 Correspondence on Congress propaganda in America, 165/186, May 23, 1932; Personal diary, 165/94, May 21, 30, 1932.

28 Letters to Elena, 165/51, Sep 19, 1940.

29 Letters to Elena, 165/51, Sep 28, 1940.

30 Letters to Elena, 165/51, Oct 15, 1940.

31 Letters to Elena, 165/51, Oct 9, Nov 16, 1940, Apr 17, Jun 4, 1941.

32 Letters to Elena, 165/51, Nov 11, 1940.

33 Letters to Elena, 165/51, Nov 16, 1940.

34 Letters to Elena, 165/51, Nov 26, 1940.

35 Letters to Elena, 165/51, Dec 30, 1941.

36 Letters to Elena, 165/51, Jan 8, 1941.

37 Letter from Ursula Blackwell, Apr 7, 1941, included in Letters to Elena, 165/51.

38 Letters to Elena, 165/51, May 11, 1931 and family information. My mother, Dick's wife, thought the story concerned the Temple Church, but I now prefer Cornelia's record that it was St Dunstan's.

39 Letters to Elena, 165/51, Apr 17, 1941.

40 Letters to Elena, 165/51, May 11, 18, 1941.

41 Letters to Elena, 165/51, Apr 17, 1941.

42 Letters to Elena, 165/51, May 18, Jun 4, Aug 4, 1941.

43 Chapter 13; Letters to Elena, 165/51, Dec 25, 1940.

44 Letters to Elena, 165/51, Aug 4, 1940.

45 Letters to Elena, 165/51, Jul 31, Aug 9, 1941; Other correspondence 1890s-1944, 165/54, pp. 207, 220, May 2, 1943.

46 Other correspondence 1890s–1944, 165/54, pp. 167–168, 225, Nov 24, 1944.

47 Other correspondence 1890s–1944, 165/54, p. 242, Sep 9, Dec 6, 1944; Correspondence with Lady Wavell, including her reply, 165/130, Jan 23, 1945.

48 Letters to Elena from and about Cornelia, 165/52, 1945.

49 Personal diary, 165/95, 96, Nov 15, 1933, Apr 8, 1934.

RETROSPECT

1 Described in Chapters 12 and 19.

2 Chapters 2 and 3.

3 Chapter 2.

4 Chapter 7.

5 Chapter 14.

6 Chapter 19.

7 Photograph Chapter 9, p. 180.

8 Cover and frontispiece.

9 William Dalrymple, *White Mughals*, London 2002; *The Last Mughal*, London 2006.

10 Chapter 16.

11 Chapters 16 and 23. See also Personal diary, 165/90, Oct 28–29, 1928.

12 Mary K. Sorabji, taped reminiscences, second set taped by Mary Matthews 1985, in Richard Sorabji collection.

13 Chapter 18.

14 Letters to Elena, 165/38, 39, 46, Apr 29, Oct 19, 1924, Nov 18, 1925, Feb 18, 1931 (to Mirabehn); *India Calling*, London pp. 3, 7, Delhi pp. 12, 15, Nottingham pp. 10, 12; Letter to Sarojini Naidu, quoted in Chapter 23. See pp. 3, 10–18, 236, 246, 278, 372–373.

15 Letter to Mrs Darling, 1897–8, 165/20, Oct 20, 1897.

16 *India Calling*, London p. 7, Delhi p. 15, Nottingham p. 12.

17 *India Calling*, London, p. 14, Nottingham p. 16, Delhi p. 19.

APPENDIX I

1 Chapter 5.

2 Letters home, 165/3, Sep 24, 1890, 165/7, Aug 1892, letters to Elena, 165/50, Dec 31, 1937.

3 Lady Ford letters, 165/203, Aug 20, 1885.

4 Cornelia letters home, 165/2, Mar 23, 1890.

5 Letter in London Metropolitan Archives, LMA/4063/003, and on website 'Moving Here'.

6 Letters home, 165/3, Oct 7, 1890.

7 Letters home, 165/7, Aug 1892.

8 Personal diary, 165/56, Jul 29, 1895.

9 Personal diary, 165/56, 57, 61, Jun–Dec 1895, Mar and Sep 1896, Apr, May, Sep 1900.

10 Dick's letters home, 165/206, Jun 6, 1895.

11 Personal diary, 165/75, Apr 26, 1914.

12 Personal diary, 165/64, Apr 28, 1903.

13 Personal diary 165/79 and 84, Dec 15–31, 1918, Apr 13–18, 1922.

14 See photograph, p. 283.

15 Letters home, 165/1 and 2, Oct 18, 1889, Mar 23, May 8 and Jun 1, 1890; Letters to Dick's family, approx. Dec 29, 1932 (only pp. 5–7 surviving), Richard Sorabji Collection.

16 He seems to have had a brother, James Thomas, with children in Buenos Aires and a sister Mrs Frances Jane Wilson, Alice, Letters home, 165/207, Mar 17, 1904.

17 Letters home, 165/3, Aug 10, 1890; Personal diary, 165/56, May 3, 1895.

18 Information on his birth from Joan King, his great grand daughter.

19 Cornelia Letters home, 165/3, Aug 10, 1890.

20 Letters home, 165/1 and 3, Sep 21 and 27, 1889, Sep 7, 1890.

21 Letters home, 165/2, May 8, 1890 (a letter to Pheroze).

22 Chapters 2 and 3.

23 Letters home, 165/3, 4, 5 and 7, Dec 4 and 11, 1890, Jun 2 and 18, Jul 8, Aug 25, Nov 8, 15 and 22, 1891, Feb 14, Nov 11, Dec 24, 1892.

24 Letters home, 165/8, Feb 16 and 22, 1893.

25 Information from Pheroze's great grand daughter, Joan King.

26 Personal diary, 165/63 and 64, Feb 4, May 6, Jun 7, Oct 15, 1902, Jan 2, 1903, Letters to Falkner Blair, 165/22, Nov 28, 1902, Jan 9, 1903, Alice, Letters home, 165/207, Apr 6, 1905.

27 Family information.

28 Personal diary, 165/73, Mar 8, 1912.

29 Pheroze was in England at least in 1905, Alice, Letters home, 165/207, Mar 30, 1905.

30 Information from Pheroze's great grand daughter, Joan King.

31 Personal diary, 165/84, Apr 26 and 30.

32 Information from Pheroze's great grand daughter, Joan King.

33 Information from my sister Francina.

34 Information from her great grand daughter, Joan King.

35 *India Calling*, London p. 14, Nottingham p. 16, Delhi p. 19.

36 Personal diary, 165/57, Feb 21, May 6, Nov 1, 1896, 165/66 and 67, Feb 5, Apr 11, 1905, May 26, 1906; Alice, Letters home, Jan 12, 1904, Feb to Apr 7, 1905. Cornelia, 'Life of Lena Sorabji', 165/211, 1935.

37 Personal diary, 165/68, 69, 70, Oct 30, 1907, Feb 3 and 16, May 2, 1908, Jan 3–4, 13–14, 1909; Cornelia, 'Life of Lena Sorabji', 165/211, 1935.

38 Work diary, 165/24, Aug 3, 1910; Letters to Elena, 165/29, Jan 27, Feb 5, 1914.

39 Work diary, 165/107, Jul 21, 1913, Personal diary, 165/77, Jan 16, Jun 24, 1916, Letters to Elena, 165/31, Jun 20 and 28, 1919.

40 Letter of Mary in Richard Sorabji collection.

41 Letters to Elena, 165/31, Jun 20 and 28, 1919, Personal diary, 165/80, Sep 22, 1919.

42 Personal diary, 165/69, Jan 5, Feb 3, 9, 16, 1908; 165/77, Jun 1–2, 1916, Cornelia, 'Life of Lena Sorabji', 165/211, 1935.

43 Cornelia, 'Life of Lena Sorabji', 165/211, 1935.

44 Letters home, 165/5, Nov 22, 1891.

45 Letters to Dick's family, approx. Dec 29, 1932 (only pp. 5–7 surviving), Richard Sorabji Collection.

46 Mary Sorabji, note (approx. 1940) on the 1884 opening of the High School for Indian Girls, Richard Sorabji collection. In Ahmedabad she was at the Mahalakshmi Training College for Women Teachers. The Poona High School was in Kibe's Wada.

47 Letters home, 165/5 and 6, Jul 12, Aug 18, 1891, Aug 18, Sep 29, Nov 1, 1892.

48 Personal diary 165/57 and 58, May 6, 1896, Jan 11 and Jul 7, 1897; Letters to Mrs Darling, 165/20, Jan 1, Oct 20, 1898; Alice, Letters home, 165/207, Mar 23, 1905.

49 Letters to Blair, 165/24, Mar 23, 1904.

50 Letters to Elena, Dec 15, 1932.

51 Mary Sorabji, note (approx. 1940) on the 1884 opening of the High School for Indian Girls, Richard Sorabji collection.

52 Personal diary, 165/68, 69 and 70, Aug 25, 1907, Nov 27, 1908, Jan 4, 1909.

53 A Canadian, Miss Young, Personal diary, 165/71 and 75, May 30, 1910, Jul 31, Aug 2, 1911, Apr 11, 1914.

54 Letters to family, 165/11, Mar 6, 1918.

55 Letters to Elena, 165/31, Mar 8, Aug 5, 1919.

56 Personal diary, 165/98–100, 1936–8.

57 Reported to me by Ewan Green, Magdalen College, Oxford.

58 Letters to Elena, 165/51, May 11 and 18, Jun 4, Aug 4, 1941.

59 Chapter 19.

60 Chapters 19 and 21.

61 Cornelia Sorabji, *The Life of Susie Sorabji*, Oxford University Press, London 1932. At pp. 20–60 this book misdates Susie's tour to 1904. For the account of Susie I am relying not only on it, but also on Cornelia, Personal Diary, 165/63, Apr 12 and Dec 2–31, 1902; Letters to Falkner Blair 165/22 and 23, Dec 3 and 24, 1902, and (misplaced at p. 496) Jan 9, 1903; on visits to Susie's school and meetings with her former pupils in 1988 and 2007, and above all on Susie's 18-page autobiography in 165/209, pp. 33–48.

62 Chapter 1.

63 Personal diary, 165/58, Oct 16, 1897.

64 That is the appraisal of Mrs Olive Das, the present Secretary of the Board of Management of the English language school that Susie went on to found, St Helena's.

65 Alice Pennell, Letters home 1904–5, 165/207; Cornelia Sorabji, Personal diary 165/66, May 23, 1905.

66 Chapter 2.

67 Also Soli Captain, Mrs Masters and Tehmi Chinnoy.

68 Oil in the school, pastel by FK in Richard Sorabji collection, given by Tehmi Chinnoy, photographs in 165/209 and in Cornelia's *Susie Sorabji*, Oxford 1932 (detail on p. 397).

69 Alice, Letter to the family on Susie's funeral, in Richard Sorabji collection.

70 Letters to Elena, 165/46, March to July 1931; Personal diary, 165/93, Jun 24, 1931.

71 3rd lot in the 1931 section.

72 See Chapter 3.

73 Letters home, 165/1, Sep 21,1889; 165/4, Jan24, 1891; 165/7, Oct 27,1892.

74 Letters to Lady Hobhouse, 165/16, Dec 10 and 27, 1895, in *Women Writing Home*.

75 Personal diary, 165/56, Dec 3,1895; 165/57, Feb 13,1896.

76 Personal diary, 165/58, Jan 9,1897.

77 Personal diary, 165/58, Feb 12; Mar 25; May 3, 6 and 27; Jun15 and 29; Jul 6,1897.

78 Personal diary, 165/59, Oct 26,1898.

79 Records from archives of Royal Holloway College and Royal Free Hospital.

80 Personal diary, 165/62, Mar 2,1901.

81 Letters to Falkner Blair 165/21, Jun 7,1901.

82 Letters to Falkner Blair 165/21, Oct and 15 Nov 1901.

83 Personal diary, 165/63, Feb 28,1902; Letters to Falkner Blair, 165/22, Jul 17,1902.

84 Alice's letters home, 165/207, Jan 12 and Feb 2 1904.

85 Personal diary, 165/65, Jun 1904; 165/66, Jan 5; Feb 8 and 14, 1905.

86 Alice's letters home, 165/207, Mar 9,1905.

87 Personal diary 165/66, Jun 17,1905; Alice's letters home 165/207, May 4, Jun 1,1905.

88 Personal diary 165/66, Nov 23, Dec 5, 1905.

89 Personal diary, 165/67, Nov 24–27, Dec 4, 1906.

90   Personal diary, 165/63, Feb 13, 1902.

91   Richard Sorabji collection, from Sheffield, Jul 30, 1908.

92   Personal diary, 165/70, Jul 14–21 1909.

93   See the similar descriptions in Alice's first novel, *Children of the Border*, John Murray, London 1926, in her report on the Mission in *Mercy and Truth* 1909, p. 174, in Cornelia's Personal diary, 165/78 May 24,1917, and in the BBC talk 'Bannu' by Veronica Cecil, 1996.

94   The married years are described in A. M. Pennell, *Pennell of the Afghan Frontier*, London 1914, esp. 345–453. A week of burglary raids at the hospital is further described by her in the Church Missionary Society magazine in 'An eventful week in Bannu', *Mercy and Truth*, 1914 and the trips to Thal in 'Two journeys to Thal', *Mercy and Truth* 1914.

95   This is described not only in *Pennell of the Afghan Frontier*, but also in *Mercy and Truth* 1909, pp. 173–174.

96   Personal diary, 165/73, Mar 20–23, Apr 10–11, 1912.

97   Personal diary 165/73, Sep 18,1912.

98   Several of the dates for this period come from a list of entries in the handwritten Bannu record book copied out for Brian Harral by Dr Ruth Coggan who worked at the Bannu Mission from 1970–1992 and who was hoping to return at the time of correspondence with me in 1996. Brian Harral very kindly let me see a paper he had written on Alice using this and minutes of the Church Missionary Society in Birmingham University Library and *Mercy and Truth*, to which he drew my attention, as well as 165/207 and 208 and *Pennell of the Afghan Frontier*. I am very grateful to him for expanding my information.

99   Brian Harral, presumably from CMS minutes.

100 Bannu record book.

101 Letters to Elena in Richard Sorabji collection Sep 23,1915. The story is spelled out by Alice in 'The kidnapping of Joel', *Mercy and Truth* 1916, pp. 63–66.

102 Cornelia, Personal diary, 165/76 Nov 1915; Alice in *Mercy and Truth* 1916, p. 283.

103 Personal diary 165/70, 84, Jun 25,1909, Nov 9, 1922; Letters to Elena, 165/37, Jan 4,1922.

104 Personal diary, 165/79, Jun 4, 1918. *Pennell of the Frontier*, pp. 182, 403.

105 So Brian Harral, drawing on CMS documents.

106 Letters to Elena, 165/31, Jul 17,1919.

107 Letter from Alice of Jan 15,1920 included in Letters to Elena, 165/33. The attack on Thal is also described in her first novel, *Children of the Border*.

108 Bannu record book; letter from Alice March 1920 in Richard Sorabji Collection.

109 Mary's reply of May 30–31, 1917 to Lena's report survives in the Richard Sorabji collection, having passed through a war-time accident at sea. For both visits see Cornelia, Personal diary 165/78 Apr 18, May 22–Jun 2 1917.

110 Personal diary, 165/78, May 26,1917.

111 Personal diary, 165/78, May 31,1917.

112 Personal diary, Feb 5–16; Letters to Elena, 165/37, Feb 13,1922.

113 Chapter 16.

114 Personal diary, 165/84, Jul 3, 1922.

115 Personal diary, 165/84, Sep 27,1922.

116 Letters to Elena 165/88, Dec 23,1926; probably 165/90, Apr 26, 1928; Bannu Record book.

117 Extract from Dr Bolton's journal supplied to Brian Harral by Dr Ruth Coggan.

118 Reported by Dick to Cornelia, Personal diary, 165/84, Oct 7,1922.

119 Bannu record book; Personal diary, 165/85, Jan 29,1923.

120 Personal diary 165/85, Jun18, Dec 11,1923.

121 Letters to Elena 165/38, May 4, 1924.

122 Letters to Elena, 165/46, 2 Apr 1931; Personal diary 165/98, Sep 12,1936.

123 Letters to Elena 165/41, Sep 8,1926; 165/43, Mar 22, 1928; 165/44, Sep 19, 1929; 165/46, Apr 2,1935.

124 Richard Sorabji collection. Internal evidence shows that the date 1941 is the date of writing, not merely of depositing in the bank for protection against the raids.

125 A comparison of the fiction of Alice and Cornelia, and comparison with Kipling, is made by C. L. Innes, *A History of Black and Asian Writing in Britain*, *1700–2000*, Cambridge University Press 2002.

126 Letters of August 1973 to the Head Master from Ram Ditta Mall, aged 85, sent me by Michael Partridge, archivist of Eastbourne College.

127 Chapter 16.

128 Personal diary, 165/95, Jan 4 and 17, 1933.

129 Richard Sorabji collection, Cornelia's letters to family from USA, Feb 1, 10 and 14, 1932.

130 Personal diary 165/100, Mar 28,1938.

131 Richard Sorabji collection, Letters to family, Dec 29, 1932 and Feb 2 and 14, 1933; Personal diary, 165/100, Jan 18,1938; cf. Letters to Elena, 165/48, Dec 5,1935.

132 For what follows, see Personal diary 165/100, 1938, Letters to Elena 165/51, 1939–41.

133 Brian Harral's unpublished memoir. For further findings on Alice, see Shane Malhotra, Open University Ph.D dissertation in preparation.

INDEX

Note: Place names are spelled as in Cornelia's time, except that in the main text the up to date spelling is supplied alongside at the first occurrence

U

University Association of Women in Calcutta, 249–250, 275 Ch. 12, n. 59

USA, Susie's lectures tours, 322, 352, 393–396; Cornelia's lecture tours, 322, 338, 352–353, 374, 380; Sarojini Naidu's lecture tour, 338, 352; Ambedkar's lecture tour, 348, 352; Tagore's lecture tour, 352

V

Vernacular in family schools, 14, 62, 390–391, 393–395; used by Cornelia, *see* Cornelia

Vickers, Hugh, 41, 43, 45, 50

Vickers, Mary, 45

Victoria High School, Poona, 12, 14, 16, 61–62, 395

Villages, 203, 319, 321–322, 328, 335, 379

Village councils (panchayats), 221, 332

Vivekananda, Swami, 388

Vosper, Dr, NW Frontier doctor, 405

W

Waddell, Helen, medievalist writer, Somervillian, 374

Wallach, 78, Ch. 16, n. 75

Ward, Mary, Mrs Humphry, novelist, educationist, sponsor of Somerville, 25, 114

Watts, G. F., 93–94, 104–106, 109–110

Watts, G. F., Mrs, 110

Wavell, Lady, Vicereine, 377–378, 380

Weld, Agnes Grace, niece of Tennyson, model for Charles Dodgson, 21, 25, 28, 39, 42, 57

Whately, Mr, solicitor mentor, 51, 60

Widowhood, 212–216, 220, 274; widowed children, 295, 316

Wigram, Dr, NW Frontier doctor, 405, 407

Willingdon, Lord, Viceroy and earlier Governor of Bombay, and Lady, 347, 400

Wills, 136, 190–192, 197–198

Wilberforce, Canon, later Archdeacon, 123, 268, 376

Williams, Ivy, 279

Women's suffrage, 316, 328

Woodrow Wilson, President USA, 271

Woolley, Leonard, archaeologist, 374

World War I, 209–210, 249, 265–271, 404, 409

World War II, and war effort, 369–378, 380

Wright, Dr Joseph, 28

Wright, Mr Justice, 44

Writers' Buildings, Calcutta, 170, 183

Y

Yatman, Rev., 395

Younghuband, Francis, and wife, 168

Z

Zenana Mission, 63, 282

Zoroastrianism, 4–8, 324

Zuleika Sorabji (Jane, Janie), 16–17, 265, 370; and marriage to 'Herbert', 387–388